Organizational Behavior

3rd EDITION

Organizational Behavior

Steven L. McShane
University of Western Australia

Mary Ann Von Glinow
Florida International University

Mc Graw Hill Education

ORGANIZATIONAL BEHAVIOR, THIRD EDITION

Published by McGraw-Hill Education, 2 Penn Plaza, New York, NY 10121. Copyright © 2016 by
McGraw-Hill Education. All rights reserved. Printed in the United States of America. Previous editions
© 2014 and 2012. No part of this publication may be reproduced or distributed in any form or by any means,
or stored in a database or retrieval system, without the prior written consent of McGraw-Hill Education,
including, but not limited to, in any network or other electronic storage or transmission, or broadcast
for distance learning.

Some ancillaries, including electronic and print components, may not be available to customers outside the
United States.

This book is printed on acid-free paper.

3 4 5 6 7 8 9 DOW 21 20 19 18 17 16

ISBN 978-0-07-772060-5
MHID 0-07-772060-1

Senior Vice President, Products & Markets: *Kurt L. Strand*
Vice President, General Manager, Products & Markets: *Michael Ryan*
Vice President, Content Design & Delivery: *Kimberly Meriwether David*
Managing Director: *Susan Gouijnstook*
Director: *Michael Ablassmeir*
Product Developer: *Heather Darr*
Marketing Manager: *Elizabeth Trepowski*
Director, Content Design & Delivery: *Terri Schiesl*
Program Manager: *Mary Conzachi*
Content Project Managers: *Christine A. Vaughan* and *Daryl Bruflodt*
Buyer: *Michael R. McCormick*
Design: *Matt Diamond*
Content Licensing Specialists: *Keri Johnson* and *Deanna Dausener*
Cover Image: *Getty Images / Martin Barraud*
Compositor: *Aptara®, Inc.*
Typeface: *10/12 Times LT*
Printer: *R. R. Donnelley*

All credits appearing on page or at the end of the book are considered to be an extension of the copyright page.

Library of Congress Control Number

2014951035

The Internet addresses listed in the text were accurate at the time of publication. The inclusion of a website does
not indicate an endorsement by the authors or McGraw-Hill Education, and McGraw-Hill Education does not
guarantee the accuracy of the information presented at these sites.

Brief Contents

Contents

part four Organizational Processes 224

What's New
in the Third Edition

Based on feedback from users and reviewers, we undertook an ambitious revision to make the book an even more effective teaching and learning tool. Following are the changes we've made for this third edition, broken out by chapter.

Overall

- Most by-the-numbers factoids have been updated or replaced.
- New real-world examples have been introduced throughout the book.
- The majority of photos illustrating or symbolizing key concepts have been replaced.

Chapter 1: Introduction to the Field of Organizational Behavior

In this edition, the opening chapter introduces an integrated model of organizational behavior to help students see the relationship among the main concepts throughout this book. This chapter has also been substantially reorganized for better conceptual flow. Furthermore, it updates and revises content on why we should study OB, the organizational learning perspective, and emerging employment relationships.

Chapter 2: Individual Behavior, Personality, and Values

This edition updates several topics in this chapter, including new information about organizational citizenship behaviors, elements of task performance, the importance of role clarity, the influence of values on individual behavior, predictors of moral sensitivity, and strategies to support ethical behavior.

Chapter 3: Perceiving Ourselves and Others in Organizations

This edition updates the topics on perceptual organization and interpretation, attribution rules, fundamental attribution error, and improving perceptions through meaningful interaction.

Chapter 4: Workplace Emotions, Attitudes, and Stress

The topics of cognitive dissonance and emotional intelligence outcomes and development have been updated. This edition also updates information on types of emotions, the relationship between emotions and attitudes, and emotional dissonance.

Chapter 5: Employee Motivation

This edition introduces social interaction and information processing demands as job characteristics that were overlooked by the traditional job design model. This chapter also updates and rewrites content on employee drives and the four-drive theory.

Chapter 6: Decision Making and Creativity

The topic of subjective expected utility (a core element of rational choice decision making) has been rewritten, including a new exhibit to illustrate the concept. This edition also updates the discussion of escalation of commitment and problem identification.

Chapter 7: Team Dynamics

This chapter has been substantially revised and updated. The team decision-making section has been substantially rewritten, including the addition of brainwriting as a team structure to improve creative decisions in teams. This edition also introduces team overconfidence (inflated team efficacy) as a team decision-making constraint. The chapter now discusses the types of teams around the emerging taxonomy of team permanence, skill differentiation, and authority differentiation. The team cohesion topic clearly explains two key contingencies (task interdependence and team norms) in how much cohesion affects team performance. The team environment topic has been rewritten to distinguish environmental resources from drivers of change within teams. The task characteristics discussion now identifies the tension between task complexity and task ambiguity. The virtual teams topic incorporates the emerging concept of virtuality.

Chapter 8: Communicating in Teams and Organizations

This edition refines and updates the topics of direct communication with top management and workplace communication through social media.

Chapter 9: Power and Influence in the Workplace

This edition has minor rewriting in the topic of impression management and ingratiation.

Chapter 10: Conflict and Negotiation in the Workplace

This edition has more detail about ways to reduce differentiation and to improve communication and mutual understanding as strategies to minimize dysfunctional conflict. Several other topics have minor revisions and updates, including task conflict, the problems with conflict, differentiation as a source of conflict, and conflict avoidance strategies.

Chapter 11: Leadership in Organizational Settings

This chapter has been completely reorganized and substantially rewritten. Transformational leadership is now presented as the first leadership perspective. Furthermore, the chapter expands discussion of strategic visions and incorporates "encourage experimentation" as one of the four elements of transformational leadership. Managerial leadership, the second leadership perspective, is described and contrasted with transformational leadership. The managerial leadership perspective incorporates earlier behavioral leadership concepts, contemporary contingency leadership theories, and servant leadership.

Chapter 12: Designing Organizational Structures

This chapter revises and updates the matrix structure topic, including the two main forms of this structure (divisional-based and project-based) and specific problems with matrix structures.

Chapter 13: Organizational Culture

The section on changing and strengthening organizational culture has been revised, particularly with the addition of supporting workforce stability and communication. The issue of espoused versus enacted values is more clearly highlighted, and the topics of organizational culture effectiveness contingencies and socialization agents have minor revisions.

Chapter 14: Organizational Change

This edition revises and updates the topic of why employees resist change. The discussion on how change agents should interpret employee resistance has also been rewritten.

Organizational
Behavior

1
chapter

Introduction to the Field of
Organizational Behavior

Learning Objectives

After studying this chapter, you should be able to:

LO1-1 Define organizational behavior and organizations, and discuss the importance of this field of inquiry.

LO1-2 Debate the organizational opportunities and challenges of globalization, workforce diversity, and emerging employment relationships.

LO1-3 Discuss the anchors on which organizational behavior knowledge is based.

LO1-4 Compare and contrast the four perspectives of organizational effectiveness.

Apple Inc. and Amazon.com are the two most admired companies in the world, according to *Fortune* magazine's annual list. Not surprising news to most of us, considering Apple's innovative products and Amazon's online retailing dominance. What is surprising is that neither company was on anyone's radar screen two decades ago. Apple was on life support in the late 1990s, barely clinging to a few percentage points of market share in the computer industry. Amazon was just a start-up company; its handful of employees were located above a retail tile store, where they developed a new website to sell books.[1] Meanwhile, some firms that were most admired back then, such as Dell and Merck, have completely disappeared from the list because they failed to innovate or fell into trouble with ethical misconduct.

The World's Most Admired Companies[2]

- **1** Apple
- **2** Amazon.com
- **3** Google
- **4** Berkshire Hathaway
- **5** Starbucks
- **6** Coca-Cola
- **7** Walt Disney
- **8** FedEx
- **9** Southwest Airlines
- **10** General Electric

BEST

WELCOME TO THE FIELD OF ORGANIZATIONAL BEHAVIOR!

Apple and Amazon are role models of how organizations can succeed in today's turbulent environment. In every sector of the economy, organizations need to be innovative, employ skilled and motivated people who can work in teams, have leaders with foresight and vision, and make decisions that consider the interests of multiple stakeholders. In other words, the best companies succeed through the concepts and practices that we discuss in this book on organizational behavior.

Our purpose is to help you understand what goes on in organizations, including the thoughts and behavior of employees and teams. We examine the factors that make companies effective, improve employee well-being, and drive successful collaboration among coworkers. We look at organizations from numerous and diverse perspectives, from the deepest foundations of employee thoughts and behavior (personality, self-concept, commitment, etc.) to the complex interplay between the organization's structure and culture and its external environment. Along this journey, we emphasize why things happen and what you can do to predict and manage organizational events.

We begin this chapter by introducing you to the field of organizational behavior and explaining why it is important to your career and to organizations. This is followed by an overview of three challenges facing organizations: globalization, increasing workforce diversity, and emerging employment relationships. We then describe four anchors that guide the development of organizational behavior knowledge. The latter part of this chapter describes the "ultimate dependent variable" in organizational behavior by presenting the four main perspectives of organizational effectiveness. The chapter closes with an integrating model of organizational behavior to help guide you through the topics in this book.

> **LO1-1** Define organizational behavior and organizations, and discuss the importance of this field of inquiry.

THE FIELD OF ORGANIZATIONAL BEHAVIOR

Organizational behavior (OB) is the study of what people think, feel, and do in and around organizations. It looks at employee behavior, decisions, perceptions, and emotional responses. It examines how individuals and teams in organizations relate to each other and to their counterparts in other organizations. OB also encompasses the study of how organizations interact with their external environments, particularly in the context of employee behavior and decisions. OB researchers systematically study these topics at multiple levels of analysis, namely, the individual, team (including interpersonal), and organization.[3]

The definition of organizational behavior begs the question: What are organizations? **Organizations** are groups of people who

work interdependently toward some purpose.[4] Notice that organizations are not buildings or government-registered entities. In fact, many organizations exist without either physical walls or government documentation to confer their legal status. Organizations have existed for as long as people have worked together. Massive temples dating back to 3500 BC were constructed through the organized actions of multitudes of people. Craftspeople and merchants in ancient Rome formed guilds, complete with elected managers. More than 1,000 years ago, Chinese factories were producing 125,000 tons of iron each year.[5]

Throughout history, these and other organizations have consisted of people who communicate, coordinate, and collaborate with each other to achieve common objectives. One key feature of organizations is that they are collective entities. They consist of human beings (typically, but not necessarily, employees and leaders try to achieve in reality. Still, imagine an organization without a collective sense of purpose. It would be a collection of people without direction or unifying force. So, whether they are designing smartphones at Apple or selling almost anything on the Internet at Amazon, people working in organizations do have some sense of collective purpose.

> "A company is one of humanity's most amazing inventions. . . . [It's] this abstract construct we've invented, and it's incredibly powerful."[6]
>
> —Steve Jobs

employees), and these people interact with each other in an *organized* way. This organized relationship requires some minimal level of communication, coordination, and collaboration to achieve organizational objectives. As such, all organizational members have degrees of interdependence with each other; they accomplish goals by sharing materials, information, or expertise with coworkers.

A second key feature of organizations is that their members have a collective sense of purpose. This collective purpose isn't always well defined or agreed on. Although most companies have vision and mission statements, these documents are sometimes out of date or don't describe what

Historical Foundations of Organizational Behavior

Organizational behavior emerged as a distinct field around the early 1940s, but organizations have been studied by experts in other fields for many centuries. The Greek philosopher Plato wrote about the essence of leadership. Around the same time, the Chinese philosopher Confucius extolled the virtues of ethics and leadership. In 1776, Adam Smith discussed the benefits of job specialization and division of labor. One hundred years later, German sociologist Max Weber wrote about rational organizations, the work ethic, and charismatic leadership. Soon after, industrial engineer Frederick Winslow Taylor proposed systematic ways to organize work processes and motivate employees through goal setting and rewards.[7]

In the 1930s, Harvard professor Elton Mayo and his colleagues established the "human relations" school of management, which emphasized the study of employee attitudes and informal group dynamics in the workplace. Around the same time, Mary Parker Follett offered new ways of thinking about constructive conflict, team dynamics, power, and leadership. Chester Barnard, another OB pioneer and respected executive, wrote insightful views regarding organizational communication, coordination, leadership and authority, organizations as open systems, and team dynamics.[8] This brief historical tour indicates that OB has been around for a long time; it just wasn't organized into a unified discipline until around World War II.

Why Study Organizational Behavior?

Organizational behavior instructors face a challenge: Students who have not yet begun their careers tend to value courses related to specific jobs, such as accounting and marketing.[9] However, OB doesn't have a specific career path—there is no "vice president of OB"—so students sometimes have difficulty recognizing the value that OB knowledge can offer to their future. Meanwhile, students with several years of work experience identify OB as one of the most important courses. Why? Because they have learned through experience that OB *does make a difference* to one's career success. OB helps us make sense of and predict the world in which we live.[10] We use OB theories to question our personal beliefs and assumptions and to adopt more accurate models of workplace behavior.

> Probably the greatest value of OB knowledge is that it helps us get things done in organizations.

But probably the greatest value of OB knowledge is that it helps us get things done in the workplace.[11] By definition, organizations are people who work together to accomplish things, so we need a toolkit of knowledge and skills to work successfully with others. Building a high-performance team, motivating coworkers, handling workplace conflicts, influencing your boss, and changing employee behavior are just a few of the areas of knowledge and skills offered in organizational behavior. No matter what career path you choose, you'll find that OB concepts play an important role in performing your job and working more effectively within organizations.

Organizational Behavior Is for Everyone A common misunderstanding is that organizational behavior is for managers. Although this knowledge is critical for effective management, this book pioneered the broader view that OB is valuable for everyone who works in and around organizations. Whether you are a software engineer, customer service representative, foreign exchange analyst, or chief executive officer, you need to understand and apply the many organizational behavior topics that are discussed in this book. Most organizations will probably always have managers, and this book recognizes the relevance of OB knowledge in these vital roles. But all employees need OB knowledge as the work environment increasingly expects us to be self-motivated and to work effectively with coworkers without management intervention. In the words of one forward-thinking OB writer more than four decades ago: Everyone is a manager.[12]

OB and the Bottom Line Up to this point, our answer to the question "Why study OB?" has focused on how organizational behavior knowledge benefits you as an individual. However, OB knowledge is just as important for the organization's financial health. Numerous studies have reported that OB practices are powerful predictors of the organization's survival and success.[13] For instance, the best 100 companies to work for in America (i.e., companies with the highest levels of employee satisfaction) have significantly higher financial performance than other businesses within the same industry. Companies with higher levels of employee engagement have significantly higher sales and profitability (see Chapter 5). OB practices are also associated with various indicators of hospital performance, such as lower patient mortality rates and higher patient satisfaction. Other studies have consistently found a positive relationship between the quality of leadership and the company's return on assets.

The bottom-line value of organizational behavior is supported by research into the best predictors of investment portfolio performance. These investigations suggest that leadership, performance-based rewards, employee development, employee attitudes, and other specific OB characteristics are important "positive screens" for selecting companies with the highest and most consistent long-term investment gains.[14] Overall, the organizational behavior concepts, theories, and practices presented throughout this book do make a positive difference to you personally, to the organization, and ultimately to society.

LO1-2 Debate the organizational opportunities and challenges of globalization, workforce diversity, and emerging employment relationships.

CONTEMPORARY CHALLENGES FOR ORGANIZATIONS

Organizational behavior knowledge has become vital because organizations are experiencing unprecedented change. As we will explain in more detail later in this chapter, organizations are deeply affected by the external environment. Consequently, they need to maintain a good organization–environment fit by anticipating and adjusting to changes in society. Over the next few pages, we highlight three of the major challenges facing organizations: globalization, increasing workforce diversity, and emerging employment relationships.

Globalization

Globalization refers to economic, social, and cultural connectivity with people in other parts of the world. Organizations globalize when they actively participate in other countries and cultures. Although businesses have traded goods across borders for centuries, the degree of globalization today is unprecedented because information technology and transportation systems allow a much more intense level of connectivity and interdependence around the planet.[15]

Globalization offers numerous benefits to organizations in terms of larger markets, lower costs, and greater access to knowledge and innovation. At the same time, there is considerable debate about whether globalization benefits developing nations and whether it is primarily responsible for increasing work intensification, as well as reducing job security and work–life balance in developed countries.[16]

Globalization is now well entrenched, so the most important issue in organizational behavior is how corporate leaders and employees alike can lead and work effectively in this emerging reality.[17] Throughout this book, we will refer to the effects of globalization on teamwork, diversity, cultural values, organizational structure, leadership, and other themes. Each topic highlights that globalization has brought more complexity to the workplace, but also more opportunities and potential benefits for individuals and organizations. Globalization requires

NEW YORK   NEW DELHI   PARIS

additional knowledge and skills that we will also discuss in this book, such as emotional intelligence, a global mindset, nonverbal communication, and conflict handling.

Increasing Workforce Diversity

In most Japanese corporations, the board of directors consists exclusively of older generation Japanese males. If the group has any diversity, it is whether the board member has an engineering or nonengineering education. Hitachi chair Takashi Kawamura recognized that this lack of diversity limited the conglomerate's potential. "Governance handled by Japanese men with homogeneous thinking is no good," says Kawamura. "To be global is to bring diversity into the company's governance." Hitachi is in the process of diversifying its board.

Hitachi's board now includes three foreign executives, including one female executive.[18]

Kawamura is increasing the **surface-level diversity** of the conglomerate's board of directors. Surface-level diversity refers to the observable demographic and other overt differences among members of a group, such as their race, ethnicity, gender, age, and physical capabilities.[19] Surface-level diversity is increasing in many other parts of the world due to more open and less discriminatory immigration policies. For instance, people with non-Caucasian or Hispanic origin currently represent one-third of the American population. Within the next 50 years, one in four Americans will be Hispanic, 14 percent will be African American, and 8 percent will be of Asian descent.[20]

Diversity also includes differences in the psychological characteristics of employees, including personalities, beliefs, values, and attitudes. We can't directly see this **deep-level diversity**, but it is evident in a person's decisions, statements, and actions. A popular example is the apparent deep-level diversity across generations.[21] Exhibit 1.1 illustrates the distribution of the American workforce by major generational cohorts: 37 percent *Baby Boomers* (born from 1946 to 1964), 28 percent *Generation Xers* (born from 1965 to 1980), and 26 percent *Millennials* (also called *Generation Yers*, born after 1980).

Some writers have made wild claims about how much employees differ across generational cohorts. Generational deep-level diversity differences do exist, but systematic research indicates that these differences are subtle. In fact, some differences are due to age, not cohort. In other words, Boomers had many of the same attitudes as Millennials when they were that age.[23] One recent investigation of 23,000 undergraduate college and university students reported that, compared with the other groups, Millennials expect more rapid career advancement regarding promotions and pay increases.[24] These observations are consistent with other studies, which have found that Millennials are more self-confident, are more self-focused, and have less work centrality (i.e., work is less of a central life interest) when compared to Baby Boomers. Generation Xers

typically average somewhere between these two cohorts.[25]

Consequences of Diversity

Diversity presents both opportunities and challenges in organizations.[26] Diversity is an advantage because it provides diverse knowledge. Furthermore, teams with some forms of diversity (particularly occupational diversity) make better decisions on complex problems than do teams whose members have similar backgrounds. There is also some evidence that companies that win diversity awards have higher financial returns, at least in the short run.[27] This is consistent with anecdotal evidence from many corporate leaders, namely that having a diverse workforce improves customer service and creativity. "As a company serving customers around the globe, we greatly value the diverse opinions and experiences that an inclusive and diverse workforce brings to the table," says a Verizon executive. The American telecommunications company has

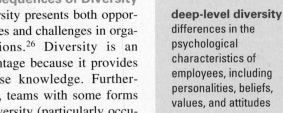

surface-level diversity
the observable demographic or physiological differences in people, such as their race, ethnicity, gender, age, and physical disabilities

deep-level diversity
differences in the psychological characteristics of employees, including personalities, beliefs, values, and attitudes

> Companies that offer an inclusive workplace are, in essence, fulfilling the ethical standard of fairness in their decisions regarding employment and the allocation of rewards.

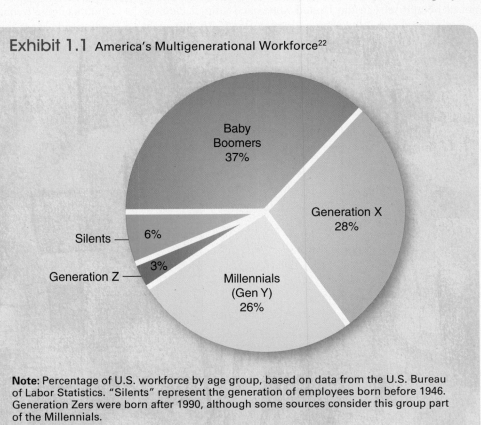

Exhibit 1.1 America's Multigenerational Workforce[22]

- Baby Boomers 37%
- Generation X 28%
- Millennials (Gen Y) 26%
- Silents 6%
- Generation Z 3%

Note: Percentage of U.S. workforce by age group, based on data from the U.S. Bureau of Labor Statistics. "Silents" represent the generation of employees born before 1946. Generation Zers were born after 1990, although some sources consider this group part of the Millennials.

work–life balance the degree to which a person minimizes conflict between work and nonwork demands

virtual work work performed away from the traditional physical workplace by using information technology

won several awards for its inclusive practices.[28]

Is workforce diversity a sound business proposition? Yes, but research indicates that the reasons are not clear-cut because most forms of diversity have both challenges and benefits.[29] Teams with diverse employees usually take longer to perform effectively because they experience numerous communication problems and create "faultlines" in informal group dynamics. Diversity is also a source of conflict, which can reduce information sharing and morale. But even with these challenges, companies need to make diversity a priority because surface-level diversity is a moral and legal imperative. Companies that offer an inclusive workplace are, in essence, fulfilling the ethical standard of fairness in their decisions regarding employment and the allocation of rewards. Fairness is a well-known predictor of employee loyalty and satisfaction.

Emerging Employment Relationships

Combine globalization with increasing workforce diversity, then add in recent developments in information technology. The resulting concoction has created incredible changes in employment relationships. A few decades ago, most (although not all) employees in the United States and similar cultures would finish their workday after eight or nine hours and could separate their personal time from work time. There were no smartphones or Internet connections to keep them tethered to work on a 24/7 schedule. Even business travel was more of an exception due to its high cost. Most competitors were located in the same country, so they had similar work practices and labor costs. Today, work hours are longer (although arguably less than 100 years ago), employees experience more work-related stress, and there is growing evidence that family and personal relations are suffering.

Little wonder that one of the most important employment issues over the past decade has been **work–life balance**. Work–life balance occurs when people are able to minimize conflict between their work and nonwork demands.[30] Most employees lack this balance because they spend too many hours each week performing or thinking about their job, whether at the workplace, at home, or on vacation. This focus on work leaves too little time to fulfill nonwork needs and obligations. Our discussion of work-related stress (Chapter 4) will examine work–life balance issues in more detail.

Another employment relationship trend is **virtual work**, whereby employees use information technology to perform their jobs away from the traditional physical workplace.[32] Some virtual work occurs when employees are connected to the office while traveling or at clients' offices. However, the most common form involves working at home rather than commuting to the office (called *telecommuting* or *teleworking*). One large-scale recent survey of employees across 24 countries reports that 17 percent of those connected from their home to the office telecommute on a frequent basis. However, less than 10 percent of connected Americans telecommute. The U.S. government reports

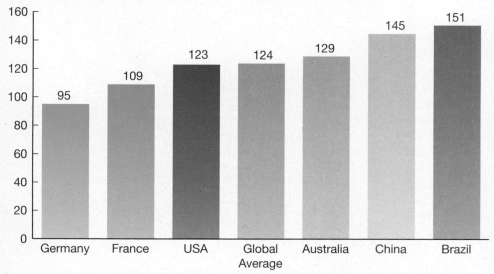

Global Work–Life Balance Index[31]

Germany: 95
France: 109
USA: 123
Global Average: 124
Australia: 129
China: 145
Brazil: 151

Based on interviews with more than 16,000 business respondents from the Regus global contacts database. This exhibit shows the Regus work–life balance index for each country listed, as well as globally (includes several countries not shown here). A higher score indicates that employees in that country experience better work–life balance. The index is standardized to 100 as the average country score in the first survey a few years ago.

that 32 percent of its employees are eligible to telecommute, but only 170,000 actually make use of that policy. More than 10 percent of Japanese employees work from home at least one day each week, a figure that the Japanese government wants to double within the next few years.[33]

The benefits and limitations of virtual work, particularly working from home, have been the subject of considerable research and discussion. One of the most consistent observations on the benefits side of the ledger is that telework is one of the most popular perks among job applicants. This work arrangement particularly attracts well-educated, tech-savvy younger generation employees. Another significant benefit is that telework improves work–life balance for most people, mainly because they have more time that previously was consumed traveling to the office. A study of 25,000 IBM employees found that female telecommuters with children were able to work 40 hours per week, whereas nontelecommuters could manage only 30 hours before feeling work–life balance tension.[34]

Telework potentially improves productivity because employees experience less stress and tend to allocate some former commuting time to work activity. Another benefit is that employees remain productive when the weather or natural

disasters block access to the office. For instance, 30 percent of U.S. federal government employees were able to continue working from home during a major snowstorm, which saved the government $30 million per day.

Telework also has environmental and financial benefits. Cisco Systems employees worldwide who telework avoid producing almost 50,000 metric tons of greenhouse gas emissions. Telus, one of Canada's largest telecommunications companies, has been able to reduce its office space by 25 percent in recent years by encouraging most of its workforce to telecommute. Its employees have also reported cost savings. One Telus employee in Vancouver recently estimated that she saves $650 each month in travel costs by working from home most days.[35]

Against these benefits are several challenges and limitations of virtual work.[36] There is fairly consistent evidence that employees who telecommute most of the time experience more social isolation and less cohesion with their coworkers. To minimize these problems, many companies require employees to work at the office at least once or twice each week. Another issue is that some employees who cannot telework (as well as some who choose not to) feel that teleworking is unfair to them (i.e., teleworkers have more freedom and benefits). At the same time, at least one study reports that teleworkers also feel an unfair disadvantage, believing that employees on company premises receive more support and promotion opportunities. For this reason, virtual work arrangements are also more successful in organizations that evaluate employees by their performance outcomes rather than "face time" (i.e., face-to-face interactions with the boss and coworkers).[37]

Telecommuting's main benefit is work–life balance, but some studies have found that family relations suffer rather than improve if employees lack sufficient space and resources for a home office. Finally, telework is better suited to people who are self-motivated, organized, can work effectively with broadband and other technology, and have sufficient fulfillment of social needs elsewhere in their life.

LO1-3 Discuss the anchors on which organizational behavior knowledge is based.

ANCHORS OF ORGANIZATIONAL BEHAVIOR KNOWLEDGE

Globalization, increasing workforce diversity, and emerging employment relationships are just a few of the trends that challenge organizations and make the field of organizational behavior more relevant than ever before. To understand these and other topics, the field of organizational behavior relies on a set of basic beliefs or knowledge structures (see Exhibit 1.2). These conceptual anchors represent the principles on which OB knowledge is developed and refined.[38]

evidence-based management the practice of making decisions and taking actions based on research evidence

The Systematic Research Anchor

A key feature of OB knowledge is that it should be based on systematic research, which typically involves forming research questions, systematically collecting data, and testing hypotheses against those data.[39] Systematic research investigation is the basis for **evidence-based management**—making decisions and taking actions guided by research evidence. It makes perfect sense that management practice should be founded on the best available systematic knowledge. Yet many of us who study organizations using systematic methods are amazed at how often corporate leaders embrace fads, consulting models, and their own pet beliefs without bothering to find out if they actually work![40]

Why don't corporate leaders and other decision makers consistently apply evidence-based management? One reason is that they are bombarded with ideas from consultant reports, popular business books, newspaper articles, and other sources, which makes it difficult to figure out which ones are based on good evidence. A second reason is that good OB research is necessarily generic; it is rarely described in the context of a specific problem in a specific organization. Managers therefore have the difficult task of figuring out which theories are relevant to their unique situation.

A third reason why organizational leaders follow popular management fads that lack research evidence is because the sources of these fads are rewarded for marketing their ideas, not for testing to see if they actually work. Indeed, some management concepts have become popular (some have even found their way into OB textbooks!) because of heavy marketing, not because of any evidence that they are valid. A fourth reason is that human beings are affected by several perceptual errors and decision-making biases, as we will learn in Chapters 3 and 6. For instance, decision makers have a natural tendency to look for evidence that supports their pet beliefs and ignore evidence that opposes those beliefs.

OB experts have proposed a few simple suggestions to create a more evidence-based organization.[41] First, be skeptical of hype, which is apparent when so-called experts say the idea is "new," "revolutionary," and "proven." In reality, most management ideas are adaptations, evolutionary, and never proven (science can disprove, but never prove; it can only find evidence to support a practice). Second, the company should embrace collective expertise rather than rely on charismatic stars and management gurus. Third, stories provide useful illustrations and possibly preliminary evidence of a useful practice, but they should never become the main foundation to support management action. Instead, rely on more systematic investigation with a larger sample. Finally, take a neutral stance toward popular trends and ideologies. Executives tend to get caught up in what their counterparts at other companies are doing without determining the validity of those trendy practices or their relevance to their own organizations.

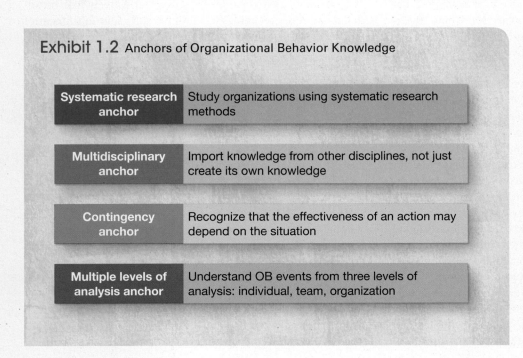

Exhibit 1.2 Anchors of Organizational Behavior Knowledge

Systematic research anchor	Study organizations using systematic research methods
Multidisciplinary anchor	Import knowledge from other disciplines, not just create its own knowledge
Contingency anchor	Recognize that the effectiveness of an action may depend on the situation
Multiple levels of analysis anchor	Understand OB events from three levels of analysis: individual, team, organization

The Multidisciplinary Anchor

Another organizational behavior anchor is that the field should welcome theories and knowledge from other disciplines, not just from its own isolated research base. For instance, psychological research has aided our understanding of individual and interpersonal behavior. Sociologists have contributed to our knowledge of team dynamics, organizational socialization, organizational power, and other aspects of the social system. OB knowledge has also benefited from knowledge in emerging fields such as communications, marketing, and information systems. This practice of borrowing theory from other disciplines is inevitable. Organizations

organizational effectiveness a broad concept represented by several perspectives, including the organization's fit with the external environment, internal subsystems configuration for high performance, emphasis on organizational learning, and ability to satisfy the needs of key stakeholders

Although OB research and writing pegs each variable within one of these levels of analysis, most variables are understood best by thinking of them from all three levels of analysis.[44] For instance, communication is located in this book as a team (interpersonal) process, but it also includes individual and organizational processes. Therefore, you should try to think about each OB topic at the individual, team, and organizational levels, not just at one of these levels.

LO1-4 Compare and contrast the four perspectives of organizational effectiveness.

have central roles in society, so they are the subject of many social sciences. Furthermore, organizations consist of people who interact with each other, so there is an inherent intersection between OB and most disciplines that study human beings.

The Contingency Anchor

People and their work environments are complex, and the field of organizational behavior recognizes this by stating that a particular action may have different consequences in different situations. In other words, no single solution is best all of the time.[42] Of course, it would be so much simpler if we could rely on "one best way" theories, in which a particular concept or practice has the same results in every situation. OB experts do search for simpler theories, but they also remain skeptical about surefire recommendations; an exception is somewhere around the corner. Thus, when faced with a particular problem or opportunity, we need to understand and diagnose the situation and select the strategy most appropriate *under those conditions*.[43]

The Multiple Levels of Analysis Anchor

Organizational behavior recognizes that what goes on in organizations can be placed into three levels of analysis: individual, team (including interpersonal), and organization. In fact, advanced empirical research currently being conducted carefully identifies the appropriate level of analysis for each variable in the study and then measures at that level of analysis. For example, team norms and cohesion are measured as team variables, not as characteristics of individuals within each team.

PERSPECTIVES OF ORGANIZATIONAL EFFECTIVENESS

Almost all organizational behavior theories have the implicit or explicit objective of making organizations more effective.[45] In fact, **organizational effectiveness** is considered the "ultimate dependent variable" in organizational behavior.[46] This means that organizational effectiveness is the outcome that most OB theories are ultimately trying to achieve. Many theories use different labels—organizational performance, success, goodness, health, competitiveness, excellence—but they are basically presenting models and recommendations that help organizations to become more effective.

Many years ago, OB experts thought the best indicator of a company's effectiveness was how well it achieved its stated objectives. According to this definition, Delta Air Lines would be an effective organization if it met or exceeded its annual sales and profit targets. Today, we know this isn't necessarily so. Any leadership team could set corporate goals that are easy to achieve yet would put the organization out of business. These goals could also be left in the dust by competitors' more aggressive objectives. Worse still, some goals might aim the organization in the wrong direction.

This book takes the view that the best yardstick of organizational effectiveness is a composite of four perspectives: open

open systems a perspective that holds that organizations depend on the external environment for resources, affect that environment through their output, and consist of internal subsystems that transform inputs to outputs

systems, organizational learning, high-performance work practices, and stakeholders.[47] Organizations are effective when they have a good fit with their external environment, are learning organizations, have efficient and adaptive internal subsystems (i.e., high-performance work practices), and satisfy the needs of key stakeholders. Let's examine each of these perspectives in more detail.

Open Systems Perspective

The **open systems** perspective of organizational effectiveness is one of the earliest and well-entrenched ways of thinking about organizations.[48] Indeed, the other major organizational effectiveness perspectives might be considered detailed extensions of the open systems model. The open systems perspective views organizations as complex organisms that "live" within an external environment, as Exhibit 1.3 illustrates. The word *open* describes this permeable relationship, whereas *closed systems* operate without dependence on or interaction with an external environment.

As open systems, organizations depend on the external environment for resources, including raw materials, job applicants, financial resources, information, and equipment. The external environment also consists of rules and expectations, such as

laws and cultural norms, that place demands on how organizations should operate. Some environmental resources (e.g., raw materials) are transformed into outputs that are exported to the external environment, whereas other resources (e.g., job applicants, equipment) become subsystems in the transformation process.

Inside the organization are numerous subsystems, such as departments, teams, informal groups, work processes, technological configurations, and other elements. Many of these subsystems are also systems with their own subsystems.[49] For example, the Nordstrom department store in Spokane, Washington, is a subsystem of the Nordstrom chain, but the Spokane store is also a system with its own subsystems of departments, teams, and work processes. An organization's subsystems are dependent on each other as they transform inputs into outputs. Some outputs (e.g., products, services, community support) may be valued by the external environment, whereas other outputs (e.g., employee layoffs, pollution) are undesirable by-products that may have adverse effects on the environment and the organization's relationship with that environment. Throughout this process, organizations receive feedback from the external environment regarding the value of their outputs and the availability of future inputs.

Organization–Environment Fit According to the open systems perspective, organizations are effective when they maintain a good "fit" with their external environment.[50] Good fit exists

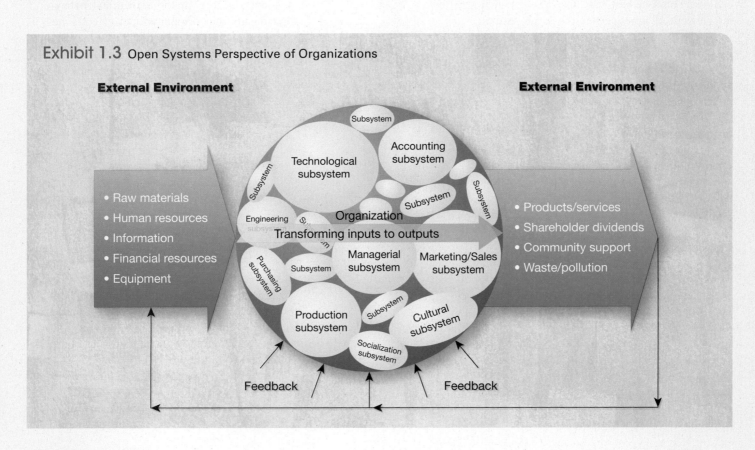

Exhibit 1.3 Open Systems Perspective of Organizations

External Environment

External Environment

- Raw materials
- Human resources
- Information
- Financial resources
- Equipment

Subsystem

Technological subsystem

Accounting subsystem

Subsystem

Subsystem

Engineering subsystem

Organization
Transforming inputs to outputs

Purchasing subsystem

Subsystem

Managerial subsystem

Marketing/Sales subsystem

Production subsystem

Subsystem

Cultural subsystem

Socialization subsystem

- Products/services
- Shareholder dividends
- Community support
- Waste/pollution

Feedback

Feedback

when the organization's inputs, processes, and outputs are aligned with the needs and expectations of the external environment. There are three ways that companies maintain a good environmental fit. The most common strategy to fit with the external environment is to change the company's products and services as well as how those outputs are produced. Zara, the world's largest fashion retailer, relies on continuous adaptation to maintain a good fit with its highly volatile external environment. The Spanish company receives continuous feedback from each of its 6,000 stores, and then uses that feedback along with ongoing creativity to rapidly design, manufacture, and deliver new styles. In contrast, fashion retailers with a poor environmental fit are overstocked with products that few people want to buy and respond slowly to changing preferences.

A second way that organizations maintain a good fit is actively managing their external environment. For instance, businesses rely on marketing to increase demand for their products or services. Some firms gain exclusive rights to particular resources (e.g., exclusive rights to sell a known brand) or restrict competitor access to valued resources. Still others lobby for legislation that strengthens their position in the marketplace or try to delay legislation that would disrupt their business activities. If the external environment is too

Zara's Open Systems Thinking

Zara has become the world's largest fashion retailer by applying the open systems perspective of organizational effectiveness. The Spanish company rapidly adapts to fashion trends by continuously experimenting with numerous new styles, receiving almost immediate feedback about which styles are most popular, making quick changes so styles are more appealing, and rapidly producing and delivering new or revised styles to better fit customer preferences.[51]

challenging, organizations rely on a third organization–environment fit strategy: they move to a new environment that can sustain them. For example, IBM exited the computer products industry when senior executives (correctly) predicted that selling computers would be less prosperous than the rapidly growing technology services business.

Internal Subsystems Effectiveness Along with the organization's fit and adaptability with the external environment, the open systems perspective views effectiveness by how well the organization internally transforms inputs into outputs. The most common indicator of this internal transformation process is **organizational efficiency** (also called productivity), which is the ratio of inputs to outcomes.[52] Companies that produce more goods or services with less labor, materials, and energy are more efficient. At the same time, organizations need transformation processes that are adaptive and innovative.[53] An adaptive transformation process enables organizations to respond better to changing conditions and customer needs. Innovation enables the company to design work processes that are superior to what competitors can offer.

An important feature of an effective transformation process is how well the internal subsystems coordinate with each other.[54] Coordination is a significant challenge as companies grow because they develop increasingly complex subsystems. This complexity increases the risk that information will get lost, ideas and resources will be hoarded, messages will be misinterpreted, and rewards will be distributed unfairly. Subsystems are also interconnected, so small changes to work practices in one subsystem may ripple through the organization and undermine the effectiveness of other subsystems. Consequently, organizations rely on coordinating mechanisms to maintain an efficient and adaptable transformation process (see Chapter 12).

Organizational Learning Perspective

The open systems perspective has traditionally focused on physical resources that enter the organization and are processed into physical goods (outputs). This was representative of the industrial economy, but at many companies knowledge is by far the most important input. Even in companies that produce physical products, knowledge is a key ingredient to success.[55] The **organizational learning** perspective takes the view that effective organizations find ways to acquire, share, use, and store knowledge. These processes build the organization's stock of knowledge, known as its **intellectual capital**.

human capital the stock of knowledge, skills, and abilities among employees that provide economic value to the organization

structural capital knowledge embedded in an organization's systems and structures

relationship capital the value derived from an organization's relationships with customers, suppliers, and others

Intellectual capital exists in three forms: human capital, structural capital, and relationship capital.[57] **Human capital** refers to the knowledge, skills, and abilities that employees carry around in their heads. Human capital is a competitive advantage because it is valuable, rare, difficult to imitate, and nonsubstitutable.[58] Specifically, human capital is valuable because employees are essential for the organization's survival and success. It is also rare and difficult to imitate, meaning that talented people are difficult to find and it is costly and challenging for competitors to duplicate another firm's human capital. Finally, human capital is nonsubstitutable because it cannot be easily replaced by technology. In spite of its competitive advantage, human capital is a huge risk for most organizations. Employees remove valuable knowledge when they leave, which makes the company less effective.[59]

Fortunately, even if every employee leaves the organization, some intellectual capital remains as structural capital. **Structural capital** includes the knowledge captured and retained in an organization's systems and structures, such as the documentation of work procedures and the physical layout of the production line.[60] Structural capital also includes the organization's finished products because knowledge can be extracted by taking them apart to discover how they work and are constructed (i.e., reverse engineering). The third form of intellectual capital is **relationship capital**, which is the value derived from an organization's relationships with customers, suppliers, and others who provide added mutual value for the organization. It includes the organization's goodwill, brand image, and combination of relationships that

> ## "An organization's ability to learn, and translate that learning into action rapidly, is the ultimate competitive advantage."[56]
>
> **—Jack Welch,** former CEO of General Electric

Exhibit 1.4 Four Organizational Learning Processes

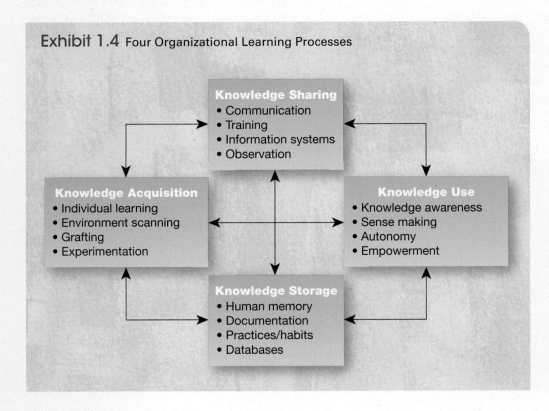

organizational members have with people outside the organization.[61]

An organization's intellectual capital develops and is maintained through the four organizational learning processes shown in Exhibit 1.4: acquiring, sharing, using, and storing knowledge.[62]

Knowledge Acquisition

Knowledge acquisition includes extracting information and ideas from the external environment as well as through insight. Many growing companies achieve this by actively recruiting talented people and buying competing businesses (called *grafting*). They also acquire knowledge through experimentation—generating new ideas and products through creative discovery and testing. A third knowledge acquisition strategy is environmental scanning, such as actively monitoring customer trends and competitor activities. A fourth strategy is individual learning, such as when employees acquire formal training from sources outside the organization.

Knowledge Sharing Knowledge sharing refers to distributing knowledge throughout the organization. This mainly occurs through communication with and learning from coworkers (training, observation, etc.). Research suggests that companies encourage informal communication through their organizational structure, physical work space, corporate culture, and social activities.[63] Company intranets and digital information repositories also support knowledge sharing.

Knowledge Use The competitive advantage of knowledge ultimately comes from using it in ways that add value to the organization and its stakeholders. To do this, employees must be aware that the knowledge exists, be able to locate it, and have

procedures, and routines. Other forms of unlearning erase attitudes, beliefs, and assumptions that are no longer valid. Organizational unlearning is particularly important for organizational change, which we discuss in Chapter 14.

high-performance work practices (HPWPs) a perspective that holds that effective organizations incorporate several workplace practices that leverage the potential of human capital

High-Performance Work Practices Perspective

The open systems perspective states that successful companies are efficient and adaptive at transforming inputs into outputs. However, that perspective does not offer guidance about specific subsystem characteristics or organizational practices that make the transformation process more effective. Consequently,

> ### Effective organizations not only learn; they also unlearn routines and patterns of behavior that are no longer appropriate.

enough freedom to apply it. This requires a culture that encourages experimentation and open communication and recognizes that learning from mistakes is part of that process.

Knowledge Storage and Organizational Memory Knowledge storage is the process of holding knowledge for later retrieval. Stored knowledge, often called *organizational memory*, includes knowledge that employees recall as well as knowledge embedded in the organization's systems and structures.[64] One way of retaining the organization's memory is motivating employees to remain with the company. Progressive businesses achieve this through pleasant work environments, engaging jobs that offer more autonomy, and managers who coach for development rather than continuous monitoring. A second organizational memory strategy is to systematically transfer knowledge to other employees. This occurs when newcomers apprentice with skilled employees, thereby acquiring knowledge that is not documented. A third strategy is to document knowledge that was previously hidden in the minds of individual employees. Some companies encourage employees to write about their successes and failures through a special intranet knowledge portal.

One last point about the organizational learning perspective: effective organizations not only learn; they also unlearn routines and patterns of behavior that are no longer appropriate.[65] Unlearning removes knowledge that no longer adds value and, in fact, may undermine the organization's effectiveness. Some forms of unlearning involve replacing dysfunctional policies,

an entire field of research has blossomed around the objective of determining specific "bundles" of **high-performance work practices (HPWPs)** that enable companies to more effectively transform inputs into outputs.[66]

The HPWP perspective states that human capital—the knowledge, skills, and abilities that employees possess—is an important source of competitive advantage for organizations.[67] This is similar to the organizational learning perspective, except

the HPWP perspective tries to figure out specific ways to generate the most value from this human capital. OB researchers have studied the effects of many work practices, but four are consistently identified as high-performance practices: employee involvement, job autonomy, competency development, and rewards for performance and competencies.[68] Each of these four work practices individually improves organizational effectiveness, but studies suggest that they have a stronger effect when bundled together.[69]

The first two factors—involving employees in decision making and giving them more autonomy over their work activities—tend to strengthen employee motivation as well as improve decisions, organizational responsiveness, and commitment to change. In high-performance workplaces, employee involvement and job autonomy often take the form of self-directed teams (see Chapter 7). The third factor, employee competence development, refers to recruiting, selecting, and training so employees are equipped with the relevant skills, knowledge, and other personal characteristics. The fourth high-performance work practice involves linking performance and skill development to various forms of financial and nonfinancial rewards valued by employees.

HPWPs improve an organization's effectiveness in at least three ways.[70] First, as we mentioned earlier, these activities develop employee skills and knowledge (human capital), which directly improve individual behavior and performance. Second, companies with superior human capital tend to adapt better to rapidly changing environments. This adaptability occurs because employees are better at performing diverse tasks in unfamiliar situations when they are highly skilled and have more freedom to perform their work. A third explanation is that HPWP practices strengthen employee motivation and positive attitudes toward the employer. HPWPs represent the company's investment in its workforce, which motivates employees to reciprocate through greater effort in their jobs and assistance to coworkers.

The HPWP perspective is still developing, but it already reveals important information about specific organizational practices that improve the input–output transformation process. Still, this perspective has been criticized for focusing on shareholder and customer needs at the expense of employee well-being.[71] This concern illustrates that the HPWP perspective offers an incomplete picture of organizational effectiveness. The remaining gaps are mostly filled by the stakeholder perspective of organizational effectiveness.

Stakeholder Perspective

The open systems perspective says that effective organizations adapt to the external environment, but it lacks details about the characteristics of the external environment. The stakeholder perspective fills this gap. **Stakeholders** include anyone with a stake in the company—employees, shareholders, suppliers, labor unions, government, communities, consumer and environmental interest groups, and so on (see Exhibit 1.5).[72] The stakeholder perspective personalizes the open systems perspective; it identifies specific people and social entities in the external environment as well as within the organization (the internal environment). This perspective also recognizes that stakeholder relations are dynamic; they can be negotiated and managed, not just taken as a fixed condition.[73] Organizations are more effective when they consider the needs and expectations of any individual, group, or other entity that affects, or is affected by, the organization's objectives and actions. In other words, the stakeholder perspective requires organizational leaders and employees to understand, manage, and satisfy the interests of their stakeholders.[74]

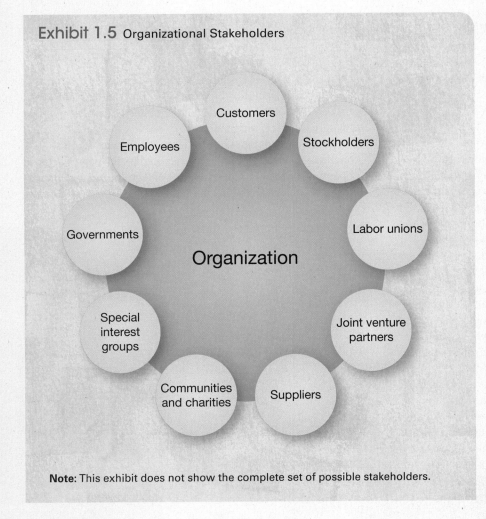

Exhibit 1.5 Organizational Stakeholders

Customers • Stockholders • Employees • Labor unions • Governments • Organization • Joint venture partners • Special interest groups • Communities and charities • Suppliers

Note: This exhibit does not show the complete set of possible stakeholders.

Understanding, managing, and satisfying the interests of stakeholders is more challenging than it sounds because stakeholders have conflicting interests and organizations don't have the resources to satisfy every stakeholder to the fullest. Therefore, organizational leaders need to decide which groups receive higher and lower priority and resources.[75]

There is some evidence that corporate leaders rely on their personal values to prioritize stakeholders. Another factor is how much power each stakeholder has over the organization. This makes sense when one considers that the most powerful stakeholders present the greatest threat and opportunity to the company's survival. Even so, organizations cannot ignore less powerful stakeholders because they may be important in the longer term. Also, ignoring less powerful stakeholders might violate the norms and standards of society, which would undermine relations with communities, government, and other powerful stakeholders.

Values, Ethics, and Corporate Social Responsibility

This brings us to one of the key strengths of the stakeholder perspective, namely, that it incorporates values, ethics, and corporate social responsibility into the organizational effectiveness equation.[76] The stakeholder perspective states that to manage the interests of diverse stakeholders, leaders ultimately need to rely on their personal and organizational values for guidance. **Values** are relatively stable, evaluative beliefs that guide our preferences for outcomes or courses of action in a variety of situations.[77] Values help us know what is right or wrong, or good or bad, in the world. Chapter 2 explains how values anchor our thoughts and to some extent motivate our actions.

Although values exist within individuals, groups of people often hold similar values, so we tend to ascribe these *shared values* to the team, department, organization, profession, or entire society. For example, Chapter 13 discusses the importance and dynamics of organizational culture, which includes shared values across the company or within subsystems. Many companies have adopted the values-driven organization model, whereby employee decisions and behavior are guided by the company's espoused values rather than by expensive and often demoralizing command-and-control management (i.e., top-down decisions with close supervision of employees).[78]

The stakeholder perspective's focus on values also brings ethics and corporate social responsibility into the organizational effectiveness equation. In fact, the stakeholder perspective emerged out of earlier writing on ethics and corporate social responsibility. **Ethics** refers to the study of moral principles or values that determine whether actions are right or wrong and outcomes are good or bad. We rely on our ethical values to determine "the right thing to do." Ethical behavior is driven by the moral principles we use to make decisions. These moral principles represent fundamental values. According to one global survey, almost 80 percent of MBA students believe a well-run company operates according to its values and code of ethics.[80] Chapter 2 provides more detail about ethical principles and related influences on moral reasoning.

Corporate social responsibility (CSR) consists of organizational activities intended to benefit society and the environment beyond the firm's immediate financial interests or legal obligations.[81] It is the view that companies have a contract

Guided by Values at **Zappos**

Zappos is a values-driven organization. The online shoe retailer's 10 core values guide employee behavior so everyone interacts effectively with stakeholders without command-and-control management. "Ideally, we want all 10 values to be reflected in everything we do, including how we interact with each other, how we interact with our customers, and how we interact with our vendors and business partners," explains Zappos CEO Tony Hsieh.[79]

with society, in which they must serve stakeholders beyond shareholders and customers. In some situations, the interests of the firm's shareholders should be secondary to those of other stakeholders.[82] As part of CSR, many companies have adopted the triple-bottom-line philosophy: They try to support or "earn positive returns" in the economic, social, and environmental spheres of sustainability. Firms that adopt the triple bottom line aim to survive and be profitable in the marketplace (economic), but they also intend to maintain or improve conditions for society (social) as well as the physical environment.[84] Companies are particularly eager to become "greener," that is, to minimize any negative effect they have on the physical environment. This activity ranges from reducing and recycling waste in the production process to using goats to mow the lawn (which is one of the many environmental initiatives at Google).

Not everyone agrees that organizations need to cater to a wide variety of stakeholders. Many years ago, economist Milton Friedman pronounced that "there is one and only one social responsibility of business—to use its resources and engage in activities designed to increase its profits."[85] Friedman is highly respected for developing economic theory, but few writers take this extreme view today. Instead, the emerging evidence is that companies with a positive CSR reputation tend to have better financial performance, more loyal employees (stronger organizational identification), and better relations with customers, job applicants, and other stakeholders.[86]

Connecting the Dots: An Integrative Model of Organizational Behavior

Open systems, organizational learning, high-performance work practices, and stakeholders represent the four perspectives of organizational effectiveness. This is the ultimate dependent variable in organizational behavior, so all other OB variables have a direct or indirect effect on overall effectiveness. This relationship between organizational effectiveness and other OB variables is shown in Exhibit 1.6. This diagram is an integrating road map for the field of organizational behavior, and for the structure of this book. You might think of it as a meta-model, because Exhibit 1.6 highlights many concepts, each of which has its own explanatory models. For instance, you will learn about models of employee motivation in Chapter 5 and models of leadership in Chapter 11. Exhibit 1.6 gives you a bird's eye view of the book and its various topics, to see how they fit together.

As Exhibit 1.6 illustrates, individual inputs and processes influence individual outcomes, which in turn have a direct effect on the organization's effectiveness. For example, how well organizations transform inputs to outputs and satisfy key stakeholders is dependent on how well employees perform their jobs and make logical and creative decisions. Individual inputs, processes, and outcomes are identified in the two left-side boxes of our integrating OB model and are the center of attention in Part 2 of this book. After introducing a model of individual behavior and results, we will learn about personality and values—two of the most important individual characteristics—and later examine various individual processes, such as self-concept, perceptions, emotions, attitudes, motivation, and self-leadership.

Part 3 of this book directs our attention to team and interpersonal inputs, processes, and outcomes. These topics are found in the two boxes on the right side of Exhibit 1.6. The chapter on team dynamics (Chapter 7) offers an integrative model for that specific topic, which shows how team inputs (i.e., team composition, size, and other team characteristics) influence team processes (team development, cohesion, and others), which then affect team performance and other outcomes. Later chapters in Part 3 examine specific interpersonal and team processes listed in Exhibit 1.6, including communication, power and influence, conflict, and leadership.

Notice in Exhibit 1.6 that team processes and outcomes affect individual processes and outcomes. For instance, an employee's personal well-being is partly affected by the mutual support he or she receives from team members and other coworkers. The opposite is also true; individual processes affect team and interpersonal dynamics in organizations. For example, we will learn that self-concept among individual team members influences the team's cohesion.

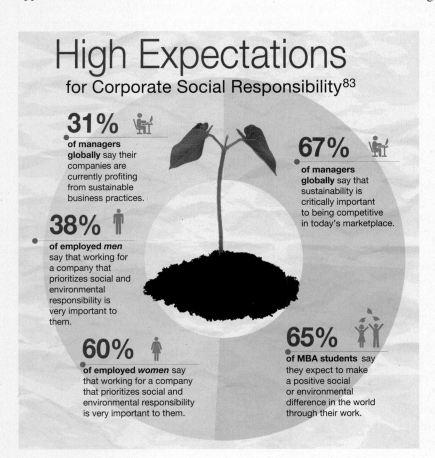

High Expectations
for Corporate Social Responsibility[83]

31%
of managers globally say their companies are currently profiting from sustainable business practices.

38%
of employed men say that working for a company that prioritizes social and environmental responsibility is very important to them.

60%
of employed women say that working for a company that prioritizes social and environmental responsibility is very important to them.

67%
of managers globally say that sustainability is critically important to being competitive in today's marketplace.

65%
of MBA students say they expect to make a positive social or environmental difference in the world through their work.

Exhibit 1.6 An Integrative Model of Organizational Behavior

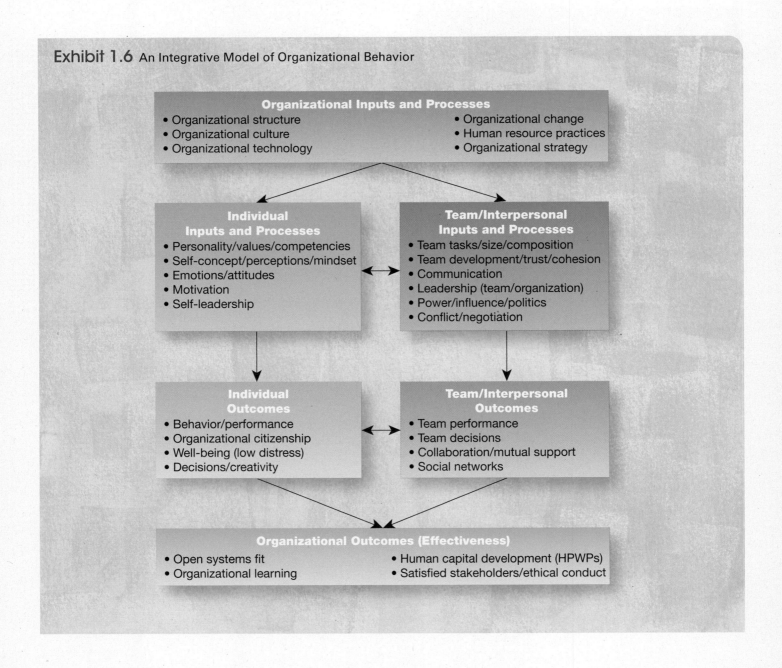

The top area of Exhibit 1.6 highlights the macro-level influence of organizational inputs and processes on both teams and individuals. These organizational-level variables are mainly discussed in Part 4, including organizational structure, organizational culture, and organizational change. However, we will also refer to human resource practices, information systems, and additional organizational-level variables throughout this book where they have a known effect on individual, interpersonal, and team dynamics.

THE JOURNEY BEGINS

This chapter gives you some background about the field of organizational behavior. But it's only the beginning of our journey. Throughout this book, we will challenge you to learn new ways of thinking about how people work in and around organizations. We begin this process in Chapter 2 by presenting a basic model of individual behavior, then introducing over the next few chapters various stable and mercurial characteristics of individuals that relate to elements of the individual behavior model. Next, this book moves to the team level of analysis. We examine a model of team effectiveness and specific features of high-performance teams. We also look at decision making and creativity, communication, power and influence, conflict, and leadership. Finally, we shift our focus to the organizational level of analysis, where the topics of organizational structure, organizational culture, and organizational change are examined in detail.

Study Checklist

- Did you tear out the perforated student review card at the back of the text to revisit learning objectives and key terms and definitions?

Connect® Management is available for *M Organizational Behavior*. Additional resources include:

- Interactive Applications:
  - **Case Analysis:** Apply concepts within the context of a real-world situation.
  - **Drag and Drop:** Work through an interactive example to test your knowledge of the concepts.
  - **Video Case:** See management in action through interactive videos.

- **SmartBook™**—SmartBook is the first and only adaptive reading experience available today. Distinguishing what you know from what you don't, and honing in on concepts you are most likely to forget, SmartBook personalizes content for you in a continuously adapting reading experience. Reading is no longer a passive and linear experience, but an engaging and dynamic one where you are more likely to master and retain important concepts and go to class better prepared.

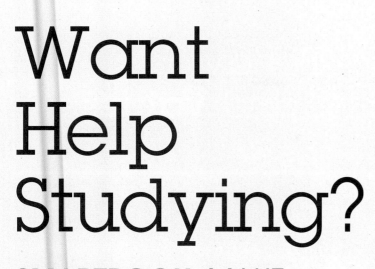

Want Help Studying?

SMARTBOOK: MAKE
EACH MINUTE COUNT.

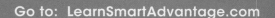

2 chapter

Individual Behavior, Personality, and **Values**

Learning Objectives

After studying this chapter, you should be able to:

LO2-1 Describe the four factors that directly influence individual behavior and performance.

LO2-2 Summarize the five types of individual behavior in organizations.

LO2-3 Describe personality and discuss how the "Big Five" personality dimensions and four MBTI types relate to individual behavior in organizations.

LO2-4 Summarize Schwartz's model of individual values and discuss the conditions where values influence behavior.

LO2-5 Describe three ethical principles and discuss three factors that influence ethical behavior.

LO2-6 Describe five values commonly studied across cultures.

Employees with average job performance don't stay very long at Netflix. The Silicon Valley leader of online video streaming has a high-performance culture that hires the best employees and quickly dismisses those who are mediocre. "At most companies, average performers get an average raise," says Netflix CEO Reed Hastings. "At Netflix, they get a generous severance package." The company decided long ago that employees work more productively when their coworkers are top performers. "The best thing you can do for employees—a perk better than foosball or free sushi—is hire only "A" players to work alongside them," explains Patty McCord, who was Netflix chief talent officer for more than a decade.

Netflix doesn't have performance appraisals, concluding that these formal sessions are usually unproductive and stressful. Instead, employees receive ongoing developmental coaching, peer feedback, and measurable indicators of their performance. "We do try to measure people by how much, how quickly, and how well they get work done," says Netflix's corporate culture document. The company hires people who are self-motivated, and gives them plenty of freedom to do their jobs. Netflix also believes in the importance of ensuring that each employee's personal values are aligned with the company's culture. "You question actions inconsistent with our values," advises Netflix's corporate culture document.[1]

This brief description about individual behavior and performance at Netflix highlights several topics that we discuss in this chapter. First, it refers to some of the four direct drivers of individual behavior and performance, such as employee abilities and motivation. It also refers to joining the organization, performing the job, and other types of individual behavior that represent the individual-level dependent variables found in most organizational behavior research. Netflix also relies on personal values, which (along with personality) is one of the two relatively stable characteristics of individuals that we discuss later in this chapter. Finally, this chapter presents the topics of ethical and cross-cultural values.

LO2-1 Describe the four factors that directly influence individual behavior and performance.

MARS MODEL OF INDIVIDUAL BEHAVIOR AND PERFORMANCE

For most of the past century, experts have investigated the direct predictors of individual behavior and performance.[2] One of the earliest formulas was *performance = person × situation*, where *person* includes individual characteristics and *situation* represents external influences on the individual's behavior. Another frequently mentioned formula is *performance = ability × motivation*.[3] Sometimes known as the "skill-and-will" model, this formula elaborates two specific characteristics within the person that influence individual performance. Ability, motivation, and situation are by far the most commonly mentioned direct predictors of individual behavior and performance, but in the 1960s researchers identified a fourth key factor: role perceptions (the individual's expected role obligations).[4]

Exhibit 2.1 illustrates these four variables—motivation, ability, role perceptions, and situational factors—which are represented by the acronym *MARS*.[5] All four factors are critical influences on an individual's voluntary behavior and performance; if any one of them is low in a given situation, the employee would perform the task poorly. For example, motivated salespeople with clear role perceptions and sufficient resources (situational factors) will not perform their jobs as well if they lack sales skills and related knowledge (ability). Motivation, ability, and role perceptions are clustered together in the model because they are located within the person. Situational factors are external to the individual but still affect his or her behavior and performance.[6] The four MARS variables are the direct predictors of employee performance, customer service, coworker collegiality, ethical behavior, and all other forms of voluntary behavior in the workplace. Let's look in more detail at each of the four factors in the MARS model.

Employee Motivation

Motivation represents the forces within a person that affect his or her direction, intensity, and persistence of voluntary behavior.[7] *Direction* refers to the path along which people steer their effort. People have choices about where they put their effort; they have a sense of what they are trying to achieve and at what level of quality, quantity, and so forth. In other words, motivation is

motivation the forces within a person that affect his or her direction, intensity, and persistence of voluntary behavior

ability the natural aptitudes and learned capabilities required to successfully complete a task

goal-directed, not random. People are motivated to arrive at work on time, finish a project a few hours early, or aim for many other targets. The second element of motivation, called *intensity,* is the amount of effort allocated to the goal. Intensity is all about how much people push themselves to complete a task. For example, two employees might be motivated to finish their project a few hours early (direction), but only one of them puts forth enough effort (intensity) to achieve this goal.

Finally, motivation involves varying levels of *persistence,* that is, continuing the effort for a certain amount of time. Employees sustain their effort until they reach their goal or give up beforehand. To help remember these three elements of motivation, consider the metaphor of driving a car in which the thrust of the engine is your effort. Direction refers to where you steer the car, intensity is how much you put your foot down on the gas pedal, and persistence is for how long you drive toward your destination. Remember that motivation is a force that exists within individuals; it is not

their actual behavior. Thus, direction, intensity, and persistence are cognitive (thoughts) and emotional conditions that directly cause us to move.

Ability

Employee abilities also make a difference in behavior and task performance. **Ability** includes both the natural aptitudes and the learned capabilities required to successfully complete a task. *Aptitudes* are the natural talents that help employees learn specific tasks more quickly and perform them better. There are many physical and mental aptitudes, and our ability to acquire skills is affected by these aptitudes. For example, finger dexterity is an aptitude by which individuals learn more quickly and potentially achieve higher performance at picking up and handling small objects with their fingers. Employees with high finger dexterity are not necessarily better than others at first; rather, their learning tends to be faster and performance potential tends to be higher. *Learned capabilities* are the skills and knowledge that you currently possess. These capabilities include the physical and mental skills and knowledge you have acquired. Learned capabilities tend to wane over time when not in use. Aptitudes and learned capabilities (skills and knowledge) are the

> "I believe the real difference between success and failure in a corporation can be very often traced to the question of how well the organization brings out the great energies and talents of its people."[8]
>
> **—Thomas J. Watson Jr.,** IBM's second CEO

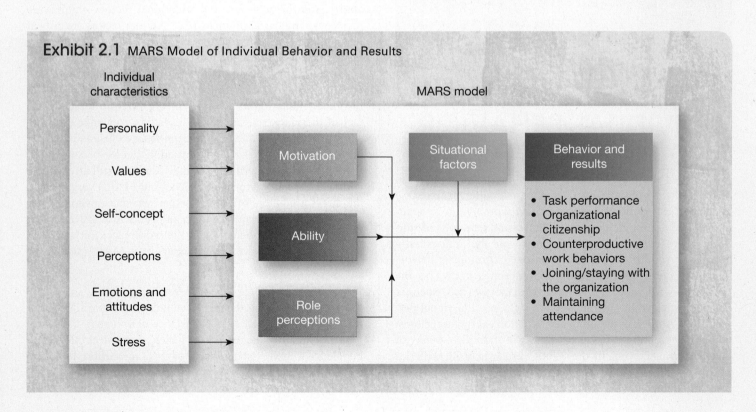

Exhibit 2.1 MARS Model of Individual Behavior and Results

Individual characteristics

- Personality
- Values
- Self-concept
- Perceptions
- Emotions and attitudes
- Stress

MARS model

- Motivation
- Ability
- Role perceptions

Situational factors

Behavior and results

- Task performance
- Organizational citizenship
- Counterproductive work behaviors
- Joining/staying with the organization
- Maintaining attendance

task might be simplified—some aspects of the work are transferred to others—so that a new employee performs only tasks that he or she is currently able to perform. As the employee becomes more competent at these tasks, other tasks are added back into the job.

Role Perceptions

Motivation and ability are important influences on individual behavior and performance, but employees also require accurate **role perceptions** to perform their jobs well. Role perceptions refer to how clearly people understand the job duties (roles) assigned to or expected of them. These perceptions range from role clarity to role ambiguity. A recent global survey suggests that most employees lack role clarity. Asked what would most improve their performance, employees identified "greater clarity about what the organization needs from me" as the first or second most important factor.[11]

Role clarity exists in three forms. First, employees have clear role perceptions when they understand the specific duties or consequences for which they are accountable. This may seem obvious, but employees are occasionally evaluated on job duties they were never told were within their zone of responsibility. Second, role clarity exists when employees understand the priority of their various tasks and performance expectations. This is illustrated in the classic dilemma of prioritizing quantity versus quality, such as how many customers to serve in an hour (quantity) versus how well the employee should serve each customer (quality). Role perception as

main elements of a broader concept called *competencies*, which are characteristics of a person that result in superior performance.[9] Some experts include personality and values as competencies, whereas others describe competencies as action-oriented results, such as serving customers and providing creative ideas.

The challenge is to match a person's abilities with the job's requirements because a good match tends to increase employee performance and well-being. One matching strategy is to select applicants who already demonstrate the required competencies. For example, companies ask applicants to perform work samples, provide references for checking their past performance, and complete various selection tests. A second strategy is to train employees who lack specific knowledge or skills needed for the job.[10] The third person–job matching strategy is to redesign the job so that employees are given tasks only within their current abilities. For example, a complex

Mind the MARS Gap
on Ability, Role Perceptions, and Situational Factors[12]

56%
of employed Americans **agree** or strongly agree that within the past year their employer gave them the opportunity to develop.

28%
of employed Americans **say** they're given a clear understanding of how their job performance impacts their employer's business results.

34%
of employed Americans **say** the feedback they receive helps them to improve their performance and succeed in their role.

23%
of employed Americans **say** they're provided with tools, resources, and/or a development plan to help them improve their performance.

prioritization also exists in the allocation of time and resources to various tasks, such as how much time you should coach employees each week versus meet with suppliers and clients. Third, role clarity is about understanding the preferred behaviors or procedures for accomplishing the assigned tasks. These are situations in which there are two or more ways to perform a task and the employee knows which approach is preferred by the company.

Role perceptions are important because they represent how well employees know where to direct their effort. Employees with role clarity perform work more accurately and efficiently, whereas those with role ambiguity waste considerable time and energy by performing the wrong tasks or in the wrong way. Furthermore, role clarity is essential for coordination with coworkers and other stakeholders. For instance, performers at Cirque du Soleil depend on one another to perform precise behaviors at exact times, such as catching each other in midair. Role clarity ensures that these expectations are met and the performances are executed safely. Finally, role clarity motivates employees because they have a higher belief that their effort will produce the expected outcomes. In other words, people are more confident exerting the required effort when they know what is expected of them.

Situational Factors

Individual behavior and performance also depend on the situation.[13] This refers to conditions beyond the employee's immediate control that constrain or facilitate behavior and performance.[14] For example, employees who are motivated, skilled, and know their role obligations will nevertheless perform poorly if they lack time, budget, physical work facilities, and other situational conditions. Situational factors also refer to

environmental cues that guide employee behavior.[15] Workplaces are safer, for example, when hazards are clearly identified. The hazard is a situational factor in employee safety, but so are the barriers and warning signs that cue employees to avoid that hazard.

LO2-2 Summarize the five types of individual behavior in organizations.

TYPES OF INDIVIDUAL BEHAVIOR

The four elements of the MARS model—motivation, ability, role perceptions, and situational factors—affect all voluntary workplace behaviors and performance. There are many varieties of individual behavior, but most can be organized into the five categories described over the next few pages: task performance, organizational citizenship, counterproductive work behaviors, joining and staying with the organization, and maintaining work attendance (Exhibit 2.2).

Task Performance

Task performance refers to goal-directed behaviors under the individual's control that support organizational objectives.[16] Most jobs require incumbents to complete several tasks. For example, foreign exchange traders at Morgan Stanley must be able to identify and execute profitable trades, work cooperatively with clients and coworkers, assist in training new staff, and work on special telecommunications equipment without error. These tasks involve various degrees of working with people, data, things, and ideas.[17] Foreign exchange traders almost continuously work with data, such as performing technical analysis of trends; they coordinate and share information with coworkers and clients throughout the day (people); and they frequently interpret and synthesize information from charts, news, and other sources (ideas). Foreign exchange traders spend little time interacting with things (e.g., manufacturing, designing, arranging) other than incidentally working with equipment.

When discussing task performance, we mainly think about performing the work efficiently and accurately. However, this *proficiency* is only one form of goal-directed behavior to support organizational objectives. A second form of behavior

Exhibit 2.2   Five Types of Individual Behavior in the Workplace

- Maintaining attendance
- Task performance
- Organizational citizenship
- Counter-productive behaviors
- Joining/staying with the organization

Types of Individual Behavior

is *adaptability*, which refers to how well the employee responds to, copes with, and supports new circumstances and work patterns. A third form of task-related behavior is *proactivity*, which refers to how well the employee anticipates environmental changes and initiates new work patterns that are aligned with those changes.[18]

Organizational Citizenship

Employee behavior extends beyond performing specific tasks. It also includes various forms of cooperation and helpfulness to others that support the organization's social and psychological context.[19] These activities are called **organizational citizenship behaviors (OCBs)**. Some OCBs are directed toward individuals, such as assisting coworkers with their work problems, adjusting your work schedules to accommodate coworkers, showing genuine courtesy toward coworkers, and sharing your work resources (supplies, technology, staff) with coworkers. Other OCBs represent cooperation and helpfulness toward the organization, such as supporting the company's public image, taking discretionary action to help the organization avoid potential problems, offering ideas beyond those required for your own job, attending voluntary functions that support the organization, and keeping up with new developments in the organization.[20]

Some experts define OCBs as discretionary behaviors (employees don't have to perform them) based on the notion that they are outside the employee's job duties. Yet, contrary to this view, research has found that many employees believe it is part of their job to engage in some OCBs. Furthermore, companies sometimes (if not always) advise employees that helping coworkers, supporting the company's public image, and engaging in other OCBs are a condition of employment.[21] Indeed, there are many cases of employees losing their jobs because they failed to engage in some of these OCBs. Therefore, OCBs are best described as behaviors that support the organization's social and psychological context through cooperation and helpfulness to others. Some of these behaviors might be discretionary behaviors, but many are work requirements.

OCBs can have a significant effect on individual, team, and organizational effectiveness. Employees who engage in more individual-directed OCBs tend to have higher task performance because they receive more support from coworkers. OCBs also increase team performance where members depend on one another.[22] However, engaging in OCBs can also have negative consequences.[23] Employees who perform more OCBs tend to have higher work–family conflict. Also, performing OCBs takes time and energy away from performing tasks, so employees who give more attention to OCBs risk lower career success in companies that reward task performance.

Counterproductive Work Behaviors

Organizational behavior is interested in all workplace behaviors, including dysfunctional activities collectively known as **counterproductive work behaviors (CWBs)**. CWBs are voluntary behaviors that have the potential to directly or indirectly harm the organization.[24] Some of the many types of CWBs include harassing coworkers, creating unnecessary conflict, deviating from preferred work methods (e.g., shortcuts that risk work quality), being untruthful, stealing, sabotaging work, avoiding work obligation (tardiness), and wasting resources. CWBs are not minor concerns; research suggests that they can substantially undermine the organization's effectiveness.

Joining and Staying with the Organization

Organizations are people working together toward common goals, so hiring and retaining talent is another critical set of behaviors.[25] Although a weak economy has increased the pool of job applicants and reduced employee turnover, employers still face challenges finding qualified applicants for specific job groups. One recent large-scale survey reported that 39 percent

organizational citizenship behaviors (OCBs) various forms of cooperation and helpfulness to others that support the organization's social and psychological context

counterproductive work behaviors (CWBs) voluntary behaviors that have the potential to directly or indirectly harm the organization

of American employers have difficulty filling jobs because applicants lack the necessary skills or knowledge. Skilled trades and sales representatives top the list of jobs with skill shortages. In another poll, 46 percent of executives in large American businesses are concerned their company won't have the skills required within the next one or two years.[26]

Even when companies are able to hire qualified staff in the face of shortages, they need to ensure that these employees stay with the company. Companies with high turnover suffer because of the high cost of replacing people who leave. More important, as was mentioned in the previous chapter, much of an organization's intellectual capital is the knowledge carried around in employees' heads. When people leave, some of this vital knowledge is lost, often resulting in lower productivity, poorer customer service, and so forth.

Maintaining Work Attendance

Along with attracting and retaining employees, organizations need everyone to show up for work at scheduled times. American employees are absent from scheduled work an average of only five days per year, but even low absenteeism can disrupt the work flow of other employees and undermine customer service. Why are employees absent or late for work?[28] Employees often point to situational factors, such as bad weather, transit strikes, personal illness, and family demands (e.g., sick children). These are usually important factors, but some people still show up for work because of their strong motivation to attend, whereas others take sick leave at the slightest sign of bad weather or illness.

Employees who experience job dissatisfaction, workplace incivility, or work-related stress are more likely to be absent or late for work because taking time off is a way of temporarily withdrawing from those difficult conditions. Absenteeism is also higher in organizations with generous sick leave because this benefit minimizes the financial loss of taking time away from work. Other factors in absenteeism are the person's values and personality. Finally, studies report that absenteeism is higher in teams with strong absence norms, meaning that team members tolerate and even expect coworkers to take time off.

Poor work attendance is an ongoing concern, but employers should also minimize presenteeism. Presenteeism is the situation whereby employees show up for work when their capacity to work is significantly diminished by illness, fatigue, personal problems, or other factors.[29] People who attend work when they are unwell or unfit may worsen their own health condition and increase health and safety risks of coworkers. Also, these employees tend to be less productive and may reduce the productivity of coworkers. Presenteeism occurs when employees lack job security, have many people dependent on their job performance, and have personality traits that motivate them to show up for work when others would gladly recover at home.[30] Personality is a widely cited predictor of most forms of individual behavior. It is also the most stable personal characteristic, so we introduce this topic next.

LO2-3 Describe personality and discuss how the "Big Five" personality dimensions and four MBTI types relate to individual behavior in organizations.

PERSONALITY IN ORGANIZATIONS

Personality is the relatively enduring pattern of thoughts, emotions, and behaviors that characterize a person, along with the psychological processes behind those characteristics.[31] It is, in essence, the bundle of characteristics that make us similar to or different from other people. We estimate an individual's personality by what they say and do, and we infer the person's internal states—including thoughts and emotions—from these observable behaviors.

People typically exhibit a wide range of behaviors, yet within that variety are discernible patterns that we refer to as *personality traits*.[32] Traits are broad concepts that allow us to label and understand individual differences. For example, you probably have some friends who are more talkative than others. You might know some people who like to take risks and others who are risk-averse. Each trait implies that there is something within the person, rather than environmental influences alone, that predicts this behavioral tendency. In fact, studies report that an individual's personality traits measured in childhood predict various behaviors and outcomes in adulthood, including educational attainment, employment success, marital relationships, illegal activities, and health-risk behaviors.[33]

Although people have behavior tendencies, they do not act the same way in all situations. Such consistency would be considered abnormal because it indicates a person's insensitivity to social norms, reward systems, and other external conditions.[35] People vary their behavior to suit the situation, even if the behavior is at odds with their personality. For example, talkative people remain relatively quiet in a library where "no talking" rules are explicit and strictly enforced. However, personality differences are still apparent in these situations because talkative people tend to do more talking in libraries relative to how much other people talk in libraries.

personality the relatively enduring pattern of thoughts, emotions, and behaviors that characterize a person, along with the psychological processes behind those characteristics

five-factor model (FFM) the five broad dimensions representing most personality traits: conscientiousness, emotional stability, openness to experience, agreeableness, and extraversion

conscientiousness a personality dimension describing people who are organized, dependable, goal-focused, thorough, disciplined, methodical, and industrious

manages goal-directed behavior—tries to keep our behavior consistent with our self-concept.[38] As self-concept becomes clearer and more stable with age, behavior and personality therefore also become more stable and consistent. We discuss self-concept in more detail in Chapter 3. The main point here is that personality is not completely determined by heredity;

> "One regrets the loss even of one's worst habits. . . . They are such an essential part of one's personality."[34]
>
> —**Oscar Wilde,** author (from *The Picture of Dorian Gray*)

Personality Determinants: Nature versus Nurture

Most experts now agree that personality is shaped by both nature and nurture, although the relative importance of each continues to be debated and studied. *Nature* refers to our genetic or hereditary origins—the genes that we inherit from our parents. Studies of identical twins, particularly those separated at birth, reveal that heredity has a very large effect on personality; up to 50 percent of variation in behavior and 30 percent of temperament preferences can be attributed to a person's genetic characteristics.[36] In other words, genetic code not only determines our eye color, skin tone, and physical shape; it also significantly affects our attitudes, decisions, and behavior.

Our personality is also affected by *nurture*—our socialization, life experiences, and other forms of interaction with the environment. Personality develops and changes mainly when people are young; it stabilizes by about 30 years of age, although some experts say personality development continues to occur through age 50.[37] The main explanation of why personality becomes more stable over time is that we form a clearer and more rigid self-concept as we get older. This increasing clarity of "who we are" serves as an anchor for our behavior because the executive function—the part of the brain that

life experiences, particularly early in life, also shape each individual's personality traits.

Five-Factor Model of Personality

Sociable, anxious, curious, dependable, suspicious, talkative, adventurous, and hundreds of other personality traits have been described over the years, so experts have tried to organize them into smaller clusters. The most researched and respected clustering of personality traits is the **five-factor model (FFM)**.[39] Several decades ago, personality experts identified more than 17,000 words that describe an individual's personality. These words were distilled down to five broad personality dimensions, each with a cluster of specific traits. Similar results were found in studies of different languages, suggesting that the five-factor model is fairly robust across cultures. These "Big Five" dimensions, represented by the handy acronym *CANOE*, are outlined in Exhibit 2.3 and described as follows:

- *Conscientiousness.* **Conscientiousness** characterizes people who are organized, dependable, goal-focused, thorough, disciplined, methodical, and industrious. People with low conscientiousness tend to be careless, disorganized, and less thorough.

- *Agreeableness*. This dimension includes the traits of being trusting, helpful, good-natured, considerate, tolerant, selfless, generous, and flexible. People with low agreeableness tend to be uncooperative and intolerant of others' needs as well as more suspicious and self-focused.

- *Neuroticism*. **Neuroticism** characterizes people who tend to be anxious, insecure, self-conscious, depressed, and temperamental. In contrast, people with low neuroticism (high emotional stability) are poised, secure, and calm.

- *Openness to experience*. This dimension is the most complex and has the least agreement among scholars. It generally refers to the extent to which people are imaginative, creative, unconventional, curious, nonconforming, autonomous, and aesthetically perceptive. Those who score low on this dimension tend to be more resistant to change, less open to new ideas, and more conventional and fixed in their ways.

- *Extraversion*. **Extraversion** characterizes people who are outgoing, talkative, energetic, sociable, and assertive. The opposite is *introversion,* which characterizes those who are quiet, cautious, and less interactive with others. Extraverts get their energy from the outer world (people and things around them), whereas introverts get their energy from the internal world, such as personal reflection on concepts and ideas. Introverts do not necessarily lack social skills. Rather, they are more inclined to direct their interests to ideas than to social events. Introverts feel quite comfortable being alone, whereas extraverts do not.

> Conscientiousness and emotional stability (low neuroticism) stand out as the best personality predictors of individual performance for most job groups.

Personality traits are fairly good at predicting a number of workplace behaviors and outcomes, particularly when we strip away the effects of employee ability and other factors. Conscientiousness and emotional stability (low neuroticism) stand out as the best personality predictors of individual performance for most job groups.[40] Various studies have reported that conscientious employees set higher personal goals for themselves, are more motivated, and have higher performance expectations compared to employees with low levels of conscientiousness. They also tend to have higher levels of organizational citizenship and work better in organizations that give employees more freedom than is found in traditional command-and-control workplaces. People with higher emotional stability have a more positive (can-do) belief system and are better at directing their energy toward the task at hand.[41]

The other three personality dimensions predict more specific types of employee behavior and performance.[42] Extraversion is associated with performance in sales and management jobs, where employees must interact with and influence people. Agreeableness is associated with performance in jobs where employees are expected to be cooperative and helpful, such as working in teams, customer relations, and other conflict-handling situations. People high on the openness-to-experience personality dimension tend to be more creative and adaptable to change.

Exhibit 2.3 Five-Factor Model of Personality Dimensions

Personality dimension	People with higher scores on this dimension tend to be more:
Conscientiousness	Organized, dependable, goal-focused, thorough, disciplined, methodical, industrious
Agreeableness	Trusting, helpful, good-natured, considerate, tolerant, selfless, generous, flexible
Neuroticism	Anxious, insecure, self-conscious, depressed, temperamental
Openness to experience	Imaginative, creative, unconventional, curious, nonconforming, autonomous, perceptive
Extraversion	Outgoing, talkative, energetic, sociable, assertive

neuroticism a personality dimension describing people who tend to be anxious, insecure, self-conscious, depressed, and temperamental

extraversion a personality dimension describing people who are outgoing, talkative, sociable, and assertive

Myers-Briggs Type Indicator (MBTI) an instrument designed to measure the elements of Jungian personality theory, particularly preferences regarding perceiving and judging information

Finally, personality influences well-being, including emotional reactions to situations and preferred coping mechanisms.[43] However, remember that the Big Five personality dimensions cluster several specific traits, and each trait's effect varies for different types of performance. Also, the relationship between a personality trait and performance is sometimes (or often) nonlinear. People with very high or very low levels of agreeableness, for example, might be less effective than those with moderate agreeableness.[44]

Jungian Personality Theory and the Myers-Briggs Type Indicator

The five-factor model of personality may have the most research support, but it is not the most popular in practice. That distinction goes to Jungian personality theory, which is measured through the **Myers-Briggs Type Indicator (MBTI)** (see Exhibit 2.4). Nearly a century ago, Swiss psychiatrist Carl Jung proposed that personality is primarily represented by the individual's preferences regarding perceiving and judging information.[45] Jung explained that perceiving, which involves how people prefer to gather information or perceive the world around them, occurs through two competing orientations: *sensing (S)* and *intuition (N)*. Sensing involves perceiving information directly through the five senses; it relies on an organized structure to acquire factual and preferably quantitative details. In contrast, intuition relies more on insight and subjective experience to see relationships among variables. Sensing types focus on the here and now, whereas intuitive types focus more on future possibilities.

Jung also proposed that judging—how people process information or make decisions based on what they have perceived—consists of two competing processes: *thinking (T)* and *feeling (F)*. People with a thinking orientation rely on rational cause–effect logic and systematic data collection to make decisions. Those with a strong feeling orientation, on the other hand, rely on their emotional responses to the options presented, as well as to how those choices affect others. Jung noted that along with differing in the four core processes of sensing, intuition, thinking, and feeling, people also differ in their degrees

of extraversion–introversion, which was introduced earlier as one of the Big Five personality traits.

Along with measuring the personality traits identified by Jung, the MBTI measures Jung's broader categories of *perceiving* and *judging*, which represents a person's attitude toward the external world. People with a perceiving orientation are open, curious, and flexible; prefer to adapt spontaneously to events as they unfold; and prefer to keep their options open. Judging types prefer order and structure and want to resolve problems quickly.

The MBTI is one of the most widely used personality tests in work settings as well as in career counseling and executive coaching.[47] Even so, the MBTI and Jung's psychological types model have received uneven support.[48] On the one hand, MBTI seems to improve self-awareness for career development and

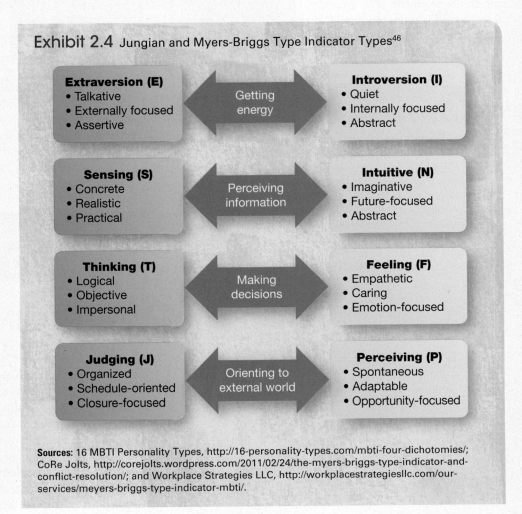

Exhibit 2.4 Jungian and Myers-Briggs Type Indicator Types[46]

Extraversion (E)
- Talkative
- Externally focused
- Assertive

Getting energy

Introversion (I)
- Quiet
- Internally focused
- Abstract

Sensing (S)
- Concrete
- Realistic
- Practical

Perceiving information

Intuitive (N)
- Imaginative
- Future-focused
- Abstract

Thinking (T)
- Logical
- Objective
- Impersonal

Making decisions

Feeling (F)
- Empathetic
- Caring
- Emotion-focused

Judging (J)
- Organized
- Schedule-oriented
- Closure-focused

Orienting to external world

Perceiving (P)
- Spontaneous
- Adaptable
- Opportunity-focused

Sources: 16 MBTI Personality Types, http://16-personality-types.com/mbti-four-dichotomies/; CoRe Jolts, http://corejolts.wordpress.com/2011/02/24/the-myers-briggs-type-indicator-and-conflict-resolution/; and Workplace Strategies LLC, http://workplacestrategiesllc.com/our-services/meyers-briggs-type-indicator-mbti/.

mutual understanding. It also does a reasonably good job of representing Jung's psychological types. On the other hand, the MBTI poorly predicts job performance and is generally not recommended for employment selection or promotion decisions. For example, although one study found that intuitive types are more common in higher level than lower level management, other research has found no relationship between any MBTI types and effective leadership. One recent large-scale study also reported that the MBTI scores of team members are not useful for predicting the team's development. Finally, the MBTI overlaps with four of the five dimensions of the five-factor personality model, yet it does so less satisfactorily than existing Big Five personality measures.[49]

Personality Testing in Organizations

Personality has gained considerable attention in OB research and in the workplace. The MBTI instrument is mostly used for team building and career development. The five-factor model is more commonly found in scholarly research, but it is increasingly used to assess job applicants. The applicant's personality is typically measured using a self-completed paper-and-pencil test. However, a few firms have discovered how to estimate applicants' personalities from their writing on blogs, Facebook pages, and other public sources.

The use of personality testing is illustrated at Amtrak. Soon after Amtrak won the Metrolink commuter service contract in Southern California, it required train engineers and conductors to complete a Big Five personality inventory as a condition of future employment. A horrendous Metrolink accident claiming two dozen lives occurred two years before Amtrak took over because a train engineer ran a red light while distracted by text messaging.[50] As a result, Amtrak apparently prefers train crew members with a "focused introverted" personality, because employees with these traits are not distracted while operating the train or performing repetitive tasks.

Personality testing wasn't always this popular in organizations. Two decades ago, companies avoided personality tests due to concerns that they do not predict job-related behavior and might unfairly discriminate against visible minorities and other identifiable groups. Personality testing slowly regained acceptance as studies reported that specific traits correlated with specific indicators of job performance (as we described earlier). Today, personality testing flourishes to such an extent that some experts warn we may have gone too far in organizational settings.

LO2-4 Summarize Schwartz's model of individual values and discuss the conditions where values influence behavior.

VALUES IN THE WORKPLACE

Colleen Abdoulah developed a strong set of personal values from her parents while she was growing up. In particular, she learned to value equality ("you're no better than anyone and they are no better than you"), to have the courage to do the right thing, and to form relationships with people so they feel a sense of ownership. Abdoulah not only practices these values every day, she has instilled them at Wide Open West, the Denver-based Internet, cable, and phone provider where she served as CEO for several years and is now its chairwoman.

"[Our employees] display the courage to do the right thing, serve each other and our customers with humility, and celebrate our learnings and success with grace," says Abdoulah. "Anyone can set values, but we have operationalized our values so that they affect everything we do every day."[52]

Colleen Abdoulah and other successful people often refer to their personal values and the critical events that formed those values earlier in life. *Values*, a concept that we introduced in Chapter 1, are stable, evaluative beliefs that guide our preferences for outcomes or courses of action in a variety of situations.[53] They are perceptions about what is good or bad, right or wrong. Values tell us to what we "ought" to do. They serve as a moral compass that directs our motivation and, potentially, our decisions and actions.

People arrange values into a hierarchy of preferences, called a *value system*. Some individuals value new challenges more than they value conformity. Others value generosity more than frugality. Each person's unique value system is developed and reinforced through socialization from parents, religious institutions, friends, personal experiences, and the society in which he or she lives. As such, a person's hierarchy of values is stable and long-lasting. For example, one study found that value

are both partly determined by heredity, values are influenced more by socialization whereas personality traits are more innate.

Types of Values

Values come in many forms, and experts on this topic have devoted considerable attention to organizing them into clusters. Several decades ago, social psychologist Milton Rokeach developed two lists of values, distinguishing means (instrumental values) from end goals (terminal values). Although Rokeach's lists are still mentioned in some organizational behavior sources, they were replaced by another model almost two decades ago. The instrumental–terminal values distinction was neither accurate nor useful, and it overlooked values that are now included in the current dominant model.

Today, the dominant model of personal values is the one developed and tested by social psychologist Shalom Schwartz and his colleagues.[56] Schwartz's list of 57 values builds on Rokeach's earlier work but does not distinguish instrumental from terminal values. Instead, research has found that human values are organized into the circular model (circumplex) shown in Exhibit 2.5. This model clusters the 57 specific values into 10 broad values categories: universalism, benevolence,

> ## Values serve as a moral compass that directs our motivation and, potentially, our decisions and actions.

systems of a sample of adolescents were remarkably similar 20 years later when they were adults.[54]

Notice that our description of values has focused on individuals, whereas executives often describe values as though they belong to the organization. In reality, values exist only within individuals—we call them *personal values*. However, groups of people might hold the same or similar values, so we tend to ascribe these *shared values* to the team, department, organization, profession, or entire society. The values shared by people throughout an organization *(organizational values)* receive fuller discussion in Chapter 13 because they are a key part of corporate culture. The values shared across a society *(cultural values)* receive attention later in this chapter.

Values and personality traits are related to each other, but the two concepts differ in a few ways.[55] The most noticeable distinction is that values are evaluative—they tell us what we *ought* to do—whereas personality traits describe what we naturally *tend* to do. A second distinction is that personality traits have minimal conflict with each other (e.g., you can have high agreeableness and high introversion), whereas some values are opposed to other values. For example, someone who values excitement and challenge would have difficulty also valuing stability and moderation. Third, although personality and values

tradition, conformity, security, power, achievement, hedonism, stimulation, and self-direction. For example, conformity includes four specific values: politeness, honoring parents, self-discipline, and obedience.

These 10 broad values categories are further clustered into four quadrants. One quadrant, called *openness to change*, refers to the extent to which a person is motivated to pursue innovative ways. This quadrant includes the value categories of self-direction (creativity, independent thought), stimulation (excitement and challenge), and hedonism (pursuit of pleasure, enjoyment, gratification of desires). The opposing quadrant is *conservation*, which is the extent to which a person is motivated to preserve the status quo. The conservation quadrant includes the value categories of conformity (adherence to social norms and expectations), security (safety and stability), and tradition (moderation and preservation of the status quo).

The third quadrant in Schwartz's circumplex model, called *self-enhancement*, refers to how much a person is motivated by self-interest. This quadrant includes the value categories of achievement (pursuit of personal success), power (dominance over others), and hedonism (a values category shared with openness to change). The opposite of self-enhancement is *self-transcendence,* which refers to motivation to promote the welfare

Exhibit 2.5 Schwartz's Values Circumplex

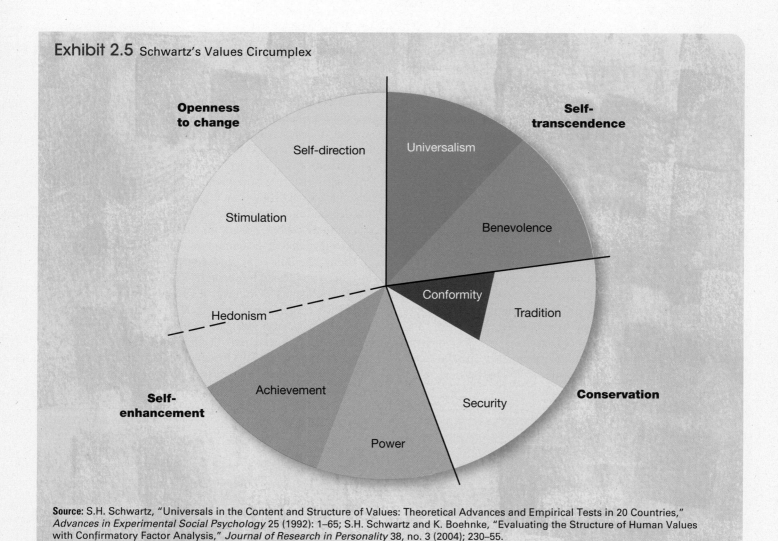

Source: S.H. Schwartz, "Universals in the Content and Structure of Values: Theoretical Advances and Empirical Tests in 20 Countries," *Advances in Experimental Social Psychology* 25 (1992): 1–65; S.H. Schwartz and K. Boehnke, "Evaluating the Structure of Human Values with Confirmatory Factor Analysis," *Journal of Research in Personality* 38, no. 3 (2004); 230–55.

of others and nature. Self-transcendence includes the value categories of benevolence (concern for others in one's life) and universalism (concern for the welfare of all people and nature).

Values and Individual Behavior

Personal values guide our decisions, behavior, and performance to some extent. For instance, one recent study found that achievement values predict a student's performance in college courses, even after controlling for personality traits. Another study reported that achievement, benevolence, and self-direction values are associated with specific forms of organizational citizenship behavior when working in student teams.[57]

Even though our decisions and behavior are guided by personal values to some degree, they deviate from our hierarchy of personal values more than we realize.[58] One reason for this "disconnect" between personal values and individual behavior is the situation. Work environments influence our behavior, at least in the short term, and this situational influence sometimes causes us to act contrary to our personal values. This values-inconsistent behavior may occur without our awareness, until

we later reflect on how coworkers, rewards, and other situational factors veered our behavior away from our core values. But people also knowingly deviate from their personal values because the situational pressures are so strong. For example, employees caught in illegal business dealings frequently blame pressure from management for their unethical activities.

Another reason why decisions and behavior deviate from our personal values is that we don't actively think about them much of the time.[59] Values are abstract concepts, so their relevance is not obvious in many situations. Furthermore, many daily decisions and actions occur routinely, so we don't actively evaluate their consistency with our values. Of course, some situations do make us conscious of our values. For example, you realize how much you value security when deciding whether to agree to perform a risky task. However, many daily events do not trigger values awareness, so we act without their guidance. We literally need to be reminded of our values so they guide our decisions and actions.

The effect of values awareness on behavior was apparent in the following study:[60] Students were given a math test and paid for each correct answer. One group submitted their results to the experimenter for scoring, so they couldn't lie about their results. A second group could lie because they scored the test themselves and told the experimenter their test score. A third group was similar to the second (they scored their own test), but that test included the following statement, and students were required to sign their name to that statement: "I understand that this short survey falls under (the university's) honor system." (The university had no such honor system.) The researchers estimated that some students cheated when they scored their own test without the "honor system" statement, whereas no one given the "honor system" form lied about their results. The message here is that people are more likely to apply their values (honesty, in this case) when they are explicitly reminded of those values and see their relevance to the situation.

Values Congruence

Values tell us what is right or wrong and what we ought to do. This evaluative characteristic affects how comfortable we are with specific organizations and individuals. The key concept here is *values congruence,* which refers to how similar a person's values hierarchy is to the values hierarchy of the organization, a coworker, or another source of comparison. *Person–organization values congruence* occurs when a person's values are similar to the organization's dominant values. This form of values congruence increases (to some extent) the chance that employees will make decisions and act in ways consistent with organizational expectations. It also leads to higher job satisfaction, loyalty, and organizational citizenship as well as lower stress and turnover.[61] "The most difficult but rewarding accomplishment in any career is 'living true' to your values and finding companies where you can contribute at the highest level while being your authentic self," says an executive in the pharmaceutical industry.[62]

Are organizations the most successful when every employee's personal values align with the company's values? Not at all! While a comfortable degree of values congruence is necessary for the reasons just noted, organizations also benefit from some level of incongruence. Employees with diverse values offer different perspectives, which potentially lead to better decision making. Also, too much congruence can create a "corporate cult" that potentially undermines creativity, organizational flexibility, and business ethics.

A second type of values congruence involves how consistent the values apparent in our actions (enacted values) are with what we say we believe in (espoused values). This *espoused–enacted values congruence* is especially important for people in leadership positions because any obvious gap between espoused and enacted values undermines their perceived integrity, a critical feature of effective leaders. One global survey reported that 55 percent of employees believe senior management behaves consistently with the company's core values.[63] Some companies try to maintain high levels of espoused–enacted values congruence by surveying subordinates and peers about whether the manager's decisions and actions are consistent with the company's espoused values.

A third category, *organization–community values congruence,* refers to the similarity of an organization's dominant values with the prevailing values of the community or society in which it conducts business.[64] Global organizations may experience higher employee turnover and difficult community relations if they try to impose their home country's values in other cultures where they do business. Thus, globalization calls for a delicate balancing act: Companies depend on shared values to maintain consistent standards and behaviors, yet they need to operate within the values of different cultures around the world.

LO2-5 Describe three ethical principles and discuss three factors that influence ethical behavior.

ETHICAL VALUES AND BEHAVIOR

When 1,000 CEOs and other top-level executives around the world were recently asked to list the most important attributes of effective leaders, the most frequently mentioned characteristic was *integrity*—the leader's ethical standards. In employee surveys, honesty/ethics is also ranked as one of the most important characteristics of effective corporate leaders.[65] *Ethics* refers to the study of moral principles or values that determine whether actions are right or wrong and outcomes are good or bad (see Chapter 1). People rely on their ethical values to determine "the right thing to do."

Three Ethical Principles

To better understand business ethics, we need to consider three distinct types of ethical principles: utilitarianism, individual rights, and distributive justice.[66] While your personal values might sway you more toward one principle than the others, all

moral intensity
the degree to which an issue demands the application of ethical principles

moral sensitivity
a person's ability to recognize the presence of an ethical issue and determine its relative importance

mindfulness
a person's receptive and impartial attention to and awareness of the present situation as well as to one's own thoughts and emotions in that moment

three should be actively considered to put important ethical issues to the test.

- *Utilitarianism.* This principle advises us to seek the greatest good for the greatest number of people. In other words, we should choose the option that provides the highest degree of satisfaction to those affected. This is sometimes known as a *consequential principle* because it focuses on the consequences of our actions, not on how we achieve those consequences. One problem with utilitarianism is that it is almost impossible to evaluate the benefits or costs of many decisions, particularly when many stakeholders have wide-ranging needs and values. Another problem is that most of us are uncomfortable engaging in behaviors that seem unethical to attain results that are ethical.

- *Individual rights.* This principle reflects the belief that everyone has entitlements that let her or him act in a certain way. Some of the most widely cited rights are freedom of movement, physical security, freedom of speech, fair trial, and freedom from torture. The individual rights principle includes more than legal rights; it also includes human rights that everyone is granted as a moral norm of society. One problem with individual rights is that certain individual rights may conflict with others. The stockholders' right to be informed about corporate activities may ultimately conflict with an executive's right to privacy, for example.

> "It takes many good deeds to build a good reputation and only one bad one to lose it."
>
> —Attributed to Benjamin Franklin

- *Distributive justice.* This principle suggests that people who are similar to each other should receive similar benefits and burdens; those who are dissimilar should receive different benefits and burdens in proportion to their dissimilarity. For example, we expect that two employees who contribute equally in their work should receive similar rewards, whereas those who make a lesser contribution should receive less. A variation of the distributive justice principle says that inequalities are acceptable when they benefit the least well-off in society. Thus, employees in risky jobs should be paid more if their work benefits others who are less well-off. One problem with the distributive justice principle is that it is difficult to agree on who is "similar" and what factors are "relevant." We discuss distributive justice further in Chapter 5.

Moral Intensity, Moral Sensitivity, and Situational Influences

Along with ethical principles and their underlying values, three other factors influence ethical conduct in the workplace: the moral intensity of the issue, the individual's moral sensitivity, and situational influences.[67]

Moral Intensity **Moral intensity** is the degree to which an issue demands the application of ethical principles. Decisions with high moral intensity have more significant ethical outcomes that affect more people, so the decision maker needs to more carefully apply ethical principles to make the best choice. Several factors influence the moral intensity of an issue.[68] Specifically, the moral intensity of a situation is higher where

a. The decision will have substantially good or bad consequences.

b. Most people view the decision outcomes as good or bad (versus diverse public opinion whether those outcomes are considered good or bad).

c. There is a high probability (rather than low probability) that the good or bad decision consequences will occur.

d. Many people will be affected by the decision and its consequences.

Moral Sensitivity **Moral sensitivity** (also called *ethical sensitivity*) is a characteristic of the person, namely his or her ability to detect a moral dilemma and estimate its relative importance. This awareness includes both cognitive (logical thinking) and emotional level awareness that something is or could become morally wrong.[69] People with high moral sensitivity can more quickly and accurately estimate the moral intensity of the issue. This awareness does not necessarily translate into more ethical behavior; it just means they are more likely to know when unethical behavior occurs.

Several factors are associated with a person's moral sensitivity.[70] Empathy is a key influence because it involves being

sensitive to the needs of others and, consequently, makes us more aware of ethical dilemmas involving others. On average, women have higher moral sensitivity compared to men, possibly because women tend to have higher empathy. Another factor is expertise or knowledge of prescriptive norms and rules. For example, accountants would be more morally sensitive regarding the appropriateness of specific accounting procedures than would someone who is not trained in this profession. A third influence on moral sensitivity is direct experience with moral dilemmas. These experiences likely generate internal cues that trigger awareness of future ethical dilemmas with similar characteristics.

A fourth predictor of moral sensitivity is the person's **mindfulness**.[71] Mindfulness refers to a person's receptive and impartial attention to and awareness of the present situation as well as to one's own thoughts and emotions in that moment. Mindfulness increases moral sensitivity because it involves actively monitoring the environment as well as being sensitive to our responses to that environment. This vigilance requires effort as well as skill to receptively evaluate our thoughts and emotions.

Unfortunately, we have a natural tendency to minimize effort, which leads to less mindfulness. For instance, research indicates that we have lower moral sensitivity when observing an organization, team, or individual assumed to have high ethical standards.[72] We assume the source is unlikely to engage in any misconduct, so we switch from mindfulness to automatic pilot. If unusual activity is detected, we are less likely to interpret that event as unethical. One of the most serious cases of accounting fraud in North America occurred because the company's chief financial officer was highly respected in the industry. He had recently been awarded the chief financial officer of the year award, so employees took longer to realize that he was engaging in fraudulent activities. Even when some of his practices seemed suspicious, accounting staff initially assumed the chief financial officer was introducing innovative—and legal—accounting procedures.[73]

Situational Factors A final reason why good people engage in unethical decisions and behavior is the situation in which the conduct occurs. Employees say they regularly experience pressure from top management that motivates them to lie to customers, breach regulations, or otherwise act unethically. Almost half of employees in one survey said they encounter situations that invite misconduct; about one-quarter of American employees said their workplace actually promotes "shoddy ethics." In

another recent study, 22 percent of Canadians agreed with the statement "I feel that I have to compromise my own personal ethics or values to keep my job."[74] Situational factors do not justify unethical conduct. Rather, we need to be aware of these factors so that organizations can reduce their influence in the future.

Observing Ethical Misconduct and Feeling Pressure to Compromise Ethical Standards[75]

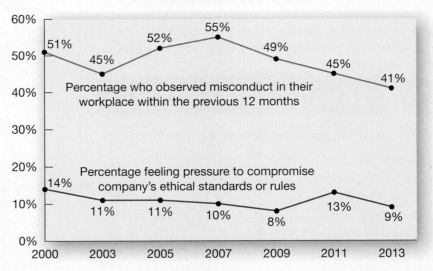

Percentage of American employees surveyed from 2000 to 2013 (N = 4,035 in the 2013 sample) who observed misconduct in their workplace within the previous 12 months and percentage who say they are feeling pressure to compromise their company's ethical standards or rules.

Supporting Ethical Behavior

Most large and medium-sized organizations in the United States and other developed countries introduce various practices to improve ethical conduct. One of the most basic steps in this direction is a code of ethical conduct—a statement about desired practices, rules of conduct, and philosophy about the organization's relationship to its stakeholders and the environment.[76] Almost all *Fortune* 500 companies in the United States and the majority of the 500 largest companies in the United Kingdom have ethics codes. These codes are supposed to motivate and guide employee behavior, signal the importance of ethical conduct, and build the firm's trustworthiness to stakeholders. However, critics suggest that they do little to reduce unethical conduct.

Another strategy to improve ethical conduct is to train and regularly evaluate employees about their knowledge of proper ethical conduct. Many large firms have annual quizzes to test employee awareness of company rules and practices on important ethical issues such as giving gifts and receiving sensitive information about competitors or governments. In some firms, employees participate in elaborate games that present increasingly challenging and complex moral dilemmas. Along with ethics codes, training programs, and ongoing ethics testing, many companies offer an ethics telephone hotline and website, typically operated by an independent organization, where employees can anonymously report suspicious behavior. A few very large businesses also employ ombudspersons who receive information confidentially from employees and proactively investigate possible wrongdoing. Ethics audits are also conducted in some organizations but are more common for evaluation of corporate social responsibility practices.[77]

Training, hotlines, audits, and related activities improve ethical conduct to some extent, but the most powerful foundation is a set of shared values that reinforces ethical conduct. As we describe in Chapter 13 (organizational culture), an ethical culture is supported by the conduct and vigilance of corporate leaders. By acting with the highest moral standards, leaders not only gain support and trust from followers; they role-model the ethical standards that employees are more likely to follow.[79]

LO2-6 Describe five values commonly studied across cultures.

VALUES ACROSS CULTURES

As the only Westerner in a 50-employee winery in China, Emilie Bourgois noticed that Chinese managers seemed to be more sensitive than European or American bosses about maintaining their authority over employees. "I was surprised to see that taking the initiative most of the time was seen as rude and as a failure to respect the executives' authority," says Bourgois, a public relations professional from Bordeaux, France. "At work, everyone had to perform well in their own tasks, but permission was required for anything other than what was expected." The power relationship was also apparent in how Chinese managers interacted with staff. "Western-style bosses tend to develop a closer relationship with employees," Bourgois suggests. "The hierarchy is much more clearly divided in Chinese-dominant companies than it is in foreign ones."[80]

Emilie Bourgois experienced the often-subtle fact that expectations and values differ around the world. Over the next few pages, we introduce five values that have cross-cultural significance: individualism, collectivism, power distance, uncertainty avoidance, and achievement-nurturing orientation. Exhibit 2.6 summarizes these values and lists countries that have high, medium, or low emphasis on these values.

Individualism and Collectivism

Two seemingly inseparable cross-cultural values are individualism and collectivism. **Individualism** is the extent to which we value independence and personal uniqueness. Highly individualist people value personal freedom, self-sufficiency, control

individualism a cross-cultural value describing the degree to which people in a culture emphasize independence and personal uniqueness

collectivism a cross-cultural value describing the degree to which people in a culture emphasize duty to groups to which they belong and to group harmony

power distance a cross-cultural value describing the degree to which people in a culture accept unequal distribution of power in a society

over their own lives, and appreciation of the unique qualities that distinguish them from others. Americans, Chileans, Canadians, and South Africans generally exhibit high individualism, whereas Taiwan and Venezuela are countries with low individualism.[81] **Collectivism** is the extent to which we value our duty to groups to which we belong and to group harmony. Highly collectivist people define themselves by their group memberships, emphasize their personal connection to others in their in-groups, and value the goals and well-being of people within those groups.[82] Low collectivism countries include the United States, Japan, and Germany, whereas Israel and Taiwan have relatively high collectivism.

Contrary to popular belief, individualism is not the opposite of collectivism. In fact, the two concepts are typically uncorrelated.[83] For example, cultures that highly value duty to one's group do not necessarily give a low priority to personal freedom and uniqueness. Generally, people across all cultures define themselves by both their uniqueness and their relationship to others. It is an inherent characteristic of everyone's self-concept, which we discuss in the next chapter. Some cultures clearly emphasize uniqueness or group obligations more than the other, but both have a place in a person's values and self-concept.

Also note that people in Japan have relatively low collectivism. This is contrary to many cross-cultural books, which claim that Japan is one of the most collectivist countries on the planet!

There are several explanations for the historical misinterpretation, ranging from problems defining and measuring collectivism to erroneous reporting of early cross-cultural research. Whatever the reasons, studies consistently report that people in Japan tend to have relatively low collectivism and moderate individualism (as indicated in Exhibit 2.6).[84]

Power Distance

Power distance refers to the extent to which people accept unequal distribution of power in a society.[85] Those with high power distance value unequal power. Those in higher positions expect obedience to authority; those in lower positions are comfortable receiving commands from their superiors without consultation or debate. People with high power distance also prefer to resolve differences through formal procedures rather than direct informal discussion. In contrast, people with low power distance expect relatively equal power sharing. They view the relationship with their boss as one of interdependence, not dependence; that is, they believe their boss is also dependent on them, so they expect power sharing and consultation before

Exhibit 2.6 Five Cross-Cultural Values

Value	Sample Countries	Representative Beliefs/Behaviors in "High" Cultures
Individualism	High: United States, Chile, Canada, South Africa Medium: Japan, Denmark Low: Taiwan, Venezuela	Defines self more by one's uniqueness; personal goals have priority; decisions have low consideration of effect on others; relationships are viewed as more instrumental and fluid.
Collectivism	High: Israel, Taiwan Medium: India, Denmark Low: United States, Germany, Japan	Defines self more by one's in-group membership; goals of self-sacrifice and harmony have priority; behavior regulated by in-group norms; in-group memberships are viewed as stable with a strong differentiation with out-groups.
Power distance	High: India, Malaysia Medium: United States, Japan Low: Denmark, Israel	Reluctant to disagree with or contradict the boss; managers are expected and preferred decision makers; perception of dependence on (versus interdependence with) the boss.
Uncertainty avoidance	High: Belgium, Greece Medium: United States, Norway Low: Denmark, Singapore	Prefer predictable situations; value stable employment, strict laws, and low conflict; dislike deviations from normal behavior.
Achievement orientation	High: Austria, Japan Medium: United States, Brazil Low: Sweden, Netherlands	Focus on outcomes (versus relationships); decisions based on contribution (equity versus equality); low empathy or showing emotions (versus strong empathy and caring).

Sources: Individualism and collectivism descriptions and results are from the meta-analysis reported in D. Oyserman, H.M. Coon, and M. Kemmelmeier, "Rethinking Individualism and Collectivism: Evaluation of Theoretical Assumptions and Meta-Analyses," *Psychological Bulletin*, 128 (2002): 3–72. The other information is from G. Hofstede, *Culture's Consequences*, 2nd ed. (Thousand Oaks, CA: Sage, 2001).

uncertainty avoidance a cross-cultural value describing the degree to which people in a culture tolerate ambiguity (low uncertainty avoidance) or feel threatened by ambiguity and uncertainty (high uncertainty avoidance)

achievement-nurturing orientation cross-cultural value describing the degree to which people in a culture emphasize competitive versus cooperative relations with other people

decisions affecting them are made. People in India and Malaysia tend to have high power distance, whereas people in Denmark and Israel generally have low power distance. Americans collectively have medium-low power distance.

Uncertainty Avoidance

Uncertainty avoidance is the degree to which people tolerate ambiguity (low uncertainty avoidance) or feel threatened by ambiguity and uncertainty (high uncertainty avoidance). Employees with high uncertainty avoidance value structured situations in which rules of conduct and decision making are clearly documented. They usually prefer direct rather than indirect or ambiguous communications. Uncertainty avoidance tends to be high in Belgium and Greece and very high in Japan. It is generally low in Denmark and Singapore. Americans collectively have medium-low uncertainty avoidance.

Achievement-Nurturing Orientation

Achievement-nurturing orientation reflects a competitive versus cooperative view of relations with other people.[86] People with a high achievement orientation value assertiveness, competitiveness, and materialism. They appreciate people who are tough, and they favor the acquisition of money and material goods. In contrast, people in nurturing-oriented cultures emphasize relationships and the well-being of others. They focus on human interaction and caring rather than competition and personal success. People in Sweden, Norway, and the Netherlands score very low on achievement orientation (i.e., they have a

high nurturing orientation). In contrast, very high achievement orientation scores have been reported in Japan and Austria. The United States is located a little above the middle of the range on achievement-nurturing orientation.

Caveats about Cross-Cultural Knowledge

Cross-cultural organizational research has gained considerable attention over the past two decades, likely due to increased globalization and cultural diversity within organizations. Our knowledge of cross-cultural dynamics has blossomed, and many of these findings will be discussed throughout this book, particularly regarding leadership, conflict handling, and influence tactics. However, we also need to raise a few warning flags about cross-cultural knowledge. One problem is that too many studies have relied on small, convenient samples (such as students attending one university) to represent an entire culture.[87] The result is that many cross-cultural studies draw conclusions that might not generalize to the cultures they intended to represent.

A second problem is that cross-cultural studies often assume that each country has one culture.[88] In reality, the United States and many other countries have become culturally diverse. As more countries embrace globalization and multiculturalism, it becomes even less appropriate to assume that an entire country has one unified culture.

A third concern is that cross-cultural research and writing continues to rely on a major study conducted almost four decades ago of 116,000 IBM employees across dozens of countries. That study helped ignite subsequent cross-cultural research, but its findings are becoming out-of-date as values in some cultures have shifted over the years. For example, value systems seem to be converging across Asia as people in these countries interact more frequently with each other and adopt standardized business practices.[89] At least one recent review has recommended that future studies should no longer rely on the IBM study to benchmark values of a particular culture.[90]

Study Checklist

- ⊘ Did you tear out the perforated student review card at the back of the text to revisit learning objectives and key terms and definitions?

Connect® Management is available for *M Organizational Behavior*. Additional resources include:

- ⊘ Interactive Applications:
  - **Decision Generator**
  - **Drag and Drop:** Work through an interactive example to test your knowledge of the concepts.

- **Video Case:** See management in action through interactive videos.

- ⊘ **SmartBook™**—SmartBook is the first and only adaptive reading experience available today. Distinguishing what you know from what you don't, and honing in on concepts you are most likely to forget, SmartBook personalizes content for you in a continuously adapting reading experience. Reading is no longer a passive and linear experience, but an engaging and dynamic one where you are more likely to master and retain important concepts and go to class better prepared.

Want
Help
Studying?

SMARTBOOK: MAKE
EACH MINUTE COUNT.

Go to: LearnSmartAdvantage.com

3 chapter

Perceiving Ourselves and Others **in Organizations**

Learning Objectives

After studying this chapter, you should be able to:

LO3-1 Describe the elements of self-concept and explain how each affects an individual's behavior and well-being.

LO3-2 Outline the perceptual process and discuss the effects of categorical thinking and mental models in that process.

LO3-3 Discuss how stereotyping, attribution, self-fulfilling prophecy, halo, false consensus, primacy, and recency influence the perceptual process.

LO3-4 Discuss three ways to improve perceptions, with specific application to organizational situations.

LO3-5 Outline the main features of a global mindset and justify its usefulness to employees and organizations.

One hundred people recently congregated along a block of Broadway and started dancing to the beat of "Party Rock Anthem." Flash mobs aren't unusual in this section of midtown Manhattan, but the group surprised many watchers because they were accountants from New Jersey. "Most people are like, 'I can't believe these are a bunch of accountants,' " recalls WithumSmith+Brown partner Jim Bourke, where the flash mob participants are employed.

The Withum accountants orchestrated the event to celebrate their merger with Manhattan CPA firm EisnerLubin. But the celebration also chipped away at the age-old stereotype by showing that accountants know how to have fun. "We play hard, and we work hard as well," said Christina Fessler, a 28-year-old CPA at Withum. "It really can be fun. And I think the era of the suit and tie at work every day is over."[1]

LO3-1 Describe the elements of self-concept and explain how each affects an individual's behavior and well-being.

SELF-CONCEPT: HOW WE PERCEIVE OURSELVES

Self-concept refers to an individual's self-beliefs and self-evaluations.[3] It is the "Who am I?" and "How do I feel about myself?" that people ask themselves and that guide their decisions and actions. When contemplating a career as an accountant, for example, we compare our images of that profession with our current (perceived self) and desired (ideal self) images of ourselves. We also evaluate our current and desired abilities to determine whether there is a good fit with that type of work. Recent studies suggest that we have an individual self (our personal traits), relational self (interpersonal relations), and collective self (our membership in identifiable social groups).[4]

> "Whenever two people meet there are really six people present. There are the two people as they see themselves, the two people as they see each other, and the two people as they really are."[2]
>
> —**Restated from Oliver Wendell Holmes Sr.,** medical scholar and author
> (in *The Autocrat of the Breakfast-Table*, 1858)

Accounting firms face two challenges in attracting and keeping talent in this occupation: (1) the perceptions (including stereotypes) that others have about accountants and (2) the self-concept accountants have about themselves. We discuss both of these related topics in this chapter. First, we examine how people perceive themselves—their self-concept—and how that self-perception affects their decisions and behavior. Next, we focus on perceptions in organizational settings, beginning with how we select, organize, and interpret information, and then reviewing several specific perceptual processes such as stereotyping, attribution, and self-fulfilling prophecy. We then identify potentially effective ways to improve perceptions. The final section of this chapter reviews the main elements of global mindset, a largely perceptual process valued in this increasingly globalized world.

Self-Concept Complexity, Consistency, and Clarity

An individual's self-concept can be described by three characteristics: complexity, consistency, and clarity (see Exhibit 3.1). *Complexity* refers to the number of distinct and important roles or identities that people perceive about themselves.[5] We all have some degree of complexity because we see ourselves in different roles at various times (student, friend, daughter, sports fan, etc.). But complexity isn't just the number of selves that define who we are; it is also the separation of those selves. A self-concept has low complexity when the individual's most important identities are highly interconnected, such as when they are all work related (manager, engineer, family income earner).

self-concept an individual's self-beliefs and self-evaluations

A second characteristic of an individual's self-concept is its internal *consistency*. High internal consistency exists when most of the individual's self-perceived roles require similar personality traits, values, and other attributes. Low consistency occurs when some self-perceptions require personal characteristics that conflict with characteristics required for other aspects of self. Low self-concept consistency would exist if you see yourself as a very meticulous accountant, but also a cavalier and risk-oriented skier.

Clarity, the third characteristic of self-concept, is the degree to which you have a clear, confidently defined, and stable self-concept.[6] Clarity occurs when we are confident about "who we are," can describe our important identities to others, and provide the same description of ourselves across time. Self-concept clarity increases with the person's age and the consistency of their multiple selves.[7]

Effects of Self-Concept Characteristics on Well-Being and Behavior Self-concept complexity, consistency, and clarity influence a person's well-being, behavior, and performance. People tend to have better psychological well-being

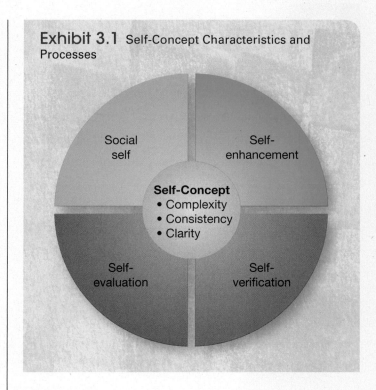

Exhibit 3.1 Self-Concept Characteristics and Processes

- Social self
- Self-enhancement
- **Self-Concept**
  - Complexity
  - Consistency
  - Clarity
- Self-evaluation
- Self-verification

when they have multiple selves (complexity) that are well established (clarity) and are similar to each other and compatible with personal traits (consistency).[9] Self-concept complexity protects our self-esteem when some roles are threatened or damaged. A complex self is rather like a ship with several compartments that can be sealed off from one another. If one compartment is damaged, the other compartments (selves) remain intact so the ship remains afloat. In contrast, people with low complexity, including when their multiple selves are interconnected, suffer severe loss when they experience failure because these events affect a large part of themselves.

People also tend to have better well-being when their multiple selves are in harmony with each other and with the individual's personality and values (consistency).[10] Some self-concept diversity helps people adapt, but too much variation causes internal tension and conflict. Finally, well-being tends to increase with self-concept clarity. People who are unsure of their self-views are more easily influenced by others, experience more stress when making decisions, and feel more threatened by social forces that undermine their self-confidence and self-esteem.[11]

Self-concept complexity, consistency, and clarity have more varied effects on behavior and performance.[12] On the one hand, people who define themselves mainly by their work (i.e., low complexity) tend to have lower absenteeism and turnover. They also tend to have better performance due to more investment in skill development, longer hours, more concentration on work, and so forth. On the other hand, low complexity commonly results in higher stress and depression when the main self aspect is damaged or threatened, which further undermines individual performance.

Self-Concept Clarity: "Acting Is Who I Am"

Hélène Joy appeared on several popular television programs, but the lack of job security as an actor motivated her to join her mother's real estate business. "It lasted a week," Joy recalls of her short-lived real estate career. "I realized that acting is what I do, and who I am." The experience helped Joy form a clearer self-concept, which provided a new determination to achieve her ideal self. "I guess I was never really committed till then, and once I did commit, I haven't stopped working." Today, Joy is a lead actor in the popular television series *Murdoch Mysteries* and has received several awards for her acting talent.[8]

Self-concept clarity tends to improve performance and is considered vital for leadership roles.[13] Clarity also focuses personal energy so employees direct their effort more efficiently toward their career objectives. Another benefit of high self-concept clarity is that people feel less threatened by interpersonal conflict, so they use more constructive problem-solving behaviors to resolve the conflict. However, those with very high clarity may have role inflexibility, with the result that they cannot adapt to changing job duties or environmental conditions.

Along with the three self-concept characteristics, Exhibit 3.1 illustrates four processes that shape self-concept and motivate a person's decisions and behavior. Let's look at each of these four "selves": self-enhancement, self-verification, self-evaluation, and social self (social identity).

Self-Enhancement

People are inherently motivated to perceive themselves (and to be perceived by others) as competent, attractive, lucky, ethical, and important.[15] This **self-enhancement** is observed in many ways. Individuals tend to rate themselves above average, believe that they have a better than average probability of success, and attribute their successes to personal motivation or ability while blaming the situation for their mistakes. For instance, 74 percent of investment fund managers claimed to be above average at their jobs. Almost 70 percent of government workers rated their performance above average compared to other coworkers in their unit; only 1 percent rated their performance below average.[16] People don't see themselves as above average in all circumstances. Instead, it is most apparent for things that are important to them and are relatively common or everyday rather than rare.[17]

Self-enhancement has both positive and negative consequences in organizational settings.[18] On the positive side, individuals tend to experience better mental and physical health and adjustment when they amplify their self-concept. Overconfidence also generates a "can-do" attitude (which we discuss later) that motivates persistence in difficult or risky tasks. On the negative side, self-enhancement causes people to overestimate future returns in investment decisions, use less conservative accounting practices, and take longer to recognize their mistakes. Some research also suggests that self-enhancement is a factor in high accident rates among novice drivers. Generally, though, successful companies strive to help employees feel they are valued and integral members of the organization.

Self-Verification

Individuals try to confirm and maintain their existing self-concept.[19] This process, called **self-verification**, stabilizes an individual's self-view, which in turn provides an important anchor that guides his or her thoughts and actions. Employees actively communicate their self-concept so coworkers understand it and provide verifying feedback when observed. For example, you might let coworkers know that you are a very organized person; later, they point out situations where you have indeed been very organized. Unlike self-enhancement, self-verification includes seeking feedback that is not necessarily flattering (e.g., "I'm a numbers person, not a people person"). Social scientists continue to debate whether and under what conditions people prefer information that supports self-enhancement or self-verification.[21] In other words, do we prefer compliments rather than accurate critique about weaknesses that we readily acknowledge? The answer is

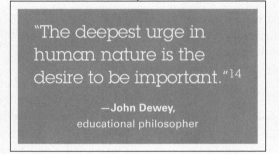

"The deepest urge in human nature is the desire to be important."[14]

—John Dewey, educational philosopher

self-enhancement
a person's inherent motivation to have a positive self-concept (and to have others perceive him or her favorably), such as being competent, attractive, lucky, ethical, and important

self-verification
a person's inherent motivation to confirm and maintain his or her existing self-concept

Many Recognition Programs, But Few Employees Feel Valued[20]

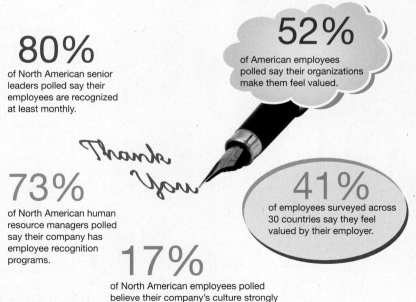

80%
of North American senior leaders polled say their employees are recognized at least monthly.

52%
of American employees polled say their organizations make them feel valued.

73%
of North American human resource managers polled say their company has employee recognition programs.

41%
of employees surveyed across 30 countries say they feel valued by their employer.

17%
of North American employees polled believe their company's culture strongly supports employee recognition.

likely an emotional tug-of-war; we enjoy compliments, but less so if they are significantly contrary to our self-view.

Self-verification has implications for organizational behavior.[22] First, it affects the perceptual process because employees are more likely to remember information that is consistent with their self-concept and nonconsciously screen out information (particularly negative information) that seems inconsistent with it. Second, the clearer their self-concept, the less people will consciously accept feedback that contradicts that self-concept. Third, employees are motivated to interact with others who affirm their self-views, and this affects how well they get along with their boss and team members. For instance, new employees are more satisfied and perform better when the socialization process allows them to affirm their authentic self—they can demonstrate and receive support for

"who they are"—rather than when the socialization process mainly steers them into the company's image of an ideal employee.[23]

Self-Evaluation

Almost everyone strives to have a positive self-concept, but some people have a more positive evaluation of themselves than do others. This *self-evaluation* is mostly defined by three elements: self-esteem, self-efficacy, and locus of control.[24]

Self-Esteem Self-esteem—the extent to which people like, respect, and are satisfied with themselves—represents a global self-evaluation. Some experts also believe that self-esteem is a person's rating of his or her success at social inclusion. In other words, people have higher self-esteem when they believe they are connected to and accepted by others. People with high self-esteem are less influenced by others, tend to persist in spite of failure, and think more rationally. Role-specific self-esteem (e.g., a good student, a good driver, a good parent) predicts attitudes and behaviors about that role, whereas a person's overall self-esteem predicts much more general attitudes and behaviors (e.g., satisfaction with self).[25]

Self-Efficacy Self-efficacy refers to a person's belief that he or she can successfully complete a task.[26] Those with high self-efficacy have a "can-do" attitude. They believe they possess the energy (motivation), ability, clear expectations (role perceptions), and resources (situational factors) to perform the task. In other words, self-efficacy is an individual's perception regarding the MARS model in a specific situation. Although originally defined in terms of specific tasks, self-efficacy is also a general trait related to self-concept.[27] General self-efficacy is a perception of one's probability of performing well across a variety of situations. People with higher general self-efficacy have a more positive overall self-evaluation.

Locus of Control Locus of control is defined as a person's general beliefs about the amount of control he or she has over personal life events.[28] Individuals with more of an internal locus of control believe their personal characteristics (i.e., motivation and abilities) mainly influence life's outcomes. Those with more of an external locus of control believe events in their life are due mainly to fate, luck, or conditions in the external environment. Locus of control is a generalized belief, so people with an external locus can feel in control in familiar situations (such as performing common tasks). However, their underlying locus of control would be apparent in new situations in which control over events is uncertain.

People with an internal locus of control have a more positive self-evaluation. They also tend to perform better in most employment situations, are more successful in their careers, earn more money, and are better suited for leadership positions. Internals are also more satisfied with their jobs, cope better in stressful situations, and are more motivated by performance-based reward systems.[29]

The Social Self

Everyone has a self-concept that includes at least a few identities (financial analyst, parent, golfer, etc.), and each identity is defined by a set of attributes. These attributes highlight both the person's uniqueness (personal identity) and association with others (social identity).[30] *Personal identity* (also known as internal self-concept) consists of attributes that make us unique and distinct from people in the social groups to which we have a connection. For instance, an unusual achievement that distinguishes you from other people typically becomes a personal identity characteristic. Personal identity refers to something about you as an individual without reference to a larger group.

At the same time, human beings are social animals; they have an inherent drive to be associated with others and to be recognized as part of social communities. This drive to belong is reflected in self-concept by the fact that all individuals define themselves to some degree by their relationships.[31] *Social identity* (also called external self-concept) is the central theme of **social identity theory**, which says that people define themselves by the groups to which they belong or have an emotional attachment. For instance, someone might have a social identity as an American, a Cleveland State University alumnus, and an employee at OhioHealth (see Exhibit 3.2).

Social identity is a complex combination of many memberships arranged in a hierarchy of importance. One factor that determines importance is how easily you are identified as a member of the reference group, such as by your gender, age, and ethnicity. A second factor is your minority status in a group. It is difficult to ignore your gender in a class where most other students are the opposite gender, for example. In that context, gender tends to become a stronger defining feature of your social identity than it is in social settings where there are many people of the same gender.

The group's status is another important social identity factor because association with the group makes us feel better about ourselves (i.e., self-enhancement). Medical doctors usually define themselves by their profession because of its high status. Some people describe themselves by where they work ("I work at Google") because their employer has a good reputation. Others never mention where they work because

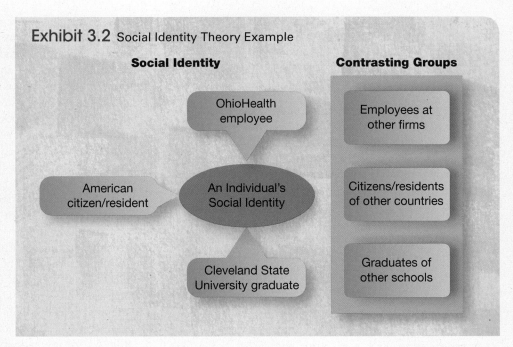

Exhibit 3.2 Social Identity Theory Example

Social Identity

- OhioHealth employee
- American citizen/resident
- An Individual's Social Identity
- Cleveland State University graduate

Contrasting Groups

- Employees at other firms
- Citizens/residents of other countries
- Graduates of other schools

their employer is noted for poor relations with employees or has a poor reputation in the community.[32]

All of us try to balance our personal and social identities, but the priority for uniqueness (personal identities) versus relatedness (social identities) differs from one person to the next. People whose self-concepts are heavily defined by social rather than personal identities are more motivated to abide by team norms and more easily influenced by peer pressure. Those who place more emphasis on personal identities, on the other hand, speak out more frequently against the majority and are less motivated to follow the team's wishes. Furthermore, expressing disagreement with others is a sign of distinctiveness and can help employees

form a clearer self-concept, particularly when that disagreement is based on differences in personal values.[33]

Self-Concept and Organizational Behavior

Self-concept has become a hot topic in the social sciences and is starting to bloom in organizational behavior research.[34] As we noted throughout this section, self-concept is a factor in perceptual and decision processes and biases, employee motivation, team dynamics, leadership development, employee stress, and several other OB topics. So, we will discuss self-concept throughout this book, including later parts of this chapter.

> **LO3-2** Outline the perceptual process and discuss the effects of categorical thinking and mental models in that process.

PERCEIVING THE WORLD AROUND US

Although we spend considerable time perceiving ourselves, most of our perceptual energy is directed toward the outer world. Whether as a structural engineer, forensic accountant, or senior executive, we need to make sense of the world around us, including the conditions that challenge the accuracy of those perceptions. **Perception** is the process of receiving information about and making sense of the world around us. It entails determining which information to notice, how to categorize this information, and how to interpret it within the framework of our existing knowledge.

This perceptual process generally follows the steps shown in Exhibit 3.3. Perception begins when environmental stimuli are received through our senses. Most stimuli that bombard our senses are screened out; the rest are organized and interpreted. The process of attending to some information received by our senses and ignoring other information is called **selective attention**. Selective attention is influenced by characteristics of the person or object being perceived, particularly size, intensity, motion, repetition, and novelty. For example, a small, flashing red light on a nurses' workstation console is immediately noticed because it is bright (intensity), flashing (motion), a rare event (novelty), and has symbolic meaning that a patient's vital signs are failing. Notice that selective attention is also influenced by the context in which the target is perceived. The selective attention process is triggered by things or people who might be out of context, such as someone with a foreign accent in a setting where most people have an American accent.

Characteristics of the perceiver also influence selective attention, usually without the perceiver's awareness.[35] When information is received through the senses, our brain quickly and nonconsciously assesses whether it is relevant or irrelevant to us and then attaches emotional markers (worry, happiness, boredom) to the retained information.[36] Emotional markers help us store information in memory; those emotions are later reproduced when recalling the perceived information. The selective attention process is far from perfect, however. The Greek philosopher Plato acknowledged this imperfection long ago when he wrote that we see reality only as shadows reflecting against the rough wall of a cave.[37]

One selective attention bias is the effect of our assumptions and expectations about future events. You are more likely to notice a particular coworker's email among the daily bombardment of messages when you expect to receive that email (even more so if it is a valuable message). Unfortunately, expectations and assumptions also cause us to screen out potentially important information. In one study, students were asked to watch a 30-second video clip in which several people passed around two basketballs. Students who were instructed just to watch

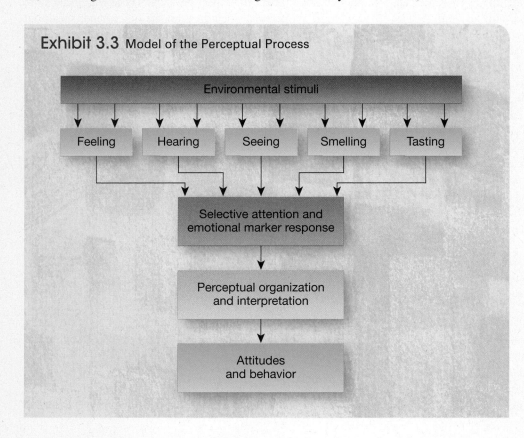

Exhibit 3.3 Model of the Perceptual Process

Environmental stimuli

Feeling   Hearing   Seeing   Smelling   Tasting

Selective attention and emotional marker response

Perceptual organization and interpretation

Attitudes and behavior

perception the process of receiving information about and making sense of the world around us

selective attention the process of attending to some information received by our senses and ignoring other information

confirmation bias the process of screening out information that is contrary to our values and assumptions and to more readily accept confirming information

categorical thinking organizing people and objects into preconceived categories that are stored in our long-term memory

mental models knowledge structures that we develop to describe, explain, and predict the world around us

the video clip easily noticed someone dressed in a gorilla suit walking among the players for nine seconds and stopping to thump his or her chest. But only half of the students who were asked to count the number of times one basketball was passed around noticed the intruding gorilla.[38]

Another selective attention problem, called **confirmation bias**, is the nonconscious tendency for people to screen out information that is contrary to their decisions, beliefs, values, and assumptions, whereas confirming information is more readily accepted through the perceptual process.[39] This bias includes overweighting positive information, perceiving only positive information, and restricting cognitive attention to a favored hypothesis. When we make important decisions, such as investing in a costly project, for example, we tend to pay attention to information that is consistent with the success of that decision and to ignore contrary or seemingly irrelevant information. In an exercise where student pilots became unsure of their location, they tried to find their true location by relying on less reliable information that was consistent with their assumptions than on more accurate information that was contrary to those assumptions. This faulty selective attention also occurs when police detectives and other forensic experts form theories too early in the investigation.[40]

Perceptual Organization and Interpretation

People make sense of information even before they become aware of it. This sense making partly includes **categorical thinking**—the mostly nonconscious process of organizing people and objects into preconceived categories that are stored in our long-term memory.[42] Categorical thinking relies on a variety of automatic perceptual grouping principles. Things are often grouped together based on their similarity or proximity to others. If you notice that a group of similar-looking people includes several professors, for instance, you will likely assume that the others

> "Theory like mist on eyeglasses. Obscure facts."[41]
>
> **—Robert Ellis and Helen Logan**
> (screenwriters of the film *Charlie Chan in Egypt,* 1935)

in that group are also professors. Another form of perceptual grouping is based on the need for cognitive closure, such as filling in missing information about what happened at a meeting that you didn't attend (e.g., who was there, where it was held). A third form of grouping occurs when we think we see trends in otherwise ambiguous information. Several studies have found that people have a natural tendency to see patterns that really are random events, such as presumed winning streaks among sports stars or in gambling.[43]

The process of "making sense" of the world around us also involves interpreting incoming information, not just organizing it. This happens as quickly as selecting and organizing because the previously mentioned emotional markers are tagged to incoming stimuli, which are essentially quick judgments about whether that information is good or bad for us. How much time does it take to make these quick judgments? Recent studies estimate that we make reliable judgments about another individual's trustworthiness based on viewing a facial image for as little as 50 milliseconds (1/20th of a second). In fact, whether we see a face for a minute or for just 200 milliseconds, our opinion of whether we like or trust that person is about the same.[44] Collectively, these studies reveal that selective attention, perceptual organization, and interpretation operate very quickly and to a large extent without our awareness.

Mental Models To achieve our goals with some degree of predictability and sanity, we need road maps of the environments in which we live. These road maps, called **mental models**, are knowledge structures that we develop to describe, explain, and predict the world around us.[45] They consist of visual or relational images in our mind, such as what the classroom looks like or what happens when we submit an assignment late. Mental models partly rely on the process of perceptual grouping to make sense of things; they fill in the missing pieces, including the causal connection among events. For example, you have a mental model about attending a class lecture or seminar, including assumptions or expectations about where the instructor and students arrange themselves in the room, how they ask and answer questions, and so forth. In other words, we create a mental image of a class in progress.

Mental models are important for sense making, yet they also make it difficult to see the world in different ways. For example, accounting professionals tend to see corporate problems from an accounting perspective, whereas marketing professionals see the same problems from a marketing perspective. Mental models also block our recognition of new opportunities. How do we change mental models? That's a tough challenge. After all, we developed these knowledge structures from several years of experience and reinforcement. The most important way to minimize the perceptual problems with mental models is to be aware of and frequently question them. We need to ask ourselves about the assumptions we make. Working with people from diverse backgrounds is another way to break out of existing mental models. Colleagues from different cultures and areas of expertise tend to have different mental models, so working with them makes our own assumptions more obvious.

SPECIFIC PERCEPTUAL PROCESSES AND PROBLEMS

Within the general perceptual process are specific subprocesses and associated biases as well as other errors. In this section of the chapter, we examine several of these perceptual processes and biases as well as their implications for organizational behavior, beginning with the most widely known one: stereotyping.

Stereotyping in Organizations

This chapter began with the story of a New Jersey accounting firm that chipped away at the widely held stereotype of accountants by holding a flash mob event on Broadway. **Stereotyping** is the perceptual process in which we assign characteristics to an identifiable group and then automatically transfer those features to anyone we believe is a member of that group.[46] The assigned characteristics tend to be difficult to observe, such as personality traits and abilities, but they can also include physical characteristics and a host of other qualities. For instance, people in most parts of the world stereotype professors and scientists in general as intelligent, absentminded, and socially inept.[47] Stereotypes are formed to some extent from personal experience, but they are mainly provided to us through media images (e.g., movie characters) and other cultural prototypes. Consequently, stereotypes are shared beliefs across an entire society and sometimes across several cultures, rather than beliefs that differ from one person to the next.

Stereotyping involves assigning a group's perceived attributes to individuals known or believed to be members of that group. Everyone identified as a member of the stereotyped group is assumed to possess these characteristics. If we learn that someone is a professor, for example, we implicitly assume the person is probably also intelligent, absentminded, and socially inept. Historically, stereotypes were defined as exaggerations or falsehoods. This is often true, but some stereotypes have kernels of truth. Some features of the stereotype are more common among people in the group than in other groups. Still, stereotypes embellish or distort the kernels of truth and include other features that are false.

Why People Stereotype

People engage in stereotyping because, as a form of categorical thinking, it is a natural and mostly nonconscious "energy-saving" process that simplifies our understanding of the world. It is easier to remember features of a stereotype than the constellation of characteristics unique to everyone we meet.[48] A second reason is that we have an innate need to understand and anticipate how others will behave. We don't have much information when first meeting someone, so we rely heavily on stereotypes to fill in the missing pieces. The higher the perceiver's need for cognitive closure, the higher the reliance on stereotypes.

A third explanation for stereotyping is that it is motivated by the observer's own self-enhancement and social identity. Earlier in this chapter we explained that people define themselves by the groups to which they belong or have an emotional attachment. They are also motivated to maintain a positive self-concept. This combination of social identity and self-enhancement leads to the process of categorization, homogenization, and differentiation:[49]

- *Categorization.* Social identity is a comparative process, and the comparison begins by categorizing people into distinct groups. By viewing someone (including yourself) as a Texan, for example, you remove that person's individuality and, instead, see him or her as a prototypical representative of the group called Texans. This categorization then allows you to distinguish Texans from people who live in, say, California or Maine.

- *Homogenization.* To simplify the comparison process, we tend to think that people within each group are very similar to each other. For instance, we think Texans collectively have similar attitudes and characteristics, whereas Californians collectively have their own set of characteristics. Of course, every individual is unique, but we tend to lose sight of this fact when thinking about our social identity and how we compare to people in other social groups.

- *Differentiation.* Along with categorizing and homogenizing people, we tend to assign more favorable characteristics to people in our groups than to people in other groups.[50] This differentiation is motivated by self-enhancement because being in a "better" group produces higher self-esteem. Differentiation is often subtle, but it can escalate into a "good guy–bad guy" contrast when groups engage in overt conflict with each other. In other words, when out-group members threaten our self-concept, we are particularly motivated (often without our awareness) to assign negative stereotypes to them. Some research suggests that men have stronger differentiation biases than do women, but we all differentiate to some extent.

Problems with Stereotyping Everyone engages in stereotyping, but this process distorts perceptions in various ways. One distortion is that stereotypes do not accurately describe every person in a social category. Consider how accountants are typically stereotyped in films and literature. Although sometimes depicted as loyal and conscientious, accountants are usually shown as boring, monotonous, cautious, unromantic, obtuse, antisocial, shy, dysfunctional, devious, calculating, and malicious.[51] The traditional accountant stereotype perhaps describes a few accountants, but it is certainly not characteristic of all—or even most—people in this profession. Nevertheless, once we categorize someone as an accountant, the stereotypic features of accountants (boring, antisocial, etc.) are transferred to that person, even though we have not attempted to verify those characteristics in that person.

Another problem with stereotyping is that it lays the foundation for discriminatory attitudes and behavior. Most of this perceptual bias occurs as *unintentional (systemic) discrimination*, whereby decision makers rely on stereotypes to establish notions of the "ideal" person in specific roles.

stereotyping the process of assigning traits to people based on their membership in a social category

A person who doesn't fit the ideal tends to receive a less favorable evaluation.

The more serious form of stereotype bias is *intentional discrimination* or *prejudice*, in which people hold unfounded negative attitudes toward people belonging to a particular stereotyped group.[53] Although it would be nice to believe that overt prejudice is disappearing, it still exists. A French study of 2,300 help-wanted ads found that job applicants with French-sounding names were much more likely to get job interviews than were applicants with North African or sub-Saharan African names, even though employers received identical résumés for both names! Furthermore, when applicants personally visited human resource staff, those with foreign names were often told the job had been filled, whereas few of the applicants with French names received this message (even when visiting afterward).[54]

If stereotyping is such a problem, shouldn't we try to avoid this process altogether? Unfortunately, it's not that simple. Most experts agree that categorical thinking (including stereotyping) is an automatic and nonconscious process. Specialized training programs can minimize stereotype activation to some extent, but for the most part the process is hardwired in our brain cells.[55] Also remember that stereotyping helps us in several valuable (although fallible) ways described earlier: minimizing mental effort, filling in missing information, and supporting our social identity. The good news is that while it is very difficult to prevent the *activation* of stereotypes, we can minimize the *application* of stereotypic information. In other words, although we automatically categorize people and assign stereotypic traits to them, we can consciously minimize the extent to which we rely on that stereotypic information. Later in this chapter, we identify ways

Perceptual Barriers to Women on Corporate Boards[52]

Women represent more than one-third of the workforce and upwards of 20 percent of middle managers in many countries, yet they comprise less than 10 percent of corporate board members worldwide. Some say the problem is mainly systemic discrimination, such as nonconsciously relying on a male prototype of the ideal board member when selecting candidates for this role. Others suggest the lack of women in the boardroom is due to more explicit prejudice. Female corporate board members are rarest (1 percent or less) in four Middle East countries and Japan; they have the highest percentage of board seats in Norway (40.1 percent), Sweden (27.3 percent), Finland (24.5 percent), and the United States (16.1 percent).

to minimize stereotyping and other perceptual biases.

Attribution Theory

Another widely discussed perceptual phenomenon in organizational settings is the **attribution process**.[56] Attribution involves forming beliefs about the causes of behavior or events. Generally, we perceive whether an observed behavior or event is caused mainly by characteristics of the person (internal factors) or by the environment (external factors). Internal factors include the person's ability or motivation, whereas external factors include resources, coworker support, or luck. If someone doesn't show up for an important meeting, for instance, we infer either internal attributions (the coworker is forgetful, lacks motivation, etc.) or external attributions (traffic, a family emergency, or other circumstances prevented the coworker from attending).

People rely on the three attribution rules—consistency, distinctiveness, consensus—to decide whether someone's behavior and performance are mainly caused by their personal characteristics or environmental influences (see Exhibit 3.4).[57] To illustrate how these three attribution rules operate, imagine a situation where an employee is making poor-quality products on a particular machine. We would probably conclude that the employee lacks skill or motivation (an internal attribution) if the employee consistently makes poor-quality products on this machine (high consistency), the employee makes poor-quality products on other machines (low distinctiveness), and other employees make good-quality products on this machine (low consensus).

In contrast, we would decide that there is something wrong with the machine (an external attribution) if the employee consistently makes poor-quality products on this machine (high consistency), the employee makes good-quality products on other machines (high distinctiveness), and other employees make poor-quality products on this machine (high consensus). Notice that consistency is high for both internal

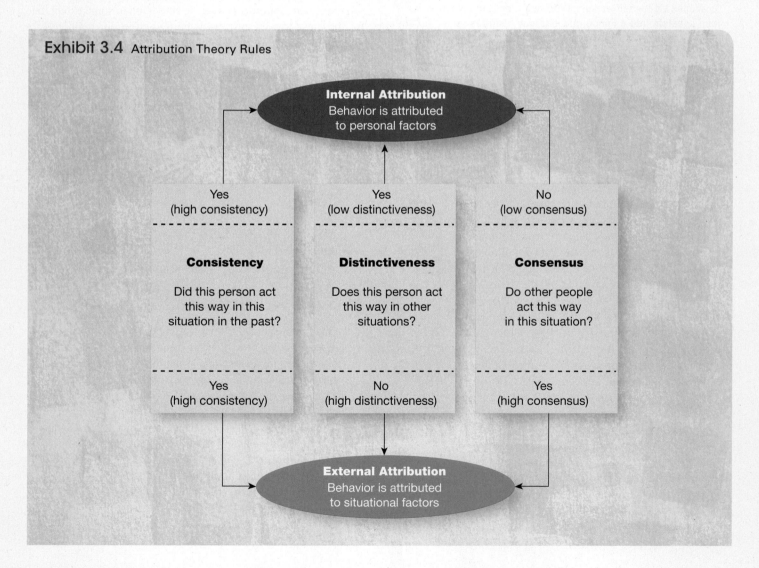

Exhibit 3.4 Attribution Theory Rules

and external attributions. This occurs because low consistency (the person's output quality on this machine is sometimes good and sometimes poor) weakens our confidence about whether the source of the problem is the person or the machine.

We rely on the attribution process to form cause–effect relationships, which enables us to work more effectively. It also helps us determine responsibility for events.[58] Suppose a coworker didn't complete his or her task on a team project. You would approach this situation differently if you believed the coworker was lazy or lacked sufficient skill (an internal attribution) than if you believed the poor performance was due to lack of time or resources available to the coworker (an external attribution). Similarly, our respect for a leader depends on whether we believe his or her actions are due to personal characteristics or the situation. We also react differently to attributions of our own behavior and performance. For instance, students who make internal attributions about their poor grades are more likely to drop out of their programs than if they make external attributions about those grades.[59]

Attribution Errors We are strongly motivated to assign internal or external attributions to someone's behavior, but this perceptual process is also susceptible to errors. One such error is **self-serving bias**—the tendency to attribute our failures to external causes (such as bad luck) more than internal causes (e.g., inefficiency), while successes are due more to internal than external factors.[60] Simply put, we take credit for our successes and blame others or the situation for our mistakes. In annual reports, for example, executives mainly refer to their personal qualities as reasons for the company's successes and to external factors as reasons for the company's failures. Similarly, entrepreneurs in one recent study overwhelmingly cited situational causes for their business failure (funding, economy), whereas they understated personal causes such as lack of vision and social skills.[61]

> We rely on the attribution process to form cause–effect relationships, which enables us to work more effectively.

fundamental attribution error the tendency to see the person rather than the situation as the main cause of that person's behavior

self-fulfilling prophecy the perceptual process in which our expectations about another person cause that person to act more consistently with those expectations

Why do people engage in self-serving bias? Fictional New York crime investigator Philo Vance gave us the answer nearly a century ago when he quipped: "Bad luck is merely a defensive and self-consoling synonym for inefficiency."[62] In other words, self-serving bias is associated with the self-enhancement process described earlier in this chapter. By pointing to external causes of their own failures (e.g., bad luck) and internal causes of their successes, people generate a more positive (and self-consoling) self-concept.

Another widely studied attribution error is **fundamental attribution error** (also called *correspondence bias*), which is the tendency to overemphasize internal causes of another person's behavior and to discount or ignore external causes of their behavior.[63] According to this perceptual error, we are more likely to think a coworker arrives late for work because he or she isn't motivated rather than because of situational constraints (such as traffic congestion). The explanation for fundamental attribution error is that observers can't easily see the external factors that constrain another person's behavior. Also, people like to think that human beings (not the situation) are the prime sources of their behavior. However, fundamental attribution error might not be as common or severe as was previously thought. There is evidence that people from Asian countries are less likely to engage in this bias because those cultures emphasize the context of behavior more than do Western cultures.[64] But a recent review of past studies suggests that fundamental attribution error isn't very noticeable in any society.[65]

Self-Fulfilling Prophecy

Self-fulfilling prophecy occurs when our expectations about another person cause that person to act in a way that is consistent with those expectations. In other words, our perceptions can influence reality. Exhibit 3.5 illustrates the four steps≈in the self-fulfilling prophecy process using the example of a supervisor and a subordinate.[66] The process begins when the supervisor forms expectations about the employee's future behavior and performance. These expectations are sometimes inaccurate, because first impressions are usually formed from limited information. The supervisor's expectations influence his or her behavior toward employees. In particular, high-expectancy employees (those expected to do well) receive more emotional support through nonverbal cues (e.g., more smiling and eye contact), more frequent and valuable feedback and reinforcement, more challenging goals, better training, and more opportunities to demonstrate good performance.

The third step in self-fulfilling prophecy includes two effects of the supervisor's behavior on the employee. First, through better training and more practice opportunities, a high-expectancy employee learns more skills and knowledge than a low-expectancy employee. Second, the employee becomes more self-confident, which results in higher motivation and willingness to set more challenging goals.[67] In the final step, high-expectancy employees have higher motivation and better skills, resulting in better performance, while the opposite is true of low-expectancy employees.

Self-fulfilling prophecy has been observed in many contexts. One of the most famous studies occurred in the Israeli Defense Force. Four combat command course instructors were told that one-third of the incoming trainees had high command potential, one-third had normal potential, and the rest had unknown potential. The trainees had been randomly placed into these categories by the researchers, but the instructors were led to believe that the information they received was accurate. Consistent with self-fulfilling prophecy, high-expectancy soldiers performed significantly better by the end of the course than did trainees in the other groups. They also had more

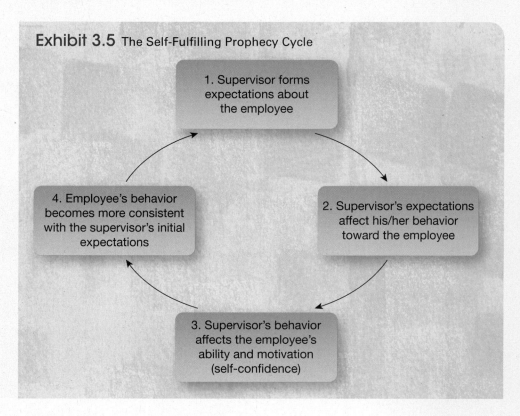

Exhibit 3.5 The Self-Fulfilling Prophecy Cycle

1. Supervisor forms expectations about the employee

2. Supervisor's expectations affect his/her behavior toward the employee

3. Supervisor's behavior affects the employee's ability and motivation (self-confidence)

4. Employee's behavior becomes more consistent with the supervisor's initial expectations

favorable attitudes toward the course and the instructor's leadership effectiveness. Other studies have reported that the initial expectations managers and teachers have of their employees and students tend to influence the self-perceptions (particularly self-efficacy) of those followers and can lead to higher or lower performance.[68]

Contingencies of Self-Fulfilling Prophecy The self-fulfilling prophecy effect is stronger in some situations than in others. It has a stronger effect at the beginning of a relationship, such as when employees are first hired. It is also stronger when several people (rather than just one person) hold the same expectations of the individual. In other words, we might be able to ignore one person's doubts about our potential but not the collective doubts of several people. The self-fulfilling prophecy effect is also stronger among people with a history of low achievement. These people tend to have

realistic, expectation toward all employees. This recommendation is consistent with the emerging philosophy of **positive organizational behavior**, which suggests that focusing on the positive rather than negative aspects of life will improve organizational success and individual well-being. Communicating hope and optimism is so important that it is identified as one of the critical success factors for physicians and surgeons. Training programs that make leaders aware of the power of positive expectations seem to have minimal effect, however. Instead, generating positive

> The main lesson from the self-fulfilling prophecy literature is that leaders need to develop and maintain a positive, yet realistic, expectation toward all employees.

lower self-esteem, so they are more easily influenced by others' opinions of them.[69]

The main lesson from the self-fulfilling prophecy literature is that leaders need to develop and maintain a positive, yet

expectations and hope depends on a corporate culture of support and learning. Hiring supervisors who are inherently optimistic toward their staff is another way of increasing the incidence of positive self-fulfilling prophecies.

Other Perceptual Effects

Self-fulfilling prophecy, attribution, and stereotyping are among the most common perceptual processes and biases in organizational settings, but there are many others. Four additional biases that have received attention in organizational settings are briefly described below.

Halo Effect The **halo effect** occurs when our general impression of a person, usually based on one prominent characteristic, distorts our perception of other characteristics of that person.[70] If a supervisor who values punctuality notices that an employee is sometimes late for work, the supervisor might form a negative image of

false-consensus effect a perceptual error in which we overestimate the extent to which others have beliefs and characteristics similar to our own

primacy effect a perceptual error in which we quickly form an opinion of people based on the first information we receive about them

recency effect a perceptual error in which the most recent information dominates our perception of others

the employee and evaluate that person's other traits unfavorably as well. The halo effect is most likely to occur when concrete information about the perceived target is missing or we are not sufficiently motivated to search for it. Instead, we use our general impression of the person to fill in the missing information.

False-Consensus Effect The **false-consensus effect** (also called *similar-to-me effect*) occurs when people overestimate the extent to which others have similar beliefs or behaviors to our own.[71] Employees who are thinking of quitting their jobs overestimate the percentage of coworkers who are also thinking about quitting, for example. There are several explanations for false-consensus effect. One is that we are comforted believing that others are similar to us, particularly regarding less acceptable or divisive behavior. Put differently, we perceive "everyone does it" to reinforce our self-concept regarding behaviors that do not have a positive image (quitting our job, parking illegally, etc.).

A second explanation for false-consensus effect is that we interact more with people who have similar views and behaviors. This frequent interaction causes us to overestimate how common those views/behaviors are in the entire organization or society. Third, as noted earlier in this chapter, we are more likely to remember information that is consistent with our own views and selectively screen out information that is contrary to our beliefs. Fourth, our social identity process homogenizes people within groups, so we tend to think that everyone in that group has similar opinions and behavior, including the false-consensus attitude or behavior.

Primacy Effect The **primacy effect** is our tendency to quickly form an opinion of people on the basis of the first information we receive about them.[72] It is the notion that first impressions are lasting impressions. This rapid perceptual organization and interpretation occurs because we need to make sense of the world around us. The problem is that first impressions—particularly negative first impressions—are difficult to change. After categorizing someone, we tend to select subsequent information that supports our first impression and screen out information that opposes that impression.

Recency Effect The **recency effect** occurs when the most recent information dominates our perceptions.[73] This perceptual bias is most common when people (especially those with limited experience) are making an evaluation involving complex information. For instance, auditors must digest large volumes of information in their judgments about financial documents, and the most recent information received prior to the decision tends to get weighted more heavily than information received at the beginning of the audit. Similarly, when supervisors evaluate the performance of employees over the previous year, the most recent performance

First Impressions Count
in Job Applications[74]

29%

of chief financial officers say job applicants make the most mistakes in their résumé or cover letter (43% say most mistakes are made during the interview).

36%

of employers say they automatically dismiss a job applicant whose résumé is generic and doesn't seem personalized for the position.

58%

of employers identified typos as the most common problems with résumés that led them to automatically dismiss a job applicant.

Some Résumé Gaffes
"Dear Sir or **Madman**."
"I'm seeking employment as an **office**."
"I'm **attacking** my résumé for you to review."
"Instrumental for **ruining** entire operation for a Midwest chain store."
"**Bilingual** in three languages."
"Received a **plague** for Salesperson of the Year."
"Hope to hear from you, **shorty**."

72%

of employers say it is somewhat or very common for applicants with promising résumés not to live up to expectations during the interview.

32%

of employers say they automatically dismiss a job applicant whose résumé includes a large amount of wording from the job posting.

information dominates the evaluation because it is the most easily recalled.

LO3-4 Discuss three ways to improve perceptions, with specific application to organizational situations.

IMPROVING PERCEPTIONS

We can't bypass the perceptual process, but we should try to minimize perceptual biases and distortions. Three potentially effective ways to improve perceptions include awareness of perceptual biases, self-awareness, and meaningful interaction.

Awareness of Perceptual Biases

One of the most obvious and widely practiced ways to reduce perceptual biases is by knowing that they exist. For example, diversity awareness training tries to minimize discrimination by making people aware of systemic discrimination as well as prejudices that occur through stereotyping. This training also attempts to dispel myths about people from various cultural and demographic groups. Awareness of perceptual biases can reduce these biases to some extent by making people more mindful of their thoughts and actions. However, awareness training has only a limited effect.[75] One problem is that teaching people to reject incorrect stereotypes has the unintended effect of reinforcing rather than reducing reliance on those stereotypes. Another problem is that diversity training is ineffective for people with deeply held prejudices against those groups.

Self-fulfilling prophecy awareness training has also failed to live up to expectations.[76] This training approach informs managers about the existence of the self-fulfilling prophecy effect and encourages them to engage in more positive rather than negative self-fulfilling prophecies. Unfortunately, research has found that managers continue to engage in negative self-fulfilling prophecies after they complete the training program.

Improving Self-Awareness

A more successful way to minimize perceptual biases is by increasing self-awareness.[77] We need to become more aware of our beliefs, values, and attitudes and, from that insight, gain a better understanding of biases in our own decisions and behavior. This self-awareness tends to reduce perceptual biases by making people more open-minded and nonjudgmental toward others. Self-awareness is equally important in other ways. The emerging concept of authentic leadership emphasizes self-awareness as the first step in a person's ability to effectively lead others (see Chapter 11). Essentially, we need to understand our own values, strengths, and biases as a foundation for building a vision and leading others toward that vision.[78]

But how do we become more self-aware? One approach is to complete formal tests that indicate any implicit biases we might have toward others. The Implicit Association Test (IAT) apparently reveals biases. Although the accuracy of the IAT is being hotly debated by scholars, it attempts to detect subtle racial, age, and gender bias by associating positive and negative words with specific demographic groups.[79] Many people are much more cautious about their stereotypes and prejudices after discovering that their test results show a personal bias against older people or individuals from different ethnic backgrounds.[80]

Another way to reduce perceptual biases through increased self-awareness is by applying the **Johari Window**.[81] Developed by Joseph Luft and Harry Ingram (hence the name "Johari"), this model of self-awareness and mutual understanding divides information about you into four "windows"—open, blind, hidden, and unknown—based on whether your own values, beliefs, and experiences are known to you and to others (see Exhibit 3.6). The *open area* includes information about

Johari Window
a model of mutual understanding that encourages disclosure and feedback to increase our own open area and reduce the blind, hidden, and unknown areas

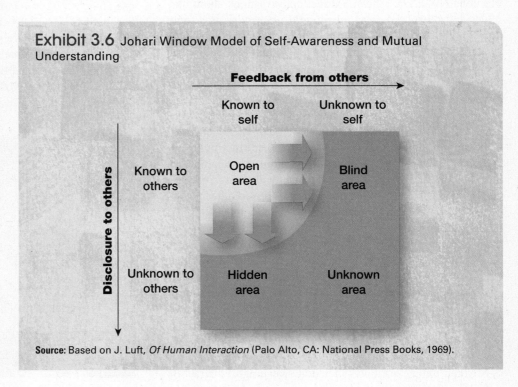

Exhibit 3.6 Johari Window Model of Self-Awareness and Mutual Understanding

Source: Based on J. Luft, *Of Human Interaction* (Palo Alto, CA: National Press Books, 1969).

you that is known both to you and to others. The *blind area* refers to information that is known to others but not to you. For example, your colleagues might notice that you are self-conscious and awkward when meeting the company chief executive, but you are unaware of this fact. Information known to you but unknown to others is found in the *hidden area.* Finally, the *unknown area* includes your values, beliefs, and experiences that aren't known to you or others.

The main objective of the Johari Window is to increase the size of the open area so that both you and your colleagues are aware of your perceptual limitations. This objective is partly accomplished by reducing the hidden area through *disclosure*—informing others of your beliefs, feelings, and experiences that may influence the work relationship. The open area also increases through *feedback* from others about your behavior. Feedback reduces your blind area because, according to recent studies, people near you are good sources of information about many (but not all) of your traits and behaviors.[82] Finally, the combination of disclosure and feedback occasionally produces revelations about you in the unknown area.

Meaningful Interaction

The Johari Window relies on direct conversations about ourselves and others, whereas *meaningful interaction* is a more indirect, yet potentially powerful, approach to improving self-awareness and mutual understanding.[83] Meaningful interaction is any activity in which people engage in valued (meaningful, not trivial) activities. The activities might be work related, such as when senior executives work alongside frontline staff. Or the activities might occur outside the workplace, such as when sales staff from several countries participate in outdoor challenges.

Meaningful interaction is founded on the **contact hypothesis**, which states that, under certain conditions, people who interact with each other will be less perceptually biased because they have a more personal understanding of the other person and their group.[84] Simply spending time with members of other groups can improve this understanding to some extent. However, meaningful interaction is strongest when people work closely and frequently with each other on a shared goal that requires mutual cooperation and reliance. Furthermore, everyone should have equal status in that context, should be engaged in a meaningful task, and should have positive experiences with each other in those interactions.

Meaningful interaction reduces dependence on stereotypes because we gain better knowledge about individuals and experience their unique attributes in action. Meaningful interaction

also potentially improves empathy toward others. **Empathy** refers to understanding and being sensitive to the feelings, thoughts, and situations of others.[85] People empathize when they visualize themselves in the other person's place as if they are the other person. This perceptual experience is both cognitive and emotional, meaning that empathy is about understanding as well as feeling what the other person feels in that context. Empathizing with others improves our sensitivity to the external causes of another person's performance and behavior, thereby reducing fundamental attribution error. A supervisor who imagines what it's like to be a single mother, for example, would become more sensitive to the external causes of lateness and other events among such employees. However, trying to empathize with others without spending time with them might actually increase rather than reduce stereotyping and other perceptual biases.[86]

> **LO3-5** Outline the main features of a global mindset and justify its usefulness to employees and organizations.

GLOBAL MINDSET: DEVELOPING PERCEPTIONS ACROSS BORDERS

Rakuten Inc. is Japan's most popular e-commerce website and one of the 10 largest Internet companies in the world. The Tokyo-based firm is rapidly expanding beyond Japanese borders, which demands a more global focus. "In the online business, which easily crosses national boundaries, domestic companies are not our sole rivals," explains Rakuten CEO Hiroshi Mikitani. Therefore, Mikitani recently made English the company's official in-house language. Even more important,

Rakuten is seeking out job applicants with international experience and a mindset to match. "Since we declared our intention to make English our official language, we've had more applicants that clearly have a global mindset," says Mikitani.[87]

Global mindset has become an important attribute of job applicants at Rakuten and other companies with international operations. A **global mindset** refers to an individual's ability to perceive, know about, and process information across cultures. It includes (a) an awareness of, openness to, and respect for other views and practices in the world; (b) the capacity to empathize and act effectively across cultures; (c) the ability to process complex information about novel environments; and (d) the ability to comprehend and reconcile intercultural matters with multiple levels of thinking.[88]

Let's look at each of these features. First, global mindset occurs as people develop more of a global than local/parochial frame of reference about their business and its environment. They also have more knowledge and appreciation of many cultures and do not judge the competence of others by their national or ethnic origins. Second, global mindset includes understanding the mental models held by colleagues from other cultures as well as their emotional experiences in a given situation. Furthermore, this empathy translates into effective use of words and behaviors that are compatible with the local culture. Third, people with a strong global mindset are able to process and analyze large volumes of information in new and diverse situations. Finally, global mindset involves the capacity to quickly develop useful mental models of situations, particularly at both a local and global level of analysis.

As you can imagine, employees who develop a global mindset offer tremendous value to organizations.[89] They develop better relationships across cultures by understanding and showing respect to distant colleagues and partners. They can sift through huge volumes of ambiguous and novel information transmitted in multinational relationships. They have a capacity to form networks and exchange resources more rapidly across borders. They also develop greater sensitivity and respond more quickly to emerging global opportunities.

Developing a Global Mindset

Developing a global mindset involves improving one's perceptions, so the practices described earlier on awareness, self-awareness, and meaningful interaction are relevant. As with most perceptual capabilities, a global mindset begins with self-awareness—understanding one's own beliefs, values, and attitudes. Through self-awareness, people are more open-minded and nonjudgmental when receiving and processing complex information for decision making. In addition, companies develop a global mindset by giving employees opportunities to compare their own mental models with those of coworkers or partners from other regions of the world. For example, employees might participate in online forums about how well the product's design or marketing strategy is received in the United States versus India or Chile. When companies engage in regular discussions about global competitors, suppliers, and other stakeholders, they eventually move the employee's sphere of awareness more toward that global level.

A global mindset develops through better knowledge of people and cultures. Some of that knowledge is acquired through formal programs, such as expatriate and diversity training, but deeper absorption results from immersion in those cultures. Just as executives need to experience frontline jobs to better understand their customers and employees, employees also need to have meaningful interaction with colleagues from other cultures in those settings. The more people embed themselves in the local environment (such as following local practices, eating local food, and using the local language), the more they tend to understand the perspectives and attitudes of their colleagues in those cultures. "We need people with a global mindset, and what better way to develop a global mindset, and what more realistic way, than for somebody to have an immersion experience with just enough safety net," says an Ernst & Young senior executive.[90]

4 chapter

Workplace Emotions, Attitudes, and Stress

Learning Objectives

After studying this chapter, you should be able to:

LO4-1 Explain how emotions and cognition (logical thinking) influence attitudes and behavior.

LO4-2 Discuss the dynamics of emotional labor and the role of emotional intelligence in the workplace.

LO4-3 Summarize the consequences of job dissatisfaction as well as strategies to increase organizational (affective) commitment.

LO4-4 Describe the stress experience and review three major stressors.

LO4-5 Identify five ways to manage workplace stress.

WestJet passengers traveling on two flights to Calgary, Canada, one November day were asked to scan their boarding passes at the departure gate using a large machine decorated as a Christmas gift box. Someone dressed as Santa Claus (but in WestJet blue rather than red) then appeared on the box's large screen, jovially asking by name what each surprised passenger would like for Christmas. The chat with Santa raised holiday spirits, but the real delight occurred several hours later on arrival at the Calgary Airport luggage carousel. Christmas lights and decorations came alive and fake snow fell as the conveyor started up. Then, instead of passenger luggage (which arrived later), the conveyor transported scarves, toys, smartphones, and other gifts, each carefully wrapped with the names of the passengers who had wished for them. WestJet employees had documented the Christmas wishes from the departure gate Santa interview and scurried around Calgary to find and wrap each gift while the four-hour flights were en route.

The WestJet Christmas Miracle event symbolizes the airline's focus on positive emotions and attitudes. "That's what WestJet is all about," explains WestJet vice president Richard Bartrem. "We like to share that fun, friendly, and caring spirit." Approximately 175 employees were directly involved, but WestJet CEO Gregg Saretsky reports that the event and its subsequent online video had a powerful effect on all WestJet employees (called WestJetters). "[We have] almost 10,000 WestJetters, who are saying they have never felt more proud than to see the reflection of our culture in that video."[1]

In less than two decades, WestJet Airlines Ltd. has grown to become one of the top-rated and most successful airlines in the world. CEO Gregg Saretsky reminds people that the airline's low fares and careful cost controls alone do not explain its success. Dozens of discount airlines have failed in Canada because they forgot the critical ingredient of having enthusiastic, energized, and loyal staff. In other words, WestJet and other organizations must pay attention to the themes discussed in this chapter: employee emotions, attitudes, and well-being.

This chapter begins by describing emotions and explaining how they influence attitudes and behavior. Next, we consider the dynamics of emotional labor, followed by the popular topic of emotional intelligence. The specific work attitudes of job satisfaction and organizational commitment are then discussed, including their association with various employee behaviors and work performance. The final section looks at work-related stress, including the stress experience, three prominent stressors, individual differences in stress, and ways to combat excessive stress.

LO4-1 Explain how emotions and cognition (logical thinking) influence attitudes and behavior.

EMOTIONS IN THE WORKPLACE

Emotions influence almost everything we do in the workplace. This is a strong statement, and one that you would rarely find a dozen years ago among organizational behavior experts. Most OB theories still assume that a person's thoughts and actions are governed primarily or exclusively by logical thinking (called *cognition*).[2] Yet groundbreaking neuroscience discoveries have revealed that our perceptions, attitudes, decisions, and behavior are influenced by emotions as well as cognitions.[3] In fact, emotions may have a greater influence because they often occur before cognitive processes and, consequently, influence the latter. By ignoring emotionality, many theories have overlooked a large piece of the puzzle about human behavior in the workplace.

Emotions are physiological, behavioral, and psychological episodes experienced toward an object, person, or event that create a state of readiness.[4] These "episodes" are very brief events that typically subside or occur in waves lasting from milliseconds to a few minutes. Emotions are directed toward someone or something. For example, we experience joy, fear, anger, and other emotional episodes toward tasks, customers, or a software program we are using. This differs from *moods*, which are not directed toward anything in particular and tend to be longer-term emotional states.[5]

Emotions are experiences. They represent changes in our physiological state (e.g., blood pressure, heart rate), psychological state

emotions physiological, behavioral, and psychological episodes experienced toward an object, person, or event that create a state of readiness

attitudes the cluster of beliefs, assessed feelings, and behavioral intentions toward a person, object, or event (called an attitude object)

(e.g., thought process), and behavior (e.g., facial expression).[7] Most of these emotional reactions are subtle; they occur without our awareness. This is an important point because the topic of emotions often conjures up images of people "getting emotional." In reality, most emotions are fleeting, low-intensity events that influence our behavior without conscious awareness.[8] Finally, emotions put us in a state of readiness. When we get worried, for example, our heart rate and blood pressure increase to make our body better prepared to engage in fight or flight. Strong emotions trigger our conscious awareness of a threat or opportunity in the external environment.

Types of Emotions

People experience many emotions and various combinations of emotions, but all of them have two common features, illustrated in Exhibit 4.1.[9] One feature is that all emotions have an associated valence (called *core affect*) signaling that the perceived object or event should be approached or avoided. In other words, all emotions evaluate environmental conditions as good or bad, helpful or harmful, positive or negative, and so forth. Furthermore, negative emotions tend to generate stronger

---

"Don't let us forget that the small emotions are the great captains of our lives, and that we obey them without knowing it."[6]

—Vincent van Gogh

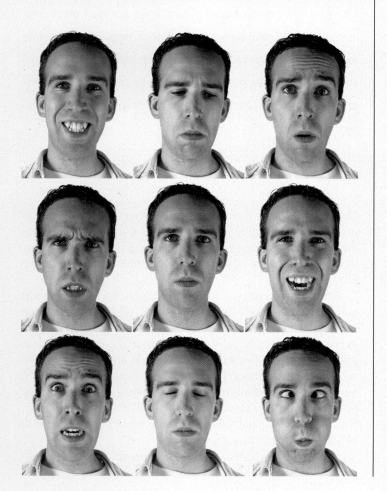

levels of activation than do positive emotions.[10] Fear and anger, for instance, are more intense experiences than are joy and delight, so they have a stronger effect on our actions. This valence asymmetry likely occurs because negative emotions protect us from harm and are therefore more critical for our survival.

The second feature is that emotions vary in their level of activation. By definition, emotions put us in a state of readiness and, as we discuss in the next chapter, are the primary source of individual motivation. Some emotional experiences, such as when we are suddenly surprised, are strong enough to consciously motivate us to act without careful thought. Most emotional experiences are more subtle, but even they activate enough to make us more aware of our environment.

Emotions, Attitudes, and Behavior

To understand how emotions influence our thoughts and behavior in the workplace, we first need to know about attitudes. **Attitudes** represent the cluster of beliefs, assessed feelings, and behavioral intentions toward a person, object, or event (called an *attitude object*).[11] Attitudes are *judgments,* whereas emotions are *experiences.* In other words, attitudes involve evaluations of an attitude object, whereas emotions operate as events, usually without our awareness. Attitudes might also operate nonconsciously, but we are usually aware of and consciously think about those evaluations. Another distinction is that we experience most emotions very briefly, whereas our attitude toward someone or something is more stable over time.[12]

Exhibit 4.1 Circumplex Model of Emotions

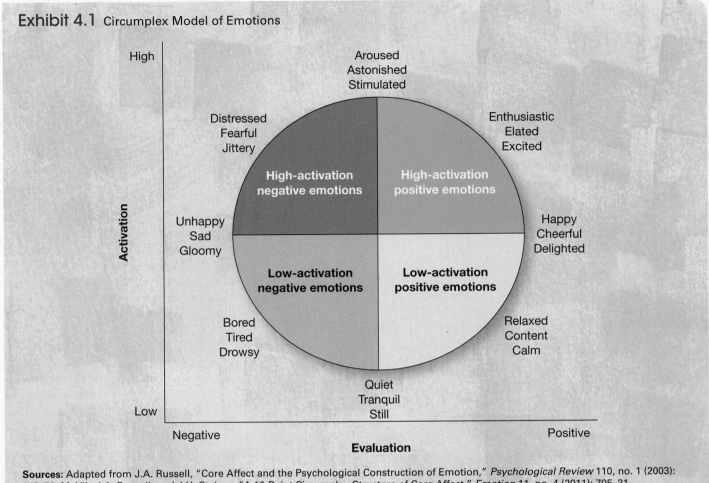

Sources: Adapted from J.A. Russell, "Core Affect and the Psychological Construction of Emotion," *Psychological Review* 110, no. 1 (2003): 145–72; M. Yik, J.A. Russell, and J.H. Steiger, "A 12-Point Circumplex Structure of Core Affect," *Emotion* 11, no. 4 (2011): 705–31.

Until recently, experts believed that attitudes could be understood just by the three cognitive components illustrated on the left side of Exhibit 4.2: beliefs, feelings, and behavioral intentions. Now evidence suggests that a parallel emotional process is also at work, shown on the right side of the exhibit.[13] Using attitude toward mergers as an example, let's look more closely at this model, beginning with the traditional cognitive perspective of attitudes.

- *Beliefs.* These are your established perceptions about the attitude object—what you believe to be true. For example, you might believe that mergers reduce job security for employees in the merged firms, or that mergers increase the company's competitiveness in this era of globalization. These beliefs are perceived facts that you acquire from experience and other forms of learning. Each of these beliefs also has a valence; that is, we have a positive or negative feeling about each belief (e.g., better job security is good).

- *Feelings.* Feelings represent your conscious positive or negative evaluations of the attitude object. Some people think mergers are good; others think they are bad. Your like or dislike of mergers represents your assessed feelings. According to the traditional cognitive perspective of attitudes (left side of the model), feelings are calculated from your beliefs about mergers and the associated

feelings about those beliefs. If you believe that mergers typically have negative consequences such as layoffs and organizational politics, you will form negative feelings toward mergers in general or about a specific planned merger in your organization. However, recent evidence suggests the opposite can also occur; your feelings about something can cause you to change your feelings about specific beliefs regarding that target.[14] For example, you might normally enjoy the challenge of hard work, but if you dislike your boss and he or she has high performance expectations, then you develop negative feelings about hard work.

- *Behavioral intentions.* Intentions represent your motivation to engage in a particular behavior regarding the attitude object.[15] Upon hearing that the company will merge with another organization, you might become motivated to look for a job elsewhere or possibly to complain to management about the merger decision. Your feelings toward mergers motivate your behavioral intentions, and which actions you choose depends on your past experience, personality, and social norms of appropriate behavior.

Several contingencies weaken the beliefs–feelings–intentions–behavior relationship. First, people with the same beliefs might form quite different feelings toward the attitude object because they have different valences for those beliefs. Two employees

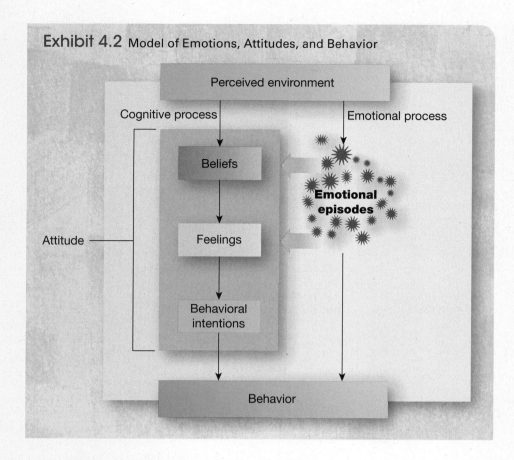

Exhibit 4.2 Model of Emotions, Attitudes, and Behavior

Perceived environment

Cognitive process / Emotional process

Beliefs

Emotional episodes

Feelings

Attitude

Behavioral intentions

Behavior

Exhibit 4.2 illustrates this process, which (like the cognitive process) also begins with perceptions of the world around us. Our brain tags incoming sensory information with emotional markers based on a quick and imprecise evaluation of whether that information supports or threatens our innate drives. These markers are not calculated feelings; they are automatic and nonconscious emotional responses based on very thin slices of sensory information.[17] The experienced emotions then influence our feelings about the attitude object. For example, at the beginning of this chapter we described how WestJet employees experienced positive emotions from the Christmas Miracle event. These positive emotions would have produced a more positive attitude toward the company.

To explain this process in more detail, consider your attitude toward mergers. You might experience worry, nervousness, or relief upon learning that your company intends to merge with a competitor. The fuzzy dots on the right side of Exhibit 4.2 illustrate the numerous emotional episodes you experience upon hearing the merger announcement, subsequently thinking about the merger, discussing the merger with coworkers, and so on. These emotions are transmitted to the reasoning process, where they are logically analyzed along with other information about the attitude object.[18] Thus, while you are consciously evaluating whether the merger is good or bad, your emotions are already sending core affect (good–bad) signals, and those emotional signals sway your conscious evaluation. In fact, we often deliberately "listen in" on our emotions to help us consciously decide whether to support or oppose something.[19]

The influence of both cognitive reasoning and emotions on attitudes is most apparent when they disagree with each other. People occasionally experience this mental tug-of-war, sensing that something isn't right even though they can't think of any logical reason to be concerned. This conflicting experience indicates that the person's logical analysis of the situation (left side of Exhibit 4.2) can't identify reasons to support the emotional reaction (right side of Exhibit 4.2).[20] Should we pay attention to our emotional response or our logical analysis? This question is not easy to answer, but some studies indicate that

might hold the common belief that their boss pushes employee performance, yet they form different feelings toward their boss because but one dislikes being pushed to perform better whereas the other employee appreciates this style of leadership.

Second, people with the same feelings toward the attitude object might develop different behavioral intentions. Suppose that two employees equally dislike their boss. One employee complains to the union or upper management while the other employee looks for a job elsewhere. They respond differently because of their unique experiences, personal values, self-concept, and so forth. Later in this chapter we describe the four main responses to dissatisfaction and other negative attitudes. Third, people with the same behavioral intention might behave differently. For example, two people might intend to quit because they dislike their boss, but only one does so because the other employee can't find better job opportunities.

> The influence of both cognitive reasoning and emotions on attitudes is most apparent when they disagree with each other.

How Emotions Influence Attitudes and Behavior The cognitive model has dominated attitude research for decades, yet we now know that emotions also have a central role in forming and changing employee attitudes.[16] The right side of

while executives tend to make quick decisions based on their gut feelings (emotional response), the best decisions tend to occur when executives spend time logically evaluating the situation.[21] Thus, we should pay attention to both the cognitive and emotional sides of the attitude model, and hope they agree with each other most of the time!

Generating Positive Emotions at Work Some companies seem to be well aware of the dual cognitive–emotional attitude process because they try to inject more positive experiences in the workplace.[22] Google Inc. is famous for its superb perks, including in-house coffee bars, gourmet cafeterias, conversation areas that look like vintage sub-

Google Offices, Dublin, Ireland

way cars, personal development courses, game rooms, free haircuts, and slides to descend to the floor below. Admiral Group, rated the best company to work for in the United Kingdom, has a "Ministry of Fun" committee that introduces plenty of positive emotions through Nintendo Wii competitions, interdepartmental Olympics, and other fun activities. "We know that our people spend a lot of time in work and we want to make sure that they enjoy this time," says Admiral CEO Henry Engelhardt.[23]

Some critics might argue that the organization's main focus should be to create positive emotions through the job itself as

well as natural everyday occurrences such as polite customers and supportive coworkers. Still, most people perform work that produces some negative emotions, and research has found that humor and fun at work—whether natural or contrived—can potentially offset some of the negative experiences.[24] Overall, corporate leaders need to keep in mind that emotions shape employee attitudes and, as we will discuss later, attitudes influence various forms of work-related behavior.

One last comment about Exhibit 4.2: Notice the arrow from the emotional episodes to behavior. It indicates that emotions

Best Employers to Work for in America, Europe, Latin America, and China[25]

Rank	Top 5 in America	Top 5 in Europe	Top 5 in Latin America	Top 5 in Greater China
1	Google	Capital One (UK)	Kimberly-Clark	Autodesk Software
2	SAS	Schoenen Torfs (Belgium)	Accor	Beijing TLScontact Consulting Co.
3	Boston Consulting Group	EnergiMidt (Denmark)	Microsoft	eBay & PayPal Technology
4	Edward Jones	DIS (Germany)	McDonald's	EMC China
5	Quicken Loans	Hygeia Hospital (Greece)	Belcorp	HDS China

None of the major "best employer" survey firms rank order companies across Asia. They rank order only for specific countries, so Greater China is shown here as an illustration. The top 5 list in Europe represents only large companies; there is a separate list for small and midsized firms. All top 5 firms in Latin America have operations across several countries; only Belcorp (Peru) is headquartered in that region.

cognitive dissonance
an emotional experience caused by a perception that our beliefs, feelings, and behavior are incongruent with one another

directly (without conscious thinking) influence a person's behavior. This occurs when we jump suddenly if someone sneaks up on us. It also occurs in everyday situations because even low-intensity emotions automatically change our facial expressions. These actions are not carefully thought out. They are automatic emotional responses that are learned or hardwired by heredity for particular situations.[26]

Cognitive Dissonance

Imagine that you have just signed a contract for new electronic whiteboards to be installed throughout the company's meeting rooms. The deal was expensive but, after consulting several staff, you felt that the technology would be valuable in this electronic age. Yet, you felt a twinge of regret soon after signing the contract. This emotional experience is **cognitive dissonance**, which occurs when people perceive that their beliefs, feelings, and behavior are incongruent with each

special markers and computer software. Or maybe you had a fleeting realization that buying electronic whiteboards costing several times more than traditional whiteboards is inconsistent with your personal values and company culture of thrift and value. Whatever the reason, the dissonance occurs because your attitude (it's good to be cost conscious) is inconsistent with your behavior (buying expensive whiteboards). Most people like to think of themselves—and be viewed by others—as rational and logical. You experience dissonance because this purchase decision is contrary to the logic of having a positive attitude about frugality and maximizing value.

How do we reduce cognitive dissonance?[28] Reversing the behavior might work, but few behaviors can be undone. In any event, dissonance still exists because others know about the behavior and that you performed it voluntarily. It would be too expensive to remove the electronic whiteboards after they have been installed and, in any event, coworkers already know that you made this purchase and did so willingly.

More often, people reduce cognitive dissonance by changing their beliefs and feelings. One dissonance-reducing strategy is to

> **When it is difficult to change behavior or reverse its consequences, people instead reduce cognitive dissonance by changing their beliefs and feelings.**

other.[27] This inconsistency generates emotions (such as feeling hypocritical) that motivate the person to create more consistency by changing one or more of these elements.

Why did you experience cognitive dissonance after purchasing the electronic whiteboards? Perhaps you remembered that some staff wanted flexibility, whereas the whiteboards require

develop more favorable attitudes toward specific features of the decision, such as forming a more positive opinion about the whiteboards' capacity to store whatever is written on them. People are also motivated to discover positive features of the decision they didn't notice earlier (e.g., the boards can change handwriting into typed text) and to discover subsequent problems with the alternatives they didn't choose (e.g., few traditional boards can be used as projection screens). A third strategy is more indirect; rather than try to overlook the high price of the electronic whiteboards, you reduce dissonance by emphasizing how your other decisions have been frugal. This framing compensates for your expensive whiteboard fling and thereby maintains your self-concept as a thrifty decision maker. Each of these mental acrobatics maintains some degree of consistency between the person's behavior (buying expensive whiteboards) and attitudes (being thrifty, appreciating good value).

Emotions and Personality

Our coverage of the dynamics of workplace emotions wouldn't be complete unless we mentioned that emotions are also partly determined by a person's personality, not just workplace experiences.[29] Some people experience positive emotions as a natural trait. People with more positive emotions typically have higher emotional stability and are extroverted (see Chapter 2). Those who experience more negative emotions tend to have higher neuroticism (lower emotional stability) and are introverted. Positive and negative emotional traits affect a person's attendance, turnover, and long-term work attitudes.[30] While positive and negative personality traits have some effect, other research concludes that the actual situation in which people work has a noticeably stronger influence on their attitudes and behavior.[31]

LO4-2 Discuss the dynamics of emotional labor and the role of emotional intelligence in the workplace.

MANAGING EMOTIONS AT WORK

People are expected to manage their emotions in the workplace. They must conceal their frustration when serving an irritating customer, display compassion to an ill patient, and hide their boredom in a long meeting with other executives. These are all forms of **emotional labor**—the effort, planning, and control needed to express organizationally desired emotions during interpersonal transactions.[32] Almost everyone is expected to abide by *display rules*—norms or explicit rules requiring us within our role to display specific emotions and to hide other emotions. Emotional labor demands are higher in jobs requiring a variety of emotions (e.g., anger as well as joy) and more intense emotions (e.g., showing delight rather than smiling weakly), as well as in jobs where interaction with clients is frequent and longer. Emotional labor also increases when employees must precisely rather than casually abide by the display rules.[33] This particularly occurs in the service industries, where employees have frequent face-to-face interaction with clients.

Emotional Display Norms across Cultures

Norms about displaying or hiding your true emotions vary considerably across cultures.[34] One major study points to Ethiopia, Japan, and Austria (among others) as cultures that discourage emotional expression. Instead, people are expected to be subdued, have relatively monotonic voice intonation, and avoid physical movement and touching that display emotions. In contrast, cultures such as Kuwait, Egypt, Spain, and Russia allow or encourage more vivid display of emotions and expect people to act more consistently with their true emotions. In these cultures, people are expected to more honestly reveal their thoughts and feelings, be dramatic in their conversational tones,

and be animated in their use of nonverbal behaviors. For example, 81 percent of Ethiopians and 74 percent of Japanese agreed that it is considered unprofessional to express emotions overtly in their culture, whereas 43 percent of Americans, 33 percent of Italians, and only 19 percent of Spaniards, Cubans, and Egyptians agreed with this statement.[35]

Emotional Dissonance

Most jobs expect employees to engage in some level of emotional labor, such as displaying courtesy to unruly passengers or maintaining civility to coworkers. Often, employees are supposed to show emotions that are quite different from the emotions they actually experience at that moment. This incongruence produces an emotional tension called **emotional dissonance**. Employees often handle these discrepancies by engaging in *surface acting*; they pretend that they feel the expected emotion even though they actually experience a different emotion.

One problem with surface acting is that it can lead to higher stress and burnout.[36] By definition, emotional labor requires effort and attention, which consume personal energy. Emotional labor also potentially requires people to act contrary to their self-view, which can lead to psychological separation from self. These problems are greater when employees need to frequently display emotions that oppose their genuine emotions. A second problem with surface acting is that pretending to feel particular emotions can be challenging. A genuine emotion automatically activates a complex set of facial muscles and body positions, all of which are difficult to replicate when pretending to have these emotions. Meanwhile, our true emotions tend to reveal themselves as subtle gestures, usually without our awareness. More often than not, observers see when we are faking and sense that we feel a different emotion.[37]

Employees can somewhat reduce psychological damage caused by surface acting by viewing their act as a natural part of their role. Flight attendants can remain pleasant to unruly passengers more easily when they define themselves by their customer service skill. By adopting this view, their faking is not deprivation of personal self-worth. Instead, it is demonstration of their skill and professionalism. The dissonant interactions are accomplishments rather than dreaded chores.[38] Another strategy is to engage in *deep acting* rather than surface acting.[39] Deep acting involves visualizing reality differently, which then produces emotions more consistent with the required emotions. Faced with an angry passenger, a flight attendant might replace hostile emotions with compassion by viewing the passenger's behavior as a sign of his or her discomfort or anxiety. Deep acting requires considerable emotional intelligence, which we discuss next.

emotional labor the effort, planning, and control needed to express organizationally desired emotions during interpersonal transactions

emotional dissonance the psychological tension experienced when the emotions people are required to display are quite different from the emotions they actually experience at that moment

EMOTIONAL INTELLIGENCE

The University of South Florida (USF) College of Medicine discovered from surveys that its graduates required emotional intelligence training to perform their jobs better. "We've created a lot of doctors that are like House," says USF's medical college dean, referring to the fictional TV physician with the caustic interpersonal style. Now, some USF students are assigned to one of America's top hospitals, where they develop their ability to understand and manage emotions through coaching and role modeling by hospital staff. "You have to have an emotionally intelligent, collaborative, interdisciplinary team practicing if you want young trainees to adopt that as their model," explains the hospital CEO.[40]

USF's College of Medicine and many other organizations increasingly recognize that **emotional intelligence (EI)** improves performance in many types of jobs. Emotional intelligence includes a set of *abilities* that enable us to recognize and regulate our own emotions as well as the emotions of other people. This definition refers to the four main dimensions shown in Exhibit 4.3.[41]

- *Awareness of our own emotions.* This is the ability to perceive and understand the meaning of our own emotions. We are more sensitive to subtle emotional responses to events and understand their message. Self-aware people are better able to eavesdrop on their emotional responses to specific situations and to use this awareness as conscious information.[42]

- *Management of our own emotions.* Emotional intelligence includes the ability to manage our own emotions, something that we all do to some extent. We keep disruptive impulses in check. We try not to feel angry or frustrated when events go against us. We try to feel and express joy and happiness toward others when the occasion calls for these emotional displays. We try to create a second wind of motivation later in the workday. Notice that management of our own emotions goes beyond displaying behaviors that represent desired emotions in a particular situation. It includes generating or suppressing emotions. In other words, the deep acting described earlier requires high levels of the self-regulation component of emotional intelligence.

- *Awareness of others' emotions.* This dimension refers to the ability to perceive and understand the emotions of other people. To a large extent, awareness of other people's emotions is represented by *empathy*—having an understanding of and sensitivity to the feelings, thoughts, and situations of others (see Chapter 3). This ability includes understanding the other person's situation, experiencing his or her emotions, and knowing his or her needs, even when unstated. Awareness of others' emotions extends beyond empathy. It also includes being organizationally aware, such as sensing office politics and understanding social networks.

- *Management of others' emotions.* This dimension of EI involves managing other people's emotions. This includes

Exhibit 4.3 Dimensions of Emotional Intelligence

	Yourself	Others
Recognition of emotions	**Awareness of own emotions**	**Awareness of others' emotions**
Regulation of emotions	**Management of own emotions**	**Management of others' emotions**

Abilities

Sources: D. Goleman, "An EI-Based Theory of Performance," in *The Emotionally Intelligent Workplace*, ed. C. Cherniss and D. Goleman (San Francisco: Jossey-Bass, 2001), 28; Peter J. Jordan and Sandra A. Lawrence, "Emotional Intelligence in Teams: Development and Initial Validation of the Short Version of the Workgroup Emotional Intelligence Profile (WEIP-S)," *Journal of Management & Organization* 15 (2009): 452–69.

consoling people who feel sad, emotionally inspiring your team members to complete a class project on time, getting strangers to feel comfortable working with you, and managing dysfunctional emotions among staff who experience conflict with customers or other employees.

These four dimensions of emotional intelligence form a hierarchy.[44] Awareness of your own emotions is lowest because you need awareness to engage in the higher levels of emotional intelligence. You can't manage your own emotions if you don't know what they are (i.e., low self-awareness). Managing other people's emotions is the highest level of EI because this ability requires awareness of your own and others' emotions. To diffuse an angry conflict between two employees, for example, you need to understand the emotions they are experiencing and manage your emotions (and display of emotions). To manage your own emotions, you also need to be aware of your current emotions.

Emotional Intelligence Outcomes and Development

Does emotional intelligence make a difference in employee performance and well-being? A few OB experts question the usefulness of the emotional intelligence concept, claiming that there is a lack of agreement on its definition and that existing concepts such as personality and general intelligence can be used instead.[45] However, a consensus is slowly emerging around the meaning of EI, and there is considerable research suggesting that this concept does help us understand what goes on in social relations.

Most jobs involve social interaction with coworkers or external stakeholders, so employees need emotional intelligence to work effectively.[46] Research suggests that people with high EI are better at interpersonal relations, perform better in jobs requiring emotional labor, are superior leaders, make better decisions involving social exchanges, are more successful in many aspects of job interviews, and are better at knowledge sharing. For example, leaders need substantial emotional intelligence because their work involves regulating their own emotions as part of emotional labor (e.g., showing patience to employees even when they might feel frustrated) as well as regulating the emotions of others (e.g., helping staff members feel optimism for the future even though they just lost an important contract). However, emotional intelligence does not improve some forms of performance, such as tasks that require minimal social interaction.[47]

Given the potential value of emotional intelligence, it's not surprising that some organizations try to measure this ability in job applicants. For instance, EI is one factor considered for entry into the elite pararescue jumper training program in the United States Air Force (USAF), which costs $250,000 per graduate and has an 80 percent failure rate. USAF research has found that trainees with high scores on several emotional intelligence dimensions are more than twice as likely to complete the pararescue jumper program.[48]

Several studies have found that companies can also increase employees' emotional intelligence through training programs designed for that purpose.[49] For instance, staff members at a Netherlands residence for people with intellectual disabilities completed an EI training program where they learned about the concept, reviewed feedback on their initial EI test scores, applied EI dimensions to case studies, developed two personal goals to improve their EI profile, and later received professional feedback based on videos showing them meeting with difficult clients. Generally, employees improve their emotional intelligence through awareness of the concept, self-awareness of their EI scores, and coaching and other forms of feedback. Emotional intelligence also increases with age; it is part of the process called maturity.

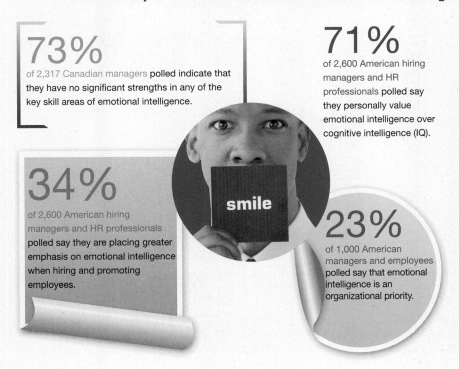

Emotional Intelligence:
Valued, but Low Skill and Low Priority[43]

73%
of 2,317 Canadian managers polled indicate that they have no significant strengths in any of the key skill areas of emotional intelligence.

71%
of 2,600 American hiring managers and HR professionals polled say they personally value emotional intelligence over cognitive intelligence (IQ).

34%
of 2,600 American hiring managers and HR professionals polled say they are placing greater emphasis on emotional intelligence when hiring and promoting employees.

23%
of 1,000 American managers and employees polled say that emotional intelligence is an organizational priority.

Improving Emotional Intelligence

1. Training programs—learn about emotional intelligence, then receive ongoing feedback in realistic situations.

2. Self-reflection—after an event, employees write a journal report on their experience in which they reflect on what happened and how it could be improved in the future.

3. Coaching—a professional coach observes the individual in work situations and listens to his or her nonobserved experiences, then provides debriefing feedback about how to improve their emotions-based behavior in those situations.

4. Maturity—people tend to improve their emotional intelligence with age due to improved self-awareness, reinforcement of emotions management, and numerous opportunities to develop their emotional intelligence skills.

So far, this chapter has introduced the model of emotions and attitudes, as well as emotional intelligence, as the means by which we manage emotions in the workplace. The next two sections look at two specific attitudes: job satisfaction and organizational commitment. These two attitudes are so important in our understanding of workplace behavior that some experts suggest the two combined should be called "overall job attitude."[50]

LO4-3 Summarize the consequences of job dissatisfaction as well as strategies to increase organizational (affective) commitment.

JOB SATISFACTION

Probably the most studied attitude in organizational behavior is **job satisfaction**, a person's evaluation of his or her job and work context.[51] It is an *appraisal* of the perceived job characteristics, work environment, and emotional experiences at work. Satisfied employees have a favorable evaluation of their jobs, based on their observations and emotional experiences. Job satisfaction is best viewed as a collection of attitudes about different aspects of the job and work context. You might like your coworkers but be less satisfied with your workload, for instance.

How satisfied are employees at work? The answer depends on the person, the workplace, and the country. Global surveys, such as the one shown in Exhibit 4.4, indicate with some consistency that job satisfaction tends to be highest in India, the United States, and some Nordic countries (such as Denmark and Sweden). The lowest levels of overall job satisfaction are usually recorded in Hungary and several Asian countries (e.g., Japan, Mainland China).[52]

Can we conclude from these surveys that most employees in Denmark and India are happy at work? Possibly, but their

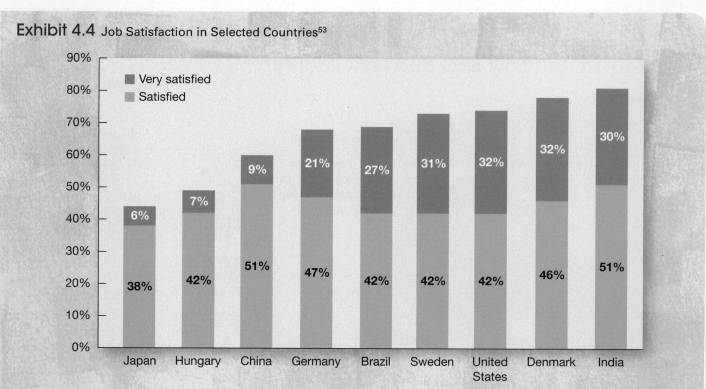

Exhibit 4.4 Job Satisfaction in Selected Countries[53]

Note: Percentage of employees in each country who said they are, in general, satisfied or very satisfied working for their current employer. Survey data were collected in 2013 for Randstad Holdings nv, with a minimum of 400 employees in each country.

overall job satisfaction probably isn't as high as these statistics suggest. One problem is that surveys often use a single direct question, such as "How satisfied are you with your job?" Many dissatisfied employees are reluctant to reveal their feelings in a direct question because this is tantamount to admitting that they made a poor job choice and are not enjoying life. This inflated result is evidenced by the fact that employees tend to report much less satisfaction with specific aspects of their work. Furthermore, studies report that many employees plan to look for work within the next year or would leave their current employer if the right opportunity came along.[54]

A second problem is that cultural values make it difficult to compare job satisfaction across countries. People in China and Japan tend to subdue their emotions in public, and there is evidence that they also avoid extreme survey ratings such as "very satisfied." A third problem is that job satisfaction changes with economic conditions. Employees with the highest job satisfaction in current surveys tend to be in countries where the economies are chugging along quite well.[55]

Job Satisfaction and Work Behavior

One of the most important organizational behavior questions is to what degree job satisfaction influences behavior in the workplace. The general answer is that job satisfaction has a considerable effect on employee behavior.[56] However, a more precise answer is that people respond differently to job dissatisfaction, and these different responses depend on the person and the situation. A useful template for organizing and understanding the consequences of job dissatisfaction is the **exit–voice–loyalty–neglect (EVLN) model**. As the name suggests, the EVLN model identifies four ways that employees respond to dissatisfaction:[57]

- *Exit.* Exit includes leaving the organization, transferring to another work unit, or at least trying to get away from the dissatisfying situation. The traditional theory is that job dissatisfaction builds over time and is eventually strong enough to motivate employees to search for better work opportunities elsewhere. This is likely true to some extent, but the most recent opinion is that specific "shock events" quickly energize employees to think about and engage in exit behavior. For example, the emotional reaction you experience to an unfair management decision or a conflict episode with a coworker motivates you to look at job ads and speak to friends about job opportunities where they work. This begins the process of realigning your self-concept more with another company than with your current employer.[58]

- *Voice.* Voice is any attempt to change, rather than escape from, the dissatisfying situation. Voice can be a constructive response, such as recommending ways for management to improve the situation, or it can be more confrontational, such as filing formal grievances or forming a coalition to oppose a decision.[59] In the extreme, some employees might engage in counterproductive behaviors to get attention and force changes in the organization.

- *Loyalty.* In the original version of this model, loyalty was not an outcome of dissatisfaction. Rather, it determined whether people chose exit or voice (i.e., high loyalty resulted in voice; low loyalty produced exit).[60] More recent writers describe loyalty as an outcome, but in various and somewhat unclear ways. Generally, they suggest that "loyalists" are employees who respond to dissatisfaction by patiently waiting—some say they "suffer in silence"—for the problem to work itself out or be resolved by others.[61]

- *Neglect.* Neglect includes reducing work effort, paying less attention to quality, and increasing absenteeism and lateness. It is generally considered a passive activity that has negative consequences for the organization.

As we mentioned, how employees respond to job dissatisfaction depends on the person and situation.[62] The individual's personality, values, and self-concept are important factors. For example, people with a high-conscientiousness personality are less likely to engage in neglect and more likely to engage in voice. Past experience also influences which EVLN action is applied. Employees who were unsuccessful with voice in the past are more likely to engage in exit or neglect when experiencing job dissatisfaction in the future. Another factor is loyalty, as it was originally intended in the EVLN model. Specifically, employees are more likely to quit when they have low loyalty to the company, and they are more likely to engage in voice when they have high loyalty. Finally, the response to dissatisfaction depends on the situation. Employees are less likely to use the exit option when there are few alternative job prospects, for example. Dissatisfied employees are more likely to use voice than the other options when they are aware that other employees are dependent on them.[63]

Job Satisfaction and Performance

Is a happy worker a more productive worker? Most corporate leaders likely think so. Yet, for most of the past century, organizational behavior scholars have challenged this "happy worker" hypothesis, concluding that job satisfaction minimally affects job performance. Now OB experts are concluding that maybe

the popular saying is correct after all; there is a *moderately* positive relationship between job satisfaction and performance. In other words, workers tend to be more productive *to some extent* when they have more positive attitudes toward their job and workplace.[64]

Why is job satisfaction associated with performance relationship only to some extent? One reason is that general attitudes (such as job satisfaction) don't predict specific behaviors very well. As the EVLN model explained, reduced performance (a form of neglect) is only one of four possible responses to dissatisfaction. A second reason is that some employees are

because many organizations do not reward good performance very well.

Job Satisfaction and Customer Satisfaction

Wegmans Food Markets in Rochester, New York, and HCL Technologies in Noida, India, are on opposite sides of the planet and in quite different industries, yet they both have the same unusual motto: *Employees first, customers second.* Why don't these companies put customers at the top of the

> ## "It just seems common sense to me that if you start with a happy, well-motivated workforce, you're much more likely to have happy customers."[66]
>
> —**Sir Richard Branson,** founder of Virgin Group

so tethered to technology or coworkers that they have little control over their performance. An assembly-line worker, for instance, installs a fixed number of windshields each hour with about the same quality of installation whether he or she is happy or unhappy with work. A third consideration is that job performance might cause job satisfaction, rather than vice versa.[65] Higher performers receive more rewards (including recognition) and, consequently, are more satisfied than low-performing employees who receive fewer rewards. The connection between job satisfaction and performance isn't stronger

stakeholder list? Their rationale is that customer satisfaction is a natural outcome of employee satisfaction. Put differently, it is difficult to keep customers happy if employee morale is low. "We really believe that if you put the employees first, they really and truly will take better care of the customer than anybody else," says Container Store chair and CEO Kip Tindell.[67]

These companies are applying the **service profit chain model**, which proposes that job satisfaction has a positive effect on customer service, which flows on to shareholder financial returns. Exhibit 4.5 diagrams this process. Specifically,

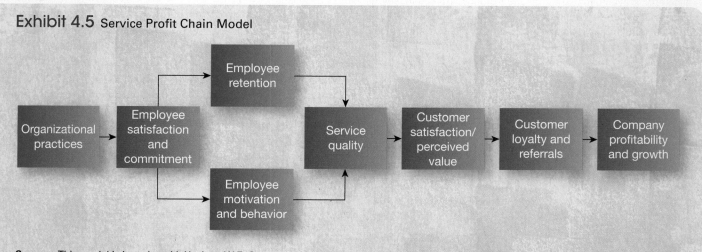

Exhibit 4.5 Service Profit Chain Model

Sources: This model is based on J.I. Heskett, W.E. Sasser, and L.A. Schlesinger, *The Service Profit Chain* (New York: Free Press, 1997); A.J. Rucci, S.P. Kirn, and R.T. Quinn, "The Employee-Customer-Profit Chain at Sears," *Harvard Business Review* 76 (1998): 83–97; S.P. Brown and S.K. Lam, "A Meta-Analysis of Relationships Linking Employee Satisfaction to Customer Responses," *Journal of Retailing* 84, no. 3 (2008): 243–55.

workplace practices affect job satisfaction, which influences employee retention, motivation, and behavior. These employee outcomes affect service quality, which then influences customer satisfaction and perceptions of value, customer referrals, and ultimately the company's profitability and growth. The service profit chain model has considerable research support. However, the benefits of job satisfaction do take considerable time to flow through to the organization's bottom line.[68]

Behind the service profit chain model are two key explanations why satisfied employees tend to produce happier and more loyal customers.[69] One explanation is that employees are usually in a more positive mood when they feel satisfied with their jobs and working conditions. Employees in a good mood more naturally and frequently display friendliness and positive emotions. When employees have good feelings, their behavior "rubs off" on most (but not all) customers, so customers feel happier and consequently form a positive evaluation of the service experience (i.e., higher service quality). The effect is also mutual—happy customers make employees happier—which can lead to a virtuous cycle of positive emotions in the service experience.

The second explanation is that satisfied employees are less likely to quit their jobs, so they have better knowledge and skills to serve clients. Lower turnover also enables customers to have the same employees serve them, so there is more consistent service. Some evidence indicates that customers build their loyalty to specific employees, not to the organization, so keeping employee turnover low tends to build customer loyalty.

Job Satisfaction and Business Ethics

Before leaving the topic of job satisfaction, we should mention that job satisfaction is also an ethical issue that influences the organization's reputation in the community. People spend a large portion of their time working in organizations, and many societies now expect companies to provide work environments that are safe and enjoyable. Indeed, employees in several countries closely monitor ratings of the best companies to work for, an indication that employee satisfaction is a virtue worth considerable goodwill to employers. This virtue is apparent when an organization has low job satisfaction. The company tries to hide this fact, and when morale problems become public, corporate leaders are usually quick to improve the situation.

ORGANIZATIONAL COMMITMENT

Organizational commitment represents the other half (with job satisfaction) of what some experts call "overall job attitude." **Affective organizational commitment** is the employee's emotional attachment to, involvement in, and identification with an organization. Affective commitment is a psychological bond whereby one chooses to be dedicated to and responsible for the organization.[70] As an example, most employees at West-Jet, the Canadian airline described at the beginning of this chapter, have high affective commitment because they feel an emotional bond to WestJet and identify with its core values.

Affective commitment is often distinguished from **continuance commitment**, which is a calculative attachment to the organization. This calculation takes two forms.[71] One form occurs where an employee has no alternative employment opportunities (e.g., "I dislike working here but there are no other jobs available"). This condition exists where unemployment is high, employees lack sufficient skills to be attractive to other employers, or the employee's skills are so specialized that there is limited demand for them nearby. The other form of continuance commitment occurs when leaving the company would be a significant financial sacrifice (e.g., "I hate this place but can't afford to quit!"). This perceived sacrifice condition occurs when the company offers high pay, benefits, and other forms of economic exchange in the employment relationship, or where quitting forfeits a large deferred financial bonus.

Affective Commitment around the Planet[72]

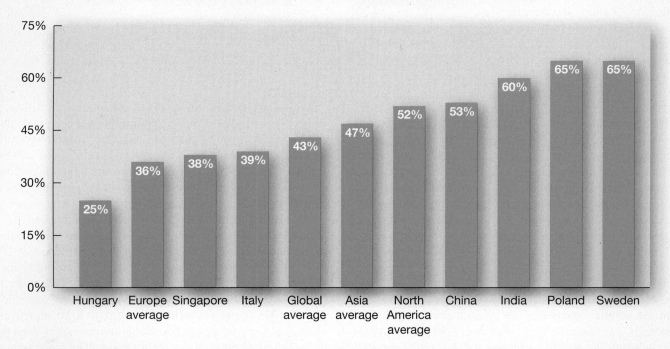

Note: Percentage of employees surveyed in selected countries who say they feel "totally committed" to their employer. More than 134,000 people in 29 countries were surveyed for Kelly Services.

Consequences of Affective and Continuance Commitment

Affective commitment can be a significant competitive advantage.[73] Employees with a strong psychological bond to the organization are less likely to quit their jobs and be absent from work. They also have higher work motivation and organizational citizenship, as well as somewhat higher job performance. Organizational commitment also improves customer satisfaction because long-tenure employees have better knowledge of work practices and because clients like to do business with the same employees. One warning is that employees with very high loyalty tend to have high conformity, which results in lower creativity. There are also cases of dedicated employees who have violated laws to defend the organization. However, most companies suffer from too little rather than too much affective commitment.

In contrast to the benefits of affective commitment, employees with high levels of continuance commitment tend to have *lower* performance and are *less* likely to engage in organizational citizenship behaviors. Furthermore, unionized employees with high continuance commitment are more likely to use formal grievances, whereas employees with high affective commitment engage in more cooperative problem solving when employee–employer relations sour.[74] Although some level of financial connection may be necessary, employers should not rely on continuance commitment instead of affective commitment. Employers still need to win employees' hearts (affective

commitment) beyond tying them financially to the organization (continuance commitment).

Building Organizational Commitment

There are almost as many ways to build affective commitment as there are topics in this textbook, but here are the most frequently mentioned strategies in the literature:

- *Justice and support.* Affective commitment is higher in organizations that fulfill their obligations to employees and abide by humanitarian values such as fairness, courtesy, forgiveness, and moral integrity. These values relate to the concept of organizational justice, which we discuss in the next chapter. Similarly, organizations that support employee well-being tend to cultivate higher levels of loyalty in return.[75]

- *Shared values.* The definition of affective commitment refers to a person's identification with the organization, and that identification is highest when employees believe their values are congruent with the organization's dominant values. Also, employees experience more comfort and predictability when they agree with the values underlying corporate decisions. This comfort increases their motivation to stay with the organization.[76]

- *Trust.* **Trust** refers to positive expectations one person has toward another person in situations involving risk.[77] Trust means putting faith in the other person or group. It is also a reciprocal activity: To receive trust, you must demonstrate trust. Employees identify with and feel obliged to work for an organization only when they trust its leaders. This explains why layoffs are one of the greatest blows to affective commitment; by reducing job security, companies reduce the trust employees have in their employer and the employment relationship.[78]

- *Organizational comprehension.* Organizational comprehension refers to how well employees understand the organization, including its strategic direction, social dynamics, and physical layout.[79] This awareness is a necessary prerequisite to affective commitment because it is difficult to identify with or feel loyal to something that you don't know very well. Furthermore, lack of information produces uncertainty, and the resulting stress can distance employees from that source of uncertainty (i.e., the organization). The practical implication here is to ensure that employees develop a reasonably clear and complete mental model of the organization. This occurs by giving staff information and opportunities to keep up to date about organizational events, interact with coworkers, discover what goes on in different parts of the organization, and learn about the organization's history and future plans.[80]

- *Employee involvement.* Employee involvement increases affective commitment by strengthening the employee's psychological ownership and social identity with the organization.[81] Employees feel that they are part of the organization when they participate in decisions that guide the organization's future (see Chapter 6). Employee involvement also builds loyalty because giving this power is a demonstration of the company's trust in its employees.

Organizational commitment and job satisfaction represent two of the most often studied and discussed attitudes in the workplace. Each is linked to emotional episodes and cognitive judgments about the workplace and relationship with the company. Emotions also play an important role in another concept that is on everyone's mind these days: stress. The final section of this chapter provides an overview of work-related stress and how it can be managed.

LO4-4 Describe the stress experience and review three major stressors.

WORK-RELATED STRESS AND ITS MANAGEMENT

When asked if they often feel stressed, most employees these days say "Yes!" Not only do most people understand the concept; they claim to have plenty of personal experience with it. **Stress** is most often described as an adaptive response to a situation that is perceived as challenging or threatening to the person's well-being.[82] It is a physiological and psychological condition that prepares us to adapt to hostile or noxious environmental conditions. Our heart rate increases, muscles tighten, breathing speeds up, and perspiration increases. Our body also moves more blood to the brain, releases adrenaline and other hormones, fuels the system by releasing more glucose and fatty acids, activates systems that sharpen our senses, and conserves resources by shutting down our immune system. One school of thought suggests that stress is a negative evaluation of the external environment. However, critics of this "cognitive appraisal" perspective point out that stress is more accurately described as an emotional experience, which may occur before or after a conscious evaluation of the situation.[83]

Whether stress is a complex emotion or a cognitive evaluation of the environment, it has become a pervasive experience in the daily lives of most people. Stress is typically described as a negative experience. This is known as *distress*—the degree of physiological, psychological, and behavioral deviation from healthy functioning. However,

Stressed Out,
Burnt Out[84]

72%
of 3,113 adult Canadians surveyed believe they experience excessive stress.

80%
of 1,004 employed American adults surveyed say they are stressed out on the job.

66%
of more than 900 Americans surveyed say their company/office does "nothing" to help alleviate stress in the workplace.

42%
of 6,700 Americans surveyed say they have left a job due to an overly stressful environment.

46%
of 7,288 American physicians surveyed report at least one of the three symptoms of professional burnout.

some level of stress—called *eustress*—is a necessary part of life because it activates and motivates people to achieve goals, change their environments, and succeed in life's challenges.[85] Our focus is on the causes and management of distress, because it has become a chronic problem in many societies.

General Adaptation Syndrome

The word *stress* was first used more than 500 years ago to describe the human response to harsh environmental conditions. However, it wasn't until the 1930s that researcher Hans Selye (often described as the father of stress research) first documented the stress experience, called the **general adaptation syndrome**. Selye determined (initially by studying rats) that people have a fairly consistent and automatic physiological response to stressful situations, which helps them cope with environmental demands.[86]

The general adaptation syndrome consists of the three stages shown in Exhibit 4.6. The *alarm reaction* stage occurs when a threat or challenge activates the physiological stress responses that were noted above. The individual's energy level and coping effectiveness decrease in response to the initial shock. The second stage, *resistance,* activates various biochemical, psychological, and behavioral mechanisms that give the individual more energy and engage coping mechanisms to overcome or remove the source of stress. To focus energy on the source of the stress, the body reduces resources to the immune system during this stage. This explains why people are more likely to catch a cold or some other illness when they experience prolonged stress. People have

a limited resistance capacity, and if the source of stress persists, the individual will eventually move into the third stage, *exhaustion*. Most of us are able to remove the source of stress or remove ourselves from that source before becoming too exhausted. However, people who frequently reach exhaustion have increased risk of long-term physiological and psychological damage.[87]

Consequences of Distress

Stress takes its toll on the human body.[88] Many people experience tension headaches, muscle pain, and related problems mainly due to muscle contractions from the stress response. Studies have found that high stress levels also contribute to cardiovascular disease, including heart attacks and strokes, and may be associated with some forms of cancer. Stress also produces various psychological consequences such as job dissatisfaction, moodiness, depression, and lower organizational commitment. Furthermore, various behavioral outcomes have been linked to high or persistent stress, including lower job performance, poor decision making, and increased workplace accidents and aggressive behavior. Most people react to stress through "fight or flight," so increased absenteeism is another outcome because it is a form of flight.[89]

A particular stress consequence, called *job burnout*, occurs when people experience emotional exhaustion, cynicism, and reduced feelings of personal accomplishment.[90] *Emotional exhaustion,* the first stage, is characterized by a lack of energy, tiredness, and a feeling that one's emotional resources are depleted. This is followed by *cynicism* (also called *depersonalization*), which is an indifferent attitude toward work, emotional detachment from clients, a cynical view of the organization, and a tendency to strictly follow rules and regulations rather than adapt to the needs of others. The final stage of burnout, called *reduced personal accomplishment,* entails feelings of diminished confidence in one's ability to perform the job well. In such situations, employees develop a sense of learned helplessness as they no longer believe that their efforts make a difference.

Stressors: The Causes of Stress

Before identifying ways to manage work-related stress, we must first understand its causes, known as stressors. **Stressors** include any environmental conditions that place a physical or emotional demand on a person.[91] There are numerous stressors in the workplace and in life in general. In this section, we'll highlight three of the most common work-related stressors: harassment and incivility, workload, and lack of task control.

Harassment and Incivility One of the fastest-growing sources of workplace stress is **psychological harassment**. Psychological harassment includes repeated hostile or unwanted conduct, verbal comments, actions,

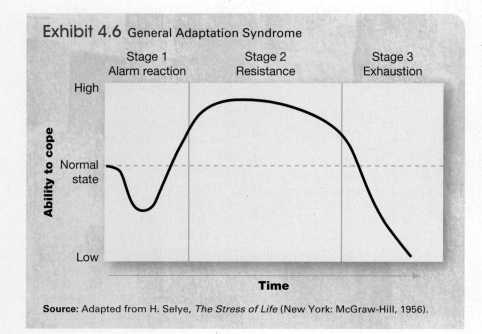

Exhibit 4.6 General Adaptation Syndrome

Source: Adapted from H. Selye, *The Stress of Life* (New York: McGraw-Hill, 1956).

and gestures that undermine an employee's dignity or psychological or physical integrity. This covers a broad landscape of behaviors, from threats and bullying to subtle yet persistent forms of incivility.[92] Some form or degree of psychological harassment exists in almost every workplace. This is apparent in one recent global survey of 16,517 employees which reported that 83 percent of Europeans, 65 percent of employees in North and South America, and 55 percent of people in Asia say they have been physically or emotionally bullied.[93]

Sexual harassment is a type of harassment in which a person's employment or job performance is conditional and depends on unwanted sexual relations (called *quid pro quo* harassment) and/or the person experiences sexual conduct from others (such as posting pornographic material) that unreasonably interferes with work performance or creates an intimidating, hostile, or offensive working environment (called *hostile work environment* harassment).[94]

Work Overload "We just keep rushing along in a confused state of never having time to do the things that seem to be pressing upon us." Sound familiar? Most of us probably had this thought over the past year. But this comment wasn't written in the past year or even in the past decade. It came from an article

called "Let's Slow Down!" in an RBC newsletter in 1949![95] The fact is, people have been struggling for more than a half century with the pace of life, including the challenges of performing too many tasks and working too many hours.

Why do employees work such long hours? One explanation is the combined effects of technology and globalization. People increasingly work with coworkers in distant time zones, and their communication habits of being constantly "on" make it difficult to separate work from personal life. A second factor is that many people are caught up in consumerism; they want to buy more goods and services, and doing so requires more income through longer work hours. A third reason, called the "ideal worker norm," is that professionals expect themselves and others to work longer work hours. For many, toiling away far beyond the normal workweek is a badge of honor, a symbol of their superhuman capacity to perform above others.[97]

Low Task Control One of the most important findings emerging from stress research is that employees are more stressed when they lack control over how and when they perform their tasks as well as lack control over the pace of work activity. Work is potentially more stressful when it is paced by a machine, involves monitoring equipment, or the work schedule is controlled by someone else. Low task control is a stressor because employees face high workloads without the ability to adjust the pace of the load to their own energy, attention span, and other resources. Furthermore, the degree to which low task control is a stressor increases with the burden of responsibility the employee must carry.[98] Assembly-line workers have low task control, but their stress can be fairly low if their level of responsibility is also low. In contrast, sports coaches are under immense pressure to win games (high responsibility), yet they have little control over what happens on the playing field (low task control).

Individual Differences in Stress

People experience different stress levels when exposed to the same stressor. One factor is the employee's physical health. Regular exercise and a healthy lifestyle produce a larger store of energy to cope with stress. A second individual difference is the coping strategy employees use to ward off a particular stressor.[99] People sometimes figure out ways to remove the stressor or to minimize its presence. Seeking support from others, reframing the stressor in a more positive light, blaming others for the stressor, and denying the stressor's existence are some other coping mechanisms. Some coping strategies work better for some stressors, and some are better across all stressors.[100] Thus, someone who uses a less effective coping mechanism in a particular situation would experience more stress in response to that situation. People have a tendency to rely on one or two coping strategies, and those who rely on

Chronic Work Overload in China[96]

Stress seems to be on the rise in China, mainly due to increasing workloads and hours of work. More than 30 percent of employees recently surveyed in China said they worked more than 10 hours every day over the previous six months. Another survey reported that 70 percent of white-collar workers in downtown Beijing show signs of overwork. "My brain doesn't seem to be working," said a 25-year-old media planner in Shanghai who had been working nonstop for 36 hours. "I don't have time to take a nap. Actually, I don't even have the energy to think if I'm tired or not."

generally poor coping strategies (such as denying the stressor exists) are going to experience more stress.

Personality is the third and possibly the most important reason why people experience different levels of stress when faced with the same stressor.[101] Individuals with low neuroticism (high emotional stability) usually experience lower stress levels because, by definition, they are less prone to anxiety, depression, and other negative emotions. Extraverts also tend to experience lower stress than do introverts, likely because extraversion includes a degree of positive thinking and extraverts interact with others, which helps buffer the effect of stressors. People with a positive self-concept—high self-esteem, self-efficacy, and internal locus of control (see Chapter 3)—feel more confident and in control when faced with a stressor. In other words, they tend to have a stronger sense of optimism.[102]

LO4-5 Identify five ways to manage workplace stress.

Managing Work-Related Stress

Many people deny the existence of their stress until it has more serious outcomes. This avoidance strategy creates a vicious cycle because the failure to cope with stress becomes another stressor on top of the one that created the stress in the first place. To prevent this vicious cycle, employers and employees need to apply one or more of the stress management strategies described next: remove the stressor, withdraw from the stressor, change stress perceptions, control stress consequences, and receive social support.[103]

How Americans Cope with Work-Related Stress[104]

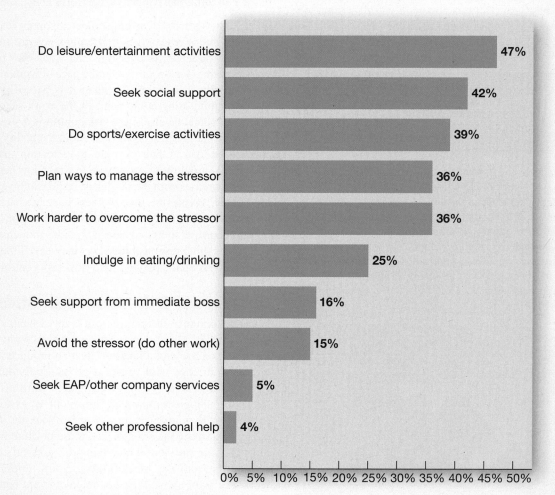

Note: This survey was conducted by Towers Watson in 2013 from 5,070 Americans working at companies employing 1,000 or more people. Leisure/entertainment examples include shopping, reading, listening to music, watching movies/TV, and playing games. Social support sources include friends, family, and coworkers. Indulgence activities include eating less healthy food and drinking more alcohol. An "EAP" is an employee assistance program. Other professional help includes family doctor and psychologist.

Remove the Stressor There are many ways to remove the stressor, but some of the more common actions involve assigning employees to jobs that match their skills and preferences, reducing excessive workplace noise, having a complaint system that takes corrective action against harassment, and giving employees more control over the work process. Another important way that companies can remove stressors is by facilitating better work–life balance. Work–life balance initiatives minimize conflict between the employee's work and nonwork demands. Five of the most common work–life balance initiatives are flexible and limited work time, job sharing, telecommuting, personal leave, and child care support.[105]

- *Flexible and limited work time.* An important way to improve work–life balance is limiting the number of hours that employees are expected to work and giving them flexibility in scheduling those hours. For example, San Jorge Children's Hospital offers a unique form of work flexibility that has dramatically reduced turnover and stress. The Puerto Rican medical center introduced a "ten month work program" in which employees can take summer months off to care for their children while out of school.[106]

- *Job sharing.* Job sharing splits a career position between two people so they experience less time-based stress between work and family. They typically work different parts of the week, with some overlapping work time in the weekly schedule to coordinate activities. This strategy gives employees the ability to work part-time in jobs that are naturally designed for full-time responsibilities.

- *Telecommuting.* Telecommuting (also called *teleworking*) involves working from home or a site close to home rather than commuting a longer distance to the office every day (see Chapter 1). By reducing or eliminating commuting time, employees can more easily fulfill family obligations such as temporarily leaving the home office to pick the kids up from school. Consequently, telecommuters tend to experience better work–life balance.[107] However, teleworking may increase stress for those who crave social interaction and who lack the space and privacy necessary to work at home.

- *Personal leave.* Employers with strong work–life values offer extended maternity, paternity, and personal leave for employees to care for a new family or take advantage of a personal experience. Most countries provide 12 to 16 weeks of paid leave, with some offering one year or more of fully or partially paid maternity leave.[108]

- *Child care support.* Many large and medium-sized employers provide on-site or subsidized child care facilities. Child care support reduces stress because employees are less rushed to drop off children and less worried during the day about how well their children are doing.[109]

Withdraw from the Stressor Removing the stressor may be the ideal solution, but it is often not feasible. An alternative strategy is to permanently or temporarily remove employees from the stressor. Permanent withdrawal occurs when employees are transferred to jobs that are more compatible with their abilities and values. Temporarily withdrawing from stressors is the most frequent way that employees manage stress. Vacations and holidays are important opportunities for employees to recover from stress and re-energize for future challenges. A small number of companies offer paid or unpaid sabbaticals.[110] Many firms also provide innovative ways for employees to withdraw from stressful work throughout the day such as game rooms, ice cream cart breaks, nap rooms, and cafeterias that include live piano recitals.

Change Stress Perceptions Earlier, we said that individuals experience different stress levels because they have different degrees of positive self-evaluation and optimism. Consequently, another way to manage stress is to help employees improve their self-concept so job challenges are not perceived as threatening. Personal goal setting and self-reinforcement can also reduce the stress that people experience when they enter new work settings. Research also suggests that some (but not all) forms of humor can improve optimism and create positive emotions by taking some psychological weight off the situation.[111]

Control Stress Consequences Regular exercise and maintaining a healthy lifestyle are effective stress management strategies because they control stress consequences. Research indicates that physical exercise reduces the physiological

consequences of stress by helping employees moderate their breathing and heart rate, muscle tension, and stomach acidity.[112] Many companies offer Pilates, yoga, and other exercise and meditation classes during the workday. Research indicates that various forms of meditation reduce anxiety, reduce blood pressure and muscle tension, and moderate breathing and heart rate.[113] Wellness programs can also help control the consequences of stress. These programs inform employees about better nutrition and fitness, regular sleep, and other good health habits. Many large companies offer *employee assistance programs (EAPs)*—counseling services that help employees resolve marital, financial, or work-related troubles, but some counseling also varies with the industry.

Receive Social Support Social support occurs when coworkers, supervisors, family members, friends, and others provide emotional and/or informational support to buffer an individual's stress experience. For instance, one recent study found that employees whose managers are good at empathizing experienced fewer stress symptoms than did employees whose managers were less empathetic. Social support potentially (but not always) improves the person's optimism and self-confidence because support makes people feel valued and worthy. Social support also provides information to help the person interpret, comprehend, and possibly remove the stressor. For instance, to reduce a new employee's stress, coworkers could describe ways to handle difficult customers. Seeking social support is called a "tend and befriend" response to stress, and research suggests that women often follow this route rather than the "fight-or-flight" response mentioned earlier.[114]

Study Checklist

✓ Did you tear out the perforated student review card at the back of the text to revisit learning objectives and key terms and definitions?

Connect® Management is available for *M Organizational Behavior*. Additional resources include:

✓ Interactive Applications:
- **Case Analysis:** Apply concepts within the context of a real-world situation.
- **Drag and Drop:** Work through an interactive example to test your knowledge of the concepts.
- **Video Case:** See management in action through interactive videos.

✓ **SmartBook™**—SmartBook is the first and only adaptive reading experience available today. Distinguishing what you know from what you don't, and honing in on concepts you are most likely to forget, SmartBook personalizes content for you in a continuously adapting reading experience. Reading is no longer a passive and linear experience, but an engaging and dynamic one where you are more likely to master and retain important concepts and go to class better prepared.

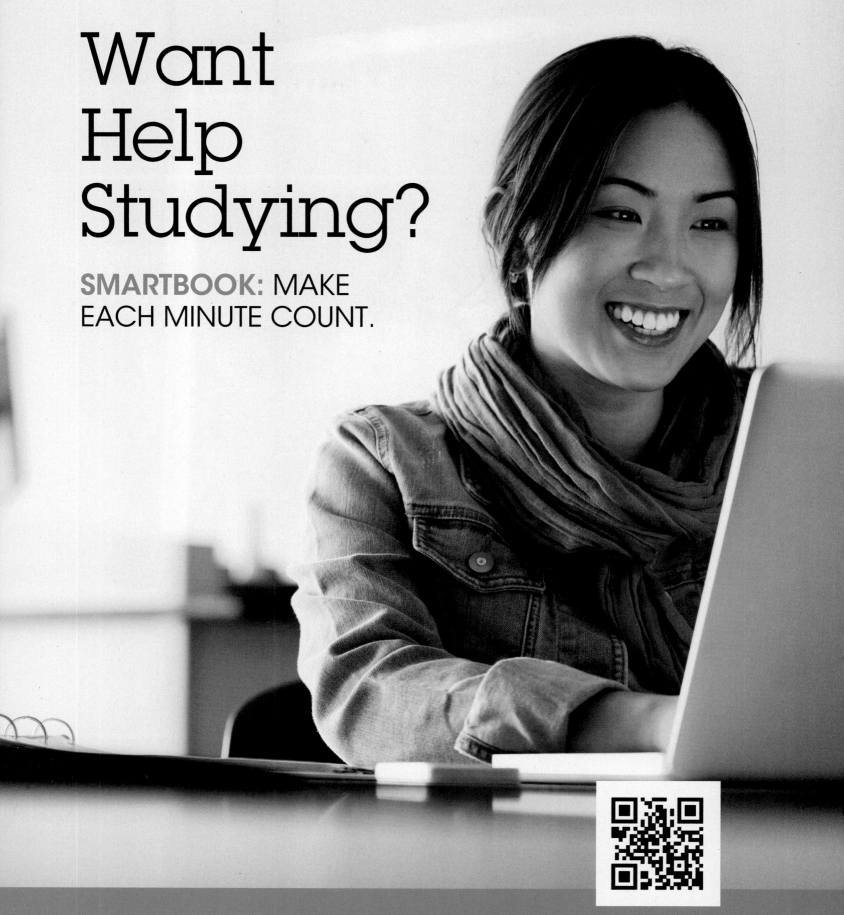

5 chapter

Employee **Motivation**

Learning Objectives

After studying this chapter, you should be able to:

LO5-1 Define employee engagement.

LO5-2 Explain how drives and emotions influence employee motivation and summarize Maslow's needs hierarchy, McClelland's learned needs theory, and four-drive theory.

LO5-3 Discuss the expectancy theory model, including its practical implications.

LO5-4 Outline organizational behavior modification (OB Mod) and social cognitive theory and explain their relevance to employee motivation.

LO5-5 Describe the characteristics of effective goal setting and feedback.

LO5-6 Summarize equity theory and describe ways to improve procedural justice.

LO5-7 List the advantages and disadvantages of job specialization and describe three ways to improve employee motivation through job design.

Frucor Beverages is the market leader of energy drinks in New Zealand and Australia. It is also one of the most energized companies in the region. "Our people are highly engaged, but they are also hungry for more success, and to be better," says Mark Callaghan, CEO of the New Zealand–based company (owned by the Japanese beverages company Suntory Group). Frucor's 800 employees are highly motivated in part because the company offers them extensive training, career development, and recognition. They are also given considerable autonomy to improve productivity and develop innovative products. This high engagement is evident in the company's action-oriented values, such as Go for it! ("Passion and self-belief help us to achieve our goals") and Trailblazing ("We innovate and move fast"). "It is common sense, to me, that if people enjoy and respect the place in which they work, and find their roles fulfilling and appropriately challenging, then they will maximize their potential and that of the business," says Carl Bergstrom, managing director of Frucor Beverages.[1]

Employee motivation has helped Frucor Beverages become one of the leading juice and energy drink companies in New Zealand and Australia. **Motivation** refers to the forces within a person that affect the direction, intensity, and persistence of voluntary behavior.[2] Motivated employees are willing to exert a particular level of effort (intensity), for a certain amount of time (persistence), toward a particular goal (direction). Motivation is one of the four essential drivers of individual behavior and performance (see Chapter 2).

The theme of this chapter is employee motivation. We begin by discussing employee engagement, an increasingly popular concept associated with motivation. Next, we look briefly at employee drives and emotions, and introduce theories that focus on drives and needs. Our attention then turns to the popular cognitive decision model of employee motivation: expectancy theory. The motivational effects of organizational behavior modification, social cognitive theory, goal setting and feedback, and organizational justice are then discussed. The last section of this chapter examines the effect of job design on employee motivation and performance.

LO5-1 Define employee engagement.

EMPLOYEE ENGAGEMENT

When executives at Frucor Beverages and other companies discuss employee motivation these days, they are just as likely to use the phrase **employee engagement**. Although its definition is still being debated,[3] we cautiously define employee engagement as an individual's emotional and cognitive (logical) motivation, particularly a focused, intense, persistent, and purposive effort toward work-related goals. It is an emotional involvement in, commitment to, and satisfaction with the work. Employee engagement also includes a high level of absorption in the work—the experience of focusing intensely on the task with limited awareness of events beyond that work. Finally, employee engagement is often described in terms of self-efficacy—the belief that you have the ability, role clarity, and resources to get the job done (see Chapter 3).

Employee engagement is on the minds of many business leaders because of evidence that it predicts employee and work unit performance. For example, Standard Chartered Bank found that branches with higher employee engagement provide significantly higher-quality customer service, have 46 percent lower employee turnover, and produce 16 percent higher profit margin growth than branches with lower employee engagement. It isn't always clear from these studies whether employee engagement makes companies more successful, or whether the company's success makes employees more engaged. However, several interventions suggest that employee engagement causes the company outcomes more than vice versa. A major British government report concluded that employee engagement is so important to the country's international competitiveness that government should urgently raise awareness of and support for employee engagement practices throughout all sectors of the economy.[4]

The challenge facing organizational leaders is that most employees aren't very engaged.[6] The numbers vary across studies, but one representative survey estimates that only 30 percent of employees in the United States are engaged, 52 percent are not engaged, and 18 percent are actively disengaged. Actively disengaged employees tend to be disruptive at work, not just

motivation forces within a person that affect the direction, intensity, and persistence of voluntary behavior

employee engagement individual's emotional and cognitive motivation, particularly a focused, intense, persistent, and purposive effort toward work-related goals

drives hardwired characteristics of the brain that correct deficiencies or maintain an internal equilibrium by producing emotions to energize individuals

needs goal-directed forces that people experience

Maslow's needs hierarchy theory a motivation theory of needs arranged in a hierarchy, whereby people are motivated to fulfill a higher need as a lower one becomes gratified

DHL Express Employees Get Engaged

Employee engagement is a foundation of business success at DHL Express, the global courier division of Germany's Deutsche Post. "Motivated and engaged employees are crucial to the success of any business and, at DHL, they form the cornerstone of our service," explains a DHL Express executive in Africa. The company builds employee engagement through goal setting, training, and ongoing recognition activities. DHL Express also strengthens employee engagement through its award-winning Certified International Specialist (CIS) program, which details how the company operates and the importance of everyone's role in the business. "CIS is not a traditional training platform," says DHL CEO Ken Allen. "It was designed first and foremost as an engagement tool."[5]

disconnected from work.[7] Employees in several Asian countries (notably Japan, China, and South Korea) and a few European countries (notably Italy, Netherlands, and France) have the lowest levels of employee engagement, whereas the highest scores are usually found in the United States, Brazil, and India.

This leads to the question: What are the drivers of employee engagement? Goal setting, employee involvement, organizational justice, organizational comprehension (knowing what's going on in the company), employee development opportunities, sufficient resources, and an appealing company vision are some of the more commonly mentioned influences.[8] In other words, building an engaged workforce calls on most topics in this book, such as the MARS model (Chapter 2), building affective commitment (Chapter 4), motivation practices (Chapter 5), organizational-level communication (Chapter 8), and leadership (Chapter 11).

LO5-2 Explain how drives and emotions influence employee motivation and summarize Maslow's needs hierarchy, McClelland's learned needs theory, and four-drive theory.

EMPLOYEE DRIVES AND NEEDS

To figure out how to nurture a more engaged and motivated workforce, we first need to understand the motivational "forces" or prime movers of employee behavior.[9] Our starting point is **drives** (also called *primary needs*), which we define as hardwired characteristics of the brain that attempt to keep us in balance by correcting deficiencies. Drives accomplish this task by producing emotions that energize us to act on our environment.[10] Drives are receiving increasing attention because recent neuroscience (brain) research has highlighted the central role of emotions in human decisions and behavior. There is no agreed-upon list of human drives, but research has consistently identified several, such as the drive for social interaction, for competence or status, to comprehend what's going on around us, and to defend ourselves against physiological and psychological harm.[11]

Drives are innate and universal, which means that everyone has them and they exist from birth. Furthermore, drives are the "prime movers" of behavior because they generate emotions, which put people in a state of readiness to act on their environment. Emotions play a central role in motivation.[12] In fact, both words (*emotion* and *motivation*) originate from the same Latin word, *movere*, which means "to move."

Exhibit 5.1 illustrates how drives and emotions translate into felt needs and behavior. Drives, and the emotions produced by these drives, produce human needs. We define **needs** as goal-directed forces that people experience. They are the motivational forces of emotions channeled toward particular goals to correct deficiencies or imbalances. As one leading neuroscientist explains: "drives express themselves directly in background emotions and we eventually become aware of their existence by means of background feelings."[13] In other words, needs are the emotions we eventually become consciously aware of.

Consider the following example: You arrive at work to discover a stranger sitting at your desk. Seeing this situation produces emotions (worry, curiosity) that motivate you to act.

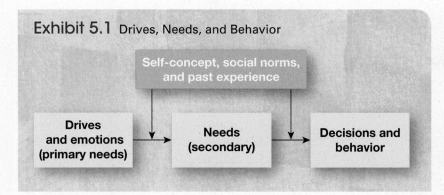

Exhibit 5.1 Drives, Needs, and Behavior

Self-concept, social norms, and past experience

Drives and emotions (primary needs) → Needs (secondary) → Decisions and behavior

These emotions are generated from drives, such as the drive to defend and drive to comprehend. When strong enough, these emotions motivate you to do something about this situation, such as finding out who that person is and possibly seeking reassurance from coworkers that your job is still safe. In this case, you have a need to make sense of (comprehend) what is going on, to feel secure, and possibly to correct a sense of personal violation. Notice that your emotional reactions to seeing the stranger sitting at your desk represent the forces that move you, but you channel those emotions toward specific goals.

Individual Differences in Needs

Everyone has the same drives; they are hardwired in us through evolution. However, people develop different intensities of needs in a particular situation. Exhibit 5.1 explains why this difference occurs. The left side of the model shows that the individual's self-concept (as well as personality and values), social norms, and past experience amplify or suppress drive-based emotions, thereby resulting in stronger or weaker needs.[14] People who define themselves as very sociable typically experience a stronger need for social interaction if alone for a while, whereas people who view themselves as less sociable would experience a less intense need to be with others over that time. These individual differences also explain why needs can be "learned" to some extent. Socialization and reinforcement may cause people to alter their self-concept somewhat, resulting in a stronger or weaker need for social interaction, achievement, and so on. We will discuss learned needs later in this chapter.

Self-concept, social norms, and past experience also regulate a person's motivated decisions and behavior, as the right side of Exhibit 5.1 illustrates. Consider the earlier example of the stranger sitting at your desk. You probably wouldn't walk up to the person and demand that he or she leave;

such blunt behavior is contrary to social norms in most cultures. Employees who view themselves as forthright might approach the stranger directly, whereas those who have a different self-concept or have had negative experiences with direct confrontation are more likely to first gather information from coworkers before approaching the intruder. In short, your drives (drive to comprehend, to defend, to bond, etc.) and resulting emotions energize you to act, and your self-concept, social norms, and past experience direct that energy into goal-directed behavior.

Exhibit 5.1 provides a useful template for understanding how drives and emotions are the prime sources of employee motivation and how individual characteristics (self-concept, experience, values) influence goal-directed behavior. You will see pieces of this theory when we discuss four-drive theory, expectancy theory, equity theory, and other concepts in this chapter. The remainder of this section describes theories that try to explain the dynamics of drives and needs.

Maslow's Needs Hierarchy Theory

The most widely known theory of human motivation is **Maslow's needs hierarchy theory**, which was developed by psychologist Abraham Maslow in the 1940s (see Exhibit 5.2). This model, which refers to primary needs (i.e., drives), condenses and integrates the long list of drives that had been previously studied into a hierarchy of five basic categories of drives (from lowest to highest):[15] *physiological* (need for food, air, water, shelter, etc.), *safety* (need for security and stability), *belongingness/love* (need for interaction with and affection from others), *esteem* (need for self-esteem and social esteem/status), and *self-actualization* (need for self-fulfillment, realization of one's potential). Along with these five categories, Maslow identified the desire to know and the desire for aesthetic beauty as two innate drives that do not fit within the hierarchy.

Maslow proposed that human beings are motivated simultaneously by several primary needs (drives), but the strongest source of motivation is the lowest unsatisfied need at the time. As the person satisfies a lower-level need, the next higher need in the hierarchy becomes the primary motivator and remains so even if never satisfied. The exception to this need fulfillment process is self-actualization; as people experience self-actualization, they desire more rather than less of this need. Thus, while the bottom four groups are *deficiency needs* because they become activated when unfulfilled, self-actualization is known as a *growth need* because it continues to develop even when fulfilled.

Exhibit 5.2 Maslow's Needs Hierarchy

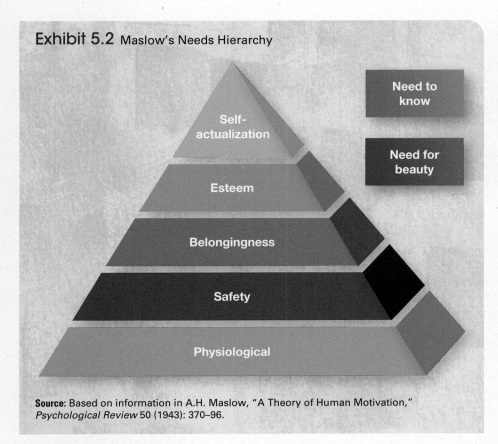

Self-actualization

Esteem

Belongingness

Safety

Physiological

Need to know

Need for beauty

Source: Based on information in A.H. Maslow, "A Theory of Human Motivation," *Psychological Review* 50 (1943): 370–96.

also have parallel differences in their needs hierarchies. If your most important values lean toward stimulation and self-direction, you probably pay more attention to self-actualization needs. If power and achievement are at the top of your value system, status needs will likely be at the top of your needs hierarchy. A person's values hierarchy can change over time, so his or her needs hierarchy also changes over time.[18]

Maslow's Contribution to Motivation

Although needs hierarchy theory has failed the reality test, Maslow deserves credit for bringing a more holistic, humanistic, and positive approach to the study of human motivation.[19]

- *Holistic perspective.* Maslow explained that the various needs should be studied together (holistically) because human behavior is typically initiated by more than one need at the same time. Previously, motivation experts had studied in isolation each of the dozens of drives and needs.[20]

> People have different hierarchies of values, so they also have parallel differences in their needs hierarchies.

Limitations of Needs Hierarchy Models In spite of its popularity, Maslow's needs hierarchy theory has been dismissed by most motivation experts.[16] Other needs hierarchy models have also failed to adequately depict human motivation. Studies have concluded that people do not progress through the hierarchy as Maslow's theory predicts. Some people fulfill their esteem needs before their safety needs, for example. Furthermore, Maslow assumed that a person's needs are fulfilled for a long time, whereas need fulfillment actually seems to last for a briefer period of time.

However, the main problem with needs hierarchy models is that people don't fit into a one-size-fits-all hierarchy of needs. Instead, one person's hierarchy of needs can be different from another person's hierarchy. Some place social status at the top of their personal hierarchy; others view personal development and growth above social relations or status. Employee needs are strongly influenced by self-concept, personal values, and personality.[17] People have different hierarchies of values (their values system—see Chapter 2), so they

- *Humanistic perspective.* Maslow introduced the then-novel idea that higher-order needs are influenced by personal and social influences, not just instincts.[21] In other words, he was among the first to recognize that human thoughts (including self-concept, social norms, past experience) play a role in motivation. Previous motivation experts had focused almost entirely on human instincts without considering that motivation could be shaped by human thought.

- *Positive perspective.* Maslow popularized the concept of *self-actualization,* suggesting that people are naturally motivated to reach their potential and that organizations and societies need to be structured to help people continue and develop this motivation.[22] This positive view of motivation contrasted with the dominant position that needs become activated by deficiencies such as hunger. Indeed, Maslow is considered a pioneer in *positive organizational behavior.* Positive OB says that focusing on the positive rather than negative aspects of life will improve organizational success and individual well-being (see Chapter 3). In other words, this approach advocates building positive qualities and perspectives within individuals or institutions as opposed to focusing on their failures and weaknesses.[23]

Falling Short
of Self-Actualization[24]

83% of human resource directors polled in UK blue-chip companies believe employees are not working to their true potential.

57% of 9,441 petroleum engineers worldwide agree or strongly agree that their job uses their full potential.

46% of 1,005 working Americans surveyed who graduated within the past two years consider themselves underemployed.

36% of 170,000 employees across 30 countries surveyed say that personal growth/advancement is the main factor driving their job choice decision (second highest factor after work–life balance).

need for achievement (nAch) a learned need in which people want to accomplish reasonably challenging goals and desire unambiguous feedback and recognition for their success

need for affiliation (nAff) a learned need in which people seek approval from others, conform to their wishes and expectations, and avoid conflict and confrontation

need for power (nPow) a learned need in which people want to control their environment, including people and material resources, to benefit either themselves (personalized power) or others (socialized power)

Learned Needs Theory

The general motivation model shown earlier in this chapter illustrated that needs are shaped, amplified, or suppressed through self-concept, social norms, and past experience. Maslow noted this when he wrote that individual characteristics influence the strength of higher-order needs, such as the need to belong. Psychologist David McClelland further investigated the idea that need strength can be altered through social influences. In particular, he recognized that a person's needs can be strengthened or weakened through reinforcement, learning, and social conditions. McClelland examined three "learned" needs: achievement, affiliation, and power.[25]

Need for Achievement People with a strong **need for achievement (nAch)** want to accomplish reasonably challenging goals through their own effort. They prefer working alone rather than in teams, and they choose tasks with a moderate degree of risk (i.e., neither too easy nor impossible to complete). High-nAch people also desire unambiguous feedback and recognition for their success. Money is a weak motivator, except when it provides feedback and recognition.[27] In contrast, employees with a low nAch perform their work better when money is used as an incentive. Successful entrepreneurs tend to have a high nAch,

> "Happiness lies not in the mere possession of money; it lies in the joy of achievement, in the thrill of creative effort."[26]
>
> —**Franklin D. Roosevelt,**
> 32nd president of the United States

possibly because they establish challenging goals for themselves and thrive on competition.[28]

Need for Affiliation **Need for affiliation (nAff)** refers to a desire to seek approval from others, conform to their wishes and expectations, and avoid conflict and confrontation. People with a strong nAff try to project a favorable image of themselves. They tend to actively support others and try to smooth out workplace conflicts. High-nAff employees generally work well in coordinating roles to mediate conflicts and in sales positions where the main task is cultivating long-term relations. However, they tend to be less effective at allocating scarce resources and making other decisions that potentially generate conflict. People in decision-making positions must have a relatively low need for affiliation so their choices and actions are not biased by a personal need for approval.[29]

Need for Power People with a high **need for power (nPow)** want to exercise control over others and are concerned about maintaining their leadership position. They frequently rely on persuasive communication, make more suggestions in meetings, and tend to publicly evaluate situations more frequently. McClelland pointed out that there are two types of nPow.

Individuals who enjoy their power for its own sake, use it to advance personal interests, and wear their power as a status symbol have *personalized power*. Others mainly have a high need for *socialized power* because they desire power as a means to help others.[30] McClelland argues that effective leaders should have a high need for socialized rather than personalized power. They must have a high degree of altruism and social responsibility and be concerned about the consequences of their own actions on others.

Learning Needs McClelland believed that needs can be learned (more accurately, strengthened or weakened), and the training programs he developed supported that proposition. In his achievement motivation program, trainees wrote achievement-oriented stories and practiced achievement-oriented behaviors in business games. They also completed a detailed achievement plan for the next two years and formed a reference group with other trainees to maintain their newfound achievement motivation.[31] Participants attending these achievement motivation programs subsequently started more new businesses, had greater community involvement, invested more in expanding their businesses, and employed twice as many people compared with a matched sample of nonparticipants. These training programs increased achievement motivation by altering participants' self-concept and reinforcing their achievement experiences. When writing an achievement plan, for example, participants were encouraged (and supported by other participants) to experience the anticipated thrill of succeeding.

Four-Drive Theory

One of the central messages of this chapter is that emotions are at the core of employee motivation. Scholars across the social sciences increasingly agree that human beings have several hardwired drives, including social interaction, learning, and getting ahead. These drives generate emotions, which represent the prime movers or sources of effort of individual behavior. Most organizational behavior theories of motivation focus on the cognitive aspects of human motivation; **four-drive theory** is one of the few to recognize the central role of human emotions in the motivation process.[32]

According to four-drive theory, everyone has four drives: the drive to acquire, drive to bond, drive to comprehend, and drive to defend. These drives are innate and universal, meaning that they are hardwired in our brains and are found in all human beings. They are also independent of one another. There is no hierarchy of drives, so one drive is neither dependent on nor inherently inferior or superior to another drive. Four-drive theory also states that these four drives are a complete set—there are no fundamental drives excluded from the model. Another key feature is that three of the four drives are proactive—we regularly try to fulfill them. Only the drive to defend is reactive—it is triggered by threat. Thus, "fulfillment" of a drive is brief.

Four-drive theory identified the four drives from earlier psychological, sociological, and anthropological research. These drives are:

- *Drive to acquire.* This is the drive to seek, take, control, and retain objects and personal experiences. The drive to acquire extends beyond basic food and water; it includes enhancing one's self-concept through relative status and recognition in society.[33] Thus, it is the foundation of competition and the basis of our need for esteem. Four-drive theory states that the drive to acquire is insatiable because the purpose of human motivation is to achieve a higher position than others, not just to fulfill one's physiological needs.

- *Drive to bond.* This is the drive to form social relationships and develop mutual caring commitments with others. It explains why people form social identities by aligning their self-concept with various social groups (see Chapter 3). It may also explain why people who lack social contact are more prone to serious health problems.[34] The drive to bond motivates people to cooperate and, consequently, is a fundamental ingredient in the success of organizations and the development of societies.

- *Drive to comprehend.* This is the drive to satisfy our curiosity, to know and understand ourselves and the environment around us.[35] When observing something that is inconsistent with or beyond our current knowledge, we experience a tension that motivates us to close that information gap. In fact, studies have revealed that people who are removed from any novel information will crave even

boring information; in one classic experiment, participants deprived of information eventually craved month-old stock reports![36] The drive to comprehend is related to the higher-order needs of growth and self-actualization described earlier.

- *Drive to defend.* This is the drive to protect ourselves physically, psychologically, and socially. Probably the first drive to develop, it creates a fight-or-flight response in the face of personal danger. The drive to defend goes beyond protecting our physical self. It includes defending our relationships, our acquisitions, and our belief systems.

How Drives Influence Motivation and Behavior Four-drive theory is derived from recent neuroscience research regarding the emotional marker process and how emotions are channeled into decisions and behavior.[37] As we described in previous chapters, our perceptions of the world around us are quickly and nonconsciously tagged with emotional markers. According to four-drive theory, the four drives determine which emotions are tagged to incoming stimuli. Most of the time, we aren't aware of our emotional experiences because they are subtle and fleeting. However, emotions do become conscious experiences when they are sufficiently strong or when they significantly conflict with one another.

Our mental skill set (social norms, past experience, and personal values) directs the motivational force of our emotions to decisions and behavior that are expected to reduce that tension (see Exhibit 5.3). In other words, our mental skill set chooses courses of action that are acceptable to society, consistent with our own moral compass, and have a high probability of achieving the goal of fulfilling those felt needs.[38] This is the process described at the beginning of this chapter: Drives produce emotions, various personal characteristics (self-concept, social norms, experience) interpret these emotions into goal-directed needs, and those personal characteristics also direct those needs into decisions and behavior.

Evaluating Four-Drive Theory Although four-drive theory was introduced recently, it is based on a deep research foundation dating back more than three decades. The drives were identified from psychological, sociological, and anthropological studies. Furthermore, four-drive theory maps well onto the 10 dimensions of Schwartz's values circumplex model (see Chapter 2).[39] The translation of drives into goal-directed behavior originates from considerable research on emotions and neural processes. The theory explains why needs vary from one person to the next, but avoids the assumption that everyone has the same needs hierarchy. Notice, too, that four-drive theory satisfies two of Maslow's criteria for any motivation theory: It is holistic (it relates to all drives, not just one or two) and humanistic (it acknowledges the role of human thought and social influences, not just instinct).

Even with its well-researched foundation, four-drive theory is far from complete. Most experts would argue that one or two other drives exist that should be included. Furthermore, social norms, personal values, and past experience probably don't represent the full set of individual characteristics that translate emotions into goal-directed effort. For example, personality and self-concept probably also moderate the effect of drives and needs on decisions and behavior.

Practical Implications of Four-Drive Theory The main recommendation from four-drive theory is that jobs and workplaces should provide a balanced opportunity to fulfill the four drives.[40] There are really two recommendations here. The first is that the best workplaces help employees fulfill all four drives. Employees continually seek fulfillment of their innate drives, so successful companies provide sufficient rewards, learning opportunities, social interaction, and so forth, for all employees.

The second recommendation is that fulfillment of the four drives must be kept in balance; that is, organizations should

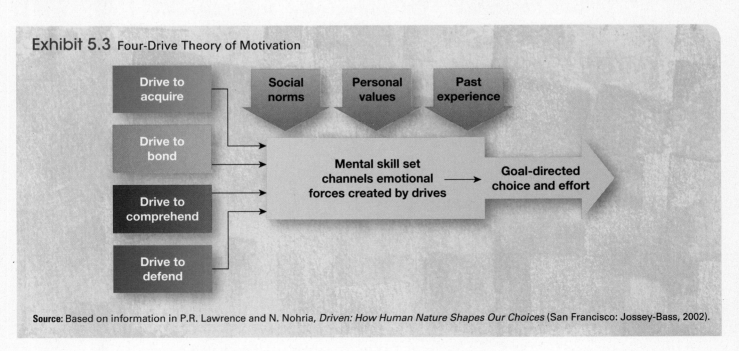

Exhibit 5.3 Four-Drive Theory of Motivation

Drive to acquire

Drive to bond

Drive to comprehend

Drive to defend

Social norms | Personal values | Past experience

Mental skill set channels emotional forces created by drives → Goal-directed choice and effort

Source: Based on information in P.R. Lawrence and N. Nohria, *Driven: How Human Nature Shapes Our Choices* (San Francisco: Jossey-Bass, 2002).

expectancy theory a motivation theory based on the idea that work effort is directed toward behaviors that people believe will lead to desired outcomes

avoid too much or too little opportunity to fulfill each drive. The reason for this advice is that the four drives counterbalance each other. The drive to bond counterbalances the drive to acquire; the drive to defend counterbalances the drive to comprehend. An organization that fuels the drive to acquire without the drive to bond may eventually suffer from organizational politics and dysfunctional conflict. Change and novelty in the workplace will aid the drive to comprehend, but too much of it will trigger the drive to defend to such an extent that employees become territorial and resistant to change. Thus, the workplace should offer enough opportunity to keep all four drives in balance.

LO5-3 Discuss the expectancy theory model, including its practical implications.

EXPECTANCY THEORY OF MOTIVATION

The theories described so far mainly explain what motivates us—the prime movers of employee motivation. But these drives and needs theories don't tell us what we are motivated to do. Four-drive theory recognizes that social norms, personal values, and past experience direct our effort, but it doesn't offer any detail about what actions people take when they are motivated.

Expectancy theory, on the other hand, predicts an individual's chosen direction, level, and persistence of effort through logical analysis of what actions would most likely satisfy the underlying needs. Essentially, the theory states that work effort is directed toward behaviors that people believe will most likely produce the desired outcomes. This is, essentially, a basic economic model of deciding which choice offers the highest expected payoff (called *subjective expected utility*, which we discuss in Chapter 6).[41] As illustrated in Exhibit 5.4, an individual's effort level depends on three factors: effort-to-performance (E-to-P) expectancy, performance-to-outcome (P-to-O) expectancy, and outcome valences. Employee motivation is influenced by all three components of the expectancy theory model. If any component weakens, motivation weakens.

- *E-to-P expectancy.* This is the individual's perception that his or her effort will result in a particular level of performance. In some situations, employees may believe that they can unquestionably accomplish the task (a probability of 1.0). In other situations, they expect that even their highest level of effort will not result in the desired performance level (a probability of 0.0). In most cases, the E-to-P expectancy falls somewhere between these two extremes.

- *P-to-O expectancy.* This is the perceived probability that a specific behavior or performance level will lead to a particular outcome. In

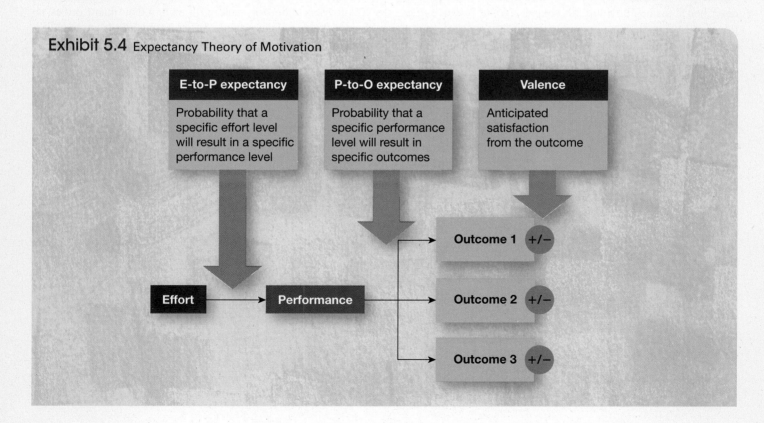

Exhibit 5.4 Expectancy Theory of Motivation

E-to-P expectancy	P-to-O expectancy	Valence
Probability that a specific effort level will result in a specific performance level	Probability that a specific performance level will result in specific outcomes	Anticipated satisfaction from the outcome

Effort → Performance

Outcome 1 +/−
Outcome 2 +/−
Outcome 3 +/−

extreme cases, employees may believe that accomplishing a particular task (performance) will definitely result in a particular outcome (a probability of 1.0), or they may believe that successful performance will have no effect on this outcome (a probability of 0.0). More often, the P-to-O expectancy falls somewhere between these two extremes.

- *Outcome valences.* A *valence* is the anticipated satisfaction or dissatisfaction that an individual feels toward an outcome. It ranges from negative to positive. (The actual range doesn't matter; it may be from −1 to +1 or from −100 to +100.) An outcome valence represents a person's anticipated satisfaction with the outcome.[42] Outcomes have a positive valence when they are consistent with our values and satisfy our needs; they have a negative valence when they oppose our values and inhibit need fulfillment.

Expectancy Theory in Practice

One of the appealing characteristics of expectancy theory is that it provides clear guidelines for increasing employee motivation.[43] Several practical applications of expectancy theory are listed in Exhibit 5.5 and described below.

Performance-to-Outcome Expectancy: the **Missing Link**[44]

31% of U.S. federal government employees surveyed agree that differences in performance are recognized in a meaningful way in their work unit.

36% of American employees surveyed say they see a clear link between performance and pay in their organization.

50% of North American employees surveyed believe high performers in their organization are rewarded for performance through incentive programs.

37% of American employees surveyed see NO link at all between their performance and their pay.

Exhibit 5.5 Practical Applications of Expectancy Theory

Expectancy Theory Component	Objective	Applications
E → P expectancies	To increase the employee's belief that she or he is capable of performing the job successfully	• Select people with the required skills and knowledge. • Provide required training and clarify job requirements. • Provide sufficient time and resources. • Assign simpler or fewer tasks until employees can master them. • Provide examples of similar employees who have successfully performed the task. • Provide coaching to employees who lack self-confidence.
P → O expectancies	To increase the employee's belief that his or her good performance will result in certain (valued) outcomes	• Measure job performance accurately. • Clearly explain the outcomes that will result from successful performance. • Describe how the employee's rewards were based on past performance. • Provide examples of other employees whose good performance has resulted in higher rewards.
Outcome valences	To increase the employee's expected satisfaction with outcomes resulting from desired performance	• Distribute rewards that employees value. • Individualize rewards. • Minimize the presence of countervalent outcomes.

organizational behavior modification (OB Mod) a theory that explains employee behavior in terms of the antecedent conditions and consequences of that behavior

Increasing E-to-P Expectancies E-to-P expectancies are influenced by the individual's belief that he or she can successfully complete the task. Some companies increase this can-do attitude by assuring employees that they have the necessary skills and knowledge, clear role perceptions, and necessary resources to reach the desired levels of performance. An important part of this process involves matching employee abilities to job requirements and clearly communicating the tasks required for the job. Similarly, E-to-P expectancies are learned, so behavior modeling and supportive feedback (positive reinforcement) typically strengthen the individual's belief that he or she is able to perform the task.

Increasing P-to-O Expectancies The most obvious ways to improve P-to-O expectancies are to measure employee performance accurately and distribute more valued rewards to those with higher job performance. P-to-O expectancies are perceptions, so employees also need to believe that higher performance will result in higher rewards. Furthermore, they need to know how that connection occurs, so leaders should use examples, anecdotes, and public ceremonies to illustrate when behavior has been rewarded.

Increasing Outcome Valences One size does not fit all when motivating and rewarding people. Organizational leaders need to find ways to individualize rewards or, where standard rewards are necessary, to identify rewards that do not have a negative valence for some staff. Consider the following story: Top-performing employees in one organization were rewarded with a one-week Caribbean cruise with the company's executive team. Many were likely delighted, but at least one top performer was aghast at the thought of going on a cruise with senior management. "I don't like schmoozing, I don't like feeling trapped. Why couldn't they just give me the money?," she complained. The employee went on the cruise, but spent most of her time working in her stateroom.[45]

One other observation about increasing outcome valences is to watch out for countervalent outcomes that offset outcomes with positive valences. For example, several employees in one work unit were individually motivated to perform well because this achievement gave them a feeling of accomplishment and rewarded them with higher pay. But their performance was considerably lower when they worked together with others because peer pressure discouraged performance above a fairly low standard. In this situation, the positive valence outcomes (feeling of accomplishment, higher pay) were offset by the negative valence outcome of peer pressure.

Overall, expectancy theory is a useful model that explains how people rationally figure out the best direction, intensity, and persistence of effort. It has been tested in a variety of situations and predicts employee motivation in different cultures.[46] However, critics have a number of concerns with how the theory has been tested. Another concern is that expectancy theory ignores the central role of emotion in employee effort and behavior. The valence element of expectancy theory captures some of this emotional process, but only peripherally.[47] Finally, expectancy theory outlines how expectancies (probability of outcomes) affect motivation, but it doesn't explain how employees develop these expectancies. Two theories that provide this explanation are organizational behavior modification and social cognitive theory, which we describe next.

> **LO5-4** Outline organizational behavior modification (OB Mod) and social cognitive theory and explain their relevance to employee motivation.

ORGANIZATIONAL BEHAVIOR MODIFICATION AND SOCIAL COGNITIVE THEORY

Expectancy theory states that motivation is determined by employee beliefs about expected performance and outcomes. But how do employees learn these expectancy beliefs? How do they learn, for example, that some work activities are more likely to produce a pay increase or promotion whereas other activities have little effect? The answer to this question directs us to two theories: organizational behavior modification (OB Mod) and social cognitive theory. These theories explain how people *learn* what to expect from their actions. Consequently, OB Mod and social cognitive theory are also theories of motivation because, as expectancy theory explains, the learned expectancies affect the person's direction, intensity, and persistence of effort.

Organizational Behavior Modification

For most of the first half of the 1900s, the dominant paradigm about managing individual behavior was *behaviorism*, which argues that a good theory should rely exclusively on behavior and the environment and ignore nonobservable cognitions and emotions.[48] Although behaviorists don't deny the existence of human thoughts and attitudes, they view them as unobservable and, therefore, irrelevant to scientific study. A variation of this paradigm, called **organizational behavior modification (OB Mod)**, eventually entered organizational studies of motivation and learning.[49]

Exhibit 5.6 A-B-Cs of Organizational Behavior Modification

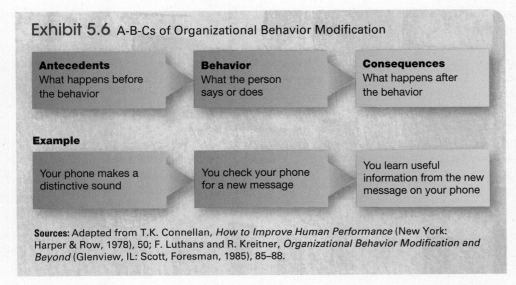

Antecedents
What happens before the behavior

Behavior
What the person says or does

Consequences
What happens after the behavior

Example

Your phone makes a distinctive sound

You check your phone for a new message

You learn useful information from the new message on your phone

Sources: Adapted from T.K. Connellan, *How to Improve Human Performance* (New York: Harper & Row, 1978), 50; F. Luthans and R. Kreitner, *Organizational Behavior Modification and Beyond* (Glenview, IL: Scott, Foresman, 1985), 85–88.

A-B-Cs of OB Mod The core elements of OB Mod are depicted in the A-B-C model shown in Exhibit 5.6. Essentially, OB Mod attempts to change behavior (B) by managing its antecedents (A) and consequences (C).[50] *Consequences* are events following a particular behavior that influence its future occurrence, such as new information you receive from an incoming text message on your smartphone, or congratulatory notes from coworkers for helping them complete a difficult task. Consequences also include no outcome at all, such as when no one says anything about how well you have been serving customers.

Antecedents are events preceding the behavior, informing employees that a particular action will produce specific consequences. An antecedent may be a sound from your smartphone signaling that a text message has arrived. Or it might be your supervisor's request to complete a specific task by tomorrow. Notice that antecedents do not cause behavior. The sound from your smartphone doesn't cause us to open the text message. Rather, the sound (antecedent) is a cue telling us that if we check the message list on our phone (behavior), we are certain to find a new message with (potentially) useful information (consequence).

OB Mod identifies four types of consequences (called the *contingencies of reinforcement*).[51] *Positive reinforcement* occurs when the introduction of a consequence increases or maintains the frequency or future probability of a specific behavior. An example of this is receiving praise after completing a project. *Punishment* occurs when a consequence decreases the frequency or future probability of a specific behavior occurring. Most of us would consider being demoted or being criticized by our coworkers as forms of punishment. A third type of consequence is *extinction*. This consequence occurs when the target behavior decreases because no consequence follows it. For instance, research suggests that performance tends to decline when managers stop congratulating employees for their good work.[52]

The fourth consequence in OB Mod, called *negative reinforcement,* is often confused with punishment. It's actually the opposite; negative reinforcement occurs when the removal or avoidance of a consequence increases or maintains the frequency or future probability of a specific behavior. For example, managers apply negative reinforcement when they *stop* criticizing employees whose substandard performance has improved.

Which of these four consequences works best? In most situations, positive reinforcement should follow desired behaviors, and extinction (do nothing) should follow undesirable behaviors. This approach is preferred because punishment and negative reinforcement generate negative emotions and attitudes toward the punisher (e.g., supervisor) and organization. However, some form of punishment (dismissal, suspension, demotion, etc.) may be necessary for extreme behaviors, such as deliberately hurting a coworker or stealing inventory. Indeed, research suggests that, under certain conditions, punishment maintains a sense of fairness.[53]

Along with the four consequences, OB Mod considers the frequency and timing of these reinforcers (called the *schedules of reinforcement*).[54] The most effective reinforcement schedule

Reinforcing Work Behavior through **Gamification**[55]

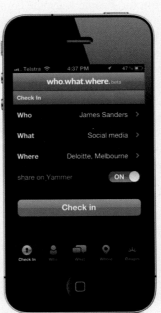

When James Sanders meets a client, he uses his phone to report the client's name, where they met, and what was the topic. Along with helping coworkers to coordinate their client visits, Sanders is motivated by Deloitte's game-based positive reinforcement (gamification) initiative that awards points and virtual "badges" for documenting client meetings, completing online training, participating in social media, and engaging in other specific behaviors. Employees with the most badges are ranked on leaderboards in various categories. "If you can gamify the process, you are rewarding the behavior and it's like a dopamine release in the brain," explains Deloitte Digital lead partner Frank Farrall.

social cognitive theory a theory that explains how learning and motivation occur by observing and modeling others as well as by anticipating the consequences of our behavior

for learning new tasks is *continuous reinforcement*—providing positive reinforcement after every occurrence of the desired behavior. The best schedule for motivating employees is a *variable ratio schedule* in which employee behavior is reinforced after a variable number of times. Salespeople experience variable ratio reinforcement because they make a successful sale (the reinforcer) after a varying number of client calls. The variable ratio schedule makes behavior highly resistant to extinction because the reinforcer is never expected at a particular time or after a fixed number of accomplishments.

Social Cognitive Theory

Social cognitive theory states that much learning occurs by observing and modeling others as well as by anticipating the consequences of our behavior.[56] Although observation and modeling (imitation) have been studied for many years as sources of motivation and learning, social scientist Albert Bandura reframed these ideas within a cognitive perspective as an alternative to the behaviorist approach. There are several pieces to social cognitive theory, but the three most relevant to employee motivation are learning behavior consequences, behavior modeling, and self-regulation.

Learning Behavior Consequences People learn the consequences of behavior by observing or hearing about what happened to other people, not just by directly experiencing the consequences.[57] Hearing that a coworker was fired for being rude to a client increases your perception that rude behavior will result in being fired. In the language of expectancy theory, learning behavior consequences changes a person's perceived P-to-O probability. Furthermore, people logically anticipate consequences in related situations. For instance, the story about the fired employee might also strengthen your P-to-O expectancy that being rude toward coworkers and suppliers (not just clients) will get you fired.

Behavior Modeling Along with observing others, people learn by imitating and practicing their behaviors.[58] Direct sensory experience helps acquire tacit knowledge and skills, such as the subtle person–machine interaction while driving a vehicle. Behavior modeling also increases self-efficacy (see Chapter 3), because people gain more self-confidence after observing others and performing the task successfully themselves. Self-efficacy particularly improves when observers

> OB Mod and social cognitive theory explain how people learn probabilities of success (E-to-P expectancies) as well as probabilities of various outcomes (P-to-O expectancies).

identify with the model, such as someone who is similar in age, experience, gender, and related features.

Self-Regulation An important feature of social cognitive theory is that human beings set goals and engage in other forms of intentional, purposive action. They establish their own short- and long-term objectives, choose their own standards of achievement, work out a plan of action, consider backup alternatives, and have the forethought to anticipate the consequences of their goal-directed behavior. Furthermore, people self-regulate by engaging in **self-reinforcement**; they reward and punish themselves for exceeding or falling short of their self-set standards of excellence.[59] For example, you might have a goal of completing the rest of this chapter, after which you reward yourself by having a snack. Raiding the refrigerator is a form of self-induced positive reinforcement for completing this reading assignment.

OB Mod and social cognitive theory explain how people learn probabilities of success (E-to-P expectancies) as well as probabilities of various outcomes (P-to-O expectancies). As such, these theories explain motivation through their relationship with expectancy theory of motivation, described earlier. Elements of these theories also help us understand other motivation processes. For instance, self-regulation is the cornerstone of motivation through goal setting and feedback, which we discuss next.

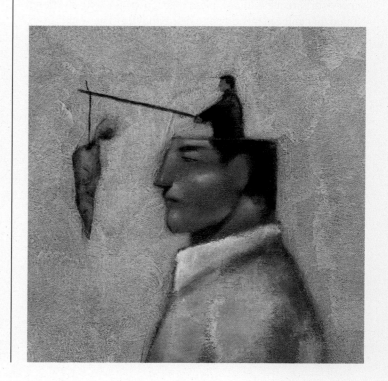

GOAL SETTING AND FEEDBACK

CalPERS—the California Public Employees' Retirement System—has challenging goals for staff at its customer contact center in Sacramento.[60] The organization aims to have 95 percent of client calls answered within 2.5 minutes. It also wants customers put on hold for no longer than 2.5 minutes. Another goal is that less than 5 percent of CalPERS clients hang up before the call is handled by someone at the contact center (called the abandonment rate). Along with these specific goals, the organization keeps track of how many calls are received (about 650,000 per year), how many callers are waiting, and how long each call takes (between 6 and 7 minutes, on average). CalPERS employees not only know these goals, they probably have some form of visual feedback. Many contact centers in other organizations have large electronic screens showing statistics for these key performance indicators.

Customer contact centers partly motivate employees through **goal setting**, which is the process of motivating employees and clarifying their role perceptions by establishing performance objectives. Goal setting potentially improves employee

---

OB THEORY TO PRACTICE

The SMARTER Approach to Goal Setting

S—Specific: state what needs to be accomplished, how it should be accomplished, and where, when, and with whom it should be accomplished.

M—Measurable: describe how much (quantity), how well (quality), and at what cost the goal should be achieved.

A—Achievable: goals should be challenging without being so difficult that employees lose their motivation to achieve them.

R—Relevant: the goal needs to be relevant to the individual's job and within his or her control.

T—Time-framed: need to specify when the goal should be completed or when it will be assessed.

E—Exciting: support employee commitment to (not just compliance with) the goal, such as by linking to the individual's growth needs and through involvement in the goal process.

R—Reviewed: provide ongoing feedback about goal progress and attainment.

---

performance in two ways: (1) by amplifying the intensity and persistence of effort and (2) by giving employees clearer role perceptions so their effort is channeled toward behaviors that will improve work performance. Goal setting is more complex than simply telling someone to "do your best." It requires several specific characteristics.[61] One popular acronym—SMARTER—captures these characteristics fairly well.[62] Effective goals are specific, measurable, achievable, relevant to the employee's job, set within a time frame, exciting to create employee commitment, and reviewed both during and after the goal has been accomplished.

Characteristics of Effective Feedback

Feedback—information that lets us know whether we have achieved the goal or are properly directing our effort toward it—is a critical partner with goal setting. Along with clarifying role perceptions and improving employee skills and knowledge, feedback motivates when it is constructive and when employees have strong self-efficacy.[63] Effective feedback has many of the same characteristics as effective goal setting. It should be *specific* and *relevant*, that is the information should refer to specific metrics (e.g., sales increased by 5 percent last month) and to the individual's behavior or outcomes within his or her control. Feedback should also be *timely;* the information should be available soon after the behavior or results occur so that employees see a clear association between their actions and the consequences. Effective feedback is also *credible.* Employees are more likely to accept feedback from trustworthy and believable sources.

The final characteristic of effective feedback is that it should be *sufficiently frequent.* How frequent is "sufficiently"? The answer depends on at least two things. One consideration is the employee's knowledge and experience with the task. Employees working on new tasks should receive more frequent feedback because they require more behavior guidance and reinforcement. Employees who perform repetitive or familiar tasks can receive less frequent feedback. The second factor is how long it takes to complete the task (i.e., its cycle time). Feedback is necessarily less frequent in jobs with a long cycle time (e.g., executives and scientists) than in jobs with a short cycle time (e.g., grocery store cashiers).

Feedback through Strengths-Based Coaching Forty years ago, Peter Drucker argued that leaders are more effective when they focus on strengths rather than weaknesses. "The effective executive builds on strengths—their own strengths, the strengths of superiors, colleagues, subordinates; and on the strength of the situation," wrote the late management guru.[64]

self-reinforcement reinforcement that occurs when an employee has control over a reinforcer but doesn't "take" it until completing a self-set goal

goal setting the process of motivating employees and clarifying their role perceptions by establishing performance objectives

strengths-based coaching a positive organizational behavior approach to coaching and feedback that focuses on building and leveraging the employee's strengths rather than trying to correct his or her weaknesses

This is the essence of **strengths-based coaching** (also known as *appreciative coaching*)—maximizing employees' potential by focusing on their strengths rather than weaknesses.[65] In strengths-based coaching, employees describe areas of work where they excel or demonstrate potential. The coach guides this discussion by asking exploratory questions that guide employees to discover ways of leveraging this strength. Situational barriers and strategies to overcome those barriers are identified to leverage the employee's potential.

Strengths-based coaching can potentially motivate employees because they inherently seek feedback about their strengths, not their flaws. Thus, strengths-based feedback is consistent with the process of self-enhancement (see Chapter 3).

Some companies set up *multisource (360-degree) feedback* which, as the name implies, is information about an employee's performance collected from a full circle of people, including subordinates, peers, supervisors, and customers. Multisource feedback tends to provide more complete and accurate information than feedback from a supervisor alone. It is particularly useful when the supervisor is unable to observe the employee's behavior or performance throughout the year. Lower-level employees also feel a greater sense of fairness and open communication when they are able to provide upward feedback about their boss's performance.[69] However, multisource feedback can be expensive and time-consuming. It also tends to produce ambiguous and conflicting feedback. A third concern is that peers may provide inflated rather than accurate feedback to minimize interpersonal conflict. A final concern is that employees experience a stronger emotional reaction when they receive critical feedback from many people rather than from just one person (such as the boss).

> "Success is achieved by developing our strengths, not by eliminating our weaknesses."[66]
>
> —Marilyn vos Savant

Strengths-based coaching also makes sense because personality becomes quite stable by the time an individual reaches his or her early career, which limits the flexibility of the person's interests, preferences, and competencies.[67]

In spite of these research observations, most bosses focus their attention on tasks that employees are performing poorly. After the initial polite compliments, many coaching or performance feedback sessions analyze the employee's weaknesses, including determining what went wrong and what the employee needs to do to improve. These inquisitions sometimes produce so much negative feedback that employees become defensive; they can also undermine self-efficacy, thereby making the employee's performance worse rather than better. By focusing on weaknesses, companies fail to realize the full potential of the employee's strengths.[68]

Sources of Feedback

Feedback can originate from nonsocial or social sources. Nonsocial sources provide feedback without someone communicating that information. Corporate intranets allow many executives to receive feedback instantaneously on their computer, usually in the form of graphic output on an executive dashboard. Employees at contact centers view electronic displays showing how many callers are waiting and the average time they have been waiting.

With so many sources of feedback—multisource feedback, executive dashboards, customer surveys, equipment gauges, nonverbal communication from your boss—which one works best under which conditions? The preferred feedback source depends on the purpose of the information. To learn about their progress toward goal accomplishment, employees usually prefer nonsocial feedback sources, such as computer printouts or

feedback directly from the job. This is because information from nonsocial sources is considered more accurate than information from social sources. Negative feedback from nonsocial sources is also less damaging to self-esteem. In contrast, social sources tend to delay negative information, leave some of it out, and distort the bad news in a positive way.[70] When employees want to improve their self-concept, they seek out positive feedback from social sources. It feels better to have coworkers say that you are performing the job well than to discover this from a computer screen.

Evaluating Goal Setting and Feedback

Goal setting represents one of the "tried-and-true" theories in organizational behavior, so much so that it is rated by experts as one of the top OB theories in terms of validity and usefulness.[71] In partnership with goal setting, feedback also has an excellent reputation for improving employee motivation and performance. At the same time, putting goal setting into practice can create problems.[72] One concern is that goal setting tends to focus employees on a narrow subset of measurable performance indicators while ignoring aspects of job performance that are difficult to measure. The saying "What gets measured, gets done" applies here.

A second problem is that when goal achievement is tied to financial rewards, many employees are motivated to set easy goals (while making the boss think they are difficult) so that they have a higher probability of receiving the bonus or pay increase. As a former Ford Motor Company CEO once quipped: "At Ford, we hire very smart people. They quickly learn how to make relatively easy goals look difficult!"[73] A third problem is that setting performance goals is effective in established jobs but seems to interfere with the learning process in new, complex jobs. Therefore, goal setting is less useful—and may be dysfunctional—where an intense learning process is occurring.

> **LO5-6** Summarize equity theory and describe ways to improve procedural justice.

ORGANIZATIONAL JUSTICE

Most organizational leaders know that treating employees fairly is both morally correct and good for employee motivation, loyalty, and well-being. Yet feelings of injustice are regular occurrences in the workplace. To minimize these incidents, we need to first understand that there are two forms of organizational justice: distributive justice and procedural justice.[74] **Distributive justice** refers to perceived fairness in the outcomes we receive compared to our contributions and the outcomes and contributions of others. **Procedural justice**, on the other hand, refers to fairness of the procedures used to decide the distribution of resources.

Equity Theory

At its most basic level, the employment relationship is about employees exchanging their time, skills, and behavior for pay, fulfilling work, skill development opportunities, and so forth. What is considered "fair" in this exchange relationship varies with each person and situation. An *equality principle* operates when we believe that everyone in the group should receive the same outcomes, such as when everyone gets subsidized meals in the company cafeteria. The *need principle* is applied when we believe that those with the greatest need should receive more outcomes than others with less need. The *equity principle* infers that people should be paid in proportion to their contribution. The equity principle is the most common distributive justice rule in organizational settings, so let's look at it in more detail.

Feelings of equity are explained by **equity theory**, which says that employees determine feelings of equity by comparing their own outcome–input ratio to the outcome–input ratio of some other person.[75] As Exhibit 5.7 illustrates, the *outcome–input ratio* is the value of the outcomes you receive divided by the value of the inputs you provide in the exchange relationship. Inputs include things such as skill, effort, reputation, performance, experience, and hours worked. Outcomes are what employees receive from the organization such as pay, promotions, recognition, interesting jobs, and opportunities to improve one's skills and knowledge.

Equity theory states that we compare our outcome–input ratio with that of a comparison other.[76] The comparison other might be another person or group of people in other jobs (e.g., comparing your pay with the CEO's pay) or another organization. Some research suggests that employees frequently collect information on several referents to form a "generalized" comparison other.[77] For the most part, however, the comparison other varies from one person to the next and is not easily identifiable.

The comparison of our own outcome–input ratio with the ratio of someone else results in perceptions of equity, underreward inequity, or overreward inequity. In the equity condition, people believe that their outcome–input ratio is similar to the ratio of the comparison other. In the underreward inequity situation, people believe their outcome–input ratio is lower than the comparison other's ratio. In the overreward inequity condition, people believe their ratio of outcomes–inputs is higher than the comparison other's ratio.

Inequity and Employee Motivation How do perceptions of equity or inequity affect employee motivation? The answer

distributive justice perceived fairness in the individual's ratio of outcomes to contributions relative to a comparison other's ratio of outcomes to contributions

procedural justice perceived fairness of the procedures used to decide the distribution of resources

equity theory a theory explaining how people develop perceptions of fairness in the distribution and exchange of resources

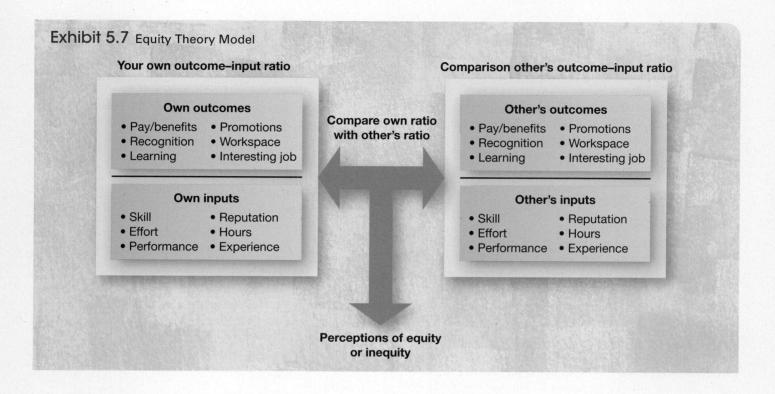

Exhibit 5.7 Equity Theory Model

Your own outcome–input ratio

Own outcomes
- Pay/benefits
- Promotions
- Recognition
- Workspace
- Learning
- Interesting job

Own inputs
- Skill
- Reputation
- Effort
- Hours
- Performance
- Experience

Compare own ratio with other's ratio

Comparison other's outcome–input ratio

Other's outcomes
- Pay/benefits
- Promotions
- Recognition
- Workspace
- Learning
- Interesting job

Other's inputs
- Skill
- Reputation
- Effort
- Hours
- Performance
- Experience

Perceptions of equity or inequity

is illustrated in Exhibit 5.8. When people believe they are under- or overrewarded, they experience negative emotions (called *inequity tension*). As we have pointed out throughout this chapter, emotions are the engines of motivation. In the case of inequity, people are motivated to reduce the emotional tension. Most people have a strong emotional response when they believe a situation is unfair, and this emotion nags at them until they take steps to correct the perceived inequity.

There are several ways to try to reduce the inequity tension.[78] Let's consider each of these in the context of underreward inequity. One action is to reduce our inputs so the outcome–input ratio is similar to the higher-paid coworker. Some employees do this by working more slowly, offering fewer suggestions, and

engaging in less organizational citizenship behavior. A second action is to increase our outcomes. Some people who think they are underpaid ask for a pay raise. Others make unauthorized use of company resources. A third behavioral response is to increase the comparison other's inputs. You might subtly ask the better-paid coworker to do a larger share of the work, for instance. A fourth action is to reduce the comparison other's outcomes. This might occur by ensuring that the coworker gets less desirable jobs or working conditions. Another action, although uncommon, is to ask the company to reduce the coworker's pay so it is the same as yours.

A fifth action is perceptual rather than behavioral. It involves changing our beliefs about the situation. For example, you might

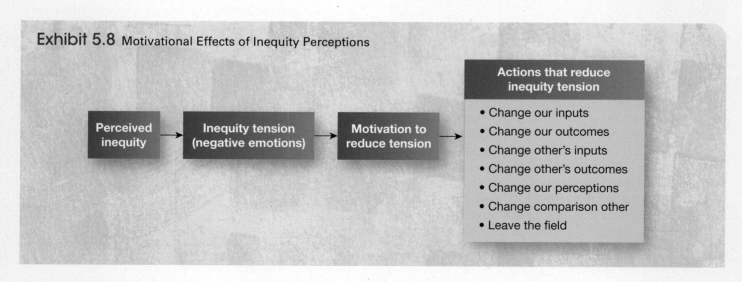

Exhibit 5.8 Motivational Effects of Inequity Perceptions

Perceived inequity → Inequity tension (negative emotions) → Motivation to reduce tension →

Actions that reduce inequity tension
- Change our inputs
- Change our outcomes
- Change other's inputs
- Change other's outcomes
- Change our perceptions
- Change comparison other
- Leave the field

Not Paid What
They're Worth[79]

61%
of 1,300 Singaporeans polled say they feel overworked and underpaid relative to the prevailing market.

38%
of 122,000 employees surveyed across 31 countries agree that the pay/compensation they receive is equitable.

43%
of 1,013 Americans polled say they are underpaid for the work they do.

77%
of 501 Canadian female executives polled say they have to work longer hours and harder than a male counterpart to attain executive positions.

4%
of 1,013 Americans polled say they are overpaid for the work they do.

3%
of 670 employed Puerto Ricans polled say they are paid more than they deserve.

Evaluating Equity Theory

Equity theory is widely studied and quite successful at predicting various situations involving feelings of workplace injustice.[81] However, equity theory isn't so easy to put into practice because it doesn't identify the comparison other and doesn't indicate which inputs or outcomes are most valuable to each employee. The best solution here is for leaders to know their employees well enough to minimize the risk of inequity feelings. Open communication is also key, enabling employees to let decision makers know when they feel decisions are unfair. A second problem is that equity theory accounts for only some of our feelings of fairness or justice in the workplace. Experts now say that procedural justice is at least as important as distributive justice.

Procedural Justice

At the beginning of this section we noted that fairness comes in two forms: distributive and procedural. *Procedural justice* refers to fairness of the procedures used to decide the distribution of resources. In other words, people evaluate fairness of the distribution of resources (distributive justice) as well as fairness of the conditions determining that distribution and its possible alteration (procedural justice).

There are several ways to improve procedural justice.[82] A good way to start is by giving employees "voice" in the process; encourage them to present their facts and perspectives on the issue. Voice also provides a "value-expressive" function; employees tend to feel better after having an opportunity to speak their mind. Procedural justice is also higher when the decision maker is perceived as unbiased, relies on complete and accurate information, applies existing policies consistently, and has listened to all sides of the dispute. If employees still feel unfairness in the allocation of resources, their feelings tend to weaken if the company has a way of appealing the decision to a higher authority.

Finally, people usually feel less injustice when they are given a full explanation of the decision and they are treated with respect throughout the complaint process. If employees

believe that the coworker really is doing more (e.g., working longer hours) for that higher pay. Alternatively, we might change our perceptions of the value of some outcomes. You might initially feel it is unfair that a coworker gets more work-related travel than you do, but later you conclude that this travel is more inconvenient than desirable. A sixth action to reduce the inequity tension is to change the comparison other. Rather than compare yourself with the higher-paid coworker, you might increasingly compare yourself with a friend or neighbor who works in a similar job. Finally, if the inequity tension is strong enough and can't be reduced through other actions, you might leave the field. This occurs by moving to another department, joining another company, or keeping away from the work site where the overpaid coworker is located.

People who feel overreward inequity would reverse these actions. Some overrewarded employees reduce their feelings of inequity by working harder; others encourage the underrewarded coworker to work at a more leisurely pace. A common reaction, however, is that the overrewarded employee changes his or her perceptions to justify the more favorable outcomes, such as believing the assigned work is more difficult or his or her skills are more valuable than the lower-paid coworker.

> "I was underpaid for the first half of my life. I don't mind being overpaid for the second half."[80]
>
> —**Pierre Berton,** journalist and popular history author

believe a decision is unfair, refusing to explain how the decision was made could fuel their feelings of inequity. For instance, one study found that nonwhite nurses who experienced racism tended to file grievances only after experiencing disrespectful treatment in their attempt to resolve the racist situation. Another study reported that employees with repetitive strain injuries were more likely to file workers' compensation claims after experiencing disrespectful behavior from management. A third recent study noted that employees have stronger feelings of injustice when the manager has a reputation of treating people unfairly most of the time.[83]

Consequences of Procedural Injustice Procedural justice has a strong influence on a person's emotions and motivation. Employees tend to experience anger toward the source of the injustice, which generates various response behaviors that scholars categorize as either withdrawal or aggression.[84] Notice how these response behaviors are similar to the fight-or-flight responses described earlier in the chapter regarding situations that activate our drive to defend. Research suggests that being treated unfairly threatens our self-concept and social status, particularly when others see that we have been unjustly treated. Employees retaliate to restore their self-esteem and reinstate their status and power in the relationship with the perpetrator of the injustice. Employees also engage in these counterproductive behaviors to educate the decision maker, thereby trying to minimize the likelihood of future injustices.[85]

LO5-7 List the advantages and disadvantages of job specialization and describe three ways to improve employee motivation through job design.

JOB DESIGN PRACTICES

How do you build a better job? That question has challenged organizational behavior experts as well as psychologists, engineers, and economists for a few centuries. Some jobs have very few tasks and usually require very little skill. Other jobs are immensely complex and require years of experience and learning to master them. From one extreme to the other, jobs have different effects on work efficiency and employee motivation. The challenge, at least from the organization's perspective, is to find the right combination so that work is performed efficiently but employees have high motivation and satisfaction.[86] This objective requires careful **job design**—the process of

assigning tasks to a job, including the interdependency of those tasks with other jobs. A *job* is a set of tasks performed by one person. To understand this issue more fully, let's begin by describing early job design efforts aimed at increasing work efficiency through job specialization.

Job Design and Work Efficiency

By any measure, supermarket cashiers have highly repetitive work. One consulting firm estimated that cashiers should be able to scan each item in an average of 4.6 seconds. A British tabloid recently reported that cashiers at five supermarket chains in that country actually took between 1.75 and 3.25 seconds to scan each item from a standardized list of 20 products. Along with scanning, cashiers process the payment, move the divider stick, and (in some stores) bag the checked groceries.[87]

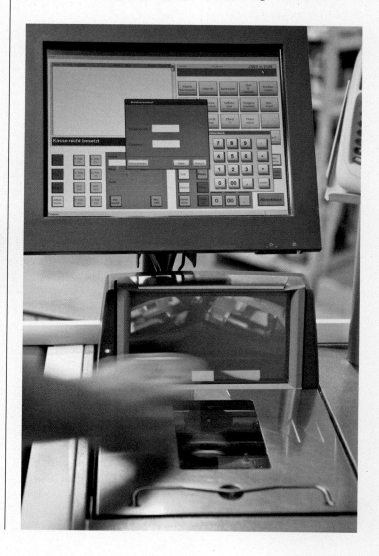

Supermarket cashiers perform jobs with a high degree of **job specialization**. Job specialization occurs when the work required to serve a customer—or provide any other product or service—is subdivided into separate jobs assigned to different people. For instance, supermarkets have separate jobs for checking out customers, stocking shelves, preparing fresh foods, and so forth. Except in the smallest family grocery stores, one person would not perform all of these tasks as part of one job. Each resulting job includes a narrow subset of tasks, usually completed in a short cycle time. *Cycle time* is the time required to complete the task before starting over with another item or client. Supermarket cashiers have a cycle time of about 4 seconds to scan each item before they repeat the activity with the next item. They also have a cycle time for serving each customer, which works out to somewhere between 20 and 40 times per hour in busy stores.

Why would companies divide work into such tiny bits? The simple answer is that job specialization potentially improves work efficiency. One reason for this higher efficiency is that employees have less variety of tasks to juggle (such as checking out customers versus stocking shelves), so there is less time lost changing over to a different type of activity. Even when people can change tasks quickly, their mental attention lingers on the previous type of work, which slows down performance on the new task.[88] A second reason for increased work efficiency is that employees can become proficient more quickly in specialized jobs. There are fewer physical and mental skills to learn and therefore less time to train and develop people for high performance. A third reason is that shorter work cycles give employees more frequent practice with the task, so jobs are mastered more quickly. A fourth reason why specialization tends to increase work efficiency is that employees with specific aptitudes or skills can be matched more precisely to the jobs for which they are best suited.[89]

The benefits of job specialization were noted more than 2,300 years ago by the Chinese philosopher Mencius and Greek philosopher Plato. Scottish economist Adam Smith wrote 250 years ago about the advantages of job specialization. Smith described a small factory where 10 pin makers collectively produced as many as 48,000 pins per day because they performed specialized tasks. One person straightened the metal, another cut it, another sharpened one end of the cut piece, yet another added a white tip to the other end, and so forth. In contrast, Smith explained that if these 10 people worked alone producing complete pins, they would collectively manufacture no more than 200 pins per day.[90]

Scientific Management One of the strongest advocates of job specialization was Frederick Winslow Taylor, an American industrial engineer who introduced the principles of **scientific management** in the early 1900s.[91] Scientific management consists of a toolkit of activities. Some of these interventions—employee selection, training, goal setting, and work incentives—are common today but were rare until Taylor popularized them. However, scientific management is mainly associated with high levels of job specialization and standardization of tasks to achieve maximum efficiency.

According to Taylor, the most effective companies have detailed procedures and work practices developed by engineers, enforced by supervisors, and executed by employees. Even the supervisor's tasks should be divided: One person manages operational efficiency, another manages inspection, and another is the disciplinarian. Taylor and other industrial engineers demonstrated that scientific management significantly improves work efficiency. No doubt, some of the increased productivity can be credited to the training, goal setting, and work incentives, but job specialization quickly became popular in its own right.

Problems with Job Specialization Frederick Winslow Taylor and his contemporaries focused on how job specialization reduces labor "waste" by improving the mechanical efficiency of work (i.e., matching skills, faster learning, less switchover time). Yet they didn't seem to notice how this extreme job specialization adversely affects employee attitudes and motivation. Some jobs—such as painting eyes on dolls—are so specialized that they soon become tedious, trivial, and socially isolating. Employee turnover and absenteeism tend to be higher in specialized jobs with very short cycle times. Companies sometimes have to pay higher wages to attract job applicants to this dissatisfying, narrowly defined work.[92]

Job specialization affects output quality, but in two opposing ways. Incumbents of specialized jobs potentially produce higher-quality results because, as we mentioned earlier, they master their work faster than do employees in jobs with many and varied tasks. But many jobs (such as supermarket cashiers) are specialized to the point that they are highly repetitive and tedious. In these repetitive jobs, the positive effect of higher proficiency is easily offset by the negative effect of lower attentiveness and motivation caused by the tedious work patterns.

Job specialization also undermines work quality by disassociating job incumbents from the overall product or service. By performing a small part of the overall work, employees have difficulty striving for better quality or even noticing flaws with that overall output. As one observer of an automobile assembly line reports: "Often [employees] did not know how their jobs related to the total picture. Not knowing, there was no incentive to strive for quality—what did quality even mean as it related to a bracket whose function you did not understand?"[93]

motivator-hygiene theory Herzberg's theory stating that employees are primarily motivated by growth and esteem needs, not by lower-level needs

job characteristics model a job design model that relates the motivational properties of jobs to specific personal and organizational consequences of those properties

Job Design and Work Motivation

Frederick Winslow Taylor may have overlooked the motivational effect of job characteristics, but it is now the central focus of many job design initiatives. Organizational behavior scholar Frederick Herzberg is credited with shifting the spotlight in the 1950s when he introduced **motivator-hygiene theory**.[94] Motivator-hygiene theory proposes that employees experience job satisfaction when they fulfill growth and esteem needs (called *motivators*) and they experience dissatisfaction when they have poor working conditions, job security, and other factors categorized as lower-order needs (called *hygienes*). Herzberg argued that only characteristics of the job itself motivate employees, whereas the hygiene factors merely prevent dissatisfaction. It might seem obvious to us today that the job itself is a source of motivation, but the concept was radical when Herzberg proposed the idea.

Motivator-hygiene theory has been soundly rejected by research studies, but Herzberg's ideas generated new thinking about the motivational potential of the job itself.[95] Out of subsequent research emerged the **job characteristics model**, shown in Exhibit 5.9. The job characteristics model identifies five core job dimensions that produce three psychological states. Employees who experience these psychological states tend to have higher levels of internal work motivation (motivation from the work itself), job satisfaction (particularly satisfaction with the work itself), and work effectiveness.[96]

Core Job Characteristics The job characteristics model identifies five core job characteristics. Under the right conditions, employees are more motivated and satisfied when jobs have higher levels of these characteristics:

- *Skill variety.* **Skill variety** refers to the use of different skills and talents to complete a variety of work activities. For example, sales

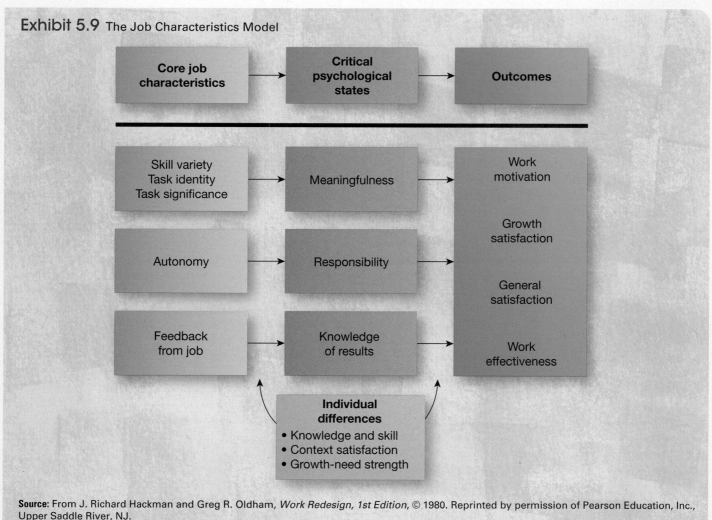

Exhibit 5.9 The Job Characteristics Model

Source: From J. Richard Hackman and Greg R. Oldham, *Work Redesign, 1st Edition*, © 1980. Reprinted by permission of Pearson Education, Inc., Upper Saddle River, NJ.

clerks who normally only serve customers might be assigned the additional duties of stocking inventory and changing storefront displays.

- *Task identity.* **Task identity** is the degree to which a job requires completion of a whole or identifiable piece of work, such as assembling an entire broadband modem rather than just soldering in the circuitry.

- *Task significance.* **Task significance** is the degree to which the job affects the organization and/or larger society. It is an observable characteristic of the job (you can see how it benefits others) as well as a perceptual awareness.

- *Autonomy.* Jobs with high levels of **autonomy** provide freedom, independence, and discretion in scheduling the work and determining the procedures to be used to complete the work. In autonomous jobs, employees make their own decisions rather than relying on detailed instructions from supervisors or procedure manuals. Autonomy is considered the core motivational element of job design.[97] As we learned in Chapter 4, autonomy is also an important mechanism to reduce stress in some situations.

- *Job feedback.* Job feedback is the degree to which employees can tell how well they are doing from direct sensory information from the job itself. Airline pilots can tell how well they land their aircraft, and road crews can see how well they have prepared the roadbed and laid the asphalt.

Critical Psychological States The five core job characteristics affect employee motivation and satisfaction through three critical psychological states, shown in Exhibit 5.9. Skill variety, task identity, and task significance directly contribute to the job's *experienced meaningfulness*—the belief that one's work is worthwhile or important. Autonomy directly contributes to feelings of *experienced responsibility*—a sense of being personally accountable for the work outcomes. The third critical psychological state is *knowledge of results*—an awareness of the work outcomes based on information from the job itself.

Individual Differences Job design doesn't increase work motivation for everyone in every situation. Employees must have the required skills and knowledge to master the more challenging work. Otherwise, job design tends to increase stress and reduce job performance. The original model also states that employees will be motivated by the five core job characteristics only when they are satisfied with their work context (e.g., working conditions, job security) and have a high *growth-need strength*. Growth-need strength refers to an individual's need for personal growth and development, such as work that offers challenge, cognitive stimulation, learning, and

independent thought and action.[98] However, research findings have been mixed, suggesting that employees might be motivated by job design no matter how they feel about their job context or how high or low they score on growth needs.[99]

Other Job Characteristics The job characteristics model overlooks two other sets of job characteristics. One of these is the extent to which the job requires employees to interact with other people (coworkers, clients, government representatives, etc.). This required social interaction is associated with emotional labor, discussed in Chapter 4, as well as with *task interdependence*, which we discuss in Chapter 7 as an element of team dynamics. The other set of job characteristics missing from the earlier model relates to the information processing demands of the work.[100] In particular, jobs differ in their task variability and task analyzability. Employees in jobs with high *task variability* have nonroutine work patterns; they would perform different types of tasks on one day than another day, and not necessarily know what tasks will be required next. Jobs with high *task analyzability* have a ready-made "cookbook" to guide job incumbents through most decisions and actions, whereas jobs with low task analyzability require employee creativity and judgment to determine the best course of action.

Job Design Practices That Motivate

The motivational potential of jobs can be increased through three strategies: job rotation, job enlargement, and job enrichment.

Job Rotation Many grocery stores reduce the tedium of checkout work by moving cashiers to other jobs during the work shift. This job rotation adds some skill variety into the workday, and many companies have found that it improves employee motivation and satisfaction to some extent. A second benefit of job rotation is that it minimizes health risks from repetitive strain and heavy lifting because employees use different muscles and physical positions in the various jobs. A third benefit is that job rotation supports multiskilling (employees learn several jobs), which increases workforce flexibility in staffing the production process and in finding replacements for employees on vacation.

Job Enlargement **Job enlargement** adds tasks to an existing job. This might involve combining two or more complete jobs into one or just adding one or two more tasks to an existing job. Either way, skill variety increases because there are more tasks to perform.

job enrichment
the practice of giving employees more responsibility for scheduling, coordinating, and planning their own work

Job Enrichment **Job enrichment** occurs when employees are given more responsibility for scheduling, coordinating, and planning their own work.[101] For example, employees have more enriched jobs when they are responsible for a variety of tasks and have enough autonomy to plan their work and choose when to perform each task. Generally, people in enriched jobs experience higher job satisfaction and work motivation, along with lower absenteeism and turnover. Productivity is also higher when task identity and job feedback are improved. Product and service quality tend to improve because job enrichment increases the jobholder's felt responsibility and sense of ownership over the product or service.[102]

One way to increase job enrichment is by combining highly interdependent tasks into one job. This *natural grouping* approach is reflected in the video journalist job. Along with being an enlarged job, video journalism is an example of job enrichment because it naturally groups tasks together to complete an entire product (i.e., a news story). By forming natural work units, jobholders have stronger feelings of responsibility for an identifiable body of work. They feel a sense of ownership and, therefore, tend to increase job quality. Forming natural work units increases task identity and task significance because employees perform a complete product or service and can more readily see how their work affects others.

A second job enrichment strategy, called *establishing client relationships,* involves putting employees in direct contact with their clients rather than using the supervisor as a go-between. By being directly responsible for specific clients, employees have more information and can make decisions affecting those clients.[103] Establishing client relationships also increases task significance because employees see a line-of-sight connection between their work and consequences for customers.

Study Checklist

- Did you tear out the perforated student review card at the back of the text to revisit learning objectives and key terms and definitions?

Connect® Management is available for *M Organizational Behavior.* Additional resources include:

- Interactive Applications:
  - **Decision Generator**
  - **Drag and Drop:** Work through an interactive example to test your knowledge of the concepts.
  - **Video Case:** See management in action through interactive videos.

- **SmartBook™**—SmartBook is the first and only adaptive reading experience available today. Distinguishing what you know from what you don't, and honing in on concepts you are most likely to forget, SmartBook personalizes content for you in a continuously adapting reading experience. Reading is no longer a passive and linear experience, but an engaging and dynamic one where you are more likely to master and retain important concepts and go to class better prepared.

Want Help Studying?

SMARTBOOK: MAKE EACH MINUTE COUNT.

Go to: LearnSmartAdvantage.com

6 chapter

Decision Making and Creativity

Learning Objectives

After studying this chapter, you should be able to:

LO6-1 Describe the rational choice paradigm of decision making.

LO6-2 Explain why people differ from the rational choice paradigm when identifying problems/opportunities, evaluating/choosing alternatives, and evaluating decision outcomes.

LO6-3 Discuss the roles of emotions and intuition in decision making.

LO6-4 Describe employee characteristics, workplace conditions, and specific activities that support creativity.

LO6-5 Describe the benefits of employee involvement and identify four contingencies that affect the optimal level of employee involvement.

"**M**y job as CEO is not to make business decisions—it's to push managers to be leaders," says Sergio Marchionne. In reality, the CEO of Fiat S.p.A. and Chrysler Group LLC makes more critical decisions in a week than most of us would make in a year. In "pushing managers to be leaders," Marchionne refers to developing their capacity to become better decision makers. At multiday weekend meetings, junior managers present their business plans to Marchionne and his 23 direct reports, who then vote on them using majority rule. Furthermore, he pushes decision making down the hierarchy, such as having Fiat and Chrysler teams work together to develop and launch new vehicles in record time. Marchionne has also brought in several people to instill more creative decision making, including Chrysler's "Imported From Detroit" brand revival. "The creativity at Chrysler had been pushed very far underground [by its previous owners]," one auto industry expert observes. "Now Marchionne is bringing it out and he will put his mark on it."[1]

Sergio Marchionne views decision making as a critical management skill. He also recognizes that decision making occurs throughout the organization, which he supports through employee involvement. Furthermore, Chrysler and other organizations depend on creativity in the decision-making process. This chapter examines each of these themes. We begin by outlining the rational choice paradigm of decision making. Next, the limitations of this paradigm are discussed, including the human limitations of rational choice. We also examine the emerging paradigm that decisions consist of a complex interaction of logic and emotion. The latter part of this chapter focuses on two topics that intertwine with decision making: creativity and employee involvement.

LO6-1 Describe the rational choice paradigm of decision making.

RATIONAL CHOICE PARADIGM OF DECISION MAKING

Decision making is the process of making choices among alternatives with the intention of moving toward some desired state of affairs.[2] This is vital to an organization's health, rather like breathing is to a human being. Indeed, leaders increasingly view themselves as physicians who resuscitate organizations by encouraging and teaching employees at all levels to make decisions more quickly, effectively, and creatively. All businesses, governments, and not-for-profit agencies depend on employees to foresee and correctly identify problems, to survey alternatives and pick the best one based on a variety of stakeholder interests, and to execute those decisions effectively.

How should people make decisions in organizations? Most business leaders would likely answer this question by saying that effective decision making involves identifying, selecting, and applying the best possible alternative. In other words, the best decisions use pure logic and all available information to choose the alternative with the highest value—such as highest expected profitability, customer satisfaction, employee well-being, or some combination of these outcomes. These decisions sometimes involve complex calculations of data to produce a formula that points to the best choice.

In its extreme form, this calculative view of decision making represents the **rational choice paradigm**, which has dominated decision-making philosophy in Western societies for most of written history.[4] It was established 2,500 years ago when Plato and his contemporaries in ancient Greece raised logical debate and reasoning to a fine art. About 400 years ago, Descartes and other European philosophers emphasized that the ability to make logical decisions is one of the most important accomplishments of human beings. In the 1700s, Scottish philosophers refined the notion that the best choice is the one that offers the greatest satisfaction or "utility."

The rational choice paradigm selects the choice with the highest utility through the calculation of **subjective expected utility (SEU)**.[5] Subjective expected utility is the probability (expectancy) of satisfaction (utility) for each alternative. SEU is the foundation of several organizational behavior theories, including the attitude

> "I am not a product of my circumstances. I am a product of my decisions."[3]
>
> —**Stephen R. Covey,**
> author and educator

decision making the conscious process of making choices among alternatives with the intention of moving toward some desired state of affairs

rational choice paradigm the view in decision making that people should—and typically do—use logic and all available information to choose the alternative with the highest value

subjective expected utility (SEU) the probability (expectancy) of satisfaction (utility) resulting from choosing a specific alternative in a decision

model in Chapter 4 and expectancy theory of motivation in Chapter 5.

To understand SEU, consider the example in Exhibit 6.1.[6] Your company wants to choose a new supplier of a particular raw material. The decision considers the three most important criteria (which are essentially outcomes of choosing a particular supplier): Does the supplier provide a high-quality product (+9) with low prices (+6) and on-time delivery (+4)?[7] The numbers, which are on a 10-point scale, indicate each outcome's valence ("utility" in subjective expected utility, which is the expected satisfaction from that outcome). Your investigations suggest that supplier A has an excellent record of on-time delivery (about 90 percent probability of exceeding the company's expectations) whereas it has a 70 percent probability

of reliably providing an exceptional-quality product. Supplier B has a 90 percent chance of providing very high product quality but a lower likelihood (40 percent) of offering the best prices. These probabilities are the "expected" in subjective expected utility and are "subjective" because they represent perceptions from available information.

Which of these two suppliers should your company choose? According to the rational choice paradigm, you would choose the supplier that will give the company the greatest satisfaction—the higher subjective expected utility. To figure out which supplier has the highest overall subjective expected utility, multiply the utility of each outcome with the probability of that outcome occurring, then add those results across all three outcomes. The supplier with the higher score is the better choice, given available information. The key point from this example is that all rational choice decisions rely primarily on two pieces of information: (a) the valence or expected satisfaction of the outcomes (utility) and (b) the probability of those good or bad outcomes occurring (expectancy).

Rational Choice Decision-Making Process

Subjective expected utility is one of two core elements of the rational choice paradigm. The other core element is that people follow the systematic decision process illustrated in Exhibit 6.2.[8] The first step is to identify the problem or recognize an opportunity. A *problem* is a deviation between the current and the desired situation—the gap between "what is" and "what ought to be." This deviation is a symptom of more fundamental causes that need to be corrected.[9] The "ought to be" refers to goals, and these goals later help to evaluate the selected choice. For instance, if the goal is to answer incoming client calls within 30 seconds, the problem is the gap between that goal and the actual time the call center takes to answer most client calls. An *opportunity* is a deviation between current expectations and a potentially better situation that was not previously expected. In other words, decision makers realize that some decisions may produce results beyond current goals or expectations.

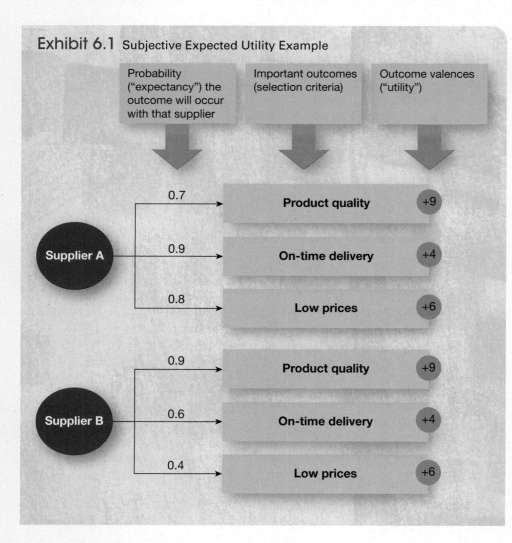

Exhibit 6.1 Subjective Expected Utility Example

Probability ("expectancy") the outcome will occur with that supplier

Important outcomes (selection criteria)

Outcome valences ("utility")

Supplier A
- 0.7 → Product quality +9
- 0.9 → On-time delivery +4
- 0.8 → Low prices +6

Supplier B
- 0.9 → Product quality +9
- 0.6 → On-time delivery +4
- 0.4 → Low prices +6

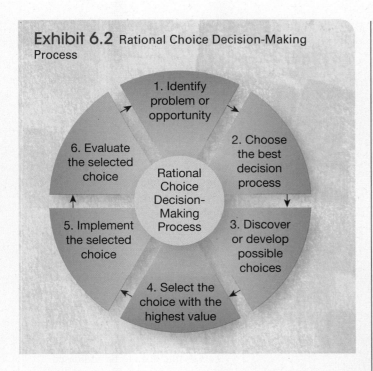

Exhibit 6.2 Rational Choice Decision-Making Process

- 1. Identify problem or opportunity
- 2. Choose the best decision process
- 3. Discover or develop possible choices
- 4. Select the choice with the highest value
- 5. Implement the selected choice
- 6. Evaluate the selected choice

Rational Choice Decision-Making Process

The second step involves choosing the best decision process. This step is really a meta-decision—deciding how to decide—because it refers to choosing among the different approaches and processes to make the decision.[10] One meta-decision is whether to solve the problem alone or involve others in the process. Later in this chapter, we'll examine the contingencies of employee involvement in the decision. Another meta-decision is whether to assume the decision is programmed or nonprogrammed. *Programmed decisions* follow standard operating procedures; they have been resolved in the past, so the optimal solution has already been identified and documented. In contrast, *nonprogrammed decisions* require all steps in the decision model because the problems are new, complex, or ill-defined.

The third step in the rational choice decision process is to identify and/or develop a list of possible choices. This usually begins by searching for ready-made solutions, such as practices that have worked well on similar problems. If an acceptable solution cannot be found, then decision makers need to design a custom-made solution or modify an existing one. The fourth step is to select the choice with the highest subjective expected utility. This calls for all possible information about all possible alternatives and their outcomes, but the rational choice paradigm assumes this can be accomplished with ease.

The fifth step in the rational choice decision process is to implement the selected alternative. Rational choice experts have little to say about this step because they assume implementation occurs without any problems. This is followed by the sixth step, evaluating whether the gap has narrowed between "what is" and "what ought to be." Ideally, this information should come from systematic benchmarks so that relevant feedback is objective and easily observed.

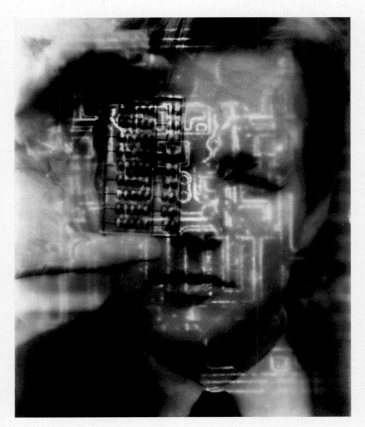

Problems with the Rational Choice Paradigm

The rational choice paradigm seems so logical, yet it is impossible to apply in reality because people are not and cannot be perfectly rational.[11] Therefore, we need to understand why people have imperfect rationality. Over the next several pages, we reexamine each step in the rational choice decision-making process, but with more detail about what really happens through the lens of "imperfect rationality."

> **LO6-2** Explain why people differ from the rational choice paradigm when identifying problems/opportunities, evaluating/choosing alternatives, and evaluating decision outcomes.

IDENTIFYING PROBLEMS AND OPPORTUNITIES

When Albert Einstein was asked how he would save the world in 1 hour, he replied that the first 55 minutes should be spent defining the problem and the last 5 minutes solving it.[12] Einstein's point is that problem identification is not just the first step in decision making; it is arguably the most *important* step. But problems and opportunities are not clearly labeled objects that appear on our desks. Instead, they are conclusions that we form from ambiguous and conflicting information.[13]

Problems with Problem Identification

The problem identification stage is, itself, filled with problems. Here are five of the most widely recognized concerns.[14]

Stakeholder Framing Employees, suppliers, customers, and other stakeholders provide (or hide) information in ways that makes the decision maker see the situation as a problem, opportunity, or steady sailing. Employees point to external factors rather than their own faults as the cause of production delays. Suppliers market their new products as unique opportunities and competitor products as problems to be avoided. Stakeholders also offer a concise statement of the situation as a problem or otherwise in the hope the decision maker will accept their verdict without further analysis. Decision makers fall prey to these constructed realities because they have a need to simplify the daily bombardment of complex and often ambiguous information.

> "When the only tool you have is a hammer, all problems begin to resemble nails."[16]
>
> —**Abraham Maslow,**
> psychologist and scholar

Decisive Leadership Various studies have found that executives are evaluated by their decisiveness, including how quickly they determine that the situation is a problem, opportunity, or nothing worth their attention.[15] Consequently, many leaders announce problems or opportunities before having a chance to logically assess the situation. The result is often a misguided effort to solve an ill-defined problem or resources wasted on a poorly identified opportunity.

Solution-Focused Problems When decision makers do recognize that the situation requires a decision, they sometimes describe the problem as a veiled solution.[17] For instance, someone might say: "The problem is that we need more control over our suppliers." This isn't a description of the problem; it is a rephrased statement of a solution to a problem that has not been adequately diagnosed. This solution-focused problem identification provides comforting closure to the otherwise ambiguous and uncertain nature of problems, but it fails to fully diagnose the underlying causes that need to be addressed.

Perceptual Defense People sometimes fail to become aware of problems because they block out bad news as a coping mechanism. Their brain refuses to see information that threatens their self-concept. The tendency to engage in perceptual defense varies from one decision maker to the next. Studies also report that perceptual defense is more common when decision makers have limited options to solve the problem.[18]

Mental Models Decision makers are victims of their own problem framing due to existing mental models. Mental models are visual or relational images in our mind of the external world; they fill in information that we don't immediately see, which helps us understand and navigate in our surrounding environment (see Chapter 3). Many mental images are also prototypes—they represent models of how things should be. Unfortunately, these mental models can blind us from seeing unique problems or opportunities because they produce a negative evaluation of things that are dissimilar to the mental model. If an idea doesn't fit the existing mental model of how things should work, then it is quickly dismissed as unworkable or undesirable.

Mental Model Myopia

Two Stanford PhD students wanted to complete their education, so they decided to sell for $1 million the new search engine they had developed. Excite, Inc., a popular search engine company at that time, turned down the search software, explaining that their mental model of successful web portals was in offering media, not searching. For similar reasons, other firms also rejected the students' invitation to buy their software. Rather than abandon their search engine creation, the students—Larry Page and Sergey Brin—decided to form a company to realize its potential. They named their company Google. Many years later, Excite cofounder Joe Kraus acknowledged the huge missed opportunity. "Let me just say that we were wrong," said Kraus. "I'll be the first to stand up and say 'whoops.' "[19]

Identifying Problems and Opportunities More Effectively

Recognizing problems and opportunities will always be a challenge, but one way to improve the process is by becoming aware of the five problem identification biases just described. For example, by recognizing that mental models restrict a person's perspective of the world, decision makers are more motivated to consider other perspectives of reality. Along with increasing their awareness of problem identification flaws, leaders require considerable

Identifying Problems and Opportunities More Effectively

▶ Be aware of the problem identification biases.

▶ Resist the temptation to look decisive.

▶ Have an aversion to complacency (practice divine discontent).

▶ Discuss the situation with others.

willpower to resist the temptation of looking decisive when a more thoughtful examination of the situation should occur.

A third way to improve problem identification is for leaders to create a norm of "divine discontent." They are never satisfied with the status quo, and this aversion to complacency creates a mindset that more actively searches for problems and opportunities.[20] Finally, employees can minimize problem identification errors by discussing the situation with colleagues. It is much easier to discover blind spots in problem identification when listening to how others perceive the situation. Opportunities also become apparent when outsiders explore this information from their different mental models.

SEARCHING FOR, EVALUATING, AND CHOOSING ALTERNATIVES

According to the rational choice paradigm of decision making, people rely on logic to evaluate and choose alternatives. This paradigm assumes that decision makers have well-articulated and agreed-on organizational goals, that they efficiently and simultaneously process facts about all alternatives and the consequences of those alternatives, and that they choose the alternative with the highest payoff.

Nobel Prize–winning organizational scholar Herbert Simon questioned these assumptions a half century ago. He argued that people engage in **bounded rationality** because they process limited and imperfect information and rarely select the best choice.[21] Simon and other OB experts demonstrated that how people evaluate and choose alternatives differs from the rational choice paradigm in several ways, as illustrated in Exhibit 6.3. These differences are so significant that many economists are now shifting from rational choice to bounded rationality assumptions in their theories. Let's look at these

Exhibit 6.3 Rational Choice Assumptions versus Organizational Behavior Findings about Choosing Alternatives

Rational choice paradigm assumptions	Observations from organizational behavior
Goals are clear, compatible, and agreed upon.	Goals are ambiguous, are in conflict, and lack full support.
Decision makers can calculate all alternatives and their outcomes.	Decision makers have limited information-processing abilities.
Decision makers evaluate all alternatives simultaneously.	Decision makers evaluate alternatives sequentially.
Decision makers use absolute standards to evaluate alternatives.	Decision makers evaluate alternatives against an implicit favorite.
Decision makers use factual information to choose alternatives.	Decision makers process perceptually distorted information.
Decision makers choose the alternative with the highest payoff.	Decision makers choose the alternative that is good enough (satisficing).

differences in terms of goals, information processing, and maximization.

Problems with Goals

The rational choice paradigm assumes that organizational goals are clear and agreed on. In fact, these conditions are necessary to identify "what ought to be" and, therefore, provide a standard against which each alternative is evaluated. Unfortunately, organizational goals are often ambiguous or in conflict with each other.

Problems with Information Processing

The rational choice paradigm also makes several assumptions about the human capacity to process information. It assumes that decision makers can process information about all alternatives and their consequences, whereas this is not possible in reality. Instead, people evaluate only a few alternatives and only some of the main outcomes of those alternatives.[22] For example, there may be dozens of computer brands to choose from and dozens of features to consider, yet people typically evaluate only a few brands and a few features.

A related problem is that decision makers typically evaluate alternatives sequentially rather than all at the same time. This sequential evaluation occurs partly because all alternatives are not usually available to the decision maker at the same time.[23] Consequently, as a new alternative comes along, it is immediately compared to an **implicit favorite**—an alternative that the decision maker prefers and that is used as a comparison with other choices. When choosing a new computer system, for example, people typically have an implicit favorite brand or model against which they compare the other brands. This sequential process of comparing alternatives with an implicit favorite occurs even when decision makers aren't consciously aware that they are doing this.[24]

The implicit favorite comparison process seems to be hardwired in human decision making (i.e., we have an innate tendency to compare things). Unfortunately, the comparison process often undermines effective decision making because people distort information to favor their implicit favorite over the alternative choices. They tend to ignore problems with the implicit favorite and advantages of the alternative. Decision makers also overweight factors on which the implicit favorite is better and underweight areas in which the alternative is superior.[25]

Biased Decision Heuristics Subjective expected utility is the cornerstone of rational choice decision making, yet psychologists

Amos Tversky and Daniel Kahneman discovered that human beings have built-in *decision heuristics* that automatically distort either the probability of outcomes or the value (utility) of those outcomes. Three of the most widely studied heuristic biases are anchoring and adjustment, availability, and representativeness:[26]

- **Anchoring and adjustment heuristic.** This heuristic states that we are influenced by an initial anchor point and do not sufficiently move away from that point as new information is provided.[27] The anchor point might be an initial offer price, initial opinion of someone, or initial estimated probability that something will occur. One explanation for this effect is that human beings tend to compare alternatives rather than evaluate them purely against objective criteria. Therefore, if someone requests a high initial price for a car we want to buy, we naturally compare—and thereby anchor—our alternative offer against that high initial price.

- **Availability heuristic.** The availability heuristic is the tendency to estimate the probability of something occurring by how easily we can recall those events. Unfortunately, how easily we recall something is due to more than just its frequency (probability).[28] For instance, we easily remember emotional events (such as earthquakes and shark attacks), so we overestimate how often these traumatic events occur. We also have an easier time recalling recent events. If the media report several incidents of air pollution, we likely give more pessimistic estimates of air quality generally than if there have been no recent reports.

- **Representativeness heuristic**. This heuristic states that we pay more attention to whether something resembles (is representative of) something else than to more precise statistics about its probability.[29] Suppose that one-fifth of the students in your class are in engineering and the others are business majors. There is only a 20 percent chance that any classmate is from engineering, yet we don't hesitate to assume a student is from engineering if they look and act like our stereotype of an engineering student. Another form of the representativeness heuristic, known as the *clustering illusion,* is the tendency to see patterns from a small sample of events when those events are, in fact, random. For example, most players and coaches believe that players are more likely to have a successful shot on the net when their previous two or three shots have been successful. The representativeness heuristic is at work here because players and coaches believe these sequences are causally connected (representative) when, in reality, they are more likely random events.

Problems with Maximization

One of the main assumptions of the rational choice paradigm is that people want to—and are able to—choose the alternative with the highest payoff (i.e., the highest "utility" in subjective expected utility). Yet rather than aiming for maximization, people engage in **satisficing**—they choose an alternative that is satisfactory or "good enough."[30] People satisfice when they select the first alternative that exceeds a standard of acceptance for their needs and preferences. Satisficing partly occurs because alternatives present themselves over time, not all at once. Consider the process of hiring new employees. It is impossible to choose the best possible job candidate because people apply over a period of time and the best candidate might not apply until next month, after earlier candidates have found other jobs. Consequently, as we mentioned earlier, decision makers rely on sequential evaluation of new alternatives against an implicit favorite. This necessarily calls for a satisficing decision rule—choose the first alternative that is "good enough."

A second reason why people engage in satisficing rather than maximization is that they lack the capacity and motivation to process the huge volume of information required to identify the best choice. Studies report that people like to have choices, but making decisions when there are many alternatives can be cognitively and emotionally draining. Consequently, when exposed to many alternatives, decision makers become cognitive misers by engaging in satisficing.[31] They also respond to a large number of choices by discarding many of them using easily identifiable factors (e.g., color, size) and by evaluating alternatives using only a handful of criteria.

When presented with a large number of choices, people often choose a decision strategy that is even less cognitively challenging than satisficing; they don't make any decision at all! One study reported that many employees delayed registering for the company's pension plan when they faced dozens of investment options, even though signing up would give them tax benefits, company contributions to that plan, and long-term financial security. The company pension plan registration rate increases dramatically when employees are given only two or three initial investment options, such as a growth fund, balanced fund, and capital stable investment. Employees learn about the dozens of other investment choices after they have signed up.[32]

> The emotional marker process shapes our preferences for each alternative before we consciously evaluate those alternatives.

Evaluating Opportunities

Opportunities are just as important as problems, but what happens when an opportunity is "discovered" is quite different from the process of problem solving. Decision makers do not evaluate several alternatives when they find an opportunity; after all, the opportunity *is* the solution, so why look for others! An opportunity is usually experienced as an exciting and rare revelation, so decision makers tend to have an emotional attachment to the opportunity. Unfortunately, this emotional preference motivates decision makers to apply the opportunity and short-circuit any detailed evaluation of it.[33]

LO6-3 Discuss the roles of emotions and intuition in decision making.

Emotions and Making Choices

Herbert Simon and many other experts have found that people do not evaluate alternatives nearly as well as is assumed by the rational choice paradigm. However, they neglected to mention another glaring weakness with rational choice: It completely ignores the effect of emotions in human decision making. Just as both the rational and emotional brain centers alert us to problems, they also influence our choice of alternatives.[34] Emotions affect the evaluation of alternatives in three ways.

Emotions Form Early Preferences
The emotional marker process described in previous chapters (Chapters 3 through 5) shapes our preference for each alternative before we consciously evaluate those alternatives. Our brain very quickly attaches specific emotions to information about each alternative, and our preferred alternative is strongly influenced by those initial emotional markers.[35] Of course, logical analysis also influences which alternative we choose, but it requires strong logical evidence to change our initial preferences (initial emotional markers). Yet even logical analysis depends on emotions to sway our decision. Specifically, neuroscientific evidence says that information produced from logical analysis is tagged with emotional markers

that then motivate us to choose or avoid a particular alternative. Ultimately, emotions, not rational logic, energize us to make the preferred choice. In fact, people with damaged emotional brain centers have difficulty making choices.

Emotions Change the Decision Evaluation Process
Moods and specific emotions influence the *process* of evaluating alternatives.[36] For instance, we pay more attention to details when in a negative mood, possibly because a negative mood signals that there is something wrong that requires attention. When in a positive mood, on the other hand, we pay less attention to details and rely on a more programmed decision routine. This phenomenon explains why executive teams in successful companies are often less vigilant about competitors and other environmental threats.[37] Research also suggests that decision makers rely on stereotypes and other shortcuts to speed up the choice process when they experience anger. Anger also makes them more optimistic about the success of risky alternatives, whereas the emotion of fear tends to make them less optimistic. Overall, emotions shape *how* we evaluate information, not just which choice we select.

Emotions Serve as Information When We Evaluate Alternatives
The third way that emotions influence the evaluation of alternatives is through a process called "emotions as information." Marketing experts have found that we listen in on our emotions to gain guidance when making choices.[38] This process is similar to having a temporary improvement in emotional intelligence. Most emotional experiences remain below the level of conscious awareness, but people actively try to be more sensitive to these subtle emotions when making a decision.

When buying a new car, for example, you not only logically evaluate each vehicle's features; you also try to gauge your emotions when visualizing what it would be like to own each of the cars on your list of choices. Even if you have solid information about the quality of each vehicle on key features (purchase price, fuel efficiency, maintenance costs, resale value, etc.), you are swayed by your emotional reaction and actively try to sense that emotional response when thinking about it. Some people pay more attention to these gut feelings, and personality tests such as the Myers-Briggs Type Indicator (see Chapter 2) identify individuals who listen in on their emotions

intuition the ability to know when a problem or opportunity exists and to select the best course of action without conscious reasoning

more than others.[39] But everyone consciously pays attention to their emotions to some degree when choosing alternatives. This phenomenon ties directly into our next topic, intuition.

Intuition and Making Choices

Do you have a gut instinct—a feeling inside—when something isn't quite right? Or perhaps a different emotional experience occurs when you sense an opportunity in front of your eyes? These emotional experiences potentially (but not necessarily) indicate your **intuition**—the ability to know when a problem or opportunity exists and to select the best course of action without conscious reasoning.[40] Intuition is both an emotional experience and a rapid nonconscious analytic process. As mentioned in the previous section, the gut feelings we experience are emotional signals that have enough intensity to make us consciously aware of them. These signals warn us of impending danger or motivate us to take advantage of an opportunity. Some intuition also directs us to preferred choices relative to other alternatives in the situation.

All gut feelings are emotional signals, but not all emotional signals are intuition. The main distinction is that intuition involves rapidly comparing our observations with deeply held patterns learned through experience.[41] These "templates of the mind" represent tacit knowledge that has been implicitly acquired over time. They are mental models that help us understand whether the current situation is good or bad, depending on how well that situation fits our mental model. When a template fits or doesn't fit the current situation, emotions are produced that motivate us to act. Studies have found that chess masters experience emotional signals when they see an opportunity through quick observation of a chessboard. They can't immediately analyze why this opportunity exists, but can do so when given time to think about the situation. Their intuition signals the opportunity long before this rational analysis takes place.

As mentioned, some emotional signals are not intuition, so gut feelings shouldn't always guide our decisions. The problem is that emotional responses are not always based on well-grounded mental models. Instead, we sometimes compare the current situation to more remote templates, which may or may not be relevant. A new employee might feel confident about relations with a supplier, whereas an experienced employee senses potential problems. The difference is that the new employee relies on templates from other experiences or industries that might not work well in this situation. Thus, the extent to which our gut feelings in a situation represent intuition depends on our level of experience in that situation.

So far, we have described intuition as an emotional experience (gut feeling) and a process in which we compare the current situation with well-established templates of the mind. Intuition also relies on *action scripts*—programmed decision routines that speed up our response to pattern matches or mismatches.[42] Action scripts effectively shorten the decision-making process by jumping from problem identification to selection of a solution. In other words, action scripting is a form of programmed decision making. Action scripts are generic, so we need to consciously adapt them to the specific situation.

Making Choices More Effectively

It is very difficult to get around the human limitations of making choices, but a few strategies help to minimize these concerns. One important discovery is that decisions tend to have a higher failure rate when leaders are decisive rather than contemplative about the available options. Of course, decisions can also be ineffective when leaders take too long to make a choice, but research indicates that a lack of logical evaluation of alternatives is a greater concern. By systematically assessing alternatives against relevant factors, decision makers minimize the implicit favorite and satisficing problems that occur when they rely on general subjective judgments. This recommendation does not suggest that we ignore intuition; rather, it suggests that we use it in combination with careful analysis of relevant information.[43]

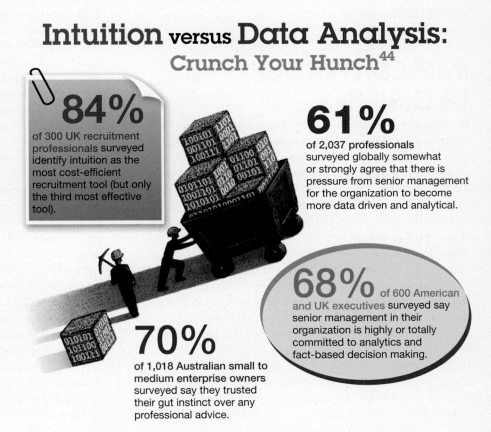

Intuition versus Data Analysis:
Crunch Your Hunch[44]

84% of 300 UK recruitment professionals surveyed identify intuition as the most cost-efficient recruitment tool (but only the third most effective tool).

61% of 2,037 professionals surveyed globally somewhat or strongly agree that there is pressure from senior management for the organization to become more data driven and analytical.

70% of 1,018 Australian small to medium enterprise owners surveyed say they trusted their gut instinct over any professional advice.

68% of 600 American and UK executives surveyed say senior management in their organization is highly or totally committed to analytics and fact-based decision making.

A second piece of advice is to remember that decisions are influenced by both rational and emotional processes. With this point in mind, some decision makers deliberately revisit important issues later so that they look at the information in different moods and have allowed their initial emotions to subside. For example, if you sense that your team is feeling somewhat too self-confident when making an important competitive decision, you might decide to have the team members revisit the decision a few days later when they are thinking more critically.

Another strategy is **scenario planning**, which is a disciplined method for imagining possible futures.[45] It typically involves thinking about what would happen if a significant environmental condition changed and what the organization should do to anticipate and react to such an outcome. Scenario planning is a useful vehicle for choosing the best solutions under possible scenarios long before they occur, because alternative courses of action are evaluated without the pressure and emotions that occur during real emergencies.

IMPLEMENTING DECISIONS

Implementing decisions is often skipped over in most writing about the decision-making process. Yet leading business writers emphasize that execution—translating decisions into action—is one of the most important and challenging tasks in the decision-making process.[46] For instance, when Bill Utt became CEO of KBR, a *Fortune* 300 engineering firm, he and his executive team fairly quickly made three strategic decisions that would improve the company's future prospects. Implementing those decisions, however, took much longer. "I expected that it would take two years to complete the three challenges," says Utt. "One thing I have learned over my career is that it is easy to develop a strategy and to find the organization's deficiencies; however, the hard part is in the implementation and having the focus, determination and stamina to see these successfully through."[47] Implementing decisions is mainly about organizational change, which we discuss in Chapter 14, but also relates to leadership (Chapter 11) and several other topics throughout this book.

EVALUATING DECISION OUTCOMES

Contrary to the rational choice paradigm, decision makers aren't completely honest with themselves when evaluating the effectiveness of their decisions. One problem is *confirmation bias* (also known as *postdecisional justification* in the context of decision evaluation), which is "unwitting selectivity in the acquisition and use of evidence."[48] When evaluating decisions, people with confirmation bias ignore or downplay the negative features of the selected alternative and overemphasize its positive features. Confirmation bias gives people an excessively optimistic evaluation of their decisions, but only until they receive very clear and undeniable information to the contrary. Unfortunately, it also inflates the decision maker's initial evaluation of the decision, so reality often comes as a painful shock when objective feedback is finally received.

Escalation of Commitment

Another reason why decision makers don't evaluate their decisions very well is due to **escalation of commitment**—the tendency to repeat an apparently bad decision or allocate more resources to a failing course of action.[49] Why are decision makers led deeper and deeper into failing projects? Several explanations have been identified and discussed over the years, but the four main influences are self-justification effect, self-enhancement effect, prospect theory effect, and sunk costs effect.

Self-Justification Effect People engage in behaviors that convey a positive public image of themselves. In decision making, this self-justification typically involves appearing to be rational and competent. People are therefore motivated to demonstrate that their decisions will be successful, and this includes continuing to support those decisions even when there is evidence that they are not having the desired outcomes. In contrast, pulling the plug symbolizes the project's failure and the decision maker's incompetence. This self-justification effect is particularly evident when decision makers are personally identified with the project, have staked their reputations to some extent on the project's success, and have low self-esteem.[50]

Self-Enhancement Effect People have a natural tendency to feel good about themselves—to feel luckier, more competent, and more successful than average—regarding things that are important to them (see Chapter 3).[51] This self-enhancement supports a positive self-concept, but it also increases the risk of escalation of commitment. When presented with evidence that a project is in trouble, the self-enhancement process biases our interpretation of the information as a temporary aberration from an otherwise positive trend line. And when we eventually realize that the project isn't going as well as planned, we continue to invest in the project because our probability of rescuing the project is above average. Self-justification and self-enhancement often occur together, but they are different mechanisms. Self-justification is a deliberate

scenario planning a systematic process of thinking about alternative futures and what the organization should do to anticipate and react to those environments

escalation of commitment the tendency to repeat an apparently bad decision or allocate more resources to a failing course of action

prospect theory effect a natural tendency to feel more dissatisfaction from losing a particular amount than satisfaction from gaining an equal amount

attempt to maintain a favorable public image, whereas self-enhancement operates mostly non-consciously, distorting information so we do not recognize the problem sooner and biasing our probabilities of success so we continue to invest in the losing project.[52]

Prospect Theory Effect **Prospect theory effect** is the tendency to experience stronger negative emotions when losing something of value than the positive emotions when gaining something of equal value. This prospect theory effect motivates us to avoid losses, which typically occurs by taking the risk of investing more in that losing project. Stopping a project is a certain loss, which is more painful to most people than the uncertainty of success associated with continuing to fund the project. Given the choice, decision makers choose escalation of commitment, which is the less painful option at the time.[53]

Sunk Costs Effect Another disincentive to axing a failing project is sunk costs—the value of resources already invested in the decision.[54] The rational choice paradigm states that investing resources should be determined by expected future gains and risk, not the size of earlier resources invested in the project. Yet people inherently feel motivated to invest more resources in projects that have high sunk costs. A variation of sunk costs is time investment. Time is a resource, so the more time decision makers have devoted to a project, the more motivated they are to continuing investing in that project. Finally, sunk costs can take the form of closing costs, that is, the financial or nonfinancial penalties associated with shutting down a project. As with other forms of sunk costs, the higher the closing costs, the more motivated decision makers are to engage in escalation of commitment.

Escalation of commitment is usually framed as poor decision making, but some experts argue that throwing more money into a failing project is sometimes a logical attempt to further understand an ambiguous situation. This strategy is essentially a variation of testing unknown waters. By adding more resources, the decision maker gains new information about the effectiveness of these funds, which provides more feedback about the project's future success. This strategy is particularly common where the project has high closing costs.[55]

Evaluating Decision Outcomes More Effectively

One of the most effective ways to minimize escalation of commitment and confirmation bias is to ensure that the people who made the original decision are not the same people who later evaluate that decision. This separation of roles minimizes the

Classics in Escalation of Commitment[56]

▶ Following the September 11, 2001, attacks, the U.S. government formed the Department of Homeland Security and decided to build a central headquarters for its many scattered units. The massive complex was supposed to cost less than $3 billion and have "final occupancy" in 2015. Instead, the project is 11 years behind schedule and its cost has ballooned to more than $4.5 billion. Supporters and critics lay the blame mainly on political infighting and underestimated costs of preserving heritage buildings on the site.

▶ In the early 1980s, the London Stock Exchange formed a project team called Taurus to build an information technology system that would replace paper-based stock settlement. The original budget of £6 million blew out to more than £400 million before the project was abandoned in 1993.

▶ During a severe drought, the state government of Queensland, Australia, decided to build the world's third largest advanced wastewater recycling project. The three treatment plants cost AUD$2.5 billion and were supposed to produce drinkable water for less than AUD$1,000 per megaliter. The facilities were mothballed a few years after completion because the drinkable water actually cost more than $4,400 per megaliter (10 times the cost of dam water). The public also opposed the idea of drinking water that had been directly converted from sewage water.

▶ In the mid-1990s, executives at health boards across Ireland funded a common payroll system with an estimated cost of US$12 million. Project costs tripled within a few years, so a major consulting firm was hired to review and make recommendations. It advised the government to fork over another $120 million to complete the payroll system. The project was officially axed a decade later with losses somewhere between $250 and $350 million.

Evaluating Decision Outcomes More Effectively

▶ Those who evaluate the success of a decision should be different from those who made the decision.

▶ Publicly establish a preset level at which the decision is abandoned or reevaluated.

▶ Seek out sources of systematic and clear feedback for the decision's outcomes.

▶ Involve several people in the decision evaluation process.

self-justification effect because the person responsible for evaluating the decision is not connected to the original decision. However, the second person might continue to escalate the project if he or she empathizes with the decision maker, has a similar mindset, or has similar attributes such as age. A second strategy is to publicly establish a preset level at which the decision is abandoned or reevaluated. This is similar to a stop-loss order in the stock market, whereby the stock is sold if it falls below a certain price. The problem with this solution is that conditions are often so complex that it is difficult to identify an appropriate point to abandon a project.[57]

A third strategy is to find a source of systematic and clear feedback.[58] At some point, even the strongest escalation and confirmation bias effects deflate when the evidence highlights the project's failings. A fourth strategy to improve the decision evaluation process is to involve several people in the evaluation. Coworkers continuously monitor each other and might notice problems sooner than someone working alone on the project.

LO6-4 Describe employee characteristics, workplace conditions, and specific activities that support creativity.

CREATIVITY

The entire decision-making process described over the preceding pages depends on **creativity**—the development of original ideas that make a socially recognized contribution.[59] Creativity is at work when imagining opportunities, such as how a company's expertise might be redirected to untapped markets. Creativity is present when developing alternatives, such as figuring out new places to look for existing solutions or working out the design of a custom-made solution. Creativity also helps us choose alternatives because we need to visualize the future in different ways and to figure out how each choice might be useful or a liability in those scenarios. In short, creativity is an essential component of decision making as well as a powerful

resource for corporate competitive advantage and individual career development.

The Creative Process

How does creativity occur? That question has puzzled experts for hundreds of years and has been the fascination of Einstein, Poincaré, and many other scientists who have reflected on the creativity that contributed to their own important discoveries. More than a century ago, German physicist Hermann von Helmholtz gave a public talk in which he described the process that led to his innovations (energy physics, instruments for examining eyes, and many others). A few decades later, London School of Economics professor Graham Wallas built on Helmholtz's ideas to construct the four-stage model shown in Exhibit 6.4.[60] Nearly a century later, this model is still considered the most elegant representation of the creative process.

The first stage is *preparation*—the process of investigating the problem or opportunity in many ways. Preparation involves developing a clear understanding of what you are trying to achieve through a novel solution and then actively studying information seemingly related to the topic. It is a process of developing knowledge and possibly skills about the issue or object of attention. The second stage, called *incubation*, is the period of reflective thought. We put the problem aside, but our mind is still working on it in the background.[61] The important condition here is to maintain a low-level awareness by frequently revisiting the problem. Incubation does not mean that you forget about the problem or issue.

Incubation assists **divergent thinking**—reframing the problem in a unique way and generating different approaches to the issue. This contrasts with *convergent thinking*—calculating the conventionally accepted "right answer" to a logical problem. Divergent thinking breaks us away from existing mental models so that we can apply concepts or processes from completely different areas of life. The invention of Velcro is a case in point. In the 1940s, Swiss engineer Georges de Mestral had just returned home from a walk with his dog through the countryside when he noticed that his clothing and the dog's fur were covered in burrs. While struggling to remove the barbed seeds, de Mestral engaged in divergent thinking by recognizing that the adhesion used by burrs could be used to attach other things together. It took another dozen years of hard work, but de Mestral eventually perfected the hook-and-loop fastener, which he trademarked as Velcro.[62]

Illumination (also called *insight*), the third stage of creativity, refers to the experience of suddenly becoming aware of a unique idea.[63] Wallas and others suggest that this stage begins with a "fringe" awareness before the idea fully enters our consciousness. Illumination is often visually depicted as a lightbulb, but a better image would be a flash of light or perhaps a briefly flickering candle—these bits of inspiration are fleeting and can be quickly lost if not documented. For this reason, many creative people keep a journal or notebook nearby so that they can jot down their ideas before they disappear. Also, flickering ideas don't keep a particular schedule; they might come to you at any time of day or night.

> Divergent thinking breaks us away from existing mental models so that we can apply concepts or processes from completely different areas of life.

Illumination presents ideas that are usually vague, roughly drawn, and untested. *Verification* therefore provides the essential final stage of creativity, whereby we flesh out the illuminated ideas and subject them to detailed logical evaluation and experimentation. This stage often calls for further creativity as the ideas evolve into finished products or services.

Thus, although verification is labeled the final stage of creativity, it is really the beginning of a long process of creative decision making toward development of an innovative product or service.

creativity the development of original ideas that make a socially recognized contribution

divergent thinking reframing a problem in a unique way and generating different approaches to the issue

Characteristics of Creative People

Everyone is creative, but some people have a higher potential for creativity. Four of the main characteristics that give individuals more creative potential are intelligence, persistence, knowledge and experience, and a cluster of personality traits and values representing independent imagination (see Exhibit 6.5).

- *Cognitive and practical intelligence.* Creative people have above-average intelligence to synthesize information, analyze ideas, and apply their ideas.[64] They recognize the significance of small bits of information and are able to connect them in ways that few others can imagine. They also have *practical intelligence*—the capacity to evaluate the potential usefulness of their ideas.

Exhibit 6.4 The Creative Process Model

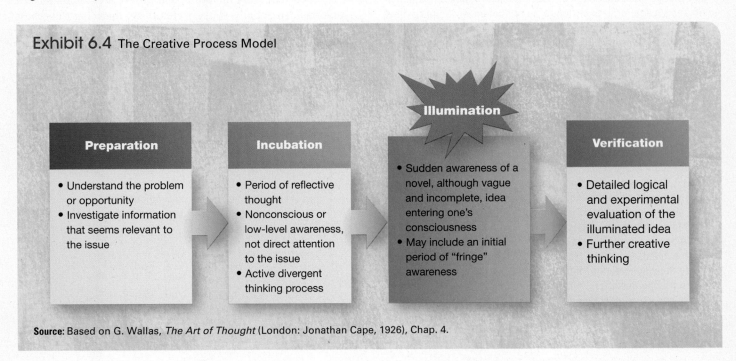

Preparation	Incubation	Illumination	Verification
• Understand the problem or opportunity • Investigate information that seems relevant to the issue	• Period of reflective thought • Nonconscious or low-level awareness, not direct attention to the issue • Active divergent thinking process	• Sudden awareness of a novel, although vague and incomplete, idea entering one's consciousness • May include an initial period of "fringe" awareness	• Detailed logical and experimental evaluation of the illuminated idea • Further creative thinking

Source: Based on G. Wallas, *The Art of Thought* (London: Jonathan Cape, 1926), Chap. 4.

Exhibit 6.5 Characteristics of Creative People

Independent Imagination
- High openness to experience
- Moderately low need for affiliation
- Strong self-direction value
- Strong stimulation value

Cognitive and Practical Intelligence
- Ability to synthesize, analyze, and apply ideas
- Ability to evaluate potential usefulness of ideas

Characteristics of Creative People

Knowledge and Experience
- Prerequisite knowledge and experience
- Not locked into a fixed knowledge mindset

Persistence
- High need for achievement
- Strong task motivation
- Moderately high self-esteem and optimism

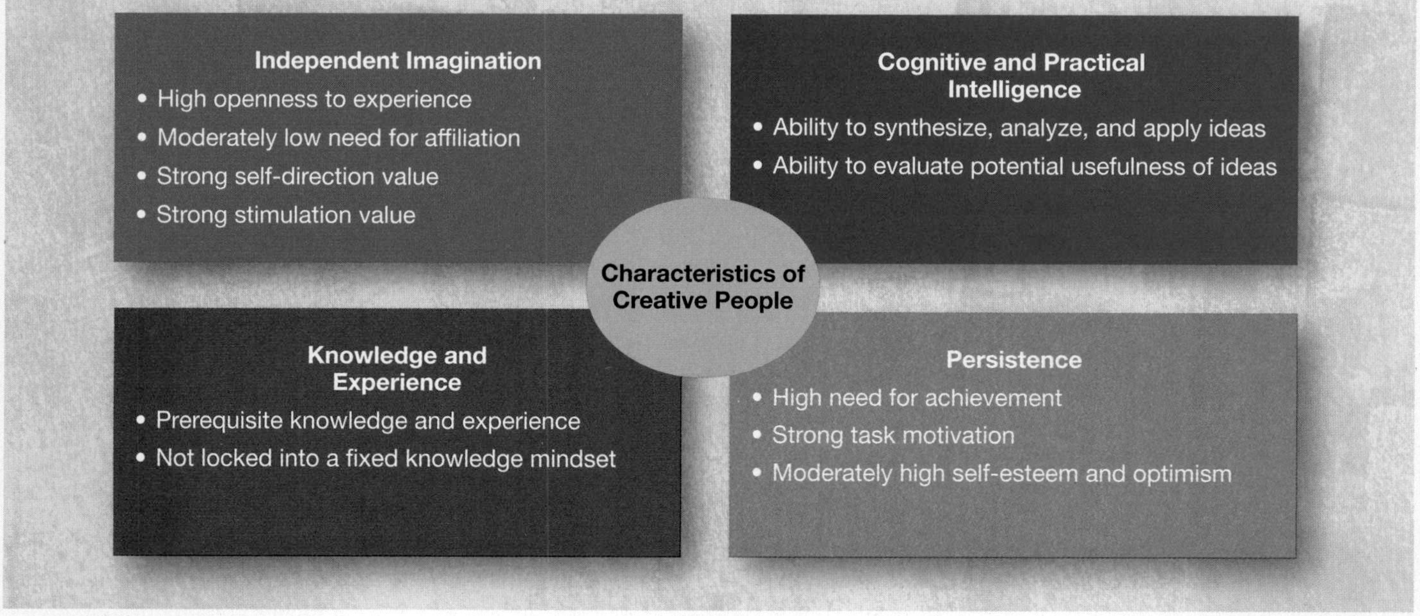

- *Persistence.* Creative people have persistence, which is based on a higher need for achievement, a strong motivation from the task itself, and a moderate or high degree of self-esteem. Persistence is vital because people need this motivation to continue working on and investing in a project in spite of failures and advice from others to quit. In fact, people have a general tendency to dismiss or criticize creative ideas, so creative people need persistence to withstand these negative social forces.[65]

- *Knowledge and Experience.* Creative people require a foundation of knowledge and experience to discover or acquire new knowledge.[66] However, this expertise is a double-edged sword. As people acquire knowledge and experience about a specific topic, their mental models tend to become more rigid. They are less adaptable to new information or rules about that knowledge domain. Some writers suggest that expertise also increases "mindless behavior" because expertise reduces the tendency to question why things happen.[67] To overcome the limitations of expertise, some corporate leaders like to hire people from other industries and areas of expertise.

- *Independent Imagination.* Creative people possess a cluster of personality traits and values that support an independent imagination: high openness to experience, moderately low need for affiliation, and strong values around self-direction and stimulation.[68] Openness to experience is a Big Five personality dimension representing the extent to which a person is imaginative, curious, sensitive, open-minded, and original (see Chapter 2). Creative people have a moderately low need for affiliation so they are less embarrassed when making mistakes. Self-direction includes the values of creativity and independent thought; stimulation includes the values of excitement and challenge. Together, these values form openness to change—representing the motivation to pursue innovative ways (see Chapter 2).

Organizational Conditions Supporting Creativity

Intelligence, persistence, expertise, and independent imagination represent a person's creative potential, but the extent to which these characteristics produce more creative output depends on how well the work environment supports the creative process.[69] Several job and workplace characteristics have been identified in the literature, and different combinations of situations can equally support creativity; there isn't one best work environment.[70]

One of the most important conditions that supports creative practice is that the organization has a *learning orientation*; that is,

OB THEORY TO PRACTICE

Features of Creative Workplaces

- Workplace has a learning-oriented culture (reasonable mistakes are viewed as learning experiences).
- Jobs have high task significance and autonomy.
- Jobs are aligned with employee competencies.
- Open communication exists across the organization.
- Employees have sufficient resources to perform their work.
- Employees experience a comfortable degree of job security.
- Workspace is nontraditional.
- Leaders and coworkers provide mutual support.

leaders recognize that employees make reasonable mistakes as part of the creative process. Motivation from the job itself is another important condition for creativity.[71] Employees tend to be more creative when they believe their work benefits the organization and/or larger society (i.e., task significance) and when they have the freedom to pursue novel ideas without bureaucratic delays (i.e., autonomy). Creativity is about changing things, and change is possible only when employees have the authority to experiment. More generally, jobs encourage creativity when they are challenging and aligned with the employee's competencies.

Along with supporting a learning orientation and intrinsically motivating jobs, companies foster creativity through open communication and sufficient resources. They also provide a comfortable degree of job security, which explains why creativity suffers during times of downsizing and corporate restructuring.[72] Some companies also support creativity by designing nontraditional workspaces, such as unique building design or unconventional office areas.[73] Google is one example. The Internet innovator has funky offices in several countries that include hammocks, gondola- and hive-shaped privacy spaces, slides, and brightly painted walls.

To some degree, creativity also improves with support from leaders and coworkers. One study reported that effective product champions provide enthusiastic support for new ideas. Other studies suggest that coworker support can improve creativity in some situations whereas competition among coworkers improves creativity in other situations.[74] Similarly, it isn't clear how much pressure should be exerted on employees to produce creative ideas. Extreme time pressures are well-known creativity inhibitors, but lack of pressure doesn't seem to produce the highest creativity either.

Activities That Encourage Creativity

Hiring people with strong creative potential and providing a work environment that supports creativity are two cornerstones of a creative workplace. The third cornerstone consists of various activities that help employees think more creatively. One set of activities involves redefining the problem. Employees might be encouraged to revisit old projects that have been set aside. After a few months of neglect, these projects might be seen in new ways.[76] Another strategy involves asking people unfamiliar with the issue (preferably with different expertise) to explore the problem with you. You would state the objectives and give some facts and then let the other person ask questions to further understand the situation. By verbalizing the problem, listening to questions, and hearing what others think, you are more likely to form new perspectives on the issue.[77]

A second set of creativity activities, known as *associative play,* attempts to bring out creativity by literally engaging in playful activities such as a team games or unusual events (such as grapefruit croquet).[78] Another associative play activity, called *morphological analysis,* involves listing different dimensions of a system and the elements of each dimension and then looking at each combination. This encourages people to carefully examine combinations that initially seem nonsensical.

A third set of activities that promote creative thinking falls under the category of *cross-pollination.*[79] Cross-pollination occurs when people from different areas of the organization exchange ideas or when new people are brought into an existing team. The 100 or so employees at Mother, the London-based creative agency, work around one monster-sized table—an 8-foot-wide reinforced-concrete slab that extends like a skateboard ramp around the entire floor. Every three weeks, employees are asked to relocate their laptop, portable telephone, and trolley to

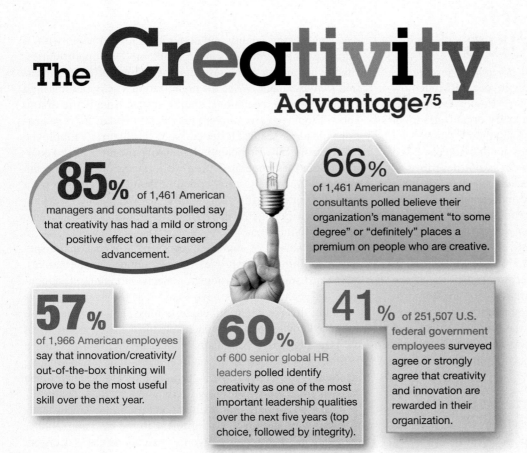

The **Creativity** Advantage[75]

85% of 1,461 American managers and consultants polled say that creativity has had a mild or strong positive effect on their career advancement.

66% of 1,461 American managers and consultants polled believe their organization's management "to some degree" or "definitely" places a premium on people who are creative.

57% of 1,966 American employees say that innovation/creativity/out-of-the-box thinking will prove to be the most useful skill over the next year.

60% of 600 senior global HR leaders polled identify creativity as one of the most important leadership qualities over the next five years (top choice, followed by integrity).

41% of 251,507 U.S. federal government employees surveyed agree or strongly agree that creativity and innovation are rewarded in their organization.

another area around the table. Why the musical-chairs exercise? "It encourages cross-pollination of ideas," explains Stef Calcraft, one of Mother's founding partners. "You have people working on the same problem from different perspectives. It makes problem-solving much more organic."[80]

Cross-pollination highlights the fact that creativity rarely occurs alone. Some creative people may be individualistic, but most creative ideas are generated through teams and informal social interaction. "This whole thing about the solitary tortured artist is nonsense I think," says John Collee, the screenwriter who penned such films as *Happy Feet* and *Master and Commander.* "All the great creative people I know have become great precisely because they know how to get along with people and swim around in the communal unconscious."[81] This notion of improving creativity through social interaction leads us to the final section of this chapter: employee involvement in decision making.

> **LO6-5** Describe the benefits of employee involvement and identify four contingencies that affect the optimal level of employee involvement.

EMPLOYEE INVOLVEMENT IN DECISION MAKING

Employee involvement (also called *participative management*) refers to the degree to which employees influence how their work is organized and carried out.[82] Employee involvement has become a natural process in every organization, but the level of involvement varies with the situation.[83] A low level of involvement occurs where employees are individually asked for specific information but the problem is not described to them. Somewhat higher involvement occurs where the problem is described and employees are asked individually or collectively for information relating to that problem.

Moving further up the involvement scale, the problem is described to employees, who are collectively given responsibility for developing recommendations. However, the decision maker is not bound to accept those recommendations. At the highest level of involvement, the entire decision-making process is handed over to employees. They identify the problem, discover alternative solutions, choose the best alternative, and implement that choice. The original decision maker serves only as a facilitator to guide the team's decision process and keep everyone on track.

Benefits of Employee Involvement

For the past half century, organizational behavior experts have advised that employee involvement potentially improves

Brasilata, the Ideas Company

Brasilata has become one of the most innovative and productive manufacturing businesses in Brazil by encouraging employee involvement. Each year, the steel can manufacturer receives more than 150,000 ideas—an average of more than 150 ideas per employee—on a wide range of themes, from how to improve production efficiency to new product designs. Ideas are so important that Brasilata employees are called "inventors," and everyone signs an "innovation contract" that reinforces their commitment to continuous improvement.[84]

decision-making quality and commitment.[85] To begin with, it improves the identification of problems and opportunities. Employees are, in many respects, the sensors of the organization's environment. When the organization's activities misalign with customer expectations, employees are usually the first to know. Employee involvement provides a conduit for organizational leaders to be alerted to such problems.[86] Employee involvement can also potentially improve the number and quality of solutions generated. In a well-managed meeting, team members create synergy by pooling their knowledge to form new alternatives. In other words, several people working together can potentially generate better solutions than the same people working alone.

A third benefit of employee involvement is that, under specific conditions, it improves the evaluation of alternatives. Numerous studies on participative decision making, task conflict, and team dynamics have found that involvement brings out more diverse perspectives, tests ideas, and provides more valuable knowledge, all of which help the decision maker select the best alternative.[87] A mathematical theorem introduced in 1785 by the Marquis de Condorcet states that the alternative selected by the team's majority is more likely to be correct than is the alternative selected by any team member individually.[88]

Along with improving decision quality, involvement tends to strengthen employee commitment to the decision. Rather than viewing themselves as agents of someone else's decision,

> ## "Tell me and I'll forget; show me and I may remember; involve me and I'll understand."
>
> **—Chinese proverb**

those who participate in a decision feel personally responsible for its success. Involvement also has positive effects on employee motivation, satisfaction, and turnover. It also increases skill variety, feelings of autonomy, and task identity, all of which increase job enrichment and potentially employee motivation. Participation is also a critical practice in organizational change because employees are more motivated to implement the decision and less likely to resist changes resulting from the decision.[89]

Contingencies of Employee Involvement

If employee involvement is so wonderful, why don't leaders leave all decisions to employees? The answer is that the optimal level of employee involvement depends on the situation. The employee involvement model shown in Exhibit 6.6 lists four contingencies: decision structure, source of decision knowledge, decision commitment, and risk of conflict in the decision process.[90]

- *Decision structure.* At the beginning of this chapter, we learned that some decisions are programmed, whereas others are nonprogrammed. Programmed decisions are less likely to need employee involvement because the solutions are already worked out from past incidents. In other words, the benefits of employee involvement increase with the novelty and complexity of the problem or opportunity.

- *Source of decision knowledge.* Subordinates should be involved in some level of decision making when the leader lacks sufficient knowledge and subordinates have additional information to improve decision quality. In many cases, employees are closer to customers and production activities, so they often know where the company can save money, improve product or service quality, and realize opportunities. This is particularly true for complex decisions where employees are more likely to possess relevant information.

- *Decision commitment.* Participation tends to improve employee commitment to the decision. If employees are

unlikely to accept a decision made without their involvement, some level of participation is usually necessary.

- *Risk of conflict.* Two types of conflict undermine the benefits of employee involvement. First, if employee goals and norms conflict with the organization's goals, only a low level of employee involvement is advisable. Second, the degree of involvement depends on whether employees will agree with each other on the preferred solution. If conflict is likely to occur, high involvement (i.e., employees make the decision) would be difficult to achieve.

Employee involvement is an important component of the decision-making process. To make the best decisions, we need to involve people who have the most valuable information and who will increase commitment to implement the decision. Employee involvement is a formative stage of team dynamics, so it carries many of the benefits and challenges of working in teams. The next chapter provides a closer look at team dynamics, including processes for making decisions in teams.

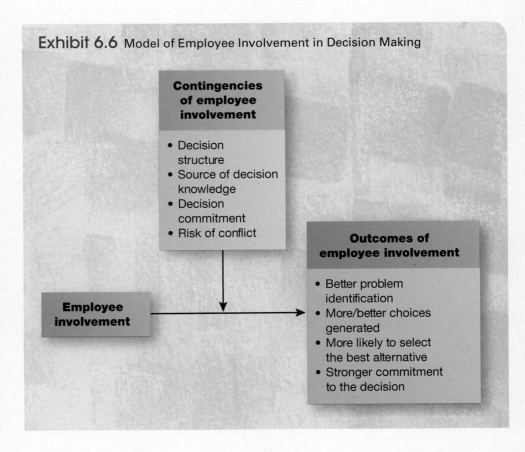

Exhibit 6.6 Model of Employee Involvement in Decision Making

Contingencies of employee involvement

- Decision structure
- Source of decision knowledge
- Decision commitment
- Risk of conflict

Employee involvement

Outcomes of employee involvement

- Better problem identification
- More/better choices generated
- More likely to select the best alternative
- Stronger commitment to the decision

Study Checklist

☑ Did you tear out the perforated student review card at the back of the text to revisit learning objectives and key terms and definitions?

Connect® Management is available for *M Organizational Behavior*. Additional resources include:

☑ Interactive Applications:
- **Drag and Drop:** Work through an interactive example to test your knowledge of the concepts.
- **Sequencing**
- **Video Case:** See management in action through interactive videos.

☑ **SmartBook™**—SmartBook is the first and only adaptive reading experience available today. Distinguishing what you know from what you don't, and honing in on concepts you are most likely to forget, SmartBook personalizes content for you in a continuously adapting reading experience. Reading is no longer a passive and linear experience, but an engaging and dynamic one where you are more likely to master and retain important concepts and go to class better prepared.

part three

7

chapter

Team Dynamics

Learning Objectives

After studying this chapter, you should be able to:

LO7-1 Explain why employees join informal groups, and discuss the benefits and limitations of teams.

LO7-2 Outline the team effectiveness model and discuss how task characteristics, team size, and team composition influence team effectiveness.

LO7-3 Discuss how the four team processes—team development, norms, cohesion, and trust—influence team effectiveness.

LO7-4 Discuss the characteristics and factors required for success of self-directed teams and virtual teams.

LO7-5 Identify four constraints on team decision making and discuss the advantages and disadvantages of four structures aimed at improving team decision making.

Teamwork is a source of competitive advantage at HFT Investment Management Co., Ltd. "HFT Investment sticks to the principle of 'value derived from teamwork' which is based on the complementary skills and cooperation of its staff," says the Shanghai, China, investment funds company, which makes all investment decisions in teams. Nextech Invest Ltd., a health care investment firm in Zurich, Switzerland, also believes in the value of teams. "Our judgment is founded on our team spirit and decisions are taken as a team."[1]

HFT, Nextech, and many other investment firms have organized employees into teams to make better investment decisions. This trend toward teamwork is, in fact, increasingly common across most industries. More than half of American organizations polled in one survey use teams to a high or very high extent to conduct day-to-day business. By comparison, only 50 percent of executives a decade ago said their work was done in teams. Two decades ago, only 20 percent of those executives said they worked in teams.[2] Teamwork has also become more important in scientific research. A study of almost 20 million research publications reported that the percentage of journal articles written by teams rather than individuals has increased substantially over the past five decades. Team-based articles also had a much higher number of subsequent citations, suggesting that journal articles written by teams are superior to articles written by individuals.[3]

Why are teams becoming so important, and how can organizations strengthen their potential for organizational effectiveness? We find the answers to these and other questions in this chapter on team dynamics. This chapter begins by defining *teams*, examining the reasons why organizations rely on teams, and explaining why people join informal groups in organizational settings. A large segment of this chapter examines a model of team effectiveness, which includes team and organizational environment, team design, and the team processes of development, norms, cohesion, and trust. We then turn our attention to two specific types of teams: self-directed teams and virtual teams. The final section of this chapter looks at the challenges and strategies for making better decisions in teams.

LO7-1 Explain why employees join informal groups, and discuss the benefits and limitations of teams.

TEAMS AND INFORMAL GROUPS

Teams are groups of two or more people who interact and influence each other, are mutually accountable for achieving common goals associated with organizational objectives, and perceive themselves as a social entity within an organization.[4] This definition has a few important components worth repeating. First, all teams exist to fulfill some purpose, such as repairing electric power lines, assembling a product, designing a new social welfare program, or making an important decision. Second, team members are held together by their interdependence and need for collaboration to achieve common goals. All teams require some form of communication so that members can coordinate and share common objectives. Third, team members influence each other, although some members may be more influential than others regarding the team's goals and activities. Finally, a team exists when its members perceive themselves to be a team.

There are many types of teams in organizations, and each type can be distinguished by three characteristics: team permanence, skill diversity, and authority dispersion (see Exhibit 7.1).[5] Team permanence refers to how long that type of team usually exists. Accounting, marketing, and other departments are usually long-lasting structures, so these teams have high permanence. In contrast, task forces usually have low permanence because most are formed temporarily to solve a problem, realize an opportunity, or design a product or service. An emerging trend is the formation of teams that exist even more briefly, sometimes only for one eight-hour shift.[6]

A second distinguishing characteristic is the team's skill diversity. A team has high skill diversity when its members possess unrelated skills and knowledge, whereas low diversity exists when team members have similar abilities and, therefore, are interchangeable. Most functional departments have low skill diversity because they organize employees around their common skill sets (e.g., people with accounting expertise are located in the accounting department). In contrast, self-directed teams, which we discuss later in this chapter, are responsible for producing an entire product or service, which often requires

teams groups of two or more people who interact and influence each other, are mutually accountable for achieving common goals associated with organizational objectives, and perceive themselves as a social entity within an organization

members with dissimilar skills and knowledge to perform the diverse tasks in that work. Cross-training increases interchangeability of team members to some extent, but moderately high skill diversity is still likely where the team's work is highly complex.

Authority dispersion, the third distinguishing characteristic of teams, refers to the degree that decision-making responsibility is distributed throughout the team (high dispersion) or is vested in one or a few members of the team (low dispersion). Departmental teams tend to have low authority dispersion because power is somewhat concentrated in a formal manager. Self-directed teams usually have high authority dispersion because the entire team makes key decisions and hierarchical authority is limited.

Informal Groups

This chapter mostly focuses on formal teams, but employees also belong to informal groups. All teams are groups; however, many groups do not satisfy our definition of teams. Groups include people assembled together, whether or not they have any interdependence or organizationally focused objective. The friends you meet for lunch are an *informal group,* but they wouldn't be called a team because they have little or no interdependence (each person could just as easily eat lunch alone) and no organizationally mandated purpose. Instead, they exist primarily for the benefit of their members. Although the terms are used interchangeably, *teams* has largely replaced *groups* in the language of business when referring to employees who work together to complete organizational tasks.[7]

Why do informal groups exist? One reason is that human beings are social animals. Our drive to bond is hardwired through evolutionary development, creating a need to belong to informal groups.[8] This is evident by the fact that people invest considerable time and effort forming and maintaining social relationships without any special circumstances or ulterior motives. A second reason why people join informal groups is provided by social identity theory, which states that individuals define themselves by their group affiliations (see Chapter 3). Thus, we join groups—particularly those that are viewed favorably by others and that have values similar to our own—because they shape and reinforce our self-concept.[9]

A third reason why informal groups exist is that they accomplish personal objectives that cannot be achieved by individuals working alone. For example, employees will sometimes congregate to oppose organizational changes because this collective effort has more power than individuals who try

Exhibit 7.1 Team Permanence, Skill Diversity, and Authority Dispersion for Selected Team Types

Team Type	Description	Typical Characteristics
Departmental teams	Teams that consist of employees who have similar or complementary skills and are located in the same unit of a functional structure; usually minimal task interdependence because each person works with clients or with employees in other departments.	*Team permanence*: High—departments continue indefinitely. *Skill diversity*: Low to medium—departments are often organized around common skills (e.g., accounting staff located in the accounting department). *Authority dispersion*: Low—departmental power is usually concentrated in the departmental manager.
Self-directed teams	Teams whose members are organized around work processes that complete an entire piece of work requiring several interdependent tasks and have substantial autonomy over the execution of those tasks (i.e., they usually control inputs, flow, and outputs with little or no supervision).	*Team permanence*: High—teams are usually assigned indefinitely to a specific cluster of production or service activities. *Skill diversity*: Medium to high—members typically perform different tasks requiring diverse skill sets, but cross-training can somewhat reduce skill diversity. *Authority dispersion*: High—team members share power, usually with limited hierarchical authority.
Task force (project) teams	Cross-functional teams whose members are usually drawn from several disciplines to solve a specific problem, realize an opportunity, or design a product or service.	*Team permanence*: Low— teams typically disband on completion of a specific project. *Skill diversity*: Medium to high—members are typically drawn from several functional specializations associated with the complexity of the problem or opportunity. *Authority dispersion*: Medium—teams often have someone with formal authority (project leader), but members also have moderate power due to their expertise and functional representation.

this shift to teamwork is that making investment decisions has become much more complex. Complex work requires skills and knowledge beyond one person's abilities. Teams are particularly well suited for complex work that can be divided into more specialized roles, and where the people in those specialized roles are able to coordinate frequently with each other.

Task complexity demands teamwork, but teams work better when the work is well structured rather than ambiguous. Assembling automobiles consists of well-structured tasks. Assembly team members perform the same set of tasks each day—they have low *task variability* (see Chapter 5)—and the work is mostly predictable so they are also guided by well-established procedures (low *task analyzability*). In contrast, a team performing a new medical procedure would have novel and less-structured work activities.

The main benefit of well-structured tasks is that it is easier to coordinate the work among several people. Teams require much more intense and ongoing coordination when the work is ambiguous and novel, which leads to process losses and errors. Fortunately, teams can perform ambiguous tasks reasonably well when their roles are well structured. The medical team members have enough role clarity and associated expertise to generally know what to expect of each other—the surgeon, scrub technicians, operating room nurses, anesthesiologist, and others—and how to coordinate most work challenges even in these unique situations.[29]

A third task-related influence on team effectiveness is **task interdependence**—the extent to which team members must share materials, information, or expertise to perform their jobs.[30] Apart from complete independence, there are three levels of task interdependence, as illustrated in Exhibit 7.3. The

lowest level of interdependence, called *pooled interdependence*, occurs when an employee or work unit shares a common resource, such as

task interdependence
the extent to which team members must share materials, information, or expertise in order to perform their jobs

machinery, administrative support, or a budget, with other employees or work units. This would occur in a team setting where each member works alone but shares raw materials or machinery to perform her or his otherwise independent tasks. Interdependence is higher under *sequential interdependence*, in which the output of one person becomes the direct input for another person or unit. Sequential interdependence occurs where team members are organized in an assembly line.

Reciprocal interdependence, in which work output is exchanged back and forth among individuals, produces the highest degree of interdependence. People who design a new product or service would typically have reciprocal interdependence because their design decisions affect others involved in the design process. Any decision made by the design engineers would influence the work of the manufacturing engineer and purchasing specialist, and vice versa. Employees with reciprocal interdependence should be organized into teams to facilitate coordination in their interwoven relationship.

As a rule, the higher the level of task interdependence, the greater the need to organize people into teams rather than have them work alone. A team structure improves interpersonal communication and thus results in better coordination. High task interdependence also motivates most people to be part of the team. However, the rule that a team should be formed when employees have high interdependence applies when team members have the same task goals, such as serving the same clients or collectively assembling the same product. When team members have different goals (such as serving different clients) but must depend on other team members to achieve those unique goals, teamwork might create excessive conflict. Under these circumstances, the company should try to reduce the level of interdependence or rely on supervision as a buffer or mediator among employees.

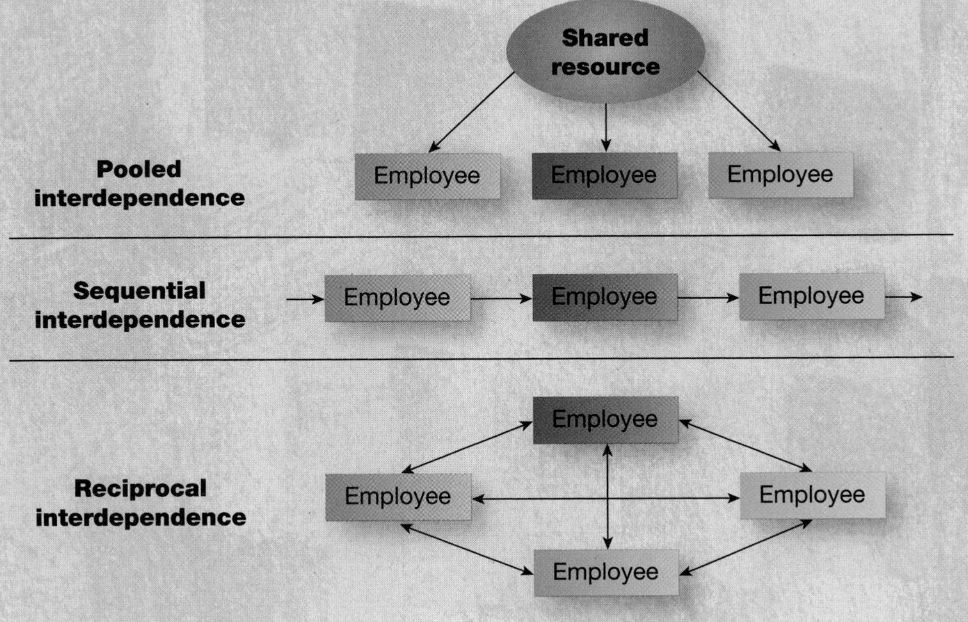

Team Size

What is the ideal size for a team? Online retailer Amazon relies on the "two-pizza team" rule, namely that a team should be small enough to be fed comfortably with two large pizzas. This works out to between five and

Exhibit 7.3 Levels of Task Interdependence

Shared resource

Pooled interdependence — Employee / Employee / Employee

Sequential interdependence — Employee → Employee → Employee

Reciprocal interdependence — Employee / Employee / Employee / Employee

seven employees. At the other extreme, a few experts suggest that tasks are becoming so complex that many teams need to have more than 100 members.[31] Unfortunately, the former piece of advice (two-pizza teams) is too simplistic, and the latter seems to have lost sight of the meaning and dynamics of real teams.

Generally, teams should be large enough to provide the necessary abilities and perspectives to perform the work, yet small enough to maintain efficient coordination and meaningful involvement of each member.[33] Small teams (say, less than a dozen members) operate effectively because they have less process loss. Members of smaller teams also tend to feel more engaged because they have more influence on the group's norms and goals and feel more responsible for the team's successes and failures. Also, members of smaller teams get to know each other better, which improves mutual trust as well as perceived support, help, and assistance from those team members.[34]

Should companies have 100-person teams if the task is highly complex? The answer is that a group this large probably isn't a team, even if management calls it one. A team exists when its members interact and influence each other, are mutually accountable for achieving common goals associated with organizational objectives, and perceive themselves as a social entity within an organization. It is very difficult for everyone in a 100-person work unit to influence each other and perceive themselves as members of the same team. However, such complex tasks can usually be divided into several smaller teams of people.

Team Composition

Teams require members with the necessary technical abilities. But their effectiveness also depends on the ability and motivation of each member to work in a team environment. Some companies go to great lengths to hire people who demonstrate effective team behaviors. The most frequently mentioned behaviors of effective team members are depicted in the "Five Cs" model illustrated in Exhibit 7.4: cooperating, coordinating, communicating, comforting, and conflict handling. The first three sets of behaviors are mainly (but

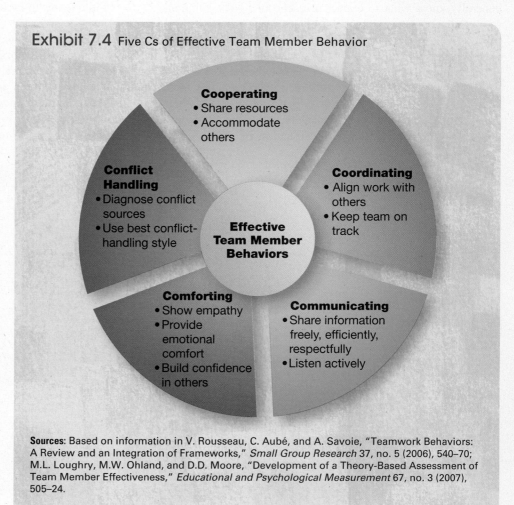

Exhibit 7.4 Five Cs of Effective Team Member Behavior

Cooperating
• Share resources
• Accommodate others

Coordinating
• Align work with others
• Keep team on track

Communicating
• Share information freely, efficiently, respectfully
• Listen actively

Comforting
• Show empathy
• Provide emotional comfort
• Build confidence in others

Conflict Handling
• Diagnose conflict sources
• Use best conflict-handling style

Effective Team Member Behaviors

Sources: Based on information in V. Rousseau, C. Aubé, and A. Savoie, "Teamwork Behaviors: A Review and an Integration of Frameworks," *Small Group Research* 37, no. 5 (2006), 540–70; M.L. Loughry, M.W. Ohland, and D.D. Moore, "Development of a Theory-Based Assessment of Team Member Effectiveness," *Educational and Psychological Measurement* 67, no. 3 (2007), 505–24.

not entirely) task-related, while the last two primarily assist team maintenance:[35]

Cooperating. Effective team members are willing and able to work together rather than alone. This includes sharing resources and being sufficiently adaptive or flexible to accommodate the needs and preferences of other team members, such as rescheduling use of machinery so that another team member with a tighter deadline can use it.

Coordinating. Effective team members actively manage the team's work so that it is performed efficiently and harmoniously. For example, effective team members keep the team on track and help integrate the work performed by different members. This typically requires that effective team members know the work of other team members, not just their own.

Communicating. Effective team members transmit information freely (rather than hoarding), efficiently (using the best channel and language), and respectfully (minimizing arousal of negative emotions).[36] They also listen actively to coworkers.

Comforting. Effective team members help coworkers maintain a positive and healthy psychological state. They show empathy, provide emotional comfort, and build coworker feelings of confidence and self-worth.

Conflict handling. Conflict is inevitable in social settings, so effective team members have the skills and motivation to resolve disagreements among team members. This requires effective use of various conflict-handling styles as well as diagnostic skills to identify and resolve the structural sources of conflict.

Which employees tend to demonstrate effective team behaviors? Top of the list are those with high conscientiousness and extraversion personality traits, as well as high emotional intelligence. Furthermore, the old saying "One bad apple spoils the barrel" seems to apply to teams; one team member who doesn't use effective team behaviors may undermine the dynamics of the entire team.[37]

Team Diversity Diversity, another important dimension of team composition, has both positive and negative effects on teams.[39] The main advantage of diverse teams is that they make better decisions than do homogeneous teams in some situations. One reason is that people from different backgrounds tend to see a problem or opportunity from different angles. Team members have different mental models, so they are more likely to identify viable solutions to difficult problems. A second reason is that diverse team members have a broader pool of technical abilities. Investment firms such as HFT Investment in Shanghai and Nextech Invest in Zurich rely on teams to make key decisions. These teams consist of people with expertise in diverse areas, such as stocks, bonds, derivatives, cash management, and other asset classes. Some teams also have diverse investment philosophies (fundamentals, technical, momentum, etc.) and expertise across regions of the world.

Another advantage of diverse teams is that they often provide better representation of the team's constituents, such as other departments or clients from similarly diverse backgrounds. This representation brings different viewpoints to the decision; it also gives stakeholders a belief that they have a voice in that decision process. As we learned in Chapter 5, voice is an important ingredient in procedural justice, so stakeholders are more likely to believe the team's decision is fair when the team mirrors the surface or deep-level diversity of its constituents.

Against these advantages are a number of challenges created by team diversity. Employees with diverse backgrounds take longer to become a high-performing team. This occurs partly because bonding is slower among people who are different from each other, especially when teams have deep-level diversity (i.e., different beliefs and values). Diverse teams are susceptible to "faultlines"—hypothetical dividing lines that may split a team into subgroups along gender, ethnic, professional, or other dimensions.[40] These faultlines undermine team effectiveness by reducing the motivation to communicate

Importance of Effective Team
Behaviors in Job Applicants,
Coworkers, and the Boss[38]

44% of more than 40,000 employees surveyed in 300 global companies identify teamwork as the most important attribute when rating their coworkers.

60% of 2,138 American hiring managers and human resource professionals surveyed say that being team-oriented is an important characteristic they look for in job applicants.

15% of 97,000 employees surveyed across 30 countries identify teamwork as the most important characteristic of a good boss.

and coordinate with teammates on the other side of the hypothetical divisions. In contrast, members of teams with minimal diversity experience higher satisfaction, less conflict, and better interpersonal relations. Consequently, homogeneous teams tend to be more effective on tasks requiring a high degree of cooperation and coordination, such as emergency response teams.

> **LO7-3** Discuss how the four team processes—team development, norms, cohesion, and trust—influence team effectiveness.

TEAM PROCESSES

The third set of elements in the team effectiveness model, collectively known as *team processes,* includes team development, norms, cohesion, and trust. These elements represent characteristics of the team that continuously evolve.

Team Development

Team members must resolve several issues and pass through several stages of development before emerging as an effective work unit. They need to get to know and trust each other, understand and agree on their respective roles, discover appropriate and inappropriate behaviors, and learn how to coordinate with each other. The longer team members work together, the better they develop common or complementary mental models, mutual understanding, and effective performance routines to complete the work.

A popular model that captures many team development activities is shown in Exhibit 7.5.[41] The diagram shows teams moving systematically from one stage to the next, while the dashed lines illustrate that teams might fall back to an earlier stage of development as new members join or other conditions disrupt the team's maturity. *Forming,* the first stage of team development, is a period of testing and orientation in which members learn about each other and evaluate the benefits and costs of continued membership. People tend to be polite, will defer to authority, and try to find out what is expected of them and how they will fit into the team. The *storming* stage is marked by interpersonal conflict as members become more proactive and compete for various team roles. Members try to establish norms of appropriate behavior and performance standards.

During the *norming* stage, the team develops its first real sense of cohesion as roles are established and a consensus forms around group objectives and a common or complementary team-based mental model. By the *performing* stage, team members have learned to efficiently coordinate and resolve conflicts. In high-performance teams, members are highly cooperative, have a high level of trust in each other, are committed to group objectives, and identify with the team. Finally, the *adjourning* stage occurs when the team is about to disband. Team members shift their attention away from task orientation to a relationship focus.

Developing Team Identities and Mental Models
Although this model depicts team development fairly well, it is not a perfect representation of the process. For instance, it does

not show that some teams remain in a particular stage longer than others and does not explain why teams sometimes regress back to earlier stages of development. The model also masks two sets of processes that are the essence of team development: developing team identity and developing team mental models and coordinating routines.[42]

Developing team identity. Team development is apparent when its members shift from viewing the team as something "out there" to something that is part of themselves. In other words, team development occurs when employees take ownership of the team's success and make the team part of their social identity.[43]

Developing team mental models and coordinating routines. Team development includes developing habitual routines with teammates and forming shared or complementary mental models.[44] Team mental models are visual or relational mental images that are shared by team members, such as what good customer service looks like. A recent meta-analysis supports the view that teams are more effective when their members share common mental models of the work.[45]

> Team development is apparent when its members shift from viewing the team as something "out there" to something that is part of themselves.

Team Roles An important part of the team development process is forming and reinforcing team roles. A **role** is a set of behaviors that people are expected to perform because they hold certain positions in a team and organization.[46] In a team setting, some roles help the team achieve its goals; other roles maintain relationships within the team. Some team roles are formally assigned to specific people. For example, team leaders are usually expected to initiate discussion, ensure that everyone has an opportunity to present his or her views, and help the team reach agreement on the issues discussed.

Team members are assigned specific roles within their formal job responsibilities. Yet, team members also assume informal roles that suit their personality and values as well as the wishes of other team members. These informal roles, which are negotiated throughout the team development process, range from supporting others

role a set of behaviors that people are expected to perform because they hold certain positions in a team and organization

Exhibit 7.5 Stages of Team Development

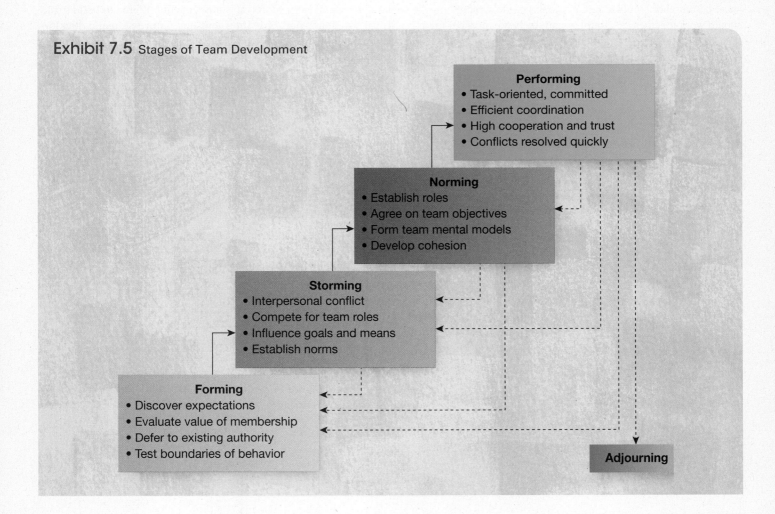

Performing
- Task-oriented, committed
- Efficient coordination
- High cooperation and trust
- Conflicts resolved quickly

Norming
- Establish roles
- Agree on team objectives
- Form team mental models
- Develop cohesion

Storming
- Interpersonal conflict
- Compete for team roles
- Influence goals and means
- Establish norms

Forming
- Discover expectations
- Evaluate value of membership
- Defer to existing authority
- Test boundaries of behavior

Adjourning

to initiating new ideas. Informal team roles are shared, but many are eventually associated with one or two people on the team.[47]

Accelerating Team Development through Team Building Team building consists of formal activities intended to improve the development and functioning of a work team.[49] To a large extent, team building attempts to speed up the team development process. This process may be applied to new teams, but it is more commonly introduced for existing teams that have regressed to earlier stages of team development due to membership turnover or loss of focus.

Some team-building interventions are task-focused. They clarify the team's performance goals, increase the team's motivation to accomplish these goals, and establish a mechanism for systematic feedback on the team's goal performance. A second type of team building tries to improve the team's problem-solving skills. A third category clarifies and reconstructs each member's perceptions of her or his role as well as the role expectations that member has of other team members. Role-definition team building also helps the team develop shared mental models—common internal representations of the external world, such as how to interact with clients, maintain machinery, and engage in meetings. Research studies indicate that team processes and performance depend on how well team members share common or complementary mental models about how they should work together.[50] A fourth—and likely the most common—type of team building is aimed at helping team members learn more about each other, build trust in each other, and develop

ways to manage conflict within the team. Popular interventions such as wilderness team activities, scavenger hunt challenges, and special team sports days are typically offered to build trust.

Do team-building interventions improve team development and effectiveness? The most effective team-building interventions seem to be those in which employees receive training on specific team skills, such as coordinating, conflict resolving, and communicating.[51] However, many team-building

OB THEORY TO PRACTICE

Popular Team-Building Activities[48]

Team-Building Activity	Description	Example
Team volunteering events	Teams of employees who spend a day providing a public service to the community.	Nicor Gas employees in Illinois volunteer their time in teams to help the community, such as building a house for Habitat for Humanity.
Team scavenger/ treasure hunt competitions	Teams that follow instructions to find clues or objects collected throughout the community.	Goldman Sachs employees work in teams ($50,000 minimum fund-raising for each team to join) to solve 24 puzzles around Manhattan over 16 hours.
Team sports/exercise competitions	A wide variety of sports or health activities, such as sports tournaments across departments.	E-commerce software developer Shopify holds an annual beach Volleyball Day, in which employee teams wear themed clothing (e.g., lumberjacks) and later enjoy a huge banquet picnic.
Team music ensemble events	A large team of employees who learn how to play drums or other musical instruments.	Employees at several GlaxoSmithKline offices in Europe and Asia have participated in drum circle team-building events.

activities are less successful.[52] One problem is that team-building interventions are used as general solutions to general team problems. A better approach is to begin with a sound diagnosis of the team's health and then select team-building interventions that address specific weaknesses.[53] Another problem is that team building is applied as a one-shot medical inoculation that every team should receive when it is formed. In truth, team building is an ongoing process, not a three-day jump start.[54] Finally, we must remember that team building occurs on the job, not just on an obstacle course or in a national park. Organizations should encourage team members to reflect on their work experiences and to experiment with just-in-time learning for team development.

Team Norms

Norms are the informal rules and shared expectations that groups establish to regulate the behavior of their members. Norms apply only to behavior, not to private thoughts or feelings. Furthermore, norms exist only for behaviors that are important to the team.[55] Norms are enforced in various ways. Coworkers grimace if we are late for a meeting, or they make sarcastic comments if we don't have our part of the project completed on time. Norms are also directly reinforced through praise from high-status members, more access to valued resources, or other rewards available to the team. But team members often conform to prevailing norms without direct reinforcement or punishment because they identify with the group and want to align their behavior with the team's expectations. The more closely the person's social identity is connected to the group, the more the individual is motivated to avoid negative sanctions from that group.[56]

How Team Norms Develop Norms develop when teams form because people need to anticipate or predict how others will act. Even subtle events during the team's formation, such as how team members initially greet each other and where they sit in the first meetings, can initiate norms that are later difficult to change. Norms also form as team members discover behaviors that help them function more effectively (such as the need to respond quickly to email).[57] In particular, a critical event in the team's history can trigger formation of a norm or sharpen a previously vague one. A third influence on team norms are the experiences and values that members bring to the team. If members of a new team value work–life balance, they will likely develop norms that discourage long hours and work overload.[58]

Preventing and Changing Dysfunctional Team Norms Team norms often become deeply anchored, so the best way to avoid norms that undermine organizational success or employee well-being is to establish desirable norms when the team is first formed. One way to do this is to clearly state desirable norms when the team is created. Another approach is to select people with appropriate values. If organizational leaders want their teams to have strong safety norms, they should hire people who already value safety and who clearly identify the importance of safety when the team is formed.

The suggestions so far refer to new teams, but how can organizational leaders maintain desirable norms in older teams? According to research, one solution is that leaders sometimes have the capacity to alter existing norms.[59] By speaking up or actively coaching the team, they may be able to subdue dysfunctional norms while developing useful norms. A second suggestion is to introduce team-based rewards that counter dysfunctional norms. However, studies report that employees might continue to adhere to a dysfunctional team norm (such as limiting output) even though this behavior reduces their paycheck. Finally, if dysfunctional norms are deeply ingrained and the previous solutions don't work, it may be necessary to disband the group and replace it with people having more favorable norms.

Team Cohesion

Team cohesion refers to the degree of attraction people feel toward the team and their motivation to remain members. It is a characteristic of the team, including the extent to which its members are attracted to the team, are committed to the team's goals or tasks, and feel a collective sense of team pride.[60] Thus, team cohesion is an emotional experience, not just a calculation of whether to stay or leave the team. It exists when team members make the team part of their social identity. Team development tends to improve cohesion because members strengthen their identity to the team during the development process.

Influences on Team Cohesion Several factors influence team cohesion, but six of the most important ones include member similarity, team size, member interaction, difficult entry, team success, and external competition or challenges. For the most part, these factors reflect the individual's social identity with the group and beliefs about how team membership will fulfill personal needs.

Member similarity. Social scientists have long known that people are attracted to others who are similar to them.[61] This similarity-attraction effect occurs because we assume that people who look like us and have similar backgrounds are more trustworthy and are more likely to accept us. We also expect to have fewer negative experiences, such as conflicts and violations of our expectations and beliefs. Thus, teams have higher cohesion or become cohesive more quickly when members are similar to each other. In contrast, it is more difficult and takes longer for teams with diverse members to become cohesive. This difficulty depends on the form of diversity, however. Teams consisting of people from different job groups seem to gel together just as well as teams of people from the same job.[62]

Team size. Smaller teams tend to have more cohesion than larger teams because it is easier for a few people to agree on goals and coordinate work activities. However, small teams have less cohesion when they lack enough members to perform the required tasks.

Member interaction. Teams tend to have more cohesion when team members interact with each other fairly regularly. This occurs when team members perform highly interdependent tasks and work in the same physical area.

Somewhat difficult entry. Teams tend to have more cohesion when entry to the team is restricted. The more elite the team, the more prestige it confers on its members, and the more they tend to value their membership in the unit. At the same time, research suggests that severe initiations can weaken team cohesion because of the adverse effects of humiliation, even for those who successfully endure the initiation.[63]

Team success. Team cohesion increases with the team's level of success because people are attracted to groups that fulfill their needs and goals.[64] Furthermore, individuals are more likely to attach their social identity to successful teams than to those with a string of failures.[65]

External competition and challenges. Team cohesion tends to increase when members face external competition or a valued objective that is challenging. This might include a threat from an external competitor or friendly competition from other teams. Employees value their membership on the team because of its ability to overcome the threat or competition and as a form of social support.

However, cohesion can dissipate when external threats are severe because these threats are stressful and cause teams to make less effective decisions.[66]

Consequences of Team Cohesion Teams with higher cohesion tend to perform better than those with low cohesion.[67] In fact, the team's existence depends on a minimal level of cohesion because it motivates team members to remain members and to help the team achieve its mutually agreed-on objectives. Members of high-cohesion teams spend more time together, share information more frequently, and are more satisfied with each other. They provide each other with better social support in stressful situations and work to minimize dysfunctional conflict.[68] When conflict does arise, high-cohesion team members tend to resolve their differences swiftly and effectively.

However, the relationship between team cohesion and team performance depends on two conditions. First, team cohesion has less effect on team performance when the team has low task interdependence.[69] High cohesion motivates employees to coordinate and cooperate with other team members. But people don't need to cooperate or coordinate as much when their work doesn't depend on other team members (low task interdependence), so the motivational effect of high cohesion is less relevant in teams with low interdependence.

Second, the effect of cohesion on team performance depends on whether the team's norms are compatible with or opposed to the organizational objectives.[70] As Exhibit 7.6 illustrates, teams with high cohesion perform better when their norms are aligned with the organization's objectives, whereas higher cohesion can potentially reduce team performance when norms are

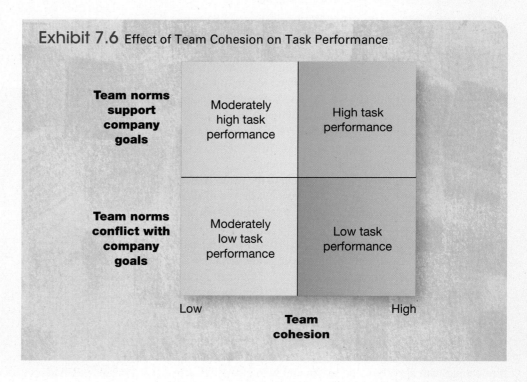

Exhibit 7.6 Effect of Team Cohesion on Task Performance

Team norms support company goals	Moderately high task performance	High task performance
Team norms conflict with company goals	Moderately low task performance	Low task performance
	Low High	
	Team cohesion	

counterproductive. This effect occurs because cohesion motivates employees to perform at a level more consistent with team norms. If a team's norm tolerates or encourages absenteeism, employees will be more motivated to take unjustified sick leave. If the team's norm discourages absenteeism, employees are more motivated to avoid taking sick leave.

One last comment about team cohesion and performance: Earlier in this section we said that team performance (success) increases cohesion, whereas we are now saying that team cohesion causes team performance. Both statements are correct, but there is some evidence that team performance has a stronger effect on cohesion than vice versa. In other words, a team's performance will likely affect its cohesion, whereas a team's cohesion has less of an effect on its performance.[71]

Team Trust

Any relationship—including the relationship among team members—depends on a certain degree of trust. *Trust* refers to positive expectations one person has toward another person in situations involving risk (see Chapter 4).[72] Trust is ultimately perceptual; we trust others on the basis of our beliefs about their ability, integrity, and benevolence. Trust is also an emotional event; we experience positive feelings toward those we trust.[73] Trust is built on three foundations: calculus, knowledge, and identification (see Exhibit 7.7).[74]

Calculus-based trust represents a logical calculation that other team members will act appropriately because they face sanctions if their actions violate reasonable expectations.[75] It offers the lowest potential trust and is easily broken by a violation of expectations. Some scholars suggest that calculus-based trust is not trust at all. Instead, it might be trust in the system rather than in the other person. In any event, calculus-based

trust alone cannot sustain a team's relationship, because it relies on deterrence. *Knowledge-based trust* is based on the predictability of another team member's behavior. This predictability refers only to "positive expectations" as the definition of trust states, because you would not trust someone who tends to engage in harmful or dysfunctional behavior. Knowledge-based trust includes our confidence in the other person's abilities, such as the confidence that exists when we trust a physician.[76] Knowledge-based trust offers a higher potential level of trust and is more stable because it develops over time.

Identification-based trust is based on mutual understanding and an emotional bond among team members. It occurs when team members think, feel, and act like each other. High-performance teams exhibit this level of trust because they share the same values and mental models. Identification-based trust is potentially the strongest and most robust of all three types of trust. The individual's self-concept is based partly on membership in the team, and he or she believes the members' values highly overlap, so any transgressions by other team members are quickly forgiven. People are more reluctant to acknowledge a violation of this high-level trust because it strikes at the heart of their self-concept.

Dynamics of Team Trust Employees typically join a team with a moderate or high level—not a low level—of trust in their new coworkers.[77] The main explanation for the initially high trust (called *swift trust*) in organizational settings is that people usually believe fellow team members are reasonably competent (knowledge-based trust) and they tend to develop some degree of social identity with the team (identification-based trust). Even when working with strangers, most of us display some level of trust, if only because it supports our self-concept of being a good person. However, trust is fragile in new relationships because it is based on assumptions rather than well-established experience. Consequently, studies report that trust tends to decrease rather than increase over time. This is unfortunate because employees become less forgiving and less cooperative toward others as their level of trust decreases, and this undermines team and organizational effectiveness.[78]

The team effectiveness model is a useful template for understanding how teams work—and don't work—in organizations. With this knowledge in hand, let's briefly investigate two types of teams that have emerged over the past couple of decades to become important forms of teamwork in organizations: self-directed teams and virtual teams.[79]

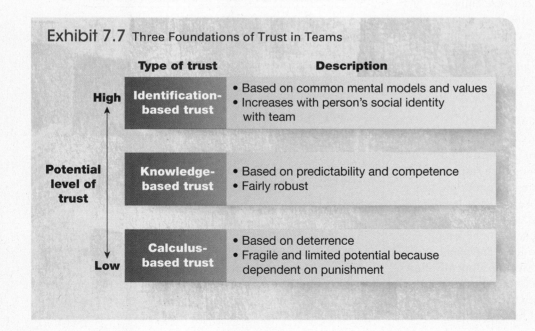

Exhibit 7.7 Three Foundations of Trust in Teams

	Type of trust	Description
High	Identification-based trust	• Based on common mental models and values • Increases with person's social identity with team
Potential level of trust	Knowledge-based trust	• Based on predictability and competence • Fairly robust
Low	Calculus-based trust	• Based on deterrence • Fragile and limited potential because dependent on punishment

SELF-DIRECTED TEAMS

Self-directed teams (SDTs) are cross-functional groups that are organized around work processes, that complete an entire piece of work requiring several interdependent tasks, and that have substantial autonomy over the execution of those tasks.[80] This definition captures two distinct features of SDTs. First, these teams complete an entire piece of work requiring several interdependent tasks. This type of work arrangement clusters the team members together while minimizing interdependence and interaction with employees outside the team. The result is a close-knit group of employees who depend on each other to accomplish their individual tasks. The second distinctive feature of SDTs is that they have substantial autonomy over the execution of their tasks. In particular, these teams plan, organize, and control work activities with little or no direct involvement of a higher-status supervisor.

Self-directed teams are found in several industries, ranging from petrochemical plants to aircraft parts manufacturing. Most of the top-rated manufacturing firms in North America apparently rely on SDTs.[81] Indeed, self-directed teams have become such a popular way to organize employees in manufacturing, services, and government work that many companies don't realize they have them. The popularity of SDTs is consistent with research indicating that they potentially increase both productivity and job satisfaction.[82] For instance, one study found that car dealership service shops that organize employees into SDTs are significantly more profitable than shops where employees work without a team structure. Another study reported that both short- and long-term measures of customer satisfaction increased after street cleaners in a German city were organized into SDTs.

Success Factors for Self-Directed Teams

The successful implementation of self-directed teams depends on several factors.[84] SDTs should be responsible for an entire work process, such as making an entire product or providing a service. This structure keeps each team sufficiently independent from other teams, yet it demands a relatively high degree of interdependence among employees within the team.[85] SDTs should also have sufficient autonomy to organize and coordinate their work. Autonomy allows them to respond more quickly and effectively to client and stakeholder demands. It also motivates team members through feelings of empowerment. Finally, SDTs are more

Self-Directed Teams at Whole Foods

Whole Foods Market operates with self-directed teams. Each store has about 10 teams, such as the prepared-foods team, the cashier/front-end team, and the seafood team. Teams are "self-directed" because team members make decisions about their work unit with minimal interference from management. "Teams make their own decisions regarding hiring, the selection of many products, merchandising, and even compensation," explains Whole Foods Market cofounder John Mackey. Employee incentives are also mostly based on team performance. The company also encourages friendly competition where, for example, the produce team in one store compares its productivity and sales against produce teams at other Whole Foods stores within the region.[83]

successful when the work site and technology support coordination and communication among team members and increase job enrichment.[86] Too often, management calls a group of employees a "team," yet the work layout, assembly-line structure, and other technologies isolate the employees from each other.

VIRTUAL TEAMS

Virtual teams are teams whose members operate across space, time, and organizational boundaries and are linked through information technologies to achieve organizational tasks.[87] Virtual teams differ from traditional teams in two ways: (1) Their members are not usually co-located (do not work in the same physical area), and (2) due to their lack of co-location, members of virtual teams depend primarily on information technologies rather than face-to-face interaction to communicate and coordinate their work effort. Teams have degrees of *virtuality*. Team virtuality increases with the geographic dispersion of team members, percentage of members who work apart, and percentage of time that members work apart. For example, a team has low virtuality when all of its members live in the same city and only one or two members work from home each day. High virtuality exists when team members are spread around the world and only a couple of members have ever met in person.

Virtual teams have become commonplace in most organizations. Two-thirds of human resource managers estimate that reliance on virtual teams will grow rapidly over the next few years.[88] In global companies such as IBM, almost everyone in knowledge work is part of a virtual team. One reason virtual teams have become so widespread is that information technologies have made it easier than ever before to communicate and coordinate with people at a distance.[89] The shift from production-based to knowledge-based work is a second reason why virtual teamwork is feasible. It isn't yet possible to make a physical product when team members are located apart, but most of us are now in jobs that mainly process knowledge.

Information technologies and knowledge-based work make virtual teams *possible*, but organizational learning and globalization are two reasons why they are increasingly *necessary*. In Chapter 1, we learned that organizational learning is one of four perspectives of organizational effectiveness. Virtual teams represent a natural part of the organizational learning process because they encourage employees to share and use knowledge where geography limits more direct forms of collaboration. Globalization makes virtual teams increasingly necessary because employees are spread around the planet rather than around one building or city. Thus, global

> **self-directed teams (SDTs)** cross-functional work groups that are organized around work processes, complete an entire piece of work requiring several interdependent tasks, and have substantial autonomy over the execution of those tasks

> **virtual teams** teams whose members operate across space, time, and organizational boundaries and are linked through information technologies to achieve organizational tasks

---

Virtual teams face all the challenges of traditional teams, as well as the issues arising from time and distance.

More Virtual Teams, More Virtual Challenges[90]

80% of managers polled in large American companies say that their firm's reliance on virtual teams will grow in importance over the next three years.

70% of American chief information officers polled indicate that managing virtual teams is a very important globalization challenge (highest-rated issue on the list).

58% of American managers say that it is somewhat or very important that all members of their department work from the *same* location.

businesses depend on virtual teamwork to leverage the potential of their employees.

Success Factors for Virtual Teams

Virtual teams face all the challenges of traditional teams, as well as the issues arising from time and distance. These challenges increase with the team's virtuality, particularly when the team exists for only a short time.[91] Fortunately, OB research has identified the following strategies to minimize most virtual team problems.[92] First, virtual team members need to apply the effective team behaviors described earlier in this chapter. They also require good communication technology skills, strong self-leadership skills to motivate and guide their behavior without peers or bosses nearby, and higher emotional intelligence so that they can decipher the feelings of other team members from email and other limited communication media.

Second, virtual teams should have a toolkit of communication channels (email,

production blocking
a time constraint in team decision making due to the procedural requirement that only one person may speak at a time

evaluation apprehension
a decision-making problem that occurs when individuals are reluctant to mention ideas that seem silly because they believe (often correctly) that other team members are silently evaluating them

team efficacy the collective belief among team members in the team's capability to successfully complete a task

processes, and agreed-on roles and responsibilities.[93] The final recommendation is that virtual team members should meet face-to-face fairly early in the team development process. This idea may seem contradictory to the entire notion of virtual teams, but so far, no technology has replaced face-to-face interaction for high-level bonding and mutual understanding.[94]

virtual whiteboards, videoconferencing, etc.) as well as the freedom to choose the channels that work best for them. This may sound obvious, but unfortunately senior management tends to impose technology on virtual teams, often based on advice from external consultants, and expects team members to use the same communication technology throughout their work. In contrast, research suggests that communication channels gain and lose importance over time, depending on the task and level of trust.

Third, virtual teams need plenty of structure. In one recent review of effective virtual teams, many of the principles for successful virtual teams related mostly to creating these structures, such as clear operational objectives, documented work

LO7-5 Identify four constraints on team decision making and discuss the advantages and disadvantages of four structures aimed at improving team decision making.

TEAM DECISION MAKING

Self-directed teams, virtual teams, and practically all other groups are expected to make decisions. Under certain conditions, teams are more effective than individuals at identifying problems, choosing alternatives, and evaluating their decisions. To

leverage these benefits, however, we first need to understand the constraints on effective team decision making. Then, we look at specific team structures that try to overcome these constraints.

Constraints on Team Decision Making

Anyone who has spent enough time in the workplace can recite several ways in which teams stumble in decision making. The four most common problems are time constraints, evaluation apprehension, pressure to conform, and overconfidence.

Time Constraints There's a saying that committees keep minutes and waste hours. This reflects the fact that teams take longer than individuals to make decisions.[95] Teams consume time organizing, coordinating, and maintaining relationships (i.e., process losses). Team members require time to build rapport, agree on rules and norms of behavior in the decision process, and understand each other's ideas.

Another time-related constraint in most team structures is that only one person can speak at a time.[96] This problem, known as **production blocking**, undermines idea generation in

Pressure to Conform Team cohesion leads employees to conform to the team's norms. This control keeps the group organized around common goals, but it may also cause team members to suppress their dissenting opinions, particularly when a strong team norm is related to the issue. When someone does state a point of view that violates the majority opinion, other members might punish the violator or try to persuade him or her that the opinion is incorrect. Conformity can also be subtle. To some extent, we depend on the opinions that others hold to validate our own views. If coworkers don't agree with us, we begin to question our own opinions even without overt peer pressure.

Overconfidence (Inflated Team Efficacy) Teams are more successful when their members have collective confidence in how well they work together and the likely success of their team effort.[98] This **team efficacy** is similar to the power of individual self-efficacy, which we discussed in Chapter 3. High-efficacy teams set more challenging goals and are more motivated to achieve them, both of which increase team performance. Unfortunately, teams make worse decisions when they become overconfident and develop a

> Overconfident teams tend to make worse decisions because they are less vigilant, engage in less constructive debate, and are less likely to seek out or accept information located outside the team.

a few ways. First, team members need to listen in on the conversation to find an opportune time to speak up, but this monitoring makes it difficult for them to concentrate on their own ideas. Second, ideas are fleeting, so the longer they wait to speak up, the more likely their flickering ideas will die out. Third, team members might remember their fleeting thoughts by concentrating on them, but this causes them to pay less attention to the conversation. By ignoring what others are saying, team members miss other potentially good ideas.

Evaluation Apprehension Team members are often reluctant to mention ideas that seem silly because they believe (often correctly) that other team members are silently evaluating them.[97] This **evaluation apprehension** is based on the individual's desire to create a favorable self-presentation and need to protect self-esteem. It is most common when meetings are attended by people with different levels of status or expertise or when members formally evaluate each other's performance throughout the year (as in 360-degree feedback). Creative ideas often sound bizarre or illogical when first presented, so evaluation apprehension tends to discourage employees from mentioning them in front of coworkers.

false sense of invulnerability.[99] In other words, the team's efficacy far exceeds reality regarding its abilities and the favorableness of the situation. Overconfident teams are less vigilant when making decisions, partly because they have more positive than negative emotions and moods during these events. They also engage in less constructive debate and are less likely to seek out or accept information located outside the team, both of which undermine the quality of team decisions.

Why do teams become overconfident? The main reason is a team-level variation of self-enhancement (see Chapter 3), whereby team members have a natural motivation to believe the team's capabilities and situation are above average. Overconfidence is more common in highly cohesive teams because people engage in self-enhancement for things that are important to them (such as a cohesive team). It is also stronger when the team has external threats or competition because these adversaries generate "us–them" differentiation. Team efficacy is further inflated by the mutually reinforcing beliefs of the team. We develop a clearer and higher opinion of the team when other team members echo that opinion.

brainstorming
a freewheeling, face-to-face meeting where team members aren't allowed to criticize but are encouraged to speak freely, generate as many ideas as possible, and build on the ideas of others

brainwriting
a variation of brainstorming whereby participants write (rather than speak about) and share their ideas

electronic brainstorming
a form of brainstorming that relies on networked computers for submitting and sharing creative ideas

Along with these general recommendations, OB studies have identified four team structures that encourage creativity in a team setting: brainstorming, brainwriting, electronic brainstorming, and nominal group technique. These four structures emphasize idea creation (the central focus of creativity), but some also include team selection of alternatives.

Improving Creative Decision Making in Teams

Team decision making is fraught with problems, but several solutions also emerge from these bad-news studies. Team members need to be confident in their decision making but not so confident that they collectively feel invulnerable. This calls for team norms that encourage critical thinking as well as team membership with sufficient diversity. Checks and balances need to be in place to prevent one or two people from dominating the discussion. The team should also be large enough to possess the collective knowledge to resolve the problem yet small enough that the team doesn't consume too much time or restrict individual input.

Brainstorming Brainstorming is a team event where participants try to think up as many ideas as possible.[100] The process was introduced by advertising executive Alex Osborn in 1939 and has four simple rules to maximize the number and quality of ideas presented: (1) Speak freely—describe even the craziest ideas; (2) don't criticize others or their ideas; (3) provide as many ideas as possible—the quality of ideas increases with the quantity of ideas; and (4) build on the ideas that others have presented.

Brainstorming rules are supposed to encourage divergent thinking while minimizing evaluation apprehension and other team dynamics problems. That thesis is not supported by lab studies with student participants, which specifically report that production blocking and evaluation apprehension undermine

creative team decision making.[101] However, field research and the experiences of several leading companies suggest that brainstorming can be effective under specific conditions, such as having an experienced facilitator and participants who work together in a supportive culture.[102]

Brainwriting **Brainwriting** is a variation of brainstorming that minimizes the problem of production blocking by removing conversation during idea generation.[103] There are many forms of brainwriting, but they all have the common feature that individuals write down their ideas rather than verbally describe them. In one version, participants write their ideas on cards and place them in the center of the table. At any time, participants can pick up one or more cards in the center to spark their thinking or further build (piggyback) on those ideas. In another variation, each person writes one idea on a card, then passes the card to the person on their right. The receiving person writes a new idea on a second card, both cards are sent to the next person, and the process is repeated. The limited research on brainwriting suggests that it produces more and better-quality ideas than brainstorming due to the lack of production blocking.

Electronic Brainstorming **Electronic brainstorming** is similar to brainwriting but uses computer technology rather than handwritten cards to document and share ideas. After receiving the question or issue, participants enter their ideas using special computer software. The ideas are distributed anonymously to other participants, who are encouraged to piggyback on those ideas. Team members eventually vote electronically on the ideas presented. Face-to-face discussion usually follows. Electronic brainstorming can be quite effective at generating creative ideas with minimal production blocking,

evaluation apprehension, or conformity problems.[104] It can be superior to brainwriting because ideas are generated anonymously and they are viewed by other participants more easily. Despite these numerous advantages, electronic brainstorming is rarely used because it is often considered too structured and technology-bound.

Nominal Group Technique **Nominal group technique** is another variation of brainwriting that adds a verbal element to the process.[105] The activity is called "nominal" because participants are a group in name only during two of the three steps. After the problem is described, team members silently and independently write down as many solutions as they can. In the second stage, participants describe their solutions to the other team members, usually in a round-robin format. As with brainstorming, there is no criticism or debate, although members are encouraged to ask for clarification of the ideas presented. In the third stage, participants silently and independently rank-order or vote on each proposed solution. Nominal group technique has been applied in numerous laboratory and real-world settings, such as identifying ways to improve tourism in various countries.[106] This method tends to generate a higher number of ideas and better-quality ideas than do traditional interacting and possibly brainstorming groups.[107] However, production blocking and evaluation apprehension still occur to some extent. Training improves this structured approach to team decision making.[108]

nominal group technique a variation of brainwriting consisting of three stages in which participants (1) silently and independently document their ideas, (2) collectively describe these ideas to the other team members without critique, and then (3) silently and independently evaluate the ideas presented

Study Checklist

☑ Did you tear out the perforated student review card at the back of the text to revisit learning objectives and key terms and definitions?

Connect® Management is available for
M Organizational Behavior. **Additional resources include:**

☑ Interactive Applications:
- **Case Analysis:** Apply concepts within the context of a real-world situation.
- **Drag and Drop:** Work through an interactive example to test your knowledge of the concepts.
- **Video Case:** See management in action through interactive videos.

☑ **SmartBook™**—SmartBook is the first and only adaptive reading experience available today. Distinguishing what you know from what you don't, and honing in on concepts you are most likely to forget, SmartBook personalizes content for you in a continuously adapting reading experience. Reading is no longer a passive and linear experience, but an engaging and dynamic one where you are more likely to master and retain important concepts and go to class better prepared.

8 chapter

Communicating in Teams and Organizations

Learning Objectives

After studying this chapter, you should be able to:

LO8-1 Explain why communication is important in organizations, and discuss four influences on effective communication encoding and decoding.

LO8-2 Compare and contrast the advantages of and problems with electronic mail, other verbal communication media, and nonverbal communication.

LO8-3 Explain how social acceptance and media richness influence the preferred communication channel.

LO8-4 Discuss various barriers (noise) to effective communication, including cross-cultural and gender-based differences in communication.

LO8-5 Explain how to get your message across more effectively, and summarize the elements of active listening.

LO8-6 Summarize effective communication strategies in organizational hierarchies, and review the role and relevance of the organizational grapevine.

Until recently, Doug Stuart was skeptical that communication technology would come anywhere close to a meeting with everyone in the same room. "If you had asked me that four years ago I would have rolled my eyes and said it is never going to work," says the chief information officer at IBM New Zealand. Today, technology quality, together with the ability to multicommunicate during meetings, has dramatically improved the communication experience of virtual meetings. "I'm looking at my screen and seeing their presentations and hearing their voices," Stuart said while he virtually attended a meeting of IBM colleagues in the United States from his workplace in Wellington. "You have the ability to raise your hand, send real-time text messaging to the chair of the meeting . . . and blogs are active during these sessions as well."[1]

Doug Stuart and many other people are experiencing a dramatic transformation in how we communicate in organizations. High-quality videoconferences, sophisticated corporate-strength social media, smartphone videos and messages, and other methods didn't exist a decade ago. Indeed, many organizations in the United States and other countries are still struggling with whether—let alone determining how—to incorporate these new ways of interacting in the workplace. These new channels offer significant potential for information sharing and social bonding. Equally important, the workforce increasingly uses and expects their organizations to provide these communication channels.

Communication refers to the process by which information is transmitted and *understood* between two or more people. We emphasize the word *understood* because transmitting the sender's intended meaning is the essence of good communication. This chapter begins by discussing the importance of effective communication, outlining the communication process model, and discussing factors that improve communication coding and decoding. Next, we identify types of communication channels, including email and social media, followed by factors to consider when choosing a communication medium. The chapter then identifies barriers to effective communication. The latter part of the chapter offers an overview of ways to communicate in organizational hierarchies and offers insight about the pervasive organizational grapevine.

> "An organization comes into being when there are persons able to communicate with each other."[3]
>
> —**Chester Barnard,** pioneering OB scholar and telecommunications CEO

LO8-1 Explain why communication is important in organizations, and discuss four influences on effective communication encoding and decoding.

THE IMPORTANCE OF COMMUNICATION

Effective communication is vital to all organizations, so much so that no company could exist without it. The reason? Recall from Chapter 1 that organizations are defined as groups of people who work interdependently toward some purpose. People work interdependently only when they can communicate with each other. Although organizations rely on a variety of coordinating mechanisms (which we discuss in Chapter 12), frequent, timely, and accurate communication remains the primary means through which employees and work units effectively synchronize their work.[2]

In addition to coordination, communication is critical for organizational learning. It is the means through which knowledge enters the organization and is distributed to employees.[4] A third function of communication is decision making. Imagine the challenge of making a decision without any information about the decision context, the alternatives available, the likely

communication

the process by which information is transmitted and understood between two or more people

outcomes of those options, or the extent to which the decision is achieving its objectives. All of these ingredients require communication from coworkers and from stakeholders in the external environment. For example, airline cockpit crews make much better decisions—and thereby cause far fewer accidents—when the captain encourages the crew to openly share information.[5]

A fourth function of communication is to change behavior.[6] When conveying information to others, we are often trying to alter their beliefs, feelings, and ultimately their behavior. This influence process might be passive, such as merely describing the situation more clearly and fully. But communication is often a deliberate attempt to change someone's thoughts and actions. We will discuss the topic of persuasion later in this chapter.

A fifth function of communication is that it supports employee well-being.[7] One way communication minimizes stress is by conveying knowledge that helps employees to better manage their work environment. For instance, research shows that new employees adjust much better to the organization when coworkers communicate subtle nuggets of wisdom, such as how to avoid office politics, complete work procedures correctly, find useful resources, handle difficult customers, and so on.[8] The second way communication minimizes stress is emotionally; talking with others can be a soothing balm during difficult times. Indeed, people are less susceptible to colds, cardiovascular disease, and other physical and mental illnesses when they have regular social interaction.[9] In essence, people have an inherent drive to bond, to validate their self-worth, and to maintain their social identity. Communication is the means through which these drives and needs are fulfilled.

A MODEL OF COMMUNICATION

To understand the key interpersonal features of effective communication, let's examine the model presented in Exhibit 8.1, which provides a useful "conduit" metaphor for thinking about the communication process.[10] According to this model, communication flows through channels between the sender and receiver. The sender forms a message and encodes it into words, gestures, voice intonations, and other symbols or signs. Next, the encoded message is transmitted to the intended receiver through one or more communication channels (media). The receiver senses the incoming message and decodes it into something meaningful. Ideally, the decoded meaning is what the sender had intended.

In most situations, the sender looks for evidence that the other person received and understood the transmitted message. This feedback may be a formal acknowledgment, such as "Yes, I know what you mean," or indirect evidence from the receiver's subsequent actions. Notice that feedback repeats the communication process. Intended feedback is encoded, transmitted, received, and decoded from the receiver to the sender of the original message. This model recognizes that communication is not a free-flowing conduit. Rather, the transmission of meaning from one person to another is hampered by *noise*—the psychological, social, and structural barriers that distort and obscure the sender's intended message. If any part of the communication process is

Exhibit 8.1 The Communication Process Model

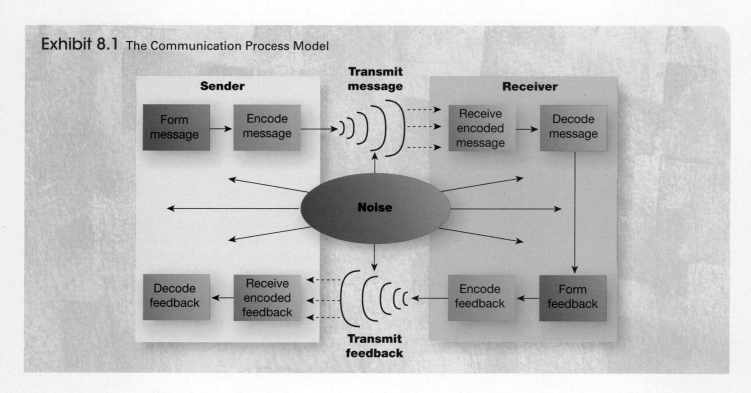

distorted or broken, the sender and receiver will not have a common understanding of the message.

Influences on Effective Encoding and Decoding

According to the communication process model, effective communication depends on the ability of sender and receiver to efficiently and accurately encode and decode information. How well this encoding–decoding process works depends on whether the sender and receiver have similar codebooks, the sender's proficiency at encoding the message to the audience, the sender and receiver's motivation and ability to transmit messages through that particular communication channel, and their common mental models of the communication context.[11]

Similar Codebooks The sender and receiver rely on "codebooks," which are dictionaries of symbols, language, gestures, idioms, and other tools used to convey information. With similar codebooks, the communication participants are able to encode and decode more accurately because they assign the same or similar meaning to the transmitted symbols and signs. Communication efficiency also improves because there is less need for redundancy (repeating the message in different ways) and less need for confirmation feedback ("So, you are saying that . . . ?").

Message Encoding Proficiency Even with the same codebooks, some people are better than others at communicating the message because, through experience, they have learned which words and gestures transmit the message best to that audience.

Suppose that you have spoken to several employee groups about the company's new product development plans. With each session, you learn which words, symbols, voice intonations, and other features transmit the message better than others. Through experience, you fine-tune the presentation so the audience receives your message more efficiently and effectively.

Communication Channel Motivation and Ability The encoding–decoding process depends on the sender's and receiver's motivation and ability to use the selected communication channel. Some people prefer face-to-face conversations, whereas others would rather prepare or receive written documentation. Some people are skilled at communicating through Twitter tweets, whereas others are more effective at writing detailed reports. So, even if both parties have the same codebooks and are skilled at using those codebooks for a particular message, message encoding and decoding can be hampered by a communication channel that the sender, receiver, or both dislike or lack proficiency in using.[12]

Shared Mental Models of the Communication Context Mental models are internal representations of the external world that allow us to visualize elements of a setting and relationships among those elements (see Chapter 3). A sender and receiver with shared mental models of the communication context have similar images and expectations regarding the location, time, layout, and other contextual features of the information. These shared mental models potentially increase the accuracy of the message content and reduce the need for communication about that context. Notice that a shared mental model of the communication context differs from a shared codebook. Codebooks are symbols used to convey message content, whereas mental models are knowledge structures of the communication setting. For example, a Russian cosmonaut and American astronaut might have shared mental models about the layout and features of the international space station (communication context), yet they experience poor communication because of language differences (i.e., different codebooks).

COMMUNICATION CHANNELS

A central feature of the communication model is the channel or medium through which information is transmitted. There are two main types of channels: verbal and nonverbal. Verbal communication uses words, so it includes spoken or written channels. Nonverbal communication is any part of communication that does not use words. Spoken and written communication are both verbal (i.e., they both use words), but they are quite different from each other and have different strengths and weaknesses in communication effectiveness, which we discuss later in this section. Also, written communication has traditionally been much slower than spoken communication at transmitting messages, although electronic mail, Twitter tweets, and other online communication channels have significantly improved written communication efficiency.

Internet-Based Communication

In the early 1960s, with funding from the U.S. Department of Defense, university researchers began discussing how to collaborate better by connecting their computers through a network. Their rough vision of connected computers became a reality in 1969 as the Advanced Research Projects Agency Network (ARPANET). ARPANET initially had only a dozen or so connections and was very slow and expensive by today's standards, but it marked the birth of the Internet. Two years later, a computer engineer developing ARPANET sent the first electronic mail (email) message between different computers on a network. By 1973, most communication on ARPANET was through email. ARPANET was mostly restricted to U.S. Defense–funded research centers, so in 1979 two graduate students at Duke University developed a public network system, called Usenet. Usenet allowed people to post information that could be retrieved by anyone else on the network, making it the first public computer-mediated social network.[13]

We have come a long way since the early days of ARPANET and Usenet. Instant messaging, social media, and other contemporary activities didn't exist in organizations a dozen years ago, whereas they are now gaining popularity. However, email remains the medium of choice in most workplaces.[14] Email messages can be written, edited, and transmitted quickly. Information can be effortlessly appended and conveyed to many people. Email is also asynchronous (messages are sent and received at different times), so there is no need to coordinate a communication session. With advances in computer search technology, email software has also become an efficient filing cabinet.[15]

Email tends to be the preferred medium for sending well-defined information for decision making. It is also central for coordinating work, although text messaging and Twitter tweets might overtake email for this objective. When email was introduced in the workplace more than two decades ago, it tended to increase the volume of communication and significantly altered the flow of that information within groups and throughout the organization.[16] Specifically, it reduced some face-to-face and telephone communication but increased communication with people further up the hierarchy. Some social and organizational status differences still exist with email,[17] but they are somewhat less apparent than in face-to-face communication. By hiding age, race, and other features, email reduces stereotype biases. However, it also tends to increase reliance on stereotypes when we are already aware of the other individual's personal characteristics.[18]

Problems with Email

In spite of the wonders of email, anyone who has used this communication medium knows that it has its limitations. Here are the top four complaints:

Email Is a Poor Medium for Communicating Emotions People rely on facial expressions and other nonverbal cues to interpret the emotional meaning of words; email lacks this parallel communication channel. Indeed, people consistently and significantly overestimate the degree to which they understand the emotional tone of email messages.[19] Senders try to clarify the

Banning Email

The firm All Western Mortgage recently decided to stop using email for internal communication. "There's a lot of uncertainty with email," explains Tory Teunis, vice president of operations at the Las Vegas financial institution. Teunis points to the communication medium's uneven reliability, lack of transparency (such as not knowing whether recipients have received or viewed the message), risk of being sent to spam folders, and a host of other problems. Clients still use email as a communication tool, but their messages are sent to a limited number of staff with email access. Instead, All Western Mortgage has shifted to an internal communication platform that combines instant messaging with social media.[20]

emotional tone of their messages by using expressive language ("Wonderful to hear from you!"), highlighting phrases in bold-face or quotation marks, and inserting graphic faces (called emot-icons or "smileys") representing the desired emotion. Recent studies suggest that writers are getting better at using these emotion symbols. Still, they do not replace the full complexity of real facial expressions, voice intonation, and hand movements.[21]

Email Reduces Politeness and Respect Email messages are often less diplomatic than written letters. Indeed, the term *flaming* has entered our language to describe email and other electronic messages that convey strong negative emotions to the receiver. People who receive email are partly to blame because they tend to infer a more negative or neutral interpretation of the email than was intended by the sender.[22] Even so, email flame wars occur mostly because senders are more likely to send disparaging messages by email than by other communication channels. One reason is that individuals can post email messages before their emotions subside, whereas the sender of a traditional memo or letter would have time for sober second thoughts. A second reason is that email has low social presence (it is impersonal); people are more likely to communicate messages through impersonal channels that they would never say in face-to-face conversation. Fortunately, research has found that flaming decreases as teams move to later stages of development and when explicit norms and rules of communication are established.[23]

Email Is a Poor Medium for Ambiguous, Complex, and Novel Situations Email is usually satisfactory for well-defined situations, such as giving basic instructions or presenting a meeting agenda, but it can be cumbersome and dysfunctional in ambiguous, complex, and novel situations. As we will describe later in this section, these circumstances require communication channels that transmit a larger volume of information with more rapid feedback. In other words, when the issue gets messy, stop emailing and start talking, preferably face-to-face.

Email Contributes to Information Overload Studies have shown that email contributes to information overload.[24] Approximately 72 trillion emails—more than half of which are in business settings—are now transmitted annually around the world, up from just 1.1 trillion in 1998. Almost two-thirds of all emails are spam![25] The email glut occurs because messages are created and copied to many people without much effort. The number of email messages will probably decrease as people become more familiar with it and as other technologies take over; until then, email volume continues to rise.

Workplace Communication through Social Media

Although email dominates most workplace communication, it may eventually be overtaken by emerging forms of social media. Social media are Internet- or mobile-based channels that allow users to generate and interactively share information. They cover a wide range of categories: social networks (Facebook, LinkedIn, Google+), microblogs (Twitter), blogs and blog communities (Typepad, BlogHer), site comments and forums (FlyerTalk, Whirlpool), multimedia sharing (YouTube, Pinterest), publishing (Wikipedia), and several others.

Unlike traditional websites that merely "push" information from the creator to the audience, social media are more conversational and reciprocally interactive between sender and receiver, resulting in a sense of community.[26] Social media typically enable users to develop a public identity through the social media content. Social media are "social" because they

Social Media Arrives in the Workplace[27]

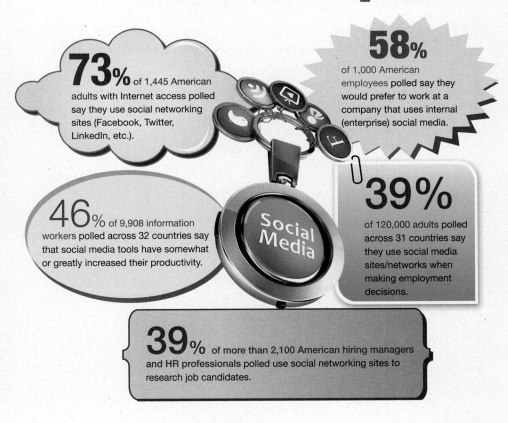

73% of 1,445 American adults with Internet access polled say they use social networking sites (Facebook, Twitter, LinkedIn, etc.).

58% of 1,000 American employees polled say they would prefer to work at a company that uses internal (enterprise) social media.

46% of 9,908 information workers polled across 32 countries say that social media tools have somewhat or greatly increased their productivity.

39% of 120,000 adults polled across 31 countries say they use social media sites/networks when making employment decisions.

39% of more than 2,100 American hiring managers and HR professionals polled use social networking sites to research job candidates.

> Social media encourage formation of communities through links, interactive conversations, and (for some platforms) common space for collaborative content development.

encourage formation of communities through links, interactive conversations, and (for some platforms) common space for collaborative content development. The audience can become participants in the conversation by contributing feedback and by linking someone else's content to their own social media spaces.

The different types of social media serve several functions, such as presenting the individual's identity, enabling conversations, sharing information, sensing the presence of others in the virtual space, maintaining relationships, revealing reputation or status, and supporting communities (see Exhibit 8.2).[28] For instance, Facebook has a strong emphasis on maintaining relationships but relatively low emphasis on sharing information or forming communities (groups). Wikis, on the other hand, focus on sharing information or forming communities but have a much lower emphasis on presenting the user's identity or reputation.

A few studies conclude (with caution) that social media offer considerable versatility and potential in the workplace.

> "The most important thing in communication is hearing what isn't said."[31]
>
> —Peter Drucker

For example, one recent study found that the introduction of an enterprise social media platform in a major credit card company improved the employees' ability to find information by 31 percent, and to find the person with the original information by 71 percent.[29] Even so, companies have been reluctant to introduce these communication tools, mainly because they lack knowledge, staff/resources, and technical support to put them into practice.[30] Indeed, a common practice is to simply ban employee access to social media (usually after discovering excess employee activity on Facebook) without thinking through the potential of this type of communication channel.

Nonverbal Communication

Nonverbal communication includes facial gestures, voice intonation, physical distance, and even silence. This communication channel is necessary where noise or physical distance prevents effective verbal exchanges and the need for immediate feedback precludes written communication. But even in quiet

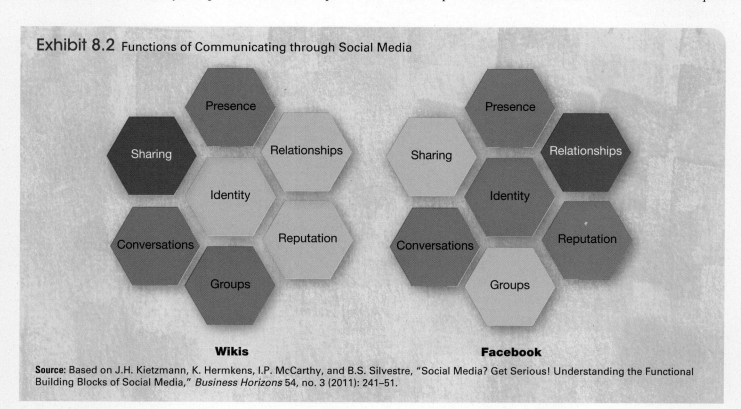

Exhibit 8.2 Functions of Communicating through Social Media

Wikis

Facebook

Source: Based on J.H. Kietzmann, K. Hermkens, I.P. McCarthy, and B.S. Silvestre, "Social Media? Get Serious! Understanding the Functional Building Blocks of Social Media," *Business Horizons* 54, no. 3 (2011): 241–51.

face-to-face meetings, most information is communicated nonverbally. Rather like a parallel conversation, nonverbal cues signal subtle information to both parties, such as reinforcing their interest in the verbal conversation or demonstrating their relative status in the relationship.[32]

Nonverbal communication differs from verbal (i.e., written and spoken) communication in a couple of ways. First, it is less rule-bound than verbal communication. We receive considerable formal training on how to understand spoken words, but very little on how to understand the nonverbal signals that accompany those words. Consequently, nonverbal cues are generally more ambiguous and susceptible to misinterpretation. At the same time, many facial expressions (such as smiling) are hardwired and universal, thereby providing the only reliable means of communicating across cultures.

The other difference between verbal and nonverbal communication is that the former is typically conscious, whereas most nonverbal communication is automatic and nonconscious. We normally plan the words we say or write, but we rarely plan every blink, smile, or other gesture during a conversation. Indeed, as we just mentioned, many of these facial expressions communicate the same meaning across cultures because they are hardwired, nonconscious responses to human emotions.[34] For example, pleasant emotions cause the brain center to widen the mouth, whereas negative emotions produce constricted facial expressions (squinting eyes, pursed lips, etc.).

Emotional Contagion One of the most fascinating aspects of nonverbal communication is **emotional contagion**, which is the automatic process of "catching" or sharing another person's

emotional contagion
the nonconscious process of "catching" or sharing another person's emotions by mimicking that person's facial expressions and other nonverbal behavior

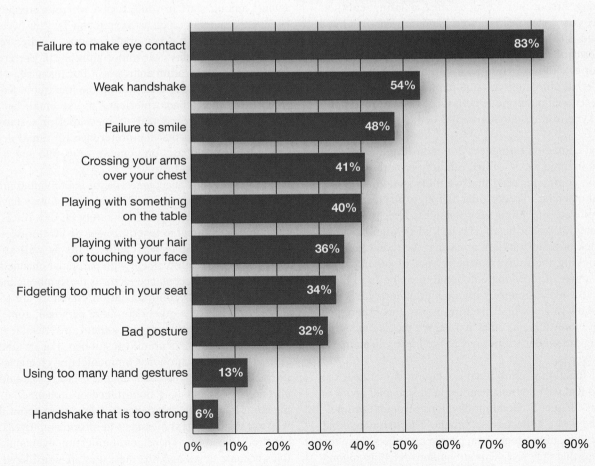

Top Ten Body Language Mistakes in Job Interviews[33]

- Failure to make eye contact — 83%
- Weak handshake — 54%
- Failure to smile — 48%
- Crossing your arms over your chest — 41%
- Playing with something on the table — 40%
- Playing with your hair or touching your face — 36%
- Fidgeting too much in your seat — 34%
- Bad posture — 32%
- Using too many hand gestures — 13%
- Handshake that is too strong — 6%

Note: Percentage of employers surveyed in the United Kingdom who reported the biggest body language turnoffs in job interviews. Similar results were found in a U.S. survey one year earlier.

emotions by mimicking that person's facial expressions and other nonverbal behavior. Technically, human beings have brain receptors that cause them to mirror what they observe. In other words, to some degree our brain causes us to act as though we are the person we are watching.[35]

Consider what happens when you see a coworker accidentally bang his or her head against a filing cabinet. Chances are, you wince and put your hand on your own head as if you had hit the cabinet. Similarly, while listening to someone describe a positive event, you tend to smile and exhibit other emotional displays of happiness. While some of our nonverbal communication is planned, emotional contagion represents nonconscious behavior—we automatically mimic and synchronize our nonverbal behaviors with other people.[36]

Emotional contagion influences communication and social relationships in three ways.[37] First, mimicry provides continuous feedback, communicating that we understand and empathize with the sender. To consider the significance of this, imagine employees remaining expressionless after watching a coworker bang his or her head! The lack of parallel behavior conveys a lack of understanding or caring. A second function is that mimicking the nonverbal behaviors of other people seems to be a way of receiving emotional meaning from those people. If a coworker is angry with a client, your tendency to frown and show anger while listening helps you experience that emotion more fully. In other words, we receive meaning by expressing the sender's emotions as well as by listening to the sender's words.

The third function of emotional contagion is to fulfill the drive to bond that we mentioned earlier in this chapter and was introduced in Chapter 5. Bonding develops through each person's awareness of a collective sentiment. Through nonverbal expressions of emotional contagion, people see others share the same emotions that they feel. This strengthens relations among team members as well as between leaders and followers by providing evidence of their similarity.

CHOOSING THE BEST COMMUNICATION CHANNEL

Which communication channel is most appropriate in a particular situation? Two important sets of factors to consider are (a) social acceptance and (b) media richness.

Social Acceptance

Social acceptance refers to how well the communication medium is approved and supported by the organization, teams, and individuals involved in the exchange.[38] One factor in social acceptance is organizational, team, and cultural norms regarding the use of specific communication channels. Norms partly explain why face-to-face meetings are daily events among staff in some firms, whereas computer-based videoconferencing (such as Skype) and Twitter tweets are the media of choice in other organizations. Studies report that national culture plays an important role in preferences for specific communication channels.[39] For instance, when communicating with people further up the hierarchy, Koreans are much less likely than Americans to use email because this medium is less respectful of the superior's status. Other research has found that the preference for email depends on the culture's emphasis on context, time, and space in social relationships.

A second social acceptance factor is individual preferences for specific communication channels.[40] You may have noticed that some coworkers ignore (or rarely check) voice mail, yet they quickly respond to text messages or Twitter tweets. These preferences are due to personality traits as well as previous experience and reinforcement with particular channels.

A third social acceptance factor is the symbolic meaning of a channel.[41] Some communication channels are viewed as impersonal whereas others are more personal; some are considered professional whereas others are casual; some are "cool" whereas others are old-fashioned. For instance, phone calls and other synchronous communication channels convey a greater sense of urgency than do text messages and other asynchronous channels. The importance of a channel's symbolic meaning is perhaps most apparent in stories about managers who use emails or text messages to inform employees that they are fired or laid off. These communication events make headlines because email and text messages are considered inappropriate (too impersonal) for transmission of that particular information.[42]

Media Richness

media richness
a medium's data-carrying capacity—that is, the volume and variety of information that can be transmitted during a specific time

Along with social acceptance, people need to determine the best level of **media richness** for their message. Media richness refers to the medium's data-carrying capacity—the volume and variety of information that can be transmitted during a specific time.[43] Exhibit 8.3 illustrates various communication channels arranged in a hierarchy of richness, with face-to-face interaction at the top and lean data-only reports at the bottom. A communication channel has high richness when it is able to convey multiple cues (such as both verbal and nonverbal information), allows timely feedback from receiver to sender, allows the sender to customize the message to the receiver, and makes use of complex symbols (such as words and phrases with multiple meanings).

Face-to-face communication is at the top of media richness because it allows us to communicate both verbally and nonverbally at the same time, to get feedback almost immediately from the receiver, to quickly adjust our message and style, and to use complex language such as metaphors and idioms (e.g., "spilling the beans").

According to media richness theory, rich media are better than lean media when the communication situation is nonroutine

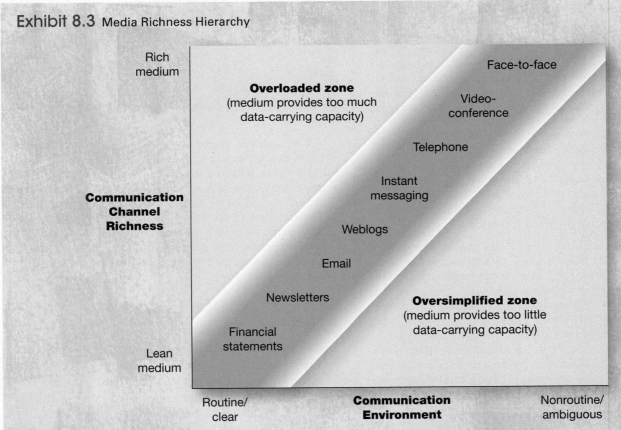

Exhibit 8.3 Media Richness Hierarchy

Rich medium

Overloaded zone
(medium provides too much data-carrying capacity)

Face-to-face

Video-conference

Telephone

Communication Channel Richness

Instant messaging

Weblogs

Email

Newsletters

Oversimplified zone
(medium provides too little data-carrying capacity)

Financial statements

Lean medium

Routine/clear   **Communication Environment**   Nonroutine/ambiguous

Sources: Based on R.H. Lengel and R.L. Daft, "The Selection of Communication Media as an Executive Skill," *Academy of Management Executive* 2, no. 3 (August 1988): 226; R.L. Daft and R.H. Lengel, "Information Richness: A New Approach to Managerial Behavior and Organization Design," *Research in Organizational Behavior* 6 (1984): 199.

and ambiguous. In nonroutine situations (such as an unexpected and unusual emergency), the sender and receiver have little common experience, so they need to transmit a large volume of information with immediate feedback. Lean media work well in routine situations because the sender and receiver have common expectations through shared mental models. Ambiguous situations also require rich media because the parties must share large amounts of information with immediate feedback to resolve multiple and conflicting interpretations of their observations and experiences.[44] Choosing the wrong medium reduces communication effectiveness. When the situation is routine or clear, using a rich medium—such as holding a special meeting—would be a waste of time. On the other hand, if a unique and ambiguous issue is handled through email or another lean medium, then issues take longer to resolve and misunderstandings are more likely to occur.

Exceptions to the Media Richness Theory Research generally supports media richness theory for traditional channels (face-to-face, written memos, etc.). However, the model doesn't fit reality nearly as well when electronic communication channels are studied.[45] Three factors seem to explain why electronic channels may have more media richness than the theory proposes:

1. *Ability to multicommunicate.* It is usually difficult (as well as rude) to communicate face-to-face with someone while simultaneously transmitting messages to someone else using another medium. Most information technologies, on the other hand, require less social etiquette and attention, so employees can easily engage in two or more communication events at the same time. In other words, they can multicommunicate.[46] For example, people routinely scan web pages while carrying on telephone conversations. Some write text messages to a client while simultaneously listening to a discussion at a large meeting. People multitask less efficiently than they think they do, but some are good enough that they likely exchange as much information through two or more lean electronic media as through one high media richness channel.

2. *Communication proficiency.* Earlier in this chapter we explained that communication effectiveness is partially determined by the sender's competency and motivation with the communication channel. People with higher proficiency can "push" more information through the channel, thereby increasing the channel's information flow. Experienced smartphone users, for instance, can whip through messages in a flash, whereas new users struggle to type notes and organize incoming messages. In contrast, there is less variation in the ability to communicate through casual conversation and other natural channels because most of us develop good levels of proficiency throughout life and possibly through hardwired evolutionary development.[47]

3. *Social presence effects.* Channels with high media richness tend to have more social presence, that is, the participants experience a stronger physical presence of each other.[48] However, high social presence also sensitizes both parties to their relative status and

self-presentation, which can distort or divert attention away from the message.[49] Face-to-face communication has very high media richness, yet its high social presence can disrupt the efficient flow of information through that medium. During a personal meeting with the company's CEO, for example, you might concentrate more on how you come across than on what the CEO is saying to you. In other words, the benefits of channels with high media richness may be offset by more social presence distractions, whereas lean media have much less social presence to distract or distort the transmitted information.

Communication Channels and Persuasion

Some communication channels are more effective than others for **persuasion**, that is, changing another person's beliefs and attitudes. Studies support the long-held view that spoken communication, particularly face-to-face interaction, is more persuasive than emails, websites, and other forms of written communication. There are three main reasons for this persuasive effect.[50] First, spoken communication is typically accompanied by nonverbal communication. People are persuaded more when they receive both emotional and logical messages, and the combination of spoken with nonverbal communication provides this dual punch. A lengthy pause, raised voice tone, and (in face-to-face interaction) animated hand gestures can amplify the emotional tone of the message, thereby signaling the vitality of the issue.

A second reason why conversations are more persuasive is that spoken communication offers the sender high-quality, immediate feedback about whether the receiver understands and accepts the message (i.e., is being persuaded). This feedback allows the sender to adjust the content and emotional tone of the message more quickly than with written communication. A third reason is that people are persuaded more under conditions of high social presence than low social presence. The sender can more easily monitor the receiver's listening in face-to-face conversations (high social presence), so listeners are more motivated to pay attention and consider the sender's ideas. When people receive persuasion attempts through a website, email, or other source of written communication, on the other hand, they experience a higher degree of anonymity and psychological distance from the persuader. These conditions reduce the motivation to think about and accept the persuasive message.

Although spoken communication tends to be more persuasive, written communication can also persuade others to some extent. Written messages have the advantage of presenting more technical detail than can occur through conversation. This factual information is valuable when the issue is important to the receiver. Also, people experience a moderate degree of social presence in written communication when they are exchanging messages with close associates, so messages from friends and coworkers can be persuasive.

> "The greatest problem with communication is the illusion that it has been accomplished."
>
> —**George Bernard Shaw**

LO8-4 Discuss various barriers (noise) to effective communication, including cross-cultural and gender-based differences in communication.

COMMUNICATION BARRIERS (NOISE)

In spite of the best intentions of sender and receiver to communicate, several barriers (called "noise" earlier in Exhibit 8.1) inhibit the effective exchange of information. One barrier is the imperfect perceptual process of both sender and receiver. As receivers, we don't listen as well as senders assume, and our needs and expectations influence what signals get noticed and ignored. We aren't any better as senders, either. Some studies suggest that we have difficulty stepping out of our own perspectives and stepping into the perspectives of others, so we overestimate how well other people understand the message we are communicating.[51]

Language issues can be huge sources of communication noise because sender and receiver might not have the same codebook. They might not speak the same language, or might have different meanings for particular words and phrases. The English language (among others) also has built-in ambiguities that cause misunderstandings. Consider the phrase "Can you close the door?" You might assume the sender is asking whether shutting the door is permitted. However, the question might be asking whether you are physically able to shut the door or whether the door is designed such that it can be shut. In fact, this question might not be a question at all; the person could be politely *telling* you to shut the door.[52]

The ambiguity of language isn't always dysfunctional noise.[53] Corporate leaders sometimes purposively use obscure language to reflect the ambiguity of the topic or to avoid unwanted emotional responses produced by more specific words. They might use metaphors to represent an abstract vision of the company's future, or use obtuse phrases such as "rightsizing" and "restructuring" to obscure the underlying message that people will be fired or laid off. One study reported that people rely on more ambiguous language when communicating with people who have different values and beliefs. In these situations, ambiguity minimizes the risk of conflict.[54]

Jargon—specialized words and phrases for specific occupations or groups—is usually designed to improve communication efficiency. However, it is a source of communication noise when transmitted to people who do not possess the jargon codebook. Furthermore, people who use jargon excessively put themselves in an unflattering light. For example, former Home Depot and Chrysler CEO Robert Nardelli announced at one news conference: "I'm blessed to have individuals with me who can take areas of responsibility and do vertical dives to really get the granularity and make sure that we're coupling horizontally across those functions so that we have a pure line of sight toward the customer." Business journalists weren't impressed, even if they did figure out what Nardelli meant.[55]

Another source of noise in the communication process is the tendency to filter messages. Filtering may involve deleting or delaying negative information or using less harsh words so the message sounds more favorable.[56] Filtering is less likely to occur when corporate leaders create a "culture of candor." This culture develops when leaders themselves communicate truthfully, seek out diverse sources for information, and protect and reward those who speak openly and truthfully.[57]

Information Overload

Start with a daily avalanche of email, then add in cell phone calls, text messages, PDF file downloads, web pages, hard copy documents, some Twitter tweets, blogs, wikis, and other sources of incoming information. Altogether, you have created a perfect recipe for **information overload**.[58] As Exhibit 8.4 illustrates, information overload occurs whenever the job's information load exceeds the individual's capacity to get through it. Employees have a certain *information-processing capacity*—the amount of information that they are able to process in a fixed unit of time. At the same time, jobs have a varying *information load*—the amount of information to be processed per unit of time. Information overload creates noise in the communication system because information gets overlooked or misinterpreted when people can't process it fast enough. The result is poorer-quality decisions as well as higher stress.[59]

Information overload problems can be minimized by increasing our information-processing capacity, reducing the job's information load, or through a combination of both. Studies suggest that employees often increase their information-processing capacity by temporarily reading faster, scanning through documents more efficiently, and removing distractions that slow information-processing speed. Time management also increases information-processing capacity. When information overload is temporary, employees can increase their information-processing capacity by

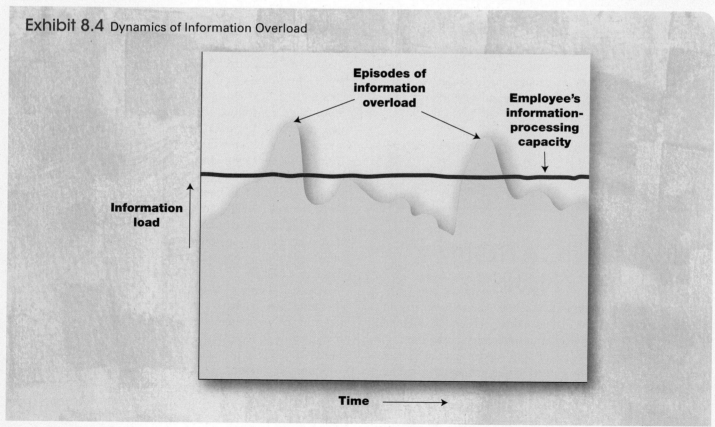

Exhibit 8.4 Dynamics of Information Overload

Episodes of information overload

Employee's information-processing capacity

Information load

Time

working longer hours. Information load can be reduced by buffering, omitting, and summarizing. Buffering involves having incoming communication filtered, usually by an assistant. Omitting occurs when we decide to overlook messages, such as using software rules to redirect emails from distribution lists to folders that we never look at. An example of summarizing would be where we read executive summaries rather than the full report.

CROSS-CULTURAL AND GENDER COMMUNICATION

Increasing globalization and cultural diversity have created more cross-cultural communication issues.[60] Voice intonation is one form of cross-cultural communication barrier. How loudly, deeply, and quickly people speak varies across cultures, and these voice intonations send secondary messages that have different meanings in different cultures.

As mentioned earlier, language is an obvious cross-cultural communication challenge. Words are easily misunderstood in verbal communication, either because the receiver has a limited vocabulary or the sender's accent distorts the usual sound of some words. In one cross-cultural seminar, for example, participants at German electronics company Siemens were reminded that a French coworker might call an event a "catastrophe" as a casual exaggeration, whereas someone in Germany usually interprets this word literally as an earth-shaking event. Similarly, KPMG staff from the United Kingdom sometimes referred to another person's suggestions as "interesting." They had to clarify to their German colleagues that "interesting" might not be complimenting the idea.[61]

Communication includes silence, but its use and meaning vary from one culture to another.[62] One study estimated that silence and pauses represented 30 percent of conversation time between Japanese doctors and patients, compared to only 8 percent of the time between American doctors and patients. Why is there more silence in Japanese conversations? One reason is that interpersonal harmony and saving face are more important in Japanese culture, and silence is a way of disagreeing without upsetting that harmony or offending the other person.[63] In addition, silence symbolizes respect and indicates that the listener is thoughtfully contemplating what has just been said.[64] Empathy is very important in Japan, and this shared understanding is demonstrated without using words. In contrast, most people in the United States and many other cultures view silence as a *lack* of communication and often interpret long breaks as a sign of disagreement.

Conversational overlaps also send different messages in different cultures. Japanese people usually stop talking when they are interrupted, whereas talking over the other person's speech is more common in Brazil, France, and some other countries. The difference in communication behavior is, again, due to interpretations. Talking while someone is speaking to you is considered quite rude in Japan, whereas Brazilians and French are more likely to interpret this as the person's interest and involvement in the conversation.

Nonverbal Differences across Cultures

Nonverbal communication represents another potential area for misunderstanding across cultures. Many nonconscious or involuntary nonverbal cues (such as smiling) have the same meaning around the world, but deliberate gestures often have different interpretations. For example, most of us shake our head from side to side to say "No," but a variation of head shaking means "I understand" to many people in India. Filipinos raise their eyebrows to give an affirmative answer, yet Arabs interpret this expression (along with clicking one's tongue) as a negative response. Most Americans are taught to maintain eye contact with the speaker to show interest and respect, whereas some North American native groups learn at an early age to show respect by looking down when an older or more senior person is talking to them.[65]

Gender Differences in Communication

Men and women have similar communication practices, but there are subtle distinctions that can occasionally lead to misunderstanding and conflict (see Exhibit 8.5).[66] One distinction is that men are more likely than women to view conversations as negotiations of relative status and power. They assert their power by directly giving advice to others (e.g., "You should do the following") and using combative language. There is also evidence that men dominate the talk time in conversations with women, as well as interrupt more and adjust their speaking style less than do women.

Men engage in more "report talk," in which the primary function of the conversation is impersonal and efficient information exchange. Women also do report talk, particularly when conversing with men, but conversations among women have a higher incidence of relationship building through "rapport talk." Women make more use of indirect requests ("Do you think you should . . ."), apologize more often, and seek advice from others more quickly than do men. Finally, research fairly consistently indicates that women are more sensitive than men to nonverbal cues in face-to-face meetings.[67] Together, these conditions can create communication conflicts. Women who describe problems get frustrated that men offer advice rather than rapport, whereas men become frustrated because they can't understand why women don't appreciate their advice.

Gender differences are also emerging in the use of social media to communicate.[68] Specifically, women are more likely

> Communication includes silence, but its use and meaning vary from one culture to another.

Exhibit 8.5 Gender Differences in Communication

When Men Communicate	When Women Communicate
• Report talk—give advice, assert power	• Rapport talk—relationship building
• Give advice directly	• Give advice indirectly
• Dominant conversation style	• Flexible conversation style
• Apologize less often	• Apologize more often
• Less sensitive to nonverbal cues	• More sensitive to nonverbal cues

to visit social networking sites like Facebook and Twitter, spend more time online, and click on more web pages than their male counterparts. Women are also more active participants in photo-sharing websites. Globally, women are outpacing men in signing up for Twitter accounts and are more active Twitter users. Their reasons for using this communication channel also differ. Women tend to use Twitter as a conversational rather than functional medium.

LO8-5 Explain how to get your message across more effectively, and summarize the elements of active listening.

IMPROVING INTERPERSONAL COMMUNICATION

Effective interpersonal communication depends on the sender's ability to get the message across and the receiver's performance as an active listener. In this section, we outline these two essential features of effective interpersonal communication.

Getting Your Message Across

This chapter began with the statement that effective communication occurs when the other person receives and understands the message. This is more difficult to accomplish than most people believe.

OB THEORY TO PRACTICE

Getting Your Message Across

Communication encoding and decoding are more effective when you:

▶ Empathize with the person receiving the message.

▶ Repeat the key points of your message a couple of times.

▶ Actively determine the best time to speak to the other person.

▶ Be descriptive by directing any negative comments toward the issue, not the person.

To get your message across to the other person, you first need to empathize with the receiver, such as being sensitive to words that may be ambiguous or trigger the wrong emotional response. Second, be sure that you repeat the message, such as by rephrasing the key points a couple of times. Third, your message competes with other messages and noise, so find a time when the receiver is less likely to be distracted by these other matters. Finally, if you are communicating bad news or criticism, focus on the problem, not the person.

Active Listening

General Electric Company (GE) recently revised its famous leadership development program to become more aligned with the cultural diversity of its employees and emerging leaders. One discovery in past programs was that U.S. managers were good at talking, but didn't always give the same priority to active listening. GE "now majors people on listening," says Susan Peters, GE's chief learning officer. "It's something we have to really work on, to equal the playing field between our American leaders and our non-American leaders."[69]

GE and other companies are increasingly recognizing that effective leadership includes active listening. Active listening is a process of mindfully sensing the sender's signals, evaluating them accurately, and responding appropriately. These three components of listening—sensing, evaluating, and responding—reflect the listener's side of the communication model described at the beginning of this chapter. Listeners receive the sender's signals, decode them as intended, and provide appropriate and timely feedback to the sender (see Exhibit 8.6). Active listeners constantly cycle through sensing, evaluating, and responding during the conversation and engage in various activities to improve these processes.[70]

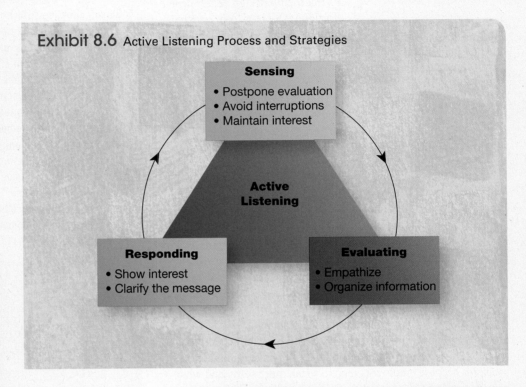

Exhibit 8.6 Active Listening Process and Strategies

Sensing
- Postpone evaluation
- Avoid interruptions
- Maintain interest

Active Listening

Responding
- Show interest
- Clarify the message

Evaluating
- Empathize
- Organize information

- *Sensing.* Sensing is the process of receiving signals from the sender and paying attention to them. Active listeners improve sensing in three ways. First, they postpone evaluation by not forming an opinion until the speaker has finished. Second, they avoid interrupting the speaker's conversation. Third, they remain motivated to listen to the speaker.

- *Evaluating.* This component of listening includes understanding the message meaning, evaluating the message, and remembering the message. To improve their evaluation of the conversation, active listeners empathize with the speaker—they try to understand and be sensitive to the speaker's feelings, thoughts, and situation. Evaluation also improves by organizing the speaker's ideas during the communication episode.

- *Responding.* This third component of listening involves providing feedback to the sender, which motivates and directs the speaker's communication. Active listeners accomplish this by maintaining sufficient eye contact and sending back channel signals (e.g., "I see"), both of which show interest. They also respond by clarifying the message—rephrasing the speaker's ideas at appropriate breaks ("So you're saying that . . . ?").

LO8-6 Summarize effective communication strategies in organizational hierarchies, and review the role and relevance of the organizational grapevine.

IMPROVING COMMUNICATION THROUGHOUT THE HIERARCHY

So far, we have focused on micro-level issues in the communication process, namely, sending and receiving information between two employees or the informal exchanges of information across several people. But in this era where knowledge is competitive advantage, corporate leaders also need to maintain an open flow of communication up, down, and across the entire organization. In this section, we discuss three organizationwide communication strategies: workspace design, Internet-based communication, and direct communication with top management.

management by walking around (MBWA)
a communication practice in which executives get out of their offices and learn from others in the organization through face-to-face dialogue

grapevine
an unstructured and informal communication network founded on social relationships rather than organizational charts or job descriptions

Workspace Design

To improve information sharing and create a more sociable work environment, Intel has torn down the cubicle walls at its microchip design center near Portland, Oregon. "We realized that we were inefficient and not as collaborative as we would have liked," acknowledges Neil Tunmore, Intel's director of corporate services. The refurbished building includes more shared space where employees set up temporary work areas. There are also more meeting rooms where employees can collaborate in private.[72]

Intel and many other companies are improving communication by redesigning the workspace and employee territorial practices in that space.[73] The location and design of hallways, offices, cubicles, and communal areas (cafeterias, elevators) all shape whom we speak to as well as the frequency of that communication. Although these open-space arrangements increase the amount of face-to-face communication, they also potentially produce more noise, distractions, and loss of privacy.[74] Employees at one eBay call center experienced too much distraction from their open-space work area, so they agreed to hush up when coworkers draped a colorful bandana on their desk lamps or around their heads.[75] Others claim that open work spaces have minimal noise problems because employees tend to speak more softly and white noise technology blocks out most voices. Still, the challenge is to increase social interaction without these stressors.

Another workspace strategy is to cloister employees into team spaces, but also encourage sufficient interaction with people from other teams. Pixar Animation Studios constructed its campus in Emeryville, California, with these principles in mind. The building encourages communication among team members. At the same time, the campus encourages happenstance interactions with people on other teams. Pixar executives call this the "bathroom effect" because team members must leave their isolated pods to fetch their mail, have lunch, or visit the restroom.[76]

Internet-Based Organizational Communication

For decades, employees received official company news through hard copy newsletters and magazines. Some firms still use these communication devices, but most have supplemented or replaced them completely with web-based sources of information. The traditional company magazine is now typically published on web pages or distributed in PDF format. The advantage of these *e-zines* is that company news can be prepared and distributed quickly.

Employees are increasingly skeptical of information that has been screened and packaged by management, so a few companies such as IBM are encouraging employees to post their own news on internal blogs and wikis. Wikis are collaborative web spaces

Welcome to the Open Office Neighborhood

GlaxoSmithKline (GSK) has transformed its traditional offices around the United States to open workspace arrangements. American employees at the London-based pharmaceutical company now work at shared tables in "neighborhoods" with coworkers in similar jobs or assigned to the same project. Electronic files stored on central servers have replaced most hard copy documents; phones are built into the laptop computers. The new work arrangement has dramatically increased face-to-face communication and cross-pollination of ideas. It also significantly reduced the amount of work space as well as email communication. However, the new work arrangements have created some problems. "There were a lot of distractions, and it was hard to stay focused," complained one GSK employee soon after moving to the company's new open-space work center in Raleigh, North Carolina (shown here).[77]

in which anyone in a group can write, edit, or remove material from the website. Wikipedia, the popular online encyclopedia, is a massive public example of a wiki. IBM's WikiCentral now hosts more than 20,000 wiki projects involving 100,000 employees. The accuracy of wikis depends on the quality of participants, but IBM experts say that errors are quickly identified by IBM's online community. Another concern is that wikis have failed to gain employee support, likely because wiki involvement takes time and the company does not reward or recognize those who provide this time to wiki development.[78]

Direct Communication with Top Management

According to various surveys, effective organizational communication includes regular interaction directly between senior executives and employees further down the hierarchy. One form of direct communication is through town hall meetings, where executives brief a large gathering of staff on the company's current strategy and results. Although the communication is mostly from executives to employees, town hall meetings are more personal and credible than video or written channels. Also, these events usually provide some opportunity for employees to ask questions. Another strategy is for senior executives to hold roundtable forums with a small representation of employees, mainly to hear their opinions on various issues. At the departmental level, some companies hold daily or weekly "huddles"—brief stand-up meetings in which staff and their managers discuss goals and hear good news stories.

A less formal approach to direct communication is **management by walking around (MBWA)**. Coined by people at Hewlett-Packard four decades ago, this is essentially the practice in which senior executives get out of their offices and casually chat with employees on a daily or regular basis. Brian Scudamore, founder and CEO of 1-800-Got-Junk?, takes MBWA one step further. "I don't have my own office, and I very often move around to different departments for a day at a time," says Scudamore.[80] These direct communication strategies potentially minimize filtering because executives listen directly to employees. They also help executives acquire a deeper meaning and quicker understanding of internal organizational problems. A third benefit of direct communication is that employees might have more empathy for decisions made further up the corporate hierarchy.

COMMUNICATING THROUGH THE GRAPEVINE

Organizational leaders may try their best to quickly communicate breaking news to employees through emails, Twitter tweets, and other direct formal channels, but employees still rely to some extent on the corporate **grapevine**. The grapevine is an unstructured and informal network founded on social relationships rather than organizational charts or job descriptions. What do employees think about the grapevine? Surveys of employees in two firms—one in Florida, the other in California—found that almost all employees use the grapevine, but very few of them prefer this source of information. The California survey also reported that only one-third of employees believe grapevine

Communicating Up and Down the Hierarchy[79]

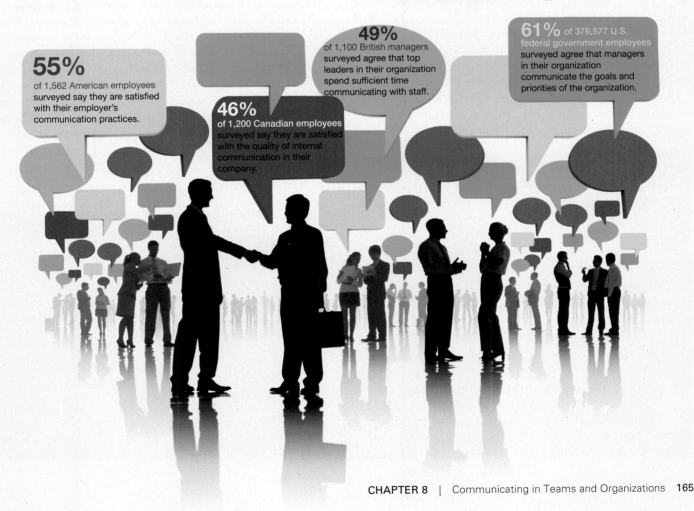

55% of 1,562 American employees surveyed say they are satisfied with their employer's communication practices.

46% of 1,200 Canadian employees surveyed say they are satisfied with the quality of internal communication in their company.

49% of 1,100 British managers surveyed agree that top leaders in their organization spend sufficient time communicating with staff.

61% of 376,577 U.S. federal government employees surveyed agree that managers in their organization communicate the goals and priorities of the organization.

information is credible. In other words, employees turn to the grapevine when they have few other options.[81]

Grapevine Characteristics

Research conducted several decades ago reported that the grapevine transmits information very rapidly in all directions throughout the organization. The typical pattern is a cluster chain, whereby a few people actively transmit rumors to many others. The grapevine works through informal social networks, so it is more active where employees have similar backgrounds and are able to communicate easily. Many rumors seem to have at least a kernel of truth, possibly because they are transmitted through media-rich communication channels (e.g., face-to-face) and employees are motivated to communicate effectively. Nevertheless, the grapevine distorts information by deleting fine details and exaggerating key points of the story.[82]

Some of these characteristics might still be true, but the grapevine almost certainly has changed as email, social networking sites, and Twitter tweets have replaced the traditional water cooler as sources of gossip. For example, several Facebook sites are unofficially themed around specific companies, allowing employees and customers to vent their complaints about the organization. Along with altering the speed and network of corporate grapevines, the Internet has expanded these networks around the globe, not just around the next cubicle.

Grapevine Benefits and Limitations

Should the grapevine be encouraged, tolerated, or quashed? The difficulty in answering this question is that the grapevine has both benefits and limitations.[83] One benefit, as was mentioned earlier, is that employees rely on the grapevine when information is not available through formal channels. It is also the main conduit through which organizational stories and other symbols of the organization's culture are communicated. A third benefit of the grapevine is that this social interaction relieves anxiety. This explains why rumor mills are most active during times of uncertainty.[84] Finally, the grapevine is associated with the drive to bond. Being a recipient of gossip is a sign of inclusion, according to evolutionary psychologists. Trying to quash the grapevine is, in some respects, an attempt to undermine the natural human drive for social interaction.[85]

While the grapevine offers these benefits, it is not a preferred communication medium. Grapevine information is sometimes so distorted that it escalates rather than reduces employee anxiety. Furthermore, employees develop more negative attitudes toward the organization when management is slower than the grapevine in communicating information. What should corporate leaders do with the grapevine? The best advice seems to be to listen to the grapevine as a signal of employee anxiety, then correct the cause of this anxiety. Some companies also listen to the grapevine and step in to correct blatant errors and fabrications. Most important, corporate leaders need to view the grapevine as a competitor and meet this challenge by directly informing employees of news before it spreads throughout the grapevine.

Study Checklist

- Did you tear out the perforated student review card at the back of the text to revisit learning objectives and key terms and definitions?

Connect® Management is available for *M Organizational Behavior.* Additional resources include:

- Interactive Applications:
  - **Case Analysis:** Apply concepts within the context of a real-world situation.
  - **Drag and Drop:** Work through an interactive example to test your knowledge of the concepts.
  - **Video Case:** See management in action through interactive videos.

- **SmartBook™**—SmartBook is the first and only adaptive reading experience available today. Distinguishing what you know from what you don't, and honing in on concepts you are most likely to forget, SmartBook personalizes content for you in a continuously adapting reading experience. Reading is no longer a passive and linear experience, but an engaging and dynamic one where you are more likely to master and retain important concepts and go to class better prepared.

9 chapter

Power and Influence in the Workplace

Learning Objectives

After studying this chapter, you should be able to:

LO9-1 Describe the dependence model of power and describe the five sources of power in organizations.

LO9-2 Discuss the four contingencies of power.

LO9-3 Explain how people and work units gain power through social networks.

LO9-4 Describe eight types of influence tactics, three consequences of influencing others, and three contingencies to consider when choosing an influence tactic.

LO9-5 Identify the organizational conditions and personal characteristics associated with organizational politics, as well as ways to minimize organizational politics.

One of the most popular topics in organizational behavior classes is about managing your boss. The theme may sound manipulative, but it is really a valuable process of gaining power and applying influence tactics for the benefit of the organization. "Managing your manager is all about going that extra step," advises photo studio director Chris Barber in Warwickshire, UK. "It doesn't mean manipulating people . . . it's about doing your job well and helping your manager to get the best results."

Managing your boss is the process of improving your relationship with your manager for the benefit of each other and the organization. Most executives say it is a key factor in everyone's career success. "It is crucial to understand how to manage your manager," says Tracey Andrews, manager of learning and development at British department store chain John Lewis. "Start by getting to know how your manager thinks and works and what his/her priorities are."[1]

There are many ways to manage your boss—or anyone else in and around organizations—such as aligning work styles, becoming a valuable resource, being solution-oriented rather than problem-oriented, and supporting their success by performing your own job well. These and other practices develop power bases and apply influence tactics that ultimately change (or stabilize) the behavior of others. These activities are not unusual. On the contrary, OB experts point out that power and influence are inherent in all organizations. They exist in every business and in every decision and action.

This chapter unfolds as follows: First, we define power and present a basic model depicting the dynamics of power in organizational settings. The chapter then discusses the five bases of power. Next, we look at the contingencies necessary to translate those sources into meaningful power. Our attention then turns to social networks and how they provide power to members through social capital. The latter part of this chapter examines the various types of influence in organizational settings as well as the contingencies of effective influence strategies. The final section of this chapter looks at situations in which influence becomes organizational politics, as well as ways of minimizing political behavior.

LO9-1 Describe the dependence model of power and describe the five sources of power in organizations.

THE MEANING OF POWER

Power is the capacity of a person, team, or organization to influence others.[2] There are a few important features of this definition. First, power is not the act of changing someone's attitudes or behavior; it is only the *potential* to do so. People frequently have power they do not use; they might not even know they have power. Second, power is based on the target's *perception* that the power holder controls (i.e., possesses, has access to, or regulates) a valuable resource that can help the target achieve his or her goals.[3] People might generate power by convincing others that they control something of value, whether or not they actually control that resource. This perception is also formed from the power holder's behavior, such as someone who is not swayed by authority or norms. For instance, one recent study found that people are perceived as more powerful just by their behavior, such as putting their feet on a table.[4] However, power is not a personal feeling of power. You might feel powerful or think you have power over others, but this is not power unless others believe you have that capacity.

power the capacity of a person, team, or organization to influence others

countervailing power the capacity of a person, team, or organization to keep a more powerful person or group in the exchange relationship

legitimate power an agreement among organizational members that people in certain roles can request certain behaviors of others

Third, power involves asymmetric (unequal) *dependence* of one party on another party.[5] This dependent relationship is illustrated in Exhibit 9.1. The line from Person B to the goal shows that he or she believes Person A controls a resource that can help or hinder Person A in achieving that goal. Person A—the power holder in this illustration—might have power over Person B by controlling a desired job assignment, useful information, rewards, or even the privilege of being associated with him or her! For example, if you believe a coworker has expertise (the resource) that would substantially help you write a better report (your goal), then that coworker has some power over you because you value that expertise to achieve your goal. Whatever the resource is, Person B is *dependent* on Person A (the power holder) to provide the resource so Person B can reach his or her goal.

Although dependence is a key element of power relationships, we use the phrase *asymmetric dependence* because the less powerful party still has some degree of power—called **countervailing power**—over the power holder. In Exhibit 9.1, Person A dominates the power relationship, but Person B has enough countervailing power to keep Person A in the exchange relationship and ensure that person or department uses its dominant power judiciously. For example, although managers have power over subordinates in many ways (e.g., controlling job security, preferred work assignments), employees have countervailing

power by possessing skills and knowledge to keep production humming and customers happy, something that management can't accomplish alone.

Finally, the power relationship depends on some minimum level of trust. Trust indicates a level of expectation that the more powerful party will deliver the resource. For example, you trust your employer to give you a paycheck at the end of each pay period. Even those in extremely dependent situations will usually walk away from the relationship if they lack a minimum level of trust in the more powerful party.

Let's look at this power dependence model in the employee–manager relationship. You depend on your boss to support your continued employment, satisfactory work arrangements, and other valued resources. At the same time, the manager depends on you to complete required tasks and to work effectively with others in the completion of their work. Managers (and the companies they represent) typically have more power, whereas employees have weaker countervailing power. But sometimes employees do have more power than their bosses in the employment relationship. Notice that the strength of your power in the employee–manager relationship doesn't depend on your actual control over valued resources; it depends on the perceptions that your boss and others have about your control of these resources. Finally, trust is an essential ingredient in this relationship. Even with strong power, the employee–manager relationship comes apart when one party no longer sufficiently trusts the other.

The dependence model reveals only the core features of power dynamics between people and work units in organizations. We also need to learn about the specific sources of power and contingencies that effectively convert power into influence. As Exhibit 9.2 illustrates, power is derived from five sources: legitimate, reward, coercive, expert, and referent.

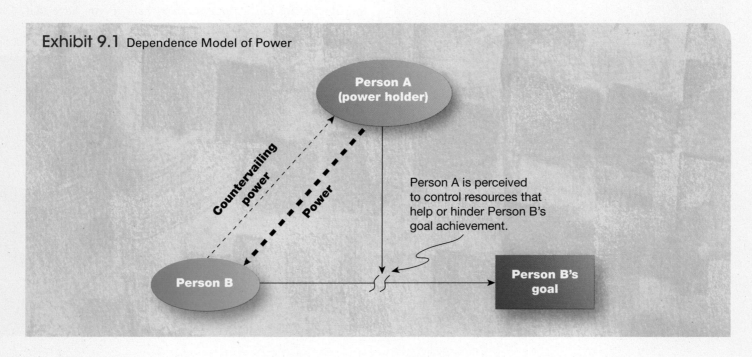

Exhibit 9.1 Dependence Model of Power

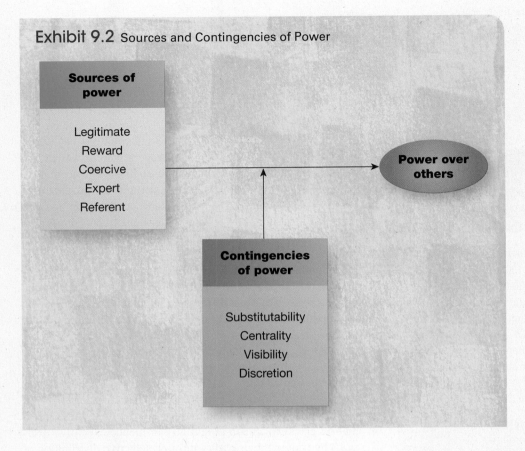

Exhibit 9.2 Sources and Contingencies of Power

Sources of power

Legitimate
Reward
Coercive
Expert
Referent

Power over others

Contingencies of power

Substitutability
Centrality
Visibility
Discretion

The model also identifies four contingencies of power: the employee's or department's substitutability, centrality, discretion, and visibility. Over the next few pages, we will discuss each of these sources and contingencies of power in the context of organizations.

SOURCES OF POWER IN ORGANIZATIONS

A half century ago, social scientists John French and Bertram Raven identified five sources of power found in organizations. Although variations of this list have been proposed over the years, the original list remains surprisingly intact.[6] Three sources of power—legitimate, reward, and coercive—originate mostly (but not completely) from the power holder's formal position or informal role. In other words, the person is granted these sources of power formally by the organization or informally by coworkers. Two other sources of power—expert and referent—originate mainly from the power holder's own characteristics; in other words, people carry these power bases around with them. However,

> Legitimate power gives the power holder only the right to ask others to perform a limited domain of behaviors.

even personal sources of power are not completely within the person because they depend on how others perceive them.

Legitimate Power

Legitimate power is an agreement among organizational members that people in certain roles can request a set of behaviors from others. This perceived right or obligation originates from formal job descriptions as well as informal rules of conduct. The most obvious example of legitimate power is a manager's right to tell employees what tasks to perform, whom to work with, what office resources they can use, and so forth. Employees follow the boss's requests because there is mutual agreement that employees will follow a range of directives from people in these positions of authority. Employees defer to this authority whether or not they will be rewarded or punished for complying with those requests.

Notice that legitimate power has restrictions; it gives the power holder only the right to ask others to perform a limited domain of behaviors. This domain—known as the "zone of indifference"—is the set of behaviors that individuals are willing to engage in at the other person's request.[7] Although most employees accept the boss's right to deny them access to Facebook during company time, some might draw the line when the boss asks them to work several hours beyond the regular workday.

The size of the zone of indifference (and, consequently, the magnitude of legitimate power) increases with the level of trust in the power holder. Some values and personality traits also make people more obedient to authority. Those who value conformity and tradition as well as have high power distance (i.e., they accept an unequal distribution of power) tend to have higher deference to authority. The organization's culture represents another influence on the willingness of employees to follow orders. A 3M scientist might continue to work on a project after being told by superiors to stop working on it because the 3M culture supports an entrepreneurial spirit, which includes ignoring your boss's authority from time to time.[8]

Managers are not the only people with legitimate power in organizations. Employees also have legitimate power over their bosses and coworkers through legal

reciprocity is a form of legitimate power because it is an informal rule of conduct that we are expected to follow.

Legitimate Power through Information Control

A particularly potent form of legitimate power occurs where people have the right to control the information that others receive.[13] These information gatekeepers gain power in two ways. First, information is a resource, so those who need information are dependent on the gatekeeper to provide that resource. For example, the map department of a mining company has incredible power when other departments are dependent on the map department to deliver maps required for exploration projects.

Second, information gatekeepers gain power by selectively distributing information so those receiving the information perceive the situation differently.[14] Executives depend on middle managers and employees to provide an accurate picture of the company's operations. Yet, as we learned in the previous chapter on communication, information is often filtered as it flows up the hierarchy. Middle managers and employees filter information so it puts them in a more positive light and allows them to steer the executive team toward one decision rather than another. In other words, these information gatekeepers can potentially influence executive decisions by framing their reality through selective distribution of information.

Reward Power

Reward power is derived from the person's ability to control the allocation of rewards valued by others and to remove negative sanctions (i.e., negative reinforcement). Managers have formal authority that gives them power over the distribution of organizational rewards such as pay, promotions, time off, vacation schedules, and work assignments. Employees also have reward power over their bosses through their feedback and ratings in 360-degree feedback systems. These ratings affect supervisors' promotions and other rewards, so supervisors tend to pay more attention to employee needs after 360-degree feedback is introduced.

Legitimate Power Takes People to the Extreme

A French television program revealed how far people are willing to follow orders. As a variation of the 1960s experiments conducted by Stanley Milgram, 80 contestants administered electric shocks whenever a volunteer (an actor who didn't receive the shocks at all) answered a question incorrectly. Shocks increased in 20-volt increments, from 20 volts for the first mistake through to 460 volts. Contestants often hesitated after hearing the volunteer screaming for them to stop, yet continued the shocks after the host reminded them of their duty. Only 16 of the 80 contestants refused to administer the strongest shocks.[9]

and administrative rights as well as informal norms.[10] For example, an organization might give employees the right to request information that is required for their job. Laws give employees the right to refuse to work in unsafe conditions. Subtler forms of legitimate power also exist. Human beings have a **norm of reciprocity**—a feeling of obligation to help someone who has helped you.[11] If a coworker previously helped you handle a difficult client, that coworker has power because you feel an obligation to help the coworker on something of similar value in the future. The norm of

> "Unthinking respect for authority is the greatest enemy of truth."[12]
>
> —**Albert Einstein,**
> theoretical physicist

Coercive Power

Coercive power is the ability to apply punishment. For many of us, the first thought is managers threatening employees with dismissal. Yet, employees also have coercive power, such as being sarcastic toward coworkers or threatening to ostracize them if they fail to conform to team norms.[15] Many firms rely on this coercive power to control coworker behavior in team settings. Nucor is one such example: "If you're not contributing with the team, they certainly will let you know about it," says an executive at the Charlotte, North Carolina, steelmaker. "The few poor players get weeded out by their peers."[16]

Expert Power

For the most part, legitimate, reward, and coercive power originate from the position.[17] Expert power, on the other hand, originates mainly from within the power holder. It is an individual's or work unit's capacity to influence others by possessing knowledge or skills valued by others. One important form of expert power is the perceived ability to manage uncertainties in the business environment. Organizations are more effective when they operate in predictable environments, so they value people who can cope with turbulence in consumer trends, societal changes, unstable supply lines, and so forth. Expertise can help companies cope with uncertainty in three ways. These coping strategies are arranged in a hierarchy of importance, with prevention being the most powerful:[18]

- *Prevention*—The most effective strategy is to prevent environmental changes from occurring. For example, financial experts acquire power by preventing the organization from experiencing a cash shortage or defaulting on loans.

- *Forecasting*—The next best strategy is to predict environmental changes or variations. In this respect, trendspotters and other marketing specialists gain power by predicting changes in consumer preferences.

- *Absorption*—People and work units also gain power by absorbing or neutralizing the impact of environmental shifts as they occur. An example is the ability of maintenance crews to come to the rescue when machines break down.

Many people respond to expertise just as they respond to authority—they mindlessly follow the guidance of these experts.[19] In one classic study, for example, a researcher posing as a hospital physician telephoned on-duty nurses to prescribe a specific dosage of medicine to a hospitalized patient. None of

the nurses knew the person calling, and hospital policy forbade them from accepting treatment by telephone (i.e., they lacked legitimate power). Furthermore, the medication was unauthorized and the prescription was twice the maximum daily dose. Yet, almost all 22 nurses who received the telephone call followed the "doctor's" orders until stopped by researchers.[20]

This doctor–nurse study is a few decades old, but the power of expertise remains just as strong today, sometimes with tragic consequences. Not long ago, the Canadian justice system discovered that one of its "star" expert witnesses—a forensic child pathology expert—had provided inaccurate cause of death evaluations in at least 20 cases, a dozen of which resulted in wrongful or highly questionable criminal convictions. The pathologist's reputation as a renowned authority was the main reason why his often-weak evidence was accepted without question. "Experts in a courtroom—we give great deference to experts," admits a Canadian defense lawyer familiar with this situation.[21]

Referent Power

People have **referent power** when others identify with them, like them, or otherwise respect them. As with expert power, referent power originates within the power holder. It is largely a function of the person's interpersonal skills. Referent power is also associated with **charisma**. Experts have difficulty agreeing on the meaning of charisma, but it is most often described as a form of interpersonal attraction whereby followers ascribe almost magical powers to the charismatic individual.[22] Some writers describe charisma as a special "gift" or trait within the charismatic person, while others say it is mainly in the eyes of the beholder. However, all agree that charisma produces a high degree of trust, respect, and devotion toward the charismatic individual.

LO9-2 Discuss the four contingencies of power.

CONTINGENCIES OF POWER

Let's say that you have expert power because of your ability to forecast and possibly even prevent dramatic changes in the organization's environment. Does this expertise mean that you are influential? Not necessarily. As was illustrated earlier in Exhibit 9.2, sources of power generate power only under certain conditions. Four important contingencies of power are substitutability, centrality, visibility, and discretion.[23]

Substitutability

Substitutability refers to the availability of alternatives. Power is strongest when someone has a monopoly over a valued

substitutability
a contingency of power
pertaining to the availability
of alternatives

resource. Conversely, power decreases as the number of alternative sources of the critical resource increases. If you—and no one else—has expertise across the organization on an important issue, you would be more powerful than if several people in your company possess this valued knowledge. Substitutability refers not only to other sources that offer the resource, but also to substitutions of the resource itself. For instance, labor unions are weakened when companies introduce technologies that replace the need for their union members. Technology is a substitute for employees and, consequently, reduces union power.

Nonsubstitutability is strengthened by controlling access to the resource. Professions and labor unions gain power by controlling knowledge, tasks, or labor to perform important activities. For instance, the medical profession is powerful because it controls who can perform specific medical procedures. Labor unions that dominate an industry effectively control access to labor needed to perform key jobs. Employees become nonsubstitutable when they possess knowledge (such as operating equipment or serving clients) that is not documented or readily available to others.

Nonsubstitutability also occurs when people differentiate their resource from the alternatives. We should all do this when developing our personal brand. Our public image and reputation should be authentic (who we really are and what we can deliver), but it also needs to be unique and valuable, which leverages the power of nonsubstitutability. "Be unique about something. Be a specialist in something. Be known for something. Drive something," advises Barry Salzberg, global chief executive of Deloitte Touche Tohmatsu Limited. "That's very, very important for success in leadership because there are so many highly talented people. What's different about you—that's your personal brand."[24]

Centrality

Centrality refers to the power holder's importance based on the degree and nature of interdependence with others.[26] Centrality increases with the number of people dependent on you as well as how quickly and severely they are affected by that dependence. Think about your own centrality for a moment: If you decided not to show up for work or school tomorrow, how many people would have difficulty performing their jobs because of your absence? How soon after they arrive at work would these coworkers notice that you are missing and have to adjust their tasks and work schedule as a result? If you have high centrality, many people in the organization would be adversely affected by your absence, and they would be affected quickly.

The power of centrality is apparent in well-timed labor union strikes, such as the New York City transit strike during the busy Christmas shopping season a few years ago. The illegal three-day work stoppage immediately clogged roads and prevented half of city workers from getting to work on time. "[The Metropolitan Transit Authority] told us we got no power, but we got power," said one striking transit worker. "We got the power to stop the city."[27]

Visibility

Lucy Shadbolt and her team members work from home and other remote locations for most of their workweek. While the manager of British Gas New Energy enjoys this freedom, she also knows that working remotely can be a career liability due to the lack of visibility. "When I go into the office, where we hot-desk, I have to make an effort to position myself near my boss," says Shadbolt. "You need to consciously build relationships when you don't have those water-cooler moments naturally occurring."[28]

Lucy Shadbolt recognizes that power does not flow to unknown people in the organization. Instead, employees gain

Developing Your Personal Brand DNA

James Davidson has read too many résumés that are so nondescript they could have been sent by almost any accounting student to any company in that industry. "It's bland, generic, blah.... If their brand isn't pronounced, I'm afraid they end up in the 'no' pile," says the senior manager of campus talent acquisition at PricewaterhouseCoopers. Your personal brand begins with your DNA (distinct and notable attributes)—a talent or expertise that is both valuable *and* unique, which gives you power through nonsubstitutability. As Davidson explains: "It's your unique promise of value; what you can bring to an organization. It needs to be authentic, different and memorable."[25]

THE POWER OF SOCIAL NETWORKS

"It's not what you know, but who you know that counts!" This often-heard statement reflects the idea that employees get ahead not just by developing their competencies, but by locating themselves within **social networks**—social structures of individuals or social units (e.g., departments, organizations) that are connected to each other through one or more forms of interdependence.[31] Some networks are held together due to common interests, such as when employees who love fancy cars spend more time together. Other networks form around common status, expertise, kinship, or physical proximity. For instance, employees are more likely to form networks with coworkers who have common educational backgrounds and occupational interests.[32]

Social networks exist everywhere because people have a drive to bond. However, there are cultural differences in the norms of active network involvement. Several writers suggest that social networking is more of a central life activity in Asian cultures that emphasize *Guanxi*, a Chinese term referring to an individual's network of social connections. Guanxi is an expressive activity because being part of a close-knit network of family and friends reinforces one's self-concept. Guanxi is also an instrumental activity because it is a strategy for receiving favors and opportunities from others. People across all cultures rely on social networks for both expressive and instrumental purposes, but these activities seem to be somewhat more explicit in Confucian cultures.[33]

Social Capital and Sources of Power

Social networks generate power through **social capital**—the goodwill and resulting resources shared among members in a

power when their talents remain in the forefront of the minds of their boss, coworkers, and others. In other words, power increases with your visibility. This visibility can occur, for example, by taking on people-oriented jobs and projects that require frequent interaction with senior executives.

Employees also gain visibility by being, quite literally, visible. Some people (such as Lucy Shadbolt) strategically locate themselves in more visible work areas, such as those closest to the boss or where other employees frequently pass by. People often use public symbols as subtle (and not-so-subtle) cues to make their power sources known to others. Many professionals display their educational diplomas and awards on office walls to remind visitors of their expertise. Medical professionals wear white coats with stethoscopes around their necks to symbolize their legitimate and expert power in hospital settings. Other people play the game of "face time"—spending more time at work and showing that they are working productively.

Discretion

The freedom to exercise judgment—to make decisions without referring to a specific rule or receiving permission from someone else—is another important contingency of power in organizations.[29] Consider the *lack* of power of many first-line supervisors. They may have legitimate, reward, and coercive power over employees, but this power is often curtailed by specific rules that supervisors must follow to use their power bases.[30]

social network.[34] Social networks produce trust, support, sympathy, forgiveness, and similar forms of goodwill among network members, and this goodwill motivates and enables network members to share resources with each other.[35]

Social networks offer a variety of resources, each of which potentially enhances the power of its members. Probably the best-known resource is information from other network members, which improves the individual's expert power.[36] The goodwill of social capital opens communication pipelines among those within the network. Network members receive valuable knowledge more easily and more quickly from fellow network members than do people outside that network.[37] With better information access and timeliness, members have more power because their expertise is a scarce resource; it is not widely available to people outside the network.

Increased visibility is a second contributor to a person's power through social networks. When asked to recommend someone for valued positions, other network members more readily think of you than people outside the network. Similarly, they are more likely to mention your name when asked to identify people with expertise in your areas of knowledge.

A third resource from social networks is increased referent power. People tend to gain referent power through networking because members of the network identify with or at least have greater trust in each other. Referent power is also apparent by the fact that reciprocity increases among network members as they become more embedded in the network.[38]

A common misperception is that social networks are free spirits that cannot be orchestrated by corporate leaders. In reality, company structures and practices can shape these networks to some extent.[39] But even if organizational leaders don't try to manage social networks, they need to be aware of them. Indeed, people gain power in organizations by knowing what the social networks around them look like.[40]

Gaining Power through Social Networks

How do individuals (and teams and organizations) gain the most social capital from social networks? To answer this question, we need to consider the number, depth, variety, and centrality of connections that people have in their networks.

OB THEORY TO PRACTICE

Introverts Can Be Effective Networkers, Too![41]

Networking requires communication and the confidence to introduce yourself to strangers. These practices come more naturally to extraverts, but networking experts say that introverts can also be good at networking. Here's how:

Networking is about listening, not just talking. Networking is two-way communication, which means that you need to listen to and develop empathy with others in your network. Introverts have a stronger preference than extraverts to listen, so it is an advantage they can use. Good listeners more quickly identify the needs of people they meet and therefore are more likely to convey information of value to others in the network.

Networking is personal, not mass production. People make the mistake of believing that they need to "work the room" by introducing themselves to as many people as possible. But networking is about personal relationships, so it's fine to meet only a handful of people at a particular event. That deeper interaction could produce clearer understanding of the potential relationship and the means to strengthen that relationship.

Network rejection is about misalignment, not personal fault. Some people you meet don't want to continue the conversation. Introverts take these networking failures more personally than do extraverts, who just move on to the next social opportunity. While we always need to reflect and learn from life's events, introverts in particular need to recognize that social interaction rejections are usually misalignments of interests, not evidence of a personal fault.

Networking is a skill, not a personality trait. Introversion is a preference and behavioral tendency, not an innate lack of ability to interact with other people. Some very notable public speakers, politicians, and business leaders are very good at intense social interaction because they have developed appropriate skills and knowledge. While introverts might not enjoy social interaction as much as do extraverts, they can learn how to effectively meet strangers and form initial social bonds that lead to network relationships.

Networking is (partly) online, not just face-to-face. The Internet has created the best of both worlds for introverts. They can engage in effective networking without the stress or awkwardness of social interaction. At the same time, introverts can't always hide behind an Internet connection. Networking ultimately thrives on plenty of face-to-face interaction, not just emails, text messaging, and social media links. "People remember faces and conversations more than the written word," advises the CEO of a career services company.

Networking can be structured, to some extent. Some experts suggest that networking isn't completely impromptu conversation. This is good news for introverts because they prefer structured social interaction. Before meeting people, introverts can think about specific questions to ask, practice ways to deliver those questions casually (not as an wooden interviewer), and practice answers to common questions that others will ask. And when someone does ask an unexpected question, a short answer can be fine when followed by asking that question or another one back to the other person.

Strong Ties, Weak Ties, Many Ties The volume of information, favors, and other social capital that people receive from networks usually increases with the number of people connected to them. Some people have an amazing capacity to maintain their connectivity with many people, and emerging communication technologies (Facebook, LinkedIn, etc.) have further amplified this capacity to maintain these numerous connections.[42] At the same time, the more people you know, the less time and energy you have to form "strong ties." Strong ties are close-knit relationships, which are evident from how often we interact with people, how much we share resources with them, and whether we have multiple- or single-purpose relationships with them (e.g., friend, coworker, sports partner). The main advantages of having strong ties are that they offer resources more quickly and sometimes more plentifully than are available from weak ties (i.e., acquaintances).

Some minimal connection strength is necessary to remain in any social network, but strong connections aren't necessarily the most valuable ties. Instead, having weak ties (i.e., being merely acquaintances) with people from diverse networks can be more valuable than having strong ties

(i.e., having close friendships) with people in similar networks.[43] Why is this so? Strong ties—our close-knit circle of friends—tend to be similar to us, and similar people tend to have the same information and connections that we already have.[44] Weak ties, on the other hand, are acquaintances who are usually different from us and therefore offer resources we do not possess. Furthermore, by serving as a "bridge" across several unrelated networks, we receive unique resources from each network rather than more of the same resources.

The strength of weak ties is most apparent in job hunting and career development.[45] People with diverse networks tend to be more successful job seekers because they have a wider net to catch new job opportunities. In contrast, people who belong to similar overlapping networks tend to receive fewer leads, many of which they already knew about. As careers require more movement across many organizations and industries, you need to establish connections with people across a diverse range of industries, professions, and other spheres of life.

Social Network Centrality Earlier in this chapter, we explained that centrality is an important contingency of power. This contingency also applies to social networks.[46] The more central a person (or team or organization) is located in the network, the more social capital and therefore more power he or she acquires. Centrality is your importance in that network.

Three factors determine your centrality in a social network. One factor is your "betweenness," which literally refers to how much you are located between others in the network. In Exhibit 9.3, Person A has high betweenness centrality because he or she is a gatekeeper who controls the flow of information to and from many other people in the network. Person G has less betweenness, whereas Person F and several other network

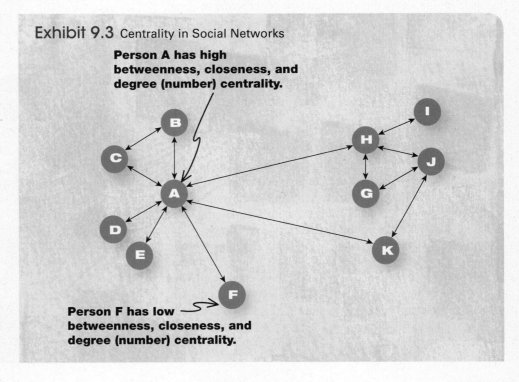

Exhibit 9.3 Centrality in Social Networks

Person A has high betweenness, closeness, and degree (number) centrality.

Person F has low betweenness, closeness, and degree (number) centrality.

members in the diagram have no betweenness. The more betweenness you have, the more you control the distribution of information and other resources to people on either side of you.

A second factor in centrality is the number or percentage of connections you have to others in the network (called *degree centrality*). Recall that the more people connected to you, the more resources (information, favors, etc.) will be available. The number of connections also increases centrality because you are more visible to other members of the network. Although being a member of a network gives you access to resources in that network, having a direct connection to people makes that resource sharing more fluid.

A third factor in centrality is the "closeness" of the relationship with others in the network. High closeness refers to strong ties. It is depicted by shorter, more direct, and efficient paths or connections with others in the network. For example, Person A has fairly high closeness centrality because he or she has direct paths to most of the network, and many of these paths are short (implying efficient and high-quality communication links). Your centrality increases with the closeness with others because they are affected more quickly and significantly by you.

One last observation is that Exhibit 9.3 illustrates two clusters of people in the network. The gap between these two clusters is called a **structural hole**.[47] Notice that Person A provides the main bridge across this structural hole (connecting to H and K in the other cluster). This bridging role gives Person A additional power in the network. By bridging this gap, Person A becomes a broker—someone who connects two independent networks and controls information flow between them. Research shows that the more brokering relationships you have, the more likely you are to get early promotions and higher pay.

The Dark Side of Social Networks Social networks are natural elements of all organizations, yet they can create a formidable barrier to those who are not actively connected to it.[48] Women are often excluded from informal management networks because they do not participate in golf games and other male-dominated social events. Several years ago, executives at Deloitte Touche Tohmatsu discovered that inaccessibility to powerful social networks partly explained why many junior female employees left the accounting and consulting firm before reaching partnership level. The global accounting and consulting firm now relies on mentoring, formal women's network groups, and measurement of career progress to ensure that female staff members have the same career development opportunities as their male colleagues.[49]

CONSEQUENCES OF POWER

How does power affect the power holder? The answer depends to some extent on the type of power.[50] When people feel empowered (high self-determination, meaning, competence, and impact), they believe they have power over themselves and freedom from being influenced by others. Empowerment tends to increase motivation, job satisfaction, organizational commitment, and job performance. However, this feeling of being in control and free from others' authority also increases automatic rather than mindful thinking. In particular, people who feel powerful usually are more likely to rely on stereotypes, have difficulty empathizing, and generally have less accurate perceptions compared with people who have less power.[51]

The other type of power is one in which an individual has power *over others*, such as the legitimate, reward, and coercive power that managers have over employees in the workplace. This type of power produces a sense of duty or responsibility for the people over whom the power holder has authority. Consequently, people who have power over others tend to be more mindful of their actions and engage in less stereotyping.

LO9-4 Describe eight types of influence tactics, three consequences of influencing others, and three contingencies to consider when choosing an influence tactic.

INFLUENCING OTHERS

So far, this chapter has focused on the sources and contingencies of power as well as power derived from social networks. But power is only the *capacity* to influence others. It represents the

potential to change someone's attitudes and behavior. **Influence**, on the other hand, refers to any behavior that attempts to alter someone's attitudes or behavior.[52] Influence is power in motion. It applies one or more sources of power to get people to alter their beliefs, feelings, and activities. Consequently, our interest in the remainder of this chapter is on how people use power to influence others.

Influence tactics are woven throughout the social fabric of all organizations. This is because influence is an essential process through which people coordinate their effort and act in concert to achieve organizational objectives. Indeed, influence is central to the definition of leadership. Influence operates down, across, and up the corporate hierarchy. Executives ensure that subordinates complete required tasks. Employees influence coworkers to help them with their job assignments.

Types of Influence Tactics

Organizational behavior researchers have devoted considerable attention to the various types of influence tactics found in organizational settings. They do not agree on a definitive list, but the most commonly discussed influence tactics are identified in Exhibit 9.4 and described over the next few pages.[53] The first five are known as "hard" influence tactics because they force behavior change through position power (legitimate, reward, and coercion). The latter three—persuasion, impression management, and exchange—are called "soft" tactics because they rely more on personal sources of power (referent, expert) and appeal to the target person's attitudes and needs.

Silent Authority The silent application of authority occurs someone complies with a request because of the requester's legitimate power as well as the target person's role expectations.[55]

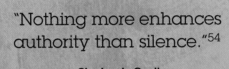

"Nothing more enhances authority than silence."[54]

—Charles de Gaulle,
French president and military leader

This deference occurs when you comply with your boss's request to complete a particular task. If the task is within your job scope and your boss has the right to make this request, then this influence strategy operates without negotiation, threats, persuasion, or other tactics. Silent authority is the most common form of influence in high power distance cultures.[56]

Assertiveness Assertiveness might be called "vocal authority" because it involves actively applying legitimate and coercive power to influence others. This includes persistently reminding the target of his or her obligations, frequently checking the target's work, confronting the target, and using threats of sanctions to force compliance. Workplace bullying is an extreme form of assertiveness because it involves explicit threats of punishment.

Information Control Earlier in this chapter we explained that people with centrality in social networks have the power to control information. This power translates into influence when the power holder selectively distributes information such that it reframes the situation and causes others to change their attitudes and/or behavior. Controlling information might include withholding information that is more critical or favorable, or distributing information to some people but not to others. According to one major survey, almost half of employees believe coworkers keep others in the dark about work issues if it helps their own cause. Another study found that CEOs influence their board of directors by selectively feeding and withholding information.[57]

Coalition Formation When people lack sufficient power alone to influence others in the organization, they might form a **coalition** of people who support the proposed change.

Exhibit 9.4 Types of Influence Tactics in Organizations

Influence Tactic	Description
Silent authority	Influencing behavior through legitimate power without explicitly referring to that power base.
Assertiveness	Actively applying legitimate and coercive power by applying pressure or threats.
Information control	Explicitly manipulating someone else's access to information for the purpose of changing their attitudes and/or behavior.
Coalition formation	Forming a group that attempts to influence others by pooling the resources and power of its members.
Upward appeal	Relying symbolically or in reality on people with higher authority or expertise to support our position.
Persuasion	Using logical arguments, factual evidence, and emotional appeals to convince people of the value of a request.
Impression management (including ingratiation)	Actively shaping, through self-presentation and other means, the perceptions and attitudes that others have of us. Includes ingratiation, which refers to the influencer's attempt to be more liked by the targeted person or group.
Exchange	Promising benefits or resources in exchange for the target person's compliance.

A coalition is influential in three ways.[58] First, it pools the power and resources of many people, so the coalition potentially has more influence than any number of people operating alone. Second, the coalition's mere existence can be a source of power by symbolizing the legitimacy of the issue. In other words, a coalition creates a sense that the issue deserves attention because it has broad support. Third, coalitions tap into the power of the social identity process introduced in Chapter 3. A coalition is an informal group that advocates a new set of norms and behaviors. If the coalition has a broad-based membership (i.e., its members come from various parts of the organization), then other employees are more likely to identify with that group and, consequently, accept the ideas the coalition is proposing.

Upward Appeal **Upward appeal** involves calling on higher authority or expertise, or symbolically relying on these sources to support the influencer's position. It occurs when someone says "The boss likely agrees with me on this matter; let's find out!" Upward appeal also occurs when relying on the authority of the firm's policies or values. By reminding others that your request is consistent with the organization's overarching goals, you are implying support from senior executives without formally involving them.

Persuasion **Persuasion** is one of the most effective influence strategies for career success. The ability to present facts, logical arguments, and emotional appeals to change another person's attitudes and behavior is not just an acceptable way to influence others; in many societies, it is a noble art and a quality of effective leaders. The effectiveness of persuasion as an influence tactic depends on characteristics of the persuader, message content, communication medium, and the audience being persuaded (see Exhibit 9.5).[60] People are more persuasive when listeners believe they have expertise and credibility, such as when the persuader does not seem to profit from the persuasion attempt and states a few points against the position.

The message is more important than the messenger when the issue is important to the audience. Persuasive message content acknowledges several points of view so the audience does not feel cornered by the speaker. The message should also be limited to a few strong arguments, which are repeated a few times, but not too frequently. The message should use emotional appeals (such as graphically showing the unfortunate consequences of a bad decision), but only in combination with logical arguments and specific recommendations to overcome the threat. Finally, message content is more persuasive when the audience is warned about opposing arguments. This **inoculation effect** causes listeners to generate counterarguments to the anticipated persuasion attempts, which makes the opponent's subsequent persuasion attempts less effective.[61]

Two other considerations when persuading people are the medium of communication and

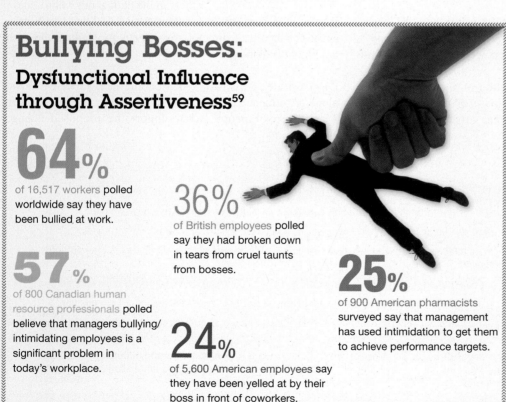

Bullying Bosses:
Dysfunctional Influence through Assertiveness[59]

64%
of 16,517 workers polled worldwide say they have been bullied at work.

57%
of 800 Canadian human resource professionals polled believe that managers bullying/intimidating employees is a significant problem in today's workplace.

36%
of British employees polled say they had broken down in tears from cruel taunts from bosses.

24%
of 5,600 American employees say they have been yelled at by their boss in front of coworkers.

25%
of 900 American pharmacists surveyed say that management has used intimidation to get them to achieve performance targets.

Exhibit 9.5 Elements of Persuasion

Persuasion Element	Characteristics of Effective Persuasion
Persuader characteristics	• Expertise • Credibility • No apparent profit motive • Appears somewhat neutral (acknowledges benefits of the opposing view)
Message content	• Multiple viewpoints (not exclusively supporting the preferred option) • Limited to a few strong arguments (not many arguments) • Repeat arguments, but not excessively • Use emotional appeals in combination with logical arguments • Offer specific solutions to overcome the stated problems • Inoculation effect—audience warned of counterarguments that opposition will present
Communication medium	• Media-rich channels are usually more persuasive
Audience characteristics	Persuasion is less effective when the audience: • has higher self-esteem • has higher intelligence • has a self-concept tied to an opposing position

characteristics of the audience. Generally, persuasion works best in face-to-face conversations and through other media-rich communication channels. The personal nature of face-to-face communication increases the persuader's credibility, and the richness of this channel provides faster feedback that the influence strategy is working. With respect to audience characteristics, it is more difficult to persuade people who have high self-esteem and intelligence, as well as a self-concept that is strongly tied to the opposing viewpoint.[62]

Impression Management (Including Ingratiation)
Silent authority, assertiveness, information control, coalitions, and upward appeals are somewhat (or very!) forceful ways to

influence other people. In contrast, a very soft influence tactic is **impression management**—actively shaping the perceptions and attitudes that others have of us.[63] Impression management mostly occurs through self-presentation. We craft our public images to communicate an identity, such as being important, vulnerable, threatening, or pleasant. For the most part, employees routinely engage in pleasant impression management behaviors to satisfy the basic norms of social behavior, such as the way they dress and how they behave toward colleagues and customers.

Impression management is a common strategy for people trying to get ahead in the workplace. In fact, career professionals encourage people to develop a personal "brand"; that is, to form and display an (accurate) impression of their own distinctive, competitive advantage.[64] Furthermore, people who master the art of personal branding rely on impression management through distinctive personal characteristics such as black shirts, tinted hair, or unique signatures. "In today's economy, your personal brand is being judged every day," says Coca-Cola senior vice president Jerry Wilson. "Either position yourself, or others will position you."[65]

One subcategory of impression management is *ingratiation*, which is any attempt to increase liking by, or perceived similarity to, some targeted person.[66] Ingratiation comes in several flavors. Employees might flatter their boss in front of others, demonstrate that they have similar attitudes as their boss (e.g., agreeing with the boss's proposal), or ask their boss for advice. Ingratiation is one of the more effective influence tactics at boosting a person's career success (i.e., performance

Impression Management in Job Interviews[67]

Interviewer Question	Impression Management Principle	Do Say . . .	Don't Say . . .
What interests you about this job?	Demonstrate your interest in and respect for this company by seeking a specific job or career here.	"There are exciting things happening at this company, and this position would be a great way for me to grow my skills."	"Well, I just need a job, and this place looks as good as any to find one."
What are your greatest weaknesses?	Demonstrate honesty, self-awareness, and an ability to develop yourself.	"Sometimes I take on more tasks than I should. I need to learn how to delegate more for better workload balance and to give others opportunities to develop their skills."	"Gee, I really don't have any weaknesses. I'm a model employee."
Why did you leave your last job?	Demonstrate that you are a positive forward-thinker who values this company's career opportunities. Avoid dwelling on negative past events.	"I have a goal to become head of marketing someday. The experience and new skills I would gain here look like an excellent fit with that aspiration."	"Working in my last job was like being on the *Titanic*. Also, I didn't like my boss. He always wanted me to work late, and it caused me to miss my favorite TV show a few times."
Describe a situation in which you had to deal with a professional disagreement or conflict.	Demonstrate that you are a good team player who is diplomatic at conflict handling and problem solving.	"My coworker and I once disagreed on (describe situation). We discussed our different methods and came up with a better way that combined the best of each of our methods."	"I've never had a disagreement. Everyone tends to know I'm right."
How many times do a clock's hands overlap in a day?	These unusual problem-solving questions test more than your technical skills; they also test your motivation and can-do attitude toward solving problems.	"Let's see, there are 24 hours in a day and every time on the clock happens twice, so . . ."	"Gosh, I have no idea. I'm not that good at math."

appraisal feedback, salaries, and promotions).[68] However, people who engage in high levels of ingratiation are less (not more) influential and less likely to get promoted.[69] Why the opposite effect? Those who engage in too much ingratiation are viewed as insincere and self-serving. The terms *apple polishing* and *brown-nosing* are applied to those who ingratiate to excess or in ways that suggest selfish motives for the ingratiation.

Exchange Exchange activities involve the promise of benefits or resources in exchange for the target person's compliance with your request. Negotiation is an integral part of exchange influence activities. For instance, you might negotiate with your boss for a day off in return for working a less desirable shift at a future date. Exchange also includes applying the norm of reciprocity that we described earlier, such as reminding the target of

past benefits or favors with the expectation that the target will now make up for that debt. Earlier in this chapter we explained how people gain power through social networks. They also use norms of reciprocity to influence others in the network. Active networkers build up "exchange credits" by helping colleagues in the short term for reciprocal benefits in the long term.

Consequences and Contingencies of Influence Tactics

Faced with a variety of influence strategies, you are probably asking: Which ones are best? To answer this question, we first need to describe how people react when others try to influence them: resistance, compliance, or commitment (see Exhibit 9.6).[70] *Resistance* occurs when people or work units

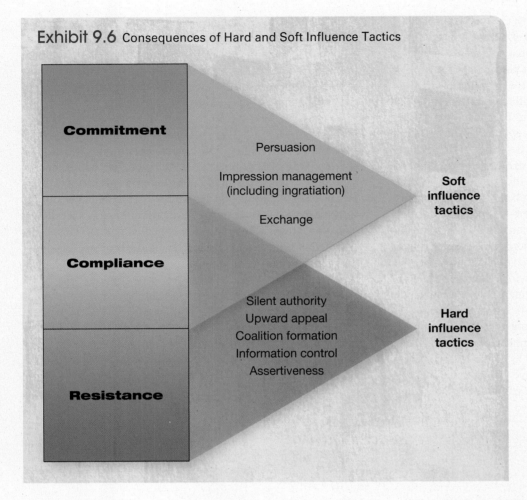

Exhibit 9.6 Consequences of Hard and Soft Influence Tactics

Commitment

Compliance

Resistance

Persuasion

Impression management (including ingratiation)

Exchange

Soft influence tactics

Silent authority
Upward appeal
Coalition formation
Information control
Assertiveness

Hard influence tactics

power are strongest. Those with expertise tend to have more influence using persuasion, whereas those with a strong legitimate power base are usually more successful applying silent authority.[71] A second contingency is whether the person being influenced is higher, lower, or at the same level in the organization. As an example, employees may face adverse career consequences by being too assertive with their boss. Meanwhile, supervisors who engage in ingratiation and impression management tend to lose the respect of their staff.

Finally, the most appropriate influence tactic depends on personal, organizational, and cultural values.[72] People with a strong power orientation might feel more comfortable using assertiveness, whereas those who value conformity would make greater use of upward appeals. At an organizational level, firms with a competitive culture might encourage more use of information control and coalition formation, whereas companies with a learning orientation would likely encourage more influence through persuasion. The preferred influence tactics also vary across societal cultures. Research indicates that ingratiation is much more common among managers in United States than in Hong Kong, possibly because this tactic disrupts the more distant roles that managers and employees expect in high power distance cultures.

LO9-5 Identify the organizational conditions and personal characteristics associated with organizational politics, as well as ways to minimize organizational politics.

oppose the behavior desired by the influencer. At the extreme, they refuse to engage in the behavior. However, there are degrees of resistance, such as when people perform the required duties yet maintain their opposition by performing the tasks poorly or continuing to complain about the imposed work. *Compliance* occurs when people are motivated to implement the influencer's request for purely instrumental reasons. Without external sources to prompt the desired behavior, compliance would not occur. Furthermore, compliance usually involves engaging in the behavior with no more effort than is required. *Commitment* is the strongest outcome of influence, whereby people identify with the influencer's request and are highly motivated to implement it even when extrinsic sources of motivation are not present.

Generally, people react more favorably to soft tactics than to hard tactics. Soft influence tactics rely on personal sources of power (expert and referent power), which tend to build commitment to the influencer's request. In contrast, hard tactics rely on position power (legitimate, reward, and coercion), so they tend to produce compliance or, worse, resistance. Hard tactics also tend to undermine trust, which can hurt future relationships.

Apart from the general preference for soft rather than hard tactics, the most appropriate influence strategy depends on a few contingencies. One obvious contingency is which sources of

ORGANIZATIONAL POLITICS

You might have noticed that organizational politics has not been mentioned yet, even though some of the practices or examples described over the past few pages are usually considered political tactics. The phrase was carefully avoided because, for the most part, organizational politics is in the eye of the beholder. You might perceive a coworker's attempt to influence the boss as acceptable behavior for the good of the organization, whereas

organizational politics behaviors that others perceive as self-serving tactics at the expense of other people and possibly the organization

Machiavellian values the beliefs that deceit is a natural and acceptable way to influence others and that getting more than one deserves is acceptable

someone else might perceive the coworker's tactic as brazen organizational politics.

This perceptual issue explains why OB experts increasingly discuss influence tactics as behaviors and organizational politics as perceptions.[74] The influence tactics described earlier are perceived as **organizational politics** when they seem to be self-serving behaviors at the expense of others and possibly contrary to the interests of the entire organization. Of course, some tactics are so blatantly selfish and counterproductive that almost everyone correctly sees them as organizational politics. In other situations, however, a person's behavior might be viewed as political or in the organization's best interest, depending on the observer's point of view.

Employees who experience organizational politics have lower job satisfaction, organizational commitment, organizational citizenship, and task performance, as well as higher levels of work-related stress and motivation to leave the organization. "A politically charged work environment can hinder productivity,

erode trust, and lead to morale and retention issues," says Renan Silva, a corporate project management office specialist at Serasa Experian, a credit bureau in São Paulo, Brazil.[75] And because political tactics serve individuals rather than organizations, they potentially divert resources away from the organization's effective functioning and may threaten its survival.

Minimizing Organizational Politics

Researchers have identified several conditions that encourage organizational politics, so we can identify corresponding strategies to keep political activities to a minimum.[77] First, organizational politics is triggered by scarce resources in the workplace. When budgets are slashed, people rely on political tactics to safeguard their resources and maintain the status quo. Although it is not easy to maintain or add resources, sometimes this action is less costly than the consequences of organizational politics.

Second, organizational politics is suppressed when resource allocation decisions are clear and simplified. Political tactics are fueled by ambiguous or complex rules, or the absence of formal rules, because those tactics help people get what they want when decisions lack structural guidelines. Third, organizational change tends to bring out more organizational politics, mainly because change creates ambiguity and threatens the

> ## "Keep your friends close and your enemies closer."[76]
> **—Attributed to Sun Tzu,**
> Chinese military general, strategist, and philosopher

OFFICE POLITICS by the Numbers[73]

68% of 1,125 Taiwanese office workers polled say they have experienced workplace politics.

43% of 3,200 Americans polled identify office politics as a significant time waster at work.

33% of 1,102 employed Americans polled who don't normally work at a desk say that an important advantage of a nondesk job is not having to deal with office politics.

19% of 7,000 American employees polled believe that office politics is more vicious than national (elected government) politics.

13% of 1,900 Australian and New Zealand professionals polled admit to engaging in office politics.

employee's power and other valued resources.[78] Consequently, leaders need to apply the organizational change strategies that we describe in Chapter 14, particularly through communication, learning, and involvement. Research has found that employees who are kept informed of what is going on in the organization and who are involved in organizational decisions are less likely to observe organizational politics.

Third, political behavior is more common in work units and organizations where it is tolerated and reinforced. Some companies seem to nurture self-serving behavior through reward systems and the role modeling of organizational leaders. To minimize political norms, the organization needs to diagnose and alter systems and role modeling that support self-serving behavior. They should support organizational values that oppose political tactics, such as altruism and focusing on the customer. One of the most important strategies is for leaders to become role models of organizational citizenship rather than symbols of successful organizational politicians.

Minimizing Organizational Politics

Clarify rules and procedures where ambiguity generates internal competition.

Provide sufficient resources before scarcity starts generating political behavior.

Manage organizational change effectively (i.e., communication, learning, and involvement).

Alter reward systems and remove leaders who reinforce and role-model self-serving behavior.

Hire and promote people with low Machiavellian values.

Personal Characteristics Several personal characteristics affect an individual's motivation to engage in self-serving behavior.[79] This includes a strong need for personal as opposed to socialized power. Those with a need for personal power seek power for its own sake and try to acquire more power. Some individuals have strong **Machiavellian values**. Machiavellianism is named after Niccolò Machiavelli, the 16th-century Italian philosopher who wrote *The Prince*, a famous treatise about political behavior. People with high Machiavellian values are comfortable with getting more than they deserve, and they believe that deceit is a natural and acceptable way to achieve this goal. They seldom trust coworkers and tend to use cruder influence tactics, such as bypassing one's boss or being assertive, to get their own way.[80]

Study Checklist

✓ Did you tear out the perforated student review card at the back of the text to revisit learning objectives and key terms and definitions?

Connect® Management is available for *M Organizational Behavior*. Additional resources include:

✓ Interactive Applications:
- **Case Analysis:** Apply concepts within the context of a real-world situation.
- **Drag and Drop:** Work through an interactive example to test your knowledge of the concepts.
- **Video Case:** See management in action through interactive videos.

✓ **SmartBook™**—SmartBook is the first and only adaptive reading experience available today. Distinguishing what you know from what you don't, and honing in on concepts you are most likely to forget, SmartBook personalizes content for you in a continuously adapting reading experience. Reading is no longer a passive and linear experience, but an engaging and dynamic one where you are more likely to master and retain important concepts and go to class better prepared.

10 chapter

Conflict and Negotiation in the Workplace

Learning Objectives

After studying this chapter, you should be able to:

LO10-1 Define conflict and debate its positive and negative consequences in the workplace.

LO10-2 Distinguish task from relationship conflict and describe three strategies to minimize relationship conflict during task conflict episodes.

LO10-3 Diagram the conflict process model and describe six structural sources of conflict in organizations.

LO10-4 Outline the five conflict-handling styles and discuss the circumstances in which each would be most appropriate.

LO10-5 Apply the six structural approaches to conflict management and describe the three types of third-party dispute resolution.

LO10-6 Describe the bargaining zone model and outline strategies skilled negotiators use to claim value and create value in negotiations.

An American Airlines flight recently returned to the gate almost as soon as it began to taxi toward its takeoff area. It was an expensive decision, but the pilots took this action because, in the airline's words, "there was a disagreement between two flight attendants." One flight attendant was using her cell phone during the predeparture preparations for the New York to Washington commuter flight. Her activities apparently prompted the other flight attendant to use the intercom and announce that everyone needed to turn off their phones and electronic devices, "including the other flight attendant." That comment led to a scuffle between the two crew members, which was serious enough for the pilots to cancel the flight. Passengers had to wait four hours for a new crew to arrive.

Exactly one week later, a United Airlines flight bound for Chicago returned to Raleigh-Durham shortly after takeoff because of a conflict between two flight attendants. The cause of the tiff seemed almost trivial. "One flight attendant had crossed their leg and accidentally brushed the other person," explained a spokesperson at Raleigh-Durham International Airport after the flight had returned. Although apparently unintentional, the other flight attendant interpreted the incident as provocation because relations between the two were already fragile. "It appears there was a disagreement before that, that became elevated," the spokesperson said. Passengers had to wait three hours for an alternative flight. United Airlines faced the costs of an abandoned flight, compensation for travelers with missed connections, possibly overtime for the replacement crew, and loss of customer goodwill.[1]

These incidents illustrate that workplace conflict can be very costly. But as we will learn in this chapter, some forms of conflict are also valuable to organizations. The challenge is to enable beneficial conflict and suppress dysfunctional conflict. We begin this chapter by defining conflict and discussing the age-old question: Is conflict good or bad? Next, we look at the conflict process and examine in detail the main factors that cause or amplify conflict. The five styles of handling conflict are then described, including the contingencies of conflict handling as well as gender and cross-cultural differences. This is followed by discussion of the most important structural approaches to conflict resolution. Next, we look at the role of managers and others in third-party conflict resolution. The final section of this chapter reviews key issues in negotiating conflict resolution.

LO10-1 Define conflict and debate its positive and negative consequences in the workplace.

THE MEANING AND CONSEQUENCES OF CONFLICT

Conflict is a fact of life in organizations. Companies are continuously adapting to their external environment, yet there is no clear road map on what changes are best. Employees disagree on the direction or form of change in individual behavior, work unit activities, and organizational-level adaptations. This conflict occurs because of clashing work goals, divergent personal values and experiences, and a variety of other reasons that we discuss in this chapter.

Conflict is a process in which one party perceives that its interests are being opposed or negatively affected by another party.[2] It may occur when one party obstructs another's goals in some way, or just from one party's perception that the other party is going to do so. Conflict is ultimately based on perceptions; it exists whenever one party *believes* that another might obstruct its efforts, regardless of whether the other party actually intends to do so.

Is Conflict Good or Bad?

One of the oldest debates in organizational behavior is whether conflict is good or bad—or, more recently, what forms of conflict are good or bad—for organizations.[3] The dominant view over most of this time has been that conflict is dysfunctional.[4] More than a century ago, European organizational theorists Henri Fayol and Max Weber emphasized that organizations work best through harmonious relations. Elton Mayo, who founded Harvard University's human relations school and is considered one of the founders of organizational behavior, was convinced that employee–management conflict undermines organizational effectiveness. These and other critics warn that even moderately low levels of disagreement tatter the fabric of workplace relations and sap energy away

conflict the process in which one party perceives that its interests are being opposed or negatively affected by another party

task conflict a type of conflict in which people focus their discussion around the issue while showing respect for people who have other points of view

relationship conflict a type of conflict in which people focus on characteristics of other individuals, rather than on the issues, as the source of conflict

distorted perceptions and stereotypes of the other party. Conflict fuels organizational politics, such as motivating employees to find ways to undermine the credibility of their opponents. Finally, conflict among team members may undermine team cohesion and performance.

from productive activities. Disagreement with one's supervisor, for example, wastes productive time, violates the hierarchy of command, and questions the efficient assignment of authority (where managers make the decisions and employees follow them).

Although the "conflict-is-bad" perspective is now considered too simplistic, conflict can indeed have negative consequences under some circumstances (see Exhibit 10.1).[5] Conflict has been criticized for reducing employee performance by consuming otherwise productive time. For instance, almost one-third of the 5,000 employees surveyed across nine countries reported that they are frequently or always dealing with workplace conflict. More than half of the employees in Germany complained that conflict was consuming their workday.[6]

Conflict is potentially dysfunctional in other ways.[7] It is often stressful, which consumes personal energy and distracts employees from their work. It also increases job dissatisfaction, resulting in higher turnover and lower customer service. People who experience conflict also tend to reduce their information sharing and other forms of coordination with each other. Ironically, with less communication, the feuding parties are more likely to escalate their disagreement because each side relies increasingly on

> "Conflict is the gadfly of thought. It stirs us to observation and memory. It instigates to invention. It shocks us out of sheeplike passivity, and sets us at noting and contriving."[9]
>
> **—John Dewey,**
> educational philosopher/psychologist

Benefits of Conflict In the 1920s, when most organizational scholars viewed conflict as inherently dysfunctional, educational philosopher and psychologist John Dewey praised its benefits by suggesting that it "shocks us out of sheeplike passivity." Three years later, political science and management theorist Mary Parker Follett similarly remarked that the "friction" of conflict should be put to use rather than treated as an unwanted consequence of differences.[8]

But it wasn't until the 1970s that conflict management experts began to embrace the notion that some level of conflict can be beneficial.[10] They formed an "optimal conflict" perspective; organizations are most effective when employees experience some level of conflict, but become less effective with high levels of conflict.[11] What are the benefits of conflict? As Dewey stated, conflict energizes people to debate issues and evaluate alternatives more thoroughly. They probe and test each other's way of thinking to better understand the underlying issues that need to be addressed. This discussion and debate tests the logic of arguments and encourages participants to reexamine their basic assumptions about the problem and its possible solution. It prevents individuals and teams from making inferior decisions and potentially helps them develop more sound and creative solutions.[12]

A second potential benefit is that moderate levels of conflict prevent organizations from becoming nonresponsive to their external environment. Differences of opinion encourage employees to engage in active thinking, and this often involves ongoing questioning and vigilance about how the organization can be more closely aligned with its customers, suppliers, and other stakeholders.[13] A third benefit of conflict occurs when team members have a dispute or competition with external sources. This form of conflict represents an external

Exhibit 10.1 Consequences of Workplace Conflict

Negative Consequences	Positive Consequences
• Lower performance	• Better decision making
• Higher stress, dissatisfaction, and turnover	— Tests logic of arguments
• Less information sharing and coordination	— Questions assumptions
• Increased organizational politics	• More responsive to changing environment
• Wasted resources	• Stronger team cohesion (conflict between the team and outside opponents)
• Weakened team cohesion (conflict among team members)	

challenge that potentially increases cohesion within the team (see Chapter 7). People are more motivated to work together when faced with an external threat, such as conflict with people outside the team.

LO10-2 Distinguish task from relationship conflict and describe three strategies to minimize relationship conflict during task conflict episodes.

The Emerging View: Task and Relationship Conflict

The "optimal conflict" perspective remains popular, but the emerging school of thought is that there are two types of conflict with opposing consequences: task conflict and relationship conflict.[14] **Task conflict** (also called *constructive conflict*) occurs when people focus their discussion around the issue (i.e., the "task") while showing respect for people with other points of view. This type of conflict debates the merits and limitations of different positions so ideas and recommendations can be clarified, redesigned, and tested for logical soundness.

By keeping the debate focused on the issue, participants calmly reexamine their assumptions and beliefs without having hostile emotions triggered by their drive to defend their self-concept. Research indicates that task conflict tends to produce the beneficial outcomes described earlier, particularly better decision making.[15] At the same time, there is likely an upper limit to the intensity of any disagreement, above which it would be difficult to remain constructive.[16]

In contrast to task conflict, **relationship conflict** focuses on interpersonal differences between or among the adversaries. The parties refer to "personality clashes" and other interpersonal incompatibilities rather than legitimate differences of opinion regarding tasks or decisions. Relationship conflict involves one party questioning or critiquing personal characteristics of the other person. As such, it attempts (or is perceived to attempt) to undermine another person's competence. These personal attacks threaten self-esteem and oppose self-enhancement and self-verification processes (see Chapter 3). Consequently, they usually trigger defense mechanisms and a competitive orientation between the parties. Relationship conflict also reduces mutual trust because it emphasizes interpersonal differences that shred any bond that existed with the other person.[17] Relationship conflict escalates more easily than task

higher emotional intelligence and stability are better able to regulate their emotions during debate, which reduces the risk of escalating perceptions of interpersonal hostility. They are also more likely to view a coworker's emotional reaction as valuable information about that person's needs and expectations, rather than as a personal attack.

- *Cohesive team.* Relationship conflict is suppressed when the conflict occurs within a highly cohesive team. The longer people work together, get to know each other, and develop mutual trust, the more latitude they give to each other to show emotions without being personally offended. This might explain why task conflict is more effective in top management teams than in teams of more junior staff.[21] Strong cohesion also allows each person to know about and anticipate the behaviors and emotions of his or her teammates. Another benefit is that cohesion produces a stronger social identity with the group, so team members are motivated to avoid escalating relationship conflict during otherwise emotionally turbulent discussions.

conflict because the adversaries become less motivated to communicate and share information, making it more difficult for them to discover common ground and ultimately resolve the conflict. Instead, they rely more on distorted perceptions and stereotypes, which tend to reinforce their perceptions of threat.

Separating Task from Relationship Conflict If there are two types of conflict, then the obvious advice is to encourage task conflict and minimize relationship conflict. This recommendation sounds good in theory, but separating these two types of conflict isn't easy in practice. Research indicates that we experience some degree of relationship conflict whenever we are engaged in constructive debate.[18] No matter how diplomatically someone questions our ideas and actions, he or she potentially threatens our self-concept (particularly our sense of competence) and our public image, which triggers our drive to defend. The stronger the level of debate and the more the issue is tied to our self-view, the more likely that task conflict will evolve into (or mix with) relationship conflict. Fortunately, three strategies or conditions potentially minimize the level of relationship conflict during task conflict episodes.[19]

> Most of us experience some degree of relationship conflict during and after any constructive debate.

- *Emotional intelligence and emotional stability.* Relationship conflict is less likely to occur, or is less likely to escalate, when team members have high levels of emotional intelligence and its associated personality characteristic: emotional stability.[20] Employees with

- *Supportive team norms.* Various team norms can hold relationship conflict at bay during task-focused debate. When team norms encourage openness, for instance, team members learn to appreciate honest dialogue without personally reacting to any emotional display during the disagreements.[22] Other norms might discourage team members from displaying negative emotions toward coworkers. Team norms also encourage tactics that diffuse relationship conflict when it first appears. For instance, research has found that teams with low relationship conflict use humor to maintain positive group emotions, which offsets negative feelings team members might develop toward some coworkers during debate.

LO10-3 Diagram the conflict process model and describe six structural sources of conflict in organizations.

CONFLICT PROCESS MODEL

Now that we have outlined the history and current perspectives of conflict and its outcomes, let's look at the model of the conflict process, shown in Exhibit 10.2.[23] This model begins with the sources of conflict, which we will describe in the next section. At some point, the sources of conflict lead one or both

Exhibit 10.2 Model of the Conflict Process

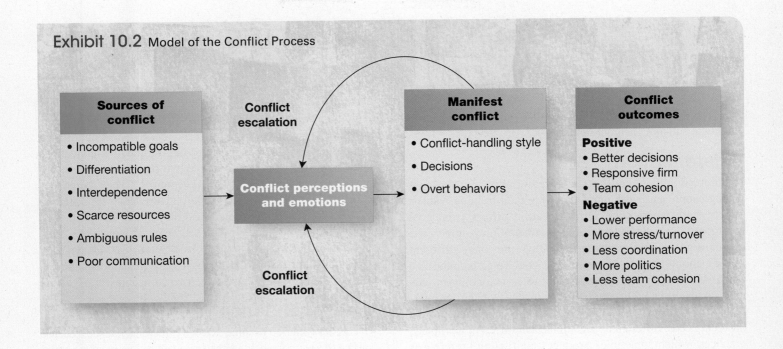

Sources of conflict
- Incompatible goals
- Differentiation
- Interdependence
- Scarce resources
- Ambiguous rules
- Poor communication

Conflict escalation

Conflict perceptions and emotions

Conflict escalation

Manifest conflict
- Conflict-handling style
- Decisions
- Overt behaviors

Conflict outcomes

Positive
- Better decisions
- Responsive firm
- Team cohesion

Negative
- Lower performance
- More stress/turnover
- Less coordination
- More politics
- Less team cohesion

---

parties to perceive that conflict exists. They become aware that one party's statements and actions are incompatible with their own goals or beliefs. These perceptions usually interact with emotions experienced about the conflict.[24] Conflict perceptions and emotions produce manifest conflict—the decisions and behaviors of one party toward the other. These *conflict episodes* may range from subtle nonverbal behaviors to warlike aggression. Particularly when people experience high levels of conflict-generated emotions, they have difficulty finding the words and expressions that communicate effectively without further irritating the relationship.[25] Conflict is also behaviorally revealed by the style each side uses to resolve the conflict. Some people tend to avoid the conflict whereas others try to defeat those with opposing views.

Exhibit 10.2 shows arrows looping back from manifest conflict to conflict perceptions and emotions. These arrows illustrate that the conflict process is really a series of episodes that potentially cycle into conflict escalation.[26] It doesn't take much to start this conflict cycle—just an inappropriate comment, a misunderstanding, or an action that lacks diplomacy. These behaviors cause the other party to perceive that conflict exists. Even if the first party did not intend to demonstrate conflict, the second party's response may create that perception.

STRUCTURAL SOURCES OF CONFLICT IN ORGANIZATIONS

The conflict model starts with the sources of conflict, so we need to understand these sources to effectively diagnose conflict episodes and subsequently resolve the conflict or occasionally to generate conflict where it is lacking. The six main conditions that cause conflict in organizational settings are incompatible goals, differentiation, interdependence, scarce resources, ambiguous rules, and communication problems.

Incompatible Goals

Goal incompatibility occurs when the goals of one person or department seem to interfere with another person's or department's goals.[27] For example, the production department strives for cost efficiency by scheduling long production runs whereas the sales team emphasizes customer service by delivering the client's product as quickly as possible. If the company runs out of a particular product, the production team would prefer to have clients wait until the next production run. This infuriates sales representatives who would rather change production quickly to satisfy consumer demand.

Differentiation

Another source of conflict is differentiation—differences among people and work units regarding their training, values, beliefs, and experiences. Differentiation differs from goal incompatibility; two people or departments may agree on a common goal (serving customers better) but have different beliefs about how to achieve that goal (e.g., standardize employee behavior versus give employees autonomy in customer interactions). Differentiation is usually a factor in intergenerational conflict. Younger and older employees have different needs, different expectations, and different workplace practices, which sometimes produces conflicting preferences and actions. Recent studies suggest that these intergenerational differences occur because people develop social identities around technological developments and other pivotal social events that are unique to their era.[28]

Differentiation also produces the classic tension between employees from two companies brought together through a merger.[31] Even when people from both companies want the integrated organization to succeed, they fight over the "right way" to do things because of their unique experiences in the separate companies. This form of conflict emerged when CenturyLink acquired Qwest, creating the third largest telecommunications company in the United States. The two companies were headquartered in different parts of the country. "Their languages were different, their food was different, answers were different. We talked fast and interrupted, and they talked slow and were polite," recalls a senior Qwest executive. "If we said up, they said down. If we said yes, they said no. If we said go, they said stop." This resulted in "unnecessary misunderstandings" as executives tried to integrate the two companies.[32]

Interdependence

All conflict is caused to some extent by interdependence, because conflict exists only when one party perceives that its interests are being opposed or negatively affected by another party. Task interdependence refers to the extent to which employees must share materials, information, or expertise to perform their jobs (see Chapter 7). Conflict is inherently about relationships because people and work units are affected by others only when they have some level of interdependence.

The risk of conflict increases with the level of interdependence.[33] Employees usually have the lowest risk of conflict when working with others in a pooled interdependence relationship. Pooled interdependence occurs where individuals operate independently except for reliance on a common resource or authority. The potential for conflict is higher in sequential interdependence work relationships, such as an assembly line. The highest risk of conflict tends to occur in reciprocal interdependence situations. With reciprocal interdependence, employees have high mutual dependence on each other as well as higher centrality. Consequently, reciprocally interdependent relationships have the strongest and most immediate risk of interfering with each other's objectives.

Scarce Resources

Resource scarcity generates conflict because each person or unit requiring the same resource necessarily undermines others who also

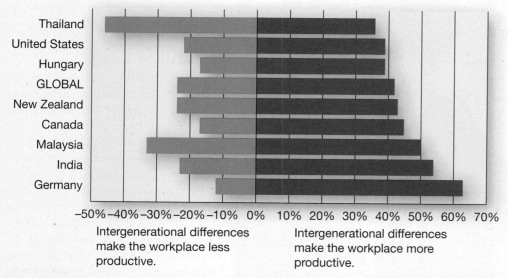

Do Intergenerational Differences Increase or Decrease Productivity?[30]

Intergenerational differences make the workplace less productive.

Intergenerational differences make the workplace more productive.

Note: Percentage of employees by country who believe that intergenerational (Baby Boomers, Gen Xers, and Gen Yers) differences have a positive or negative effect on workplace productivity. Percentages do not add up to 100 percent because some respondents reported that generational differences have no effect on productivity. Based on a survey of 100,000 employees in 33 countries.

need that resource to fulfill their goals. Most labor strikes, for instance, occur because there aren't enough financial and other resources for employees and company owners to each receive the outcomes they seek, such as higher pay (employees) and higher investment returns (stockholders). Budget deliberations within organizations also produce conflict because there aren't enough funds to satisfy the goals of each work unit. The more resources one group receives, the fewer resources other groups will receive. Fortunately, these interests aren't perfectly opposing in complex negotiations, but limited resources are typically a major source of friction.

Ambiguous Rules

Ambiguous rules—or the complete lack of rules—breed conflict. This occurs because uncertainty increases the risk that one party intends to interfere with the other party's goals. Ambiguity also encourages political tactics and, in some cases, employees enter a free-for-all battle to win decisions in their favor. This explains why conflict is more common during mergers and acquisitions. Employees from both companies have conflicting practices and values, and few rules have developed to minimize the maneuvering for power and resources.[34] When clear rules

exist, on the other hand, employees know what to expect from each other and have agreed to abide by those rules.

Communication Problems

Conflict often occurs due to the lack of opportunity, ability, or motivation to communicate effectively. Let's look at each of these causes. First, when two parties lack the opportunity to communicate, they tend to rely more on stereotypes to understand the other party in the conflict. Unfortunately, stereotypes are sufficiently subjective that emotions can negatively distort the meaning of an opponent's actions, thereby escalating perceptions of conflict. Second, some people lack the necessary skills to communicate in a diplomatic, nonconfrontational manner. When one party communicates its disagreement arrogantly, opponents are more likely to heighten their perception of the conflict. This may lead opponents to reciprocate with a similar response, which further escalates the conflict.[35]

A third problem is that relationship conflict is uncomfortable, so people are less motivated to communicate with others in a disagreement. Unfortunately, less communication can further escalate the conflict because each side has less accurate information about the other side's intentions. To fill in the missing pieces, they rely on distorted images and stereotypes of the other party. Perceptions are further distorted because people in conflict situations tend to engage in more differentiation with those who are different from them (see Chapter 3). This differentiation creates a more positive self-concept and a more negative image of the opponent. We begin to see competitors less favorably so our self-concept remains positive during these conflict episodes.[36]

LO10-4 Outline the five conflict-handling styles and discuss the circumstances in which each would be most appropriate.

INTERPERSONAL CONFLICT-HANDLING STYLES

The six sources of conflict lead to conflict perceptions and emotions which, in turn, motivate people to respond in some way to the conflict. Mary Parker Follett (who argued that conflict can be beneficial) observed more than 70 years ago that people respond to perceived and felt conflict through various conflict-handling strategies. Follett's original list was expanded and refined over the years into the five-category model shown in Exhibit 10.3. This model recognizes that how people respond behaviorally to a conflict situation depends on the relative importance they place on maximizing outcomes for themselves and for the other party.[37]

Exhibit 10.3 Interpersonal Conflict-Handling Styles

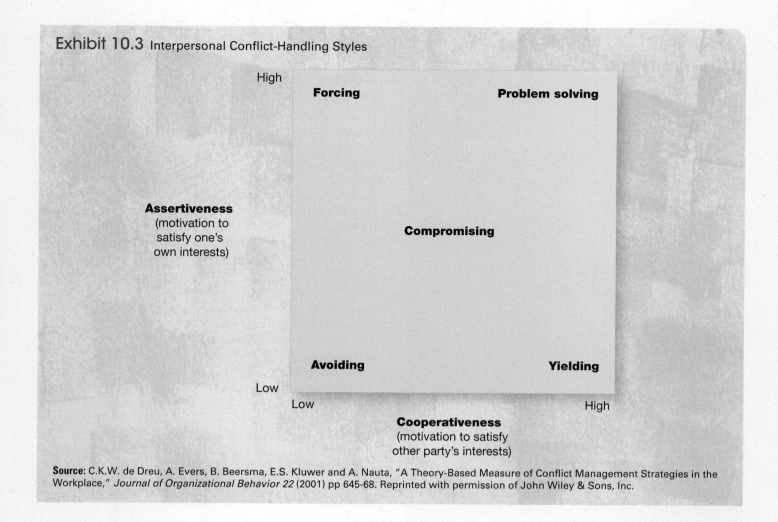

Source: C.K.W. de Dreu, A. Evers, B. Beersma, E.S. Kluwer and A. Nauta, "A Theory-Based Measure of Conflict Management Strategies in the Workplace," *Journal of Organizational Behavior 22* (2001) pp 645-68. Reprinted with permission of John Wiley & Sons, Inc.

> "The more arguments you win, the fewer friends you will have."[38]
>
> —Mid-20th-century American proverb

- *Problem solving.* Problem solving tries to find a solution that is beneficial for both parties. This is known as the **win–win orientation** because people using this style believe the resources at stake are expandable rather than fixed if the parties work together to find a creative solution. Information sharing is an important feature of this style because both parties collaborate to identify common ground and potential solutions that satisfy everyone involved.

- *Forcing.* Forcing tries to win the conflict at the other's expense. People who use this style typically have a **win–lose orientation**— they believe the parties are drawing from a fixed pie, so the more one party receives, the less the other party will receive. Consequently, this style relies on assertiveness and other hard influence tactics (see Chapter 9) to get one's own way.

- *Avoiding.* Avoiding tries to smooth over or evade conflict situations altogether. A common avoidance strategy is to minimize interaction with certain coworkers. A second avoidance strategy is to steer clear of the sensitive topic when interacting with the other person in the conflict. Notice from these examples that avoidance does not necessarily mean that we have a low concern for both one's own and the other party's interest. We might be very concerned about the issue but conclude that avoidance is the best solution, at least in the short term.[39]

- *Yielding.* Yielding involves giving in completely to the other side's wishes, or at least cooperating with little or no attention to your own interests. This style involves making unilateral concessions and unconditional promises, as well as offering help with no expectation of reciprocal help.

- *Compromising.* Compromising involves looking for a position in which your losses are offset by equally valued gains. It involves matching the other party's concessions, making conditional promises or threats, and actively searching for a middle ground between the interests of the two parties.

Choosing the Best Conflict-Handling Style

Chances are that you prefer one or two conflict-handling styles more than the others. You might typically engage in avoiding or yielding because disagreement makes you feel uncomfortable and is contrary to your self-view as someone who likes to get along with everyone. Or perhaps you prefer the compromising and forcing strategies because they reflect your strong need for achievement and to control your environment. People usually gravitate toward one or two conflict-handling styles that match their personality, personal and cultural values, and past experience.[40] However, the best style depends on the situation, so we need to understand and develop the capacity to use any of the five styles for the appropriate occasions.[41]

Exhibit 10.4 summarizes the main contingencies, as well as problems with using each conflict-handling style. Problem solving is widely recognized as the preferred conflict-handling style, whenever possible. Why? This approach calls for dialogue and clever thinking, both of which help the parties discover a win–win solution. In addition, the problem-solving style tends to improve long-term relationships, reduce stress, and minimize emotional defensiveness and other indications of relationship conflict.[42]

However, problem solving assumes there are opportunities for mutual gains, such as when the conflict is complex with multiple elements. If the conflict is simple and perfectly opposing (each party wants more of a single fixed pie), then this style will waste time and increase frustration. The problem-solving approach also takes more time and requires a fairly high degree of trust, because there is a risk that the other party will take advantage of the information you have openly shared. As one study recently found, the problem-solving style is more stressful when people experience strong feelings of conflict, likely because these negative emotions undermine trust in the other party.[43]

> The best conflict-handling style depends on the situation, so we need to understand and develop the capacity to use any of the five styles for the appropriate occasions.

win–win orientation
the belief that conflicting parties will find a mutually beneficial solution to their disagreement

win–lose orientation
the belief that conflicting parties are drawing from a fixed pie, so the more one party receives, the less the other party will receive

Exhibit 10.4 Conflict-Handling Style Contingencies and Problems

Conflict-Handling Style	Preferred Style When . . .	Problems with This Style
Problem solving	• Interests are not perfectly opposing (i.e., not pure win–lose) • Parties have trust, openness, and time to share information • Issues are complex	• Sharing information that the other party might use to his or her advantage
Forcing	• You have a deep conviction about your position (e.g., believe other person's behavior is unethical) • Dispute requires a quick solution • Other party would take advantage of more cooperative strategies	• Highest risk of relationship conflict • May damage long-term relations, reducing future problem solving
Avoiding	• Conflict has become too emotionally charged • Cost of trying to resolve the conflict outweighs the benefits	• Doesn't usually resolve the conflict • May increase other party's frustration
Yielding	• Other party has substantially more power • Issue is much less important to you than to the other party • The value and logic of your position isn't as clear	• Increases other party's expectations in future conflict episodes
Compromising	• Parties have equal power • Time pressure to resolve the conflict • Parties lack trust/openness for problem solving	• Suboptimal solution where mutual gains are possible

The conflict avoidance style is often ineffective because it doesn't resolve the conflict and may increase the other party's frustration. However, avoiding may be the best strategy where conflict has become emotionally charged or where conflict resolution would cost more than its benefits.[44] The forcing style is usually inappropriate because it frequently generates relationship conflict more quickly or intensely than other conflict-handling styles. However, forcing may be necessary when you know you are correct (e.g., the other party's position is unethical or based on obviously flawed logic), the dispute requires a quick solution, or the other party would take advantage of a more cooperative conflict-handling style.

The yielding style may be appropriate when the other party has substantially more power, the issue is not as important to you as to the other party, and you aren't confident that your position has superior logical or ethical justification.[46] On the other hand, yielding behaviors may give the other side unrealistically high expectations, thereby motivating them to seek more from you in the future. In the long run, yielding may produce more conflict, rather than resolve it. "Raised voices, red faces, and table thumping is a far less dysfunctional way of challenging each other than withdrawal, passivity and sullen acceptance," argues one conflict management consultant. "It doesn't mean that people agree with you: they just take their misgivings underground and spread them throughout the organization, which has a corrosive effect."[47]

The compromising style may be best when there is little hope for mutual gain through problem solving, both parties have equal power, and both are under time pressure to settle their differences. However, we rarely know whether the parties have perfectly opposing interests, yet the compromise approach assumes this win–lose orientation. Therefore, entering a conflict with the compromising style may cause the parties to overlook better solutions because they have not attempted to share enough information and creatively look for win–win alternatives.

Cultural and Gender Differences in Conflict-Handling Styles

Cultural differences are more than just a source of conflict. They also influence the preferred conflict-handling style.[48] Some research suggests that people from high collectivism cultures—where group goals are valued more than individual goals—are motivated to maintain harmonious relations and, consequently, are more likely than those from low collectivism cultures to manage disagreements through avoidance or problem solving. However, this view may be somewhat simplistic. Collectivism motivates harmony within the group but not necessarily with people outside the group. Indeed, research indicates that managers in some collectivist cultures are more likely to publicly shame those whose actions oppose their own.[49] Cultural values and norms influence the conflict-handling style used most often in a society, so they also represent an important contingency when choosing the preferred conflict-handling approach in that culture. For example, people who frequently use the conflict avoidance style might have more problems in cultures where the forcing style is common.

According to some writers, men and women tend to rely on different conflict-handling styles.[50] Compared to men,

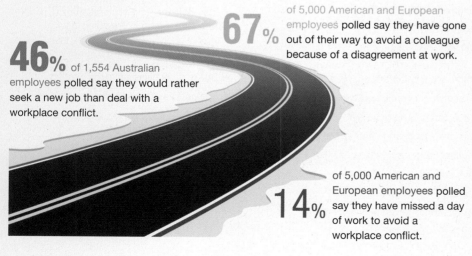

Steering Clear
of Workplace Conflict[45]

82% of 1,554 Australian employees polled say they felt uncomfortable approaching human resource staff about a workplace conflict.

67% of 5,000 American and European employees polled say they have gone out of their way to avoid a colleague because of a disagreement at work.

46% of 1,554 Australian employees polled say they would rather seek a new job than deal with a workplace conflict.

14% of 5,000 American and European employees polled say they have missed a day of work to avoid a workplace conflict.

women pay more attention to the relationship between the parties. Consequently, women tend to adopt a compromising or occasionally problem-solving style in business settings and are more willing to compromise to protect the relationship. Women are also slightly more likely to use the avoiding style. Men tend to be more competitive and take a short-term orientation to the relationship. In low collectivism cultures, men are more likely than women to use the forcing approach to conflict handling. We must be cautious about these observations, however, because women and men differ only to a small degree on preferred conflict-handling styles.

LO10-5 Apply the six structural approaches to conflict management and describe the three types of third-party dispute resolution.

STRUCTURAL APPROACHES TO CONFLICT MANAGEMENT

Conflict-handling styles describe how we approach the other party in a conflict situation. But conflict management also involves altering the underlying structural causes of potential conflict. The main structural approaches parallel the sources of conflict discussed earlier. These structural approaches include emphasizing superordinate goals, reducing differentiation, improving communication and understanding, reducing task interdependence, increasing resources, and clarifying rules and procedures.

Emphasizing Superordinate Goals

One of the oldest recommendations for resolving conflict is to refocus the parties' attention around superordinate goals and away from the conflicting subordinate goals.[51] **Superordinate goals** are goals that the conflicting employees or departments value and whose attainment requires the joint resources and effort of those parties.[52] These goals are called superordinate because they are higher-order aspirations such as the organization's strategic objectives rather than objectives specific to the individual or work unit. Research indicates that the most effective executive teams frame their decisions as superordinate goals that rise above each executive's departmental or divisional goals. Similarly, one recent study reported that effective leaders reduce conflict through an

> One of the oldest recommendations for resolving conflict is to focus attention on common superordinate goals.

inspirational vision that unifies employees and makes them less preoccupied with their subordinate goal differences.[53]

Suppose that marketing staff members want a new product released quickly whereas engineers want more time to test and add new features. Leaders can potentially reduce this interdepartmental conflict by reminding both groups of the company's mission to serve customers, or by pointing out that competitors currently threaten the company's leadership in the industry. By increasing commitment to companywide goals (customer focus, competitiveness), engineering and marketing employees pay less attention to their competing departmental-level goals, which reduces their perceived conflict with each other. Superordinate goals also potentially reduce the problem of differentiation because they establish feelings of a shared social identity (work for the same company).[54]

superordinate goals goals that the conflicting parties value and whose attainment requires the joint resources and effort of those parties

Reducing Differentiation

Differentiation—differences regarding training, values, beliefs, and experiences—was identified earlier as one of the main sources of workplace conflict. Therefore, reducing differentiation is a logical approach to reducing dysfunctional conflict. As people develop common experiences and beliefs, they become more motivated to coordinate activities and resolve their disputes through constructive discussion.[55] One way to reduce differentiation is to rotate key staff to different departments or regions throughout their career. This career development process develops common experiences around the entire company rather than within different areas. Another way to reduce differentiation is to have employees from different parts of the organization work together on important (and hopefully successful) projects. These projects become a common ground for otherwise diverse employee groups. A third strategy is to build and maintain a strong organizational culture. Employees have shared values and assumptions in a company with a strong culture, and Chapter 13 describes specific activities to support a strong culture.

Improving Communication and Mutual Understanding

A third way to resolve dysfunctional conflict is to give the conflicting parties more opportunities to communicate and understand each other. This recommendation applies two principles and practices introduced in Chapter 3: the Johari Window model and meaningful interaction. Although both were previously described as ways to improve self-awareness, they are equally valuable to improve other-awareness.

In the Johari Window process, individuals disclose more about themselves so others have a better understanding of the underlying causes of their behavior. A variation of Johari Window occurs in "lunch and learn" sessions, where employees in one functional area describe work and its challenges to coworkers in other areas. Houston-based Brookstone Construction introduced these information meetings, which helped reduce frustrations between the field and office staff.[57]

Meaningful interaction potentially improves mutual understanding through the contact hypothesis, which says that we develop a more person-specific and accurate understanding of others by working closely with them.[58] For example, more than 18,000 employees and managers at the various companies of System Capital Management recently participated in the "Let's Make Ukraine Clean" campaign. In addition to improving the environment—each person picked up an average of about 100 kilograms (220 pounds) of garbage—this volunteering improved relations among management and employees at the Ukraine's leading financial and industrial group.[59]

Although communication and mutual understanding can work well, there are two important warnings. First, these interventions should be applied only where differentiation is sufficiently low or *after* differentiation has been reduced. If perceived differentiation remains high, attempts to manage conflict through dialogue might escalate rather than reduce relationship conflict. The reason is that when forced to interact with people who we believe are quite different and in conflict with us, we tend to select information that reinforces that view.[60] The second warning is that people in collectivist and high power distance cultures are less comfortable with the practice of resolving differences

Applying the **Johari Window** to Minimize Intergenerational Conflict

L'Oréal Canada's award-winning workshop, called Valorizing Intergenerational Differences, minimizes intergenerational conflict by helping employees understand coworkers across generational cohorts. One part of the workshop applies Johari Window principles to improve mutual understanding. Participants are grouped into generational cohorts, and each cohort answers questions from the others about what is important to them (such as security, performance, and collaboration). "The Valorizing Intergenerational Differences training really helped me understand where people from each generation are coming from," says Ashley Bancroft, a L'Oréal Canada key account manager.[56]

third-party conflict resolution any attempt by a relatively neutral person to help conflicting parties resolve their differences

through direct and open communication.[61] Recall that people in collectivist cultures prefer an avoidance conflict-handling style because it is the most consistent with harmony and face saving. Direct communication is a high-risk strategy because it easily threatens the need to save face and maintain harmony.

Reducing Interdependence

Conflict occurs where people are dependent on each other, so another way to reduce dysfunctional conflict is to minimize the level of interdependence between the parties. Three ways to reduce interdependence among employees and work units are to create buffers, use integrators, and combine jobs.

- *Create buffers.* A buffer is any mechanism that loosens the coupling between two or more people or work units. This decoupling reduces the potential for conflict because the buffer reduces the effect of one party on the other. Building up inventories between people in an assembly line would be a buffer, for example, because each employee is less dependent in the short term on the previous person along that line.

- *Use integrators.* Integrators are employees who coordinate the activities of work units toward the completion of a common task. For example, an individual might be responsible for coordinating the efforts of the research, production, advertising, and marketing departments in launching a new product line. In some respects, integrators are human buffers; they reduce the frequency of direct interaction among work units that have diverse goals and perspectives. Integrators rarely have direct authority over the departments they integrate, so they must rely on referent power and persuasion to manage conflict and accomplish the work.

- *Combine jobs.* Combining jobs is both a form of job enrichment and a way to reduce task interdependence. Consider a toaster assembly system where one person inserts the heating element, another adds the sides, and so on. By combining these tasks so that each person assembles an entire toaster, the employees now have a pooled rather than sequential form of task interdependence and the likelihood of dysfunctional conflict is reduced.

Increasing Resources

Resource scarcity is a source of conflict, so increasing the amount of resources available would have the opposite effect. This might not be a feasible strategy for minimizing dysfunctional conflict due to the costs involved. However, these costs need to be compared against the costs of dysfunctional conflict due to the resource scarcity.

Clarifying Rules and Procedures

Conflicts that arise from ambiguous rules can be minimized by establishing rules and procedures. If two departments are fighting over the use of a new laboratory, a schedule might be established that allocates the lab exclusively to each team at certain times of the day or week.

THIRD-PARTY CONFLICT RESOLUTION

Most of this chapter has focused on people directly involved in a conflict, yet many disputes among employees and departments are resolved with the assistance of a manager. **Third-party conflict resolution** is any attempt by a relatively neutral person to help the parties resolve their differences. There are three main third-party dispute resolution activities: arbitration, inquisition, and mediation. These interventions can be classified by their level of control over the process and control over the decision (see Exhibit 10.5).[62]

- *Arbitration*—Arbitrators have high control over the final decision, but low control over the process. Executives engage in this strategy by following previously agreed-upon rules of due process, listening to arguments from the disputing employees, and making a binding decision. Arbitration is applied as the final stage of grievances by unionized employees in many countries, but it is also becoming more common in nonunion conflicts.

- *Inquisition*—Inquisitors control all discussion about the conflict. Like arbitrators, they have high decision control because they determine how to resolve the conflict. However, they also have high process control because they choose which information to examine and how to examine it, and they generally decide how the conflict resolution process will be handled.

When **Managers** Try to Resolve **Employee Conflict**[63]

42% of 1,279 employees surveyed in the United States and several other countries say their leader sometimes or never handles workplace conflict effectively.

30% of 1,279 employees surveyed in the United States and several other countries say their boss doesn't remain calm and constructive when discussing a conflict.

16% is the average percentage of work time that 300 senior Canadian managers say they spend intervening in employee disputes.

18% is the average percentage of work time that 1,000 senior American managers say they spend intervening in employee disputes (compared with 18%, 13%, and 9% when the same question was asked 15, 20, and 25 years earlier, respectively).

Exhibit 10.5 Types of Third-Party Intervention

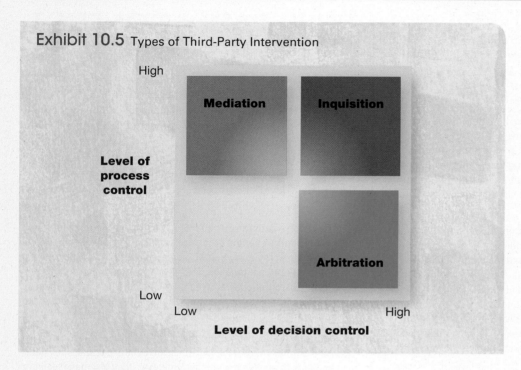

- *Mediation*—Mediators have high control over the intervention process. In fact, their main purpose is to manage the process and context of interaction between the disputing parties. However, the parties make the final decision about how to resolve their differences. Thus, mediators have little or no control over the conflict resolution decision.[64]

Choosing the Best Third-Party Intervention Strategy

Team leaders, executives, and coworkers regularly intervene in workplace disputes. Sometimes they adopt a mediator role; other times they serve as arbitrators. Occasionally, they begin with one approach then switch to another. However, research suggests that people in positions of authority (e.g., managers) usually adopt an inquisitional approach whereby they dominate the intervention process as well as make a binding decision.[65]

Managers tend to rely on the inquisition approach because it is consistent with the decision-oriented nature of managerial jobs, gives them control over the conflict process and outcome, and tends to resolve disputes efficiently. However, inquisition is usually the least effective third-party conflict resolution method in organizational settings.[66] One problem is that leaders who take an inquisitional role tend to collect limited information about the problem, so their imposed decision may produce an ineffective solution to the conflict. Another problem is that

employees often view inquisitional procedures and outcomes as unfair because they have little control over this approach. In particular, the inquisitional approach potentially violates several practices required to support procedural justice (see Chapter 5).

Which third-party intervention is most appropriate in organizations? The answer partly depends on the situation, such as the type of dispute, the relationship between the manager and employees, and cultural values such as power distance.[67] Also, any third-party approach has more favorable results when it applies the procedural justice practices described in Chapter 5.[68] But generally speaking, for everyday disagreements between two employees, the mediation approach is usually best because this gives employees more responsibility for resolving their own disputes. The third-party representative merely establishes an appropriate context for conflict resolution. Although not as efficient as other strategies, mediation potentially offers the highest level of employee satisfaction with the conflict process and outcomes.[69] When employees cannot resolve their differences through mediation, arbitration seems to work best because the predetermined rules of evidence and other processes create a higher sense of procedural fairness.[70] Arbitration is also preferred where the organization's goals should take priority over individual goals.

LO10-6 Describe the bargaining zone model and outline strategies skilled negotiators use to claim value and create value in negotiations.

RESOLVING CONFLICT THROUGH NEGOTIATION

Think back through yesterday's events. Maybe you had to work out an agreement with other students about what tasks to complete for a team project. Chances are you shared transportation with someone, so you had to agree on the timing of the ride. Then perhaps there was the question of who made dinner. Each of these daily events created potential conflict, and they were resolved through negotiation. **Negotiation** occurs whenever two or more conflicting parties attempt to resolve their divergent goals by redefining the terms of their interdependence. In other words, people negotiate when they think that discussion can produce a more satisfactory arrangement (at least for them) in their exchange of goods or services.

As you can see, negotiation is not an obscure practice reserved for labor and management bosses when hammering out a collective agreement. Everyone negotiates, every day. Most of the time, you don't even realize that you are in negotiations. Negotiation is particularly evident in the workplace because employees work interdependently with each other. They negotiate with their supervisors over next month's work assignments, with customers over the sale and delivery schedules of their product, and with coworkers over when to have lunch. And yes, they occasionally negotiate with each other in labor disputes and collective agreements.

Bargaining Zone Model of Negotiations

One way to view the negotiation process is that each party moves along a continuum in opposite directions with an area of potential overlap called the *bargaining zone*.[71] Exhibit 10.6 displays one possible bargaining zone situation. This linear diagram illustrates a purely win–lose situation—one side's gain will be the other's loss. However, a variation of the bargaining zone model can depict situations in which both sides potentially gain from the negotiations. As this model illustrates, the parties typically establish three main negotiating points. The *initial offer point* is the team's opening offer to the other party. This may be its best expectation or a pie-in-the-sky starting point. The *target point* is the team's realistic goal or expectation for a final agreement. The *resistance point* is the point beyond which the team will make no further concessions.

negotiation the process whereby two or more conflicting parties attempt to resolve their divergent goals by redefining the terms of their interdependence

The parties begin negotiations by describing their initial offer point for each item on the agenda. In most cases, the participants know that this is only a starting point that will change as both sides offer concessions. In win–lose situations, neither the target nor the resistance point is revealed to the other party. However, people try to discover the other side's resistance point because this knowledge helps them determine how much they can gain without breaking off negotiations.

The bargaining zone model implies that the parties compete against each other to reach their target point. Competition does exist to varying degrees because negotiators try to *claim value*, that is, to get the best possible outcomes for themselves. Yet, the hallmark of successful negotiation is a combination of competition and cooperation. Negotiators also need to cooperate with each other to *create value*, that is, to discover ways to achieve mutually satisfactory outcomes for both parties.[72] Cooperation maintains a degree of trust necessary to share information. To some degree, it may also improve concessions so the negotiations are resolved more quickly and with greater mutual gains.

Strategies for Claiming Value

Claiming value involves trying to obtain the best possible outcomes for yourself and your constituents. A purely competitive approach, in which you forcefully influence the other party and assert your power (such as threatening to walk away from the negotiation), typically leads to failure because it generates negative emotions and undermines trust. Even so, some degree of value claiming is necessary to achieve a favorable outcome. Here are four skills to effectively claim value in negotiations.

Prepare and Set Goals People negotiate more successfully when they carefully think through their three key positions in the bargaining zone model (initial, target, and resistance), consider alternative strategies to achieve those objectives, and test their underlying assumptions about the situation.[73] Equally important, they need to research what the other party wants from the negotiation. "You have to be prepared every which way about the people, the subject, and your fallback position," advises Paul Tellier, chair of Global Container Terminals and the former CEO of CN Railway and Bombardier, Inc. "Before walking into the room for the actual negotiation, I ask my colleagues to throw some curve balls at me."[74]

Exhibit 10.6 Bargaining Zone Model of Negotiations

Your initial point — Your target point — Your resistance point

Area of potential agreement →

Opponent's resistance point — Opponent's target point — Opponent's initial offer point

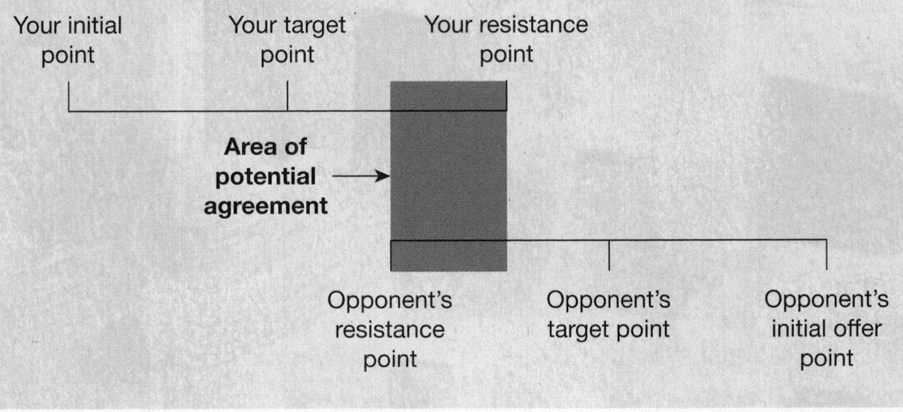

Know Your BATNA To determine whether the opponent's offers are favorable, negotiators need to understand what outcome they might achieve through some other means (such as negotiating with someone else). This comparison is called the **best alternative to a negotiated agreement (BATNA)**. BATNA estimates your power in the negotiation because it represents the estimated cost of walking away from the relationship. If others are willing to negotiate with you for the product or service you need, then you have a high BATNA and considerable power in the negotiation because it would not cost you much to walk away from the current negotiation. A common problem in negotiations, however, is that people tend to overestimate their BATNA; they wrongly believe there are plenty of other ways to achieve their objective rather than through this negotiation.

Manage Time Negotiators make more concessions as the deadline gets closer.[75] This can be a liability if you are under time pressure, or it can be an advantage if the other party alone is under time pressure. Negotiators with more power in the relationship sometimes apply time pressure through an "exploding offer" whereby they give their opponent a very short time to accept their offer.[76] These time-limited offers are frequently found in consumer sales ("on sale today only!") and in some job offers. They produce time pressure, which can motivate the other party to accept the offer and forfeit the opportunity to explore their BATNA. Another time factor is that the more time someone has invested in the negotiation, the more committed they become to ensuring an agreement is reached. This commitment increases the tendency to make unwarranted concessions so that the negotiations do not fail.

Manage First Offers and Concessions Negotiators who make the first offer have the advantage of creating a position around which subsequent negotiations are anchored. As we explained in Chapter 6, people tend to adjust their expectations around the initial point, so if your first offer is high, opponents might move more quickly toward their resistance point along the bargaining zone.[77] It may even cause opponents to lower their resistance point.

After the first offer, negotiators need to make concessions.[78] Concessions serve at least three important purposes: They (1) enable the parties to move toward the area of potential agreement, (2) symbolize each party's motivation to bargain in good faith, and (3) tell the other party of the relative importance of the negotiating items. However, concessions need to be clearly labeled as such and should be accompanied by an expectation that the other party will reciprocate. They should also be offered in installments because people experience more positive emotions from a few smaller concessions than from one large concession.[79] Generally, the best strategy is to be moderately tough and give just enough concessions to communicate sincerity and motivation to resolve the conflict.[80]

Strategies for Creating Value

Earlier in this section we pointed out that negotiations involve more than just claiming value; they also involve creating value—trying to obtain the best possible outcomes for both parties. In other words, negotiators need to apply the problem-solving approach to conflict handling. Information exchange is a critical feature of creating value, but it is also a potential pitfall. Information is power in negotiations, so information sharing gives the other party more power to leverage a better deal if the opportunity occurs.[81] Skilled negotiators address this dilemma by adopting a cautious problem-solving style at the outset. They begin by sharing information slowly and determining whether the other side will reciprocate. In this way, they try to establish trust with the other party. Here are several ways that skilled negotiators reap the benefits of problem solving and value creation.

Gather Information Information is the cornerstone of effective value creation.[82] Therefore, skilled negotiators heed the advice of the late management guru Stephen Covey: "Seek first to understand, then to be understood."[83] This means that we should present our case only after spending more time listening closely to the other party and asking for details. It is particularly important to look beyond the opponent's stated justifications to the unstated motivation for their claims. Probing questions (such as asking "why") and listening intently can reveal better solutions for both parties. Nonverbal communication can also convey important information about the other party's priorities. Negotiating in teams can also aid the information gathering process because some team members will hear information that others have ignored.

Discover Priorities through Offers and Concessions

Some types of offers and concessions are better than others at creating value. The key objective is to discover and signal which issues are more and less important to each side. Suppose that you have been asked to "second" (temporarily transfer) some of your best staff to projects in another division, whereas you need these people on-site for other assignments and to coach junior staff. Through problem-solving negotiation, you discover that the other division doesn't need those staff at their site; rather, the division head mainly needs some guarantee that these people will be available. The result is that your division keeps the staff (important to you) while the other division has some guarantee these people will be available at specific times for their projects (important to them).

One way to figure out the relative importance of the issues to each party is to make multi-issue offers rather than discuss one issue at a time.[84] You might offer a client a specific price, delivery date, and guarantee period, for example. The other party's counteroffer to multiple items signals which are more and which are less important to them. Your subsequent concessions similarly signal how important each issue is to your group.

Build the Relationship
Trust is critical for the problem-solving style of conflict handling as well as in the value creation objective of negotiations.[85] How do you build trust in negotiations? One approach is to discover common backgrounds and interests, such as places you have lived, favorite hobbies and sports teams, and so forth. If there are substantial differences between the parties (age, gender, etc.), consider having team members who more closely match the backgrounds of the other party. First impressions are also important. Recall from earlier chapters in this book that people attach emotions to incoming stimuli in a fraction of a second. Therefore, you need to be sensitive to your nonverbal cues, appearance, and initial statements.

Signaling that we are trustworthy also helps strengthen the relationship. We can do this by demonstrating that we are reliable, will keep our promises, and have shared goals and values with the other party. Trustworthiness also increases by developing a shared understanding of the negotiation process, including its norms and expectations about speed and timing.[86] Finally, relationship building demands emotional intelligence.[87] This includes managing the emotions you display to the other party, particularly avoiding an image of superiority, aggressiveness, or insensitivity. Emotional intelligence also involves managing the

other party's emotions. We can use well-placed flattery, humor, and other methods to keep everyone in a good mood and to break unnecessary tension.[88]

Situational Influences on Negotiations

The effectiveness of negotiating depends to some extent on the environment in which the negotiations occur. Three key situational factors are location, physical setting, and audience.

Location
It is easier to negotiate on your own turf because you are familiar with the negotiating environment and are able to maintain comfortable routines.[89] Also, there is no need to cope with travel-related stress or depend on others for resources during the negotiation. Of course, you can't walk out of negotiations as easily when the event occurs on your own turf, but this is usually a minor issue. Considering the strategic benefits of home turf, many negotiators agree to neutral territory. Phone calls, videoconferences, email, and other forms of information technology potentially avoid territorial issues, but skilled negotiators usually prefer the media richness of face-to-face meetings. Frank Lowy, cofounder of retail property giant Westfield Group, says that telephones are "too cold" for negotiating. "From a voice I don't get all the cues I need. I go by touch and feel and I need to see the other person."[90]

Physical Setting
The physical distance between the parties and formality of the setting can influence their orientation toward each other and the disputed issues. So can the seating arrangements. People who sit face-to-face are more likely to develop a win–lose orientation toward the conflict situation. In contrast, some negotiation groups deliberately intersperse participants around the table to convey a win–win orientation. Others arrange the seating so that both parties face a whiteboard, reflecting the notion that both parties face the same problem or issue.

Audience Characteristics
Most negotiators have audiences—anyone with a vested interest in the negotiation outcomes, such as executives, other team members, or the general public. Negotiators tend to act differently when their audience observes the negotiation or has detailed information about the process, compared to situations in which the audience sees only the end results.[91] When the audience has direct surveillance over the proceedings, negotiators tend to be more competitive, less willing to make concessions, and more likely to engage in assertive tactics against the other party. This "hard-line" behavior shows the audience that the negotiator is working for their interests. With their audience watching, negotiators also have more interest in saving face.

Study Checklist

- Did you tear out the perforated student review card at the back of the text to revisit learning objectives and key terms and definitions?

Connect® Management is available for *M Organizational Behavior*. Additional resources include:

- Interactive Applications:
  - **Case Analysis:** Apply concepts within the context of a real-world situation.
  - **Drag and Drop:** Work through an interactive example to test your knowledge of the concepts.
  - **Video Case:** See management in action through interactive videos.

- **SmartBook™**—SmartBook is the first and only adaptive reading experience available today. Distinguishing what you know from what you don't, and honing in on concepts you are most likely to forget, SmartBook personalizes content for you in a continuously adapting reading experience. Reading is no longer a passive and linear experience, but an engaging and dynamic one where you are more likely to master and retain important concepts and go to class better prepared.

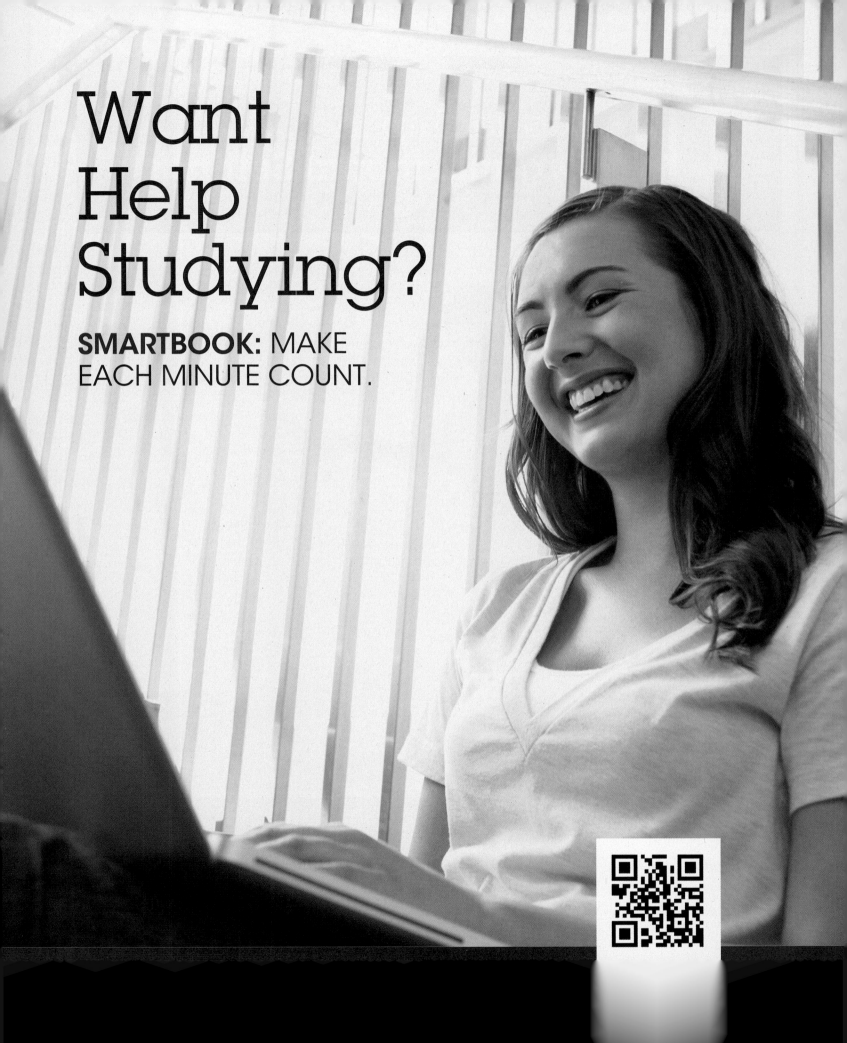

11 chapter

Leadership in Organizational Settings

Learning Objectives

After studying this chapter, you should be able to:

LO11-1 Define leadership and shared leadership.

LO11-2 Describe the four elements of transformational leadership and explain why they are important for organizational change.

LO11-3 Compare managerial leadership with transformational leadership and describe the features of task-oriented, people-oriented, and servant leadership.

LO11-4 Discuss the elements of path–goal theory, Fiedler's contingency model, and leadership substitutes.

LO11-5 Describe the two components of the implicit leadership perspective.

LO11-6 Identify eight personal attributes associated with effective leaders and describe authentic leadership.

LO11-7 Discuss cultural and gender similarities and differences in leadership.

Leadership is one of the most researched and discussed topics in the field of organizational behavior.[1] Google returns a whopping 306 million web pages where *leadership* is mentioned. Google Scholar lists 216,000 journal articles and books with *leader* or *leadership* in the title. Amazon lists more than 27,000 books in the English language with *leadership* in the title. From 2000 to 2009, the U.S. Library of Congress catalog added 7,336 books or documents with the words *leader* or *leadership* in the citation, compared with 3,054 items added in the 1990s and only 146 items with these words (many of which were newspaper names) added during the first decade of the 1900s.

The topic of leadership captivates us because we are awed by individuals who influence and motivate a group of people beyond expectations. This chapter explores leadership from four perspectives: transformational, managerial, implicit, and personal attributes.[2] Although some of these perspectives are currently more popular than others, each helps us to more fully understand the complex issue of leadership. The final section of this chapter looks at cross-cultural and gender issues in organizational leadership. But first, we learn about the meaning of leadership as well as shared leadership.

LO11-1 Define leadership and shared leadership.

WHAT IS LEADERSHIP?

Several years ago, 54 leadership experts from 38 countries reached a consensus that **leadership** is about influencing, motivating, and enabling others to contribute toward the effectiveness and success of the organizations of which they are members.[3] This definition has two key components. First, leaders motivate others through persuasion and other influence tactics. They use their communication skills, rewards, and other resources to energize the collective toward the achievement of challenging objectives. Second, leaders are enablers. They arrange the work environment—such as allocating resources, altering work relationships, and buffering from outside interferences—so employees can achieve organizational objectives more easily.

Filling the U.S. Library of Congress with Leadership Books and Materials

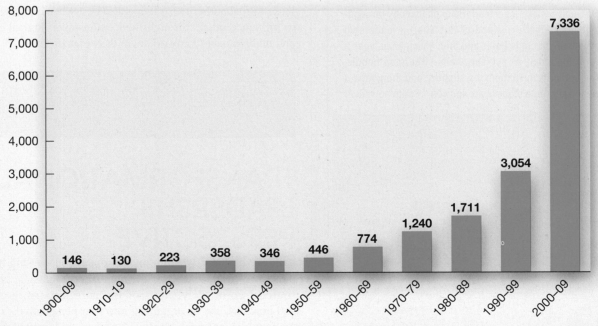

Note: Number of books and other materials with *leader* or *leadership* in the title or citation cataloged by the U.S. Library of Congress and currently listed in its catalog, by decade that the item was published or produced. The U.S. Library of Congress is the world's largest library.

Shared Leadership

Organizational behavior experts have long argued that leadership is not about specific positions in the organizational hierarchy. Of course, formal leaders are responsible for "leading" others, but companies are far more effective when everyone assumes leadership responsibilities in various ways and at various times. This emerging view, called **shared leadership**, is based on the idea that leadership is a role, not a position.[5] As such, employees lead each other as the occasion arises. Shared leadership exists when employees champion the introduction of new technologies and products.[6] It also exists when employees engage in organizational citizenship behaviors to assist the performance and well-being of coworkers and the overall team.

John Gardner, the former White House cabinet member who introduced Medicare, wrote more than two decades ago that organizations depend on employees across all levels of the organization to seek out opportunities and solutions rather than rely on formal leaders to do so.[7] Shared leadership is now gaining acceptance in the business community. For example, Fiat and Chrysler CEO Sergio Marchionne recently said: "We've abandoned the Great Man model of leadership that long characterized Fiat and have created a culture where everyone is expected to lead."[8]

Shared leadership typically supplements formal leadership; that is, employees lead along with the formal manager, rather than replace the manager. However, W. L. Gore & Associates, Semco SA, Valve Corporation, and a few other unique companies rely almost completely on shared leadership because they don't have any formal managers on the organizational chart.[10] In fact, when Gore employees are asked "Are you a leader?" in annual surveys, more than 50 percent of them answer yes.

Shared leadership flourishes in organizations where the formal leaders are willing to delegate power and encourage employees to take initiative and risks without fear of failure (i.e., a learning orientation culture). Shared leadership also calls for a collaborative rather than internally competitive culture because employees take on shared leadership roles when coworkers support them for their initiative. Furthermore, shared leadership lacks formal authority, so it operates best when employees learn to influence others through their enthusiasm, logical analysis, and involvement of coworkers in their idea or vision.

EllisDon: The Leaderful Construction Services Company

At EllisDon, leaders aren't just people in management jobs. The Canadian construction services giant believes that leadership extends to every employee in the organization. "Everyone is a leader, everyone is accountable to each other, and everyone is involved in the success of the company as a whole," says EllisDon CEO Geoff Smith. "It's a leadership philosophy throughout our company." EllisDon supports this shared leadership approach by setting outcome goals and then giving employees a high degree of autonomy to achieve them. "Get good people, give them the authority, give them the support, and then get out of their way so you create leaders around you," Smith advises.[9]

> **LO11-2** Describe the four elements of transformational leadership and explain why they are important for organizational change.

TRANSFORMATIONAL LEADERSHIP PERSPECTIVE

A huge volume of writing on the topic of leadership has been published in journals, books, magazines, websites, and other sources. Fortunately, most of the core leadership concepts and practices can be organized into four perspectives: transformational, managerial, implicit, and personal attributes. By far the most popular of these perspectives today—and arguably the

most important in the domain of leadership—is transformational leadership. **Transformational leadership** views leaders as change agents. They create, communicate, and model a shared vision for the team or organization. They encourage experimentation so employees find a better path to the future. Through these and other activities, transformational leaders also build commitment in followers to strive for that vision.

There are several models of transformational leadership, but four elements that are common throughout most of them and represent the core concepts of this leadership perspective are to develop and communicate a strategic vision, model the vision, encourage experimentation, and build commitment to the vision (see Exhibit 11.1).[11]

Develop and Communicate a Strategic Vision

The heart of transformational leadership is a strategic *vision*.[12] A vision is a positive image or model of the future that energizes and unifies employees.[13] Sometimes this vision is created by the leader; at other times, it is formed by employees or other stakeholders and then adopted and championed by the formal leader. An effective strategic vision has several identifiable features.[14] It refers to an idealized future with a higher purpose. This purpose is associated with personal values that directly or indirectly fulfill the needs of multiple stakeholders. A values-based vision is also meaningful and appealing to employees,

leadership
influencing, motivating, and enabling others to contribute toward the effectiveness and success of the organizations of which they are members

shared leadership
the view that leadership is a role, not a position assigned to one person; consequently, people within the team and organization lead each other

transformational leadership
a leadership perspective that explains how leaders change teams or organizations by creating, communicating, and modeling a vision for the organization or work unit and inspiring employees to strive for that vision

which energizes them to strive for that ideal. A vision needs to energize employees because it is usually a distant goal that is both challenging and abstract. A vision is challenging because it requires substantial transformation, such as new work practices and belief systems.

A strategic vision is necessarily abstract for two reasons. One reason is that it hasn't yet been experienced (at least, not in this company or industry), so it isn't possible to detail what the vision looks like. The other reason is that an abstract description enables the vision to remain stable over time, yet is sufficiently flexible to accommodate operational adjustments in a shifting external environment. As such, a vision describes a broad noble cause related to fulfilling the needs of one or more stakeholder groups.

Another feature of an effective vision is that it is unifying. It is a superordinate objective that bonds employees together and aligns their personal values with the organization's values. In fact, a successful vision is really a shared vision because employees collectively define themselves by this aspirational image of the future as part of their identification with the organization.

Communicate the Vision A strategic vision's effectiveness depends on how leaders convey it to followers and other stakeholders.[15] Words shape how we view the world, so successful transformational leaders carefully choose phrases that "frame" the vision and evoke desired images of the ideal future. Leaders also communicate the vision with a sincerity and level of passion that reflects their personal belief in the vision and optimism that it can be reached. In other words, leaders communicate the vision nonverbally as well as verbally.

A third way leaders communicate the vision is through symbols, metaphors, stories, and other vehicles that transcend plain language.[16] These tools often borrow images from other experiences, thereby creating richer meaning of the not-yet-experienced vision. Borrowing from existing experiences also generates

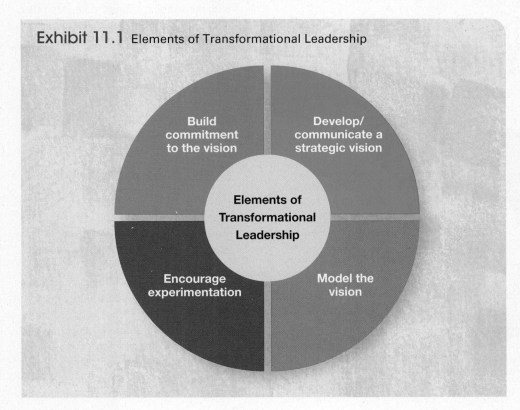

Exhibit 11.1 Elements of Transformational Leadership

- Build commitment to the vision
- Develop/communicate a strategic vision
- Encourage experimentation
- Model the vision

Elements of Transformational Leadership

desired emotions, which motivates people to pursue the vision. For instance, when McDonald's faced the daunting challenge of opening the company's first restaurants in Russia (back when it was the USSR), CEO George Cohen frequently reminded his team members that they were establishing "hamburger diplomacy."[17]

Model the Vision

Transformational leaders not only talk about a vision; they enact it. They "walk the talk" by stepping outside the executive suite and doing things that symbolize the vision.[19] Leaders model the vision through significant events such as visiting customers, moving their offices closer to (or further from) employees, and holding ceremonies to symbolize significant change. However, they also enact the vision by ensuring that the more mundane daily activities—meeting agendas, dress codes, executive schedules—are consistent with the vision and its underlying values.

Modeling the vision is important because it legitimizes and demonstrates what the vision looks like in practice. Modeling is also important because it builds employee trust in the leader. The greater the consistency between the leader's words and actions, the more employees will believe in and be willing to follow the leader. In fact, one survey reported that leading by example is the most important characteristic of a leader.[20] "We hold our leaders to an even higher standard than our employees," says Nathan Bigler, human resource director at Eastern Idaho Regional Medical Center. "Leaders have to consistently walk the talk."[21]

Encourage Experimentation

Transformational leadership is about change, and central to any change is discovering new behaviors and practices that are better aligned with the desired vision. Thus, effective transformational leaders encourage employees to question current practices and to experiment with new ways that are potentially more consistent with the visionary future state.[23] In other words, transformational leaders support a learning orientation (see Chapter 6). They encourage employees to continuously question the way things are currently done, actively experiment with new ideas and practices, and view reasonable mistakes as a natural part of the learning process.[24]

Build Commitment toward the Vision

Transforming a vision into reality requires employee commitment, and transformational leaders build this commitment in several ways.[25] Their words, symbols, and stories build a contagious enthusiasm that energizes people to adopt the vision as their own. Leaders demonstrate a can-do attitude by enacting and behaving consistently with their vision. This persistence and consistency reflect an image of honesty, trust, and integrity. By encouraging experimentation, leaders

Leading without Vision?[18]

47%
of 1,200 Canadian employees surveyed strongly or somewhat agree that senior management in their organization communicates a clear vision.

40%
of 1,061 American employees surveyed say they don't get (understand) the company's vision or have never seen it.

42%
of more than 40,000 employees surveyed in 300 global companies say they know their organization's vision, mission, and values.

38%
of 168,000 employees surveyed across 30 countries say they either do not believe in their employer's mission/purpose (vision) or don't understand it.

involve employees in the change process so it is a collective activity. Leaders also build commitment through rewards, recognition, and celebrations as they pass milestones along the road to the desired vision.

Transformational Leadership and Charisma

Some experts believe that charisma is an element of transformational leadership. They describe charismatic leadership either as an essential ingredient of transformational leadership or as transformational leadership in its highest form of excellence.[26] However, the emerging view, which this book adopts, is that charisma is distinct from transformational leadership. Charisma is a personal trait or relational quality that provides referent power over followers, whereas transformational leadership is a set of behaviors that engage followers toward a better future.[27]

Transformational leadership motivates followers through behaviors that persuade and earn trust, whereas charismatic leadership motivates followers directly through the leader's inherent referent power. For instance, communicating an inspiring vision is a transformational leadership behavior that motivates followers to strive for that vision. This motivational effect exists separate from the leader's charismatic appeal. If the leader is highly charismatic, however, his or her charisma will amplify follower motivation.

Being charismatic is not inherently good or bad, but several research studies have concluded that charismatic leaders can produce negative consequences.[28] One concern with charismatic leadership is that it tends to produce dependent followers. Transformational leadership has the opposite effect—it builds follower empowerment, which tends to reduce dependence on the leader.

Another concern is that leaders who possess the gift of charisma may become intoxicated by this power, which leads to a greater focus on self-interest than on the common good. "Charisma becomes the undoing of leaders," warned Peter Drucker many years ago. "It makes them inflexible, convinced of their own infallibility, unable to change."[29] The late management guru witnessed the destructive effects of charismatic political leaders in Europe a century ago and foresaw that this personal or relational characteristic would create similar problems for organizations. The main point here is that transformational leaders are not necessarily charismatic, and charismatic leaders are not necessarily transformational.

Evaluating the Transformational Leadership Perspective

Transformational leaders do make a difference.[30] Subordinates are more satisfied and have higher affective organizational commitment under transformational leaders. They also perform their jobs better, engage in more organizational citizenship behaviors, and make better or more creative decisions. One study of bank branches reported that organizational commitment and financial performance increased when the branch manager completed a transformational leadership training program.[31]

Transformational leadership is currently the most popular leadership perspective, but it faces a number of challenges.[32] One problem is that some models engage in circular logic. They define and measure transformational leadership by its effects on employees (e.g., inspire employees), then (not surprisingly) report that this leadership is effective because it inspires employees. Instead, transformational leadership needs to be defined purely as a set of behaviors that people use to lead others through the change process. A second concern is that some transformational leadership theories combine leader behaviors with the personal characteristics of leaders. For instance, transformational leaders are described as visionary, imaginative, sensitive, and thoughtful, yet these personal characteristics are really predictors of transformational leadership behaviors.

A third concern is that transformational leadership is usually described as a universal concept, that is, it is good in all situations. Only a few studies have investigated whether this form of leadership is more valuable in some situations than others.[33] For instance, transformational leadership is probably more appropriate when organizations need to continuously adapt to a rapidly changing external environment than when the environment is stable. Preliminary evidence suggests that the transformational leadership perspective is relevant across cultures. However, there may be specific elements of transformational leadership, such as the way visions are communicated and modeled, that are more appropriate in North America than in other cultures.

MANAGERIAL LEADERSHIP PERSPECTIVE

Leaders don't spend all (or even most) of their time transforming the organization or work unit. They also engage in **managerial leadership**—daily activities that support and guide the performance and well-being of individual employees and the work unit toward current objectives and practices. Leadership experts recognize that leading (transformational leadership) differs from managing (managerial leadership).[34] Although the distinction between these two perspectives remains somewhat fuzzy, each cluster has a reasonably clear set of activities and strong research foundation.

One distinction between these two perspectives is that managerial leadership assumes the organization's (or department's) objectives are stable and aligned with the external environment.[36]

> "Managers are people who do things right and leaders are people who do the right thing."[35]
>
> —**Warren Bennis,** leadership scholar

It focuses on continuously developing or maintaining the effectiveness of employees and work units toward those established objectives and practices. In contrast, transformational leadership assumes the organization's current direction is misaligned and therefore needs to change toward a better future. This distinction is captured in the often-cited statement that managers are people who do things right and leaders are people who do the right thing. Managers (more correctly, managerial leadership behaviors) "do things right" by enabling employees to perform established goals more effectively. Leaders (more correctly, transformational leadership behaviors) "do the right thing" by redirecting the organization toward a path that is better aligned with the external environment.

A second distinction is that managerial leadership is more micro-focused and concrete, because it relates to the specific performance and well-being objectives of individual employees and the immediate work unit. Transformational leadership is more macro-focused and abstract. It is directed toward an abstract strategic vision for an entire organization, department, or team.

Although transformational and managerial leadership are discussed as two leadership perspectives, they are better described as *interdependent* perspectives.[37] In other words, transformational leadership and managerial leadership depend on each other. Transformational leadership identifies, communicates, and builds commitment to a better future for the collective. But these transformational leadership behaviors are not enough for organizational success. That success also requires managerial leadership to translate the abstract vision into more specific operational behaviors and practices, and to continuously improve employee performance and well-being in the pursuit of that future ideal.

Managerial leadership also depends on transformational leadership to set the right direction. Otherwise, managers produce operational excellence toward long-range goals that are misaligned with the organization's long-term survival and for which employees lack commitment. For instance, the leaders at Dell Inc. relied on managerial excellence to produce low-cost computers, yet the company subsequently suffered because the external environment shifted toward higher-priced, innovative products.[38] In other words, successful managerial leadership (operational efficiency with reasonably happy employees) was not enough to make Dell successful. It also needed transformational leadership to develop a vision that aligned the company's products more closely with the marketplace and inspired employees to work toward that vision.

An important message here is that managerial and transformational leadership are not embodied in different people or positions in the organization. As you might expect, senior executive positions require more transformational leadership behavior than do management positions further down the hierarchy,

likely because transformational leadership requires more discretion to enable macro-level change. However, every manager needs to apply both transformational and managerial leadership behaviors to varying degrees. Indeed, frontline employees who engage in shared leadership may be managerial (helping coworkers through a difficult project) or transformational (championing a more customer-friendly culture in the work unit).

Task-Oriented and People-Oriented Leadership

Managerial leadership research began in the 1940s and 1950s, when research teams at several universities launched intensive investigations to answer the question "What behaviors make leaders effective?" They studied first-line supervisors by asking subordinates to rate their bosses on many behaviors. These independent research teams essentially produced the same two clusters of leadership behavior from literally thousands of items (Exhibit 11.2).[39]

One cluster, called *task-oriented leadership*, includes behaviors that define and structure work roles. Task-oriented leaders assign employees to specific tasks, set goals and deadlines, clarify work duties and procedures, define work procedures, and plan work activities. The other cluster represents *people-oriented leadership*. This cluster includes behaviors such as listening to employees for their opinions and ideas, creating a pleasant physical work environment, showing interest in staff, complimenting and recognizing employees for their effort, and showing consideration of employee needs.

These early studies tried to find out whether effective managers are more task-oriented or more people-oriented. This proved to be a difficult

> Servant leaders have a natural desire or "calling" to serve others—a deep commitment to help others in their personal growth for that purpose alone.

question to answer because each style has its advantages and disadvantages. In fact, recent evidence suggests that effective leaders rely on both styles, but in different ways.[40] When leaders apply high levels of people-oriented leadership behavior, their employees tend to have more positive attitudes as well as lower absenteeism, grievances, and turnover. For instance, one recent study reported that followers have fewer stress symptoms when leaders show empathy toward employees.[41] When leaders have more task-oriented leadership, their employees tend to have higher job performance. Not surprisingly, employees generally prefer people-oriented bosses and they form negative attitudes toward bosses who are mostly task-oriented. However, task-oriented leadership is also appreciated to some degree. For example, college students value task-oriented instructors because they want clear expectations and well-prepared lectures that abide by the course objectives.[42]

Servant Leadership

Servant leadership is an extension or variation of people-oriented leadership because it defines leadership as serving others. In particular, servant leaders assist others in their need fulfillment, personal development, and growth.[43] Servant leaders ask "How can I help you?" rather than expecting employees to serve them. Servant leaders have been described as selfless, egalitarian, humble, nurturing, empathetic, and ethical coaches. The main objective of servant leadership is to help followers and other stakeholders fulfill their needs and potential, particularly "to become healthier, wiser, freer, more autonomous, more likely themselves to become servants."[44]

Servant leadership research suffers from ambiguous and conflicting definitions, but writers agree on a few features.[45] First, servant leaders have a natural desire or "calling" to serve others. This natural desire is a deep commitment to help others in their personal growth for that purpose alone. It goes beyond the leader's role

managerial leadership a leadership perspective stating that effective leaders help employees improve their performance and well-being toward current objectives and practices

servant leadership the view that leaders serve followers, rather than vice versa; leaders help employees fulfill their needs and are coaches, stewards, and facilitators of employee development

Exhibit 11.2 Task- and People-Oriented Leadership Styles

Leaders are task-oriented when they . . .	Leaders are people-oriented when they . . .
• Assign work and clarify responsibilities. • Set goals and deadlines. • Evaluate and provide feedback on work quality. • Establish well-defined best work procedures. • Plan future work activities.	• Show interest in others as people. • Listen to employees. • Make the workplace more pleasant. • Show appreciation to employees for their performance contribution. • Are considerate of employee needs.

path–goal leadership theory a leadership theory stating that effective leaders choose the most appropriate leadership style(s), depending on the employee and situation, to influence employee expectations about desired results and their positive outcomes

obligation to help others and is not merely an instrument to achieve company objectives. Second, servant leaders maintain a relationship with others that is humble, egalitarian, and accepting. Servant leaders do not view leadership as a position of power. Rather, they serve without drawing attention to themselves, without evoking superior status, and without being judgmental about others or defensive of criticisms received. Third, servant leaders anchor their decisions and actions in ethical principles and practices. They display sensitivity to and enactment of moral values and are not swayed by social pressures or expectations to deviate from those values.

Servant Leadership Ingrained in **Military Leadership**

Servant leadership has recently gained the attention of organizational behavior scholars, but it has been ingrained in military leadership for decades. "If you look at our Army Values, the center of that is selfless service," explains General Daniel Allyn, commander of United States Army Forces Command (front right in photo). "The idea of servant leadership is you put others before yourself. That, to me, is an inherent quality of leadership, and our Warrior Ethos also speaks to it in 'I'll never leave a fallen comrade.' That implies that we're going to do all we can to ensure that we're always looking after the needs of our Soldiers."[46]

In this respect, servant leadership relies heavily on the idea of authentic leadership that we discuss later in this chapter.

Servant leadership was introduced four decades ago and has since had a steady following, particularly among practitioners and religious leaders. Scholarly interest in this topic has bloomed within the past few years, but the concept still faces a number of conceptual hurdles. Although servant leadership writers generally agree on the three features we described earlier, many have included other characteristics that lack agreement and might confound the concept with its predictors and outcomes. Still, the notion of leader as servant has considerable currency and for many centuries has been embedded in the principles of major religions. One recent study also found that companies have higher performance (return on assets) when their chief executive officer exhibits servant leadership behaviors.[47]

> **LO11-4** Discuss the elements of path–goal theory, Fiedler's contingency model, and leadership substitutes.

Path–Goal Leadership Theory

The servant leadership model implies that leaders should be servants in all circumstances. However, the broader literature on task-oriented and people-oriented leadership has concluded that the best style is contingent on the situation.[48] This "it depends" view is more consistent with the contingency anchor of organizational behavior discussed in Chapter 1. In other words, the most appropriate leadership style depends on the characteristics of the employees, work setting, the leader–follower relationship, and other factors.

Path–goal leadership theory is the dominant model that applies this contingency approach to managerial leadership. The main premise of path–goal theory is that effective leaders choose one or more leadership styles to influence employee expectations (their preferred path) regarding achievement of desired results (their work-related goals), as well as their perceived satisfaction with those results (outcome valences). In other words, path–goal theory recognizes that leadership is an important influence in the expectancy theory of motivation (Chapter 5) and its underlying formula, subjective expected utility (Chapter 6).[49] Leaders clarify the link between employee behaviors and outcomes, influence the value of those outcomes, provide a work environment to facilitate goal accomplishment, and so forth.[50]

Path–Goal Leadership Styles Exhibit 11.3 presents the path–goal theory of leadership. This model specifically highlights four leadership styles and several contingency factors leading to three indicators of leader effectiveness. The four leadership styles are:[51]

- *Directive.* Directive leadership is the same as task-oriented leadership, described earlier. This leadership style consists of clarifying behaviors that provide a psychological structure for subordinates.

Exhibit 11.3 Path–Goal Leadership Theory

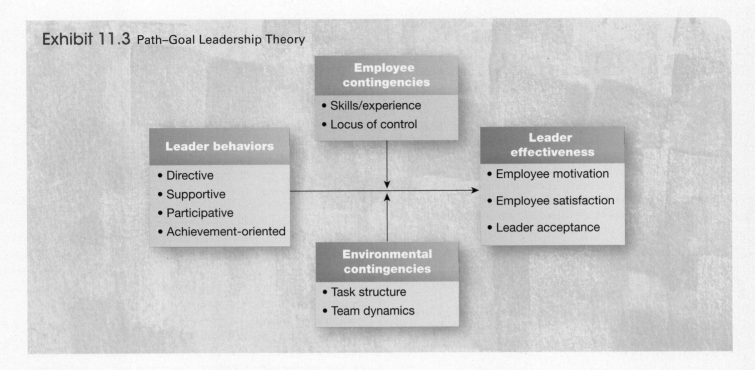

This includes clarifying performance goals, the means to reach those goals, and the standards against which performance will be judged. It also includes judicious use of rewards and disciplinary actions.

- *Supportive.* Supportive leadership is the same as people-oriented leadership, described earlier. This style provides psychological support for subordinates. The leader is friendly and approachable; makes the work more pleasant; treats employees with equal respect; and shows concern for the status, needs, and well-being of employees.

- *Participative.* Participative leadership behaviors encourage and facilitate subordinate involvement in decisions beyond their normal work activities. The leader consults with employees, asks for their suggestions, and takes these ideas into serious consideration before making a decision. Participative leadership relates to involving employees in decisions (see Chapter 6).

- *Achievement-oriented.* This leadership style emphasizes behaviors that encourage employees to reach their peak performance. The leader sets challenging goals, expects employees to perform at their highest level, continuously seeks improvement in employee performance, and shows a high degree of confidence that employees will assume responsibility and accomplish challenging goals. Achievement-oriented leadership applies goal-setting theory as well as positive expectations in self-fulfilling prophecy.

The path–goal model contends that effective leaders are capable of selecting the most appropriate behavioral style (or styles) for each situation. Also, leaders often use two or more styles at the same time, if these styles are appropriate for the circumstances.

Contingencies of Path–Goal Theory As a contingency theory, path–goal theory states that each of the four leadership styles will be more effective in some situations than in others. The path–goal leadership model specifies two sets of situational variables that moderate the relationship between a

How Satisfied Are Employees with Their Management's Leadership Style?[52]

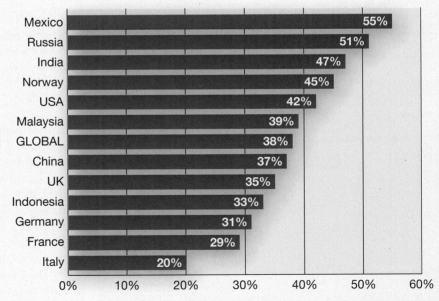

Note: Percentage of employees surveyed in selected countries who indicated that they are satisfied with their management's leadership style. Data were collected for Kelly Services in 2012 from more than 168,000 people in 30 countries. The global average includes respondents from all 30 countries, not just those shown in this chart.

leader's style and effectiveness: (1) employee characteristics and (2) characteristics of the employee's work environment. Several contingencies have already been studied within the path–goal framework, and the model is open for more variables in the future.[53] However, only four contingencies are reviewed here.

- *Skill and experience.* A combination of directive and supportive leadership is best for employees who are (or perceive themselves to be) inexperienced and unskilled.[54] Directive leadership gives subordinates information about how to accomplish the task, whereas supportive leadership helps them cope with the uncertainties of unfamiliar work situations. Directive leadership is detrimental when employees are skilled and experienced because it introduces too much supervisory control.

- *Locus of control.* People with an internal locus of control believe that they have control over their work environment (see Chapter 3). Consequently, these employees prefer participative and achievement-oriented leadership styles and may become frustrated with a directive style. In contrast, people with an external locus of control believe that their performance is due more to luck and fate, so they tend to be more satisfied with directive and supportive leadership.

- *Task structure.* Leaders should adopt the directive style when the task is nonroutine, because this style minimizes the role ambiguity that tends to occur in complex work situations (particularly for inexperienced employees).[55] The directive style is ineffective when employees have routine and simple tasks because the manager's guidance serves no purpose and may be viewed as unnecessarily close control. Employees in highly routine and simple jobs may require supportive leadership to help them cope with the tedious nature of the work and lack of control over the pace of work. Participative leadership is preferred for employees performing nonroutine tasks because the lack of rules and procedures gives them more discretion to achieve challenging goals. The participative style is ineffective for employees in routine tasks because they lack discretion over their work.

- *Team dynamics.* Cohesive teams with performance-oriented norms act as a substitute for most leader interventions. High team cohesion

substitutes for supportive leadership, whereas performance-oriented team norms substitute for directive and possibly achievement-oriented leadership. Thus, when team cohesion is low, leaders should use a supportive style. Leaders should apply a directive style to counteract team norms that oppose the team's formal objectives. For example, the team leader may need to exert authority if team members have developed a norm to "take it easy" rather than get a project completed on time.

Evaluating Path–Goal Theory Path–goal theory has received more research support than other managerial leadership models. In fact, one study reported that path–goal theory explained more about effective leadership than did the transformational leadership model.[56] This stronger effect is likely because most managers spend more of their time engaging in managerial rather than transformational leadership.[57]

Support for the path–goal model is far from ideal, however. A few contingencies (e.g., task structure) have limited research support. Other contingencies and leadership styles in the path–goal leadership model haven't been investigated at all.[58] Another concern is that as path–goal theory expands, the model may become too complex for practical use. Few people would be able to remember all the contingencies and the appropriate leadership styles for those contingencies.

Another limitation of path–goal theory is its assumption that effective leaders can adapt their behaviors and styles to the immediate situation. In reality, leaders typically have a preferred style. It takes considerable effort for leaders to choose and enact different styles to match the situation. In spite of these limitations, path–goal theory remains a relatively robust theory of managerial leadership.

Other Managerial Leadership Theories

Several other managerial leadership theories have developed over the years. Some overlap with the path–goal model's leadership styles, but most use simpler and more abstract contingencies. We will briefly mention only two here because of their popularity and historical significance to the field.

Situational Leadership Theory One of the most popular managerial leadership theories among practitioners is the **situational leadership theory (SLT)**, developed by Paul Hersey and Ken Blanchard.[59] SLT suggests that effective leaders vary their style with the ability and motivation (or commitment) of followers. The most recent version uses four labels to describe followers, such as "enthusiastic beginner" (low ability, high motivation) and "disillusioned learner" (moderate ability and low motivation).

The situational leadership model also identifies four leadership styles—telling, selling, participating, and delegating—that Hersey and Blanchard distinguish by the amount of task-oriented and people-oriented behavior provided. For example, "telling" has high task behavior and low supportive behavior. The situational leadership model has four quadrants, with each quadrant showing the leadership style that is most appropriate under different circumstances.

In spite of its popularity, several studies and at least three reviews have concluded that the situational leadership model lacks empirical support.[60] Only one part of the model apparently works, namely, that leaders should use "telling" (i.e., task-oriented style) when employees lack motivation and ability. This relationship is also documented in path–goal theory. The model's elegant simplicity is attractive and entertaining, but most parts don't represent reality very well.

Fiedler's Contingency Model **Fiedler's contingency model**, developed by Fred Fiedler and his associates, is the earliest managerial leadership theory that adopted the contingency approach.[62] According to this model, leader effectiveness depends on whether the person's natural leadership style is appropriately matched to the situation. The theory examines two leadership styles that essentially correspond to the previously described people-oriented and task-oriented styles. Unfortunately, Fiedler's model relies on a questionnaire that does not measure either leadership style very well.

Fiedler's model suggests that the best leadership style depends on the level of *situational control,* that is, the degree of power and influence that the leader possesses in a particular situation. Situational control is affected by three factors in the following order of importance: leader–member relations, task structure, and position power.[63] *Leader–member relations* refers to how much employees trust and respect the leader and are willing to follow his or her guidance. *Task structure* refers to the clarity or ambiguity of operating procedures. *Position power* is the extent to which the leader possesses legitimate, reward, and coercive power over subordinates. These three contingencies form the eight possible combinations of *situation favorableness* from the leader's viewpoint. Good leader–member relations, high task structure, and strong position power create the most favorable situation for the leader because he or she has the most power and influence under these conditions.

> ## Contrary to the assumptions of most leadership theories, leaders might not be able to change their style easily to fit the situation.

Situational Leadership Theory:
Widely Adopted in Spite of the Evidence[61]

1972
Year that Hersey and Blanchard introduced situational leadership theory (then known as "life-cycle leadership").

70
Percentage of *Fortune* 500 companies that currently use one or more situational leadership training products.

14 **million**
Estimated number of people who have received situational leadership training (as of 2010).

3 **million**
Estimated number of people who have received situational leadership training (as of 1997).

Fiedler's theory lacks research support, mainly due to flaws with its leadership-style scale, its limited focus on only two leadership styles, and its creation of a single contingency variable (leader–member relations) based on an unexplainable arrangement of three situational factors in a hierarchy.[64] However, Fiedler's model makes two lasting contributions to leadership knowledge. One contribution is that it recognizes the importance of the leader's power in determining the best leadership style. Leader power is not explicit in other managerial leadership models.

Second, contrary to the assumptions of most leadership theories, Fiedler argues that leaders might not be able to change their style easily to fit the situation. Instead, they tend to rely mainly on one style that is most consistent with their personality and values. Leaders with high agreeableness personality and benevolence values tend to prefer supportive leadership, for example, whereas leaders with high conscientiousness personality and achievement values feel more comfortable with the

high-involvement team structures.[68] Coworkers instruct new employees, thereby providing directive leadership. They also provide social support, which reduces stress among fellow employees. Teams with norms that support organizational goals may substitute for achievement-oriented leadership, because employees encourage (or pressure) coworkers to stretch their performance levels.[69]

The leadership substitutes model has intuitive appeal, but the evidence so far is mixed. Some studies show that a few substitutes do replace the need for task- or people-oriented leadership, but others do not. The difficulties of statistically testing for leadership substitutes may account for some problems, but a few writers contend that the limited support is evidence that leadership plays a critical role regardless of the situation.[70] At this point, we can conclude that leadership substitutes might reduce the need for leaders, but they do not completely replace leaders in these situations.

LO11-5 Describe the two components of the implicit leadership perspective.

IMPLICIT LEADERSHIP PERSPECTIVE

The transformational and managerial leadership perspectives make the basic assumption that leaders "make a difference." Certainly, there is evidence that leaders do influence the performance of their departments and organizations. However, leadership also involves followers' perceptions about the characteristics and attributions of people in formal leadership positions. This perceptual perspective of leadership, called **implicit leadership theory**, has two components: leader prototypes and the romance or attribution of leadership.[71]

Prototypes of Effective Leaders

One aspect of implicit leadership theory states that everyone has *leadership prototypes*—preconceived beliefs about the features and behaviors of effective leaders.[72] These prototypes, which develop through socialization within the family and society, shape the follower's expectations and acceptance of others as leaders, and this in turn affects their willingness to remain as a follower. Leadership prototypes not only support a person's role as leader; they also influence our perception of the leader's effectiveness. In other words, leaders are often perceived as more effective when they look and act consistently like observers' prototype of a leader.[73]

directive style of leadership.[65] Recently, other scholars have also proposed that leadership styles are "hardwired" more than most contingency leadership theories assume.[66] Leaders might be able to alter their style temporarily, but they tend to rely mainly on one style that is most consistent with their personality and values.

Leadership Substitutes

So far, we have looked at managerial leadership theories that recommend using different leadership styles in various situations. But one theory, called **leadership substitutes**, identifies conditions that either limit the leader's ability to influence subordinates or make a particular leadership style unnecessary. The literature identifies several conditions that possibly substitute for task-oriented or people-oriented leadership. Task-oriented leadership might be less important when performance-based reward systems keep employees directed toward organizational goals. Similarly, increasing employee skill and experience might reduce the need for task-oriented leadership. This proposition is consistent with path–goal leadership theory, which states that directive leadership is unnecessary—and may be detrimental—when employees are skilled or experienced.[67]

Some research suggests that effective leaders help team members learn to lead themselves through leadership substitutes; in other words, coworkers substitute for leadership in

> Leaders are often perceived as more effective when they look and act consistently like observers' prototype of a leader.

Why does this prototype comparison process occur? People want to trust their leader before they are willing to serve as followers, yet the leader's actual effectiveness usually isn't known for several months or possibly years. The prototype comparison process is a quick (although faulty) way of estimating the leader's effectiveness.

The Romance of Leadership

Along with relying on implicit prototypes of effective leaders, followers tend to distort their perception of the influence that leaders have on the organization's success. This "romance of leadership" effect exists because people in most cultures want to believe that leaders make a difference.

There are two basic reasons why people inflate their perceptions of the leader's influence over the environment.[74] First, leadership is a useful way for us to simplify life events. It is easier to explain organizational successes and failures in terms of the leader's ability than by analyzing a complex array of other forces. Second, there is a strong tendency in the United States and other Western cultures to believe that life events are generated more by people than by uncontrollable natural forces.[75] This illusion of control is satisfied by believing that events result from the rational actions of leaders. In other words, employees feel better believing that leaders make a difference, so they actively look for evidence that this is so.

One way that followers support their perceptions that leaders make a difference is through fundamental attribution error (see Chapter 3). Research has found that (at least in Western cultures) leaders are given credit or blame for the company's success or failure because employees do not readily see the external forces that also influence these events. Leaders reinforce this belief by taking credit for organizational successes.[76]

The implicit leadership perspective provides valuable advice to improve leadership acceptance. It highlights the fact that leadership is a perception of followers as much as the actual behaviors and formal roles of people calling themselves leaders. Potential leaders must be sensitive to this fact, understand what followers expect, and act accordingly. Individuals who do not naturally fit leadership prototypes need to provide more direct evidence of their effectiveness as leaders.

leadership substitutes a theory identifying conditions that either limit a leader's ability to influence subordinates or make a particular leadership style unnecessary

implicit leadership theory a theory stating that people evaluate a leader's effectiveness in terms of how well that person fits preconceived beliefs about the features and behaviors of effective leaders (leadership prototypes) and that people tend to inflate the influence of leaders on organizational events

LO11-6 Identify eight personal attributes associated with effective leaders and describe authentic leadership.

PERSONAL ATTRIBUTES PERSPECTIVE OF LEADERSHIP

Since the beginning of recorded civilization, people have been interested in the personal characteristics that distinguish great leaders from the rest of us.[77] One groundbreaking review in the late 1940s concluded that no consistent list of leadership traits could be distilled from previous research. This conclusion was revised a decade later, suggesting that a few traits are associated with effective leaders.[78] These nonsignificant findings caused many scholars to give up their search for the personal characteristics of effective leaders.

Over the past two decades, leadership experts have returned to the notion that effective leaders possess specific personal attributes.[79] Most scholarly studies long ago were apparently plagued by methodological problems, lack of theoretical foundation, and inconsistent definitions of leadership. The emerging research has largely addressed these problems, with the result that several attributes are consistently identified with effective leadership or leader emergence. The main leadership attributes are listed in Exhibit 11.4 and described as follows:[80]

Personality. Most of the Big Five personality dimensions (see Chapter 2) are associated with effective leadership to some extent, but the strongest predictors are high levels of extraversion (outgoing, talkative, sociable, and assertive) and conscientiousness (careful, dependable, and self-disciplined). With high extraversion, effective leaders are comfortable having an influential role in social settings. With higher

Exhibit 11.4 Attributes of Effective Leaders

Leadership Attribute	Description
Personality	Effective leaders have higher levels of extraversion (outgoing, talkative, sociable, and assertive) and conscientiousness (careful, dependable, and self-disciplined).
Self-concept	Effective leaders have strong self-beliefs and a positive self-evaluation about their own leadership skills and ability to achieve objectives.
Drive	Effective leaders have an inner motivation to pursue goals.
Integrity	Effective leaders have strong moral principles, which are demonstrated through truthfulness and consistency of words with deeds.
Leadership motivation	Effective leaders have a need for socialized power (not personalized power) to accomplish team or organizational goals.
Knowledge of the business	Effective leaders have tacit and explicit knowledge about the company's environment, enabling them to make more intuitive decisions.
Cognitive and practical intelligence	Effective leaders have above-average cognitive ability to process information (cognitive intelligence) and ability to solve real-world problems by adapting to, shaping, or selecting appropriate environments (practical intelligence).
Emotional intelligence	Effective leaders have the ability to recognize and regulate their own emotions and the emotions of others.

> "To succeed as a business leader, you must have the bravery to give it a go. One needs resolve and conviction to overcome hurdles and give people confidence to follow you."[83]
>
> —**Sir Richard Branson,** founder of Virgin Group

conscientiousness, effective leaders set higher goals for themselves (and others), are organized, and have a strong sense of duty to fulfill work obligations.

Self-concept. Successful leaders have a complex, internally consistent, and clear self-concept as a leader (see Chapter 3). This "leader identity" also includes a positive self-evaluation, including high self-esteem, self-efficacy, and internal locus of control.[81] While many people in leadership positions default to daily managerial leadership and define themselves as managers, effective leaders view themselves as both transformational and managerial, and are confident with both of these self-views.[82]

Leadership motivation. Effective leaders don't just see themselves as leaders. They are also motivated to lead others. They have a strong need for *socialized power*, meaning that they want power to lead others in accomplishing organizational objectives and similar good deeds. This contrasts with a need for *personalized power*, which is the desire to have power for personal gain or for the thrill one might experience from wielding power over others (see Chapter 5).[84] Leadership motivation is also necessary because, even in collegial firms, leaders are in contests for positions further up the hierarchy. Effective leaders thrive rather than wither in the face of this competition.[85]

Drive. Related to their high conscientiousness, extraversion, and self-evaluation, successful leaders have a moderately high need for achievement (see Chapter 5). This drive represents the inner motivation that leaders possess to pursue their goals and encourage others to move forward with theirs. Drive inspires inquisitiveness, an action orientation, and measured boldness to take the organization or team into uncharted waters.

Integrity. Integrity involves having strong moral principles, which supports the tendency to be truthful and to be consistent in words and deeds. Leaders have a high moral capacity to judge dilemmas using sound values and to act accordingly. Notice that integrity is ultimately based on the leader's values, which provide an anchor for consistency. Several large-scale studies have reported that integrity and honesty are the most important characteristics of effective leaders.[86] Unfortunately, surveys also report that employees don't believe their leaders have integrity and, consequently, don't trust those leaders.

Knowledge of the business. Effective leaders possess tacit and explicit knowledge of the business environment in which they operate, including subtle indications of emerging trends. Knowledge of the business also includes a good understanding of how their organization works effectively.

Cognitive and practical intelligence. Leaders have above-average cognitive ability to process enormous amounts of information. Leaders aren't necessarily geniuses; rather, they have a superior ability to analyze a variety of complex alternatives and opportunities. Furthermore, leaders have practical intelligence. This means that they can think through the relevance and application of ideas in real-world settings. Practical intelligence is particularly evident where problems are poorly defined, information is missing, and more than one solution may be plausible.[87]

Emotional intelligence. Effective leaders have a high level of emotional intelligence.[88] They are able to recognize and regulate emotions in themselves and in other people (see Chapter 4). For example, effective leaders can tell when their conversations are having the intended emotional effect on employees. They are also able to recognize and change their own emotional state to suit the situation, such as feeling optimistic and determined in spite of recent business setbacks.

Authentic Leadership

A few paragraphs ago, we said that successful leaders have a complex, internally consistent, and clear self-concept as a leader, and that they have a strong positive self-evaluation. These characteristics lay the foundation for **authentic leadership**, which refers to how well leaders are aware of, feel comfortable with, and act consistently with their self-concept.[89] Authenticity is mainly about knowing yourself and being yourself (see Exhibit 11.5). Leaders learn more about their personality, values, thoughts, and habits by reflecting on various situations and personal experiences. They also improve this self-awareness by receiving feedback from trusted people inside and outside the organization. Both self-reflection and receptivity to feedback require high levels of emotional intelligence.

As people learn more about themselves, they gain a greater understanding of their inner purpose which, in turn, generates a long-term passion for achieving something worthwhile for the organization or society. Some leadership experts suggest that this inner purpose emerges from a life story, typically a transformative event or experience earlier in life that provides guidance for their later career and energy.[90]

Authentic leadership is more than self-awareness; it also involves behaving in ways that are consistent with that self-concept rather than pretending to be someone else. To be themselves, great leaders regulate their decisions and behavior in several ways. First, they develop their own style and, where appropriate, move into positions where that style is most effective. Although effective leaders adapt their behavior to the situation to some extent, they invariably understand and rely on decision methods and interpersonal styles that feel most comfortable to them.

Second, effective leaders continually think about and consistently apply their stable hierarchy of personal values to those decisions and behaviors. Leaders face many pressures and temptations, such as achieving short-term stock price targets at the cost of long-term profitability. Experts note that authentic leaders demonstrate self-discipline by remaining anchored to their values. Third, leaders maintain consistency around their self-concept by having a strong, positive core self-evaluation. They have high self-esteem and self-efficacy as well as an internal locus of control (Chapter 3).

Personal Attributes Perspective Limitations and Practical Implications

Personality, experience, self-concept, and other personal characteristics potentially contribute to a leader's effectiveness. Still, the leadership attributes perspective has a few limitations.[91] First, it assumes that all effective leaders have the same personal characteristics that are equally

authentic leadership the view that effective leaders need to be aware of, feel comfortable with, and act consistently with their values, personality, and self-concept

Exhibit 11.5 Authentic Leadership

Know yourself:
- Engage in self-reflection.
- Receive feedback from trusted sources.
- Understand your life story.

Be yourself:
- Develop your own style.
- Apply your values.
- Maintain a positive core self-evaluation.

important in all situations. This is probably a false assumption; leadership is far too complex to have a universal list of traits that apply to every condition. Some attributes might not be important all the time. Second, alternative combinations of attributes may be equally successful; two people with different sets of personal characteristics might be equally good leaders. Third, the attribute perspective views leadership as something within a person, yet experts emphasize that leadership is relational. People are effective leaders because of their favorable relationships with followers, so effective leaders cannot be identified without considering the quality of these relationships.[92]

Also remember from our discussion earlier in this chapter that, in the short term, followers tend to define others as effective or ineffective leaders based on their personal characteristics rather than whether the leader actually makes a difference to the organization's success. People who exhibit self-confidence, extraversion, and other traits are called leaders because they fit the widely held prototype of an effective leader. Alternatively, if someone is successful, observers might assign several nonobservable personal characteristics to them, such as intelligence, confidence, and drive. In short, the link between personal characteristics and effective leadership is muddied by several perceptual distortions.

One important final point: The personal attribute perspective of leadership does not necessarily imply that leadership is a talent acquired at birth rather than developed throughout life. On the contrary, attributes indicate only leadership *potential*, not leadership performance. People with these characteristics become effective leaders only after they have developed and mastered the necessary leadership behaviors. People with somewhat lower leadership attributes may become very effective leaders because they have worked harder to apply their lower potential more fully.

LO11-7 Discuss cultural and gender similarities and differences in leadership.

CROSS-CULTURAL AND GENDER ISSUES IN LEADERSHIP

Along with the four perspectives of leadership presented throughout this chapter, cultural values and practices affect what leaders do. Culture shapes the leader's values and norms, which influence his or her decisions and actions. Cultural values also shape the expectations that followers have of their leaders. An executive who acts inconsistently with cultural expectations is more likely to be perceived as an ineffective leader. Furthermore, leaders who deviate from those values may experience various forms of influence to get them to conform to the leadership norms and expectations of the society.

In other words, implicit leadership theory, described in a previous section of this chapter, explains differences in leadership practices across cultures.

Over the past several years, 150 researchers from dozens of countries have worked together on Project GLOBE (Global Leadership and Organizational Behavior Effectiveness) to identify the effects of cultural values on leadership.[93] The project organized countries into 10 regional clusters, of which the United States, Great Britain, and similar countries are grouped into the "Anglo" cluster. The results of this massive investigation suggest that some features of leadership are universal and some differ across cultures. Specifically, the GLOBE project reports that "charismatic visionary" is a universally recognized concept and that middle managers around the world believe that it is characteristic of effective leaders. *Charismatic visionary* represents a cluster of concepts including visionary, inspirational, performance orientation, integrity, and decisiveness.[94]

In contrast, participative leadership is perceived as characteristic of effective leadership in low power distance cultures but less so in high power distance cultures. For instance, one study reported that Mexican employees expect managers to make decisions affecting their work. Mexico is a high power distance culture, so followers expect leaders to apply their authority rather than delegate their power most of the time.[95] In summary, there are similarities and differences in the concept and preferred practice of leadership across cultures.

Gender and Leadership

Studies in field settings have generally found that male and female leaders do not differ in their levels of task-oriented or people-oriented leadership. The main explanation is that real-world jobs require similar behavior from male and female job incumbents.[96] However, women do adopt a participative leadership style more readily than their male counterparts. One possible reason is that, compared to boys, girls are often raised to

be more egalitarian and less status-oriented, which is consistent with being participative. There is also some evidence that women have somewhat better interpersonal skills than men, and this translates into their relatively greater use of the participative leadership style. A third explanation is that employees, on the basis of their own gender stereotypes, expect female leaders to be more participative, so female leaders comply with follower expectations to some extent.

Surveys report that women are rated higher than men on the emerging leadership qualities of coaching, teamwork, and empowering employees.[97] Yet research also suggests that women are evaluated negatively when they try to apply the full range of leadership styles, particularly more directive and autocratic approaches. Thus, ironically, women may be well suited to contemporary leadership roles, yet they often continue to face limitations of leadership through the gender stereotypes and prototypes of leaders that are held by followers.[98] Overall, both male and female leaders must be sensitive to the fact that followers have expectations about how leaders should act, and negative evaluations may go to leaders who deviate from those expectations.

Study Checklist

- Did you tear out the perforated student review card at the back of the text to revisit learning objectives and key terms and definitions?

Connect® Management is available for *M Organizational Behavior.* Additional resources include:

- Interactive Applications:
  - **Decision Generator**
  - **Drag and Drop:** Work through an interactive example to test your knowledge of the concepts.
  - **Video Case:** See management in action through interactive videos.

- **SmartBook™**—SmartBook is the first and only adaptive reading experience available today. Distinguishing what you know from what you don't, and honing in on concepts you are most likely to forget, SmartBook personalizes content for you in a continuously adapting reading experience. Reading is no longer a passive and linear experience, but an engaging and dynamic one where you are more likely to master and retain important concepts and go to class better prepared.

part four

12 chapter

Designing Organizational Structures

Learning Objectives

After studying this chapter, you should be able to:

LO12-1   Describe three types of coordination in organizational structures.

LO12-2   Discuss the role and effects of span of control, centralization, and formalization and relate these elements to organic and mechanistic organizational structures.

LO12-3   Identify and evaluate five types of departmentalization.

LO12-4   Explain how the external environment, organizational size, technology, and strategy are relevant when designing an organizational structure.

Toyota Motor Company received scathing criticism a few years ago from the National Highway Traffic Safety Administration (NHTSA) for the automaker's slow response to alleged faults in some models of its cars. In fact, the NHTSA penalized Toyota on four separate occasions (some were the maximum fine allowed) for failing to act quickly enough. How could one of the largest and most respected automakers in the world get into this situation? Toyota commissioned a special panel of independent experts to find the answer. The panel offered recommendations regarding mechanical and electrical engineering, supplier product quality, and processes to address issues of quality and safety. But the panel's main conclusion was that Toyota's slow and inappropriate responses were mostly due to its organizational structure.

In particular, the review panel reported that Toyota was mainly organized around functional units (sales, engineering, manufacturing), and that the heads of these units in each region reported directly to headquarters in Japan. Toyota did not have structural integration around regions, so its centralized functional structure resulted in silos of knowledge and slower decision making. Toyota has since redesigned its organizational structure around regions. "Dealing with our overseas operations on a regional basis, rather than a functional basis, will enable us to conduct decision making on a more-comprehensive basis," said Toyota CEO Akio Toyoda when announcing the new structure.[1]

The recent events at Toyota Motor Company illustrate the importance of organizational structure. **Organizational**

structure refers to the division of labor as well as the patterns of coordination, communication, workflow, and formal power that direct organizational activities. It formally dictates what activities receive the most attention as well as financial, power, and information resources. At Toyota, for example, power and resources previously flowed mainly through the functional units (manufacturing, marketing, etc.) to the head office in Japan. With the new design, power is redirected to the regional headquarters (e.g., United States) so the company can anticipate and respond to local issues more quickly.

Although the topic of organizational structure typically conjures up images of an organizational chart, this diagram is only part of the puzzle. Organizational structure includes these reporting relationships, but it also relates to job design, information flow, work standards and rules, team dynamics, and power relationships. As such, the organization's structure is an important instrument in an executive's toolkit for organizational change because it establishes new communication patterns and aligns employee behavior with the corporate vision.[2]

This chapter begins by introducing the two fundamental processes in organizational structure: division of labor and coordination. This is followed by a detailed investigation of the four main elements of organizational structure: span of control, centralization, formalization, and departmentalization. The latter part of this chapter examines the contingencies of organizational design, including external environment, organizational size, technology, and strategy.

LO12-1 Describe three types of coordination in organizational structures.

DIVISION OF LABOR AND COORDINATION

All organizational structures include two fundamental requirements: the division of labor into distinct tasks and the coordination of that labor so employees are able to accomplish common

goals.[3] Organizations are groups of people who work interdependently toward some purpose. To efficiently accomplish their goals, these groups typically divide the work into manageable chunks, particularly when there are many different tasks to perform. They also introduce various coordinating mechanisms to ensure that everyone is working effectively toward the same objectives.

Division of Labor

Division of labor refers to the subdivision of work into separate jobs assigned to different people. Subdivided work leads to job

organizational structure the division of labor as well as the patterns of coordination, communication, workflow, and formal power that direct organizational activities

specialization, because each job now includes a narrow subset of the tasks necessary to complete the product or service. As companies get larger, this horizontal division of labor is usually accompanied by vertical division of labor. Some people are assigned the task of supervising employees, others are responsible for managing those supervisors, and so on.

Why do companies divide the work into several jobs? As we described in Chapter 5, job specialization increases work efficiency.[4] Job incumbents can master their tasks quickly because work cycles are shorter. Less time is wasted changing from one task to another. Training costs are reduced because employees require fewer physical and mental skills to accomplish the assigned work. Finally, job specialization makes it easier to match people with specific aptitudes or skills to the jobs for which they are best suited. For instance, Toyota and other automakers divide design and manufacturing work into thousands of specific jobs clustered around highly specialized knowledge and skills—design engineering, assembler, instrumentation technician, software programmer, and so forth. Even if someone learns many of these diverse jobs, his or her natural aptitudes are likely much better suited to some of these than others.

Coordination of Work Activities

When people divide work among themselves, they require coordinating mechanisms to ensure that everyone works in concert. Coordination is so closely connected to division of labor that the optimal level of specialization is limited by the feasibility of coordinating the work. In other words, an organization's ability to divide work among people depends on how well those

people can coordinate with each other. Otherwise, individual effort is wasted due to misalignment, duplication, and mistiming of tasks. Coordination also tends to become more expensive and difficult as the division of labor increases. Therefore, companies specialize jobs only to the point where it isn't too costly or challenging to coordinate the people in those jobs.[5]

Every organization—from the two-person corner convenience store to the largest corporate entity—uses one or more of the following coordinating mechanisms:[6] informal communication, formal hierarchy, and standardization (see Exhibit 12.1). These forms of coordination align the work of staff within the same department as well as across work units. These coordinating mechanisms are also critical when several organizations work together, such as in joint ventures and humanitarian aid programs.[7]

Coordination through Informal Communication All organizations rely on informal communication as a coordinating mechanism. This process includes sharing information on

---

Exhibit 12.1 Coordinating Mechanisms in Organizations

Form of Coordination	Description	Subtypes/Strategies
Informal communication	Sharing information on mutual tasks; forming common mental models to synchronize work activities	Direct communication Liaison roles Integrator roles Temporary teams
Formal hierarchy	Assigning legitimate power to individuals, who then use this power to direct work processes and allocate resources	Direct supervision Formal communication channels
Standardization	Creating routine patterns of behavior or output	Standardized skills Standardized processes Standardized output

Sources: Based on information in J. Galbraith, *Designing Complex Organizations* (Reading, MA: Addison-Wesley, 1973), 8–19; H. Mintzberg, *The Structuring of Organizations* (Englewood Cliffs, NJ: Prentice Hall, 1979), Chap. 1; D.A. Nadler and M.L. Tushman, *Competing by Design: The Power of Organizational Architecture* (New York: Oxford University Press, 1997), Chap. 6.

Informal communication is the most flexible form of coordination, but it can become chaotic as the number of employees increases.

mutual tasks as well as forming common mental models so that employees synchronize work activities using the same mental road map.[8] Informal communication is vital in nonroutine and ambiguous situations because employees need to exchange a large volume of information through face-to-face communication and other media-rich channels.

Although coordination through informal communication is easiest in small firms, information technologies have further enabled this coordinating mechanism in large organizations.[9] Companies employing thousands of people also support informal communication by keeping each production site small. Magna International follows this principle by keeping most of its plants to no more than 200 employees. The global auto-parts manufacturer has found that employees have difficulty remembering each other's names in plants that are any larger, a situation that makes informal communication more difficult as a coordinating mechanism.[10]

Larger organizations also encourage coordination through informal communication by assigning *liaison roles* to employees, who are expected to communicate and share information with coworkers in other work units. Where coordination is required among several work units, companies create *integrator roles*. These people are responsible for coordinating a work process by encouraging employees in each work unit to share information and informally coordinate work activities. Integrators do not have authority over the people involved in that process, so they must rely on persuasion and commitment. Brand managers for luxury perfumes have integrator roles because they ensure that the work of fragrance developers, bottle designers, advertising creatives, production, and other groups are aligned with the brand's image and meaning.[11]

Another way that larger organizations encourage coordination through informal communication is by organizing employees from several departments into temporary teams. Temporary cross-functional teams give employees more authority and opportunity to coordinate through informal communication. This process is now common in vehicle design, which Toyota pioneered more than two decades ago. As the design engineer begins work on product specifications, team members from manufacturing, engineering, marketing, purchasing, and other departments are able to provide immediate feedback as well as begin their contribution to the process. Without the informal coordination available through teams, the preliminary car design would pass from one department to the next—a much slower process.[12]

Coordination through Formal Hierarchy Informal communication is the most flexible form of coordination, but it can become chaotic as the number of employees increases. Consequently, as organizations grow, they rely increasingly on a second coordinating mechanism: formal hierarchy.[13] Hierarchy assigns legitimate power to individuals, who then use this power to direct work processes and allocate resources. In other words, work is coordinated through direct supervision—the chain of command. For instance, Walmart stores have managers and assistant managers who are responsible for ensuring that employees are properly trained, perform their respective tasks, and coordinate effectively with other staff.

A century ago, management scholars applauded the formal hierarchy as the best coordinating mechanism for large organizations. They argued that organizations are most effective when managers exercise their authority and employees receive orders from only one supervisor. The chain of command—in which information flows across work units only through supervisors and managers—was viewed as the backbone of organizational strength.

Coordination through Micromanagement[14]

44% of 434 American human resource professionals polled identify micromanaging as a major complaint or concern that younger employees have about older managers.

37% of 524 American employees surveyed say they occasionally or frequently feel micromanaged by their boss.

31% of 97,000 employees surveyed in 30 countries describe their company's leadership as oppressive or authoritative.

18% of 300 American human resource managers say that micromanaging employees has the most negative effect on employee morale (second only to lack of open, honest communication).

25% of 500 American employees surveyed say they work for a "micromanager."

Although still important, formal hierarchy is much less popular today. One problem is that hierarchical organizations are not as agile for coordination in complex and novel situations. Communicating through the chain of command is rarely as fast or accurate as direct communication between employees. Another concern with formal hierarchy is that managers are able to closely supervise only a limited number of employees. As the business grows, the number of supervisors and layers of management must increase, resulting in a costly bureaucracy. A third problem is that today's workforce demands more autonomy over work and more involvement in company decisions. Formal hierarchy coordination processes tend to limit employee autonomy and involvement.

Coordination through Standardization Standardization, the third means of coordination, involves creating routine patterns of behavior or output. This coordinating mechanism takes three distinct forms:

- *Standardized processes.* Quality and consistency of a product or service can often be improved by standardizing work activities through job descriptions and procedures.[15] For example, flowcharts represent a standardized process coordinating mechanism. This coordinating mechanism works best when the task is routine (such as mass production) or simple (such as stocking shelves), but it is less effective in nonroutine and complex work such as product design.

- *Standardized outputs.* This form of standardization involves ensuring that individuals and work units have clearly defined goals and output measures (e.g., customer satisfaction, production efficiency). For instance, to coordinate the work of salespeople, companies assign sales targets rather than specific behaviors.

- *Standardized skills.* When work activities are too complex to standardize through processes or goals, companies often coordinate work effort by ensuring that job incumbents have the necessary

knowledge and skills. This occurs by carefully hiring people for their skills and experience, so they can perform tasks without job descriptions or precise guidelines. Training is also a form of standardization through skills. Many companies have in-house training programs where employees learn how to perform tasks consistent with company expectations.

Division of labor and coordination of work represent the two fundamental ingredients of all organizations. But how work is divided, which coordinating mechanisms are emphasized, who makes decisions, and other issues are related to the four elements of organizational structure that we discuss over the next two sections of this chapter.

LO12-2 Discuss the role and effects of span of control, centralization, and formalization and relate these elements to organic and mechanistic organizational structures.

ELEMENTS OF ORGANIZATIONAL STRUCTURE

Organizational structure has four elements that apply to every organization. This section introduces three of them: span of control, centralization, and formalization. The fourth element—departmentalization—is presented in the next section.

Span of Control

Span of control (also called *span of management*) refers to the number of people directly reporting to the next level in the hierarchy. A narrow span of control exists when very few people report directly to a manager, whereas a wide span exists when a manager has many direct reports.[16] A century ago, French engineer and management scholar Henri Fayol strongly recommended a relatively narrow span of control, typically no more than 20 employees per supervisor and 6 supervisors per manager. Fayol championed formal hierarchy as the primary coordinating mechanism, so he believed that supervisors should closely monitor and coach employees. His views were similar to those of Napoleon, who declared that senior military leaders should have no more than five officers directly reporting to them. These prescriptions were based on the belief that managers simply could not monitor and control any more subordinates closely enough.[17]

Today, we know better. The best-performing manufacturing plants currently have an average of 38 production employees per supervisor (see Exhibit 12.2).[18] What's the secret here? Did Fayol, Napoleon, and others miscalculate the optimal span of control? The answer is that those sympathetic to hierarchical control believed that employees should perform the physical tasks, whereas supervisors and other management personnel

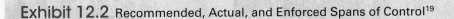

Exhibit 12.2 Recommended, Actual, and Enforced Spans of Control[19]

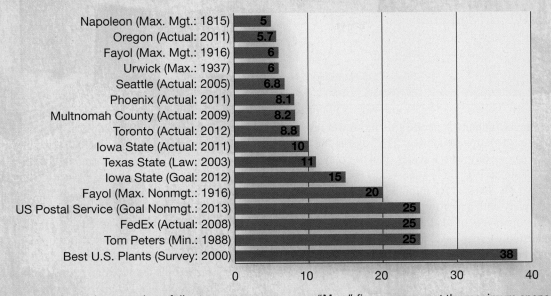

Note: Figures represent the average number of direct reports per manager. "Max." figures represent the maximum spans of control recommended by Napoleon Bonaparte, Henri Fayol, and Lyndall Urwick. "Min." figure represents the minimum span of control recommended by Tom Peters. "Goal" figures represent span of control targets that the U.S. Postal Service and State of Iowa are trying to achieve. (USPS currently exceeds its goal.) The State of Texas figure represents the span of control mandated by law. The Best U.S. Plants figure is the average span of control in American manufacturing facilities identified by *Industry Week* magazine as the most effective. "Actual" figures are spans of control in the cities of Toronto, Phoenix, Seattle, and Portland (Multnomah County), the U.S. states of Oregon and Iowa, and FedEx Corporation in the years indicated. The City of Toronto excludes firefighters and parks, which have unusually high spans of control. When these units are included, Toronto's span of control is 16.29.

should make the decisions and monitor employees to make sure they performed their tasks. In contrast, the best-performing manufacturing operations today rely on self-directed teams, so direct supervision (formal hierarchy) is supplemented with other coordinating mechanisms. Self-directed teams coordinate mainly through informal communication and various forms of standardization (i.e., training and processes), so formal hierarchy plays more of a supporting role.

Many firms that employ doctors, lawyers, and other professionals also have a wider span of control because these staff members coordinate their work mainly through standardized skills. For example, more than two dozen people report directly to Cindy Zollinger, cofounder and president of litigation-consulting firm Cornerstone Research. Zollinger explains that this large number of direct reports is possible because she leads professional staff who don't require close supervision. "They largely run themselves," Zollinger explains. "I help them in dealing with obstacles they face, or in making the most of opportunities that they find."[20]

A second factor influencing the best span of control is whether employees perform routine tasks. A wider span of control is possible when employees perform routine jobs, because they require less direction or advice from supervisors. A narrow span of control is necessary when employees perform novel or complex tasks, because these employees tend to require more supervisory decisions and coaching. This principle is illustrated

in a survey of property and casualty insurers. The average span of control in commercial-policy processing departments is around 15 employees per supervisor, whereas the span of control is 6.1 in claims service and 5.5 in commercial underwriting. Staff members in the latter two departments perform more technical work, so they have more novel and complex tasks, which requires more supervisor involvement. Commercial-policy processing, on the other hand, is like production work. Tasks are routine and have few exceptions, so managers have less coordinating to do with each employee.[21]

A third influence on span of control is the degree of interdependence among employees within the department or team.[22] Generally, a narrow span of control is necessary where employees perform highly interdependent work with others. More supervision is required for highly interdependent jobs because employees tend to experience more conflict with each other, which requires more of a manager's time to resolve. Also, employees are less clear on their personal work performance in highly interdependent tasks, so supervisors spend more time providing coaching and feedback.

Tall versus Flat Structures Span of control is interconnected with organizational size (number of employees) and the number of layers in the organizational hierarchy. Consider two companies with the same number of employees. If Company A has a wider span of control (more direct reports per manager)

> "Any new idea condemned to struggle upward through multiple levels of rigidly hierarchical, risk-averse management is an idea that won't see daylight . . . until it's too late."[24]
>
> —**Sergio Marchionne,** CEO of Fiat and Chrysler Corporation

than Company B, then Company A necessarily has fewer layers of management (i.e., a flatter structure). The reason for this relationship is that a company with a wider span of control has more employees per supervisor, more supervisors for each middle manager, and so on. This larger number of direct reports, compared to a company with a narrower span of control, is possible only by removing layers of management.

The interconnection of span of control, organizational size (number of employees), and number of management layers has important implications for companies. Organizations employ more people as they grow, which means they must widen the span of control, build a taller hierarchy, or both. Most companies end up building taller structures because they rely on direct supervision to some extent as a coordinating mechanism and there are limits to how many people each manager can coordinate.

Unfortunately, building a taller hierarchy (more layers of management) creates problems. One concern is that executives in tall structures tend to receive lower-quality and less timely information. People tend to filter, distort, and simplify information before it is passed to higher levels in the hierarchy because they are motivated to frame the information in a positive light or to summarize it more efficiently. In contrast, information receives less manipulation in flat hierarchies, and is often received much more quickly than in tall hierarchies.

A second problem is that taller structures have higher overhead costs. With more managers per employee, tall hierarchies necessarily have more people administering the company, thereby reducing the percentage of staff who are actually making the product or providing the service. A third issue with tall hierarchies is that employees usually feel less empowered and engaged in their work. Hierarchies are power structures, so more levels of hierarchy tend to draw power away from people at the bottom of that hierarchy. Indeed, the size of the hierarchy itself tends to focus power around managers rather than employees.[25]

These problems have prompted companies to remove one or more levels in the organizational hierarchy.[26] KenGen had more than 15 layers of hierarchy a few years ago. Today, the 1,500 employees at Kenya's leading electricity generation company are organized in a hierarchy with only six layers. Sandvik also recently "delayered" its hierarchy. "We had as much as 13 layers in the Company between me as CEO and the most junior worker in the Company," says Olof Faxander, CEO of the Swedish manufacturer of tools and equipment for mining and other industries. "We've flattened that [so we] only have up to seven layers in the Company."[27] Although flattening the hierarchy has advantages, critics warn that it can also lead to problems.

Wider Span of Control Keeps CEOs Busy

In the 1980s, chief executive officers of *Fortune* 500 companies had about five people (typically vice presidents), on average, who reported directly to them. By the end of the 1990s, this span of control increased to an average of 6.5 direct reports. Today, CEOs of the largest firms have an average of 10 direct reports, double the number a few decades earlier. This increase reflects the fact that most *Fortune* 500 companies are far more complex today. They operate in many markets, have more variety of products, and employ people with a broader array of technical specialties. Each type of variation demands top-level attention, so CEOs need to have more vice presidents than ever before reporting directly to them. In other words, they have a wider span of control.[23]

Centralization and Decentralization

Centralization means that formal decision-making authority is held by a small group of people, typically those at the top of the organizational hierarchy. Most organizations begin with centralized structures, as the founder makes most of the decisions and tries to direct the business toward his or her vision. As organizations grow, however, they diversify and their environments become more complex. Senior executives aren't able to process all the decisions that significantly influence the business. Consequently, larger organizations typically *decentralize;* that is, they disperse decision authority and power throughout the organization.

The optimal level of centralization or decentralization depends on several contingencies that we will examine later in this chapter. However, different degrees of decentralization can occur simultaneously in different parts of an organization. For instance, 7-Eleven centralizes decisions about information technology and supplier purchasing to improve buying power, increase cost efficiencies, and minimize complexity across the organization. Yet it decentralizes local inventory decisions to store managers because they have the best information about their customers and can respond quickly to local market needs. "We could never predict a busload of football players on a Friday night, but the store manager can," explains a 7-Eleven executive.[28]

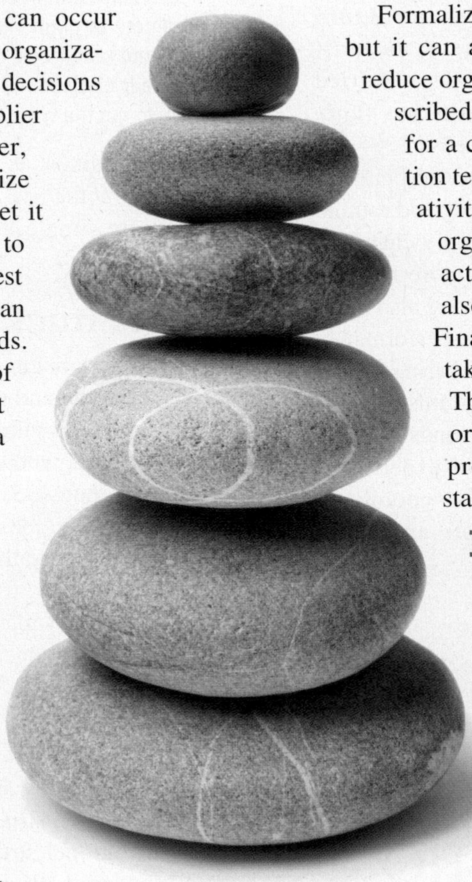

Formalization

Formalization is the degree to which organizations standardize behavior through rules, procedures, formal training, and related mechanisms.[29] In other words, companies become more formalized as they increasingly rely on various forms of standardization to coordinate work. McDonald's restaurants and most other efficient fast-food chains typically have a high degree of formalization because they rely on standardization of work processes as a coordinating mechanism. Employees have precisely defined roles, right down to how much mustard should be dispensed, how many pickles should be applied, and how long each hamburger should be cooked.

Older companies tend to become more formalized because work activities become routinized, making them easier to document into standardized practices. Larger companies also tend to have more formalization because direct supervision and informal communication among employees do not operate as easily when large numbers of people are involved.

External influences, such as government safety legislation and strict accounting rules, also encourage formalization.

Formalization may increase efficiency and compliance, but it can also create problems.[30] Rules and procedures reduce organizational flexibility, so employees follow prescribed behaviors even when the situation clearly calls for a customized response. High levels of formalization tend to undermine organizational learning and creativity. Some work rules become so convoluted that organizational efficiency would decline if they were actually followed as prescribed. Formalization is also a source of job dissatisfaction and work stress. Finally, rules and procedures have been known to take on a life of their own in some organizations. They become the focus of attention rather than the organization's ultimate objectives of producing a product or service and serving its dominant stakeholders.

Mechanistic versus Organic Structures

We discussed span of control, centralization, and formalization together because they cluster around two broader organizational forms: mechanistic and organic structures (see Exhibit 12.3).[31] A **mechanistic structure** is characterized by a narrow span of control and high degree of formalization and centralization. Mechanistic structures have many

Exhibit 12.3 Contrasting Mechanistic and Organic Organizational Structures

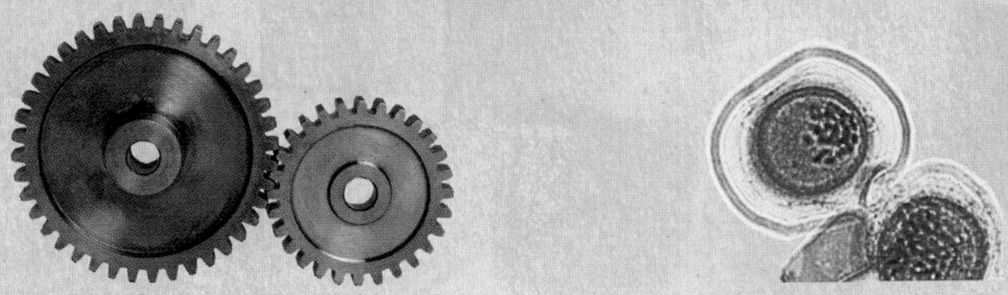

Mechanistic Structure	Organic Structure
• Narrow span of control	• Wide span of control
• High centralization	• High decentralization
• High formalization	• Low formalization

rules and procedures, limited decision making at lower levels, tall hierarchies of people in specialized roles, and vertical rather than horizontal communication flows. Tasks are rigidly defined and are altered only when sanctioned by higher authorities. Companies with an **organic structure** have the opposite characteristics. They operate with a wide span of control, decentralized decision making, and little formalization. Tasks are fluid, adjusting to new situations and organizational needs.

As a general rule, mechanistic structures operate better in stable environments because they rely on efficiency and routine behaviors. Organic structures work better in rapidly changing (i.e., dynamic) environments because they are more flexible and responsive to the changes. Organic structures are also more compatible with organizational learning and high-performance workplaces because they emphasize information sharing and an empowered workforce rather than hierarchy and status.[32] However, the effectiveness of organic structures depends on how well employees have developed their roles and expertise.[33] Without these conditions, employees are unable to coordinate effectively with each other, resulting in errors and gross inefficiencies.

LO12-3 Identify and evaluate five types of departmentalization.

FORMS OF DEPARTMENTALIZATION

Span of control, centralization, and formalization are important elements of organizational structure, but most people think about organizational charts when the discussion of organizational structure arises. The organizational chart represents the fourth element in the structuring of organizations, called *departmentalization*. Departmentalization specifies how employees and their activities are grouped together. It is a fundamental strategy for coordinating organizational activities because it influences organizational behavior in the following ways:[34]

- Departmentalization establishes the chain of command—the system of common supervision among positions and units within the organization. It frames the membership of formal work teams and typically determines which positions and units must share resources. Thus, departmentalization establishes interdependencies among employees and subunits.

- Departmentalization focuses people around common mental models or ways of thinking, such as serving clients, developing products, or supporting a particular skill set. This focus is typically anchored around the common budgets and measures of performance assigned to employees within each departmental unit.

- Departmentalization encourages specific people and work units to coordinate through informal communication. With common supervision and resources, members within each configuration typically work near each other, so they can use frequent and informal interaction to get the work done.

There are almost as many organizational charts as there are businesses, but the five most common pure types of departmentalization are simple, functional, divisional, team-based, and matrix.

Simple Structure

Most companies begin with a *simple structure*.[35] They employ only a few people and typically offer only one distinct product or service. There is minimal hierarchy—usually just employees reporting to the owners. Employees perform broadly defined roles because there are insufficient economies of scale to assign them to specialized jobs. The simple structure is highly flexible and minimizes the walls that form between employees in other structures. However, the simple structure usually depends on the owner's direct supervision to coordinate work activities, so it is very difficult to operate as the company grows and becomes more complex.

Functional Structure

As organizations grow, they typically shift from a simple structure to a functional structure. Even after they adopt more complex organizational structures that we discuss later, they will have a functional structure at some level of the hierarchy. A **functional structure** organizes employees around specific knowledge or other resources (see Exhibit 12.4). Employees with marketing expertise are grouped into a marketing unit, those with production skills are located in manufacturing,

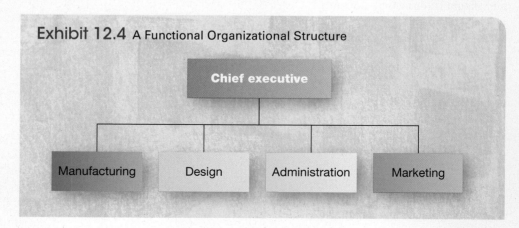

Exhibit 12.4 A Functional Organizational Structure

Chief executive

Manufacturing | Design | Administration | Marketing

engineers are found in product development, and so on. Organizations with functional structures are typically centralized to coordinate their activities effectively.

Evaluating the Functional Structure The functional structure creates specialized pools of talent that typically serve everyone in the organization. This provides more economies of scale than are possible if functional specialists are spread over different parts of the organization. It increases employee identity with the specialization or profession. Direct supervision is easier in functional structures because managers oversee people with common issues and expertise.[36]

The functional structure also has limitations.[37] Grouping employees around their skills tends to focus attention on those skills and related professional needs rather than on the company's products, services, or client needs. Unless people are transferred from one function to the next, they might not develop a broader understanding of the business. Compared with other structures, the functional structure usually produces more dysfunctional conflict and poorer coordination in serving clients or developing products. These problems occur because employees need to work with coworkers in other departments to complete organizational tasks, yet they have different subgoals and mental models of ideal work. Together, these problems require substantial formal controls and

> Compared with other structures, the functional structure usually produces more dysfunctional conflict and poorer coordination in serving clients or developing products.

coordination when people are organized around functions.

Divisional Structure

The **divisional structure** (sometimes called the *multidivisional* or *M-form* structure) groups employees around geographic areas, outputs (products or services), or clients. Exhibit 12.5 illustrates these three variations of divisional structure.[38] The *geographic divisional structure* organizes employees around distinct regions of the country or world. Exhibit 12.5(a) illustrates a geographic divisional structure adopted by Barrick Gold Corporation, the world's largest gold-mining company. The *product/service divisional structure* organizes employees around distinct outputs. Exhibit 12.5(b) illustrates a simplified version of this type of structure at Philips. The Dutch electronics company divides its workforce mainly into three divisions: health care products, lighting products, and consumer products. (Philips also has a fourth organizational group consisting of the research and design functions.) The *client divisional structure* organizes employees around specific customer groups. Exhibit 12.5(c) illustrates a customer-focused divisional structure adopted by JPMorgan Chase bank.[39]

Which form of divisional structure should large organizations adopt? The answer depends mainly on the primary source of environmental diversity or uncertainty.[40] Suppose an organization has one type of product sold to people across the country. If customers have different needs across regions, or if state governments impose different regulations on the product, then a geographic structure would be best to be more vigilant about this diversity.

On the other hand, if the company sells several types of products across the country and customer preferences and government regulations are similar everywhere, then a product structure would likely work best.

Coca-Cola, Nestlé, and many other food and beverage companies are organized mainly around geographic regions because consumer tastes and preferred marketing strategies vary considerably around the world. Even though McDonald's makes the same Big Mac throughout the world, the company has more fish products in Hong Kong and more vegetarian products in India, in line with traditional diets in those countries. Philips, on the other hand, is organized around products because consumer preferences around the world are similar within each product group. Hospitals from Geneva, Switzerland, to Santiago, Chile, buy similar medical equipment from Philips, whereas the manufacturing and marketing of these products are quite different from Philips' consumer electronics business.

Exhibit 12.5 Three Types of Divisional Structure

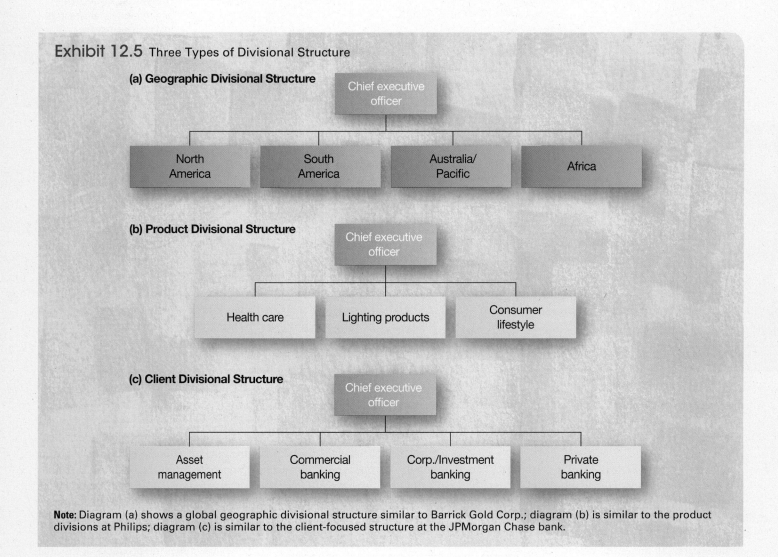

(a) Geographic Divisional Structure

Chief executive officer

- North America
- South America
- Australia/ Pacific
- Africa

(b) Product Divisional Structure

Chief executive officer

- Health care
- Lighting products
- Consumer lifestyle

(c) Client Divisional Structure

Chief executive officer

- Asset management
- Commercial banking
- Corp./Investment banking
- Private banking

Note: Diagram (a) shows a global geographic divisional structure similar to Barrick Gold Corp.; diagram (b) is similar to the product divisions at Philips; diagram (c) is similar to the client-focused structure at the JPMorgan Chase bank.

Many companies are moving away from structures that organize people around geographic clusters.[41] One reason is that clients can purchase products online and communicate with businesses from almost anywhere in the world, so local representation is becoming less important. Reduced geographic variation is another reason for the shift away from geographic structures; freer trade has reduced government intervention, and consumer preferences for many products and services are becoming more similar (converging) around the world. The third reason is that large companies increasingly have global business customers who demand one global point of purchase, not one in every country or region.

Evaluating the Divisional Structure The divisional organizational structure is a building-block structure; it accommodates growth relatively easily and focuses employee attention on products or customers rather than tasks. As the company develops new products, services, or clients, it can sprout new divisions. This structure also directs employee attention to customers and products, rather than to their own specialized knowledge.[42]

These advantages are offset by a number of limitations. First, the divisional structure tends to duplicate resources, such as production equipment and engineering or information technology expertise. Also, unless the division is quite large, resources are not used as efficiently as they are in functional structures where resources are pooled across the entire organization. The divisional structure also creates silos of knowledge. Expertise is spread across several autonomous business units, and this reduces the ability and perhaps motivation of the people in one division to share their knowledge with counterparts in other divisions. In contrast, a functional structure groups experts together, thereby supporting knowledge sharing.

Finally, the preferred divisional structure depends on the company's primary source of environmental diversity or uncertainty. This principle seems to be applied easily enough at Coca-Cola, McDonald's, and Philips, but many global organizations experience diversity and uncertainty in terms of geography, product, *and* clients. Consequently, some organizations revise their structures back and forth or create complex structures that attempt to give all three dimensions equal status. This ambivalence generates further complications, because organizational

Valve Corporation's Team-Based Structure on Wheels

Valve Corporation's organizational structure literally operates on wheels. The Bellevue, Washington, software and entertainment company has an extreme team-based structure with no bosses or departments to determine employee job duties or location. Instead, Valve's 300 engineers, artists, and other professionals move their desks (which have wheels) to the team that can best use their talents. "Think of those wheels as a symbolic reminder that you should always be considering where you could move yourself to be more valuable," says Valve's quirky handbook. "There is no organizational structure keeping you from being in close proximity to the people who you'd help or be helped by most."[43]

structure decisions shift power and status among executives. If the company switches from a geographic to a product structure, people who lead the geographic fiefdoms suddenly get demoted under the product chiefs. In short, leaders of global organizations struggle to find the best divisional structure, often resulting in the departure of some executives and frustration among those who remain.

Team-Based Structure

A **team-based organizational structure** is built around self-directed teams that complete an entire piece of work, such as manufacturing a product or developing an electronic game. This type of structure is usually organic. There is a wide span of control because teams operate with minimal supervision. In its most extreme variation, there is no formal leader, just someone selected by other team members to help coordinate the work and liaise with top management.

Team structures are highly decentralized because almost all day-to-day decisions are made by team members rather than someone further up the organizational hierarchy. Many team-based structures also have low formalization because teams are given relatively few rules about how to organize their work. Instead, executives assign quality and quantity output targets, and often productivity improvement goals, to each team. Teams are then encouraged to use available resources and their own initiative to achieve those objectives.

Team-based structures are usually found within the manufacturing or service operations of larger divisional structures. Several GE Aircraft Engines plants are organized as team-based structures, but these plants operate within GE's larger divisional structure. However, a small number of firms apply the team-based structure from top to bottom, including W. L. Gore & Associates, Semco SA, and Valve Corporation, where almost all associates work in teams.

Evaluating the Team-Based Structure The team-based structure has gained popularity because it tends to be flexible and responsive in turbulent environments.[44] It tends to reduce costs because teams have less reliance on formal hierarchy (direct supervision). A cross-functional team structure improves communication and cooperation across traditional boundaries. With greater autonomy, this structure also allows quicker and more informed decision making.[45] For this reason, some hospitals have shifted from functional departments to cross-functional teams. Teams composed of nurses, radiologists, anesthetists, a pharmacology representative, possibly social workers, a rehabilitation therapist, and other specialists communicate and coordinate more efficiently, thereby reducing delays and errors.[46]

Contrasted with these benefits, the team-based structure can be costly to maintain due to the need for ongoing interpersonal skills training. Teamwork potentially takes more time to coordinate than formal hierarchy during the early stages of team development. Employees may experience more stress due to increased ambiguity in their roles. Team leaders also experience more stress due to increased conflict, loss of functional power, and unclear career progression ladders. In addition, team structures suffer from duplication of resources and potential competition (and lack of resource sharing) across teams.[47]

Matrix Structure

ABB Group, one of the world's largest power and automation technology engineering firms,

team-based organizational structure an organizational structure built around self-directed teams that complete an entire piece of work

matrix structure

an organizational structure that overlays two structures (such as a geographic divisional and a product structure) in order to leverage the benefits of both

has five product divisions, such as power products and process automation. It employs more than 140,000 people across 100 countries, so the global giant also has eight regional groups (North America, IMEA, and so forth). What organizational structure would work best for ABB? For example, should the head of power products in North America report to the worldwide head of power products in Zurich, Switzerland, or to the head of North American operations?

For ABB, the answer is to have the regional product leaders report to both the regional chiefs and the product chiefs back at global headquarters. In other words, ABB has a **matrix structure**, which overlays two structures (in this case, a geographic divisional and product structure) to leverage the benefits of both.[48] Exhibit 12.6 shows a geographic-product matrix structure, which is a simplified version of ABB's structure. The dots represent the individuals who have two bosses. For example, the head of power products in North America reports to both the worldwide head of the product group and to the head of North American operations.

A common mistake is to assume that everyone in this type of matrix organizational structure reports to two bosses. In reality, in this type of matrix design only managers at one level in the organization (typically country-specific product managers) have two bosses. For example, the manager responsible for power products in North America reports to both the worldwide head of the product group as well as to the head of North American operations. However, employees below that country product leader report to only a manager in North America.

The geographic-product matrix structure is the most common matrix design among global companies. For instance, Nestlé, Procter & Gamble, and Shell have variations of this matrix structure because these firms recognize that regional groups and product/services groups are equally important. Other variations of matrix structures also exist in global businesses, however. Investment bank Macquarie Group overlays client groups (such as securities, investment funds, and currencies/commodities) with four functional groups (risk management, legal/governance, financial management, and corporate operations).[49]

Global organizations tend to have complex designs that combine different types of structures, so a "pure" matrix design is relatively uncommon. A pure matrix gives equal power to

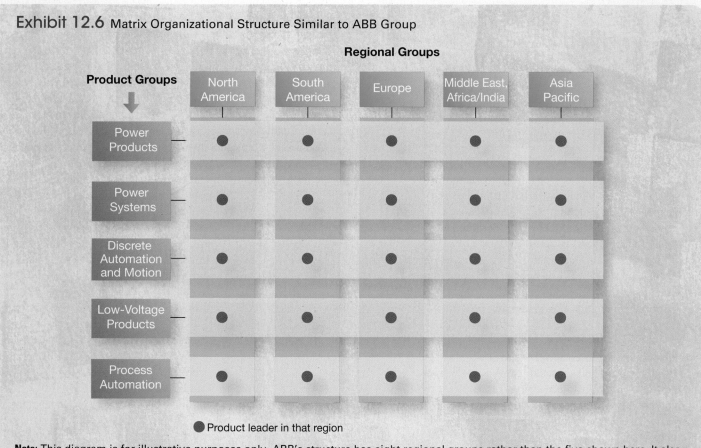

Exhibit 12.6 Matrix Organizational Structure Similar to ABB Group

Regional Groups

Product Groups

| | North America | South America | Europe | Middle East, Africa/India | Asia Pacific |

Power Products

Power Systems

Discrete Automation and Motion

Low-Voltage Products

Process Automation

● Product leader in that region

Note: This diagram is for illustrative purposes only. ABB's structure has eight regional groups rather than the five shown here. It also has four nonmatrixed functional groups reporting directly to the CEO. In addition, this diagram assumes ABB has a pure matrix structure, where both product and regional chiefs have equal power, whereas either the regional or product groups might have more direct line authority.

leaders of both groups (regions and products, for example), whereas in reality companies often give more power to one set of groups while the other set of groups has "dotted line" or advisory authority. So, although ABB's head of power products has two bosses, one of them might have more final say or line authority than the other.

Some companies also deviate from the pure matrix structure by applying it only to some regions. One such example is Cummins Inc., which is mainly organized around product divisions but has a matrix structure in China, India, and Russia. These markets are large, have high potential, and are potentially less visible to headquarters, so the country leaders are given as much authority as the product leaders within those regions. "I think in China there's still enough lack of transparency, there's still enough uniqueness to the market that having some kind of coordination across business units gets the greatest synergies," explains Michael Barbalas, China president of Goodrich Corporation.[50]

A second type of matrix structure, which can be applied to small or large companies, overlays functional units with project teams.[51] BioWare adopted this project–functional matrix structure soon after the electronic games company was born a decade ago. Most BioWare employees have two managers. One manager leads the specific project to which employees are assigned, such as *Star Wars*, *Baldur's Gate*, and *Dragon Age*; the other manager is head of the employee's functional specialization, such as art, programming, audio, quality assurance, and design.[52] Employees are assigned permanently to their functional unit but physically work with the temporary project team. When the project nears completion, the functional boss reassigns employees in his or her functional specialization to another project.

Evaluating the Matrix Structure The functional-project matrix structure usually makes very good use of resources and expertise, making it ideal for project-based organizations with fluctuating workloads. When properly managed, it improves communication efficiency, project flexibility, and innovation, compared to purely functional or divisional designs. It focuses employees on serving clients or creating products yet keeps people organized around their specialization, so knowledge sharing improves and human resources are used more efficiently. Matrix structures for global organizations (e.g., geographic-product structures) are also a logical choice when, as in the case of ABB Group, two different dimensions (regions and products) are equally important. Structures determine executive power and what should receive priority; the matrix structure works best when the business environment is complex and two different dimensions deserve equal attention and integration. Executives who have worked in a global matrix also say they have more freedom, likely because their two bosses are more advisory and less command and control focused.[53]

In spite of these advantages, the matrix structure has several well-known problems.[54] One concern is that it increases conflict among managers who equally share power. Employees working at the matrix level have two bosses and, consequently, two sets of priorities that aren't always aligned with each other. Project leaders might squabble with functional leaders regarding the assignment of specific employees to projects as well as regarding the employee's technical competence. However, successful companies manage this conflict by developing and promoting leaders who can work effectively in matrix structures. "Of course there's potential for friction," says an executive at IBM India. "In fact, one of the prerequisites to attaining a leadership position at IBM is the ability to function in a matrix structure."[55]

Ambiguous accountability is another challenge with matrix structures. In a functional or divisional structure, one manager is responsible for everything, even the most unexpected issues. But in a matrix structure, the unusual problems don't get resolved because neither manager takes ownership of them.[56] Due to this ambiguous accountability, matrix structures have been blamed for corporate ethical misconduct, such as embezzlement at Hana Financial Group in Korea and massive bribes at Siemens AG in Germany. Oracle president Mark Hurd warned of this problem a few years ago when he was CEO of Hewlett-Packard: "The more accountable I can make you, the easier it is for you to show you're a great performer," says Hurd. "The more I use a matrix, the easier I make it to blame someone else."[57] The combination of dysfunctional conflict and ambiguous accountability in matrix structures also explains why some employees experience more stress and some managers are less satisfied with their work arrangements.

> The more complex the environment, the more decentralized the organization should become.

LO12-4 Explain how the external environment, organizational size, technology, and strategy are relevant when designing an organizational structure.

CONTINGENCIES OF ORGANIZATIONAL DESIGN

Most organizational behavior theories and concepts have contingencies: Ideas that work well in one situation might not work as well in another situation. This contingency approach is certainly relevant when choosing the most appropriate organizational structure.[58] In this section, we introduce four contingencies of organizational design: external environment, size, technology, and strategy.

External Environment

The best structure for an organization depends on its external environment. The external environment includes anything outside the organization, including most stakeholders (e.g., clients, suppliers, government), resources (e.g., raw materials, human resources, information, finances), and competitors. Four characteristics of external environments influence the type of organizational structure best suited to a particular situation: dynamism, complexity, diversity, and hostility.[59]

Dynamic versus Stable Environments Dynamic environments have a high rate of change, leading to novel situations and a lack of identifiable patterns. Organic structures in which employees are experienced and coordinate well in teams are better suited to dynamic environments, so the organization can adapt more quickly to changes.[60] In contrast, stable environments are characterized by regular cycles of activity and steady changes in supply and demand for inputs and outputs. Events are more predictable, enabling the firm to apply rules and procedures. Mechanistic structures are more efficient when the environment is predictable, so they tend to be more profitable than organic structures under these conditions.

Complex versus Simple Environments Complex environments have many elements, whereas simple environments have few things to monitor. As an example, a major university library operates in a more complex environment than a small-town public library. The university library's clients require several types of services—book borrowing, online full-text databases, research centers, course reserve collections, and so on. A small-town public library has fewer of these demands placed on it. The more complex the environment, the more decentralized the organization should become. Decentralization is a logical choice for complex environments because decisions are pushed down to people and subunits with the necessary information to make informed choices.

OB THEORY TO PRACTICE

Choosing the Best Organizational Structure for the Environment

▶ Organic structures are better suited for dynamic environments; mechanistic structures are usually more effective for stable environments.

▶ Organizations should be more decentralized as environments become more complex.

▶ Diverse environments call for a divisional structure aligned with the highest form of diversity.

▶ Organic structures are better suited for hostile environments; mechanistic structures are usually more effective in munificent environments.

Organizational Size

organizational strategy
the way the organization positions itself in its setting in relation to its stakeholders, given the organization's resources, capabilities, and mission

Larger organizations have different structures than do smaller organizations, for good reason.[62] As the number of employees increases, job specialization increases due to a greater division of labor. The greater division of labor requires more elaborate coordinating mechanisms. Thus, larger firms make greater use of standardization (particularly work processes and outcomes) to coordinate work activities. These coordinating mechanisms create an administrative hierarchy and greater formalization. Historically, larger organizations make less use of informal communication as a coordinating mechanism. However, emerging information technologies and increased emphasis on empowerment have caused informal communication to regain its importance in large firms.[63]

Larger organizations also tend to be more decentralized than smaller organizations. Executives have neither sufficient time nor expertise to process all the decisions that significantly influence the business as it grows. Therefore, decision-making authority is pushed down to lower levels, where employees are able to make decisions on issues within their narrower range of responsibility.

Technology

Technology is another factor to consider when designing the best organizational structure for the situation.[64] *Technology* refers to the mechanisms or processes an organization relies on to make its products or services. In other words, technology isn't just the equipment used to make something; it also includes how the production process is physically arranged and how the production work is divided among employees. The two main technological contingencies are variability and analyzability, both of which we described as job characteristics in Chapter 5. *Variability* refers to the number of exceptions to standard procedure that tend to occur. In work processes with low variability, jobs are routine and follow standard operating procedures. *Analyzability* refers to the predictability or difficulty of the required work. The less analyzable the work, the more it requires experts with sufficient discretion to address the work challenges.

An organic, rather than a mechanistic, structure should be introduced where employees perform tasks with high variability and low analyzability, such as in a research setting. The reason is that employees face unique situations with little opportunity for repetition. In contrast, a mechanistic structure is preferred where the technology has low variability and high analyzability, such as an assembly line. The work is routine and highly predictable, an ideal situation for a mechanistic structure to operate efficiently.

Organizational Strategy

Organizational strategy refers to the way the organization positions itself in its setting in relation to its stakeholders, given

Diverse versus Integrated Environments Organizations located in diverse environments have a greater variety of products or services, clients, and regions. In contrast, an integrated environment has only one client, product, and geographic area. The more diversified the environment, the more the firm needs to use a divisional structure aligned with that diversity. If it sells a single product around the world, a geographic divisional structure would align best with the firm's geographic diversity, for example. Diverse environments also call for decentralization. By pushing decision making further down the hierarchy, the company can adapt better and more quickly to diverse clients, government requirements, and other circumstances related to that diversity.

Hostile versus Munificent Environments Firms located in a hostile environment face resource scarcity and more competition in the marketplace. Hostile environments are typically dynamic ones because they reduce the predictability of access to resources and demand for outputs. Organic structures tend to be best in hostile environments. However, when the environment is extremely hostile—such as a severe shortage of supplies or tumbling market share—organizations tend to temporarily centralize so that decisions can be made more quickly and executives feel more comfortable being in control.[61] Ironically, centralization may result in lower-quality decisions during organizational crises, because top management has less information, particularly when the environment is complex.

the organization's resources, capabilities, and mission.[65] In other words, strategy represents the decisions and actions applied to achieve the organization's goals. Although size, technology, and environment influence the optimal organizational structure, these contingencies do not necessarily determine structure. Instead, corporate leaders formulate and implement strategies that shape both the characteristics of these contingencies as well as the organization's resulting structure.

This concept is summed up with the simple phrase "structure follows strategy."[66] Organizational leaders decide how large to grow and which technologies to use. They take steps to define and manipulate their environments, rather than let the organization's fate be entirely determined by external influences.

Furthermore, organizational structures don't evolve as a natural response to environmental conditions; they result from conscious human decisions. Thus, organizational strategy influences both the contingencies of structure and the structure itself.

If a company's strategy is to compete through innovation, a more organic structure would be preferred because it is easier for employees to share knowledge and be creative. If a company chooses a low-cost strategy, a mechanistic structure is preferred because it maximizes production and service efficiency.[67] Overall, it is now apparent that organizational structure is influenced by size, technology, and environment, but the organization's strategy may reshape these elements and loosen their connection to organizational structure.

Study Checklist

- Did you tear out the perforated student review card at the back of the text to revisit learning objectives and key terms and definitions?

Connect® Management is available for *M Organizational Behavior*. Additional resources include:

- Interactive Applications:
  - **Decision Generator**
  - **Drag and Drop:** Work through an interactive example to test your knowledge of the concepts.
  - **Video Case:** See management in action through interactive videos.

- **SmartBook™**—SmartBook is the first and only adaptive reading experience available today. Distinguishing what you know from what you don't, and honing in on concepts you are most likely to forget, SmartBook personalizes content for you in a continuously adapting reading experience. Reading is no longer a passive and linear experience, but an engaging and dynamic one where you are more likely to master and retain important concepts and go to class better prepared.

13 chapter

Organizational **Culture**

Learning Objectives

After studying this chapter, you should be able to:

LO13-1 Describe the elements of organizational culture and discuss the importance of organizational subcultures.

LO13-2 Describe four categories of artifacts through which corporate culture is deciphered.

LO13-3 Discuss the importance of organizational culture and the conditions under which organizational culture strength improves organizational performance.

LO13-4 Compare and contrast four strategies for merging organizational cultures.

LO13-5 Describe five strategies for changing and strengthening an organization's culture, including the application of attraction–selection–attrition theory.

LO13-6 Describe the organizational socialization process and identify strategies to improve that process.

Due to its global popularity, Facebook has quickly expanded its operations to Ireland, India, and many other worldwide locations. In each country, the social networking platform company has instilled its unique corporate culture: focus on impact, move fast, be bold, be open, and build social value. "There is a really great culture of empowerment here," says a Facebook employee at the company's recently opened site in Austin, Texas. "We want people to take risks and be bold and really strive to make a huge impact, because that is what the company is trying to do."

To maintain its unique culture in far-flung locations, Facebook dispatches a "landing team" of current employees to each new site. The main objective of the landing teams is "a transfer of knowledge and of culture to make sure we're spreading our own unique Facebook culture in different offices around the world," says a landing team member who opened the office in Hyderabad, India. "The India landing team had seven members across three different teams in operations—advertisers, developers and testers." The landing team embeds Facebook's culture at each site by carefully selecting applicants for their compatibility with that culture and coaching newcomers on the Facebook way of life.[1]

To build the world's best platform for social networking, Facebook pays close attention to developing and maintaining its organizational culture. **Organizational culture** consists of the values and assumptions shared within an organization.[2] It defines what is important and unimportant in the company and, consequently, directs everyone in the organization toward the "right way" of doing things. You might think of organizational culture as the company's DNA—invisible to the naked eye, yet a powerful template that shapes what happens in the workplace.

This chapter begins by identifying the elements of organizational culture and then describing how culture is deciphered through artifacts. This is followed by a discussion of the relationship between organizational culture and performance, including the effects of cultural strength, fit, and adaptability. We then turn our attention to the challenges of and solutions to merging organizational cultures. The latter part of this chapter examines ways to change and strengthen organizational culture, including a closer look at the related topic of organizational socialization.

> "The thing I have learned at IBM is that culture is everything."[3]
>
> —**Louis V. Gerstner Jr.,** business leader (former IBM CEO, American Express executive)

LO13-1 Describe the elements of organizational culture and discuss the importance of organizational subcultures.

ELEMENTS OF ORGANIZATIONAL CULTURE

Organizational culture consists of shared values and assumptions. Exhibit 13.1 illustrates how these shared values and assumptions relate to each other and are associated with artifacts, which are discussed later in this chapter. *Values* are stable, evaluative beliefs that guide our preferences for outcomes or courses of action in a variety of situations (see Chapters 1 and 2).[4] They are conscious perceptions about what is good or bad, right or wrong. In the context of organizational culture, values are discussed as *shared values,* which are values that people within the organization or work unit have in common and place near the top of their hierarchy of values.[5] For example, Facebook employees embrace five shared values: focus on impact, move fast, be bold, be open, and build social value.

Organizational culture also consists of *shared assumptions*—a deeper element that some experts believe is the essence of corporate culture. Shared assumptions are nonconscious, taken-for-granted perceptions or ideal prototypes of behavior that are

organizational culture the values and assumptions shared within an organization

considered the correct way to think and act toward problems and opportunities. Shared assumptions are so deeply ingrained that you probably wouldn't discover them by surveying employees. Only by observing employees, analyzing their decisions, and debriefing them on their actions would these assumptions rise to the surface.

Espoused versus Enacted Values

Most corporate websites have "Careers" web pages for job candidates, and many of these sites proudly list the company's core values. Do these values really represent the organization's culture? They probably do to some degree, but these pages more likely describe *espoused values*—the values that corporate leaders want others to believe guide the organization's decisions and actions.[6] Espoused values are usually socially desirable, so they present a positive public image. Even if top management acts consistently with the espoused values, lower-level employees might not do so. Employees bring diverse personal values to the organization, some of which might conflict with the organization's espoused values.

BP is a case in point.[7] The British energy giant lists responsibility as one of its core values, which means that "we aim for no accidents, no harm to people and no damage to the environment." Yet BP was at the center of the Gulf of Mexico oil spill, now considered the worst environmental disaster in recent history. A few months before the spill occurred, the U.S. government penalized BP with the largest health and safety fine in history for failing to sufficiently improve safety at its Texas City refinery. Four years earlier, 15 employees died in an explosion at that refinery. A U.S. government report on that explosion concluded that BP "did not provide effective safety culture leadership."

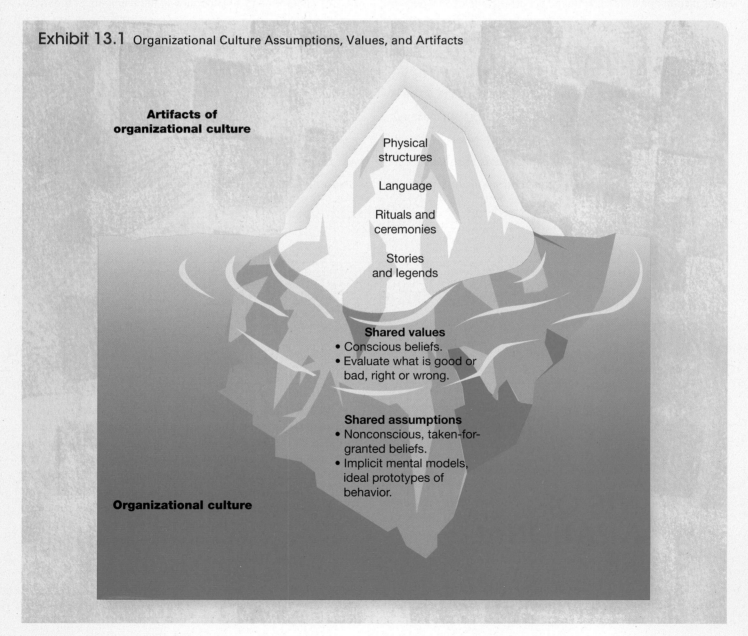

Exhibit 13.1 Organizational Culture Assumptions, Values, and Artifacts

Artifacts of organizational culture

Physical structures

Language

Rituals and ceremonies

Stories and legends

Shared values
• Conscious beliefs.
• Evaluate what is good or bad, right or wrong.

Shared assumptions
• Nonconscious, taken-for-granted beliefs.
• Implicit mental models, ideal prototypes of behavior.

Organizational culture

A few years earlier, officials in Norway and Alaska also reported problems with BP's "safety culture." In short, the energy company says it values responsibility, but the evidence suggests that this is only an espoused value.

The main point here is that an organization's culture is not defined by its espoused values. Instead, corporate culture consists of shared *enacted values*—the values that most leaders and employees truly rely on to guide their decisions and behavior. These "values-in-use" are apparent when watching executives and other employees in action, including their decisions, where they focus their attention and resources, how they behave toward stakeholders, and the outcomes of those decisions and behavior.

Exhibit 13.2 Organizational Culture Profile Dimensions and Characteristics

Organizational Culture Dimension	Characteristics of the Dimension
Innovation	Experimenting, opportunity seeking, risk taking, few rules, low cautiousness
Stability	Predictability, security, rule-oriented
Respect for people	Fairness, tolerance
Outcome orientation	Action-oriented, high expectations, results-oriented
Attention to detail	Precise, analytic
Team orientation	Collaboration, people-oriented
Aggressiveness	Competitive, low emphasis on social responsibility

Source: Based on information in C.A. O'Reilly III, J. Chatman, and D.F. Caldwell, "People and Organizational Culture: A Profile Comparison Approach to Assessing Person-Organization Fit," *Academy of Management Journal* 34, no. 3 (1991): 487–518.

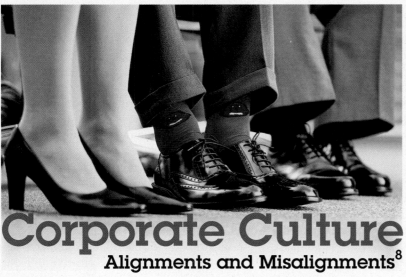

Corporate Culture
Alignments and Misalignments[8]

94% of 303 American corporate executives surveyed believe a distinct workplace culture is important to business success.

88% of 1,005 American employees surveyed believe a distinct workplace culture is important to business success.

84% of 2,219 executives and employees surveyed across several countries agree that their organization's culture is "critical" to business success.

75% of junior managers surveyed in the UK believe there is a mismatch between their company's "espoused values" and what actually goes on in the company.

51% of 2,219 executives and employees surveyed across several countries think their organization's culture is in need of a major overhaul.

25% of board of directors surveyed in the UK believe there is a mismatch between their company's "espoused values" and what actually goes on in the company.

Content of Organizational Culture

Organizations differ in their cultural content, that is, the relative ordering of shared values.[9] How many corporate cultures are there? Several models and measures classify organizational culture into a handful of easy-to-remember categories. One of these, shown in Exhibit 13.2, identifies seven corporate cultures. Another popular model identifies four organizational cultures organized in a two-by-two table representing internal versus external focus and flexibility versus control. Other models organize cultures around a circle with 8 or 12 categories. These circumplex models suggest that some cultures are opposite to others, such as an avoidance culture versus a self-actualization culture, or a power culture versus a collegial culture.[10]

These organizational culture models and surveys are popular with corporate leaders faced with the messy business of diagnosing their company's culture and identifying what kind of culture they want to develop. Unfortunately, they oversimplify the diversity of cultural values in organizations. The fact is, there are dozens of individual values, and many more combinations of values, so the number of organizational cultures that these models describe likely falls considerably short of the full set. A second concern is that organizational culture includes shared assumptions, not just shared values. Most organizational culture measures ignore assumptions because they represent a more subterranean aspect of culture.

A third concern is that many organizational culture models and measures incorrectly assume that organizations have a fairly clear, unified culture that is easily decipherable.[11] This "integration" perspective, as it is called, further assumes that when an organization's culture changes, it shifts from one unified condition to a new unified condition with only temporary ambiguity or weakness during the transition. These assumptions are probably incorrect or, at best, oversimplified. An organization's culture is usually quite blurry, so much so that it cannot be estimated through employee surveys alone. As we discuss next, organizations consist of diverse subcultures because employees across the organization have different clusters of experiences and backgrounds that have shaped their values and priorities.

Even these subcultural clusters can be ill-defined because values and assumptions ultimately vary from one employee to the next. As long as employees differ, an organization's culture will have noticeable variability. Thus, many of the popular organizational culture models and measures oversimplify the variety of organizational cultures and falsely presume that organizations can easily be identified within these categories.

Organizational Subcultures

When discussing organizational culture, we are really referring to the *dominant culture,* that is, the values and assumptions shared most consistently and widely by the organization's members. The dominant culture is usually supported by senior management, but not always. Cultural values and assumptions can also persist in spite of senior management's desire for another culture. Furthermore, organizations are composed of *subcultures* located throughout their various divisions, geographic regions,

and occupational groups.[12] Some subcultures enhance the dominant culture by espousing parallel assumptions and values. Others differ from but do not conflict with the dominant culture. Still others are called *countercultures* because they embrace values or assumptions that directly oppose the organization's dominant culture. It is also possible that some organizations (including some universities, according to one study) consist of subcultures with no decipherable dominant culture at all.[13]

Subcultures, particularly countercultures, potentially create conflict and dissension among employees, but they also serve two important functions.[14] First, they maintain the organization's standards of performance and ethical behavior. Employees who hold countercultural values are an important source of surveillance and critical review of the dominant order. They encourage constructive conflict and more creative thinking about how the organization should interact with its environment. Subcultures potentially support ethical conduct by preventing employees from blindly following one set of values. Subculture members continually question the "obvious" decisions and actions of the majority, thereby making everyone more mindful of the consequences of their actions.

The second function of subcultures is to act as spawning grounds for emerging values that keep the firm aligned with the evolving needs and expectations of customers, suppliers, communities, and other stakeholders. Companies eventually need to replace their dominant values with ones that are more appropriate for the changing environment. Those emerging cultural values and assumptions usually exist in subcultures long before they are ideal for the organization. If subcultures are suppressed, the organization may take longer to discover, develop, and adopt the emerging desired culture.

LO13-2 Describe four categories of artifacts through which corporate culture is deciphered.

DECIPHERING ORGANIZATIONAL CULTURE THROUGH ARTIFACTS

Shared values and assumptions are not easily measured through surveys and might not be accurately reflected in the organization's values statements. Instead, as Exhibit 13.1 illustrated earlier, an organization's culture needs to be deciphered through a detailed investigation of artifacts. **Artifacts** are the observable symbols and signs of an organization's culture, such as the way visitors are greeted, the organization's physical layout, and how employees are rewarded.[15] A few experts suggest that artifacts are the essence of organizational culture, whereas most others (including the authors of this book) view artifacts as symbols or indicators of

culture. In other words, culture is cognitive (values and assumptions inside people's heads) whereas artifacts are observable manifestations of that culture. Either way, artifacts are important because they represent and reinforce an organization's culture.

Artifacts provide valuable evidence about a company's culture.[16] An organization's ambiguous (fragmented) culture is best understood by observing workplace behavior, listening to everyday conversations among staff and with customers, studying written documents and emails, viewing physical structures and settings, and interviewing staff about corporate stories. In other words, to truly understand an organization's culture, we need to sample information from a variety of organizational artifacts.

The Mayo Clinic conducted such an assessment a few years ago. An anthropologist was hired to decipher the medical organization's culture at its headquarters in Minnesota and to identify ways of transferring that culture to its two newer sites in Florida and Arizona. For six weeks, the anthropologist shadowed employees, posed as a patient in waiting rooms, did countless interviews, and accompanied physicians on patient visits. The final report outlined Mayo's dominant culture and how its satellite operations varied from that culture.[17] Over the next few pages, we review four broad categories of artifacts: organizational stories and legends, language, rituals and ceremonies, and physical structures and symbols.

Organizational Stories and Legends

Stories and legends about the company's founders and past events permeate strong organizational cultures. Some tales recount heroic deeds, whereas others ridicule past events that deviate from the firm's core values. Organizational stories and legends serve as powerful social prescriptions of the way things should (or should not) be done. They add human realism to corporate expectations, individual performance standards, and the criteria for getting fired. Stories also produce emotions in listeners, and these emotions tend to improve listeners' memory of the lesson within the story.[18] Stories communicate corporate culture most effectively when they describe real people, are assumed to be true, and are known by employees throughout the organization. Stories are also prescriptive—they advise people what to do or not to do.[19]

Organizational Language

The language of the workplace speaks volumes about the company's culture. How employees talk to each other, describe customers, express anger, and greet stakeholders are all verbal symbols of cultural values. The language of culture is apparent at The Container Store, where employees compliment each other about "being Gumby," meaning that they are being as flexible as the once-popular green toy to help a customer or another employee.[20] Language also highlights values held by organizational subcultures. Consultants working at Whirlpool kept hearing employees talk about the appliance company's "PowerPoint culture." This phrase, which names Microsoft's presentation software, implied that Whirlpool has a hierarchical culture in which communication is one-way (from executives to employees).[21]

When Clients Are **Muppets**

According to former Goldman Sachs manager Greg Smith, employees at the investment firm routinely described their clients as muppets. "My muppet client didn't put me in comp on the trade we just printed," said one salesperson, meaning that the client was an idiot because he didn't compare prices, so the salesperson overcharged him. The "muppet" label seems to reveal a culture with a derogatory view of clients. "Being a muppet meant being an idiot, a fool, manipulated by someone else," Smith explains. Goldman Sachs subsequently scanned its internal emails for the muppet label and warned employees not to use the term.[22]

Rituals and Ceremonies

Rituals are the programmed routines of daily organizational life that dramatize an organization's culture.[23] They include how visitors are greeted, how often senior executives visit subordinates, how people communicate with each other, how much time employees take for lunch, and so on. These rituals are repetitive, predictable events that have symbolic meaning of underlying cultural values and assumptions. For instance, BMW's fast-paced culture is quite literally apparent in the way employees walk around the German automaker's offices. "When you move through the corridors and hallways of other companies' buildings, people kind of crawl, they walk slowly," observes a BMW executive. "But BMW people tend to move faster."[24] **Ceremonies** are more formal artifacts than rituals. Ceremonies are planned activities conducted specifically for the benefit of an audience. This would include publicly rewarding (or punishing) employees or celebrating the launch of a new product or newly won contract.

Physical Structures and Symbols

The size, shape, location, and age of buildings both reflect and influence an organization's culture. They might suggest a company's emphasis on teamwork, environmental friendliness, hierarchy, or any other set of values.[26] Even if the building doesn't make much of a statement, there is a treasure trove of physical artifacts inside. Desks, chairs, office space, and wall hangings (or lack of them) are just a few of the items that might convey cultural meaning.[27] Each physical artifact alone might not say much, but put enough of them together and you can see how they symbolize the organization's culture.

> **LO13-3** Discuss the importance of organizational culture and the conditions under which organizational culture strength improves organizational performance.

IS ORGANIZATIONAL CULTURE IMPORTANT?

In less than a dozen years, Coastal.com and its subsidiaries (including Clearly Contacts) has become North America's largest online retailer of eyeglasses and contact lenses. According to founder and CEO Roger Hardy, corporate culture is the main reason for the company's success. "Our corporate culture has allowed us to do that," says Hardy. "I think of it [the company's culture] as having been our competitive advantage for a long time." He adds that the company's culture was developed strategically, not haphazardly. "We defined our core values early on: hardworking, team work, bias to action, do more with less, always be innovating, agents of change."[28]

Roger Hardy and many other leaders believe that an organization's success partly depends on its culture. Many writers of popular-press management books also assert that the most successful companies have strong cultures. In fact, one popular management book, *Built to Last,* suggests that successful companies are "cultlike" (although not actually cults, the authors are careful to point out).[29] Does OB research support this view that companies are more effective when they have a strong culture? Yes, potentially, but the evidence indicates that the relationship depends on a few conditions.[30]

Before discussing these contingencies, let's examine the meaning of a "strong" organizational culture and its potential benefits. The strength of an organization's culture refers to how widely and deeply employees hold the company's dominant values and assumptions. In a strong organizational culture, most employees across all subunits understand and embrace the dominant values. These values and assumptions are also institutionalized through well-established artifacts, which further entrench the culture. In addition, strong cultures tend to be long-lasting; some can be traced back to the values and assumptions established by the company's founder. In contrast, companies have weak cultures when the dominant values are held mainly by a few people at the top of the organization, are barely discernible from artifacts, and are in flux.

A few paragraphs ago we said that companies with stronger cultures are *potentially* more effective; this occurs through the three important functions listed in Exhibit 13.3 and described as follows:

1. *Control system.* Organizational culture is a deeply embedded form of social control that influences employee decisions and behavior.[32] Culture is pervasive and operates nonconsciously. Think of it as an automatic pilot, nonconsciously directing employees so their behavior is consistent with organizational expectations. For this reason, some writers describe organizational culture as a compass that points everyone in the same direction.

2. *Social glue.* Organizational culture is the social glue that bonds people together and makes them feel part of the organizational experience.[33] Employees are motivated to internalize the organization's dominant culture because it fulfills their need for social identity. This social glue attracts new staff and retains top performers. It also becomes the common thread that holds employees together in global organizations. "The values of the company are really the bedrock—the glue which holds the firm together," says Nandan Nilekani, the head of the government of India's technology committee and former CEO of Infosys.[34]

3. *Sense making.* Organizational culture helps employees make sense of what goes on and why things happen in the company.[35] Corporate culture also makes it easier for them to understand what is expected of them. For instance, research has found that sales employees in companies with stronger organizational cultures have clearer role perceptions and less role-related stress.[36]

rituals the programmed routines of daily organizational life that dramatize the organization's culture

ceremonies planned displays of organizational culture, conducted specifically for the benefit of an audience

> "Culture is one of the most precious things a company has, so you must work harder on it than anything else."[31]
>
> —**Herb Kelleher,** cofounder and former CEO of Southwest Airlines

Contingencies of Organizational Culture and Effectiveness

Studies have found only a moderately positive relationship between culture strength and organizational effectiveness. The reason for this weak link is that strong cultures improve organizational effectiveness only under specific conditions (see Exhibit 13.3). The three main contingencies are (1) whether the culture content is aligned with the environment, (2) whether the culture is moderately strong, not cultlike, and (3) whether the culture incorporates an adaptive culture.

Culture Content Is Aligned with the External Environment The benefits of a strong culture depend on whether the

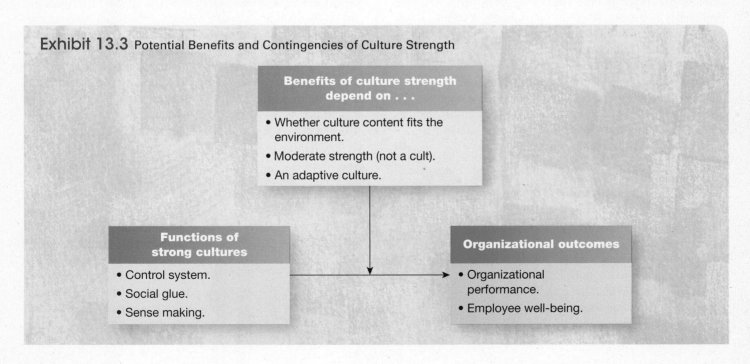

Exhibit 13.3 Potential Benefits and Contingencies of Culture Strength

Benefits of culture strength depend on . . .
- Whether culture content fits the environment.
- Moderate strength (not a cult).
- An adaptive culture.

Functions of strong cultures
- Control system.
- Social glue.
- Sense making.

Organizational outcomes
- Organizational performance.
- Employee well-being.

culture content—its dominant values and assumptions—is aligned with the external environment. Companies require an employee-centric culture in environments where business success depends mainly on employee talent, whereas an efficiency-focused culture may be more critical for companies in environments with strong competition and standardized products. If the dominant values are congruent with the environment, then employees are more likely to engage in behaviors that improve the organization's interaction with that environment. But when the dominant values are misaligned with the environment, a strong culture encourages behaviors that can undermine the organization's connection with its stakeholders.

For example, Coles became a successful competitor in the Australian retail food industry after it was acquired by Wesfarmers, which injected a strong culture around performance and customer service. Wesfarmers is a highly successful Australian conglomerate, but it doesn't nurture the same culture in all of its businesses (food, hardware, clothing, office supplies, insurance, fertilizers, mining, and so on). Instead, Wesfarmers ensures each company maintains a strong culture around the values that matter most for that industry and its stakeholders. "It would be a huge mistake if we tried to impose one culture over all these businesses," explains Wesfarmers CEO Richard Goyder. "Bunnings (Australia's largest home improvement retailer) and Coles have to be customer-centric, whereas our coal business has to be absolutely focused on safety."[37]

> "You have to create a culture that not only accepts change but seeks out how to change."[40]
>
> **—Dan Akerson,**
> former General Motors CEO

Culture Strength Is Not the Level of a Cult A second contingency is the degree of culture strength. Various experts suggest that companies with very strong cultures (i.e., corporate "cults") may be less effective than companies with moderately strong cultures.[38] One reason why corporate cults may undermine organizational effectiveness is that they lock people into mental models, which can blind them to new opportunities and unique problems. The effect of these very strong cultures is that people overlook or incorrectly define subtle misalignments between the organization's activities and the changing environment.

The other reason why very strong cultures may be dysfunctional is that they suppress dissenting subcultures. The challenge for organizational leaders is to maintain not only a strong culture but one that allows subcultural diversity. Subcultures encourage task-oriented conflict, which improves creative thinking and offers some level of ethical vigilance over the dominant culture. In the long run, a subculture's nascent values could become important dominant values as the environment changes. Corporate cults suppress subcultures, thereby undermining these benefits.

Culture Is an Adaptive Culture A third factor determining whether cultural strength improves organizational effectiveness is whether the culture content includes an **adaptive culture**.[39] An adaptive culture embraces change, creativity, open-mindedness, growth, and learning. Organizational leaders across many industries increasingly view an adaptive culture as an important ingredient for the organization's long-term success.

What does an adaptive culture look like? Employees who embrace an adaptive culture view the organization's survival and success in terms of ongoing adaptation to the external environment, which itself is continuously changing. They assume that their future depends on monitoring the external environment and serving stakeholders with the resources available. Thus, employees in adaptive cultures see things from an open systems perspective and take responsibility for the organization's performance and alignment with the external environment.

In an adaptive culture, receptivity to change extends to internal processes and roles. Employees believe that satisfying stakeholder needs requires continuous improvement of internal work processes. They also recognize the importance of remaining flexible in their own work roles. The phrase "That's not my job" is found in nonadaptive cultures. Finally, an adaptive culture has a strong *learning orientation* because being receptive to change necessarily means that the company also supports action-oriented discovery. With a learning orientation, employees welcome new learning opportunities, actively experiment with new ideas and practices, view reasonable mistakes as a natural part of the learning process, and continuously question past practices (see Chapter 6).[41]

Organizational Culture and Business Ethics

An organization's culture influences the ethical conduct of its employees. This makes sense because good behavior is driven by ethical values, and ethical values become embedded in an organization's dominant culture. For example, aerospace giant

Lockheed Martin has a strong culture that emphasizes "do what's right." This cultural value states that the company believes in practicing the highest standards of ethical conduct, maintaining trust with stakeholders, being good citizens, and taking responsibility for their actions.[42]

An organization's culture can also motivate unethical conduct. For example, critics claim that News Corp's news tabloids have had a culture that rewards aggressive, partisan, and sensationalistic tactics. This culture may have uncovered news, but it allegedly also pushed some journalists and executives over the ethical line, including illegally hacking into the phones of celebrities, crime victims, and politicians. A British parliamentary committee (among others) concluded that News Corp's wrongdoing was caused by a wayward culture that "permeated from the top throughout the organization." As one journalist concluded: "Phone hacking is done by employees within the corporate culture of 'whatever it takes.' "[43] The point here is that organizational culture and ethics go hand-in-hand, so leaders need to nurture a culture that guides and reinforces ethical conduct.

> **LO13-4** Compare and contrast four strategies for merging organizational cultures.

MERGING ORGANIZATIONAL CULTURES

Mergers and acquisitions often fail to add financial gains when the merging organizations have incompatible cultures.[44] Unless the acquired firm is left to operate independently, companies with clashing cultures tend to undermine employee performance and customer service. Organizational leaders can minimize cultural collisions in corporate mergers and fulfill their duty of due diligence by conducting a bicultural audit and then applying one of four main strategies to merge the two cultures.

Bicultural Audit

A **bicultural audit** diagnoses cultural relations between the companies and determines the extent to which cultural clashes will likely occur.[46] The process begins by identifying cultural differences between the merging companies. This might occur by surveying employees or through an extended series of meetings where executives and staff of both firms discuss how they think through important decisions in their business. From the survey data or meetings, the parties determine which differences between the two firms will result in conflict and which cultural values provide common ground on

which to build a cultural foundation in the merged organization. The final stage involves identifying strategies and preparing action plans to bridge the two organizations' cultures.

Strategies for Merging Different Organizational Cultures

In some cases, the bicultural audit results in a decision to end merger talks because the two cultures are too different to merge effectively. However, even with substantially different cultures, two companies may form a workable union if they apply the appropriate merger strategy. The four main strategies for merging different corporate cultures are assimilation, deculturation, integration, and separation (see Exhibit 13.4).[47]

Assimilation Assimilation occurs when employees at the acquired company willingly embrace the cultural values of the acquiring organization. Typically, this strategy works best when the acquired company has a weak, dysfunctional culture and the

adaptive culture
an organizational culture in which employees are receptive to change, including the ongoing alignment of the organization to its environment and continuous improvement of internal processes

bicultural audit
a process of diagnosing cultural relations between companies and determining the extent to which cultural clashes will likely occur

Losing Value **and** Talent **with** Mergers and Acquisitions[45]

85% of executives of failed mergers identify organizational culture differences as the major cause of the failure.

71% of acquisitions (on average across three major studies) destroyed rather than enhanced shareholder value.

75% of executives interviewed believed their acquisition was successful.

40% of executives in acquired firms left within two years after the acquisition (twice the usual executive turnover rate).

Exhibit 13.4 Strategies for Merging Different Organizational Cultures

Merger Strategy	Description	Works Best When . . .
Assimilation	Acquired company embraces acquiring firm's culture.	Acquired firm has a weak culture.
Deculturation	Acquiring firm imposes its culture on unwilling acquired firm.	Rarely works—may be necessary only when acquired firm's culture doesn't work but employees don't realize it.
Integration	Merging companies combine the two or more cultures into a new composite culture.	Existing cultures can be improved.
Separation	Merging companies remain distinct entities with minimal exchange of culture or organizational practices.	Firms operate successfully in different businesses requiring different cultures.

Sources: Based on ideas in A.R. Malekzadeh and A. Nahavandi, "Making Mergers Work by Managing Cultures," *Journal of Business Strategy* 11 (May/June 1990): 55–57; K.W. Smith, "A Brand-New Culture for the Merged Firm," *Mergers and Acquisitions* 35 (June 2000): 45–50.

acquiring company's culture is strong and aligned with the external environment. The cultural assimilation strategy seldom produces cultural clashes because the acquiring firm's culture is highly respected and the acquired firm's culture is either weak or relatively similar to the other culture. A recent example of the assimilation strategy is the Southwest Airlines acquisition of AirTran Airways. The two firms already had similar cultures, but Southwest's legendary "Southwest way" culture also made the acquisition relatively free of culture clashes. "It's helpful that Southwest has a great cultural reputation," says a Southwest executive about the AirTran Airways acquisition.[48]

Deculturation Assimilation is rare. Employees usually resist organizational change, particularly when they are asked to throw away personal and cultural values. Under these conditions, some acquiring companies apply a *deculturation* strategy by imposing their culture and business practices on the acquired organization. The acquiring firm strips away artifacts and reward systems that support the old culture. People who cannot adopt the acquiring company's culture often lose their jobs. Deculturation may be necessary when the acquired firm's culture doesn't work, even when employees in the acquired company aren't convinced of this. However, this strategy is difficult to apply effectively because the acquired firm's employees resist the cultural intrusions from the buying firm, thereby delaying or undermining the merger process.

Integration A third strategy is to combine the two or more cultures into a new composite culture that preserves the best features of the previous cultures. Integration is slow and potentially risky because there are many forces preserving the existing cultures. Still, this strategy should be considered when the companies have relatively weak cultures or when their cultures include several overlapping values. Integration also works best when people realize that their company's existing culture is ineffective, which motivates them to adopt a new set of dominant values.

Separation A separation strategy occurs when the merging companies agree to remain distinct entities with minimal exchange of culture or organizational practices. This strategy is most appropriate when the two merging companies are in unrelated industries or operate in different countries, because the most appropriate cultural values tend to differ by industry and national culture. This strategy is also relevant advice for the corporate cultures of diversified conglomerates. The cultural separation approach is rare, however. Executives in acquiring firms usually have difficulty keeping their hands off the acquired firm. According to one estimate, only 15 percent of mergers leave the acquired company as a stand-alone unit.[49]

> **LO13-5** Describe five strategies for changing and strengthening an organization's culture, including the application of attraction–selection–attrition theory.

CHANGING AND STRENGTHENING ORGANIZATIONAL CULTURE

Is it possible to change an organization's culture? Yes, but doing so isn't easy, the change rarely occurs quickly, and often the culture ends up changing (or replacing) corporate leaders. A few experts argue that an organization's culture "cannot be managed," so attempting to change the company's values and assumptions is a waste of time.[50] This may be an extreme view, but organizational culture experts generally agree that changing an organization's culture is a monumental challenge. At the

> ## "Unconsciously or consciously, senior people leave their marks on an organization's culture and legacy."[53]
>
> **—Max De Pree**, business author and former Herman Miller CEO

same time, the external environment changes over time, so organizations need to shift their culture to maintain alignment with the emerging environment.

Over the next few pages, we will highlight five strategies that have had some success at altering corporate cultures. These strategies, illustrated in Exhibit 13.5, are not exhaustive, but each seems to work well under the right circumstances.

Actions of Founders and Leaders

An organization's culture begins with its founders and leaders.[51] Whether deliberately or haphazardly, the company's founder shapes an organization's culture during its early stages.[52] The company's culture sometimes reflects the founder's personality, and this cultural imprint can remain with the organization for decades. The founder's activities are also later retold as organizational stories to further reinforce the culture.

Subsequent leaders can further reinforce or, with considerable effort, shift the dominant culture. In fact, an organization's culture can drift away from the founder's values, so leaders must continuously monitor and reinforce the desired values. This advice was recently echoed by Bill Emerson, CEO of Quicken Loans. "If you don't spend time to create a culture in your organization, one will create itself," warns Emerson. "And the one that creates itself is probably not going to be good."[54] The process of leading cultural change applies both transformational leadership and authentic leadership (see Chapter 11). In each of those models, leaders base their words and actions on personal values, and those values potentially become a reflection of the organization's values.

Align Artifacts with the Desired Culture

Artifacts represent more than just the visible indicators of a company's culture. They are also mechanisms that keep the culture in place or shift the culture to a new set of values and assumptions. As we discuss in the next chapter on organizational change, systems and structures are powerful mechanisms to support the desired state of affairs. These systems and structures are artifacts, such as the workplace layout, reporting structure, office rituals, type of information distributed, and language that is reinforced or discouraged. Corporate cultures are also altered and strengthened through the artifacts of stories and behaviors. According to Max De Pree, former CEO of furniture manufacturer Herman Miller Inc., every organization needs "tribal storytellers" to keep the organization's history and culture alive.[55] Leaders play a role by creating memorable events that symbolize the cultural values they want to develop or maintain.

Introduce Culturally Consistent Rewards and Recognition

Reward systems and informal recognition practices are artifacts, but they deserve separate discussion because of their powerful effect on strengthening or reshaping an organization's culture.[56] For example, to change Home Depot's freewheeling culture, Robert Nardelli introduced precise measures of corporate performance and drilled managers with weekly performance objectives related to those metrics. A two-hour weekly conference call became a ritual in which Home Depot's top executives were held accountable for the previous week's goals. These actions

Exhibit 13.5 Strategies for Changing and Strengthening Organizational Culture

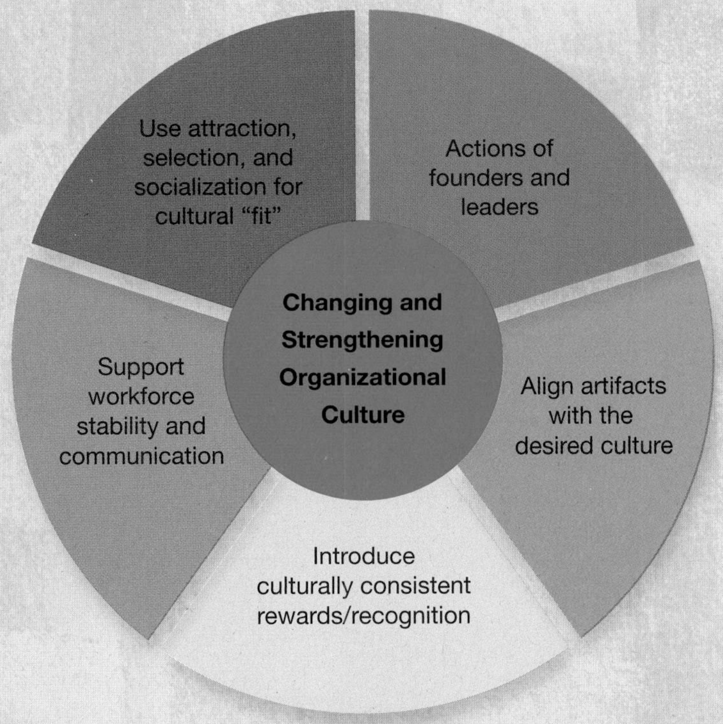

- Use attraction, selection, and socialization for cultural "fit"
- Actions of founders and leaders
- Align artifacts with the desired culture
- Introduce culturally consistent rewards/recognition
- Support workforce stability and communication

Changing and Strengthening Organizational Culture

reinforced a more disciplined (and centralized) performance-oriented culture.[58]

Support Workforce Stability and Communication

An organization's culture is embedded in the minds of its employees. Organizational stories are rarely written down; rituals and ceremonies do not usually exist in procedure manuals; organizational metaphors are not found in corporate directories. Thus, a strong culture depends on a stable workforce. Workforce stability is also important because it takes time for employees to fully understand the organization's culture and how to enact it in their daily work lives. The organization's culture can literally disintegrate during periods of high turnover and precipitous downsizing because the corporate memory leaves with these employees. Along with workforce stability, a strong organizational culture depends on a workplace where employees regularly communicate with each other. This ongoing communication enables employees to develop shared language, stories, and other artifacts.

Leaders Communicate and
Enact the Organization's Culture[57]

51%
of employees surveyed* say their immediate boss speaks to them often about the company's culture.

81%
of executives surveyed say senior leadership acts in accordance with the company's core values and beliefs.

69%
of employees surveyed say senior leadership acts in accordance with the company's core values and beliefs.

67%
of employees surveyed say senior leadership regularly communicates their company's core values and beliefs.

*All statistics based on a survey of 1,005 U.S. adults employed full-time and 303 corporate executives.

Use Attraction, Selection, and Socialization for Cultural Fit

Organizational culture is strengthened by attracting and hiring people who already embrace the organization's dominant values and assumptions. This process, along with weeding out people who don't fit the culture, is explained by **attraction–selection–attrition (ASA) theory**.[59] ASA theory states that organizations have a natural tendency to attract, select, and retain people with values and personality characteristics that are consistent with the organization's character, resulting in a more homogeneous organization and a stronger culture.

Ensuring the Cultural Shoe Fits at **Zappos**

Online shoe and clothing retailer Zappos has a strong organizational culture, thanks to its widely acclaimed attraction, selection, and attrition practices. Zappos describes its culture in recruiting material, so job applicants quickly learn about its core values such as "Deliver WOW through Service," "Embrace and Drive Change," and "Create Fun and A Little Weirdness." The company also carefully selects applicants whose personal values are aligned with the company's values. For example, they find out how well applicants treat others during their interview visit. And to encourage attrition, Zappos pays $2,000 to any new recruit who quits because they discover their personal values don't fit the company's culture.[60]

- *Attraction.* Job applicants engage in self-selection by avoiding employment in companies whose values seem incompatible with their own values.[62] They look for subtle artifacts during interviews and through public information that communicate the company's culture. Some organizations often encourage this self-selection by actively describing their cultures. At Reckitt Benckiser, for instance, applicants can complete an online simulation that estimates their fit with the British household products company's hard-driving culture. Participants indicate how they would respond to a series of business scenarios. The exercise then calculates their cultural fit score and asks them to decide whether to continue pursuing employment with the company.[63]

- *Selection.* How well the person "fits in" with the company's culture is often a factor in deciding which job applicants to hire.[64] For example, job applicants at G Adventures go through a special interview to determine their cultural fit. A few current employees at the adventure travel company are randomly selected to conduct each interview. They listen carefully to the applicant's responses to five unusual questions, and then collectively decide whether the individual's personal values are sufficiently aligned with G Adventures' core values.

- *Attrition.* People are motivated to seek environments that are sufficiently congruent with their personal values and to leave environments that are a poor fit. This occurs because person–organization values congruence supports their social identity and minimizes internal role conflict. Even if employees aren't forced out, many quit when values incongruence is sufficiently high.[65] Zappos, G Adventures, and a few other companies will even pay newcomers to quit within the first few weeks of employment if they think there is a cultural mismatch.

LO13-6 Describe the organizational socialization process and identify strategies to improve that process.

ORGANIZATIONAL SOCIALIZATION

Organizational socialization is another process that companies use to maintain a strong corporate culture and, more generally, help people to adjust to new employment. **Organizational socialization** is the process by which individuals learn the values, expected behaviors, and social knowledge necessary to assume their roles in the organization.[66] This process can potentially change employee values to become more aligned with the company's culture. However, changing an employee's personal values is much more difficult than is often assumed, because personal values are fairly stable beyond an individual's young adulthood. More likely, effective socialization gives newcomers a clearer understanding about the company's values and how they are translated into specific on-the-job behaviors.[67]

Organizational socialization not only strengthens the company's culture; it is also valuable for helping newcomers adjust to work procedures, coworkers, and other corporate realities. Research indicates that when employees are guided through the evidence-based organizational socialization practices, they tend to perform better, have higher job satisfaction, and remain longer with the organization.[68]

Organizational Socialization as a Learning and Adjustment Process

Organizational socialization is a process of both learning and adjustment. It is a learning process because newcomers try to make sense of the company's physical workplace, social dynamics, and strategic and cultural environment. They learn about the organization's performance expectations, power dynamics, corporate culture,

Organizational Culture
during the Hiring Process[61]

82%
of 500 managers surveyed (most in Europe and Oceania) say it is important to measure job applicants for their cultural fit.

44%
of *Fortune* 500 companies say they take steps to describe their corporate culture to job seekers.

32%
of 500 managers surveyed (most in Europe and Oceania) say their organization measures the cultural fit of job applicants.

51%
of 2,303 American managers surveyed say they search social network sites to determine if the job candidate is a good fit for the company's culture.

34%
of 230,000 employees surveyed across 31 countries say that corporate culture is an important factor that would drive their decision to accept one job/position over another.

company history, and jargon. They also need to form successful and satisfying relationships with other people from whom they can learn the ropes.[69] Thus, effective socialization enables new employees to form a cognitive map of the physical, social, strategic, and cultural dynamics of the organization without experiencing information overload.

Organizational socialization is also an adjustment process because individuals need to adapt to their new work environment. They develop new work roles that reconfigure their social identity, adopt new team norms, and practice new behaviors.[70] The adjustment process is fairly rapid for many people, usually occurring within a few months. However, newcomers with diverse work experience seem to adjust better than those with limited previous experience, possibly because they have a larger toolkit of knowledge and skills to make the adjustment possible.[71]

Stages of Organizational Socialization

Organizational socialization is a continuous process, beginning long before the first day of employment and continuing throughout one's career within the company. However, it is most intense when people move across organizational boundaries, such as when they first join a company or get transferred to an international assignment. Each of these transitions is a process that can be divided into three stages. Our focus here is on the socialization of new employees, so the three stages are called preemployment socialization, encounter, and role management (see Exhibit 13.6). These stages parallel the individual's transition from outsider to newcomer and then to insider.[72]

Stage 1: Preemployment Socialization Think back to the months and weeks before you began working in a new job (or attending a new school). You actively searched for information about the company, formed expectations about working there, and felt some anticipation about fitting into that environment. The preemployment socialization stage encompasses all the learning and adjustment that occurs before the first day of work. In fact, a large part of the socialization adjustment process occurs during this stage.[73]

The main problem with preemployment socialization is that outsiders rely on indirect information about what it is like to work in the organization. This information is often distorted by inherent conflicts during the mating dance between employer and applicant.[74] One conflict occurs between the employer's need to attract qualified applicants and the applicant's need for complete information to make accurate employment decisions. Many firms describe only positive aspects of the job and company, causing applicants to accept job offers with incomplete or false expectations. Another conflict occurs because applicants want to convey a favorable image to their prospective employer, so they avoid asking important questions about the company that may cast a shadow over that public image. For instance, applicants usually don't like to ask about starting salaries and promotion opportunities because it makes them seem greedy or aggressive. Yet, unless the employer provides this information, applicants might fill in the missing details with false assumptions that produce inaccurate expectations.

Two other types of conflict tend to distort preemployment information for employers. Applicants engage in impression management when seeking employment, and this tends to motivate them to hide negative information, act out of character, and occasionally embellish information about their past accomplishments. At the same time, employers are sometimes reluctant to ask certain questions or use potentially valuable selection devices because they might scare off applicants. Unfortunately, employers form inaccurate expectations about job candidates because of exaggerated résumés as well as reluctance by managers to dig further in interviews for more delicate information about those applicants.

Stage 2: Encounter The first day on the job typically marks the beginning of the encounter stage of organizational socialization. This is the stage in which newcomers test how well

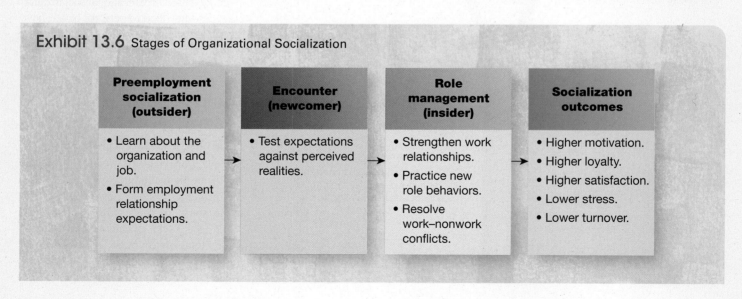

Exhibit 13.6 Stages of Organizational Socialization

Preemployment socialization (outsider)	Encounter (newcomer)	Role management (insider)	Socialization outcomes
• Learn about the organization and job. • Form employment relationship expectations.	• Test expectations against perceived realities.	• Strengthen work relationships. • Practice new role behaviors. • Resolve work–nonwork conflicts.	• Higher motivation. • Higher loyalty. • Higher satisfaction. • Lower stress. • Lower turnover.

their preemployment expectations fit reality. Many companies fail that test, resulting in **reality shock**—the stress that results when employees perceive discrepancies between their preemployment expectations and on-the-job reality.[75] Reality shock doesn't necessarily occur on the first day; it might develop over several weeks or even months as newcomers form a better understanding of their new work environment.

Reality shock is common in many organizations.[76] Unmet expectations sometimes occur because the employer is unable to live up to its promises, such as failing to provide challenging projects or the resources to get the work done. Reality shock also occurs because new hires develop distorted work expectations through the information exchange conflicts described earlier. Whatever the cause, reality shock impedes the socialization process because the newcomer's energy is directed toward managing the stress rather than learning and accepting organizational knowledge and roles.[77]

Stage 3: Role Management Role management, the third stage of organizational socialization, really begins during preemployment socialization, but it is most active as employees make the transition from newcomers to insiders. They strengthen relationships with coworkers and supervisors, practice new role behaviors, and adopt attitudes and values consistent with their new positions and the organization. Role management also involves resolving the conflicts between work and nonwork activities, including resolving discrepancies between their personal values and those emphasized by the organizational culture.

Improving the Socialization Process

As we mentioned earlier, many companies overpromise to job applicants. They often exaggerate positive features of the job and neglect to mention the undesirable elements in the hope that the best applicants will get "stuck" on the organization. In contrast, a **realistic job preview (RJP)** offers a balance of positive and negative information about the job and work context.[78] This balanced description of the company and work helps job

applicants decide for themselves whether their skills, needs, and values are compatible with the job and organization.

RJPs scare away some applicants, but they also tend to reduce turnover and increase job performance.[79] This occurs because RJPs help applicants develop more accurate preemployment expectations, which, in turn, minimize reality shock. RJPs represent a type of vaccination by preparing employees for the more challenging and troublesome aspects of work life. There is also some evidence that RJPs increase affective organizational commitment. This effect might occur because companies providing candid information are easier to trust. They also show respect for employee expectations and concern for their well-being.[80]

Socialization Agents Ask new employees what most helped them to adjust to their jobs and chances are they will mention helpful coworkers, bosses, or maybe even friends who work elsewhere in the organization. The fact is, socialization occurs mainly through these socialization agents.[81] Supervisors tend to provide technical information, performance feedback, and information about job duties. They also improve the socialization process by giving newcomers reasonably challenging first assignments, buffering them from excessive demands, helping them form social ties with coworkers, and generating positive emotions around their new work experience.[82]

Coworkers are important socialization agents because they are easily accessible, can answer questions when problems arise, and serve as role models for appropriate behavior. New employees tend to receive this information and support when coworkers welcome them into the work team. Coworkers also aid the socialization process by being flexible and tolerant in their interactions with new hires.

Coworkers play a more valuable role in newcomer socialization when companies help to strengthen social bonds with the new hires. At Clear Channel Communications, Inc., in San Antonio, Texas, newcomers are paired with "peer coaches" before their first day of work, so they have someone to contact about their questions and guide them through the organizational entry process. Lupin Limited also has a popular buddy system for new hires. The buddy system not only improves socialization of newcomers at the Mumbai, India, pharmaceutical company; it has also become a valuable form of leadership development for the buddy coworker. "A happy by-product of the buddy program is the biggest supervisor training program the company has ever conducted in its history," says Divakar Kaza, Lupin's president of human resources.[83]

Study Checklist

- Did you tear out the perforated student review card at the back of the text to revisit learning objectives and key terms and definitions?

Connect® Management is available for *M Organizational Behavior.* Additional resources include:

- Interactive Applications:
  - **Decision Generator**
  - **Sequencing**
  - **Video Case:** See management in action through interactive videos.

- **SmartBook™**—SmartBook is the first and only adaptive reading experience available today. Distinguishing what you know from what you don't, and honing in on concepts you are most likely to forget, SmartBook personalizes content for you in a continuously adapting reading experience. Reading is no longer a passive and linear experience, but an engaging and dynamic one where you are more likely to master and retain important concepts and go to class better prepared.

Want Help Studying?

SMARTBOOK: MAKE
EACH MINUTE COUNT.

Go to: LearnSmartAdvantage.com

14 chapter

Organizational **Change**

Learning Objectives

After studying this chapter, you should be able to:

LO14-1 Describe the elements of Lewin's force field analysis model.

LO14-2 Discuss the reasons why people resist organizational change and how change agents should view this resistance.

LO14-3 Outline six strategies for minimizing resistance to change, and debate ways to effectively create an urgency to change.

LO14-4 Discuss how leadership, coalitions, social networks, and pilot projects assist organizational change.

LO14-5 Describe and compare action research and appreciative inquiry as formal approaches to organizational change.

LO14-6 Discuss two cross-cultural and three ethical issues in organizational change.

ouis Gerstner Jr. led the legendary turnaround of IBM in the 1990s, but Sam Palmisano may have orchestrated an equally breathtaking transformation of the company over the past decade. Soon after taking over from Gerstner as CEO, Palmisano (who recently stepped down as IBM's chair) frankly warned staff that although IBM was good, it still wasn't an industry-leading business. He asked four questions—about whether the business satisfied customers, employees, society, and stockholders—whose answers would transform IBM beyond expectations. "The hardest thing is answering those four questions," says Palmisano. "You've got to answer all four and work at answering all four to really execute with excellence."

The change process didn't come easily. In particular, the master stroke decision to sell IBM's PC business met with strong internal opposition and subtler forms of resistance. Palmisano eased these concerns by explaining how the PC business failed to deliver on the four questions. He also regularly cited the founding principle of Thomas J. Watson Jr. (IBM's second CEO) that IBM's ultimate purpose is to help solve society's challenges. "It's old-fashioned, but it's motivational," says Palmisano. This message and the four questions drove the change process, catapulting IBM to the top of the league once again.[1]

IBM's continuous transformation and reinvention illustrates many of the strategies and practices necessary to successfully change organizations. It reveals how leaders create an urgency for change, revise systems and structures to support the change, and continuously communicate the change process. Although IBM's ongoing change process sounds simple on paper, in reality it is a complex process, requiring considerable leadership effort and vigilance. As we will describe throughout this chapter, the challenge of change is not just in deciding which way to go; the challenge is in the execution of this strategy. When leaders discover the need for change and identify some ideas about the preferred route to a better future, the change process involves navigating around the numerous obstacles and gaining organizationwide support for that change.

How Effectively Do Organizations around the World Handle Change?[2]

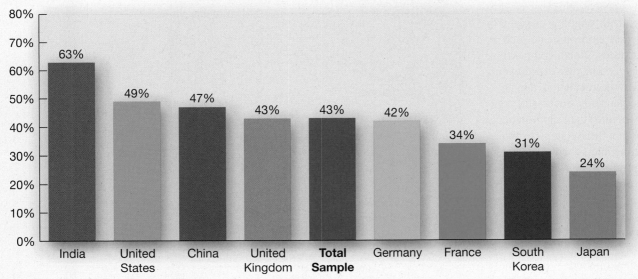

Note: Percentage of employees, by selected countries, who agree or strongly agree that "change is handled effectively in my organization." Not all 28,810 employees across the 15 countries surveyed are shown here, but all are included in the "total sample" figure.

This chapter unfolds as follows. We begin by introducing Lewin's model of change and its component parts. This discussion includes sources of resistance to change, ways to minimize this resistance, and ways to stabilize desired behaviors.

Next, the chapter examines two approaches to organizational change—action research and appreciative inquiry. The last section of this chapter considers both cross-cultural and ethical issues in organizational change.

> "I've always believed that when the rate of change inside an institution becomes slower than the rate of change outside, the end is in sight."[4]
>
> —**Jack Welch,** former General Electric CEO

LO14-1 Describe the elements of Lewin's force field analysis model.

LEWIN'S FORCE FIELD ANALYSIS MODEL

"The velocity of change is so rapid, so quick, that if you don't accept the change and move with the change, you're going to be left behind."[3] This statement by BHP Billiton chair Jacques Nasser highlights one of the messages throughout this book: organizations operate as open systems that need to keep pace with ongoing changes in their external environment, such as consumer needs, global competition, technology, community expectations, government (de)regulation, and environmental standards. Successful organizations monitor their environments and take appropriate steps to maintain a compatible fit with new external conditions. Rather than resisting change, employees in successful companies embrace change as an integral part of organizational life.

It is easy to see environmental forces pushing companies to change the way they operate. What is more difficult to see is the complex interplay of these forces on the internal dynamics of organizations. Social

psychologist Kurt Lewin developed the force field analysis model to describe this process using the metaphor of a force field (see Exhibit 14.1).[5] Although it was developed more than 50 years ago, recent reviews affirm that Lewin's **force field analysis** model remains one of the most widely respected ways of viewing the change process.[6]

One side of the force field model represents the *driving forces* that push organizations toward a new state of affairs. These might include new competitors or technologies, evolving workforce expectations, or a host of other environmental changes. Corporate leaders also produce driving forces even when external forces for change aren't apparent. For instance,

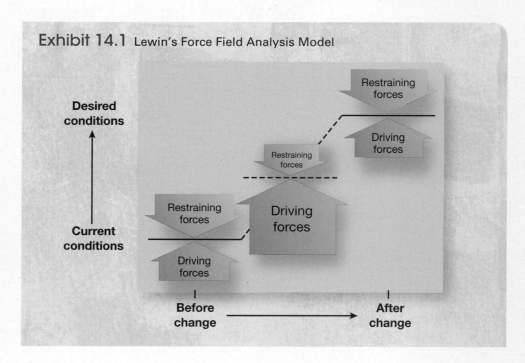

Exhibit 14.1 Lewin's Force Field Analysis Model

some experts call for "divine discontent" as a key feature of successful organizations, meaning that leaders continually urge employees to strive for higher standards or better practices. Even when the company outshines the competition, employees believe they can do better. "We have a habit of divine discontent with our performance," says creative agency Ogilvy & Mather about its corporate culture. "It is an antidote to smugness."[7]

The other side of Lewin's model represents the *restraining forces* that maintain the status quo. These restraining forces are commonly called "resistance to change" because they appear to block the change process. Stability occurs when the driving and restraining forces are roughly in equilibrium—that is, they are of approximately equal strength in opposite directions.

Lewin's force field model emphasizes that effective change occurs by **unfreezing** the current situation, moving to a desired condition, and then **refreezing** the system so it remains in the desired state. Unfreezing involves producing disequilibrium between the driving and restraining forces. As we will describe later, this may occur by increasing the driving forces, reducing the restraining forces, or having a combination of both. Refreezing occurs when the organization's systems and structures are aligned with the desired behaviors. They must support and reinforce the new role patterns and prevent the organization from slipping back into the old way of doing things. Over the next few pages, we use Lewin's model to understand why change is blocked and how the process can evolve more smoothly.

force field analysis Kurt Lewin's model of systemwide change that helps change agents diagnose the forces that drive and restrain proposed organizational change

unfreezing the first part of the change process, in which the change agent produces disequilibrium between the driving and restraining forces

refreezing the latter part of the change process, in which systems and structures are introduced that reinforce and maintain the desired behaviors

LO14-2 Discuss the reasons why people resist organizational change and how change agents should view this resistance.

UNDERSTANDING RESISTANCE TO CHANGE

Robert Nardelli pushed hard to transform Home Depot from a loose configuration of fiefdoms to a more performance-oriented operation that delivered a consistent customer experience. Change did occur at the world's largest home improvement

Resistance to Change in United–Continental Merger

Four years after it merged with Continental Airlines, United Airlines continues to suffer from operational and customer service problems. United executives say the poor results are partly due to the challenges of combining complex reservation and operational systems. But they also admit that subtle forms of employee resistance to change are also at work. Some Continental employees have opposed United Airlines' operational practices, while some United Airlines employees have failed to embrace Continental's customer service standards. "You know, the cultural change takes time," explains United Airlines CEO Jeffery Smisek. "And people resist change. People are sort of set in their ways."[8]

retailer, but at a price. Many talented managers and employees left the company, and some of those remaining continued to resent Nardelli's transformation. Disenchanted staff referred to the company as "Home Despot" because the changes took away their autonomy. Others named it "Home GEpot," a disparaging reference to the many former GE executives that Nardelli hired into top positions. After five years, the Home Depot board decided to replace Nardelli, partly because he made some unsuccessful strategic decisions and partly because some changes he introduced were unsuccessful.[9]

Robert Nardelli experienced considerable *resistance to change* at Home Depot. Resistance to change takes many forms, ranging from overt work stoppages to subtle attempts to continue the old ways.[10] A study of bank employees reported that subtle resistance is much more common than overt resistance. Some employees in that study avoided the desired changes by moving into different jobs. Others continued to perform tasks the old way as long as management didn't notice. Even when employees complied with the planned changes, they showed resistance by performing the new task while letting customers know that they disapproved of these changes forced on them![11]

Resistance is a form of conflict, but unfortunately change agents sometimes interpret that disagreement as relationship conflict (see Chapter 10). They describe the people who oppose change as unreasonable, dysfunctional, and irrational reactionaries to a desirable initiative. This perspective shapes the change agent's response to resistance, which tends to escalate the conflict, producing even stronger resistance to the change initiative. A more productive approach is to view resistance to change as task conflict. From the task conflict perspective, resistance is a signal that the change agent has not sufficiently prepared employees for change.[13]

Employees might not feel a sufficiently strong urgency to change, or they might feel the change strategy is ill-conceived. Even if they recognize the need for change and agree with the strategy, employees might resist because they lack confidence to change or believe the change will make them worse off than the current situation. Resistance takes many forms, and change agents need to decipher those different types of resistance to understand their underlying causes.[14]

Resistance is also a form of voice, so discussion potentially improves procedural justice through voice (see Chapter 5) as well as decision making through involvement (see Chapter 6). By redirecting initial forms of resistance into constructive conversations, change agents can increase employee perceptions and feelings of fairness. Furthermore, resistance is motivational; it potentially engages people to think about the change strategy

Facing the Challenge of
Resistance to Resistance[15]

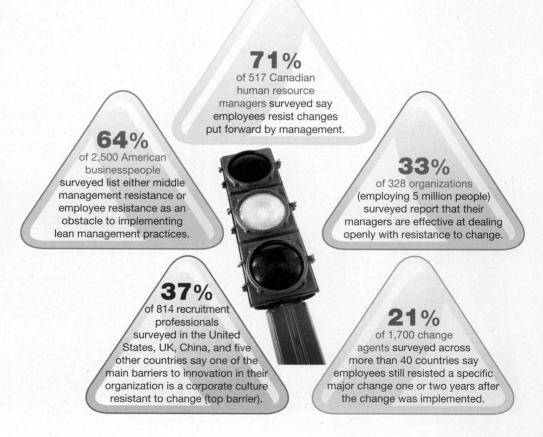

71% of 517 Canadian human resource managers surveyed say employees resist changes put forward by management.

64% of 2,500 American businesspeople surveyed list either middle management resistance or employee resistance as an obstacle to implementing lean management practices.

33% of 328 organizations (employing 5 million people) surveyed report that their managers are effective at dealing openly with resistance to change.

37% of 814 recruitment professionals surveyed in the United States, UK, China, and five other countries say one of the main barriers to innovation in their organization is a corporate culture resistant to change (top barrier).

21% of 1,700 change agents surveyed across more than 40 countries say employees still resisted a specific major change one or two years after the change was implemented.

and process. Change agents can harness that motivational force to ultimately strengthen commitment to the change initiative.

Why Employees Resist Change

Change management experts have developed a long list of reasons why people resist change.[16] Some people inherently oppose change because of their personality and values.[17] Aside from these dispositional factors, employees typically oppose organizational change because they lack sufficient motivation, ability, role clarity, or situational support to change their attitudes, decisions, and behavior.[18] In other words, an employee's readiness for change depends on all four elements of the MARS model. These MARS elements are the foundations of the six most commonly cited reasons why people resist change: (1) negative valence of change, (2) fear of the unknown, (3) not-invented-here syndrome, (4) breaking routines, (5) incongruent team dynamics, and (6) incongruent organizational systems and structures.

Negative Valence of Change

Employees tend to resist change when they believe the new work environment will have more negative than positive outcomes, particularly when the negative outcomes have a high probability of occurring and the positive outcomes have a low probability of occurring.[19] In other words, they apply (although imperfectly) the subjective expected utility formula (Chapter 6) to estimate whether the change will make them better or worse off. This cost–benefit analysis mainly considers personal outcomes. However, resistance also increases when employees believe the change will do more harm than good to the team and organization.[20]

Fear of the Unknown

Organizational change usually has a degree of uncertainty, and employees tend to assume the worst when they are unsure whether the change will have good or bad outcomes. Uncertainty is also associated with lack of personal control, which is another source of negative emotions.[21] Consequently, the uncertainty inherent in most organizational change is usually considered less desirable than the relative certainty of the status quo. This condition adds more negative valence to the cost–benefit calculation we described earlier.

Not-Invented-Here Syndrome

Employees sometimes oppose or even discreetly undermine organizational change initiatives that originate elsewhere. This "not-invented-here" syndrome is most apparent among employees who are usually responsible for the knowledge or initiative, rather than the external sources.[22] For example, information technology staff are more likely to resist implementing new technology championed by marketing or finance employees. If the IT staff support the change, they are implicitly acknowledging another group's superior knowledge or initiative within IT's own area of expertise. To protect their self-worth, some employees deliberately inflate problems with changes that they did not initiate, just to "prove" that those ideas were not superior to their own. As one consultant warned: "Unless they're scared enough to listen, they'll never forgive you for being right and for knowing something they don't."[23]

Breaking Routines

People typically resist initiatives that force them out of their comfort zones and require them to invest time and energy in learning new role patterns. Indeed, most employees in one survey admitted they don't follow through with organizational changes because they "like to keep things the way they are" or the changes seem to be too complicated or time wasting.[24]

Incongruent Team Dynamics

Teams develop and enforce conformity to a set of norms that guide behavior. However, conformity to existing team norms may discourage employees from accepting organizational change. For instance, organizational initiatives to improve customer service may be thwarted by team norms that discourage the extra effort expected to serve customers at this higher standard.

Incongruent Organizational Systems

Rewards, information systems, patterns of authority, career paths, selection criteria, and other systems and structures are both friends and foes of organizational change. When properly aligned, they reinforce desired behaviors. When misaligned, they pull people back into their old attitudes and behavior. Even enthusiastic employees lose momentum after failing to overcome the structural confines of the past.

> "Even when we want to change, and do change, we tend to relax and the rubber band snaps us back into our comfort zones."[25]
>
> —**Ray Davis**, CEO of Umpqua Bank

LO14-3 Outline six strategies for minimizing resistance to change, and debate ways to effectively create an urgency to change.

UNFREEZING, CHANGING, AND REFREEZING

According to Lewin's force field analysis model, effective change occurs by unfreezing the current situation, moving to a desired condition, and then refreezing the system so it remains in this desired state. Unfreezing occurs when the driving forces are stronger than the restraining forces. This happens by making the driving forces stronger, weakening or removing the restraining forces, or doing both.

The first option is to increase the driving forces, motivating employees to change through fear or threats (real or contrived). This strategy rarely works, however, because the action of increasing the driving forces alone is usually met with an equal and opposing increase in the restraining forces. A useful metaphor is pushing against the coils of a mattress. The harder corporate leaders push for change, the stronger the restraining forces push back. This antagonism threatens the change effort by producing tension and conflict within the organization.

The second option is to weaken or remove the restraining forces. The problem with this change strategy is that it provides no motivation for change. To some extent, weakening the restraining forces is like clearing a pathway for change. An unobstructed road makes it easier to travel to the destination but does not motivate anyone to go there. The preferred option, therefore, is to both increase the driving forces and reduce or remove the restraining forces. Increasing the driving forces creates an urgency for change, while reducing the restraining forces lessens motivation to oppose the change and removes obstacles such as lack of ability and situational constraints.

Creating an Urgency for Change

A few months after he became CEO of Nokia Corporation, Stephen Elop sent employees a scorching email, warning them about the urgency for change. "I have learned that we are standing on a burning platform," wrote Elop. "And, we have more than one explosion—we have multiple points of scorching heat that are fuelling a blazing fire around us." Elop specifically described strong competition from Apple and Google, Nokia's tumbling brand preference, and its falling credit rating.[26]

Nokia has since sold its mobile phone division to Microsoft, where Elop is currently executive vice president. But this incident illustrates Elop's strong belief that Nokia employees needed a stronger urgency for change.[27] Developing an urgency for change typically occurs by informing or reminding employees about competitors, changing consumer trends, impending government regulations, and other forms of turbulence in the external environment. These are the main driving forces in Lewin's model. They push people out of their comfort zones, energizing them to face the risks

> Leaders often need to create an urgency for change long before problems come knocking at the company's door.

that change creates. In many organizations, however, leaders buffer employees from the external environment to such an extent that these driving forces are hardly felt by anyone below the top executive level. The result is that employees don't understand why they need to change and leaders are surprised when their change initiatives do not have much effect.

Some companies fuel the urgency to change by putting employees in direct contact with customers. Dissatisfied customers represent a compelling driving force for change because the organization's survival typically depends on having customers who are satisfied with the product or service. Customers also provide a human element that further energizes employees to change current behavior patterns.[28]

Creating an Urgency for Change without External Forces Exposing employees to external forces can strengthen the urgency for change, but leaders often need to begin the change process before problems come knocking at the company's door. The challenge is greatest when companies are successful in their markets. Studies have found that when the organization is performing well, decision makers become less vigilant about external threats and are more resistant to change. "The biggest risk is that complacency can also come with that success," warns Richard Goyder, CEO of Wesfarmers, Australia's largest conglomerate. "That complacency may result in risk-aversion, or it may simply show up as a lack of urgency, as people take the foot off the accelerator and just assume that success will come as it always has."[29]

Creating an urgency for change when the organization is ahead of the competition requires a lot of persuasive influence that helps employees visualize future competitive threats and environmental shifts. Experts warn, however, that employees may see this strategy as manipulative—a view that produces cynicism about change and undermines trust in the change agent.[30] Fortunately, the urgency for change doesn't need to originate from problems or threats to the company; this motivation can also develop through a change champion's vision of a more appealing future. By creating a future vision of a better organization, leaders effectively make the current situation less appealing. When the vision connects to employee values and needs, it can be a motivating force for change even when external problems are insignificant.

Reducing the Restraining Forces

Earlier, we used the mattress metaphor to explain that increasing the driving forces alone will not bring about change because employees often push back harder to offset the opposing forces. Instead, change agents need to address each of the sources of resistance. Six of the main strategies are outlined in Exhibit 14.2. If feasible, communication, learning, employee involvement, and stress management should be attempted first.[31] However, negotiation and coercion are necessary for people who will clearly lose something from the change and in cases where the speed of change is critical.

Communication Communication is the highest priority and first strategy required for any organizational change. According to one recent survey, communication (together with involvement) is considered the top strategy for engaging employees in the change process.[32] Communication improves the change process in at least two ways.[33] One way is that communication is necessary to generate the urgency for change that we described previously. Leaders motivate employees to support the change by candidly telling them about the external threats and opportunities that make change so important. Whether through town hall meetings with senior management or by directly meeting with disgruntled customers, employees become energized to change when they understand and visualize those external forces.

The second way that communication minimizes resistance to change is by illuminating the future and thereby reducing fear of the unknown. The more leaders communicate their vision, particularly details about that future and milestones already achieved toward that future, the more easily employees can understand their own roles in that future. "No. 1 is to

Exhibit 14.2 Strategies for Minimizing Resistance to Change

Strategy	Example	When Applied	Problems
Communication	Customer complaint letters are shown to employees.	When employees don't feel an urgency for change, don't know how the change will affect them, or resist change due to a fear of the unknown.	Time-consuming and potentially costly.
Learning	Employees learn how to work in teams as company adopts a team-based structure.	When employees need to break old routines and adopt new role patterns.	Time-consuming, potentially costly, and some employees might not be able to learn the new skills.
Employee involvement	Company forms a task force to recommend new customer service practices.	When the change effort needs more employee commitment, some employees need to protect their self-worth, and/or employee ideas would improve decisions about the change strategy.	Very time-consuming. Might lead to conflict and poor decisions if employees' interests are incompatible with organizational needs.
Stress management	Employees attend sessions to discuss their worries about the change.	When communication, training, and involvement do not sufficiently ease employee worries.	Time-consuming and potentially expensive. Some methods may not reduce stress for all employees.
Negotiation	Employees agree to replace strict job categories with multiskilled job clusters in return for increased job security.	When employees will clearly lose something of value from the change and would not otherwise support the new conditions. Also necessary when the company must change quickly.	May be expensive, particularly if other employees want to negotiate their support. Also tends to produce compliance but not commitment to the change.
Coercion	Company president tells managers to "get on board" the change or leave.	When other strategies are ineffective and the company needs to change quickly.	Can lead to subtler forms of resistance, as well as long-term antagonism with the change agent.

Sources: Adapted from J.P. Kotter and L.A. Schlesinger, "Choosing Strategies for Change," *Harvard Business Review* 57 (1979): 106–14; P.R. Lawrence, "How to Deal with Resistance to Change," *Harvard Business Review* (May/June 1954): 49–57.

always communicate, communicate, communicate," advises Randall Dearth, CEO of the purification technology company Calgon Carbon Corporation. "If you're bringing in change, you need to be able to make a very compelling case of what change looks like and why change is necessary."[34]

Learning Learning is an important process in most organizational change initiatives because employees need new knowledge and skills to fit the organization's evolving requirements. Learning not only helps employees perform better following the change; it also increases their readiness for change because they develop a stronger self-efficacy or confidence in their ability to function effectively following the change (called *change self-efficacy*). And when employees develop stronger change self-efficacy, they develop a stronger acceptance of and commitment to the change related to those acquired skills and knowledge.[36]

Employee Involvement Unless the change must occur quickly or employee interests are highly incompatible with the organization's needs, employee involvement is almost an essential part of the change process. In the chapter on decision making (Chapter 6), we described several potential benefits of employee involvement, all of which are relevant to organizational change. Employees who participate in decisions about a change tend to feel more personal responsibility for its

successful implementation, rather than being disinterested agents of someone else's decisions.[37] This sense of ownership also minimizes the not-invented-here syndrome and fear of the unknown. Furthermore, the complexity of today's work environment demands that more people provide ideas regarding the best direction of the change effort.

Stress Management Organizational change is a stressful experience for many people because it threatens self-esteem and creates uncertainty about the future.[38] Communication, learning, and employee involvement can reduce some of the stressors.[39] However, research indicates that companies also need to introduce stress management practices to help employees cope with changes.[40] In particular, stress management minimizes resistance by removing some of the negative valence and fear of the unknown about the change process. Stress also saps energy, so minimizing stress potentially increases employee motivation to support the change process.

Negotiation As long as people resist change, organizational change strategies will require a variety of influence tactics. Negotiation is a form of influence that involves the promise of benefits or resources in exchange for the target person's compliance with the influencer's request. This strategy potentially gains support from those who would otherwise lose out from the change. However, this support is mostly compliance with,

At What Stage in the Change Process Do Companies Begin Communicating with Employees about the Change?[35]

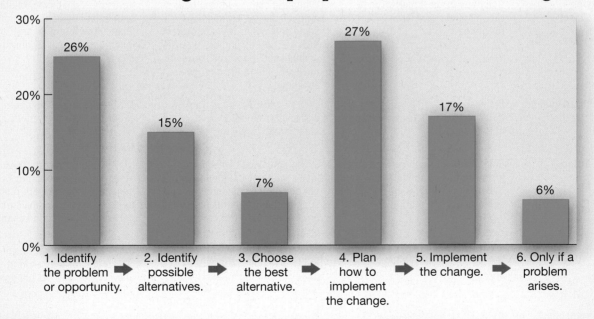

Note: Figures indicate percentage of 651 organizations surveyed globally (half in Asia-Pacific region) that "activate the internal communication function" (i.e., begin involving staff responsible for communicating with employees) at each stage of the change process. Half (50 percent) do not begin communicating the change with employees until after the change strategy has been selected.

rather than commitment to, the change effort, so negotiation might not be effective in the long term.

Coercion If all else fails, leaders rely on coercion to change organizations. Coercion can include persistently reminding people of their obligations, frequently monitoring behavior to ensure compliance, confronting people who do not change, and using threats of punishment (including dismissal) to force compliance. Replacing or threatening to replace staff who will not support the change is an extreme step, but it is fairly common in major organizational change.

For instance, one year after Robert Nardelli was hired as CEO of Home Depot, most of the retailer's top management team had voluntarily or involuntarily left the company. Several years earlier, StandardAero CEO Bob Hamaberg threatened to fire senior managers who opposed his initiative to introduce lean management. "You must have senior management commitment," Hamaberg said bluntly at the time. "I had some obstacles. I removed the obstacles." Today, StandardAero is a world leader in the aircraft engine repair and overhaul business thanks largely to the lean management changes that Hamaberg introduced.[41]

Firing people is the least desirable way to change organizations. However, dismissals and other forms of coercion are sometimes necessary when speed is essential and other tactics are ineffective. The previous examples illustrate that it may be necessary to remove several members of an executive team who are unwilling or unable to change their existing mental models of the ideal organization. This is also a radical form of organizational "unlearning" (see Chapter 1) because when executives leave, they remove knowledge of the organization's past routines that have become dysfunctional.[42] Even so, coercion is a risky strategy because survivors (employees who do not leave) may have less trust in corporate leaders and engage in more political tactics to protect their own job security.

Refreezing the Desired Conditions

Unfreezing and changing behavior won't produce lasting change. People are creatures of habit, so they easily slip back into past patterns. Therefore, leaders need to refreeze the new behaviors by realigning organizational systems and team dynamics with the desired changes.[43] The desired patterns of behavior can be "nailed down" by changing the physical structure and situational conditions. Organizational rewards are also

powerful systems that refreeze behaviors.[44] If the change process is supposed to encourage efficiency, then rewards should be realigned to motivate and reinforce efficient behavior. Information systems play a complementary role in the change process, particularly as conduits for feedback.[45] Feedback mechanisms help employees learn how well they are moving toward the desired objectives, and they provide a permanent architecture to support the new behavior patterns in the long term. The adage "What gets measured, gets done" applies here. Employees concentrate on the new priorities when they receive a continuous flow of feedback about how well they are achieving those goals.

LO14-4 Discuss how leadership, coalitions, social networks, and pilot projects assist organizational change.

LEADERSHIP, COALITIONS, AND PILOT PROJECTS

Kurt Lewin's force field analysis model is a useful template to explain the dynamics of organizational change. But it overlooks four other ingredients in effective change processes: leadership, coalitions, social networks, and pilot projects.

Transformational Leadership and Change

Change is difficult unless one or more people take leadership roles in the change process. Successful change initiatives rely on the elements of transformational leadership that were discussed in Chapter 11. Specifically, effective change agents develop and champion a vision of the desired future state, communicate that vision in ways that are meaningful to others, make decisions and act in ways that are consistent with that vision, and encourage employees to experiment with ways to align work activities more closely with the vision.[46]

A key element of leading change is a strategic vision.[48] A leader's vision provides a sense of direction and establishes the critical success factors against which the real changes are evaluated. Furthermore, a vision provides an emotional foundation for the change because it links the individual's values and self-concept to the desired change.[49] A strategic vision also minimizes employee fear of the unknown and provides a better understanding of what behaviors employees must learn for the desired future.

Coalitions, Social Networks, and Change

One of the great truths of organizational change is that change agents cannot lead the initiative alone. They need the assistance

Driving Change through a "One Ford" Vision

Alan Mulally, who recently retired as Ford Motor Company CEO, has been hailed as a turnaround champion by transforming the company into a successful and competitive automaker. Mulally's vision for change ("One Ford—One Team, One Plan, One Goal") focused everyone on one brand (Ford) with a few models that have global platforms. He held numerous town hall meetings, drumming the same message that everyone needs to cooperate as One Ford across divisions and focus more on customers than personal fiefdoms. To demonstrate his One Ford vision, Mulally created a pilot project—a special global task force that designed and engineered a new Focus with the same chassis, features, and name around the world. Today, the Ford Focus is Mulally's "proof point"—a beacon of his One Ford vision.[47]

of several people with a similar degree of commitment to the change.[50] Indeed, one recent study concluded that this group—often called a *guiding coalition*—may be the most important factor in the success of public sector organizational change programs.[51]

Membership in the guiding coalition extends beyond the executive team. Ideally, it includes a diagonal swath of employees representing different functions and most levels of the organization. The guiding coalition is sometimes formed from a special task force that initially investigates the opportunities for change. Members of the guiding coalition should also be influence leaders; that is, they should be highly respected by peers in their area of the organization. At the same time, one recent report on organizational change warned that it takes more than a few dedicated disciples to generate widespread change.[52] Guiding coalitions may be very important, but they alone do not generate commitment to change in the rest of the workforce.

> Social networks have an important role in communication and influence, both of which are key ingredients of organizational change.

Social Networks and Viral Change While a guiding coalition is a formally structured group, change also occurs more informally through social networks. To some extent, coalition members support the change process by feeding into these networks. But social networks play a role in organizational change whether or not the change process includes a formal coalition. Social networks are social structures of individuals or social units (e.g., departments, organizations) that are connected to each other through one or more forms of interdependence (see Chapter 9). They have an important role in communication and influence, both of which are key ingredients for organizational change.

The problem is that social networks are not easily controlled. Even so, some change agents have tapped into social networks to build a groundswell of support for a change initiative. This *viral change* process adopts principles found in word-of-mouth and viral marketing.[53] Viral and word-of-mouth marketing occur when information seeded to a few people is transmitted to others through their friendship connections. Within organizations, social networks represent the channels through which news and opinions about change initiatives are transmitted. Participants in that network have relatively high trust, so their information and views are more persuasive than when communication occurs through more formal channels of communication. Social networks also provide opportunities for behavior observation—employees observe each other's behavior and often adopt that behavior themselves. So, when a change initiative causes change in the behavior of some employees, the social network potentially spreads this behavior change to others in that network.[54]

Pilot Projects and Diffusion of Change

Many companies introduce change through a pilot project. This cautious approach tests the effectiveness of the change as well as the strategies to gain employee support for the change without the enormous costs and risks of companywide initiatives. Unlike centralized, systemwide changes, pilot projects are more flexible and less risky.[55] They also make it easier to select organizational groups that are most ready for change, thus increasing the pilot project's success.

Procter & Gamble (P&G) relied on a pilot project as a first step in shifting the consumer products company to "design thinking." Design thinking takes the view that new ideas emerge through discovery of the unknown rather than through structured surveys and other data collection methods that are framed from existing knowledge. This "abductive" approach is neither easy nor comfortable for most businesspeople, which is the main reason why P&G began the change process through a pilot project at the company's global hair-care business in London, England. Participants in the program learned the meaning of design thinking and were coached in applying it to real-world issues, such as how women actually use styling products. These participants learned about design thinking and developed skills to teach coworkers about this unique business decision-making approach. Eventually, more than 150 people across many areas of P&G's global business became trained facilitators, developing the practice in everyday meetings. "These things are literally going on every day, and we don't even know where or when," says the P&G executive who initiated the change program.[56]

How do we diffuse the pilot project's change to other parts of the organization? The MARS model (see Chapter 2)

OB THEORY TO PRACTICE

Strategies for Diffusing Change from a Pilot Project

Motivation

- Widely communicate and celebrate the pilot project's success.
- Reward and recognize pilot project employees as well as those who work at transferring that change to other parts of the organization.
- Ensure that managers support and reinforce the desired behaviors related to the pilot project's success.
- Identify and address potential sources of resistance to change.

Ability

- Give employees the opportunity to interact with and learn from those in the pilot project.
- Reassign or temporarily transfer some pilot project employees to other work units, where they can coach and serve as role models.
- Give employees technical training to implement practices identified in the pilot project.

Role Perceptions

- Communicate and teach employees how the pilot project practices are relevant for their own functional areas.
- Ensure that the pilot project is described in a way that is neither too specific nor too general.

Situational Factors

- Give staff sufficient time and resources to learn and implement the pilot project practices in their work units.

provides a useful template for identifying strategies to diffuse pilot projects to other parts of the organization. First, employees are more likely to adopt the practices of a pilot project when they are motivated to do so.[57] This occurs when they see that the pilot project is successful and people in the pilot project receive recognition and rewards for changing their previous work practices. Diffusion also occurs more successfully when managers support and reinforce the desired behaviors. More generally, change agents need to minimize the sources of resistance to change that we discussed earlier in this chapter.

Second, employees must have the ability—the required skills and knowledge—to adopt the practices introduced in the pilot project. According to innovation diffusion studies, people adopt ideas more readily when they have an opportunity to interact with and learn from others who have already applied the new practices.[58] For instance, Procter & Gamble's design thinking pilot project was diffused by having the original participants learn how to train coworkers and serve as role models and knowledge sources across the organization.

Third, pilot projects get diffused when employees have clear role perceptions—that is, when they understand how the practices in a pilot project apply to them even though they are in a completely different functional area. For instance, accounting department employees won't easily recognize how they can adopt quality improvement practices developed by employees in the production department. The challenge here is for change agents to provide guidance that is not too specific (not too narrowly defined around the pilot project environment) because it might not seem relevant to other areas of the organization. At the same time, the pilot project intervention should not be described too broadly or abstractly to other employees because this makes the information and role model too vague. Finally, employees require supportive situational factors, including the resources and time necessary to adopt the practices demonstrated in the pilot project.

LO14-5 Describe and compare action research and appreciative inquiry as formal approaches to organizational change.

TWO APPROACHES TO ORGANIZATIONAL CHANGE

So far, this chapter has examined the dynamics of change that occur every day in organizations. However, organizational change agents and consultants also apply various structured approaches to organizational change. This section introduces two of the leading approaches: action research and appreciative inquiry.

Action Research Approach

Along with introducing the force field model, Kurt Lewin recommended an **action research** approach to the change process. The philosophy of action research is that meaningful change is a combination of action orientation (changing attitudes and behavior) and research orientation (testing theory).[59] On one hand, the change process needs to be action-oriented because the ultimate goal is to change the workplace. An action orientation involves diagnosing current problems and applying interventions that resolve those problems. On the other hand, the change process is a research study because change agents apply a conceptual framework (such as team dynamics or organizational culture) to a real situation. As with any good research, the change process involves collecting data to diagnose problems more effectively and to systematically evaluate how well the theory works in practice.[60]

Within this dual framework of action and research, the action research approach adopts an open systems view. It recognizes that organizations have many interdependent parts, so change agents need to anticipate both the intended and the unintended consequences of their interventions. Action research is also a highly participative process because open systems change requires both the knowledge and the commitment of members within that system. Indeed, employees are essentially co-researchers as well as participants in the intervention. Overall, action research is a data-based, problem-oriented process that diagnoses the need for change, introduces the intervention, and then evaluates and stabilizes the desired

changes. The main phases of action research are illustrated in Exhibit 14.3 and described here:[61]

1. *Form client–consultant relationship.* Action research usually assumes that the change agent originates outside the system (such as a consultant), so the process begins by forming the client–consultant relationship. Consultants need to determine the client's readiness for change, including whether people are motivated to participate in the process, are open to meaningful change, and possess the abilities to complete the process.

2. *Diagnose the need for change.* Action research is a problem-oriented activity that carefully diagnoses the problem through systematic analysis of the situation. Organizational diagnosis identifies the appropriate direction for the change effort by gathering and analyzing data about an ongoing system, such as through interviews and surveys of employees and other stakeholders. Organizational diagnosis also includes employee involvement in agreeing on the appropriate change method, the schedule for the actions involved, and the expected standards of successful change.

3. *Introduce intervention.* This stage in the action research model applies one or more actions to correct the problem. It may include any of the prescriptions mentioned in this book, such as building more effective teams, managing conflict, building a better organizational structure, or changing the corporate culture. An important issue is how quickly the changes should occur.[62] Some experts recommend *incremental change*, in which the organization fine-tunes the system and takes small steps toward a desired state. Others claim that *rapid change* is often required, in which the system is overhauled decisively and quickly.

4. *Evaluate and stabilize change.* Action research recommends evaluating the effectiveness of the intervention against the standards established in the diagnostic stage. Unfortunately, even when these standards are clearly stated, the effectiveness of an intervention might not be apparent for several years or might be difficult to separate from other factors. If the activity has the desired effect, the change agent and participants need to stabilize the new conditions. This refers to the refreezing process that was described earlier. Rewards, information systems, team norms, and other conditions are redesigned so they support the new values and behaviors.

The action research approach has dominated organizational change thinking since it was introduced in the 1940s. However, some experts are concerned that the problem-oriented nature of action research—in which something is wrong that must be fixed—focuses on the negative dynamics of the group or system rather than its positive opportunities and potential. This concern with action research has led to the development of a more positive approach to organizational change, called *appreciative inquiry.*[63]

Appreciative Inquiry Approach

Appreciative inquiry tries to break out of the problem-solving mentality of traditional change management practices by reframing relationships around the positive and the possible. It searches for organizational (or team) strengths and capabilities and then applies that knowledge for further success and well-being. Appreciative inquiry is therefore deeply grounded in the emerging philosophy of *positive organizational behavior,* which suggests that focusing on the positive rather than the negative aspects of life will improve organizational success and individual well-being. In other words, this approach emphasizes building on strengths rather than trying to directly correct problems.[64]

Appreciative inquiry typically examines successful events, organizations, and work units. This focus becomes a form of behavioral modeling, but it also increases open dialogue by redirecting the group's attention away from its own problems. Appreciative inquiry is especially useful when participants are aware of their problems or already suffer from negativity in their relationships. The positive orientation of appreciative inquiry enables groups to overcome these negative tensions and build a more hopeful perspective of their future by focusing on what is possible.[65]

Appreciative inquiry's positive focus is illustrated by the intervention conducted a few years ago at Heidelberg USA. The American arm of the world's largest printing press manufacturer (Heidelberger Druckmaschinen AG) experienced morale-busting product setbacks as well as downsizing due to the economic recession. To rebuild employee morale and

appreciative inquiry an organizational change strategy that directs the group's attention away from its own problems and focuses participants on the group's potential and positive elements

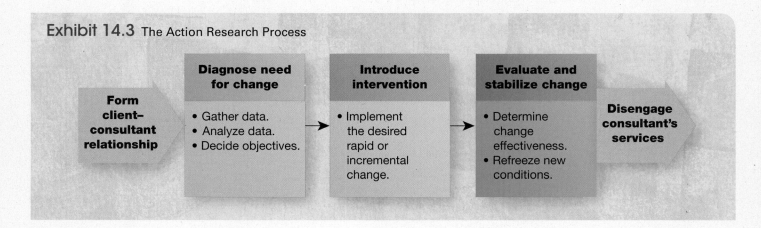

Exhibit 14.3 The Action Research Process

Form client–consultant relationship → **Diagnose need for change**
- Gather data.
- Analyze data.
- Decide objectives.

→ **Introduce intervention**
- Implement the desired rapid or incremental change.

→ **Evaluate and stabilize change**
- Determine change effectiveness.
- Refreeze new conditions.

→ **Disengage consultant's services**

situation depends on the questions we ask and the language we use. Therefore, appreciative inquiry uses words and language carefully because it is sensitive to the thoughts and feelings behind that communication. This relates to a third principle, called the *simultaneity principle*, which states that inquiry and change are simultaneous, not sequential. The moment we ask questions of others, we are changing those people. Furthermore, the questions we ask determine the information we receive, which in turn affects which change intervention we choose. The key learning point from this principle is to be mindful of effects that the inquiry has on the direction of the change process.

A fourth principle, called the *poetic principle*, states that organizations are open books, so we have choices in how they may be perceived, framed, and described. The poetic principle is reflected in the notion that a glass of water can be viewed as half full or half empty. Therefore, appreciative inquiry actively frames reality in a way that provides constructive value for future development. *The anticipatory principle*, the fifth principle of appreciative inquiry, emphasizes the importance of a positive collective vision of the future state. People are motivated and guided by the vision they see and believe in for the future. Images that are mundane or disempowering will affect current effort and behavior differently than will images that are inspiring and engaging. We noted the importance of visions earlier in this chapter (change agents) and in our discussion of transformational leadership (Chapter 11).

The Four-D Model of Appreciative Inquiry These five principles lay the foundation for appreciative inquiry's "Four-D" process. The model's name refers to its four stages, shown in Exhibit 14.5. Appreciative inquiry begins with *discovery*—identifying the positive elements of the observed events or organization.[68] This might involve documenting positive customer experiences elsewhere in the organization. Or it might include interviewing members of another organization to discover its fundamental strengths. As participants discuss their findings, they shift into the *dreaming* stage by envisioning what

engagement, Heidelberg held a two-day appreciative inquiry summit involving one-third of its staff. Organized into diverse groups from across the organization, participants envisioned what Heidelberg would ideally look like in the future. From these sessions emerged a new vision and greater autonomy for employees to serve customers. "Appreciative inquiry can energize an organization even in tough times because it begins the conversation with possibilities instead of problems," says a senior executive at Heidelberg USA.[66]

Appreciative Inquiry Principles Appreciative inquiry embraces five key principles (see Exhibit 14.4).[67] One of these is the positive principle, which we have just described. A second principle, called the *constructionist principle*, takes the position that conversations don't describe reality; they shape that reality. The understanding we form of an event, group, or

Exhibit 14.4 Five Principles of Appreciative Inquiry

Appreciative Inquiry Principle	Description
Positive principle	Focusing on positive events and potential produces more positive, effective, and enduring change.
Constructionist principle	How we perceive and understand the change process depends on the questions we ask and language we use throughout that process.
Simultaneity principle	Inquiry and change are simultaneous, not sequential.
Poetic principle	Organizations are open books, so we have choices in how they may be perceived, framed, and described.
Anticipatory principle	People are motivated and guided by the vision they see and believe in for the future.

Sources: Based on D.L. Cooperrider and D.K. Whitney, *Appreciative Inquiry: A Positive Revolution in Change* (San Francisco: Berrett-Koehler, 2005), Chap. 7; D.K. Whitney and A. Trosten-Bloom. *The Power of Appreciative Inquiry: A Practical Guide to Positive Change*, 2nd ed. (San Francisco: Berrett-Koehler, 2010), Chap. 3.

Exhibit 14.5 The Four-D Model of Appreciative Inquiry

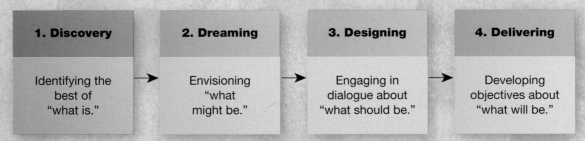

1. Discovery	2. Dreaming	3. Designing	4. Delivering
Identifying the best of "what is."	Envisioning "what might be."	Engaging in dialogue about "what should be."	Developing objectives about "what will be."

Sources: Based on F.J. Barrett and D.L. Cooperrider, "Generative Metaphor Intervention: A New Approach for Working with Systems Divided by Conflict and Caught in Defensive Perception," *Journal of Applied Behavioral Science* 26 (1990): 229; D. Whitney and C. Schau, "Appreciative Inquiry: An Innovative Process for Organization Change," *Employment Relations Today* 25 (Spring 1998): 11–21; D.L. Cooperrider and D.K. Whitney, *Appreciative Inquiry: A Positive Revolution in Change* (San Francisco: Berrett-Koehler, 2005), Chap. 3.

Appreciative Inquiry Guides Hospital Leadership

Toronto Western Hospital (TWH) held an appreciative inquiry (AI) retreat at which staff discussed the hospital's past successes and crafted a vision for its future. TWH's executive team believed the AI philosophy should guide daily leadership behavior, so they developed and taught a positive leadership program, which has since been completed by almost 100 leaders at the hospital. Senior vice president Kathy Sabo says the leadership program tries to "embed [AI] in our daily work differently than we do now—not just focused on a particular initiative but how do we enact it daily." The positive leadership program has apparently improved balanced scorecard results, patient satisfaction, and staff engagement. "We've seen really positive outcomes in how people apply the [AI] theory, how they behave as leaders, how that has impacted their staff," says Sabo.[69]

might be possible in an ideal organization. By pointing out a hypothetical ideal organization or situation, participants feel safer revealing their hopes and aspirations than they would if they were discussing their own organization or predicament.

As participants make their private thoughts public to the group, the process shifts into the third stage, called *designing*. Designing involves dialogue in which participants listen with selfless receptivity to each other's models and assumptions and eventually form a collective model for thinking within the team. In effect, they create a common image of what should be. As this model takes shape, group members shift the focus back to their own situation. In the final stage of appreciative inquiry, called *delivering* (also known as *destiny*), participants establish specific objectives and direction for their own organization on the basis of their model of what will be.

Appreciative inquiry was introduced more than two decades ago, but it really gained popularity only within the past few years. Several success stories of organizational change from appreciative inquiry have emerged in a variety of organizational settings, including Heidelberg USA, Toronto Western Hospital, British Broadcasting Corporation, and Hunter Douglas.

Appreciative inquiry has much to offer, but it is not always the best approach to changing teams or organizations and, indeed, has not always been successful. This approach depends on participants' ability to let go of the problem-oriented approach, including the "blame game" of determining who may have been responsible for past failures. It also requires leaders who are willing to accept appreciative inquiry's less structured process.[70] Another concern is that research has not yet examined the contingencies of this approach.[71] In other words, we don't yet know under what conditions appreciative inquiry is a useful approach to organizational change and under what conditions it is less effective. Overall, appreciative inquiry can be an effective approach to organizational change, but we are still discovering its potential and limitations.

CROSS-CULTURAL AND ETHICAL ISSUES IN ORGANIZATIONAL CHANGE

Throughout this chapter, we have emphasized that change is inevitable and often continuous because organizations need to remain aligned with the dynamic external environment. Yet, we also need to be aware of cross-cultural and ethical issues with any change process. Many organizational change practices are built around Western cultural assumptions and values, which may differ from and sometimes conflict with assumptions and values in other cultures.[72] One possible cross-cultural limitation is that Western organizational change models, such as Lewin's force field analysis, often assume that change has a beginning and an ending in a logical linear sequence (that is, a straight line from point A to point B). Yet change is viewed more as a cyclical phenomenon in some cultures, such as the earth's revolution around the sun or a pendulum swinging back and forth. Other cultures have more of an interconnected view of change, whereby one change leads to another (often unplanned) change, which leads to another change, and so on until the change objective is ultimately achieved in a more circuitous way.

Another cross-cultural issue with some organizational change interventions is the assumption that effective organizational change is necessarily punctuated by tension and overt conflict. Indeed, some change interventions encourage such conflict. But this direct confrontation view is incompatible with cultures that emphasize harmony and equilibrium. These cross-cultural differences suggest that a more contingency-oriented perspective is required for organizational change to work effectively in this era of globalization.

Some organizational change practices also face ethical issues.[73] One ethical concern is the risk of violating individual privacy rights. The action research model is built on the idea of collecting information from organizational members, yet this requires that employees provide personal information and reveal emotions they may not want to divulge.[74] A second ethical concern is that some change activities potentially increase management's power by inducing compliance and conformity in organizational members. For instance, action research is a systemwide activity that requires employee participation rather than allowing individuals to get involved voluntarily. A third concern is that some organizational change interventions undermine the individual's self-esteem. The unfreezing process requires that participants disconfirm their existing beliefs, sometimes including their own competence at certain tasks or interpersonal relations.

Organizational change is usually more difficult than it initially seems. Yet the dilemma is that most organizations operate in hyperfast environments that demand continuous and rapid adaptation. Organizations survive and gain competitive advantage by mastering the complex dynamics of moving people through the continuous process of change as quickly as the external environment is changing.

ORGANIZATIONAL BEHAVIOR: THE JOURNEY CONTINUES

Nearly 100 years ago, industrialist Andrew Carnegie said: "Take away my people, but leave my factories, and soon grass will grow on the factory floors. Take away my factories, but leave my people, and soon we will have a new and better factory."[75] Carnegie's statement reflects the message woven throughout this textbook: Organizations are not buildings or machinery or financial assets; rather, they are the people in them. Organizations are human entities—full of life, sometimes fragile, and always exciting.

Study Checklist

☑ Did you tear out the perforated student review card at the back of the text to revisit learning objectives and key terms and definitions?

Connect® Management is available for *M Organizational Behavior*. Additional resources include:

☑ Interactive Applications:
- **Case Analysis:** Apply concepts within the context of a real-world situation.
- **Drag and Drop:** Work through an interactive example to test your knowledge of the concepts.
- **Video Case:** See management in action through interactive videos.

☑ **SmartBook™**—SmartBook is the first and only adaptive reading experience available today. Distinguishing what you know from what you don't, and honing in on concepts you are most likely to forget, SmartBook personalizes content for you in a continuously adapting reading experience. Reading is no longer a passive and linear experience, but an engaging and dynamic one where you are more likely to master and retain important concepts and go to class better prepared.

Endnotes

Chapter 1

1. W. Isaacson, *Steve Jobs* (New York: Simon & Schuster, 2013), Chap. 24; B. Stone, *The Everything Store: Jeff Bezos and the Age of Amazon* (New York: Little, Brown, 2013).

2. S.N. Mehta and C. Fairchild, "The World's Most Admired Companies," *Fortune*, March 17, 2014, 123–27.

3. M. Warner, "Organizational Behavior Revisited," *Human Relations* 47 (1994): 1151–66; R. Westwood and S. Clegg, "The Discourse of Organization Studies: Dissensus, Politics, and Paradigms," in *Debating Organization: Point-Counterpoint in Organization Studies*, ed. R. Westwood and S. Clegg (Malden, MA: Wiley-Blackwell, 2003), 1–42.

4. R.N. Stern and S.R. Barley, "Organizations as Social Systems: Organization Theory's Neglected Mandate," *Administrative Science Quarterly* 41 (1996): 146–62; D. Katz and R.L. Kahn, *The Social Psychology of Organizations* (New York: Wiley, 1966), Chap. 2.

5. L.E. Greiner, "A Recent History of Organizational Behavior," in *Organizational Behavior*, ed. S. Kerr (Columbus, OH: Grid, 1979), 3–14; J. Micklethwait and A. Wooldridge, *The Company: A Short History of a Revolutionary Idea* (New York: Random House, 2003).

6. B. Schlender, "The Three Faces of Steve," *Fortune*, November 9, 1998, 96–101.

7. J.A. Conger, "Max Weber's Conceptualization of Charismatic Authority: Its Influence on Organizational Research," *The Leadership Quarterly* 4, no. 3/4 (1993): 277–88; R. Kanigel, *The One Best Way: Frederick Winslow Taylor and the Enigma of Efficiency* (New York: Viking, 1997); T. Takala, "Plato on Leadership," *Journal of Business Ethics* 17 (1998): 785–98; J.A. Fernandez, "The Gentleman's Code of Confucius: Leadership by Values," *Organizational Dynamics* 33, no. 1 (2004): 21–31.

8. W.L.M. King, *Industry and Humanity: A Study in the Principles Underlying Industrial Reconstruction* (Toronto: Thomas Allen, 1918); H.C. Metcalf and L. Urwick, *Dynamic Administration: The Collected Papers of Mary Parker Follett* (New York: Harper & Brothers, 1940); J. Smith, "The Enduring Legacy of Elton Mayo," *Human Relations* 51, no. 3 (1998): 221–49; E. O'Connor, "Minding the Workers: The Meaning of 'Human' and 'Human Relations' in Elton Mayo," *Organization* 6, no. 2 (1999): 223–46; K. Hallahan, "W.L. Mackenzie King: Rockefeller's 'Other' Public Relations Counselor in Colorado," *Public Relations Review* 29, no. 4 (2003): 401–14.

9. S.L. Rynes et al., "Behavioral Coursework in Business Education: Growing Evidence of a Legitimacy Crisis," *Academy of Management Learning & Education* 2, no. 3 (2003): 269–83; R.P. Singh and A.G. Schick, "Organizational Behavior: Where Does It Fit in Today's Management Curriculum?," *Journal of Education for Business* 82, no. 6 (2007): 349.

10. P.R. Lawrence and N. Nohria, *Driven: How Human Nature Shapes Our Choices* (San Francisco: Jossey-Bass, 2002), Chap. 6.

11. OB scholars have been debating the field's relevance to practitioners. See, for example: P.R. Lawrence, "Historical Development of Organizational Behavior," in *Handbook of Organizational Behavior*, ed. L.W. Lorsch (Englewood Cliffs, NJ: Prentice Hall, 1987), 1–9; S.A. Mohrman, C.B. Gibson, and A.M. Mohrman Jr., "Doing Research That Is Useful to Practice: A Model and Empirical Exploration," *Academy of Management Journal* 44 (2001): 357–75; J.P. Walsh et al., "On the Relationship between Research and Practice: Debate and Reflections," *Journal of Management Inquiry* 16, no. 2 (2007): 128–54; F. Vermeulen, "'I Shall Not Remain Insignificant': Adding a Second Loop to Matter More," *Academy of Management Journal* 50, no. 4 (2007): 754–61; R. Gulati, "Tent Poles, Tribalism, and Boundary Spanning: The Rigor-Relevance Debate in Management Research," *Academy of Management Journal* 50, no. 4 (2007): 775–82; D. Palmer, B. Dick, and N. Freiburger, "Rigor and Relevance in Organization Studies," *Journal of Management Inquiry* 18, no. 4 (2009): 265–72; A. Nicolai and D. Seidl, "That's Relevant! Different Forms of Practical Relevance in Management Science," *Organization Studies* 31, no. 9/10 (2010): 1257–85.

12. M.S. Myers, *Every Employee a Manager* (New York: McGraw-Hill, 1970).

13. M.A. West et al., "Reducing Patient Mortality in Hospitals: The Role of Human Resource Management," *Journal of Organizational Behavior* 27, no. 7 (2006): 983–1002; A. Edmans, "The Link between Job Satisfaction and Firm Value, with Implications for Corporate Social Responsibility," *Academy of Management Perspectives* 26, no. 4 (2012): 1–19; A.M. Baluch, T.O. Salge, and E.P. Piening, "Untangling the Relationship between HRM and Hospital Performance: The Mediating Role of Attitudinal and Behavioural HR Outcomes," *The International Journal of Human Resource Management* 24, no. 16 (2013): 3038–61; I.S. Fulmer and R.E. Ployhart, "'Our Most Important Asset': A Multidisciplinary/Multilevel Review of Human Capital Valuation for Research and Practice," *Journal of Management* 40, no. 1 (2014): 161–92; D.C. Hambrick and T.J. Quigley, "Toward More Accurate Contextualization of the CEO Effect on Firm Performance," *Strategic Management Journal* 35, no. 4 (2014): 473–91.

14. J. Roberts et al., "In the Mirror of the Market: The Disciplinary Effects of Company/Fund Manager Meetings," *Accounting, Organizations and Society* 31, no. 3 (2006): 277–94; J.T. Comeault and D. Wheeler, "Human Capital–Based Investment Criteria for Total Shareholder Returns," in *Pensions at Work: Socially Responsible Investment of Union-Based Pension Funds*, ed. J. Quarter, I. Carmichael, and S. Ryan (Toronto: University of Toronto Press, 2008); R. Barker et al., "Can Company-Fund Manager Meetings Convey Informational Benefits? Exploring the Rationalisation of Equity Investment Decision Making by UK Fund Managers," *Accounting, Organizations and Society* 37, no. 4 (2012): 207–22.

15. S. Fischer, "Globalization and Its Challenges," *American Economic Review* (2003): 1–29. For discussion of the diverse meanings of *globalization*, see M.F. Guillén, "Is Globalization Civilizing, Destructive or Feeble? A Critique of Five Key Debates in the Social Science Literature," *Annual Review of Sociology* 27 (2001): 235–60.

16. The ongoing debate regarding the advantages and disadvantages of globalization is discussed in Guillén, "Is Globalization Civilizing,

Destructive or Feeble?"; J. Bhagwati, *In Defense of Globalization* (New York: Oxford University Press, 2004); M. Wolf, *Why Globalization Works* (New Haven, CT: Yale University Press, 2004).

17. K. Ohmae, *The Next Global Stage* (Philadelphia: Wharton School Publishing, 2005).

18. "Japan Real Time: Dear Successful Female Foreign CEO, Hitachi Wants You!," *Dow Jones International News*, April 27, 2012.

19. D.A. Harrison et al., "Time, Teams, and Task Performance: Changing Effects of Surface- and Deep-Level Diversity on Group Functioning," *Academy of Management Journal* 45, no. 5 (2002): 1029–46; W.J. Casper, J.H. Wayne, and J.G. Manegold, "Who Will We Recruit? Targeting Deep- and Surface-Level Diversity with Human Resource Policy Advertising," *Human Resource Management* 52, no. 3 (2013): 311–32; J.E. Mathieu et al., "A Review and Integration of Team Composition Models: Moving toward a Dynamic and Temporal Framework," *Journal of Management* 40, no. 1 (2014): 130–60.

20. M.F. Riche, "America's Diversity and Growth: Signposts for the 21st Century," *Population Bulletin* (2000): 3–43; U.S. Census Bureau, *Statistical Abstract of the United States: 2004–2005* (Washington, DC: U.S. Census Bureau, May 2005).

21. R. Zemke, C. Raines, and B. Filipczak, *Generations at Work: Managing the Clash of Veterans, Boomers, Xers, and Nexters in Your Workplace* (New York: Amacom, 2000); N. Howe and W. Strauss, "The Next 20 Years: How Customer and Workforce Attitudes Will Evolve," *Harvard Business Review* (2007): 41–52.

22. U.S. Bureau of Labor Statistics, *Household Data, Annual Averages: Employment Status of the Civilian Noninstitutional Population by Age, Sex, and Race* (Washington, DC: U.S. Bureau of Labor Statistics, 2010).

23. E. Parry and P. Urwin, "Generational Differences in Work Values: A Review of Theory and Evidence," *International Journal of Management Reviews* 13 (2011): 79–96.

24. E. Ng, L. Schweitzer, and S. Lyons, "New Generation, Great Expectations: A Field Study of the Millennial Generation," *Journal of Business and Psychology* 25, no. 2 (2010): 281–92.

25. M. Wong et al., "Generational Differences in Personality and Motivation," *Journal of Managerial Psychology* 23, no. 8 (2008): 878–90; J.M. Twenge and S.M. Campbell, "Generational Differences in Psychological Traits and Their Impact on the Workplace," *Journal of Managerial Psychology* 23, no. 8 (2008): 862–77; J.M. Twenge, "A Review of the Empirical Evidence on Generational Differences in Work Attitudes," *Journal of Business and Psychology* 25, no. 2 (2010): 201–10; B. Kowske, R. Rasch, and J. Wiley, "Millennials' (Lack of) Attitude Problem: An Empirical Examination of Generational Effects on Work Attitudes," *Journal of Business and Psychology* 25, no. 2 (2010): 265–79; J. Deal, D. Altman, and S. Rogelberg, "Millennials at Work: What We Know and What We Need to Do (If Anything)," *Journal of Business and Psychology* 25, no. 2 (2010): 191–99.

26. T. Kochan et al., "The Effects of Diversity on Business Performance: Report of the Diversity Research Network," *Human Resource Management* 42 (2003): 3–21; R.J. Burke and E. Ng, "The Changing Nature of Work and Organizations: Implications for Human Resource Management," *Human Resource Management Review* 16 (2006): 86–94; M.-E. Roberge and R. van Dick, "Recognizing the Benefits of Diversity: When and How Does Diversity Increase Group Performance?," *Human Resource Management Review* 20, no. 4 (2010): 295–308.

27. D. Porras, D. Psihountas, and M. Griswold, "The Long-Term Performance of Diverse Firms," *International Journal of Diversity* 6, no. 1 (2006): 25–34; R.A. Weigand, "Organizational Diversity, Profits and Returns in U.S. Firms," *Problems & Perspectives in Management* 5, no. 3 (2007): 69–83.

28. "*Working Mother Magazine* Ranks Verizon among the Best Companies for Multicultural Women," news release for Verizon (New York: PR Newswire, May 26, 2011).

29. Kochan et al., "The Effects of Diversity on Business Performance: Report of the Diversity Research Network"; G.K. Stahl et al., "A Look at the Bright Side of Multicultural Team Diversity," *Scandinavian Journal of Management* 26, no. 4 (2010): 439–47; L.M. Shore et al., "Inclusion and Diversity in Work Groups: A Review and Model for Future Research," *Journal of Management* 37, no. 4 (2011): 1262–89; S.T. Bell et al., "Getting Specific about Demographic Diversity Variable and Team Performance Relationships: A Meta-Analysis," *Journal of Management* 37, no. 3 (2011): 709–43; S.M.B. Thatcher and P.C. Patel, "Group Faultlines: A Review, Integration, and Guide to Future Research," *Journal of Management* 38, no. 4 (2012): 969–1009.

30. E. Greenblatt, "Work/Life Balance: Wisdom or Whining," *Organizational Dynamics* 31, no. 2 (2002): 177–93; W.G. Bennis and R.J. Thomas, *Geeks and Geezers* (Boston: Harvard Business School Press, 2002), 74–79.

31. Regus, *A Better Balance: Regus Work-Life Balance Index* (Luxembourg: Regus, May 2012).

32. T.L. Johns, "The Third Wave of Virtual Work," *Harvard Business Review* 91, no. 1 (2013): 66–73.

33. WorldatWork, *Telework Trendlines 2009*, WorldatWork (Scottsdale, AZ: February 2009); E. Corkill, "Teleworking: Home Sweet . . . Office," *Japan Times*, September 30, 2012; Ipsos, "Global Study of Online Employees Shows One in Five (17%) Work from Elsewhere," news release for Ipsos (New York: Ipsos, January 23, 2012); "Telework and the Federal Government," *The Wall Street Journal*, April 11, 2013.

34. E.J. Hill et al., "Workplace Flexibility, Work Hours, and Work–Life Conflict: Finding an Extra Day or Two," *Journal of Family Psychology* 24, no. 3 (2010): 349–58; A. Bourhis and R. Mekkaoui, "Beyond Work–Family Balance: Are Family-Friendly Organizations More Attractive?," *Relations Industrielles/Industrial Relations* 65, no. 1 (2010): 98–117.

35. "Increased Productivity Due to Telecommuting Generates an Estimated $277 Million in Annual Savings for Company," news release (San Jose, CA: Cisco Systems, June 25, 2009); D. Meinert, "Make Telecommuting Pay Off," *HRMagazine*, June 2011, 33; M. McQuigge, "A Panacea for Some, Working from Home Still a Tough Sell for Some Employers," *Canadian Press* (Toronto), June 26, 2013.

36. G.W. Marshall, C.E. Michaels, and J.P. Mulki, "Workplace Isolation: Exploring the Construct and Its Measurement," *Psychology and Marketing* 24, no. 3 (2007): 195–223; V.J. Morganson et al., "Comparing Telework Locations and Traditional Work Arrangements," *Journal of Managerial Psychology* 25, no. 6 (2010): 578–95; S.M.B. Thatcher and J. Bagger, "Working in Pajamas: Telecommuting, Unfairness Sources, and Unfairness

Perceptions," *Negotiation and Conflict Management Research* 4, no. 3 (2011): 248–76; J. Mahler, "The Telework Divide: Managerial and Personnel Challenges of Telework," *Review of Public Personnel Administration* 32, no. 4 (2012): 407–18.

37. D.E. Bailey and N.B. Kurland, "A Review of Telework Research: Findings, New Directions, and Lessons for the Study of Modern Work," *Journal of Organizational Behavior* 23 (2002): 383–400; D.W. McCloskey and M. Igbaria, "Does 'Out of Sight' Mean 'Out of Mind'? An Empirical Investigation of the Career Advancement Prospects of Telecommuters," *Information Resources Management Journal* 16 (2003): 19–34.

38. Most of these anchors are mentioned in J.D. Thompson, "On Building an Administrative Science," *Administrative Science Quarterly* 1, no. 1 (1956): 102–11.

39. This anchor has a colorful history dating back to critiques of business schools in the 1950s. Soon after, systematic research became a mantra for many respected scholars. See, for example: Thompson, "On Building an Administrative Science."

40. J. Pfeffer and R.I. Sutton, *Hard Facts, Dangerous Half-Truths, and Total Nonsense* (Boston: Harvard Business School Press, 2006); D.M. Rousseau and S. McCarthy, "Educating Managers from an Evidence-Based Perspective," *Academy of Management Learning & Education* 6, no. 1 (2007): 84–101; R.B. Briner and D.M. Rousseau, "Evidence-Based I–O Psychology: Not There Yet," *Industrial and Organizational Psychology* 4, no. 1 (2011): 3–22.

41. Pfeffer and Sutton, *Hard Facts, Dangerous Half-Truths, and Total Nonsense*.

42. D.M. Rousseau and Y. Fried, "Location, Location, Location: Contextualizing Organizational Research," *Journal of Organizational Behavior* 22, no. 1 (2001): 1–13; C.M. Christensen and M.E. Raynor, "Why Hard-Nosed Executives Should Care about Management Theory," *Harvard Business Review* (September 2003): 66–74. For excellent critique of the "one best way" approach in early management scholarship, see P.F. Drucker, "Management's New Paradigms," *Forbes* (1998): 152–77.

43. H.L. Tosi and J.W. Slocum Jr., "Contingency Theory: Some Suggested Directions," *Journal of Management* 10 (1984): 9–26.

44. D.M. Rousseau, R.J. House, "Meso Organizational Behavior: Avoiding Three Fundamental Biases," in *Trends in Organizational Behavior*, ed. C.L. Cooper and D.M. Rousseau (Chichester, UK: Wiley, 1994), 13–30.

45. Mohrman, Gibson, and Mohrman Jr., "Doing Research That Is Useful to Practice"; Walsh et al., "On the Relationship between Research and Practice." Similarly, in 1961, Harvard business professor Fritz Roethlisberger proposed that the field of OB is concerned with human behavior "from the points of view of both (a) its determination . . . and (b) its improvement." See P.B. Vaill, "F. J. Roethlisberger and the Elusive Phenomena of Organizational Behavior," *Journal of Management Education* 31, no. 3 (2007): 321–38.

46. R.H. Hall, "Effectiveness Theory and Organizational Effectiveness," *Journal of Applied Behavioral Science* 16, no. 4 (1980): 536–45; K. Cameron, "Organizational Effectiveness: Its Demise and Re-Emergence through Positive Organizational Scholarship," in *Great Minds in Management*, ed. K.G. Smith and M.A. Hitt (New York: Oxford University Press, 2005), 304–30.

47. S.C. Selden and J.E. Sowa, "Testing a Multi-Dimensional Model of Organizational Performance: Prospects and Problems," *Journal of Public Administration Research and Theory* 14, no. 3 (2004): 395–416.

48. Chester Barnard gives one of the earliest descriptions of organizations as systems interacting with external environments and that are composed of subsystems. See C. Barnard, *The Functions of the Executive* (Cambridge, MA: Harvard University Press, 1938), esp. Chap. 6. Also see F.E. Kast and J.E. Rosenzweig, "General Systems Theory: Applications for Organization and Management," *Academy of Management Journal* 15, no. 4 (1972): 447–65; P.M. Senge, *The Fifth Discipline: The Art and Practice of the Learning Organization* (New York: Doubleday Currency, 1990); G. Morgan, *Images of Organization*, 2nd ed. (Newbury Park: Sage, 1996); A. de Geus, *The Living Company* (Boston: Harvard Business School Press, 1997).

49. D.P. Ashmos and G.P. Huber, "The Systems Paradigm in Organization Theory: Correcting the Record and Suggesting the Future," *Academy of Management Review* 12, no. 4 (1987): 607–21.

50. Katz and Kahn, *The Social Psychology of Organizations*; J. McCann, "Organizational Effectiveness: Changing Concepts for Changing Environments," *Human Resource Planning* 27, no. 1 (2004): 42–50; A.H. Van de Ven, M. Ganco, and C.R. Hinings, "Returning to the Frontier of Contingency Theory of Organizational and Institutional Designs," *Academy of Management Annals* 7, no. 1 (2013): 391–438.

51. N. Tokatli, "Global Sourcing: Insights from the Global Clothing Industry—the Case of Zara, a Fast Fashion Retailer," *Journal of Economic Geography* 8, no. 1 (2008): 21–38; L. Osborne, "High Street Fashion Chain Zara Is Hit by 'Slave Labour' Outcry," *Daily Mail (London, UK)*, April 4, 2013, 25; S.R. Levine, "How Zara Took Customer Focus to New Heights," *Credit Union Times,* April 9, 2013, 10; C. Nogueir, "How Inditex Rules the Weaves, and Plans to Carry on Doing So," *El Pais* (Madrid, Spain), April 24, 2013, 4; G. Ruddick, "Spain's Leader in Fast Fashion Has Much to Teach British Store Rivals," *Daily Telegraph* (London), March 15, 2013, 2; "The Cult of Zara," *Sunday Independent* (Dublin, Ireland), February 10, 2013, 24.

52. C. Ostroff and N. Schmitt, "Configurations of Organizational Effectiveness and Efficiency," *Academy of Management Journal* 36, no. 6 (1993): 1345–61.

53. P.S. Adler et al., "Performance Improvement Capability: Keys to Accelerating Performance Improvement in Hospitals," *California Management Review* 45, no. 2 (2003): 12–33; J. Jamrog, M. Vickers, and D. Bear, "Building and Sustaining a Culture That Supports Innovation," *Human Resource Planning* 29, no. 3 (2006): 9–19.

54. K.E. Weick, *The Social Psychology of Organizing* (Reading, MA: Addison-Wesley, 1979); S. Brusoni and A. Prencipe, "Managing Knowledge in Loosely Coupled Networks: Exploring the Links between Product and Knowledge Dynamics," *Journal of Management Studies* 38, no. 7 (2001): 1019–35.

55. W.C. Bogner and P. Bansal, "Knowledge Management as the Basis of Sustained High Performance," *Journal of Management Studies* 44, no. 1 (2007): 165–88; L. Argote and E. Miron-Spektor, "Organizational Learning: From Experience to Knowledge," *Organization Science* 22, no. 5 (2011): 1123–37.

56. R. Slater, *Jack Welch & the G.E. Way: Management Insights and Leadership Secrets of the Legendary CEO* (New York: McGraw-Hill, 1999).

57. T.A. Stewart, *Intellectual Capital: The New Wealth of Organizations* (New York: Currency/Doubleday, 1997); H. Saint-Onge and D. Wallace, *Leveraging Communities of Practice for Strategic Advantage* (Boston: Butterworth-Heinemann), 9–10; J.-A. Johannessen, B. Olsen, and J. Olaisen, "Intellectual Capital as a Holistic Management Philosophy: A Theoretical Perspective," *International Journal of Information Management* 25, no. 2 (2005): 151–71; L. Striukova, J. Unerman, and J. Guthrie, "Corporate Reporting of Intellectual Capital: Evidence from UK Companies," *British Accounting Review* 40, no. 4 (2008): 297–313.

58. J. Barney, "Firm Resources and Sustained Competitive Advantage," *Journal of Management* 17, no. 1 (1991): 99–120.

59. J.P. Hausknecht and J.A. Holwerda, "When Does Employee Turnover Matter? Dynamic Member Configurations, Productive Capacity, and Collective Performance," *Organization Science* 24, no. 1 (2013): 210–25.

60. S.-C. Kang and S.A. Snell, "Intellectual Capital Architectures and Ambidextrous Learning: A Framework for Human Resource Management," *Journal of Management Studies* 46, no. 1 (2009): 65–92; L.-C. Hsu and C.-H. Wang, "Clarifying the Effect of Intellectual Capital on Performance: The Mediating Role of Dynamic Capability," *British Journal of Management* 23, no. 2 (2012): 179–205.

61. Some organizational learning researchers use the label "social capital" instead of relationship capital. Social capital is discussed later in this book as the goodwill and resulting resources shared among members in a social network. The two concepts may be identical (as those writers suggest). However, we continue to use "relationship capital" for intellectual capital because social capital typically refers to individual relationships whereas relationship capital also includes value not explicit in social capital, such as the organization's goodwill and brand value.

62. G. Huber, "Organizational Learning: The Contributing Processes and Literature," *Organizational Science* 2 (1991): 88–115; D.A. Garvin, *Learning in Action: A Guide to Putting the Learning Organization to Work* (Boston: Harvard Business School Press, 2000); H. Shipton, "Cohesion or Confusion? Towards a Typology for Organizational Learning Research," *International Journal of Management Reviews* 8, no. 4 (2006): 233–52; D. Jiménez-Jiménez and J.G. Cegarra-Navarro, "The Performance Effect of Organizational Learning and Market Orientation," *Industrial Marketing Management* 36, no. 6 (2007): 694–708. One recent study suggests that these organizational learning processes aren't always beneficial because they may be more costly or burdensome than the value they create. See S.S. Levine and M.J. Prietula, "How Knowledge Transfer Impacts Performance: A Multilevel Model of Benefits and Liabilities," *Organization Science* 23, no. 6 (2012): 1748–66.

63. B. van den Hooff and M. Huysman, "Managing Knowledge Sharing: Emergent and Engineering Approaches," *Information & Management* 46, no. 1 (2009): 1–8.

64. M.N. Wexler, "Organizational Memory and Intellectual Capital," *Journal of Intellectual Capital* 3, no. 4 (2002): 393–414; M. Fiedler and I. Welpe, "How Do Organizations Remember? The Influence of Organizational Structure on Organizational Memory," *Organization Studies* 31, no. 4 (2010): 381–407.

65. M.E. McGill and J.W. Slocum Jr., "Unlearn the Organization," *Organizational Dynamics* 22, no. 2 (1993): 67–79; A.E. Akgün, G.S. Lynn, and J.C. Byrne, "Antecedents and Consequences of Unlearning in New Product Development Teams," *Journal of Product Innovation Management* 23 (2006): 73–88.

66. L. Sels et al., "Unravelling the HRM-Performance Link: Value-Creating and Cost-Increasing Effects of Small Business HRM," *Journal of Management Studies* 43, no. 2 (2006): 319–42; G.S. Benson, S.M. Young, and E.E. Lawler III, "High-Involvement Work Practices and Analysts' Forecasts of Corporate Earnings," *Human Resource Management* 45, no. 4 (2006): 519–37.

67. M.A. Huselid, "The Impact of Human Resource Management Practices on Turnover, Productivity, and Corporate Financial Performance," *Academy of Management Journal* 38, no. 3 (1995): 635–70; B.E. Becker and M.A. Huselid, "Strategic Human Resources Management: Where Do We Go from Here?," *Journal of Management* 32, no. 6 (2006): 898–925; J. Combs et al., "How Much Do High-Performance Work Practices Matter? A Meta-Analysis of Their Effects on Organizational Performance," *Personnel Psychology* 59, no. 3 (2006): 501–28.

68. E.E. Lawler III, S.A. Mohrman, and G.E. Ledford Jr., *Strategies for High Performance Organizations* (San Francisco: Jossey-Bass, 1998); S.H. Wagner, C.P. Parker, and D. Neil, "Employees That Think and Act Like Owners: Effects of Ownership Beliefs and Behaviors on Organizational Effectiveness," *Personnel Psychology* 56, no. 4 (2003): 847–71; Y. Liu et al., "The Value of Human Resource Management for Organizational Performance," *Business Horizons* 50 (2007): 503–11; P. Tharenou, A.M. Saks, and C. Moore, "A Review and Critique of Research on Training and Organizational-Level Outcomes," *Human Resource Management Review* 17, no. 3 (2007): 251–73.

69. M. Subramony, "A Meta-Analytic Investigation of the Relationship between HRM Bundles and Firm Performance," *Human Resource Management* 48, no. 5 (2009): 745–68.

70. L.-Q. Wei and C.-M. Lau, "High Performance Work Systems and Performance: The Role of Adaptive Capability," *Human Relations* 63, no. 10 (2010): 1487–511; J. Camps and R. Luna-Arocas, "A Matter of Learning: How Human Resources Affect Organizational Performance," *British Journal of Management* 23, no. 1 (2012): 1–21; R.R. Kehoe and P.M. Wright, "The Impact of High-Performance Human Resource Practices on Employees' Attitudes and Behaviors," *Journal of Management* 39, no. 2 (2013): 366–91.

71. G. Murray et al., eds., *Work and Employment Relations in the High-Performance Workplace* (London: Continuum, 2002); B. Harley, "Hope or Hype? High Performance Work Systems," in *Participation and Democracy at Work: Essays in Honour of Harvie Ramsay*, ed. B. Harley, J. Hyman, and P. Thompson (Houndmills, UK: Palgrave Macmillan, 2005), 38–54.

72. J. Tullberg, "Stakeholder Theory: Some Revisionist Suggestions," *The Journal of Socio-Economics* 42 (2013): 127–35.

73. C. Eden and F. Ackerman, *Making Strategy: The Journey of Strategic Management* (London: Sage, 1998).

74. A.L. Friedman and S. Miles, *Stakeholders: Theory and Practice* (New York: Oxford University Press, 2006); M.L. Barnett, "Stakeholder Influence Capacity and the Variability of Financial Returns to Corporate Social Responsibility," *Academy of Management Review* 32, no. 3 (2007): 794–816; R.E. Freeman, J.S. Harrison,

and A.C. Wicks, *Managing for Stakeholders: Survival, Reputation, and Success* (New Haven, CT: Yale University Press, 2007).

75. G.R. Salancik and J. Pfeffer, *The External Control of Organizations: A Resource Dependence Perspective* (New York: Harper & Row, 1978); N. Roome and F. Wijen, "Stakeholder Power and Organizational Learning in Corporate Environmental Management," *Organization Studies* 27, no. 2 (2005): 235–63; R.B. Adams, A.N. Licht, and L. Sagiv, "Shareholders and Stakeholders: How Do Directors Decide?," *Strategic Management Journal* 32, no. 12 (2011): 1331–55; A. Santana, "Three Elements of Stakeholder Legitimacy," *Journal of Business Ethics* 105, no. 2 (2012): 257–65.

76. R.E. Freeman, A.C. Wicks, and B. Parmar, "Stakeholder Theory and 'the Corporate Objective Revisited,'" *Organization Science* 15, no. 3 (2004): 364–69; B.R. Agle et al., "Dialogue: Toward Superior Stakeholder Theory," *Business Ethics Quarterly* 18, no. 2 (2008): 153–90; B.L. Parmar et al., "Stakeholder Theory: The State of the Art," *Academy of Management Annals* 4, no. 1 (2010): 403–45.

77. B.M. Meglino and E.C. Ravlin, "Individual Values in Organizations: Concepts, Controversies, and Research," *Journal of Management* 24, no. 3 (1998): 351–89; A. Bardi and S.H. Schwartz, "Values and Behavior: Strength and Structure of Relations," *Personality and Social Psychology Bulletin* 29, no. 10 (2003): 1207–20; S. Hitlin and J.A. Pilavin, "Values: Reviving a Dormant Concept," *Annual Review of Sociology* 30 (2004): 359–93.

78. Some popular books that emphasize the importance of personal and organizational values include J.C. Collins and J.I. Porras, *Built to Last: Successful Habits of Visionary Companies* (London: Century, 1995); C.A. O'Reilly III and J. Pfeffer, *Hidden Value* (Cambridge, MA: Harvard Business School Press, 2000); R. Barrett, *Building a Values-Driven Organization: A Whole System Approach to Cultural Transformation* (Burlington, MA: Butterworth-Heinemann, 2006); R. Tocquigny and A. Butcher, *When Core Values Are Strategic* (Upper Saddle River, NJ: FT Press, 2012).

79. T. Hsieh, *Delivering Happiness: A Path to Profits, Passion, and Purpose* (New York: Hachette Book Group, 2010), 155–59.

80. Aspen Institute, *Where Will They Lead? MBA Student Attitudes about Business & Society* (Washington, DC: Aspen Institute, April 2008).

81. M. van Marrewijk, "Concepts and Definitions of CSR and Corporate Sustainability: Between Agency and Communion," *Journal of Business Ethics* 44 (2003): 95–105; Barnett, "Stakeholder Influence Capacity and the Variability of Financial Returns to Corporate Social Responsibility."

82. L.S. Paine, *Value Shift* (New York: McGraw-Hill, 2003); A. Mackey, T.B. Mackey, and J.B. Barney, "Corporate Social Responsibility and Firm Performance: Investor Preferences and Corporate Strategies," *Academy of Management Review* 32, no. 3 (2007): 817–35.

83. D. Kiron et al., "Sustainability Nears a Tipping Point," *MIT Sloan Management Review* 53, no. 2 (Winter 2012): 69–74; Net Impact, *Talent Report: What Workers Want in 2012*, (San Francisco: Net Impact, 2012).

84. S. Zadek, *The Civil Corporation: The New Economy of Corporate Citizenship* (London: Earthscan, 2001); S. Hart and M. Milstein, "Creating Sustainable Value," *Academy of Management Executive* 17, no. 2 (2003): 56–69.

85. M. Friedman, *Capitalism and Freedom*, 40th Anniversary ed. (Chicago: University of Chicago Press, 2002), Chap. 8; N. Vorster, "An Ethical Critique of Milton Friedman's Doctrine on Economics and Freedom," *Journal for the Study of Religions and Ideologies* 9, no. 26 (2010): 163–88.

86. A.B. Carroll and K.M. Shabana, "The Business Case for Corporate Social Responsibility: A Review of Concepts, Research and Practice," *International Journal of Management Reviews* 12, no. 1 (2010): 85–105; H. Aguinis and A. Glavas, "What We Know and Don't Know about Corporate Social Responsibility: A Review and Research Agenda," *Journal of Management* 38, no. 4 (2012): 932–68.

Chapter 2

1. M. Conlin, "Netflix: Flex to the Max," *BusinessWeek*, September 24, 2007, 72; R. Hastings and P. McCord, *Netflix Culture: Freedom and Responsibility*, (Los Gatos, CA: Netflix, August 2009); P. McCord, "How Netflix Reinvented HR," *Harvard Business Review* 92, no. 1/2 (2014): 70–76.

2. L.L. Thurstone, "Ability, Motivation, and Speed," *Psychometrika* 2, no. 4 (1937): 249–54; N.R.F. Maier, *Psychology in Industry*, 2nd ed. (Boston: Houghton Mifflin, 1955); V.H. Vroom, *Work and Motivation* (New York: Wiley, 1964); J.P. Campbell et al., *Managerial Behavior, Performance, and Effectiveness* (New York: McGraw-Hill, 1970).

3. U.-C. Klehe and N. Anderson, "Working Hard and Working Smart: Motivation and Ability during Typical and Maximum Performance," *Journal of Applied Psychology* 92, no. 4 (2007): 978–92; J.S. Gould-Williams and M. Gatenby, "The Effects of Organizational Context and Teamworking Activities on Performance Outcomes—a Study Conducted in England Local Government," *Public Management Review* 12, no. 6 (2010): 759–87.

4. E.E. Lawler III and L.W. Porter, "Antecedent Attitudes of Effective Managerial Performance," *Organizational Behavior and Human Performance* 2 (1967): 122–42; M.A. Griffin, A. Neal, and S.K. Parker, "A New Model of Work Role Performance: Positive Behavior in Uncertain and Interdependent Contexts," *Academy of Management Journal* 50, no. 2 (2007): 327–47.

5. Only a few sources have included all four factors. These include J.P. Campbell and R.D. Pritchard, "Motivation Theory in Industrial and Organizational Psychology," in *Handbook of Industrial and Organizational Psychology*, ed. M.D. Dunnette (Chicago: Rand McNally, 1976), 62–130; T.R. Mitchell, "Motivation: New Directions for Theory, Research, and Practice," *Academy of Management Review* 7, no. 1 (1982): 80–88; G.A.J. Churchill et al., "The Determinants of Salesperson Performance: A Meta-Analysis," *Journal of Marketing Research (JMR)* 22, no. 2 (1985): 103–18; R.E. Plank and D.A. Reid, "The Mediating Role of Sales Behaviors: An Alternative Perspective of Sales Performance and Effectiveness," *Journal of Personal Selling & Sales Management* 14, no. 3 (1994): 43–56. The "MARS" acronym was coined by senior officers in the Singapore Armed Forces during a senior officer program taught by Steve McShane. Chris Perryer at the University of Western Australia suggests the full model should be called the "MARS BAR" because the outcomes might be labeled "behavior and results"!

6. Technically, the model proposes that situation factors moderate the effects of the three within-person factors. For instance, the effect of employee motivation on behavior and performance depends on (is moderated by) the situation.

7. C.C. Pinder, *Work Motivation in Organizational Behavior* (Upper Saddle River, NJ: Prentice Hall, 1998); G.P. Latham and C.C. Pinder, "Work Motivation Theory and Research at the Dawn of the Twenty-First Century," *Annual Review of Psychology* 56 (2005): 485–516.

8. T.J. Watson Jr., *A Business and Its Beliefs* (New York: McGraw-Hill, 2003), 4.

9. L.M. Spencer and S.M. Spencer, *Competence at Work: Models for Superior Performance* (New York: Wiley, 1993); R. Kurz and D. Bartram, "Competency and Individual Performance: Modelling the World of Work," in *Organizational Effectiveness: The Role of Psychology*, ed. I.T. Robertson, M. Callinan, and D. Bartram (Chichester, UK: Wiley, 2002), 227–58; D. Bartram, "The Great Eight Competencies: A Criterion-Centric Approach to Validation," *Journal of Applied Psychology* 90, no. 6 (2005): 1185–203; H. Heinsman et al., "Competencies through the Eyes of Psychologists: A Closer Look at Assessing Competencies," *International Journal of Selection and Assessment* 15, no. 4 (2007): 412–27.

10. P. Tharenou, A.M. Saks, and C. Moore, "A Review and Critique of Research on Training and Organizational-Level Outcomes," *Human Resource Management Review* 17, no. 3 (2007): 251–73; T. W.H. Ng and D.C. Feldman, "How Broadly Does Education Contribute to Job Performance?," *Personnel Psychology* 62, no. 1 (2009): 89–134.

11. "Canadian Organizations Must Work Harder to Productively Engage Employees," news release for Watson Wyatt Canada (Toronto: January 25, 2005); BlessingWhite, *Employee Engagement Report 2011* (Princeton, NJ: BlessingWhite, January 2011).

12. J.N. Roy, "The Great Talent Migration," *Talent Management*, May 4, 2012. Based on interviews with 1,143 employed U.S. adults in September 2011.

13. W.H. Cooper and M.J. Withey, "The Strong Situation Hypothesis," *Personality and Social Psychology Review* 13, no. 1 (2009): 62–72; D.C. Funder, "Persons, Behaviors and Situations: An Agenda for Personality Psychology in the Postwar Era," *Journal of Research in Personality* 43, no. 2 (2009): 120–26; R.D. Meyer, R.S. Dalal, and R. Hermida, "A Review and Synthesis of Situational Strength in the Organizational Sciences," *Journal of Management* 36, no. 1 (2010): 121–40; R.A. Sherman, C.S. Nave, and D.C. Funder, "Situational Similarity and Personality Predict Behavioral Consistency," *Journal of Personality and Social Psychology* 99, no. 2 (2010): 330–43.

14. K.F. Kane, "Special Issue: Situational Constraints and Work Performance," *Human Resource Management Review* 3 (1993): 83–175; S.B. Bacharach and P. Bamberger, "Beyond Situational Constraints: Job Resources Inadequacy and Individual Performance at Work," *Human Resource Management Review* 5, no. 2 (1995): 79–102; G. Johns, "Commentary: In Praise of Context," *Journal of Organizational Behavior* 22 (2001): 31–42.

15. Meyer, Dalal, and Hermida, "A Review and Synthesis of Situational Strength in the Organizational Sciences."

16. J.P. Campbell, "The Definition and Measurement of Performance in the New Age," in *The Changing Nature of Performance: Implications for Staffing, Motivation, and Development*, ed. D.R. Ilgen and E.D. Pulakos (San Francisco: Jossey-Bass, 1999), 399–429; R.D. Hackett, "Understanding and Predicting Work Performance in the Canadian Military," *Canadian Journal of Behavioural Science* 34, no. 2 (2002): 131–40.

17. L. Tay, R. Su, and J. Rounds, "People-Things and Data-Ideas: Bipolar Dimensions?," *Journal of Counseling Psychology* 58, no. 3 (2011): 424–40.

18. Griffin, Neal, and Parker, "A New Model of Work Role Performance"; A. Charbonnier-Voirin and P. Roussel, "Adaptive Performance: A New Scale to Measure Individual Performance in Organizations," *Canadian Journal of Administrative Sciences* 29, no. 3 (2012): 280–93.

19. D.W. Organ, "Organizational Citizenship Behavior: It's Construct Clean-up Time," *Human Performance* 10 (1997): 85–97; J.A. LePine, A. Erez, and D.E. Johnson, "The Nature and Dimensionality of Organizational Citizenship Behavior: A Critical Review and Meta-Analysis," *Journal of Applied Psychology* 87 (2002): 52–65; M.C. Bolino, J. Harvey, and D.G. Bachrach, "A Self-Regulation Approach to Understanding Citizenship Behavior in Organizations," *Organizational Behavior and Human Decision Processes* 119, no. 1 (2012): 126–39.

20. K. Lee and N.J. Allen, "Organizational Citizenship Behavior and Workplace Deviance: The Role of Affect and Cognitions," *Journal of Applied Psychology* 87, no. 1 (2002): 131–42.

21. E.W. Morrison, "Role Definitions and Organizational Citizenship Behavior: The Importance of the Employee's Perspective," *Academy of Management Journal* 37, no. 6 (1994): 1543–67; E. Vigoda-Gadot, "Compulsory Citizenship Behavior: Theorizing Some Dark Sides of the Good Soldier Syndrome in Organizations," *Journal for the Theory of Social Behaviour* 36, no. 1 (2006): 77–93; M.C. Bolino et al., "Exploring the Dark Side of Organizational Citizenship Behavior," *Journal of Organizational Behavior* 34, no. 4 (2013): 542–59.

22. M. Ozer, "A Moderated Mediation Model of the Relationship between Organizational Citizenship Behaviors and Job Performance," *Journal of Applied Psychology* 96, no. 6 (2011): 1328–36; T.M. Nielsen et al., "Utility of OCB: Organizational Citizenship Behavior and Group Performance in a Resource Allocation Framework," *Journal of Management* 38, no. 2 (2012): 668–94.

23. A.C. Klotz and M.C. Bolino, "Citizenship and Counterproductive Work Behavior: A Moral Licensing View," *Academy of Management Review* 38, no. 2 (2013): 292–306; Bolino et al., "Exploring the Dark Side of Organizational Citizenship Behavior."

24. M. Rotundo and P. Sackett, "The Relative Importance of Task, Citizenship, and Counterproductive Performance to Global Ratings of Job Performance: A Policy-Capturing Approach," *Journal of Applied Psychology* 87 (2002): 66–80; P.D. Dunlop and K. Lee, "Workplace Deviance, Organizational Citizenship Behaviour, and Business Unit Performance: The Bad Apples Do Spoil the Whole Barrel," *Journal of Organizational Behavior* 25 (2004): 67–80; R.S. Dalal, "A Meta-Analysis of the Relationship between Organizational Citizenship Behavior and Counterproductive Work Behavior," *Journal of Applied Psychology* 90, no. 6 (2005): 1241–55; N.A. Bowling and M.L. Gruys, "Overlooked Issues in the Conceptualization and Measurement of Counterproductive Work Behavior," *Human Resource Management Review* 20, no. 1 (2010): 54–61.

25. The relationship between employee turnover and firm performance is actually very low, but this is due to moderators and is stronger for some forms of firm performance. See J.I. Hancock et al., "Meta-Analytic Review of Employee Turnover as a Predictor of Firm Performance," *Journal of Management* 39, no. 3 (2013): 573–603.

26. ManpowerGroup, *Talent Shortage Survey: Research Results* (Milwaukee, WI: ManpowerGroup, May 25, 2013); Accenture, *Accenture 2013 Skills and Employment Trends Survey: Perspectives on Training* (New York: Accenture, October 14, 2013).

27. P. Brotherton, "Social Media and Referrals Are Best Sources for Talent," *T&D*, January 2012, 24; A.D. Wright, "Your Social Media Is Showing," *HRMagazine*, March 2012, 16; "Social Recruiting Survey 2011" (Burlingame, CA: Jobvite, 2012), www.jobvite.com (accessed June 15, 2012).

28. A. Väänänen et al., "The Role of Work Group in Individual Sickness Absence Behavior," *Journal of Health and Social Behavior* 49, no. 4 (2008): 452–67; W. Beemsterboer et al., "A Literature Review on Sick Leave Determinants (1984–2004)," *International Journal of Occupational Medicine and Environmental Health* 22, no. 2 (2009): 169–79; C.M. Berry, A.M. Lelchook, and M.A. Clark, "A Meta-Analysis of the Interrelationships between Employee Lateness, Absenteeism, and Turnover: Implications for Models of Withdrawal Behavior," *Journal of Organizational Behavior* 33, no. 5 (2012): 678–99; S. Störmer and R. Fahr, "Individual Determinants of Work Attendance: Evidence on the Role of Personality," *Applied Economics* 45, no. 19 (2012): 2863–75; M. Sliter, K. Sliter, and S. Jex, "The Employee as a Punching Bag: The Effect of Multiple Sources of Incivility on Employee Withdrawal Behavior and Sales Performance," *Journal of Organizational Behavior* 33, no. 1 (2012): 121–39; M. Biron and P. Bamberger, "Aversive Workplace Conditions and Absenteeism: Taking Referent Group Norms and Supervisor Support into Account," *Journal of Applied Psychology* 97, no. 4 (2012): 901–12.

29. G. Johns, "Presenteeism in the Workplace: A Review and Research Agenda," *Journal of Organizational Behavior* 31, no. 4 (2010): 519–42; E. Gosselin, L. Lemyre, and W. Corneil, "Presenteeism and Absenteeism: Differentiated Understanding of Related Phenomena," *Journal of Occupational Health Psychology* 18, no. 1 (2013): 75–86.

30. G. Johns, "Attendance Dynamics at Work: The Antecedents and Correlates of Presenteeism, Absenteeism, and Productivity Loss," *Journal of Occupational Health Psychology* 16, no. 4 (2011): 483–500; D. Baker-McClearn et al., "Absence Management and Presenteeism: The Pressures on Employees to Attend Work and the Impact of Attendance on Performance," *Human Resource Management Journal* 20, no. 3 (2010): 311–28.

31. Personality researchers agree on one point about the definition of personality: It is difficult to pin down. A definition necessarily captures one perspective of the topic more than others, and the concept of personality is itself very broad. The definition presented here is based on C.S. Carver and M.F. Scheier, *Perspectives on Personality*, 6th ed. (Boston: Allyn & Bacon, 2007); D.C. Funder, *The Personality Puzzle*, 4th ed. (New York: Norton, 2007).

32. D.P. McAdams and J.L. Pals, "A New Big Five: Fundamental Principles for an Integrative Science of Personality," *American Psychologist* 61, no. 3 (2006): 204–17.

33. B.W. Roberts and A. Caspi, "Personality Development and the Person-Situation Debate: It's Déjà Vu All over Again," *Psychological Inquiry* 12, no. 2 (2001): 104–09.

34. O. Wilde, *The Picture of Dorian Gray* (New York: Barnes & Noble, 2003), 340.

35. B. Reynolds and K. Karraker, "A Big Five Model of Disposition and Situation Interaction: Why a "Helpful" Person May Not Always Behave Helpfully," *New Ideas in Psychology* 21, no. 1 (2003): 1–13; W. Mischel, "Toward an Integrative Science of the Person," *Annual Review of Psychology* 55 (2004): 1–22.

36. K.L. Jang, W.J. Livesley, and P.A. Vernon, "Heritability of the Big Five Personality Dimensions and Their Facets: A Twin Study," *Journal of Personality* 64, no. 3 (1996): 577–91; N.L. Segal, *Entwined Lives: Twins and What They Tell Us about Human Behavior* (New York: Plume, 2000); G. Lensvelt-Mulders and J. Hettema, "Analysis of Genetic Influences on the Consistency and Variability of the Big Five across Different Stressful Situations," *European Journal of Personality* 15, no. 5 (2001): 355–71; T. Bouchard and J. Loehlin, "Genes, Evolution, and Personality," *Behavior Genetics* 31, no. 3 (2001): 243–73; P. Borkenau et al., "Genetic and Environmental Influences on Person × Situation Profiles," *Journal of Personality* 74, no. 5 (2006): 1451–80.

37. B.W. Roberts and W.F. DelVecchio, "The Rank-Order Consistency of Personality Traits from Childhood to Old Age: A Quantitative Review of Longitudinal Studies," *Psychological Bulletin* 126, no. 1 (2000): 3–25; A. Terracciano, P.T. Costa, and R.R. McCrae, "Personality Plasticity after Age 30," *Personality and Social Psychology Bulletin* 32, no. 8 (2006): 999–1009.

38. M. Jurado and M. Rosselli, "The Elusive Nature of Executive Functions: A Review of Our Current Understanding," *Neuropsychology Review* 17, no. 3 (2007): 213–33.

39. J.M. Digman, "Personality Structure: Emergence of the Five-Factor Model," *Annual Review of Psychology* 41 (1990): 417–40; O.P. John and S. Srivastava, "The Big Five Trait Taxonomy: History, Measurement, and Theoretical Perspectives," in *Handbook of Personality: Theory and Research*, ed. L.A. Pervin and O.P. John (New York: Guilford Press, 1999), 102–38; R.R. McCrae, J.F. Gaines, and M.A. Wellington, "The Five-Factor Model in Fact and Fiction," in *Handbook of Psychology*, ed. I.B. Weiner (2012), 65–91.

40. M.R. Barrick and M.K. Mount, "Yes, Personality Matters: Moving on to More Important Matters," *Human Performance* 18, no. 4 (2005): 359–72; S.J. Perry et al., "P = F (Conscientiousness × Ability): Examining the Facets of Conscientiousness," *Human Performance* 23, no. 4 (2010): 343–60; A. Neal et al., "Predicting the Form and Direction of Work Role Performance from the Big 5 Model of Personality Traits," *Journal of Organizational Behavior* 33, no. 2 (2012): 175–92.

41. M.R. Barrick, M.K. Mount, and T.A. Judge, "Personality and Performance at the Beginning of the New Millennium: What Do We Know and Where Do We Go Next?," *International Journal of Selection and Assessment* 9, no. 1/2 (2001): 9–30; T.A. Judge and R. Ilies, "Relationship of Personality to Performance Motivation: A Meta-Analytic Review," *Journal of Applied Psychology* 87, no. 4 (2002): 797–807; A. Witt, L.A. Burke, and M.R. Barrick, "The Interactive Effects of Conscientiousness and Agreeableness on Job Performance," *Journal of Applied Psychology* 87 (2002): 164–69; J. Moutafi, A. Furnham, and J. Crump, "Is Managerial Level Related to Personality?," *British Journal of Management* 18, no. 3 (2007): 272–80.

42. R. Ilies, M.W. Gerhardt, and H. Le, "Individual Differences in Leadership Emergence: Integrating Meta-Analytic Findings and Behavioral Genetics Estimates," *International Journal of Selection and Assessment* 12, no. 3 (2004): 207–19; I.-S. Oh and

C.M. Berry, "The Five-Factor Model of Personality and Managerial Performance: Validity Gains through the Use of 360 Degree Performance Ratings," *Journal of Applied Psychology* 94, no. 6 (2009): 1498–513; A. Minbashian, J.E.H. Bright, and K.D. Bird, "Complexity in the Relationships among the Subdimensions of Extraversion and Job Performance in Managerial Occupations," *Journal of Occupational and Organizational Psychology* 82, no. 3 (2009): 537–49.

43. K.M. DeNeve and H. Cooper, "The Happy Personality: A Meta-Analysis of 137 Personality Traits and Subjective Well-Being," *Psychological Bulletin* 124 (1998): 197–229; M.L. Kern and H.S. Friedman, "Do Conscientious Individuals Live Longer? A Quantitative Review," *Health Psychology* 27, no. 5 (2008): 505–12; F.C.M. Geisler, M. Wiedig-Allison, and H. Weber, "What Coping Tells about Personality," *European Journal of Personality* 23, no. 4 (2009): 289–306; P.S. Fry and D.L. Debats, "Perfectionism and the Five-Factor Personality Traits as Predictors of Mortality in Older Adults," *Journal of Health Psychology* 14, no. 4 (2009): 513–24; H.S. Friedman, M.L. Kern, and C.A. Reynolds, "Personality and Health, Subjective Well-Being, and Longevity," *Journal of Personality* 78, no. 1 (2010): 179–216.

44. H. Le et al., "Too Much of a Good Thing: Curvilinear Relationships between Personality Traits and Job Performance," *Journal of Applied Psychology* 96, no. 1 (2011): 113–33.

45. C.G. Jung, *Psychological Types*, trans. H.G. Baynes (Princeton, NJ: Princeton University Press, 1971); I.B. Myers, *The Myers-Briggs Type Indicator* (Palo Alto, CA: Consulting Psychologists Press, 1987).

46. Adapted from an exhibit found at www.16-personality-types.com.

47. M. Gladwell, "Personality Plus," *New Yorker*, September 20, 2004, 42–48; R.B. Kennedy and D.A. Kennedy, "Using the Myers-Briggs Type Indicator in Career Counseling," *Journal of Employment Counseling* 41, no. 1 (2004): 38–44.

48. J. Michael, "Using the Myers-Briggs Type Indicator as a Tool for Leadership Development? Apply with Caution," *Journal of Leadership & Organizational Studies* 10 (2003): 68–81; R.M. Capraro and M.M. Capraro, "Myers-Briggs Type Indicator Score Reliability across Studies: A Meta-Analytic Reliability Generalization Study," *Educational and Psychological Measurement* 62 (2002): 590–602; Moutafi, Furnham, and Crump, "Is Managerial Level Related to Personality?"; B.S. Kuipers et al., "The Influence of Myers-Briggs Type Indicator Profiles on Team Development Processes," *Small Group Research* 40, no. 4 (2009): 436–64; F.W. Brown and M.D. Reilly, "The Myers-Briggs Type Indicator and Transformational Leadership," *Journal of Management Development* 28, no. 10 (2009): 916–32.

49. R.R. McCrae and P.T. Costa, "Reinterpreting the Myers-Briggs Type Indicator from the Perspective of the Five-Factor Model of Personality," *Journal of Personality* 57 (1989): 17–40; A. Furnham, "The Big Five Versus the Big Four: The Relationship between the Myers-Briggs Type Indicator (MBTI) and NEO-PI Five Factor Model of Personality," *Personality and Individual Differences* 21, no. 2 (1996): 303–7.

50. R.J. Lopez, D. Weikel, and R. Connell, "NTSB Blames Engineer for 2008 Metrolink Crash," *Los Angeles Times*, January 22, 2010; "Metrolink Train Crews in Southern California Threaten Boycott over New Personality Tests," *Associated Press*, April 1, 2010.

51. S. Vazire and S.D. Gosling, "E-Perceptions: Personality Impressions Based on Personal Websites," *Journal of Personality and Social Psychology* 87, no. 1 (2004): 123–32; C. Ross et al., "Personality and Motivations Associated with Facebook Use," *Computers in Human Behavior* 25, no. 2 (2009): 578–86; A.J. Gill, J. Oberlander, and E. Austin, "Rating E-Mail Personality at Zero Acquaintance," *Personality and Individual Differences* 40, no. 3 (2006): 497–507; R.E. Guadagno, B.M. Okdie, and C.A. Eno, "Who Blogs? Personality Predictors of Blogging," *Computers in Human Behavior* 24, no. 5 (2008): 1993–2004; D.H. Kluemper and P.A. Rosen, "Future Employment Selection Methods: Evaluating Social Networking Web Sites," *Journal of Managerial Psychology* 24, no. 6 (2009): 567–80; M.D. Back et al., "Facebook Profiles Reflect Actual Personality, Not Self-Idealization," *Psychological Science* (2010); T. Yarkoni, "Personality in 100,000 Words: A Large-Scale Analysis of Personality and Word Use among Bloggers," *Journal of Research in Personality* 44, no. 3 (2010): 363–73.

52. K.C. Neel, "Abdoulah Sets WOW Apart," *Multichannel News*, January 29, 2007, 2; D. Graham, "She Walks the Talk," *Denver Woman*, April 2009; "WOW! Management Team," (Denver, 2010), www.wowway.com (accessed December 6, 2010).

53. B.M. Meglino and E.C. Ravlin, "Individual Values in Organizations: Concepts, Controversies, and Research," *Journal of Management* 24, no. 3 (1998): 351–89; B.R. Agle and C.B. Caldwell, "Understanding Research on Values in Business," *Business and Society* 38, no. 3 (1999): 326–87; S. Hitlin and J.A. Pilavin, "Values: Reviving a Dormant Concept," *Annual Review of Sociology* 30 (2004): 359–93.

54. D. Lubinski, D.B. Schmidt, and C.P. Benbow, "A 20-Year Stability Analysis of the Study of Values for Intellectually Gifted Individuals from Adolescence to Adulthood," *Journal of Applied Psychology* 81 (1996): 443–51.

55. L. Parks and R.P. Guay, "Personality, Values, and Motivation," *Personality and Individual Differences* 47, no. 7 (2009): 675–84.

56. S.H. Schwartz, "Universals in the Content and Structure of Values: Theoretical Advances and Empirical Tests in 20 Countries," *Advances in Experimental Social Psychology* 25 (1992): 1–65; D. Spini, "Measurement Equivalence of 10 Value Types from the Schwartz Value Survey across 21 Countries," *Journal of Cross-Cultural Psychology* 34, no. 1 (2003): 3–23; S.H. Schwartz and K. Boehnke, "Evaluating the Structure of Human Values with Confirmatory Factor Analysis," *Journal of Research in Personality* 38, no. 3 (2004): 230–55; S.H. Schwartz, "Studying Values: Personal Adventure, Future Directions," *Journal of Cross-Cultural Psychology* 42, no. 2 (2011): 307–19. Schwartz's model is currently being revised, but the new model is similar in overall design and still requires refinement. See S.H. Schwartz et al., "Refining the Theory of Basic Individual Values," *Journal of Personality and Social Psychology* 103, no. 4 (2012): 663–88.

57. L. Parks and R.P. Guay, "Can Personal Values Predict Performance? Evidence in an Academic Setting," *Applied Psychology* 61, no. 1 (2012): 149–73; M.L. Arthaud-Day, J.C. Rode, and W.H. Turnley, "Direct and Contextual Effects of Individual Values on Organizational Citizenship Behavior in Teams," *Journal of Applied Psychology* 97, no. 4 (2012): 792–807.

58. G.R. Maio et al., "Addressing Discrepancies between Values and Behavior: The Motivating Effect of Reasons," *Journal of Experimental Social Psychology* 37, no. 2 (2001): 104–17; B. Verplanken and R.W. Holland, "Motivated Decision Making: Effects of Activation and Self-Centrality of Values on Choices and Behavior," *Journal of Personality and Social Psychology* 82, no. 3 (2002): 434–47; A. Bardi and S.H. Schwartz, "Values and Behavior: Strength and Structure of Relations," *Personality and Social Psychology Bulletin* 29, no. 10 (2003): 1207–20; G.R. Maio et al., "Changing, Priming, and Acting on Values: Effects Via Motivational Relations in a Circular Model," *Journal of Personality and Social Psychology* 97, no. 4 (2009): 699–715; L. Sagiv, N. Sverdlik, and N. Schwarz, "To Compete or to Cooperate? Values' Impact on Perception and Action in Social Dilemma Games," *European Journal of Social Psychology* 41, no.1 (2011): 64–77.

59. E. Dreezens et al., "The Missing Link: On Strengthening the Relationship between Values and Attitudes," *Basic and Applied Social Psychology* 30, no. 2 (2008): 142–52.

60. N. Mazar, O. Amir, and D. Ariely, "The Dishonesty of Honest People: A Theory of Self-Concept Maintenance," *Journal of Marketing Research* 45 (2008): 633–44.

61. M.L. Verquer, T.A. Beehr, and S.H. Wagner, "A Meta-Analysis of Relations between Person-Organization Fit and Work Attitudes," *Journal of Vocational Behavior* 63 (2003): 473–89; J.W. Westerman and L.A. Cyr, "An Integrative Analysis of Person-Organization Fit Theories," *International Journal of Selection and Assessment* 12, no. 3 (2004): 252–61; J.R. Edwards and D.M. Cable, "The Value of Value Congruence," *Journal of Applied Psychology* 94, no. 3 (2009): 654–77; B.J. Hoffman et al., "Person-Organization Value Congruence: How Transformational Leaders Influence Work Group Effectiveness," *Academy of Management Journal* 54, no. 4 (2011): 779–96.

62. K. Hornyak, "Upward Move: Cynthia Schwalm," *Medical Marketing & Media*, June 2008, 69. For research on the consequences on values congruence, see A.L. Kristof, "Person-Organization Fit: An Integrative Review of Its Conceptualizations, Measurement, and Implications," *Personnel Psychology* 49, no. 1 (1996): 1–49; Verquer, Beehr, and Wagner, "A Meta-Analysis of Relations between Person-Organization Fit and Work Attitudes"; Westerman and Cyr, "An Integrative Analysis of Person-Organization Fit Theories"; D. Bouckenooghe et al., "The Prediction of Stress by Values and Value Conflict," *Journal of Psychology* 139, no. 4 (2005): 369–82.

63. T. Simons, "Behavioral Integrity: The Perceived Alignment between Managers' Words and Deeds as a Research Focus," *Organization Science* 13, no. 1 (2002): 18–35; Watson Wyatt, "Employee Ratings of Senior Management Dip, Watson Wyatt Survey Finds" (New York: Watson Wyatt, 2007).

64. Z. Aycan, R.N. Kanungo, and J.B.P. Sinha, "Organizational Culture and Human Resource Management Practices: The Model of Culture Fit," *Journal of Cross-Cultural Psychology* 30 (1999): 501–26; M. Naor, K. Linderman, and R. Schroeder, "The Globalization of Operations in Eastern and Western Countries: Unpacking the Relationship between National and Organizational Culture and Its Impact on Manufacturing Performance," *Journal of Operations Management* 28, no. 3 (2010): 194–205. This type of values incongruence can occur even when the company is founded in that country, that is, when a local company tries to introduce a culture incompatible with the national culture. See, for example, A. Danisman, "Good Intentions and Failed Implementations: Understanding Culture-Based Resistance to Organizational Change," *European Journal of Work and Organizational Psychology* 19, no. 2 (2010): 200–20.

65. J.M. Kouzes and B.Z. Posner, *The Leadership Challenge*, 4th ed. (San Francisco: Jossey-Bass, 2010), pp. 32–33; The Conference Board, *CEO Challenge 2014* (New York: The Conference Board, January 2014).

66. P.L. Schumann, "A Moral Principles Framework for Human Resource Management Ethics," *Human Resource Management Review* 11 (2001): 93–111; J. Boss, *Analyzing Moral Issues*, 3rd ed. (New York: McGraw-Hill, 2005), Chap. 1; M.G. Velasquez, *Business Ethics: Concepts and Cases*, 6th ed. (Upper Saddle River, NJ: Prentice-Hall, 2006), Chap. 2.

67. For analysis of these predictors of ethical conduct, see: J.J. Kish-Gephart, D.A. Harrison, and L.K. Treviño, "Bad Apples, Bad Cases, and Bad Barrels: Meta-Analytic Evidence about Sources of Unethical Decisions at Work," *Journal of Applied Psychology* 95, no. 1 (2010): 1–31.

68. T.M. Jones, "Ethical Decision Making by Individuals in Organizations: An Issue-Contingent Model," *Academy of Management Review* 16 (1991): 366–95; T. Barnett, "Dimensions of Moral Intensity and Ethical Decision Making: An Empirical Study," *Journal of Applied Social Psychology* 31, no. 5 (2001): 1038–57; J. Tsalikis, B. Seaton, and P. Shepherd, "Relative Importance Measurement of the Moral Intensity Dimensions," *Journal of Business Ethics* 80, no. 3 (2008): 613–26; S. Valentine and D. Hollingworth, "Moral Intensity, Issue Importance, and Ethical Reasoning in Operations Situations," *Journal of Business Ethics* 108, no. 4 (2012): 509–23.

69. K. Weaver, J. Morse, and C. Mitcham, "Ethical Sensitivity in Professional Practice: Concept Analysis," *Journal of Advanced Nursing* 62, no. 5 (2008): 607–18; L.J.T. Pedersen, "See No Evil: Moral Sensitivity in the Formulation of Business Problems," *Business Ethics: A European Review* 18, no. 4 (2009): 335–48. According to one recent neuroscience study, the emotional aspect of moral sensitivity declines and the cognitive aspect increases between early childhood and young adulthood. See: J. Decety, K.J. Michalska, and K.D. Kinzler, "The Contribution of Emotion and Cognition to Moral Sensitivity: A Neurodevelopmental Study," *Cerebral Cortex* 22, no. 1 (2012): 209–20.

70. D. You, Y. Maeda, and M.J. Bebeau, "Gender Differences in Moral Sensitivity: A Meta-Analysis," *Ethics & Behavior* 21, no. 4 (2011): 263–82; A.H. Chan and H. Cheung, "Cultural Dimensions, Ethical Sensitivity, and Corporate Governance," *Journal of Business Ethics* 110, no. 1 (2012): 45–59; G. Desautels and S. Jacob, "The Ethical Sensitivity of Evaluators: A Qualitative Study Using a Vignette Design," *Evaluation* 18, no. 4 (2012): 437–50.

71. N. Ruedy and M. Schweitzer, "In the Moment: The Effect of Mindfulness on Ethical Decision Making," *Journal of Business Ethics* 95, no. 1 (2010): 73–87.

72. S.J. Reynolds, K. Leavitt, and K.A. DeCelles, "Automatic Ethics: The Effects of Implicit Assumptions and Contextual Cues on Moral Behavior," *Journal of Applied Psychology* 95, no. 4 (2010): 752–60.

73. D.R. Beresford, N.d. Katzenbach, and C.B. Rogers Jr., *Report of Investigation by the Special Investigative Committee of the Board of Directors of Worldcom, Inc.* (March 31, 2003).

74. J. Harper, "Government in 'an Ethics Crisis,' Survey Finds," *Washington Times*, January 30, 2008, A5; Ipsos Reid, "Four in Ten (42%) Employed Canadians Have Observed Some Form of Workplace Misconduct," news release (Toronto: Ipsos Reid, July 3, 2013).

75. Ethics Resource Center, *2013 National Business Ethics Survey* (Arlington, VA: Ethics Resource Center, 2014).

76. H. Donker, D. Poff, and S. Zahir, "Corporate Values, Codes of Ethics, and Firm Performance: A Look at the Canadian Context," *Journal of Business Ethics* 82, no. 3 (2008): 527–37; G. Svensson et al., "Ethical Structures and Processes of Corporations Operating in Australia, Canada, and Sweden: A Longitudinal and Cross-Cultural Study," *Journal of Business Ethics* 86, no. 4 (2009): 485–506; L. Preuss, "Codes of Conduct in Organisational Context: From Cascade to Lattice-Work of Codes," *Journal of Business Ethics* 94, no. 4 (2010): 471–87.

77. Svensson et al., "Ethical Structures and Processes of Corporations Operating in Australia, Canada, and Sweden: A Longitudinal and Cross-Cultural Study."

78. Texas Instruments, *The Values and Ethics of TI*, (Dallas: Texas Instruments, February 18, 2011).

79. S.L. Grover, T. Nadisic, and D.L. Patient, "Bringing Together Different Perspectives on Ethical Leadership," *Journal of Change Management* 12, no. 4 (2012): 377–81; J. Jordan et al., "Someone to Look Up To: Executive–Follower Ethical Reasoning and Perceptions of Ethical Leadership," *Journal of Management* 39, no. 3 (2013): 660–83; J. Jaeger, "Compliance Culture Depends on Middle Management," *Compliance Week*, February 2014, 47–61.

80. "Rolling Up the Sleeves," *Shanghai Daily*, September 3, 2012.

81. Individualism and collectivism information is from the meta-analysis by Oyserman et al., not the earlier findings by Hofstede. See D. Oyserman, H.M. Coon, and M. Kemmelmeier, "Rethinking Individualism and Collectivism: Evaluation of Theoretical Assumptions and Meta-Analyses," *Psychological Bulletin* 128 (2002): 3–72. Consistent with Oyserman et al., a recent study found high rather than low individualism among Chileans. See A. Kolstad and S. Horpestad, "Self-Construal in Chile and Norway," *Journal of Cross-Cultural Psychology* 40, no. 2 (2009): 275–81.

82. F.S. Niles, "Individualism-Collectivism Revisited," *Cross-Cultural Research* 32 (1998): 315–41; C.P. Earley and C.B. Gibson, "Taking Stock in Our Progress on Individualism-Collectivism: 100 Years of Solidarity and Community," *Journal of Management* 24 (1998): 265–304; C.L. Jackson et al., "Psychological Collectivism: A Measurement Validation and Linkage to Group Member Performance," *Journal of Applied Psychology* 91, no. 4 (2006): 884–99.

83. Oyserman, Coon, and Kemmelmeier, "Rethinking Individualism and Collectivism."Also see F. Li and L. Aksoy, "Dimensionality of Individualism–Collectivism and Measurement Equivalence of Triandis and Gelfand's Scale," *Journal of Business and Psychology* 21, no. 3 (2007): 313–29. The "vertical–horizontal" distinction does not account for the lack of correlation between individualism and collectivism. See J.H. Vargas and M. Kemmelmeier, "Ethnicity and Contemporary American Culture: A Meta-Analytic Investigation of Horizontal–Vertical Individualism–Collectivism," *Journal of Cross-Cultural Psychology* 44, no. 2 (2013): 195–222.

84. M. Voronov and J.A. Singer, "The Myth of Individualism-Collectivism: A Critical Review," *Journal of Social Psychology* 142 (2002): 461–80; Y. Takano and S. Sogon, "Are Japanese More Collectivistic Than Americans?," *Journal of Cross-Cultural Psychology* 39, no. 3 (2008): 237–50; D. Dalsky, "Individuality in Japan and the United States: A Cross-Cultural Priming Experiment," *International Journal of Intercultural Relations* 34, no. 5 (2010): 429–35. Japan scored 46 on individualism in Hofstede's original study, placing it a little below the middle of the range and around the 60th percentile among the countries studied.

85. G. Hofstede, *Culture's Consequences: Comparing Values, Behaviors, Institutions, and Organizations across Nations*, 2nd ed. (Thousand Oaks, CA: Sage, 2001).

86. Hofstede, *Culture's Consequences: Comparing Values, Behaviors, Institutions, and Organizations across Nations*. Hofstede used the terms *masculinity* and *femininity* for *achievement* and *nurturing orientation*, respectively. We (along with other writers) have adopted the latter two terms to minimize the sexist perspective of these concepts. Also, readers need to be aware that achievement orientation is assumed to be opposite of nurturing orientation, but this opposing relationship might be questioned.

87. V. Taras, J. Rowney, and P. Steel, "Half a Century of Measuring Culture: Review of Approaches, Challenges, and Limitations Based on the Analysis of 121 Instruments for Quantifying Culture," *Journal of International Management* 15, no. 4 (2009): 357–73.

88. R.L. Tung and A. Verbeke, "Beyond Hofstede and GLOBE: Improving the Quality of Cross-Cultural Research," *Journal of International Business Studies* 41, no. 8 (2010): 1259–74.

89. W.K.W. Choy, A.B.E. Lee, and P. Ramburuth, "Multinationalism in the Workplace: A Myriad of Values in a Singaporean Firm," *Singapore Management Review* 31, no. 1 (2009): 1–31.

90. N. Jacob, "Cross-Cultural Investigations: Emerging Concepts," *Journal of Organizational Change Management* 18, no. 5 (2005): 514–28; V. Taras, B.L. Kirkman, and P. Steel, "Examining the Impact of Culture's Consequences: A Three-Decade, Multilevel, Meta-Analytic Review of Hofstede's Cultural Value Dimensions," *Journal of Applied Psychology* 95, no. 3 (2010): 405–39.

Chapter 3

1. M. Johnson, "Why Accounting Is Cool," *NJBIZ*, February 24, 2014, 13.

2. O.W. Holmes, *The Autocrat of the Breakfast-Table* (Boston: Phillips, Sampson, 1858), 58–59. This quotation, which Steve McShane slightly rewrote to remove sexist language, has a long and convoluted history. Pioneering psychology professor William James is almost always cited as the source, yet there is no evidence that he wrote this statement or anything similar. The first attribution of this quotation to William James may have been a 1958 *Rand Memoranda* publication (p. 925), and later in *Reader's Digest* (1962). Even if James did publish something similar, it is a highly condensed version of the humorous discussion of "six persons" that Oliver Wendell Holmes Sr. published decades before James began writing. Most likely, a Rand Corporation editor crafted this quotation from vague memory of Holmes's story and misattributed William James as the author because one of Holmes's characters in the story was "James." We cite Holmes as the source because he wrote the story from which this quotation is derived.

3. D. Cooper and S.M.B. Thatcher, "Identification in Organizations: The Role of Self-Concept Orientations and Identification Motives," *Academy of Management Review* 35, no. 4 (2010): 516–38; J. Schaubroeck, Y.J. Kim, and A.C. Peng, "The Self-Concept in Organizational Psychology: Clarifying and Differentiating the Constructs," in *International Review of Industrial and Organizational Psychology* (New York: Wiley, 2012): 1–38.

4. L. Gaertner et al., "A Motivational Hierarchy within: Primacy of the Individual Self, Relational Self, or Collective Self?," *Journal of Experimental Social Psychology* 48, no. 5 (2012): 997–1013; R.E. Johnson et al., "Leader Identity as an Antecedent of the Frequency and Consistency of Transformational, Consideration, and Abusive Leadership Behaviors," *Journal of Applied Psychology* 97, no. 6 (2012): 1262–72.

5. E. Rafaeli-Mor and J. Steinberg, "Self-Complexity and Well-Being: A Review and Research Synthesis," *Personality and Social Psychology Review* 6, no. 1 (2002): 31–58; E.J. Koch and J.A. Shepperd, "Is Self-Complexity Linked to Better Coping? A Review of the Literature," *Journal of Personality* 72, no. 4 (2004): 727–60; A.R. McConnell, R.J. Rydell, and C.M. Brown, "On the Experience of Self-Relevant Feedback: How Self-Concept Organization Influences Affective Responses and Self-Evaluations," *Journal of Experimental Social Psychology* 45, no. 4 (2009): 695–707.

6. J.D. Campbell et al., "Self-Concept Clarity: Measurement, Personality Correlates, and Cultural Boundaries," *Journal of Personality and Social Psychology* 70, no. 1 (1996): 141–56.

7. J. Lodi-Smith and B.W. Roberts, "Getting to Know Me: Social Role Experiences and Age Differences in Self-Concept Clarity During Adulthood," *Journal of Personality* 78, no. 5 (2010): 1383–410.

8. G. Quill, "Hélène Joy: Successful—and Ignored," *Toronto Star*, January 10, 2009; "Canada Wins Aussie Joy," *West Australian*, June 29, 2011, 5.

9. Koch and Shepperd, "Is Self-Complexity Linked to Better Coping? A Review of the Literature"; T.D. Ritchie et al., "Self-Concept Clarity Mediates the Relation between Stress and Subjective Well-Being," *Self and Identity* 10, no. 4 (2010): 493–508.

10. A.T. Brook, J. Garcia, and M.A. Fleming, "The Effects of Multiple Identities on Psychological Well-Being," *Personality and Social Psychology Bulletin* 34, no. 12 (2008): 1588–600.

11. J.D. Campbell, "Self-Esteem and Clarity of the Self-Concept," *Journal of Personality and Social Psychology* 59, no. 3 (1990).

12. T.W.H. Ng, K.L. Sorensen, and D.C. Feldman, "Dimensions, Antecedents, and Consequences of Workaholism: A Conceptual Integration and Extension," *Journal of Organizational Behavior* 28 (2007): 111–36; S. Pachulicz, N. Schmitt, and G. Kuljanin, "A Model of Career Success: A Longitudinal Study of Emergency Physicians," *Journal of Vocational Behavior* 73, no. 2 (2008): 242–53; M.N. Bechtoldt et al., "Self-Concept Clarity and the Management of Social Conflict," *Journal of Personality* 78, no. 2 (2010): 539–74.

13. B. George, *Authentic Leadership* (San Francisco: Jossey-Bass, 2004); S.T. Hannah and B.J. Avolio, "Ready or Not: How Do We Accelerate the Developmental Readiness of Leaders?," *Journal of Organizational Behavior* 31, no. 8 (2010): 1181–87.

14. This quotation has been cited since the 1930s, yet we were unable to find it in any of Dewey's writing. The earliest known reference to this quotation is Dale Carnegie's famous self-help book, where the statement is attributed to Dewey. See D. Carnegie, *How to Win Friends and Influence People*, 1st ed. (New York: Simon & Schuster, 1936), 43–44 (19 in later editions).

15. C.L. Guenther and M.D. Alicke, "Deconstructing the Better-Than-Average Effect," *Journal of Personality and Social Psychology* 99, no. 5 (2010): 755–70; S. Loughnan et al., "Universal Biases in Self-Perception: Better and More Human Than Average," *British Journal of Social Psychology* 49 (2010): 627–36; H.C. Boucher, "Understanding Western-East Asian Differences and Similarities in Self-Enhancement," *Social and Personality Psychology Compass* 4, no. 5 (2010): 304–17; A. Gregg, C. Sedikides, and J. Gebauer, "Dynamics of Identity: Between Self-Enhancement and Self-Assessment," in *Handbook of Identity Theory and Research*, ed. S.J. Schwartz, K. Luyckx, and V.L. Vignoles (New York: Springer, 2011), 305–27.

16. U.S. Merit Systems Protection Board, *Accomplishing Our Mission: Results of the 2005 Merit Principles Survey*, U.S. Merit Systems Protection Board (Washington, DC: December 6, 2007); J. Montier, *Behavioural Investing* (Chichester, UK: Wiley, 2007), 82–83.

17. D. Dunning, C. Heath, and J.M. Suls, "Flawed Self-Assessment: Implications for Health, Education, and the Workplace," *Psychological Science in the Public Interest* 5, no. 3 (2004): 69–106; D.A. Moore, "Not So above Average after All: When People Believe They Are Worse Than Average and Its Implications for Theories of Bias in Social Comparison," *Organizational Behavior and Human Decision Processes* 102, no. 1 (2007): 42–58.

18. J.A. Doukas and D. Petmezas, "Acquisitions, Overconfident Managers and Self-Attribution Bias," *European Financial Management* 13, no. 3 (2007): 531–77; N. Harrè and C.G. Sibley, "Explicit and Implicit Self-Enhancement Biases in Drivers and Their Relationship to Driving Violations and Crash-Risk Optimism," *Accident Analysis & Prevention* 39, no. 6 (2007): 1155–61; D.A. Moore and P.J. Healy, "The Trouble with Overconfidence," *Psychological Review* 115, no. 2 (2008): 502–17; F. Jiang et al., "Managerial Hubris, Firm Expansion and Firm Performance: Evidence from China," *The Social Science Journal* 48, no. 3 (2011): 489–99; A.S. Ahmed and S. Duellman, "Managerial Overconfidence and Accounting Conservatism," *Journal of Accounting Research* 51, no. 1 (2013): 1–30.

19. W.B. Swann Jr., "To Be Adored or to Be Known? The Interplay of Self-Enhancement and Self-Verification," in *Foundations of Social Behavior*, ed. R.M. Sorrentino and E.T. Higgins (New York: Guilford, 1990), 408–48; W.B. Swann Jr., P.J. Rentfrow, and J.S. Guinn, "Self-Verification: The Search for Coherence," in *Handbook of Self and Identity*, ed. M.R. Leary and J. Tagney (New York: Guilford, 2002), 367–83; D.M. Cable and V.S. Kay, "Striving for Self-Verification during Organizational Entry," *Academy of Management Journal* 55, no. 2 (2012): 360–80.

20. Kelly Services, *Acquisition and Retantion in the War for Talent*, Kelly Global Workforce Index, Kelly Services (Troy, MI: April 2012); S.S. Garr, *The State of Employee Recognition in 2012*, Bersin & Associates (Oakland, CA: June 2012); American Psychological Association, *2014 Work and Well-Being Survey*, American Psychological Association (New York: April 2014); Kelly Services, *Engaging Active and Passive Job Seekers*, Kelly Services (Troy, MI: 5 May 2014).

21. F. Anseel and F. Lievens, "Certainty as a Moderator of Feedback Reactions? A Test of the Strength of the Self-Verification Motive," *Journal of Occupational & Organizational Psychology* 79, no. 4

(2006): 533–51; T. Kwang and W.B. Swann, "Do People Embrace Praise Even When They Feel Unworthy? A Review of Critical Tests of Self-Enhancement versus Self-Verification," *Personality and Social Psychology Review* 14, no. 3 (2010): 263–80.

22. M.R. Leary, "Motivational and Emotional Aspects of the Self," *Annual Review of Psychology* 58, no. 1 (2007): 317–44.

23. D.M. Cable, F. Gino, and B. Staats, "Breaking Them In or Eliciting Their Best? Reframing Socialization around Newcomers' Authentic Self-Expression," *Administrative Science Quarterly* 58, no. 1 (2013): 1–36.

24. T.A. Judge and J.E. Bono, "Relationship of Core Self-Evaluations Traits—Self-Esteem, Generalized Self-Efficacy, Locus of Control, and Emotional Stability—with Job Satisfaction and Job Performance: A Meta-Analysis," *Journal of Applied Psychology* 86, no. 1 (2001): 80–92; T.A. Judge and C. Hurst, "Capitalizing on One's Advantages: Role of Core Self-Evaluations," *Journal of Applied Psychology* 92, no. 5 (2007): 1212–27. We have described the three most commonly identified components of self-evaluation. The full model also includes emotional stability (low neuroticism), but it is a behavior tendency (personality dimension), whereas the other three components are self-evaluations. Generally, the core self-evaluation model has received limited research and its dimensions continue to be debated. For example, see T.W. Self, "Evaluating Core Self-Evaluations: Application of a Multidimensional, Latent-Construct, Evaluative Framework to Core Self-Evaluations Research" (PhD, University of Houston, 2007); R.E. Johnson, C.C. Rosen, and P.E. Levy, "Getting to the Core of Core Self-Evaluation: A Review and Recommendations," *Journal of Organizational Behavior* 29 (2008): 391–413.

25. R.F. Baumeister and J.M. Twenge, *The Social Self, Handbook of Psychology* (New York: Wiley, 2003); W.B. Swann Jr., C. Chang-Schneider, and K.L. McClarty, "Do People's Self-Views Matter?: Self-Concept and Self-Esteem in Everyday Life," *American Psychologist* 62, no. 2 (2007): 84–94.

26. A. Bandura, *Self-Efficacy: The Exercise of Control* (New York: W. H. Freeman, 1997). However, one review found that self-efficacy's effect on task and job performance is much lower when also including the effects of personality traits on performance. See T.A. Judge et al., "Self-Efficacy and Work-Related Performance: The Integral Role of Individual Differences," *Journal of Applied Psychology* 92, no. 1 (2007): 107–27.

27. G. Chen, S.M. Gully, and D. Eden, "Validation of a New General Self-Efficacy Scale," *Organizational Research Methods* 4, no. 1 (2001): 62–83.

28. J.B. Rotter, "Generalized Expectancies for Internal Versus External Control of Reinforcement," *Psychological Monographs* 80, no. 1 (1966): 1–28.

29. P.E. Spector, "Behavior in Organizations as a Function of Employee's Locus of Control," *Psychological Bulletin* 91 (1982): 482–97; K. Hattrup, M.S. O'Connell, and J.R. Labrador, "Incremental Validity of Locus of Control after Controlling for Cognitive Ability and Conscientiousness," *Journal of Business and Psychology* 19, no. 4 (2005): 461–81; T.W.H. Ng, K.L. Sorensen, and L.T. Eby, "Locus of Control at Work: A Meta-Analysis," *Journal of Organizational Behavior* 27 (2006): 1057–87; Q. Wang, N.A. Bowling, and K.J. Eschleman, "A Meta-Analytic Examination of Work and General Locus of Control," *Journal of Applied Psychology* 95, no. 4 (2010): 761–68.

30. M.A. Hogg and D.J. Terry, "Social Identity and Self-Categorization Processes in Organizational Contexts," *Academy of Management Review* 25 (2000): 121–40; L.L. Gaertner et al., "The "I," the "We," and the "When": A Meta-Analysis of Motivational Primacy in Self-Definition," *Journal of Personality and Social Psychology* 83, no. 3 (2002): 574; S.A. Haslam, R.A. Eggins, and K.J. Reynolds, "The Aspire Model: Actualizing Social and Personal Identity Resources to Enhance Organizational Outcomes," *Journal of Occupational and Organizational Psychology* 76 (2003): 83–113; S.A. Haslam, S.D. Reicher, and M.J. Platow, *The New Psychology of Leadership* (Hove, UK: Psychology Press, 2011).

31. C. Sedikides and A.P. Gregg, "Portraits of the Self," in *The Sage Handbook of Social Psychology*, ed. M.A. Hogg and J. Cooper (London: Sage, 2003), 110–38. The history of the social self in human beings is described in M.R. Leary and N.R. Buttermore, "The Evolution of the Human Self: Tracing the Natural History of Self-Awareness," *Journal for the Theory of Social Behaviour* 33, no. 4 (2003): 365–404.

32. M.R. Edwards, "Organizational Identification: A Conceptual and Operational Review," *International Journal of Management Reviews* 7, no. 4 (2005): 207–30; D.A. Whetten, "Albert and Whetten Revisited: Strengthening the Concept of Organizational Identity," *Journal of Management Inquiry* 15, no. 3 (2006): 219–34.

33. M.B. Brewer, "The Social Self: On Being the Same and Different at the Same Time," *Personality and Social Psychology Bulletin* 17, no. 5 (1991): 475–82; R. Imhoff and H.-P. Erb, "What Motivates Nonconformity? Uniqueness Seeking Blocks Majority Influence," *Personality and Social Psychology Bulletin* 35, no. 3 (2009): 309–20; K.R. Morrison and S.C. Wheeler, "Nonconformity Defines the Self: The Role of Minority Opinion Status in Self-Concept Clarity," *Personality and Social Psychology Bulletin* 36, no. 3 (2010): 297–308; M.G. Mayhew, J. Gardner, and N.M. Ashkanasy, "Measuring Individuals' Need for Identification: Scale Development and Validation," *Personality and Individual Differences* 49, no. 5 (2010): 356–61.

34. See, for example, W.B. Swann Jr., R.E. Johnson, and J.K. Bosson, "Identity Negotiation at Work," *Research in Organizational Behavior* 29 (2009): 81–109; H.-L. Yang and C.-Y. Lai, "Motivations of Wikipedia Content Contributors," *Computers in Human Behavior* 26, no. 6 (2010): 1377–83; Bechtoldt et al., "Self-Concept Clarity and the Management of Social Conflict"; Hannah and Avolio, "Ready or Not: How Do We Accelerate the Developmental Readiness of Leaders?"

35. E.I. Knudsen, "Fundamental Components of Attention," *Annual Review of Neuroscience* 30, no. 1 (2007): 57–78. For an evolutionary psychology perspective of selective attention and organization, see L. Cosmides and J. Tooby, "Evolutionary Psychology: New Perspectives on Cognition and Motivation," *Annual Review of Psychology* 64, no. 1 (2013): 201–29.

36. A. Bechara and A.R. Damasio, "The Somatic Marker Hypothesis: A Neural Theory of Economic Decision," *Games and Economic Behavior* 52, no. 2 (2005): 336–72; T.S. Saunders and M.J. Buehner, "The Gut Chooses Faster Than the Mind: A Latency Advantage of Affective over Cognitive Decisions," *Quarterly Journal of Experimental Psychology* 66, no. 2 (2012): 381–88; A. Aite et al., "Impact of Emotional Context Congruency on Decision Making under Ambiguity," *Emotion* 13, no. 2 (2013): 177–82.

37. Plato, *The Republic*, trans. D. Lee (Harmondsworth, UK: Penguin, 1955).

38. D.J. Simons and C.F. Chabris, "Gorillas in Our Midst: Sustained Inattentional Blindness for Dynamic Events," *Perception* 28 (1999): 1059–74.

39. R.S. Nickerson, "Confirmation Bias: A Ubiquitous Phenomenon in Many Guises," *Review of General Psychology* 2, no. 2 (1998): 175–220; A. Gilbey and S. Hill, "Confirmation Bias in General Aviation Lost Procedures," *Applied Cognitive Psychology* 26, no. 5 (2012): 785–95; A.M. Scherer, P.D. Windschitl, and A.R. Smith, "Hope to Be Right: Biased Information Seeking Following Arbitrary and Informed Predictions," *Journal of Experimental Social Psychology* 49, no. 1 (2013): 106–12.

40. E. Rassin, A. Eerland, and I. Kuijpers, "Let's Find the Evidence: An Analogue Study of Confirmation Bias in Criminal Investigations," *Journal of Investigative Psychology and Offender Profiling* 7, no. 3 (2010): 231–46; C. Wastell et al., "Identifying Hypothesis Confirmation Behaviors in a Simulated Murder Investigation: Implications for Practice," *Journal of Investigative Psychology and Offender Profiling* 9, no. 2 (2012): 184–98.

41. Earl Derr Biggers, the author of the Charlie Chan novels, is sometimes cited as the source of this quotation. However, this statement is found only in the 1935 film *Charlie Chan in Egypt*, which is based on Biggers's character. It does not appear in any Charlie Chan novels.

42. C.N. Macrae and G.V. Bodenhausen, "Social Cognition: Thinking Categorically about Others," *Annual Review of Psychology* 51 (2000): 93–120. For literature on the automaticity of the perceptual organization and interpretation process, see J.A. Bargh, "The Cognitive Monster: The Case against the Controllability of Automatic Stereotype Effects," in *Dual Process Theories in Social Psychology*, ed. S. Chaiken and Y. Trope (New York: Guilford, 1999), 361–82; J.A. Bargh and M.J. Ferguson, "Beyond Behaviorism: On the Automaticity of Higher Mental Processes," *Psychological Bulletin* 126, no. 6 (2000): 925–45; M. Gladwell, *Blink: The Power of Thinking without Thinking* (New York: Little, Brown, 2005).

43. E.M. Altmann and B.D. Burns, "Streak Biases in Decision Making: Data and a Memory Model," *Cognitive Systems Research* 6, no. 1 (2005): 5–16. For a discussion of cognitive closure and perception, see A.W. Kruglanski, *The Psychology of Closed Mindedness* (New York: Psychology Press, 2004).

44. J. Willis and A. Todorov, "First Impressions: Making Up Your Mind after a 100-Ms Exposure to a Face," *Psychological Science* 17, no. 7 (2006): 592–98; A. Todorov, M. Pakrashi, and N.N. Oosterhof, "Evaluating Faces on Trustworthiness after Minimal Time Exposure," *Social Cognition* 27, no. 6 (2009): 813–33; C. Olivola and A. Todorov, "Elected in 100 Milliseconds: Appearance-Based Trait Inferences and Voting," *Journal of Nonverbal Behavior* 34, no. 2 (2010): 83–110. For related research on thin slices, see N. Ambady et al., "Surgeons' Tone of Voice: A Clue to Malpractice History," *Surgery* 132, no. 1 (2002): 5–9; D.J. Benjamin and J.M. Shapiro, "Thin-Slice Forecasts of Gubernatorial Elections," *Review of Economics and Statistics* 91, no. 3 (2009): 523–36.

45. P.M. Senge, *The Fifth Discipline: The Art and Practice of the Learning Organization* (New York: Doubleday Currency, 1990), Chap. 10; T.J. Chermack, "Mental Models in Decision Making and Implications for Human Resource Development," *Advances in Developing Human Resources* 5, no. 4 (2003): 408–22; P.N. Johnson-Laird, "Mental Models and Deductive Reasoning," in *Reasoning: Studies of Human Inference and Its Foundations*, ed. J.E. Adler and L.J. Rips (Cambridge: Cambridge University Press, 2008); S. Ross and N. Allen, "Examining the Convergent Validity of Shared Mental Model Measures," *Behavior Research Methods* 44, no. 4 (2012): 1052–62.

46. G.W. Allport, *The Nature of Prejudice* (Reading, MA: Addison-Wesley, 1954); J.C. Brigham, "Ethnic Stereotypes," *Psychological Bulletin* 76, no. 1 (1971): 15–38; D.J. Schneider, *The Psychology of Stereotyping* (New York: Guilford, 2004); S. Kanahara, "A Review of the Definitions of Stereotype and a Proposal for a Progressional Model," *Individual Differences Research* 4, no. 5 (2006): 306–21.

47. V. Christidou, V. Hatzinikita, and G. Samaras, "The Image of Scientific Researchers and Their Activity in Greek Adolescents' Drawings," *Public Understanding of Science* 21, no. 5 (2012): 626–47; S. Cheryan et al., "The Stereotypical Computer Scientist: Gendered Media Representations as a Barrier to Inclusion for Women," *Sex Roles* 69, no. 1/2 (2013): 58–71.

48. C.N. Macrae, A.B. Milne, and G.V. Bodenhausen, "Stereotypes as Energy-Saving Devices: A Peek inside the Cognitive Toolbox," *Journal of Personality and Social Psychology* 66 (1994): 37–47; J.W. Sherman et al., "Stereotype Efficiency Reconsidered: Encoding Flexibility under Cognitive Load," *Journal of Personality and Social Psychology* 75 (1998): 589–606; Macrae and Bodenhausen, "Social Cognition: Thinking Categorically about Others."

49. J.C. Turner and S.A. Haslam, "Social Identity, Organizations, and Leadership," in *Groups at Work: Theory and Research*, ed. M.E. Turner (Mahwah, NJ: Erlbaum, 2001), 25–65; J. Jetten, R. Spears, and T. Postmes, "Intergroup Distinctiveness and Differentiation: A Meta-Analytic Integration," *Journal of Personality and Social Psychology* 86, no. 6 (2004): 862–79; M.A. Hogg et al., "The Social Identity Perspective: Intergroup Relations, Self-Conception, and Small Groups," *Small Group Research* 35, no. 3 (2004): 246–76; K. Hugenberg and D.F. Sacco, "Social Categorization and Stereotyping: How Social Categorization Biases Person Perception and Face Memory," *Social and Personality Psychology Compass* 2, no. 2 (2008): 1052–72.

50. N. Halevy, G. Bornstein, and L. Sagiv, "'In-Group Love' and 'Out-Group Hate' as Motives for Individual Participation in Intergroup Conflict: A New Game Paradigm," *Psychological Science* 19, no. 4 (2008): 405–11; T. Yamagishi and N. Mifune, "Social Exchange and Solidarity: In-Group Love or Out-Group Hate?," *Evolution and Human Behavior* 30, no. 4 (2009): 229–37; N. Halevy, O. Weisel, and G. Bornstein, "'In-Group Love' and 'Out-Group Hate' in Repeated Interaction between Groups," *Journal of Behavioral Decision Making* 25, no. 2 (2012): 188–95; M. Parker and R. Janoff-Bulman, "Lessons from Morality-Based Social Identity: The Power of Outgroup 'Hate,' Not Just Ingroup 'Love,'" *Social Justice Research* 26, no. 1 (2013): 81–96.

51. S.N. Cory, "Quality and Quantity of Accounting Students and the Stereotypical Accountant: Is There a Relationship?," *Journal of Accounting Education* 10, no. 1 (1992): 1–24; P.D. Bougen, "Joking Apart: The Serious Side to the Accountant Stereotype," *Accounting, Organizations and Society* 19, no. 3 (1994): 319–35; A.L. Friedman and S.R. Lyne, "The Beancounter Stereotype: Towards a General Model of Stereotype Generation," *Critical*

Perspectives on Accounting 12, no. 4 (2001): 423–51; A. Hoffjan, "The Image of the Accountant in a German Context," *Accounting and the Public Interest* 4 (2004): 62–89; T. Dimnik and S. Felton, "Accountant Stereotypes in Movies Distributed in North America in the Twentieth Century," *Accounting, Organizations and Society* 31, no. 2 (2006): 129–55.

52. K. Gladman and M. Lamb, *GMI Ratings' 2012 Women on Boards Survey*, GovernanceMetrics International (New York: 2012); Catalyst, *Quick Takes: Women on Boards* (New York: April 9, 2012).

53. S.O. Gaines and E.S. Reed, "Prejudice: From Allport to Dubois," *American Psychologist* 50 (1995): 96–103; S.T. Fiske, "Stereotyping, Prejudice, and Discrimination," in *Handbook of Social Psychology*, ed. D.T. Gilbert, S.T. Fiske, and G. Lindzey (New York: McGraw-Hill, 1998), 357–411; M. Hewstone, M. Rubin, and H. Willis, "Intergroup Bias," *Annual Review of Psychology* 53 (2002): 575–604.

54. E. Cediey and F. Foroni, *Discrimination in Access to Employment on Grounds of Foreign Origin in France*, International Labour Organization (Geneva: 2008); P. Gumbel, "The French Exodus," *Time International*, April 16, 2007, 18; "Study Finds Major Discrimination against Turkish Job Applicants," *The Local (Berlin)*, February 9, 2010.

55. J.A. Bargh and T.L. Chartrand, "The Unbearable Automaticity of Being," *American Psychologist* 54, no. 7 (1999): 462–79; S.T. Fiske, "What We Know Now about Bias and Intergroup Conflict, the Problem of the Century," *Current Directions in Psychological Science* 11, no. 4 (2002): 123–28; R. Krieglmeyer and J.W. Sherman, "Disentangling Stereotype Activation and Stereotype Application in the Stereotype Misperception Task," *Journal of Personality and Social Psychology* 103, no. 2 (2012): 205–24. On the limitations of some stereotype training, see B. Gawronski et al., "When 'Just Say No' Is Not Enough: Affirmation versus Negation Training and the Reduction of Automatic Stereotype Activation," *Journal of Experimental Social Psychology* 44 (2008): 370–77.

56. H.H. Kelley, *Attribution in Social Interaction* (Morristown, NJ: General Learning Press, 1971); B.F. Malle, "Attribution Theories: How People Make Sense of Behavior," in *Theories of Social Psychology*, ed. D. Chadee (Chichester, UK: Blackwell, 2011), 72–95. This "internal–external" or "person–situation" perspective of the attribution process differs somewhat from the original "intentional–unintentional" perspective, which says that we try to understand the deliberate or accidental/involuntary reasons why people engage in behaviors, as well as the reasons for behavior. Some writers suggest the original perspective is more useful. See B.F. Malle, "Time to Give Up the Dogmas of Attribution: An Alternative Theory of Behavior Explanation," in *Advances in Experimental Social Psychology*, Vol. 44, ed. K.M. Olson and M.P. Zanna (San Diego: Elsevier Academic, 2011), 297–352.

57. H.H. Kelley, "The Processes of Causal Attribution," *American Psychologist* 28 (1973): 107–28.

58. J.M. Schaubroeck and P. Shao, "The Role of Attribution in How Followers Respond to the Emotional Expression of Male and Female Leaders," *The Leadership Quarterly* 23, no. 1 (2012): 27–42; D. Lange and N.T. Washburn, "Understanding Attributions of Corporate Social Irresponsibility," *Academy of Management Review* 37, no. 2 (2012): 300–26.

59. J.M. Crant and T.S. Bateman, "Assignment of Credit and Blame for Performance Outcomes," *Academy of Management Journal* 36 (1993): 7–27; B. Weiner, "Intrapersonal and Interpersonal Theories of Motivation from an Attributional Perspective," *Educational Psychology Review* 12 (2000): 1–14; N. Bacon and P. Blyton, "Worker Responses to Teamworking: Exploring Employee Attributions of Managerial Motives," *International Journal of Human Resource Management* 16, no. 2 (2005): 238–55.

60. D.T. Miller and M. Ross, "Self-Serving Biases in the Attribution of Causality: Fact or Fiction?," *Psychological Bulletin* 82, no. 2 (1975): 213–25; J. Shepperd, W. Malone, and K. Sweeny, "Exploring Causes of the Self-Serving Bias," *Social and Personality Psychology Compass* 2, no. 2 (2008): 895–908.

61. E.W.K. Tsang, "Self-Serving Attributions in Corporate Annual Reports: A Replicated Study," *Journal of Management Studies* 39, no. 1 (2002): 51–65; N.J. Roese and J.M. Olson, "Better, Stronger, Faster: Self-Serving Judgment, Affect Regulation, and the Optimal Vigilance Hypothesis," *Perspectives on Psychological Science* 2, no. 2 (2007): 124–41; R. Hooghiemstra, "East–West Differences in Attributions for Company Performance: A Content Analysis of Japanese and U.S. Corporate Annual Reports," *Journal of Cross-Cultural Psychology* 39, no. 5 (2008): 618–29; M. Franco and H. Haase, "Failure Factors in Small and Medium-Sized Enterprises: Qualitative Study from an Attributional Perspective," *International Entrepreneurship and Management Journal* 6, no. 4 (2010): 503–21.

62. S.S. Van Dine (Willard Huntington Wright), *The Benson Murder Mystery* (New York: Scribner's, 1926), Chap. 6.

63. D.T. Gilbert and P.S. Malone, "The Correspondence Bias," *Psychological Bulletin* 117, no. 1 (1995): 21–38.

64. I. Choi, R.E. Nisbett, and A. Norenzayan, "Causal Attribution across Cultures: Variation and Universality," *Psychological Bulletin* 125, no. 1 (1999): 47–63; R.E. Nisbett, *The Geography of Thought: How Asians and Westerners Think Differently—and Why* (New York: Free Press, 2003), Chap. 5; S.G. Goto et al., "Cultural Differences in Sensitivity to Social Context: Detecting Affective Incongruity Using the N400," *Social Neuroscience* 8, no. 1 (2012): 63–74.

65. B.F. Malle, "The Actor–Observer Asymmetry in Attribution: A (Surprising) Meta-Analysis," *Psychological Bulletin* 132, no. 6 (2006): 895–919; C.W. Bauman and L.J. Skitka, "Making Attributions for Behaviors: The Prevalence of Correspondence Bias in the General Population," *Basic and Applied Social Psychology* 32, no. 3 (2010): 269–77.

66. Similar models are presented in D. Eden, "Self-Fulfilling Prophecy as a Management Tool: Harnessing Pygmalion," *Academy of Management Review* 9 (1984): 64–73; R.H.G. Field and D.A. Van Seters, "Management by Expectations (MBE): The Power of Positive Prophecy," *Journal of General Management* 14 (1988): 19–33; D.O. Trouilloud et al., "The Influence of Teacher Expectations on Student Achievement in Physical Education Classes: Pygmalion Revisited," *European Journal of Social Psychology* 32 (2002): 591–607.

67. D. Eden, "Interpersonal Expectations in Organizations," in *Interpersonal Expectations: Theory, Research, and Applications* (Cambridge: Cambridge University Press, 1993), 154–78.

68. K.S. Crawford, E.D. Thomas, and J.J.A. Fink, "Pygmalion at Sea: Improving the Work Effectiveness of Low Performers," *Journal of Applied Behavioral Science* 16 (1980): 482–505; D. Eden, "Pygmalion Goes to Boot Camp: Expectancy, Leadership, and Trainee Performance," *Journal of Applied Psychology*

67 (1982): 194–99; C.M. Rubie-Davies, "Teacher Expectations and Student Self-Perceptions: Exploring Relationships," *Psychology in the Schools* 43, no. 5 (2006): 537–52; P. Whiteley, T. Sy, and S.K. Johnson, "Leaders' Conceptions of Followers: Implications for Naturally Occurring Pygmalion Effects," *Leadership Quarterly* 23, no. 5 (2012): 822–34.

69. S. Madon, L. Jussim, and J. Eccles, "In Search of the Powerful Self-Fulfilling Prophecy," *Journal of Personality and Social Psychology* 72, no. 4 (1997): 791–809; A.E. Smith, L. Jussim, and J. Eccles, "Do Self-Fulfilling Prophecies Accumulate, Dissipate, or Remain Stable over Time?," *Journal of Personality and Social Psychology* 77, no. 3 (1999): 548–65; S. Madon et al., "Self-Fulfilling Prophecies: The Synergistic Accumulative Effect of Parents' Beliefs on Children's Drinking Behavior," *Psychological Science* 15, no. 12 (2005): 837–45.

70. W.H. Cooper, "Ubiquitous Halo," *Psychological Bulletin* 90 (1981): 218–44; P. Rosenzweig, *The Halo Effect . . . and the Eight Other Business Delusions That Deceive Managers* (New York: Free Press, 2007); J.W. Keeley et al., "Investigating Halo and Ceiling Effects in Student Evaluations of Instruction," *Educational and Psychological Measurement* 73, no. 3 (2013): 440–57.

71. B. Mullen et al., "The False Consensus Effect: A Meta-Analysis of 115 Hypothesis Tests," *Journal of Experimental Social Psychology* 21, no. 3 (1985): 262–83; G. Marks and N. Miller, "Ten Years of Research on the False-Consensus Effect: An Empirical and Theoretical Review," *Psychological Bulletin* 102, no. 1 (1987): 72–90; F.J. Flynn and S.S. Wiltermuth, "Who's with Me? False Consensus, Brokerage, and Ethical Decision Making in Organizations," *Academy of Management Journal* 53, no. 5 (2010): 1074–89.

72. C.L. Kleinke, *First Impressions: The Psychology of Encountering Others* (Englewood Cliffs, NJ: Prentice Hall, 1975); E.A. Lind, L. Kray, and L. Thompson, "Primacy Effects in Justice Judgments: Testing Predictions from Fairness Heuristic Theory," *Organizational Behavior and Human Decision Processes* 85 (2001): 189–210; O. Ybarra, "When First Impressions Don't Last: The Role of Isolation and Adaptation Processes in the Revision of Evaluative Impressions," *Social Cognition* 19 (2001): 491–520.

73. D.D. Steiner and J.S. Rain, "Immediate and Delayed Primacy and Recency Effects in Performance Evaluation," *Journal of Applied Psychology* 74 (1989): 136–42; K.T. Trotman, "Order Effects and Recency: Where Do We Go from Here?," *Accounting & Finance* 40 (2000): 169–82; W. Green, "Impact of the Timing of an Inherited Explanation on Auditors' Analytical Procedures Judgements," *Accounting and Finance* 44 (2004): 369–92.

74. "Survey: Candidates with Strong Resumes Often Fail to Meet Expectations in Interview," News release for Accountemps (Menlo Park, CA: PR News, 23 July 2009); "Careerbuilder Releases Study of Common and Not-So-Common Resume Mistakes That Can Cost You the Job," News release for CareerBuilder (Chicago: 11 September 2013); "Survey: Job Interview Trips up More Candidates Than Any Other Step in Hiring Process," News release for Accountemps (Menlo Park, CA: 2 April 2014).

75. L. Roberson, C.T. Kulik, and M.B. Pepper, "Using Needs Assessment to Resolve Controversies in Diversity Training Design," *Group & Organization Management* 28, no. 1 (2003): 148–74; D.E. Hogan and M. Mallott, "Changing Racial Prejudice through Diversity Education," *Journal of College Student Development* 46, no. 2 (2005): 115–25; Gawronski et al., "When 'Just Say No' Is Not Enough."

76. Eden, "Self-Fulfilling Prophecy as a Management Tool: Harnessing Pygmalion"; S.S. White and E.A. Locke, "Problems with the Pygmalion Effect and Some Proposed Solutions," *Leadership Quarterly* 11 (2000): 389–415.

77. T.W. Costello and S.S. Zalkind, *Psychology in Administration: A Research Orientation* (Englewood Cliffs, NJ: Prentice Hall, 1963), 45–46; J.M. Kouzes and B.Z. Posner, *The Leadership Challenge*, 4th ed. (San Francisco: Jossey-Bass, 2007), Chap. 3.

78. George, *Authentic Leadership*; W.L. Gardner et al., " 'Can You See the Real Me?' A Self-Based Model of Authentic Leader and Follower Development," *Leadership Quarterly* 16 (2005): 343–72; B. George, *True North* (San Francisco: Jossey-Bass, 2007).

79. W. Hofmann et al., "Implicit and Explicit Attitudes and Interracial Interaction: The Moderating Role of Situationally Available Control Resources," *Group Processes Intergroup Relations* 11, no. 1 (2008): 69–87; A.G. Greenwald et al., "Understanding and Using the Implicit Association Test: III. Meta-Analysis of Predictive Validity," *Journal of Personality and Social Psychology* 97, no. 1 (2009): 17–41; J.D. Vorauer, "Completing the Implicit Association Test Reduces Positive Intergroup Interaction Behavior," *Psychological Science* 23, no. 10 (2012): 1168–75.

80. Hofmann et al., "Implicit and Explicit Attitudes and Interracial Interaction: The Moderating Role of Situationally Available Control Resources"; J.T. Jost et al., "The Existence of Implicit Bias Is Beyond Reasonable Doubt: A Refutation of Ideological and Methodological Objections and Executive Summary of Ten Studies That No Manager Should Ignore," *Research in Organizational Behavior* 29 (2009): 39–69.

81. J. Luft, *Of Human Interaction* (Palo Alto, CA: National Press, 1969). For a variation of this model, see J. Hall, "Communication Revisited," *California Management Review* 15 (1973): 56–67.

82. S. Vazire and M.R. Mehl, "Knowing Me, Knowing You: The Accuracy and Unique Predictive Validity of Self-Ratings and Other-Ratings of Daily Behavior," *Journal of Personality and Social Psychology* 95, no. 5 (2008): 1202–16; S. Vazire, "Who Knows What about a Person? The Self-Other Knowledge Asymmetry (SOKA) Model," *Journal of Personality and Social Psychology* 98, no. 2 (2010): 281–300.

83. P.J. Henry and C.D. Hardin, "The Contact Hypothesis Revisited: Status Bias in the Reduction of Implicit Prejudice in the United States and Lebanon," *Psychological Science* 17, no. 10 (2006): 862–68; T.F. Pettigrew and L.R. Tropp, "A Meta-Analytic Test of Intergroup Contact Theory," *Journal of Personality and Social Psychology* 90, no. 5 (2006): 751–83; T.F. Pettigrew, "Future Directions for Intergroup Contact Theory and Research," *International Journal of Intercultural Relations* 32, no. 3 (2008): 187–99; F.K. Barlow et al., "The Contact Caveat: Negative Contact Predicts Increased Prejudice More Than Positive Contact Predicts Reduced Prejudice," *Personality and Social Psychology Bulletin* 38, no. 12 (2012): 1629–43.

84. The contact hypothesis was first introduced in Allport, *The Nature of Prejudice*, Chap. 16.

85. C. Duan and C.E. Hill, "The Current State of Empathy Research," *Journal of Counseling Psychology* 43 (1996): 261–74; W.G. Stephen and K.A. Finlay, "The Role of Empathy in Improving Intergroup Relations," *Journal of Social Issues* 55 (1999): 729–43; S.K. Parker and C.M. Axtell, "Seeing Another Viewpoint: Antecedents and Outcomes of Employee Perspective Taking,"

Academy of Management Journal 44 (2001): 1085–100; G.J. Vreeke and I.L. van der Mark, "Empathy, an Integrative Model," *New Ideas in Psychology* 21, no. 3 (2003): 177–207.

86. M. Tarrant, R. Calitri, and D. Weston, "Social Identification Structures the Effects of Perspective Taking," *Psychological Science* 23, no. 9 (2012): 973–78; J.L. Skorinko and S.A. Sinclair, "Perspective Taking Can Increase Stereotyping: The Role of Apparent Stereotype Confirmation," *Journal of Experimental Social Psychology* 49, no. 1 (2013): 10–18.

87. A. Sugimoto, "English Is Vital, Rakuten Boss Says—but It Isn't Everything," *Nikkei Weekly* (Tokyo), April 22, 2013.

88. There is no consensus on the meaning of global mindset. The elements identified in this book are common among most of the recent writing on this subject. See, for example, S.J. Black, W.H. Mobley, and E. Weldon, "The Mindset of Global Leaders: Inquisitiveness and Duality," in *Advances in Global Leadership* (Greenwich, CT: JAI, 2006), 181–200; O. Levy et al., "What We Talk about When We Talk about 'Global Mindset': Managerial Cognition in Multinational Corporations," *Journal of International Business Studies* 38, no. 2 (2007): 231–58; S. Beechler and D. Baltzley, "Creating a Global Mindset," *Chief Learning Officer* 7, no. 6 (2008): 40–45; M. Javidan and D. Bowen, "The 'Global Mindset' of Managers: What It Is, Why It Matters, and How to Develop It," *Organizational Dynamics* 42, no. 2 (2013): 145–55.

89. A.K. Gupta and V. Govindarajan, "Cultivating a Global Mindset," *Academy of Management Executive* 16, no. 1 (2002): 116–26.

90. M. Jackson, "Corporate Volunteers Reaching Worldwide," *Boston Globe*, May 4, 2008, 3.

Chapter 4

1. S. Deveau, "WestJet Expansion Worth a Few Ruffled Feathers," *National Post*, December 14, 2013, FP3; "WestJet Head Talks Effective Employee Engagement," *CEO Series* (Vancouver: Simon Fraser University, April 25, 2013), http://beedie.sfu.ca/blog/2013/04/westjet-head-talks-effective-employee-engagement-ceo-series/ (accessed March 3, 2014); WestJet, "WestJet Christmas Miracle: Real-Time Giving" (Calgary: YouTube, December 8, 2013), https://www.youtube.com/watch?v=zIEIvi2MuEk, Video 5:25 (accessed March 4, 2014); "WestJet Named Value Airline of the Year," *Canada Newswire* (Calgary), January 14, 2014.

2. Emotions are also cognitive processes. However, we use the narrow definition of cognition as a well-used label referring only to reasoning processes. Also, this and other chapters emphasize that emotional and cognitive processes are intertwined.

3. For discussion of emotions in marketing, economics, and sociology, see M. Hubert, "Does Neuroeconomics Give New Impetus to Economic and Consumer Research?," *Journal of Economic Psychology* 31, no. 5 (2010): 812–17; D.D. Franks, "Introduction," in *Neurosociology: The Nexus between Neuroscience and Social Psychology* (New York: Springer, 2010); N. Martins, "Can Neuroscience Inform Economics? Rationality, Emotions and Preference Formation," *Cambridge Journal of Economics* 35, no. 2 (2011): 251–67; H. Plassmann, T.Z. Ramsøy, and M. Milosavljevic, "Branding the Brain: A Critical Review and Outlook," *Journal of Consumer Psychology* 22, no. 1 (2012): 18–36.

4. The definition presented here is constructed from the following sources: N.M. Ashkanasy, W.J. Zerbe, and C.E.J. Hartel, "Introduction: Managing Emotions in a Changing Workplace," in *Managing Emotions in the Workplace*, ed. N.M. Ashkanasy, W.J. Zerbe, and C.E.J. Hartel (Armonk, NY: M. E. Sharpe, 2002), 3–18; H.M. Weiss, "Conceptual and Empirical Foundations for the Study of Affect at Work," in *Emotions in the Workplace*, ed. R.G. Lord, R.J. Klimoski, and R. Kanfer (San Francisco: Jossey-Bass, 2002), 20–63. However, the meaning of emotions is still being debated. See, for example, M. Cabanac, "What Is Emotion?," *Behavioral Processes* 60 (2002): 69–83; B. Russell and J. Eisenberg, "The Role of Cognition and Attitude in Driving Behavior: Elaborating on Affective Events Theory," in *Experiencing and Managing Emotions in the Workplace*, ed. N.M. Ashkanasy, C.E.J. Hartel, and W.J. Zerbe, *Research on Emotion in Organizations* (Bingley, UK: Emerald Group, 2012), 203–24.

5. R. Kanfer and R.J. Klimoski, "Affect and Work: Looking Back to the Future," in *Emotions in the Workplace*, ed. R.G. Lord, R.J. Klimoski, and R. Kanfer (San Francisco: Jossey-Bass, 2002), 473–90; J.A. Russell, "Core Affect and the Psychological Construction of Emotion," *Psychological Review* 110, no. 1 (2003): 145–72.

6. V. van Gogh, T. van Gogh, and I. Stone, *Dear Theo: The Autobiography* (New York: Doubleday, 1937; repr., 1995), 441. This quotation originally appeared in a letter sent by Vincent van Gogh to his brother Théo in 1889.

7. R. Reisenzein, M. Studtmann, and G. Horstmann, "Coherence between Emotion and Facial Expression: Evidence from Laboratory Experiments," *Emotion Review* 5, no. 1 (2013): 16–23.

8. R.B. Zajonc, "Emotions," in *Handbook of Social Psychology*, ed. D.T. Gilbert, S.T. Fiske, and L. Gardner (New York: Oxford University Press, 1998), 591–634; P. Winkielman, "Bob Zajonc and the Unconscious Emotion," *Emotion Review* 2, no. 4 (2010): 353–62.

9. R.J. Larson, E. Diener, and R.E. Lucas, "Emotion: Models, Measures, and Differences," in *Emotions in the Workplace*, ed. R.G. Lord, R.J. Klimoski, and R. Kanfer (San Francisco: Jossey-Bass, 2002), 64–113; L.F. Barrett et al., "The Experience of Emotion," *Annual Review of Psychology* 58, no. 1 (2007): 373–403; M. Yik, J.A. Russell, and J.H. Steiger, "A 12-Point Circumplex Structure of Core Affect," *Emotion* 11, no. 4 (2011): 705–31.

10. R.F. Baumeister, E. Bratslavsky, and C. Finkenauer, "Bad Is Stronger Than Good," *Review of General Psychology* 5, no. 4 (2001): 323–70; A. Vaish, T. Grossmann, and A. Woodward, "Not All Emotions Are Created Equal: The Negativity Bias in Social-Emotional Development," *Psychological Bulletin* 134, no. 3 (2008): 383–403; B.E. Hilbig, "Good Things Don't Come Easy (to Mind): Explaining Framing Effects in Judgments of Truth," *Experimental Psychology* 59, no. 1 (2012): 38–46.

11. A.P. Brief, *Attitudes in and around Organizations* (Thousand Oaks, CA: Sage, 1998); A.H. Eagly and S. Chaiken, "The Advantages of an Inclusive Definition of Attitude," *Social Cognition* 25, no. 5 (2007): 582–602; G. Bohner and N. Dickel, "Attitudes and Attitude Change," *Annual Review of Psychology* 62, no. 1 (2011): 391–417. The definition of attitudes is still being debated. First, it is unclear whether an attitude includes emotions (affect), or whether emotions influence an attitude. We take the latter view. Although emotions influence and are closely connected to attitudes, an attitude is best defined as an evaluation of an attitude object. That evaluation is not always conscious, however. Second, a few writers argue that attitudes are formed each time one thinks about the attitude object, which is contrary to the traditional view that attitudes are fairly stable predispositions toward

the attitude object. Third, although less of an issue now, some attitude models refer only to the "feelings" component, whereas we view attitude as a three-component construct (beliefs, feelings, behavioral intentions). For various definitions of attitude and discussion of these variations, see I. Ajzen, "Nature and Operation of Attitudes," *Annual Review of Psychology* 52 (2001): 27–58; D. Albarracín et al., "Attitudes: Introduction and Scope," in *The Handbook of Attitudes*, ed. D. Albarracín, B.T. Johnson, and M.P. Zanna (Mahwah, NJ: Erlbaum, 2005), 3–20; W.A. Cunningham and P.D. Zelazo, "Attitudes and Evaluations: A Social Cognitive Neuroscience Perspective," *TRENDS in Cognitive Sciences* 11, no. 3 (2007): 97–104; B. Gawronski, "Editorial: Attitudes Can Be Measured! But What Is an Attitude?," *Social Cognition* 25, no. 5 (2007): 573–81; R.S. Dalal, "Job Attitudes: Cognition and Affect," in *Handbook of Psychology*, 2nd ed. (Wiley, 2012).

12. Neuroscience has a slightly more complicated distinction in that conscious awareness is "feeling a feeling" whereas "feeling" is a nonconscious sensing of the body state created by emotion, which itself is a nonconscious neural reaction to a stimulus. However, this distinction is not significant for scholars focused on human behavior rather than brain activity, and the labels collide with popular understanding of "feeling." See A.R. Damasio, *The Feeling of What Happens: Body and Emotion in the Making of Consciousness* (New York: Harcourt Brace, 1999); F. Hansen, "Distinguishing between Feelings and Emotions in Understanding Communication Effects," *Journal of Business Research* 58, no. 10 (2005): 1426–36; T. Bosse, C.M. Jonker, and J. Treur, "Formalisation of Damasio's Theory of Emotion, Feeling and Core Consciousness," *Consciousness and Cognition* 17, no. 1 (2008): 94–113.

13. Cunningham and Zelazo, "Attitudes and Evaluations,"; M.D. Lieberman, "Social Cognitive Neuroscience: A Review of Core Processes," *Annual Review of Psychology* 58, no. 1 (2007): 259–89; M. Fenton-O'Creevy et al., "Thinking, Feeling and Deciding: The Influence of Emotions on the Decision Making and Performance of Traders," *Journal of Organizational Behavior* 32 (2011): 1044–61. The dual emotion–cognition processes are likely the same as the implicit–explicit attitude processes reported by several scholars, as well as tacit knowledge structures. See B. Gawronski and G.V. Bodenhausen, "Unraveling the Processes Underlying Evaluation: Attitudes from the Perspective of the Ape Model," *Social Cognition* 25, no. 5 (2007): 687–717; W.J. Becker and R. Cropanzano, "Organizational Neuroscience: The Promise and Prospects of an Emerging Discipline," *Journal of Organizational Behavior* 31, no. 7 (2010): 1055–59.

14. D. Trafimow et al., "It Is Irrelevant, but It Matters: Using Confluence Theory to Predict the Influence of Beliefs on Evaluations, Attitudes, and Intentions," *European Journal of Social Psychology* 42, no. 4 (2012): 509–20.

15. S. Orbell, "Intention-Behavior Relations: A Self-Regulation Perspective," in *Contemporary Perspectives on the Psychology of Attitudes*, ed. G. Haddock and G.R. Maio (East Sussex, UK: Psychology Press, 2004), 145–68.

16. H.M. Weiss and R. Cropanzano, "Affective Events Theory: A Theoretical Discussion of the Structure, Causes and Consequences of Affective Experiences at Work," *Research in Organizational Behavior* 18 (1996): 1–74; A. Bechara et al., "Deciding Advantageously before Knowing the Advantageous Strategy," *Science* 275, no. 5304 (1997): 1293–95; H.A. Elfenbein, "Chapter 7: Emotion in Organizations," *The Academy of Management Annals* 1 (2007): 315–86.

17. J.A. Bargh and M.J. Ferguson, "Beyond Behaviorism: On the Automaticity of Higher Mental Processes," *Psychological Bulletin* 126, no. 6 (2000): 925–45; J.M. George, "The Illusion of Will in Organizational Behavior Research: Nonconscious Processes and Job Design," *Journal of Management* 35, no. 6 (2009): 1318–39; K.I. Ruys and D.A. Stapel, "The Unconscious Unfolding of Emotions," *European Review of Social Psychology* 20 (2009): 232–71; P. Winkielman and K.C. Berridge, "Unconscious Emotion," *Current Directions in Psychological Science* 13, no. 3 (2004): 120–23.

18. A.R. Damasio, *Descartes' Error: Emotion, Reason, and the Human Brain* (New York: Putnam Sons, 1994); P. Ekman, "Basic Emotions," in *Handbook of Cognition and Emotion*, ed. T. Dalgleish and M. Power (San Francisco: Jossey-Bass, 1999), 45–60; J.E. LeDoux, "Emotion Circuits in the Brain," *Annual Review of Neuroscience* 23 (2000): 155–84; Damasio, *The Feeling of What Happens: Body and Emotion in the Making of Consciousness*; R.J. Dolan, "Emotion, Cognition, and Behavior," *Science* 298, no. 5596 (2002): 1191–94.

19. N. Schwarz, "Emotion, Cognition, and Decision Making," *Cognition and Emotion* 14, no. 4 (2000): 433–40; M.T. Pham, "The Logic of Feeling," *Journal of Consumer Psychology* 14, no. 4 (2004): 360–69. One recent proposition is that a person's confidence in his or her beliefs is also influenced by the person's emotional experiences regarding those beliefs. See Z. Memon and J. Treur, "On the Reciprocal Interaction between Believing and Feeling: An Adaptive Agent Modelling Perspective," *Cognitive Neurodynamics* 4, no. 4 (2010): 377–94.

20. G.R. Maio, V.M. Esses, and D.W. Bell, "Examining Conflict between Components of Attitudes: Ambivalence and Inconsistency Are Distinct Constructs," *Canadian Journal of Behavioural Science* 32, no. 2 (2000): 71–83.

21. P.C. Nutt, *Why Decisions Fail* (San Francisco: Berrett-Koehler, 2002); S. Finkelstein, *Why Smart Executives Fail* (New York: Viking, 2003); P.C. Nutt, "Search during Decision Making," *European Journal of Operational Research* 160 (2005): 851–76.

22. S.C. Bolton and M. Houlihan, "Are We Having Fun Yet? A Consideration of Workplace Fun and Engagement," *Employee Relations* 31, no. 6 (2009): 556–68.

23. R. Evans, "'Our Success at Admiral Is All Thanks to Brilliant Staff,'" *Western Mail* (Cardiff, Wales), January 2, 2013, 1; J.B. Stewart, "Looking for a Lesson in Google's Perks," *The New York Times*, March 15, 2013.

24. N. Wijewardena, C.E.J. Hartel, and R. Samaratunge, "A Laugh a Day Is Sure to Keep the Blues Away: Managers' Use of Humor and the Construction and Destruction of Employees' Resilience," in *Emotions and Organizational Dynamism*, ed. W.J. Zerbe, C.E.J. Hartel, and N.M. Ashkanasy, *Research on Emotion in Organizations* (Bradford: Emerald Group, 2010), 259–78; C. Robert and J.E. Wilbanks, "The Wheel Model of Humor: Humor Events and Affect in Organizations," *Human Relations* 65, no. 9 (2012): 1071–99; J. Mesmer-Magnus, D.J. Glew, and C. Viswesvaran, "A Meta-Analysis of Positive Humor in the Workplace," *Journal of Managerial Psychology* 27, no. 2 (2012): 155–90.

25. These lists are found at www.greatplacetowork.com. They present the top listed companies for 2014 in the United States and 2013 elsewhere. Hewitt Associates produces a related list, particularly for Asia, Europe, and the Middle East. See https://ceplb03.hewitt.com/bestemployers/pages/index.htm.

26. Weiss and Cropanzano, "Affective Events Theory."

27. L. Festinger, *A Theory of Cognitive Dissonance* (Evanston, IL: Row, Peterson, 1957); A.D. Galinsky, J. Stone, and J. Cooper, "The Reinstatement of Dissonance and Psychological Discomfort Following Failed Affirmation," *European Journal of Social Psychology* 30, no. 1 (2000): 123–47; J. Cooper, *Cognitive Dissonance: Fifth Years of a Classic Theory* (London: Sage, 2007).

28. G.R. Salancik, "Commitment and the Control of Organizational Behavior and Belief," in *New Directions in Organizational Behavior*, ed. B.M. Staw and G.R. Salancik (Chicago: St. Clair, 1977), 1–54; J.M. Jarcho, E.T. Berkman, and M.D. Lieberman, "The Neural Basis of Rationalization: Cognitive Dissonance Reduction during Decision-Making," *Social Cognitive and Affective Neuroscience* 6, no. 4 (2011): 460–67.

29. T.A. Judge, E.A. Locke, and C.C. Durham, "The Dispositional Causes of Job Satisfaction: A Core Evaluations Approach," *Research in Organizational Behavior* 19 (1997): 151–88; T.W.H. Ng and K.L. Sorensen, "Dispositional Affectivity and Work-Related Outcomes: A Meta-Analysis," *Journal of Applied Social Psychology* 39, no. 6 (2009): 1255–87.

30. C.M. Brotheridge and A.A. Grandey, "Emotional Labor and Burnout: Comparing Two Perspectives of 'People Work,'" *Journal of Vocational Behavior* 60 (2002): 17–39; P.G. Irving, D.F. Coleman, and D.R. Bobocel, "The Moderating Effect of Negative Affectivity in the Procedural Justice-Job Satisfaction Relation," *Canadian Journal of Behavioural Science* 37, no. 1 (2005): 20–32.

31. J. Schaubroeck, D.C. Ganster, and B. Kemmerer, "Does Trait Affect Promote Job Attitude Stability?," *Journal of Organizational Behavior* 17 (1996): 191–96; C. Dormann and D. Zapf, "Job Satisfaction: A Meta-Analysis of Stabilities," *Journal of Organizational Behavior* 22 (2001): 483–504.

32. J.A. Morris and D.C. Feldman, "The Dimensions, Antecedents, and Consequences of Emotional Labor," *Academy of Management Review* 21 (1996): 986–1010. This is a person-centered definition, which is supplemented by other approaches to the topic. For recent reviews, see A.S. Wharton, "The Sociology of Emotional Labor," *Annual Review of Sociology* 35, no. 1 (2009): 147–65; F.M. Peart, A.M. Roan, and N.M. Ashkanasy, "Trading in Emotions: A Closer Examination of Emotional Labor," in *Experiencing and Managing Emotions in the Workplace*, ed. N.M. Ashkanasy, C.E.J. Hartel, and W.J. Zerbe, *Research on Emotion in Organizations* (Bingley, UK: Emerald Group, 2012), 279–304; A.A. Grandey, J.M. Diefendorff, and D.E. Rupp, "Bringing Emotional Labor in Focus: A Review and Integration of Three Research Issues," in *Emotional Labor in the 21st Century: Diverse Perspectives on Emotion Regulation at Work*, ed. A.A. Grandey, J.M. Diefendorff, and D.E. Rupp, *Series in Organization and Management* (Hove, UK: Routledge, 2013), 3–28.

33. Morris and Feldman, "The Dimensions, Antecedents, and Consequences of Emotional Labor"; D. Zapf, "Emotion Work and Psychological Well-Being: A Review of the Literature and Some Conceptual Considerations," *Human Resource Management Review* 12 (2002): 237–68.

34. A.E. Raz and A. Rafaeli, "Emotion Management in Cross-Cultural Perspective: 'Smile Training' in Japanese and North American Service Organizations," *Research on Emotion in Organizations* 3 (2007): 199–220; D. Matsumoto, S.H. Yoo, and J. Fontaine, "Mapping Expressive Differences around the World," *Journal of Cross-Cultural Psychology* 39, no. 1 (2008): 55–74; S. Ravid, A. Rafaeli, and A. Grandey, "Expressions of Anger in Israeli Workplaces: The Special Place of Customer Interactions," *Human Resource Management Review* 20, no. 3 (2010): 224–34. Emotional display norms might also explain differences in aggression across cultures. See N. Bergeron and B.H. Schneider, "Explaining Cross-National Differences in Peer-Directed Aggression: A Quantitative Synthesis," *Aggressive Behavior* 31, no. 2 (2005): 116–37.

35. F. Trompenaars and C. Hampden-Turner, *Riding the Waves of Culture*, 2nd ed. (New York: McGraw-Hill, 1998), Chap. 6. Also see S. Safdar et al., "Variations of Emotional Display Rules within and across Cultures: A Comparison between Canada, USA, and Japan," *Canadian Journal of Behavioural Science* 41, no. 1 (2009): 1–10.

36. W.J. Zerbe, "Emotional Dissonance and Employee Well-Being," in *Managing Emotions in the Workplace*, ed. N.M. Ashkanasy, W.J. Zerbe, and C.E.J. Hartel (Armonk, NY: M. E. Sharpe, 2002), 189–214; F. Cheung and C. Tang, "The Influence of Emotional Dissonance on Subjective Health and Job Satisfaction: Testing the Stress–Strain–Outcome Model," *Journal of Applied Social Psychology* 40, no. 12 (2010): 3192–217; Grandey, Diefendorff, and Rupp, "Bringing Emotional Labor in Focus."

37. N.-W. Chi et al., "Want a Tip? Service Performance as a Function of Emotion Regulation and Extraversion," *Journal of Applied Psychology* 96, no. 6 (2011): 1337–46; S. Côté, I. Hideg, and G.A. van Kleef, "The Consequences of Faking Anger in Negotiations," *Journal of Experimental Social Psychology* 49, no. 3 (2013): 453–63.

38. S.D. Pugh, M. Groth, and T. Hennig-Thurau, "Willing and Able to Fake Emotions: A Closer Examination of the Link between Emotional Dissonance and Employee Well-Being," *Journal of Applied Psychology* 96, no. 2 (2011): 377–90; R.S. Rubin et al., "A Reconceptualization of the Emotional Labor Construct: On the Development of an Integrated Theory of Perceived Emotional Dissonance and Emotional Labor," in *Emotions in Organizational Behavior*, ed. C. Hartel, N.M. Ashkanasy, and W. Zerbe (Hoboken, NJ: Taylor and Francis, 2012), 189–211.

39. Zapf, "Emotion Work and Psychological Well-Being"; J.D. Kammeyer-Mueller et al., "A Meta-Analytic Structural Model of Dispositonal Affectivity and Emotional Labor," *Personnel Psychology* 66, no. 1 (2013): 47–90; H. Ozcelik, "An Empirical Analysis of Surface Acting in Intra-Organizational Relationships," *Journal of Organizational Behavior* 34, no. 3 (2013): 291–309. Deep acting is considered an adaptation of method acting used by professional actors.

40. L. Peterson, "USF Seeking Medical Students Nicer Than 'House,'" *Tampa Tribune*, June 20, 2011; A.D.H. Monroe and A. English, "Fostering Emotional Intelligence in Medical Training: The SELECT Program," *Virtual Mentor* 15, no. 6 (2013): 509–13.

41. This model is very similar to Goleman's revised emotional intelligence model. See D. Goleman, R. Boyatzis, and A. McKee,

Primal Leadership (Boston: Harvard Business School Press, 2002), Chap. 3. Recent studies indicate that this model (when framed as abilities) provides the best fit to data. See R.P. Tett and K.E. Fox, "Confirmatory Factor Structure of Trait Emotional Intelligence in Student and Worker Samples," *Personality and Individual Differences* 41 (2006): 1155–68; P.J. Jordan and S.A. Lawrence, "Emotional Intelligence in Teams: Development and Initial Validation of the Short Version of the Workgroup Emotional Intelligence Profile (WEIP-S)," *Journal of Management & Organization* 15 (2009): 452–69; D.L. Joseph and D.A. Newman, "Emotional Intelligence: An Integrative Meta-Analysis and Cascading Model," *Journal of Applied Psychology* 95, no. 1 (2010): 54–78.

42. H.A. Elfenbein and N. Ambady, "Predicting Workplace Outcomes from the Ability to Eavesdrop on Feelings," *Journal of Applied Psychology* 87, no. 5 (2002): 963–71.

43. "Seventy-One Percent of Employers Say They Value Emotional Intelligence over IQ, according to CareerBuilder Survey," news release for CareerBuilder (Chicago: August 18, 2011); "Nine in Ten (91%) Managers and Supervisors Agree It's Important to Improve Their Emotional Intelligence in the Workplace," news release for Ipsos Reid (Toronto: October 18, 2012); "Crossing the Gap: From Science to Practice," sixseconds, June 10, 2013, www.6seconds.org/2013/06/10/emotional-intelligence-change-3/ (accessed May 14, 2014).

44. The hierarchical nature of the four EI dimensions is discussed by Goleman, but it is more explicit in the Salovey and Mayer model. See D.R. Caruso and P. Salovey, *The Emotionally Intelligent Manager* (San Francisco: Jossey-Bass, 2004). This hierarchy is also identified (without the self-other distinction) as a sequence in Joseph and Newman, "Emotional Intelligence."

45. E.A. Locke, "Why Emotional Intelligence Is an Invalid Concept," *Journal of Organizational Behavior* 26 (2005): 425–31; J. Antonakis, "'Emotional Intelligence': What Does It Measure and Does It Matter for Leadership?," in *LMX Leadership—Game-Changing Designs: Research-Based Tools*, ed. G.B. Graen (Greenwich, CT: Information Age, 2009), 163–92; J. Antonakis, N.M. Ashkanasy, and M.T. Dasborough, "Does Leadership Need Emotional Intelligence?," *Leadership Quarterly* 20 (2009): 247–61; M. Fiori and J. Antonakis, "The Ability Model of Emotional Intelligence: Searching for Valid Measures," *Personality and Individual Differences* 50, no. 3 (2011): 329–34.

46. D.L. Reis et al., "Emotional Intelligence Predicts Individual Differences in Social Exchange Reasoning," *NeuroImage* 35, no. 3 (2007): 1385–91; C. Cherniss, "Emotional Intelligence: Toward Clarification of a Concept," *Industrial and Organizational Psychology* 3, no. 2 (2010): 110–26; F. Walter, M.S. Cole, and R.H. Humphrey, "Emotional Intelligence: Sine Qua Non of Leadership or Folderol?," *Academy of Management Perspectives* 25, no. 1 (2011): 45–59.

47. Some studies have reported situations where EI has a limited effect on individual performance. For example, see A.L. Day and S.A. Carroll, "Using an Ability-Based Measure of Emotional Intelligence to Predict Individual Performance, Group Performance, and Group Citizenship Behaviors," *Personality and Individual Differences* 36 (2004): 1443–58; Z. Ivcevic, M.A. Brackett, and J.D. Mayer, "Emotional Intelligence and Emotional Creativity," *Journal of Personality* 75, no. 2 (2007): 199–236;

J.C. Rode et al., "Emotional Intelligence and Individual Performance: Evidence of Direct and Moderated Effects," *Journal of Organizational Behavior* 28, no. 4 (2007): 399–421.

48. R. Bar-On, *Preliminary Report: A New US Air Force Study Explores the Cost-Effectiveness of Applying the Bar-On EQ-i*, eiconsortium, August 2010; W. Gordon, "Climbing High for EI," *T+D* 64, no. 8 (2010): 72–73; "Randolph's Occupational Analysts Influence Air Force Decision Makers," *US Fed News*, November 3, 2010.

49. H.A. Elfenbein, "Learning in Emotion Judgments: Training and the Cross-Cultural Understanding of Facial Expressions," *Journal of Nonverbal Behavior* 30, no. 1 (2006): 21–36; D. Nelis et al., "Increasing Emotional Intelligence: (How) Is It Possible?," *Personality and Individual Differences* 47, no. 1 (2009): 36–41; L.J.M. Zijlmans et al., "Training Emotional Intelligence Related to Treatment Skills of Staff Working with Clients with Intellectual Disabilities and Challenging Behaviour," *Journal of Intellectual Disability Research* 55, no. 2 (2011): 219–30; D. Blanch-Hartigan, "An Effective Training to Increase Accurate Recognition of Patient Emotion Cues," *Patient Education and Counseling* 89, no. 2 (2012): 274–80; J. Shaw, S. Porter, and L. ten Brinke, "Catching Liars: Training Mental Health and Legal Professionals to Detect High-Stakes Lies," *Journal of Forensic Psychiatry & Psychology* 24, no. 2 (2013): 145–59.

50. D.A. Harrison, D.A. Newman, and P.L. Roth, "How Important Are Job Attitudes? Meta-Analytic Comparisons of Integrative Behavioral Outcomes and Time Sequences," *Academy of Management Journal* 49, no. 2 (2006): 305–25. Another recent study concluded that job satisfaction and organizational commitment are so highly correlated that they represent the same construct. See H. Le et al., "The Problem of Empirical Redundancy of Constructs in Organizational Research: An Empirical Investigation," *Organizational Behavior and Human Decision Processes* 112, no. 2 (2010): 112–25. They are also considered the two central work-related variables in the broader concept of happiness at work. See C.D. Fisher, "Happiness at Work," *International Journal of Management Reviews* 12, no. 4 (2010): 384–412.

51. E.A. Locke, "The Nature and Causes of Job Satisfaction," in *Handbook of Industrial and Organizational Psychology*, ed. M. Dunnette (Chicago: Rand McNally, 1976), 1297–350; H.M. Weiss, "Deconstructing Job Satisfaction: Separating Evaluations, Beliefs and Affective Experiences," *Human Resource Management Review*, no. 12 (2002): 173–94. Some definitions still include emotion as an element of job satisfaction, whereas the definition presented in this book views emotion as a cause of job satisfaction. Also, this definition views job satisfaction as a "collection of attitudes," not several "facets" of job satisfaction.

52. Ipsos-Reid, "Ipsos-Reid Global Poll Finds Major Differences in Employee Satisfaction around the World," in *Ipsos-Reid* news release (Toronto, 2001); International Survey Research, *Employee Satisfaction in the World's 10 Largest Economies: Globalization or Diversity?*, International Survey Research (Chicago: 2002); Watson Wyatt Worldwide, "Malaysian Workers More Satisfied with Their Jobs Than Their Companies' Leadership and Supervision Practices" (Kuala Lumpur: Watson Wyatt Worldwide, 2004); Kelly Global Workforce Index, *American Workers Are Happy with Their Jobs and Their Bosses* (Troy, MI: Kelly Services, November 2006).

53. Randstad, *Skills Shortage*, Randstad Holding nv (Amsterdam: August 2013). Survey data were collected from a minimum of 400 interviews per country of adults working 24 hours or more per week. Respondents were asked: "How satisfied are you in general working for your current employer?"

54. L. Saad, *Job Security Slips in U.S. Worker Satisfaction Rankings*, Gallup, Inc. (Princeton, NJ: August 27, 2009); *Employee Engagement Report 2011*, BlessingWhite (Princeton, NJ: 2011). A recent Kelly Services Workforce Index survey reported that 66 percent of the 170,000 respondents in 30 countries plan to look for a job with another organization within the next year. See Kelly Services, *Acquisition and Retention in the War for Talent*, Kelly Global Workforce Index (Troy, MI: Kelly Services, April 2012).

55. The problems with measuring attitudes and values across cultures is discussed in L. Saari and T.A. Judge, "Employee Attitudes and Job Satisfaction" *Human Resource Management* 43, no. 4 (2004): 395–407; A.K. Uskul et al., "How Successful You Have Been in Life Depends on the Response Scale Used: The Role of Cultural Mindsets in Pragmatic Inferences Drawn from Question Format," *Social Cognition* 31, no. 2 (2013): 222–36.

56. For a review of the various job satisfaction outcome theories, see Dalal, "Job Attitudes: Cognition and Affect."

57. M.J. Withey and W.H. Cooper, "Predicting Exit, Voice, Loyalty, and Neglect," *Administrative Science Quarterly* 34, no. 4 (1989): 521–39; W.H. Turnley and D.C. Feldman, "The Impact of Psychological Contract Violations on Exit, Voice, Loyalty, and Neglect," *Human Relations* 52, no. 7 (1999): 895–922. Subdimensions of silence and voice also exist. See L. van Dyne, S. Ang, and I.C. Botero, "Conceptualizing Employee Silence and Employee Voice as Multidimensional Constructs," *Journal of Management Studies* 40, no. 6 (2003): 1359–92.

58. T.R. Mitchell, B.C. Holtom, and T.W. Lee, "How to Keep Your Best Employees: Developing an Effective Retention Policy," *Academy of Management Executive* 15 (2001): 96–108; C.P. Maertz and M.A. Campion, "Profiles of Quitting: Integrating Process and Content Turnover Theory," *Academy of Management Journal* 47, no. 4 (2004): 566–82; K. Morrell, J. Loan-Clarke, and A. Wilkinson, "The Role of Shocks in Employee Turnover," *British Journal of Management* 15 (2004): 335–49; B.C. Holtom, T.R. Mitchell, and T.W. Lee, "Increasing Human and Social Capital by Applying Job Embeddedness Theory," *Organizational Dynamics* 35, no. 4 (2006): 316–31.

59. B.S. Klaas, J.B. Olson-Buchanan, and A.-K. Ward, "The Determinants of Alternative Forms of Workplace Voice: An Integrative Perspective," *Journal of Management* 38, no. 1 (2012): 314–45. For a critique and explanation for historical errors in the EVLN model's development, see S.L. McShane, "Reconstructing the Meaning and Dimensionality of Voice in the Exit–Voice–Loyalty–Neglect Model," paper presented at the Voice and Loyalty Symposium, Annual Conference of the Administrative Sciences Association of Canada, Organizational Behaviour Division, Halifax, 2008.

60. A.O. Hirschman, *Exit, Voice, and Loyalty: Responses to Decline in Firms, Organizations, and States* (Cambridge, MA: Harvard University Press, 1970); E.A. Hoffmann, "Exit and Voice: Organizational Loyalty and Dispute Resolution Strategies," *Social Forces* 84, no. 4 (2006): 2313–30.

61. J.D. Hibbard, N. Kumar, and L.W. Stern, "Examining the Impact of Destructive Acts in Marketing Channel Relationships," *Journal of Marketing Research* 38 (2001): 45–61; J. Zhou and J.M. George, "When Job Dissatisfaction Leads to Creativity: Encouraging the Expression of Voice," *Academy of Management Journal* 44 (2001): 682–96.

62. M.J. Withey and I.R. Gellatly, "Situational and Dispositional Determinants of Exit, Voice, Loyalty and Neglect," *Proceedings of the Administrative Sciences Association of Canada, Organizational Behaviour Division*, 1998; D.C. Thomas and K. Au, "The Effect of Cultural Differences on Behavioral Responses to Low Job Satisfaction," *Journal of International Business Studies* 33, no. 2 (2002): 309–26; S.F. Premeaux and A.G. Bedeian, "Breaking the Silence: The Moderating Effects of Self-Monitoring in Predicting Speaking Up in the Workplace," *Journal of Management Studies* 40, no. 6 (2003): 1537–62; D.J. Travis, R.J. Gomez, and M.E. Mor Barak, "Speaking Up and Stepping Back: Examining the Link between Employee Voice and Job Neglect," *Children and Youth Services Review* 33, no. 10 (2011): 1831–41.

63. V. Venkataramani and S. Tangirala, "When and Why Do Central Employees Speak Up? An Examination of Mediating and Moderating Variables," *Journal of Applied Psychology* 95, no. 3 (2010): 582–91.

64. T.A. Judge et al., "The Job Satisfaction-Job Performance Relationship: A Qualitative and Quantitative Review," *Psychological Bulletin* 127, no. 3 (2001): 376–407; C.D. Fisher, "Why Do Lay People Believe That Satisfaction and Performance Are Correlated? Possible Sources of a Commonsense Theory," *Journal of Organizational Behavior* 24, no. 6 (2003): 753–77; Saari and Judge, "Employee Attitudes and Job Satisfaction." Other studies report stronger correlations with job performance when both the belief and feeling components of job satisfaction are consistent with each other and when overall job attitude (satisfaction and commitment combined) is being measured. See D.J. Schleicher, J.D. Watt, and G.J. Greguras, "Reexamining the Job Satisfaction-Performance Relationship: The Complexity of Attitudes," *Journal of Applied Psychology* 89, no. 1 (2004): 165–77; Harrison, Newman, and Roth, "How Important Are Job Attitudes?" The positive relationship between job satisfaction and employee performance is also consistent with emerging research on the outcomes of positive organizational behavior. For example, see J.R. Sunil, "Enhancing Employee Performance through Positive Organizational Behavior," *Journal of Applied Social Psychology* 38, no. 6 (2008): 1580–600.

65. However, panel studies suggest that satisfaction has a stronger effect on performance than the other way around. For a summary, see Fisher, "Happiness at Work."

66. "The Greatest Briton in Management and Leadership," *Personnel Today* (March 2003): 20.

67. V. Naidu, "HCL Tech: Leaders of Indian Companies Are amongst the Sharpest, Smartest in the World," *Times of India* (Mumbai, India), April 25, 2013; E. Sapong, "Wegmans Ranked among Best Places to Work for 16th Straight Year," *Buffalo News*, January 16, 2013; L. Wirthman, "Container Store Moves Ahead with Superb Communications among Employees," *Denver Post*, April 21, 2013.

68. J.I. Heskett, W.E. Sasser, and L.A. Schlesinger, *The Service Profit Chain* (New York: Free Press, 1997); S.P. Brown and

S.K. Lam, "A Meta-Analysis of Relationships Linking Employee Satisfaction to Customer Responses," *Journal of Retailing* 84, no. 3 (2008): 243–55; T.J. Gerpott and M. Paukert, "The Relationship between Employee Satisfaction and Customer Satisfaction: A Meta-Analysis (Der Zusammenhang Zwischen Mitarbeiter-Und Kundenzufriedenheit: Eine Metaanalyse)," *Zeitschrift für Personalforschung* 25, no. 1 (2011): 28–54; R.W.Y. Yee, A.C.L. Yeung, and T.C.E. Cheng, "The Service-Profit Chain: An Empirical Analysis in High-Contact Service Industries," *International Journal of Production Economics* 130, no. 2 (2011): 236–45; H. Evanschitzky, F.V. Wangenheim, and N.V. Wünderlich, "Perils of Managing the Service Profit Chain: The Role of Time Lags and Feedback Loops," *Journal of Retailing* 88, no. 3 (2012): 356–66; Y. Hong et al., "Missing Link in the Service Profit Chain: A Meta-Analytic Review of the Antecedents, Consequences, and Moderators of Service Climate," *Journal of Applied Psychology* 98, no. 2 (2013): 237–67.

69. W.-C. Tsai and Y.-M. Huang, "Mechanisms Linking Employee Affective Delivery and Customer Behavioral Intentions," *Journal of Applied Psychology* 87, no. 5 (2002): 1001–08; P. Guenzi and O. Pelloni, "The Impact of Interpersonal Relationships on Customer Satisfaction and Loyalty to the Service Provider," *International Journal of Service Industry Management* 15, no. 3/4 (2004): 365–84; S.J. Bell, S. Auh, and K. Smalley, "Customer Relationship Dynamics: Service Quality and Customer Loyalty in the Context of Varying Levels of Customer Expertise and Switching Costs," *Journal of the Academy of Marketing Science* 33, no. 2 (2005): 169–83; P.B. Barger and A.A. Grandey, "Service with a Smile and Encounter Satisfaction: Emotional Contagion and Appraisal Mechanisms," *Academy of Management Journal* 49, no. 6 (2006): 1229–38. On the reciprocal effect, see E. Kim and D.J. Yoon, "Why Does Service with a Smile Make Employees Happy? A Social Interaction Model," *Journal of Applied Psychology* 97, no. 5 (2012): 1059–67.

70. R.T. Mowday, L.W. Porter, and R.M. Steers, *Employee Organization Linkages: The Psychology of Commitment, Absenteeism, and Turnover* (New York: Academic Press, 1982); J.P. Meyer, "Organizational Commitment," *International Review of Industrial and Organizational Psychology* 12 (1997): 175–228. The definition and dimensions of organizational commitment continue to be debated. Some writers even propose that "affective commitment" refers only to one's psychological attachment to and involvement in the organization, whereas "identification" with the organization is a distinct concept further along a continuum of bonds. See O.N. Solinger, W. van Olffen, and R.A. Roe, "Beyond the Three-Component Model of Organizational Commitment," *Journal of Applied Psychology* 93, no. 1 (2008): 70–83; H.J. Klein, J.C. Molloy, and C.T. Brinsfield, "Reconceptualizing Workplace Commitment to Redress a Stretched Construct: Revisiting Assumptions and Removing Confounds," *Academy of Management Review* 37, no. 1 (2012): 130–51.

71. M. Taing et al., "The Multidimensional Nature of Continuance Commitment: Commitment Owing to Economic Exchanges versus Lack of Employment Alternatives," *Journal of Business and Psychology* 26, no. 3 (2011): 269–84; C. Vandenberghe and A. Panaccio, "Perceived Sacrifice and Few Alternatives Commitments: The Motivational Underpinnings of Continuance Commitment's Subdimensions," *Journal of Vocational Behavior* 81, no. 1 (2012): 59–72.

72. Data provided in several country-specific news releases from Kelly Services. For a white paper summary of the survey, see Kelly Services, *Employee Loyalty Rises during Global Economic Recession, Kelly International Workforce Survey Finds*, Kelly Services (Troy, MI: March 8, 2010).

73. J.P. Meyer et al., "Affective, Continuance, and Normative Commitment to the Organization: A Meta-Analysis of Antecedents, Correlates, and Consequences," *Journal of Vocational Behavior* 61 (2002): 20–52; M. Riketta, "Attitudinal Organizational Commitment and Job Performance: A Meta-Analysis," *Journal of Organizational Behavior* 23 (2002): 257–66; J.P. Meyer and E.R. Maltin, "Employee Commitment and Well-Being: A Critical Review, Theoretical Framework and Research Agenda," *Journal of Vocational Behavior* 77, no. 2 (2010): 323–37.

74. J.P. Meyer et al., "Organizational Commitment and Job Performance: It's the Nature of the Commitment That Counts," *Journal of Applied Psychology* 74 (1989): 152–56; A.A. Luchak and I.R. Gellatly, "What Kind of Commitment Does a Final-Earnings Pension Plan Elicit?," *Relations Industrielles* 56 (2001): 394–417; Z.X. Chen and A.M. Francesco, "The Relationship between the Three Components of Commitment and Employee Performance in China," *Journal of Vocational Behavior* 62, no. 3 (2003): 490–510; H. Gill et al., "Affective and Continuance Commitment and Their Relations with Deviant Workplace Behaviors in Korea," *Asia Pacific Journal of Management* 28, no. 3 (2011): 595–607. The negative effect on performance might depend on the type of continuance commitment. See Taing et al., "The Multidimensional Nature of Continuance Commitment."

75. J.E. Finegan, "The Impact of Person and Organizational Values on Organizational Commitment," *Journal of Occupational and Organizational Psychology* 73 (2000): 149–69; A. Panaccio and C. Vandenberghe, "Perceived Organizational Support, Organizational Commitment and Psychological Well-Being: A Longitudinal Study," *Journal of Vocational Behavior* 75, no. 2 (2009): 224–36.

76. A.L. Kristof-Brown, R.D. Zimmerman, and E.C. Johnson, "Consequences of Individuals' Fit at Work: A Meta-Analysis of Person-Job, Person-Organization, Person-Group, and Person-Supervisor Fit," *Personnel Psychology* 58, no. 2 (2005): 281–342; J.R. Edwards, "Chapter 4: Person-Environment Fit in Organizations: An Assessment of Theoretical Progress," *The Academy of Management Annals* 2 (2008): 167–230; M.E. Bergman et al., "An Event-Based Perspective on the Development of Commitment," *Human Resource Management Review* 23, no. 2 (2013): 148–60.

77. D.M. Rousseau et al., "Not So Different after All: A Cross-Discipline View of Trust," *Academy of Management Review* 23 (1998): 393–404.

78. D.K. Datta et al., "Causes and Effects of Employee Downsizing: A Review and Synthesis," *Journal of Management* 36, no. 1 (2010): 281–348.

79. Similar concepts on information acquisition are found in socialization and organizational change research. See, for example, P. Bordia et al., "Uncertainty during Organizational Change: Types, Consequences, and Management Strategies," *Journal of Business and Psychology* 18, no. 4 (2004): 507–32; H.D. Cooper-Thomas and N. Anderson, "Organizational Socialization: A Field Study into Socialization Success and Rate," *International Journal*

of Selection and Assessment 13, no. 2 (2005): 116–28; T.N. Bauer, "Newcomer Adjustment during Organizational Socialization: A Meta-Analytic Review of Antecedents, Outcomes, and Methods," *Journal of Applied Psychology* 92, no. 3 (2007): 707–21.

80. T.S. Heffner and J.R. Rentsch, "Organizational Commitment and Social Interaction: A Multiple Constituencies Approach," *Journal of Vocational Behavior* 59 (2001): 471–90.

81. J.L. Pierce, T. Kostova, and K.T. Dirks, "Toward a Theory of Psychological Ownership in Organizations," *Academy of Management Review* 26, no. 2 (2001): 298–310; M. Mayhew et al., "A Study of the Antecedents and Consequences of Psychological Ownership in Organizational Settings," *The Journal of Social Psychology* 147, no. 5 (2007): 477–500; T.-S. Han, H.-H. Chiang, and A. Chang, "Employee Participation in Decision Making, Psychological Ownership and Knowledge Sharing: Mediating Role of Organizational Commitment in Taiwanese High-Tech Organizations," *The International Journal of Human Resource Management* 21, no. 12 (2010): 2218–33.

82. J.C. Quick et al., *Preventive Stress Management in Organizations* (Washington, DC: American Psychological Association, 1997), 3–4; R.S. DeFrank and J.M. Ivancevich, "Stress on the Job: An Executive Update," *Academy of Management Executive* 12 (1998): 55–66; A.L. Dougall and A. Baum, "Stress, Coping, and Immune Function," in *Handbook of Psychology*, ed. M. Gallagher and R.J. Nelson (Hoboken, NJ: Wiley, 2003), 441–55. There are at least three schools of thought regarding the meaning of stress, and some reviews of the stress literature describe these schools without pointing to any one as the preferred definition. One reviewer concluded that the stress concept is so broad that it should be considered an umbrella concept, capturing a broad array of phenomena and providing a simple term for the public to use. See T.A. Day, "Defining Stress as a Prelude to Mapping Its Neurocircuitry: No Help from Allostasis," *Progress in Neuro-Psychopharmacology and Biological Psychiatry* 29, no. 8 (2005): 1195–200; R. Cropanzano and A. Li, "Organizational Politics and Workplace Stress," in *Handbook of Organizational Politics*, ed. E. Vigoda-Gadot and A. Drory (Cheltenham, UK: Edward Elgar, 2006), 139–60; R.L. Woolfolk, P.M. Lehrer, and L.A. Allen, "Conceptual Issues Underlying Stress Management," in *Principles and Practice of Stress Management*, ed. P.M. Lehrer, R.L. Woolfolk, and W.E. Sime (New York: Guilford Press, 2007), 3–15.

83. Finegan, "The Impact of Person and Organizational Values on Organizational Commitment"; Dougall and Baum, "Stress, Coping, and Immune Function"; R.S. Lazarus, *Stress and Emotion: A New Synthesis* (New York: Springer, 2006); L.W. Hunter and S.M.B. Thatcher, "Feeling the Heat: Effects of Stress, Commitment, and Job Experience on Job Performance," *Academy of Management Journal* 50, no. 4 (2007): 953–68.

84. T.D. Shanafelt et al., "Burnout and Satisfaction with Work-Life Balance among US Physicians Relative to the General US Population," *Archives of Internal Medicine* 172, no. 18 (2012): 1377–85; "National Survey Reveals 90 Per Cent of Young Canadians Are Stressed Out in Today's Economy," news release for Sun Life Financial (Toronto, November 5, 2012); "Low Pay, Commute Top Reasons 80% of Americans Stressed at Work," news release for Corinthian Colleges (Los Angeles: Globe Newswire, April 9, 2014); "Dangerously Stressful Work Environments Force Workers to Seek New Employment," news release for Monster Worldwide (Weston, MA: April 16, 2014).

85. Quick et al., *Preventive Stress Management in Organizations*, 5–6; B.L. Simmons and D.L. Nelson, "Eustress at Work: The Relationship between Hope and Health in Hospital Nurses," *Health Care Management Review* 26, no. 4 (2001): 7ff.

86. H. Selye, "A Syndrome Produced by Diverse Nocuous Agents," *Nature* 138, no. 1 (1936): 32; H. Selye, *Stress without Distress* (Philadelphia: J. B. Lippincott, 1974). For the history of the word *stress*, see R.M.K. Keil, "Coping and Stress: A Conceptual Analysis," *Journal of Advanced Nursing* 45, no. 6 (2004): 659–65.

87. S.E. Taylor, R.L. Repetti, and T. Seeman, "Health Psychology: What Is an Unhealthy Environment and How Does It Get under the Skin?," *Annual Review of Psychology* 48 (1997): 411–47.

88. D. Ganster, M. Fox, and D. Dwyer, "Explaining Employees' Health Care Costs: A Prospective Examination of Stressful Job Demands, Personal Control, and Physiological Reactivity," *Journal of Applied Psychology* 86 (2001): 954–64; M. Kivimaki et al., "Work Stress and Risk of Cardiovascular Mortality: Prospective Cohort Study of Industrial Employees," *British Medical Journal* 325 (2002): 857–60; A. Rosengren et al., "Association of Psychosocial Risk Factors with Risk of Acute Myocardial Infarction in 11119 Cases and 13648 Controls from 52 Countries (the Interheart Study): Case-Control Study," *The Lancet* 364, no. 9438 (2004): 953–62; S. Andrew and S. Ayers, "Stress, Health, and Illness," in *The Sage Handbook of Health Psychology*, ed. S. Sutton, A. Baum, and M. Johnston (London: Sage, 2004), 169–96.

89. R.C. Kessler, "The Effects of Stressful Life Events on Depression," *Annual Review of Psychology* 48 (1997): 191–214; M.S. Hershcovis et al., "Predicting Workplace Aggression: A Meta-Analysis," *Journal of Applied Psychology* 92, no. 1 (2007): 228–38.

90. C. Maslach, W.B. Schaufeli, and M.P. Leiter, "Job Burnout," *Annual Review of Psychology* 52 (2001): 397–422; J.R.B. Halbesleben and M.R. Buckley, "Burnout in Organizational Life," *Journal of Management* 30, no. 6 (2004): 859–79; G.M. Alarcon, "A Meta-Analysis of Burnout with Job Demands, Resources, and Attitudes," *Journal of Vocational Behavior* 79, no. 2 (2011): 549–62.

91. K. Danna and R.W. Griffin, "Health and Well-Being in the Workplace: A Review and Synthesis of the Literature," *Journal of Management* 25, no. 3 (1999): 357–84.

92. This is a slight variation of the definition in the Quebec antiharassment legislation. See www.cnt.gouv.qc.ca/en/in-case-of/psychological-harassment-at-work/index.html. For related definitions and discussion of workplace incivility, see H. Cowiea et al., "Measuring Workplace Bullying," *Aggression and Violent Behavior* 7 (2002): 33–51; C.M. Pearson and C.L. Porath, "On the Nature, Consequences and Remedies of Workplace Incivility: No Time for 'Nice'? Think Again," *Academy of Management Executive* 19, no. 1 (2005): 7–18. For recent discussion of workplace harassment legislation in the United States, see D.C. Yamada, "Workplace Bullying and American Employment Law: A Ten-Year Progress Report and Assessment," *Comparative Labor Law and Policy Journal* 32, no. 1 (2010): 251–84.

93. "Monster Global Poll Reveals Workplace Bullying Is Endemic" (London: OnRec, 2011), www.onrec.com (accessed June 26, 2012).

94. P. McDonald, "Workplace Sexual Harassment 30 Years On: A Review of the Literature," *International Journal of Management Reviews* 14, no. 1 (2012): 1–17.

95. "Let's Slow Down!," *The Royal Bank of Canada Monthly Letter*, September 1949.

96. L. Xu, "A Hard Day's Night," *China Daily*, July 12, 2012, 20; Y. Yuan, "White Collars Overworked," *Beijing Review*, June 20, 2013.

97. R. Drago, D. Black, and M. Wooden, *The Persistence of Long Work Hours*, Melbourne Institute Working Paper Series, Melbourne Institute of Applied Economic and Social Research, University of Melbourne (Melbourne: August 2005); L. Golden, "A Brief History of Long Work Time and the Contemporary Sources of Overwork," *Journal of Business Ethics* 84, no. S2 (2009): 217–27.

98. R. Karasek and T. Theorell, *Healthy Work: Stress, Productivity, and the Reconstruction of Working Life* (New York: Basic Books, 1990); N. Turner, N. Chmiel, and M. Walls, "Railing for Safety: Job Demands, Job Control, and Safety Citizenship Role Definition," *Journal of Occupational Health Psychology* 10, no. 4 (2005): 504–12.

99. Lazarus, *Stress and Emotion: A New Synthesis*, Chap. 5.

100. M. Zuckerman and M. Gagne, "The COPE Revised: Proposing a 5-Factor Model of Coping Strategies," *Journal of Research in Personality* 37 (2003): 169–204; S. Folkman and J.T. Moskowitz, "Coping: Pitfalls and Promise," *Annual Review of Psychology* 55 (2004): 745–74; C.A. Thompson et al., "On the Importance of Coping: A Model and New Directions for Research on Work and Family," *Research in Occupational Stress and Well-Being* 6 (2007): 73–113.

101. S.E. Taylor et al., "Psychological Resources, Positive Illusions, and Health," *American Psychologist* 55, no. 1 (2000): 99–109; F. Luthans and C.M. Youssef, "Emerging Positive Organizational Behavior," *Journal of Management* 33, no. 3 (2007): 321–49; P. Steel, J. Schmidt, and J. Shultz, "Refining the Relationship between Personality and Subjective Well-Being," *Psychological Bulletin* 134, no. 1 (2008): 138–61; G. Alarcon, K.J. Eschleman, and N.A. Bowling, "Relationships between Personality Variables and Burnout: A Meta-Analysis," *Work & Stress* 23, no. 3 (2009): 244–63; R. Kotov et al., "Linking "Big" Personality Traits to Anxiety, Depressive, and Substance Use Disorders: A Meta-Analysis," *Psychological Bulletin* 136, no. 5 (2010): 768–821.

102. G.A. Bonanno, "Loss, Trauma, and Human Resilience: Have We Underestimated the Human Capacity to Thrive after Extremely Aversive Events?," *American Psychologist* 59, no. 1 (2004): 20–28; F. Luthans, C.M. Youssef, and B.J. Avolio, *Psychological Capital: Developing the Human Competitive Edge* (New York: Oxford University Press, 2007).

103. M. Siegall and L.L. Cummings, "Stress and Organizational Role Conflict," *Genetic, Social, and General Psychology Monographs* 12 (1995): 65–95.

104. From 2013/2014 Staying@Work Survey Report, Towers Watson/National Business Group on Health, p. 19. http://www.slideshare.net/TowersWatson/towers-watsonstayingatworkreport2014unitedstates Reprinted with permission of Towers Watson.

105. L.T. Eby et al., "Work and Family Research in IO/OB: Content Analysis and Review of the Literature (1980–2002)," *Journal of Vocational Behavior* 66, no. 1 (2005): 124–97.

106. N. Davidson, "Vancouver Developer Looks to Make Video Games without Burning Out Staff," *Canadian Press*, February 21, 2006; F. Jossi, "Clocking Out," *HRMagazine*, June 2007, 46–50; American Psychological Association, "San Jorge Children's Hospital: A Culture of Collaboration and Care," news release for A.P. Association (Washington, DC: 2011).

107. S.R. Madsen, "The Effects of Home-Based Teleworking on Work-Family Conflict," *Human Resource Development Quarterly* 14, no. 1 (2003): 35–58; S. Raghuram and B. Wiesenfeld, "Work-Nonwork Conflict and Job Stress among Virtual Workers," *Human Resource Management* 43, no. 2/3 (2004): 259–77.

108. Organization for Economic Co-operation and Development, *Babies and Bosses: Reconciling Work and Family Life*, vol. 4 (Canada, Finland, Sweden and the United Kingdom) (Paris: OECD Publishing, 2005); J. Heymann et al., *The Work, Family, and Equity Index: How Does the United States Measure Up?*, Project on Global Working Families, Institute for Health and Social Policy (Montreal: June 2007).

109. M. Secret, "Parenting in the Workplace: Child Care Options for Consideration," *Journal of Applied Behavioral Science* 41, no. 3 (2005): 326–47.

110. A.E. Carr and T.L.-P. Tang, "Sabbaticals and Employee Motivation: Benefits, Concerns, and Implications," *Journal of Education for Business* 80, no. 3 (2005): 160–64; S. Overman, "Sabbaticals Benefit Companies as Well as Employees," *Employee Benefit News*, April 15, 2006; O.B. Davidson et al., "Sabbatical Leave: Who Gains and How Much?," *Journal of Applied Psychology* 95, no. 5 (2010): 953–64. For discussion of psychological detachment and stress management, see C. Fritz et al., "Happy, Healthy, and Productive: The Role of Detachment from Work during Nonwork Time," *Journal of Applied Psychology* 95, no. 5 (2010): 977–83.

111. M.H. Abel, "Humor, Stress, and Coping Strategies," *Humor: International Journal of Humor Research* 15, no. 4 (2002): 365–81; N.A. Kuiper et al., "Humor Is Not Always the Best Medicine: Specific Components of Sense of Humor and Psychological Well-Being," *Humor: International Journal of Humor Research* 17, no. 1/2 (2004): 135–68; E.J. Romero and K.W. Cruthirds, "The Use of Humor in the Workplace," *Academy of Management Perspectives* 20, no. 2 (2006): 58–69; M. McCreaddie and S. Wiggins, "The Purpose and Function of Humor in Health, Health Care and Nursing: A Narrative Review," *Journal of Advanced Nursing* 61, no. 6 (2008): 584–95.

112. W.M. Ensel and N. Lin, "Physical Fitness and the Stress Process," *Journal of Community Psychology* 32, no. 1 (2004): 81–101.

113. S. Armour, "Rising Job Stress Could Affect Bottom Line," *USA Today*, July 29, 2003; V.A. Barnes, F.A. Treiber, and M.H. Johnson, "Impact of Transcendental Meditation on Ambulatory Blood Pressure in African-American Adolescents," *American Journal of Hypertension* 17, no. 4 (2004): 366–69; P. Manikonda et al., "Influence of Non-Pharmacological Treatment (Contemplative Meditation and Breathing Technique) on Stress Induced Hypertension—a Randomized Controlled Study," *American Journal of Hypertension* 18, no. 5, Supplement 1 (2005): A89–A90.

114. C. Viswesvaran, J.I. Sanchez, and J. Fisher, "The Role of Social Support in the Process of Work Stress: A Meta-Analysis," *Journal of Vocational Behavior* 54, no. 2 (1999): 314–34; S.E. Taylor et al., "Biobehavioral Responses to Stress in

Females: Tend-and-Befriend, Not Fight-or-Flight," *Psychological Review* 107, no. 3 (2000): 411–29; R. Eisler and D.S. Levine, "Nurture, Nature, and Caring: We Are Not Prisoners of Our Genes," *Brain and Mind* 3 (2002): 9–52; T.A. Beehr, N.A. Bowling, and M.M. Bennett, "Occupational Stress and Failures of Social Support: When Helping Hurts," *Journal of Occupational Health Psychology* 15, no. 1 (2010): 45–59; B.A. Scott et al., "A Daily Investigation of the Role of Manager Empathy on Employee Well-Being," *Organizational Behavior and Human Decision Processes* 113, no. 2 (2010): 127–40.

Chapter 5

1. "Investing in People and Business Pays Off for Frucor," *Scoop .co.nz*, June 5, 2013; "Frucor Beverages: A Top Employer with Continued Growth," *Six Degrees Executive—Our Thoughts*, July 29, 2013, www.sixdegreesexecutive.com.au/blogs/our-thoughts/frucor-beverages/.

2. C.C. Pinder, *Work Motivation in Organizational Behavior* (Upper Saddle River, NJ: Prentice Hall, 1998); R.M. Steers, R.T. Mowday, and D.L. Shapiro, "The Future of Work Motivation Theory," *Academy of Management Review* 29 (2004): 379–87.

3. W.H. Macey and B. Schneider, "The Meaning of Employee Engagement," *Industrial and Organizational Psychology* 1 (2008): 3–30; A.B. Bakker and W.B. Schaufeli, "Positive Organizational Behavior: Engaged Employees in Flourishing Organizations," *Journal of Organizational Behavior* 29, no. 2 (2008): 147–54.

4. J. Engen, "Are Your Employees Truly Engaged?," *Chief Executive*, March 2008, 42; S. Flander, "Terms of Engagement," *Human Resource Executive Online*, January 2008; D. Macleod and N. Clarke, *Engaging for Success: Enhancing Performance through Employee Engagement* (London: UK Government. Department for Business Innovation and Skills, July 2009).

5. K. Allen, "The Art of Engagement" (Bonn, Germany: Deutsche Post DHL, August 12, 2013), www.dpdhl.com/en/logistics_around_us/from_our_divisions/ken_allen_the_art_of_engagement. html (accessed August 21, 2013); "Rewards to Spur on Latent Talent," *Cape Argus* (South Africa), February 13, 2013, E1; "DHL Africa Puts Employee Recognition at the Centre of Its Business," press release by *African Press Organization*, June 19, 2013.

6. Gallup Consulting, *The Gallup Q12—Employee Engagement-Poll 2008 Results*, Gallup Consulting (February 2009); A. Fox, "Raising Engagement," *HRMagazine*, May 2010, 34; Blessing-White, *Employee Engagement Report 2011*, BlessingWhite (Princeton, NJ: January 2011).

7. *State of the American Workplace: Employee Engagement Insights for U.S. Business Leaders*, Gallup (Washington, DC: June 13, 2013).

8. Several sources attempt to identify and organize the drivers of employee engagement. See, for example, D. Robinson, S. Perryman, and S. Hayday, *The Drivers of Employee Engagement*, Institute for Employment Studies (Brighton, UK: 2004); W.H. Macey et al., *Employee Engagement: Tools for Analysis, Practice, and Competitive Advantage* (Malden, MA: Wiley-Blackwell, 2009); Macleod and Clarke, *Engaging for Success: Enhancing Performance through Employee Engagement*; M. Stairs and M. Galpin, "Positive Engagement: From Employee Engagement to Workplace Happiness," in *Oxford Handbook of Positive Psychology of Work*, ed. P.A. Linley, S. Harrington, and N. Garcea (New York: Oxford University Press, 2010), 155–72.

9. The confusing array of definitions about drives and needs has been the subject of criticism for a half century. See, for example, R.S. Peters, "Motives and Motivation," *Philosophy* 31 (1956): 117–30; H. Cantril, "Sentio, Ergo Sum: 'Motivation' Reconsidered," *Journal of Psychology* 65, no. 1 (1967): 91–107; G.R. Salancik and J. Pfeffer, "An Examination of Need-Satisfaction Models of Job Attitudes," *Administrative Science Quarterly* 22, no. 3 (1977): 427–56.

10. D.W. Pfaff, *Drive: Neurobiological and Molecular Mechanisms of Sexual Motivation* (Cambridge, MA: MIT Press, 1999); A. Blasi, "Emotions and Moral Motivation," *Journal for the Theory of Social Behaviour* 29, no. 1 (1999): 1–19; T.V. Sewards and M.A. Sewards, "Fear and Power-Dominance Drive Motivation: Neural Representations and Pathways Mediating Sensory and Mnemonic Inputs, and Outputs to Premotor Structures," *Neuroscience and Biobehavioral Reviews* 26 (2002): 553–79; K.C. Berridge, "Motivation Concepts in Behavioral Neuroscience," *Physiology & Behavior* 81, no. 2 (2004): 179–209. We distinguish drives from emotions, but future research may find that the two concepts are not so different as is stated here. Woodworth is credited with either coining or popularizing the term "drives" in the context of human motivation. His classic book is certainly the first source to discuss the concept in detail. See R.S. Woodworth, *Dynamic Psychology* (New York: Columbia University Press, 1918).

11. G. Loewenstein, "The Psychology of Curiosity: A Review and Reinterpretation," *Psychological Bulletin* 116, no. 1 (1994): 75–98; A.E. Kelley, "Neurochemical Networks Encoding Emotion and Motivation: An Evolutionary Perspective," in *Who Needs Emotions? The Brain Meets the Robot*, ed. J.M. Fellous and M.A. Arbib (New York: Oxford University Press, 2005), 29–78; M.R. Leary, "Motivational and Emotional Aspects of the Self," *Annual Review of Psychology* 58, no. 1 (2007): 317–44; L.A. Leotti, S.S. Iyengar, and K.N. Ochsner, "Born to Choose: The Origins and Value of the Need for Control," *Trends in Cognitive Sciences* 14, no. 10 (2010): 457–63.

12. K. Passyn and M. Sujan, "Self-Accountability Emotions and Fear Appeals: Motivating Behavior," *Journal of Consumer Research* 32, no. 4 (2006): 583–89; S.G. Barsade and D.E. Gibson, "Why Does Affect Matter in Organizations?," *Academy of Management Perspectives* 21, no. 2 (2007): 36–59.

13. A.R. Damasio, *The Feeling of What Happens: Body and Emotion in the Making of Consciousness* (New York: Harcourt Brace, 1999), 286.

14. S. Hitlin, "Values as the Core of Personal Identity: Drawing Links between Two Theories of Self," *Social Psychology Quarterly* 66, no. 2 (2003): 118–37; B. Monin, D.A. Pizarro, and J.S. Beer, "Deciding versus Reacting: Conceptions of Moral Judgment and the Reason-Affect Debate," *Review of General Psychology* 11, no. 2 (2007): 99–111; D.D. Knoch and E.E. Fehr, "Resisting the Power of Temptations. The Right Prefrontal Cortex and Self-Control," *Annals of the New York Academy of Sciences* 1104, no. 1 (2007): 123.

15. A.H. Maslow, "A Theory of Human Motivation," *Psychological Review* 50 (1943): 370–96; A.H. Maslow, *Motivation and Personality* (New York: Harper & Row, 1954).

16. D.T. Hall and K.E. Nougaim, "An Examination of Maslow's Need Hierarchy in an Organizational Setting," *Organizational Behavior and Human Performance* 3, no. 1 (1968): 12; M.A. Wahba and

L.G. Bridwell, "Maslow Reconsidered: A Review of Research on the Need Hierarchy Theory," *Organizational Behavior and Human Performance* 15 (1976): 212–40; E.L. Betz, "Two Tests of Maslow's Theory of Need Fulfillment," *Journal of Vocational Behavior* 24, no. 2 (1984): 204–20; P.A. Corning, "Biological Adaptation in Human Societies: A 'Basic Needs' Approach," *Journal of Bioeconomics* 2, no. 1 (2000): 41–86. For a recent proposed revision of the model, see D.T. Kenrick et al., "Renovating the Pyramid of Needs: Contemporary Extensions Built upon Ancient Foundations," *Perspectives on Psychological Science* 5, no. 3 (2010): 292–314.

17. L. Parks and R.P. Guay, "Personality, Values, and Motivation," *Personality and Individual Differences* 47, no. 7 (2009): 675–84.

18. B.A. Agle and C.B. Caldwell, "Understanding Research on Values in Business," *Business and Society* 38 (1999): 326–87; B. Verplanken and R.W. Holland, "Motivated Decision Making: Effects of Activation and Self-Centrality of Values on Choices and Behavior," *Journal of Personality and Social Psychology* 82, no. 3 (2002): 434–47; S. Hitlin and J.A. Pilavin, "Values: Reviving a Dormant Concept," *Annual Review of Sociology* 30 (2004): 359–93.

19. K. Dye, A.J. Mills, and T.G. Weatherbee, "Maslow: Man Interrupted—Reading Management Theory in Context," *Management Decision* 43, no. 10 (2005): 1375–95.

20. A.H. Maslow, "A Preface to Motivation Theory," *Psychosomatic Medicine* 5 (1943): 85–92.

21. S. Kesebir, J. Graham, and S. Oishi, "A Theory of Human Needs Should Be Human-Centered, Not Animal-Centered," *Perspectives on Psychological Science* 5, no. 3 (2010): 315–19.

22. A.H. Maslow, *Maslow on Management* (New York: Wiley, 1998).

23. F.F. Luthans, "Positive Organizational Behavior: Developing and Managing Psychological Strengths," *Academy of Management Executive* 16, no. 1 (2002): 57–72; S.L. Gable and J. Haidt, "What (and Why) Is Positive Psychology?," *Review of General Psychology* 9, no. 2 (2005): 103–10; M.E.P. Seligman et al., "Positive Psychology Progress: Empirical Validation of Interventions," *American Psychologist* 60, no. 5 (2005): 410–21.

24. Society of Petroleum Engineers, "SPE Survey Rates Employee Satisfaction," *Talent & Technology* 2007; Kelly Services, *Acquisition and Retention in the War for Talent*, Kelly Global Workforce Index, Kelly Services (Troy, MI: April 2012); InStep, "HR Professionals Cite Improvement in Employee Performance," news release for InStep (Cheshire, UK: April 4, 2012); Accenture, *Great Expectations: Insights from the Accenture 2014 College Graduate Employment Survey*, Accenture (New York: May 6, 2014).

25. D.C. McClelland, *The Achieving Society* (New York: Van Nostrand Reinhold, 1961); D.C. McClelland and D.H. Burnham, "Power Is the Great Motivator," *Harvard Business Review* 73 (1995): 126–39; D. Vredenburgh and Y. Brender, "The Hierarchical Abuse of Power in Work Organizations," *Journal of Business Ethics* 17 (1998): 1337–47; S. Shane, E.A. Locke, and C.J. Collins, "Entrepreneurial Motivation," *Human Resource Management Review* 13, no. 2 (2003): 257–79.

26. F.D. Roosevelt, "First Inaugural Address, Washington, D.C., March 4, 1933," in *Franklin Delano Roosevelt: Great Speeches*, ed. J. Grafton (Mineola, NY: Dover, 1999), 28–31.

27. McClelland, *The Achieving Society*.

28. Shane et al., "Entrepreneurial Motivation."

29. McClelland and Burnham, "Power Is the Great Motivator"; J.L. Thomas, M.W. Dickson, and P.D. Bliese, "Values Predicting Leader Performance in the U.S. Army Reserve Officer Training Corps Assessment Center: Evidence for a Personality-Mediated Model," *The Leadership Quarterly* 12, no, 2 (2001): 181–96.

30. Vredenburgh and Brender, "The Hierarchical Abuse of Power in Work Organizations."

31. D. Miron and D.C. McClelland, "The Impact of Achievement Motivation Training on Small Business," *California Management Review* 21 (1979): 13–28.

32. P.R. Lawrence and N. Nohria, *Driven: How Human Nature Shapes Our Choices* (San Francisco: Jossey-Bass, 2002); N. Nohria, B. Groysberg, and L.E. Lee, "Employee Motivation: A Powerful New Model," *Harvard Business Review* (2008): 78–84. On the application of four-drive theory to leadership, see P.R. Lawrence, *Driven to Lead* (San Francisco: Jossey-Bass, 2010).

33. The drive to acquire is likely associated with research on getting ahead, desire for competence, the selfish gene, and desire for social distinction. See R.H. Frank, *Choosing the Right Pond: Human Behavior and the Quest for Status* (New York: Oxford University Press, 1985); L. Gaertner et al., "The 'I,' the 'We,' and the 'When': A Meta-Analysis of Motivational Primacy in Self-Definition," *Journal of Personality and Social Psychology* 83, no. 3 (2002): 574–91; J. Hogan and B. Holland, "Using Theory to Evaluate Personality and Job-Performance Relations: A Socioanalytic Perspective," *Journal of Applied Psychology* 88, no. 1 (2003): 100–12; R. Dawkins, *The Selfish Gene*, 30th Anniversary Ed. (Oxford, UK: Oxford University Press, 2006); Leary, "Motivational and Emotional Aspects of the Self"; B.S. Frey, "Awards as Compensation," *European Management Journal* 4 (2007): 6–14.

34. R.E. Baumeister and M.R. Leary, "The Need to Belong: Desire for Interpersonal Attachments as a Fundamental Human Motivation," *Psychological Bulletin* 117 (1995): 497–529.

35. J. Litman, "Curiosity and the Pleasures of Learning: Wanting and Liking New Information," *Cognition and Emotion* 19, no. 6 (2005): 793–814; T.G. Reio Jr. et al., "The Measurement and Conceptualization of Curiosity," *Journal of Genetic Psychology* 167, no. 2 (2006): 117–35.

36. W.H. Bexton, W. Heron, and T.H. Scott, "Effects of Decreased Variation in the Sensory Environment," *Canadian Journal of Psychology* 8 (1954): 70–76; Loewenstein, "The Psychology of Curiosity."

37. A.R. Damasio, *Descartes' Error: Emotion, Reason, and the Human Brain* (New York: Putnam Sons, 1994); A. Bechara et al., "Deciding Advantageously before Knowing the Advantageous Strategy," *Science* 275, no. 5304 (1997): 1293–95; J.E. LeDoux, "Emotion Circuits in the Brain," *Annual Review of Neuroscience* 23 (2000): 155–84; P. Winkielman and K.C. Berridge, "Unconscious Emotion," *Current Directions in Psychological Science* 13, no. 3 (2004): 120–23; M. Reimann and A. Bechara, "The Somatic Marker Framework as a Neurological Theory of Decision-Making: Review, Conceptual Comparisons, and Future Neuroeconomics Research," *Journal of Economic Psychology* 31, no. 5 (2010): 767–76.

38. Lawrence and Nohria, *Driven*, 145–47; R.F. Baumeister, E.J. Masicampo, and K.D. Vohs, "Do Conscious Thoughts Cause Behavior?," *Annual Review of Psychology* 62, no. 1 (2011): 331–61.

39. S.H. Schwartz, B.A. Hammer, and M. Wach, "Les Valeurs De Base De La Personne: Théorie, Mesures Et Applications [Basic Human Values: Theory, Measurement, and Applications]," *Revue française de sociologie* 47, no. 4 (2006): 929–68.

40. Lawrence and Nohria, *Driven*, Chap. 11.

41. Expectancy theory of motivation in work settings originated in V.H. Vroom, *Work and Motivation* (New York: Wiley, 1964). The version of expectancy theory presented here was developed by Edward Lawler. Lawler's model provides a clearer presentation of the model's three components. P-to-O expectancy is similar to "instrumentality" in Vroom's original expectancy theory model. The difference is that instrumentality is a correlation whereas P-to-O expectancy is a probability. See J.P. Campbell et al., *Managerial Behavior, Performance, and Effectiveness* (New York: McGraw-Hill, 1970); E.E. Lawler III, *Motivation in Work Organizations* (Monterey, CA: Brooks-Cole, 1973); D.A. Nadler and E.E. Lawler, "Motivation: A Diagnostic Approach," in *Perspectives on Behavior in Organizations*, ed. J.R. Hackman, E.E. Lawler III, and L.W. Porter (New York: McGraw-Hill, 1983), 67–78.

42. M. Zeelenberg et al., "Emotional Reactions to the Outcomes of Decisions: The Role of Counterfactual Thought in the Experience of Regret and Disappointment," *Organizational Behavior and Human Decision Processes* 75, no. 2 (1998): 117–41; B.A. Mellers, "Choice and the Relative Pleasure of Consequences," *Psychological Bulletin* 126, no. 6 (2000): 910–24; R.P. Bagozzi, U.M. Dholakia, and S. Basuroy, "How Effortful Decisions Get Enacted: The Motivating Role of Decision Processes, Desires, and Anticipated Emotions," *Journal of Behavioral Decision Making* 16, no. 4 (2003): 273–95. The neuropsychology of valences and its associated "expected utility" is discussed in A. Bechara and A.R. Damasio, "The Somatic Marker Hypothesis: A Neural Theory of Economic Decision," *Games and Economic Behavior* 52, no. 2 (2005): 336–72.

43. Nadler and Lawler, "Motivation: A Diagnostic Approach," 70–73.

44. A. Fisher, "Expecting a Fat Year-End Bonus? Don't Get Your Hopes Up," *Fortune*, December 5, 2012; J.M. Jones, *Talent Town Hall: A Presentation to OESA*, Towers Watson (New York: October 25, 2012); "Infographic #2: 2013 Talent Management and Rewards Study—North America" (New York: Towers Watson, August 7, 2013), www.towerswatson.com (accessed May 18, 2014); United States Office of Personnel Management, *Federal Employee Viewpoint Survey Results*, Office of Personnel Management (Washington, DC: November 12, 2013).

45. B. Moses, "Time to Get Serious about Rewarding Employees," *Globe & Mail*, April 28, 2010, B16.

46. T. Matsui and T. Terai, "A Cross-Cultural Study of the Validity of the Expectancy Theory of Motivation," *Journal of Applied Psychology* 60 (1975): 263–65; D.H.B. Welsh, F. Luthans, and S.M. Sommer, "Managing Russian Factory Workers: The Impact of U.S.-Based Behavioral and Participative Techniques," *Academy of Management Journal* 36 (1993): 58–79.

47. This limitation was recently acknowledged by Victor Vroom, who had introduced expectancy theory in his 1964 book.

See G.P. Latham, *Work Motivation: History, Theory, Research, and Practice* (Thousand Oaks, CA: Sage, 2007), 47–48.

48. J.B. Watson, *Behavior: An Introduction to Comparative Psychology* (New York: Henry Holt, 1914).

49. B.F. Skinner, *About Behaviorism* (New York: Knopf, 1974); J. Komaki, T. Coombs, and S. Schepman, "Motivational Implications of Reinforcement Theory," in *Motivation and Leadership at Work*, ed. R.M. Steers, L.W. Porter, and G.A. Bigley (New York: McGraw-Hill, 1996), 34–52; R.G. Miltenberger, *Behavior Modification: Principles and Procedures* (Pacific Grove, CA: Brooks/Cole, 1997).

50. T.K. Connellan, *How to Improve Human Performance* (New York: Harper & Row, 1978), 48–57; F. Luthans and R. Kreitner, *Organizational Behavior Modification and Beyond* (Glenview, IL: Scott, Foresman, 1985), 85–88.

51. B.F. Skinner, *Science and Human Behavior* (New York: Free Press, 1965); Miltenberger, *Behavior Modification: Principles and Procedures*, Chap. 4–6.

52. T.R. Hinkin and C.A. Schriesheim, "'If You Don't Hear from Me You Know You Are Doing Fine,'" *Cornell Hotel & Restaurant Administration Quarterly* 45, no. 4 (2004): 362–72.

53. L.K. Trevino, "The Social Effects of Punishment in Organizations: A Justice Perspective," *Academy of Management Review* 17 (1992): 647–76; L.E. Atwater et al., "Recipient and Observer Reactions to Discipline: Are Managers Experiencing Wishful Thinking?," *Journal of Organizational Behavior* 22, no. 3 (2001): 249–70.

54. G.P. Latham and V.L. Huber, "Schedules of Reinforcement: Lessons from the Past and Issues for the Future," *Journal of Organizational Behavior Management* 13 (1992): 125–49; B.A. Williams, "Challenges to Timing-Based Theories of Operant Behavior," *Behavioural Processes* 62 (2003): 115–23.

55. L. Brousell, "Gamification Boosts Class Participation," *CIO*, February 5, 2013; J.C. Meister, "How Deloitte Made Learning a Game," *HBR Blog Network*, January 2, 2013, http://blogs.hbr.org/cs/2013/01/how_deloitte_made_learning_a_g.html; Z. Bodnar, "Using Game Mechanics to Enhance Leadership Education," *eLearn Magazine*, February 2014.

56. A. Bandura, *Social Foundations of Thought and Action: A Social Cognitive Theory* (Englewood Cliffs, NJ: Prentice Hall, 1986); A. Bandura, "Social Cognitive Theory of Self-Regulation," *Organizational Behavior and Human Decision Processes* 50, no. 2 (1991): 248–87; A. Bandura, "Social Cognitive Theory: An Agentic Perspective," *Annual Review of Psychology* 52, no. 1 (2001): 1–26.

57. M.E. Schnake, "Vicarious Punishment in a Work Setting," *Journal of Applied Psychology* 71 (1986): 343–45; Trevino, "The Social Effects of Punishment in Organizations: A Justice Perspective"; J. Malouff et al., "Effects of Vicarious Punishment: A Meta-Analysis," *Journal of General Psychology* 136, no. 3 (2009): 271–86.

58. A. Pescuric and W.C. Byham, "The New Look of Behavior Modeling," *Training & Development* 50 (1996): 24–30.

59. A. Bandura, "Self-Reinforcement: Theoretical and Methodological Considerations," *Behaviorism* 4 (1976): 135–55; C.A. Frayne and J.M. Geringer, "Self-Management Training for Improving Job Performance: A Field Experiment Involving Salespeople,"

Journal of Applied Psychology 85, no. 3 (2000): 361–72; J.B. Vancouver and D.V. Day, "Industrial and Organisation Research on Self-Regulation: From Constructs to Applications," *Applied Psychology: An International Journal* 54, no. 2 (2005): 155–85.

60. *Case Study Government: CalPERS*, VHT (Akron, OH: August 25, 2012).

61. E.A. Locke and G.P. Latham, *A Theory of Goal Setting and Task Performance* (Englewood Cliffs, NJ: Prentice Hall, 1990); G.P. Latham, "Goal Setting: A Five-Step Approach to Behavior Change," *Organizational Dynamics* 32, no. 3 (2003): 309–18.

62. There are several variations of the SMARTER goal-setting model; "achievable" is sometimes "acceptable," "reviewed" is sometimes "recorded," and "exciting" is sometimes "ethical." Based on the earlier SMART model, the SMARTER goal-setting model seems to originate in British sports psychology writing around the mid-1990s. For early examples, see P. Butler, *Performance Profiling* (Leeds, UK: The National Coaching Foundation, 1996), 36; R.C. Thelwell and I.A. Greenlees, "The Effects of a Mental Skills Training Program Package on Gymnasium Triathlon Performance," *The Sports Psychologist* 15, no. 2 (2001): 127–41.

63. S.P. Brown, S. Ganesan, and G. Challagalla, "Self-Efficacy as a Moderator of Information-Seeking Effectiveness," *Journal of Applied Psychology* 86, no. 5 (2001): 1043–51; D. Van-Dijk and A.N. Kluger, "Feedback Sign Effect on Motivation: Is It Moderated by Regulatory Focus?," *Applied Psychology: An International Review* 53, no. 1 (2004): 113–35; P.A. Heslin and G.P. Latham, "The Effect of Upward Feedback on Managerial Behaviour," *Applied Psychology: An International Review* 53, no. 1 (2004): 23–37; J.E. Bono and A.E. Colbert, "Understanding Responses to Multi-Source Feedback: The Role of Core Self-Evaluations," *Personnel Psychology* 58, no. 1 (2005): 171–203.

64. P. Drucker, *The Effective Executive* (Oxford, UK: Butterworth-Heinemann, 2007), 22. Drucker's emphasis on strengths was also noted in D.K. Whitney and A. Trosten-Bloom, *The Power of Appreciative Inquiry: A Practical Guide to Positive Change*, 2nd ed. (San Francisco: Berrett-Koehler, 2010), xii.

65. M. Buckingham, *Go Put Your Strengths to Work* (New York: Free Press, 2007); S.L. Orem, J. Binkert, and A.L. Clancy, *Appreciative Coaching: A Positive Process for Change* (San Francisco: Jossey-Bass, 2007); S. Gordon, "Appreciative Inquiry Coaching," *International Coaching Psychology Review* 3, no. 2 (2008): 19–31.

66. H. Aguinis, R.K. Gottfredson, and H. Joo, "Delivering Effective Performance Feedback: The Strengths-Based Approach," *Business Horizons* 55, no. 2 (2012): 105–11.

67. A. Terracciano, P.T. Costa, and R.R. McCrae, "Personality Plasticity after Age 30," *Personality and Social Psychology Bulletin* 32, no. 8 (2006): 999–1009; Leary, "Motivational and Emotional Aspects of the Self."

68. A.N. Kluger and D. Nir, "The Feedforward Interview," *Human Resource Management Review* 20, no. 3 (2010): 235–46; Aguinis et al., "Delivering Effective Performance Feedback: The Strengths-Based Approach."

69. F.P. Morgeson, T.V. Mumford, and M.A. Campion, "Coming Full Circle: Using Research and Practice to Address 27 Questions about 360-Degree Feedback Programs," *Consulting Psychology Journal* 57, no. 3 (2005): 196–209; J.W. Smither, M. London,

and R.R. Reilly, "Does Performance Improve Following Multisource Feedback? A Theoretical Model, Meta-Analysis, and Review of Empirical Findings," *Personnel Psychology* 58, no. 1 (2005): 33–66; L.E. Atwater, J.F. Brett, and A.C. Charles, "Multisource Feedback: Lessons Learned and Implications for Practice," *Human Resource Management* 46, no. 2 (2007): 285–307.

70. S.J. Ashford and G.B. Northcraft, "Conveying More (or Less) Than We Realize: The Role of Impression Management in Feedback Seeking," *Organizational Behavior and Human Decision Processes* 53 (1992): 310–34; J.R. Williams et al., "Increasing Feedback Seeking in Public Contexts: It Takes Two (or More) to Tango," *Journal of Applied Psychology* 84 (1999): 969–76.

71. J.B. Miner, "The Rated Importance, Scientific Validity, and Practical Usefulness of Organizational Behavior Theories: A Quantitative Review," *Academy of Management Learning and Education* 2, no. 3 (2003): 250–68. Also see Pinder, *Work Motivation in Organizational Behavior*, 384.

72. P.M. Wright, "Goal Setting and Monetary Incentives: Motivational Tools That Can Work Too Well," *Compensation and Benefits Review* 26 (1994): 41–49; E.A. Locke and G.P. Latham, "Building a Practically Useful Theory of Goal Setting and Task Motivation: A 35-Year Odyssey," *American Psychologist* 57, no. 9 (2002): 705–17.

73. Latham, *Work Motivation*, 188.

74. J. Greenberg and E.A. Lind, "The Pursuit of Organizational Justice: From Conceptualization to Implication to Application," in *Industrial and Organizational Psychology: Linking Theory with Practice*, ed. C.L. Cooper and E.A. Locke (London: Blackwell, 2000), 72–108; D.T. Miller, "Disrespect and the Experience of Injustice," *Annual Review of Psychology* 52 (2001): 527–53; R. Cropanzano and M. Schminke, "Using Social Justice to Build Effective Work Groups," in *Groups at Work: Theory and Research*, ed. M.E. Turner (Mahwah, NJ: Erlbaum, 2001), 143–71.

75. J.S. Adams, "Toward an Understanding of Inequity," *Journal of Abnormal and Social Psychology* 67 (1963): 422–36; R.T. Mowday, "Equity Theory Predictions of Behavior in Organizations," in *Motivation and Work Behavior*, ed. L.W. Porter and R.M. Steers (New York: McGraw-Hill, 1991), 111–31; R.G. Cropanzano and J. Greenberg, "Progress in Organizational Justice: Tunneling through the Maze," in *International Review of Industrial and Organizational Psychology*, ed. C.L. Cooper and I.T. Robertson (New York: Wiley, 1997), 317–72; L.A. Powell, "Justice Judgments as Complex Psychocultural Constructions: An Equity-Based Heuristic for Mapping Two- and Three-Dimensional Fairness Representations in Perceptual Space," *Journal of Cross-Cultural Psychology* 36, no. 1 (2005): 48–73.

76. C.T. Kulik and M.L. Ambrose, "Personal and Situational Determinants of Referent Choice," *Academy of Management Review* 17 (1992): 212–37; G. Blau, "Testing the Effect of Level and Importance of Pay Referents on Pay Level Satisfaction," *Human Relations* 47 (1994): 1251–68.

77. T.P. Summers and A.S. DeNisi, "In Search of Adams' Other: Reexamination of Referents Used in the Evaluation of Pay," *Human Relations* 43 (1990): 497–511.

78. Y. Cohen-Charash and P.E. Spector, "The Role of Justice in Organizations: A Meta-Analysis," *Organizational Behavior and Human Decision Processes* 86 (2001): 278–321.

79. L. Saad, "More Workers OK with Their Pay in 2010," *Gallup Daily News*, August 19, 2010; Kelly Services, *Workplace Performance*, Kelly Global Workforce Index, Kelly Services (Troy, MI: June 26, 2013); Randstad Canada, *Women Shaping Business: Challenges and Opportunities in 2013*, Randstad Canada (Toronto: October 2013); "6 in 10 Singaporean Employees Claim They Are Overworked, Underpaid," *Singapore Business Review*, March 21, 2014; R. Fajardo, "36% of Working Respondents Believe They Are Overqualified for Their Current Positions," *Caribbean Business*, February 6, 2014.

80. Canadian Press, "Pierre Berton, Canadian Cultural Icon, Enjoyed Long and Colourful Career," *Times Colonist* (Victoria, BC), November 30, 2004.

81. J. Fizel, A.C. Krautman, and L. Hadley, "Equity and Arbitration in Major League Baseball," *Managerial and Decision Economics* 23, no. 7 (2002): 427–35; M. Ezzamel and R. Watson, "Pay Comparability across and within UK Boards: An Empirical Analysis of the Cash Pay Awards to CEOs and Other Board Members," *Journal of Management Studies* 39, no. 2 (2002): 207–32.

82. Greenberg and Lind, "The Pursuit of Organizational Justice"; K. Roberts and K.S. Markel, "Claiming in the Name of Fairness: Organizational Justice and the Decision to File for Workplace Injury Compensation," *Journal of Occupational Health Psychology* 6 (2001): 332–47; J.B. Olson-Buchanan and W.R. Boswell, "The Role of Employee Loyalty and Formality in Voicing Discontent," *Journal of Applied Psychology* 87, no. 6 (2002): 1167–74.

83. R. Hagey et al., "Immigrant Nurses' Experience of Racism," *Journal of Nursing Scholarship* 33 (2001): 389–95; Roberts and Markel, "Claiming in the Name of Fairness: Organizational Justice and the Decision to File for Workplace Injury Compensation"; D.A. Jones and D.P. Skarlicki, "The Effects of Overhearing Peers Discuss an Authority's Fairness Reputation on Reactions to Subsequent Treatment," *Journal of Applied Psychology* 90, no. 2 (2005): 363–72.

84. Miller, "Disrespect and the Experience of Injustice."

85. M.L. Ambrose, M.A. Seabright, and M. Schminke, "Sabotage in the Workplace: The Role of Organizational Injustice," *Organizational Behavior and Human Decision Processes* 89, no. 1 (2002): 947–65.

86. J.R. Edwards, J.A. Scully, and M.D. Brtek, "The Nature and Outcomes of Work: A Replication and Extension of Interdisciplinary Work-Design Research," *Journal of Applied Psychology* 85, no. 6 (2000): 860–68; F.P. Morgeson and M.A. Campion, "Minimizing Tradeoffs When Redesigning Work: Evidence from a Longitudinal Quasi-Experiment," *Personnel Psychology* 55, no. 3 (2002): 589–612.

87. A. Shinnar et al., "Survey of Ergonomic Features of Supermarket Cash Registers," *International Journal of Industrial Ergonomics* 34, no. 6 (2004): 535–41; V. O'Connell, "Stores Count Seconds to Trim Labor Costs," *The Wall Street Journal*, November 13, 2008; A. Kihlstedt and G.M. Hägg, "Checkout Cashier Work and Counter Design—Video Movement Analysis, Musculoskeletal Disorders and Customer Interaction," *International Journal of Industrial Ergonomics* 41, no. 3 (2011): 201–07; "One Checkout Item Every Three Seconds," *Mail Online* (London), July 8, 2012. Average scanning times vary considerably with the scanning technology, product standardization, and ergonomic design of the cashier station.

88. S. Leroy, "Why Is It So Hard to Do My Work? The Challenge of Attention Residue When Switching between Work Tasks," *Organizational Behavior and Human Decision Processes* 109, no. 2 (2009): 168–81.

89. H. Fayol, *General and Industrial Management*, trans. C. Storrs (London: Pitman, 1949); Lawler III, *Motivation in Work Organizations*, Chap. 7; M.A. Campion, "Ability Requirement Implications of Job Design: An Interdisciplinary Perspective," *Personnel Psychology* 42 (1989): 1–24.

90. A. Smith, *An Inquiry into the Nature and Causes of the Wealth of Nations*, ed. E. Cannan, 5th ed. (London: Methuen, 1904), 8–9.

91. F.W. Taylor, *The Principles of Scientific Management* (New York: Harper & Row, 1911); R. Kanigel, *The One Best Way: Frederick Winslow Taylor and the Enigma of Efficiency* (New York: Viking, 1997).

92. C.R. Walker and R.H. Guest, *The Man on the Assembly Line* (Cambridge, MA: Harvard University Press, 1952); W.F. Dowling, "Job Redesign on the Assembly Line: Farewell to Blue-Collar Blues?," *Organizational Dynamics* (1973): 51–67; E.E. Lawler III, *High-Involvement Management* (San Francisco: Jossey-Bass, 1986).

93. M. Keller, *Rude Awakening: The Rise, Fall, and Struggle for Recovery of General Motors* (New York: Harper Perennial, 1989), 128.

94. F. Herzberg, B. Mausner, and B.B. Snyderman, *The Motivation to Work* (New York: Wiley, 1959).

95. S.K. Parker, T.D. Wall, and J.L. Cordery, "Future Work Design Research and Practice: Toward an Elaborated Model of Work Design," *Journal of Occupational and Organizational Psychology* 74 (2001): 413–40. For a decisive critique of motivator-hygiene theory, see N. King, "Clarification and Evaluation of the Two Factor Theory of Job Satisfaction," *Psychological Bulletin* 74 (1970): 18–31.

96. J.R. Hackman and G. Oldham, *Work Redesign* (Reading, MA: Addison-Wesley, 1980).

97. M. Gagné and D. Bhave, "Autonomy in the Workplace: An Essential Ingredient to Employee Engagement and Well-Being in Every Culture," in *Human Autonomy in Cross-Cultural Context* (Cross-Cultural Advancements in Positive Psychology), ed. V.I. Chirkov, R.M. Ryan, and K.M. Sheldon (Dordrecht, Netherlands: Springer Netherlands, 2011), 163–87.

98. C.E. Shalley, L.L. Gilson, and T.C. Blum, "Interactive Effects of Growth Need Strength, Work Context, and Job Complexity on Self-Reported Creative Performance," *Academy of Management Journal* 52, no. 3 (2009): 489–505.

99. R.B. Tiegs, L.E. Tetrick, and Y. Fried, "Growth Need Strength and Context Satisfactions as Moderators of the Relations of the Job Characteristics Model," *Journal of Management* 18, no. 3 (1992): 575–93; J.E. Champoux, "A Multivariate Test of the Job Characteristics Theory of Work Motivation," *Journal of Organizational Behavior* 12, no. 5 (1991): 431–46.

100. C. Perrow, "A Framework for the Comparative Analysis of Organizations," *American Sociological Review* 32, no. 2 (1967): 194–208; R.L. Daft and N.B. Macintosh, "A Tentative Exploration into the Amount and Equivocality of Information Processing in Organizational Work Units," *Administrative Science Quarterly* 26, no. 2 (1981): 207–24. This job characteristics category is part of "job complexity," the latter of which has too

many dimensions and interpretations. See P. Liu and Z. Li, "Task Complexity: A Review and Conceptualization Framework," *International Journal of Industrial Ergonomics* 42, no. 6 (2012): 553–68.

101. J.R. Hackman et al., "A New Strategy for Job Enrichment," *California Management Review* 17, no. 4 (1975): 57–71; R.W. Griffin, *Task Design: An Integrative Approach* (Glenview, IL: Scott, Foresman, 1982).

102. P.E. Spector and S.M. Jex, "Relations of Job Characteristics from Multiple Data Sources with Employee Affect, Absence, Turnover Intentions, and Health," *Journal of Applied Psychology* 76 (1991): 46–53; P. Osterman, "How Common Is Workplace Transformation and Who Adopts It?," *Industrial and Labor Relations Review* 47 (1994): 173–88; R. Saavedra and S.K. Kwun, "Affective States in Job Characteristics Theory," *Journal of Organizational Behavior* 21 (2000): 131–46.

103. Hackman and Oldham, *Work Redesign*, 137–38.

Chapter 6

1. J. Reed, "High Stakes for Fiat's Sergio Marchionne," *Financial Times* (London), February 19, 2010; S. Marchionne, "Fiat's Extreme Makeover," *Harvard Business Review* (2008): 45–48; B. Wernie and L. Ciferri, "Life under Marchionne: New Stars, Hasty Exits," *Automotive News*, October 12, 2009, 1, 42; D. Welch, D. Kiley, and C. Matlack, "Tough Love at Chrysler," *BusinessWeek*, 24 August 2009; "Marchionne's Weekend Warriors," *Automotive News*, June 22, 2009; "Marchionne Faces Tough Challenge to Match Ghosn's Success," *Automotive News*, April 28, 2010; D. Kiley, "Imported from France," *Advertising Age*, February 21, 2011, 1; E. Mayne, "Chrysler-Fiat Merger under Consideration, Says CEO Marchionne," *Ward's Dealer Business*, March 2011, 12.

2. F.A. Shull Jr., A.L. Delbecq, and L.L. Cummings, *Organizational Decision Making* (New York: McGraw-Hill, 1970), 31.

3. S.R. Covey, *The Wisdom and Teachings of Stephen R. Covey* (New York: Free Press, 2012).

4. M.V. White, "Jevons in Australia: A Reassessment," *The Economic Record* 58 (1982): 32–45; R.E. Nisbett, *The Geography of Thought: How Asians and Westerners Think Differently—and Why* (New York: Free Press, 2003); R. Hanna, "Kant's Theory of Judgment" (Stanford Encyclopedia of Philosophy, 2004), http://plato.stanford.edu/entries/kant-judgment/(accessed March 31, 2008); D. Baltzly, "Stoicism" (Stanford Encyclopedia of Philosophy, 2008), http://plato.stanford.edu/entries/stoicism/ (accessed March 30, 2008).

5. J.G. March and H.A. Simon, *Organizations* (New York: Wiley, 1958); K. Manktelow, *Thinking and Reasoning: An Introduction to the Psychology of Reason, Judgment and Decision Making* (Hoboken, NJ: Taylor & Francis, 2012), Chap. 8.

6. This example differs from the game theory model in classic economic theory. In classic economic theory, the "outcomes" are alternatives, so the probabilities must add up to 1.0. For example, if there is a 30 percent probability that your company will choose supplier A, then there is necessarily a 70 percent chance that the company will choose supplier B (if those are the only choices). The current example, which is much more relevant to business decisions, differs because subjective expected utility calculates each alternative's composite valence from a set of criteria (outcomes) associated with all alternatives. These probabilities do not add up to 1.0 because they refer to entities that are not perfectly correlated (e.g., a supplier might have a high probability of offering quality products, reliable delivery, and low prices). The current application of subjective expected utility may be more consistent with the founding theories of utilitarianism.

7. These criteria are commonly used in supplier selection modeling. See, for example, H. Karimi and A. Rezaeinia, "Supplier Selection Using Revised Multi-Segment Goal Programming Model," *International Journal of Advanced Manufacturing Technology* 70, no. 5/8 (2014): 1227–34.

8. This model is adapted from several sources, including H.A. Simon, *The New Science of Management Decision* (New York: Harper & Row, 1960); H. Mintzberg, D. Raisinghani, and A. Théorét, "The Structure of 'Unstructured' Decision Processes," *Administrative Science Quarterly* 21 (1976): 246–75; W.C. Wedley and R.H.G. Field, "A Predecision Support System," *Academy of Management Review* 9 (1984): 696–703.

9. P.F. Drucker, *The Practice of Management* (New York: Harper & Brothers, 1954), 353–57; B.M. Bass, *Organizational Decision Making* (Homewood, IL: Irwin, 1983), Chap. 3.

10. L.R. Beach and T.R. Mitchell, "A Contingency Model for the Selection of Decision Strategies," *Academy of Management Review* 3 (1978): 439–49; I.L. Janis, *Crucial Decisions* (New York: Free Press, 1989), 35–37; W. Zhongtuo, "Meta-Decision Making: Concepts and Paradigm," *Systematic Practice and Action Research* 13, no. 1 (2000): 111–15.

11. J. de Jonge, *Rethinking Rational Choice Theory: A Companion on Rational and Moral Action* (Basingstoke, UK: Palgrave Macmillan, 2011).

12. A. Howard, "Opinion," *Computing* (1999): 18.

13. For a recent discussion on problem finding in organizations, see M.A. Roberto, *Know What You Don't Know: How Great Leaders Prevent Problems before They Happen* (Saddle River, NJ: Wharton School Publishing, 2009).

14. T.K. Das and B.S. Teng, "Cognitive Biases and Strategic Decision Processes: An Integrative Perspective," *Journal of Management Studies* 36, no. 6 (1999): 757–78; P. Bijttebier, H. Vertommen, and G.V. Steene, "Assessment of Cognitive Coping Styles: A Closer Look at Situation-Response Inventories," *Clinical Psychology Review* 21, no. 1 (2001): 85–104; P.C. Nutt, "Expanding the Search for Alternatives during Strategic Decision-Making," *Academy of Management Executive* 18, no. 4 (2004): 13–28.

15. P.C. Nutt, *Why Decisions Fail* (San Francisco: Berrett-Koehler, 2002); S. Finkelstein, *Why Smart Executives Fail* (New York: Viking, 2003).

16. A.H. Maslow, *The Psychology of Science: A Reconnaissance* (Chapel Hill, NC: Maurice Bassett, 2002).

17. E. Witte, "Field Research on Complex Decision-Making Processes—the Phase Theorum," *International Studies of Management and Organization*, no. 56 (1972): 156–82; J.A. Bargh and T.L. Chartrand, "The Unbearable Automaticity of Being," *American Psychologist* 54, no. 7 (1999): 462–79.

18. M. Hock and H.W. Krohne, "Coping with Threat and Memory for Ambiguous Information: Testing the Repressive Discontinuity Hypothesis," *Emotion* 4, no. 1 (2004): 65–86; J. Brandtstadter,

A. Voss, and K. Rothermund, "Perception of Danger Signals: The Role of Control," *Experimental Psychology* 51, no. 1 (2004): 24–32.

19. D. O'Brien, "The Fine Art of Googling," *Sunday Times* (London), July 20, 2000; K.J. Delaney and A. Grimes, "For Some Who Passed on Google Long Ago, Wistful Thinking," *The Wall Street Journal*, August 23, 2004, A1; "Google Wanted to Sell for $1 Million and Got Rejected," *Softpedia* (September 30, 2010), http://news.softpedia.com/news/Google-Wanted-to-Sell-for-1-Million-and-Got-Rejected-158828.shtml (accessed August 27, 2013).

20. R. Rothenberg, "Ram Charan: The Thought Leader Interview," *strategy + business*, Fall 2004.

21. H.A. Simon, *Administrative Behavior*, 2nd ed. (New York: Free Press, 1957); H.A. Simon, "Rational Decision Making in Business Organizations," *American Economic Review* 69, no. 4 (1979): 493–513.

22. Simon, *Administrative Behavior*, xxv, 80–84.

23. S. Sacchi and M. Burigo, "Strategies in the Information Search Process: Interaction among Task Structure, Knowledge, and Source," *Journal of General Psychology* 135, no. 3 (2008): 252–70.

24. P.O. Soelberg, "Unprogrammed Decision Making," *Industrial Management Review* 8 (1967): 19–29; J.E. Russo, V.H. Medvec, and M.G. Meloy, "The Distortion of Information during Decisions," *Organizational Behavior & Human Decision Processes* 66 (1996): 102–10; K.H. Ehrhart and J.C. Ziegert, "Why Are Individuals Attracted to Organizations?," *Journal of Management* 31, no. 6 (2005): 901–19. This is consistent with the observations by Milton Rokeach, who famously stated, "Life is ipsative, because decisions in everyday life are inherently and phenomenologically ipsative decisions." M. Rokeach, "Inducing Changes and Stability in Belief Systems and Personality Structures," *Journal of Social Issues* 41, no. 1 (1985): 153–71.

25. A.L. Brownstein, "Biased Predecision Processing," *Psychological Bulletin* 129, no. 4 (2003): 545–68.

26. T. Gilovich, D. Griffin, and D. Kahneman, *Heuristics and Biases: The Psychology of Intuitive Judgment* (Cambridge: Cambridge University Press, 2002); D. Kahneman, "Maps of Bounded Rationality: Psychology for Behavioral Economics," *American Economic Review* 93, no. 5 (2003): 1449–75; F.L. Smith et al., "Decision-Making Biases and Affective States: Their Potential Impact on Best Practice Innovations," *Canadian Journal of Administrative Sciences* 27, no. 4 (2010): 277–91.

27. A. Tversky and D. Kahneman, "Judgment under Uncertainty: Heuristics and Biases," *Science* 185, no. 4157 (1974): 1124–31; I. Ritov, "Anchoring in Simulated Competitive Market Negotiation," *Organizational Behavior and Human Decision Processes* 67, no. 1 (1996): 16; D. Ariely, G. Loewenstein, and A. Prelec, "'Coherent Arbitrariness': Stable Demand Curves without Stable Preferences," *Quarterly Journal of Economics* 118 (2003): 73; N. Epley and T. Gilovich, "Are Adjustments Insufficient?," *Personality and Social Psychology Bulletin* 30, no. 4 (2004): 447–60; J.D. Jasper and S.D. Christman, "A Neuropsychological Dimension for Anchoring Effects," *Journal of Behavioral Decision Making* 18 (2005): 343–69; S.D. Bond et al., "Information Distortion in the Evaluation of a Single Option," *Organizational Behavior & Human Decision Processes* 102 (2007): 240–54.

28. A. Tversky and D. Kahneman, "Availability: A Heuristic for Judging Frequency and Probability," *Cognitive Psychology* 5 (1973): 207–32.

29. D. Kahneman and A. Tversky, "Subjective Probability: A Judgment of Representativeness," *Cognitive Psychology* 3, no. 3 (1972): 430; T. Gilovich, *How We Know What Isn't So: The Fallibility of Human Reason in Everyday Life* (New York: Free Press, 1991); B.D. Burns, "Heuristics as Beliefs and as Behaviors: The Adaptiveness of the 'Hot Hand,'" *Cognitive Psychology* 48 (2004): 295–331; E.M. Altmann and B.D. Burns, "Streak Biases in Decision Making: Data and a Memory Model," *Cognitive Systems Research* 6, no. 1 (2005): 5–16.

30. H.A. Simon, "Rational Choice and the Structure of Environments," *Psychological Review* 63 (1956): 129–38.

31. S. Botti and S.S. Iyengar, "The Dark Side of Choice: When Choice Impairs Social Welfare," *Journal of Public Policy and Marketing* 25, no. 1 (2006): 24–38; K.D. Vohs et al., "Making Choices Impairs Subsequent Self-Control: A Limited-Resource Account of Decision Making, Self-Regulation, and Active Initiative," *Journal of Personality and Social Psychology* 94, no. 5 (2008): 883–98.

32. J. Choi, D. Laibson, and B. Madrian, *Reducing the Complexity Costs of 401(k) Participation through Quick Enrollment™*, National Bureau of Economic Research, Inc. (January 2006); J. Beshears et al., "Simplification and Saving" (SSRN, 2006); S. Iyengar, *The Art of Choosing* (New York: Hachette, 2010), 194–200.

33. P.C. Nutt, "Search during Decision Making," *European Journal of Operational Research* 160 (2005): 851–76.

34. P. Winkielman et al., "Affective Influence on Judgments and Decisions: Moving towards Core Mechanisms," *Review of General Psychology* 11, no. 2 (2007): 179–92.

35. A.R. Damasio, *Descartes' Error: Emotion, Reason, and the Human Brain* (New York: Putnam Sons, 1994); P. Winkielman and K.C. Berridge, "Unconscious Emotion," *Current Directions in Psychological Science* 13, no. 3 (2004): 120–23; A. Bechara and A.R. Damasio, "The Somatic Marker Hypothesis: A Neural Theory of Economic Decision," *Games and Economic Behavior* 52, no. 2 (2005): 336–72.

36. J.P. Forgas and J.M. George, "Affective Influences on Judgments and Behavior in Organizations: An Information Processing Perspective," *Organizational Behavior and Human Decision Processes* 86 (2001): 3–34; G. Loewenstein and J.S. Lerner, "The Role of Affect in Decision Making," in *Handbook of Affective Sciences*, ed. R.J. Davidson, K.R. Scherer, and H.H. Goldsmith (New York: Oxford University Press, 2003), 619–42; M.T. Pham, "Emotion and Rationality: A Critical Review and Interpretation of Empirical Evidence," *Review of General Psychology* 11, no. 2 (2007): 155–78; H.J.M. Kooij-de Bode, D. Van Knippenberg, and W.P. Van Ginkel, "Good Effects of Bad Feelings: Negative Affectivity and Group Decision-Making," *British Journal of Management* 21, no. 2 (2010): 375–92; J.P. Forgas and A.S. Koch, "Mood Effects on Cognition," in *Handbook of Cognition and Emotion*, ed. M.D. Robinson, E.R. Watkins, and E. Harmon-Jones (New York: Guilford, 2013), 231–51.

37. D. Miller, *The Icarus Paradox* (New York: HarperBusiness, 1990); D. Miller, "What Happens after Success: The Perils of Excellence," *Journal of Management Studies* 31, no. 3 (1994): 325–68;

A.C. Amason and A.C. Mooney, "The Icarus Paradox Revisited: How Strong Performance Sows the Seeds of Dysfunction in Future Strategic Decision-Making," *Strategic Organization* 6, no. 4 (2008): 407–34.

38. M.T. Pham, "The Logic of Feeling," *Journal of Consumer Psychology* 14 (2004): 360–69; N. Schwarz, "Feelings-as-Information Theory," in *Handbook of Theories of Social Psychology*, ed. P. Van Lange, A. Kruglanski, and E.T. Higgins (London: Sage, 2012), 289–308.

39. L. Sjöberg, "Intuitive vs. Analytical Decision Making: Which Is Preferred?," *Scandinavian Journal of Management* 19 (2003): 17–29.

40. W.H. Agor, "The Logic of Intuition," *Organizational Dynamics* (1986): 5–18; H.A. Simon, "Making Management Decisions: The Role of Intuition and Emotion," *Academy of Management Executive* (1987): 57–64; O. Behling and N.L. Eckel, "Making Sense out of Intuition," *Academy of Management Executive* 5 (1991): 46–54. This process is also known as naturalistic decision making. For a discussion of research on naturalistic decision making, see the special issue in *Organization Studies*: R. Lipshitz, G. Klein, and J.S. Carroll, "Introduction to the Special Issue: Naturalistic Decision Making and Organizational Decision Making: Exploring the Intersections," *Organization Studies* 27, no. 7 (2006): 917–23.

41. M.D. Lieberman, "Intuition: A Social Cognitive Neuroscience Approach," *Psychological Bulletin* 126 (2000): 109–37; G. Klein, *Intuition at Work* (New York: Currency/Doubleday, 2003); E. Dane and M.G. Pratt, "Exploring Intuition and Its Role in Managerial Decision Making," *Academy of Management Review* 32, no. 1 (2007): 33–54.

42. Klein, *Intuition at Work*, 12–13, 16–17.

43. Y. Ganzach, A.H. Kluger, and N. Klayman, "Making Decisions from an Interview: Expert Measurement and Mechanical Combination," *Personnel Psychology* 53 (2000): 1–20; A.M. Hayashi, "When to Trust Your Gut," *Harvard Business Review* 79 (2001): 59–65. Evidence of high failure rates from quick decisions is reported in Nutt, *Why Decisions Fail*; Nutt, "Search during Decision Making"; P.C. Nutt, "Investigating the Success of Decision Making Processes," *Journal of Management Studies* 45, no. 2 (2008): 425–55.

44. "Organizations Make Strides in Adoption of Analytics, but Struggle to Capitalize on Investments, Accenture Research Finds," news release for Accenture (New York: March 5, 2013); "Survey Finds Most SMEs Shun Professional Advice, Possibly at Their Peril," news release for W. Kluwer (Sydney: April 11, 2013); *The Recruitment Reality Check*, Monster UK and University College London (London: March 17, 2014); D. Kiron, K. Prentice, and R.B. Ferguson, *The Analytics Mandate*, MIT Sloan Management Review and SAS Institute (Cambridge, MA: May 12, 2014).

45. R. Bradfield et al., "The Origins and Evolution of Scenario Techniques in Long Range Business Planning," *Futures* 37, no. 8 (2005): 795–812; G. Wright, G. Cairns, and P. Goodwin, "Teaching Scenario Planning: Lessons from Practice in Academe and Business," *European Journal of Operational Research* 194, no. 1 (2009): 323–35; T.J. Chermack, *Scenario Planning in Organizations* (San Francisco: Berrett-Koehler, 2011).

46. J. Pfeffer and R.I. Sutton, "Knowing 'What' to Do Is Not Enough: Turning Knowledge into Action," *California Management Review* 42, no. 1 (1999): 83–108; R. Charan, C. Burke, and L. Bossidy, *Execution: The Discipline of Getting Things Done* (New York: Crown Business, 2002).

47. R.F. Bruner, "In Defense of Reorganizations," *The Washington Post*, May 13, 2013, A22.

48. R.S. Nickerson, "Confirmation Bias: A Ubiquitous Phenomenon in Many Guises," *Review of General Psychology* 2, no. 2 (1998): 175–220; O. Svenson, I. Salo, and T. Lindholm, "Post-Decision Consolidation and Distortion of Facts," *Judgment and Decision Making* 4, no. 5 (2009): 397–407.

49. B.M. Staw and J. Ross, "Behavior in Escalation Situations: Antecedents, Prototypes, and Solutions," in *Research in Organizational Behavior*, ed. L.L. Cummings and B.M. Staw (Greenwich, CT: JAI, 1987), 39–78; J. Brockner, "The Escalation of Commitment to a Failing Course of Action: Toward Theoretical Progress," *Academy of Management Review* 17, no. 1 (1992): 39–61; D.J. Sleesman et al., "Cleaning up the Big Muddy: A Meta-Analytic Review of the Determinants of Escalation of Commitment," *Academy of Management Journal* 55, no. 3 (2012): 541–62.

50. F.D. Schoorman and P.J. Holahan, "Psychological Antecedents of Escalation Behavior: Effects of Choice, Responsibility, and Decision Consequences," *Journal of Applied Psychology* 81 (1996): 786–93; N. Sivanathan et al., "The Promise and Peril of Self-Affirmation in De-Escalation of Commitment," *Organizational Behavior and Human Decision Processes* 107, no. 1 (2008): 1–14.

51. N.J. Roese and J.M. Olson, "Better, Stronger, Faster: Self-Serving Judgment, Affect Regulation, and the Optimal Vigilance Hypothesis," *Perspectives on Psychological Science* 2, no. 2 (2007): 124–41; C.L. Guenther and M.D. Alicke, "Deconstructing the Better-Than-Average Effect," *Journal of Personality and Social Psychology* 99, no. 5 (2010): 755–70; S. Loughnan et al., "Universal Biases in Self-Perception: Better and More Human Than Average," *British Journal of Social Psychology* 49 (2010): 627–36.

52. M. Keil, G. Depledge, and A. Rai, "Escalation: The Role of Problem Recognition and Cognitive Bias," *Decision Sciences* 38, no. 3 (2007): 391–421.

53. G. Whyte, "Escalating Commitment in Individual and Group Decision Making: A Prospect Theory Approach," *Organizational Behavior and Human Decision Processes* 54 (1993): 430–55; D. Kahneman and J. Renshon, "Hawkish Biases," in *American Foreign Policy and the Politics of Fear: Threat Inflation since 9/11*, ed. T. Thrall and J. Cramer (New York: Routledge, 2009), 79–96.

54. Sleesman et al., "Cleaning up the Big Muddy."

55. J.D. Bragger et al., "When Success Breeds Failure: History, Hysteresis, and Delayed Exit Decisions " *Journal of Applied Psychology* 88, no. 1 (2003): 6–14. A second logical reason for escalation, called the Martingale strategy, is described in J.A. Aloysius, "Rational Escalation of Costs by Playing a Sequence of Unfavorable Gambles: The Martingale," *Journal of Economic Behavior & Organization* 51 (2003): 111–29.

56. H. Drummond, *Escalation in Decision-Making: The Tragedy of Taurus* (Oxford: Oxford University Press, 1996); M. Sheehan, "Throwing Good Money after Bad," *Sunday Independent* (Dublin), October 9, 2005; "Good Sense Ran Dry in Costly Water

Solutions," *Courier-Mail* (Brisbane), September 13, 2013, 32; D. Houghton, "Billions Down Drain as Plug Pulled on Scheme," *Courier-Mail* (Brisbane), September 13, 2013, 2; K. Riddell, "DHS under Fire with St. Elizabeths Plan over Budget, Woefully Behind," *The Washington Times*, March 24, 2014; J. Markon, "Planned Homeland Security Headquarters, Long Delayed and over Budget, Now in Doubt," *The Washington Post*, May 21, 2014.

57. I. Simonson and B.M. Staw, "De-Escalation Strategies: A Comparison of Techniques for Reducing Commitment to Losing Courses of Action," *Journal of Applied Psychology* 77 (1992): 419–26; W. Boulding, R. Morgan, and R. Staelin, "Pulling the Plug to Stop the New Product Drain," *Journal of Marketing Research*, no. 34 (1997): 164–76; B.M. Staw, K.W. Koput, and S.G. Barsade, "Escalation at the Credit Window: A Longitudinal Study of Bank Executives' Recognition and Write-Off of Problem Loans," *Journal of Applied Psychology* 82, no. 1 (1997): 130–42; M. Keil and D. Robey, "Turning around Troubled Software Projects: An Exploratory Study of the Deescalation of Commitment to Failing Courses of Action," *Journal of Management Information Systems* 15 (1999): 63–87; B.C. Gunia, N. Sivanathan, and A.D. Galinsky, "Vicarious Entrapment: Your Sunk Costs, My Escalation of Commitment," *Journal of Experimental Social Psychology* 45, no. 6 (2009): 1238–44.

58. D. Ghosh, "De-Escalation Strategies: Some Experimental Evidence," *Behavioral Research in Accounting* 9 (1997): 88–112.

59. M.I. Stein, "Creativity and Culture," *Journal of Psychology* 36 (1953): 311–22; M.A. Runco and G.J. Jaeger, "The Standard Definition of Creativity," *Creativity Research Journal* 24, no. 1 (2012): 92–96.

60. G. Wallas, *The Art of Thought* (London: Jonathan Cape, 1926). For recent applications of Wallas's classic model, see T. Kristensen, "The Physical Context of Creativity," *Creativity and Innovation Management* 13, no. 2 (2004): 89–96; U.E. Haner, "Spaces for Creativity and Innovation in Two Established Organizations," *Creativity and Innovation Management* 14, no. 3 (2005): 288–98.

61. R.S. Nickerson, "Enhancing Creativity," in *Handbook of Creativity*, ed. R.J. Sternberg (New York: Cambridge University Press, 1999), 392–430.

62. E. Oakes, *Notable Scientists: A to Z of STS Scientists* (New York: Facts on File, 2002), 207–09.

63. For a thorough discussion of illumination or insight, see R.J. Sternberg and J.E. Davidson, *The Nature of Insight* (Cambridge, MA: MIT Press, 1995).

64. R.J. Sternberg and L.A. O'Hara, "Creativity and Intelligence," in *Handbook of Creativity*, ed. R.J. Sternberg (New York: Cambridge University Press, 1999), 251–72; S. Taggar, "Individual Creativity and Group Ability to Utilize Individual Creative Resources: A Multilevel Model," *Academy of Management Journal* 45 (2002): 315–30.

65. G.J. Feist, "The Influence of Personality on Artistic and Scientific Creativity," in *Handbook of Creativity*, ed. R.J. Sternberg (New York: Cambridge University Press, 1999), 273–96; T. Åsterbro, S.A. Jeffrey, and G.K. Adomdza, "Inventor Perseverance after Being Told to Quit: The Role of Cognitive Biases," *Journal of Behavioral Decision Making* 20 (2007): 253–72;

J.S. Mueller, S. Melwani, and J.A. Goncalo, "The Bias against Creativity: Why People Desire but Reject Creative Ideas," *Psychological Science* 23, no. 1 (2012): 13–17.

66. R.W. Weisberg, "Creativity and Knowledge: A Challenge to Theories," in *Handbook of Creativity*, ed. R.J. Sternberg (New York: Cambridge University Press, 1999), 226–50.

67. E. Dane, "Reconsidering the Trade-Off between Expertise and Flexibility: A Cognitive Entrenchment Perspective," *Academy of Management Review* 35, no. 4 (2010): 579–603; R.I. Sutton, *Weird Ideas That Work* (New York: Free Press, 2002), 53–54, 121.

68. Feist, "The Influence of Personality on Artistic and Scientific Creativity"; C.E. Shalley, J. Zhou, and G.R. Oldham, "The Effects of Personal and Contextual Characteristics on Creativity: Where Should We Go from Here?," *Journal of Management* 30, no. 6 (2004): 933–58; S.J. Dollinger, K.K. Urban, and T.A. James, "Creativity and Openness to Experience: Validation of Two Creative Product Measures," *Creativity Research Journal* 16, no. 1 (2004): 35–47; T.S. Schweizer, "The Psychology of Novelty-Seeking, Creativity and Innovation: Neurocognitive Aspects within a Work-Psychological Perspective," *Creativity and Innovation Management* 15, no. 2 (2006): 164–72; S. Acar and M.A. Runco, "Creative Abilities: Divergent Thinking," in *Handbook of Organizational Creativity*, ed. M. Mumford (Waltham, MA: Academic Press, 2012), 115–39.

69. Shalley et al., "The Effects of Personal and Contextual Characteristics on Creativity"; T.M. Amabile et al., "Leader Behaviors and the Work Environment for Creativity: Perceived Leader Support," *The Leadership Quarterly* 15, no. 1 (2004): 5–32; S.T. Hunter, K.E. Bedell, and M.D. Mumford, "Climate for Creativity: A Quantitative Review," *Creativity Research Journal* 19, no. 1 (2007): 69–90; T.C. DiLiello and J.D. Houghton, "Creative Potential and Practised Creativity: Identifying Untapped Creativity in Organizations," *Creativity and Innovation Management* 17, no. 1 (2008): 37–46.

70. R. Westwood and D.R. Low, "The Multicultural Muse: Culture, Creativity and Innovation," *International Journal of Cross Cultural Management* 3, no. 2 (2003): 235–59.

71. T.M. Amabile, "Motivating Creativity in Organizations: On Doing What You Love and Loving What You Do," *California Management Review* 40 (1997): 39–58; A. Cummings and G.R. Oldham, "Enhancing Creativity: Managing Work Contexts for the High Potential Employee," *California Management Review*, no. 40 (1997): 22–38; F. Coelho and M. Augusto, "Job Characteristics and the Creativity of Frontline Service Employees," *Journal of Service Research* 13, no. 4 (2010): 426–38.

72. T.M. Amabile, "Changes in the Work Environment for Creativity During Downsizing," *Academy of Management Journal* 42 (1999): 630–40.

73. J. Moultrie et al., "Innovation Spaces: Towards a Framework for Understanding the Role of the Physical Environment in Innovation," *Creativity & Innovation Management* 16, no. 1 (2007): 53–65.

74. J.M. Howell and K. Boies, "Champions of Technological Innovation: The Influence of Contextual Knowledge, Role Orientation, Idea Generation, and Idea Promotion on Champion Emergence," *The Leadership Quarterly* 15, no. 1 (2004): 123–43; Shalley et al., "The Effects of Personal and Contextual Characteristics on Creativity"; S. Powell, "The Management and Consumption of

Organisational Creativity," *Journal of Consumer Marketing* 25, no. 3 (2008): 158–66.

75. Innovation Tools, *2009 Creativity Survey*, InnovationTools.com (Milwaukee: July 2009); *Working Beyond Borders*, IBM Institute for Business Value (Somers, NY: September 2010); "Though 57% Say Innovation Is Key in 2011, Few Have Applied It to Drive Personal Growth," news release for FPC (New York: May 25, 2011); *2010 Federal Employee Viewpoint Survey Results* (Washington, DC: 2011).

76. A. Hiam, "Obstacles to Creativity—and How You Can Remove Them," *Futurist* 32 (1998): 30–34.

77. M.A. West, *Developing Creativity in Organizations* (Leicester, UK: BPS Books, 1997), 33–35.

78. For discussion of how play affects creativity, see S. Brown, *Play: How It Shapes the Brain, Opens the Imagination, and Invigorates the Soul* (New York: Avery, 2009).

79. A. Hargadon and R.I. Sutton, "Building an Innovation Factory," *Harvard Business Review* 78 (2000): 157–66; T. Kelley, *The Art of Innovation* (New York: Currency Doubleday, 2001), 158–62; P.F. Skilton and K.J. Dooley, "The Effects of Repeat Collaboration on Creative Abrasion," *Academy of Management Review* 35, no. 1 (2010): 118–34.

80. M. Burton, "Open Plan, Open Mind," *Director* (2005): 68–72; A. Benady, "Mothers of Invention," *The Independent* (London), November 27, 2006; B. Murray, "Agency Profile: Mother London," *Ihaveanidea*, January 28, 2007.

81. "John Collee—Biography" (Internet Movie Database, 2009), www.imdb.com/name/nm0171722/bio (accessed April 27, 2009).

82. M. Fenton-O'Creevy, "Employee Involvement and the Middle Manager: Saboteur or Scapegoat?," *Human Resource Management Journal*, no. 11 (2001): 24–40. Also see V.H. Vroom and A.G. Jago, *The New Leadership: Managing Participation in Organizations* (Englewood Cliffs, NJ: Prentice Hall, 1988).

83. Vroom and Jago, *The New Leadership*.

84. J.C. Barbieri and A.C.T. Álvares, "Innovation in Mature Industries: The Case of Brasilata S.A Metallic Packaging," in *4th International Conference on Technology Policy and Innovation* (Curitiba, Brazil: 2000); "Participação É Desafio Nas Empresas (Participation Is a Challenge in Business)," *Gazeta do Povo*, November 16, 2008; "Brasilata Internal Suggestion System Is a Benchmark in Innovation in the Brazilian Market" (São Paulo, Brazil: Brasilata, 2010), http://brasilata.jp/en/noticias_detalhada.php?cd_noticia=219 (accessed June 10, 2011); "Simplification Project" (São Paulo, Brazil: Brasilata, 2011), http://brasilata.jp/en/projeto_cronologia.php (accessed June 10, 2011); "Business Management" (São Paulo, Brazil: Brasilata, 2011), http://brasilata.jp/en/pessoal_negocios.php (accessed June 14, 2011).

85. Some of the early OB writing on employee involvement includes C. Argyris, *Personality and Organization* (New York: Harper & Row, 1957); D. McGregor, *The Human Side of Enterprise* (New York: McGraw-Hill, 1960); R. Likert, *New Patterns of Management* (New York: McGraw-Hill, 1961).

86. A.G. Robinson and D.M. Schroeder, *Ideas Are Free* (San Francisco: Berrett-Koehler, 2004).

87. R.J. Ely and D.A. Thomas, "Cultural Diversity at Work: The Effects of Diversity Perspectives on Work Group Processes and Outcomes," *Administrative Science Quarterly* 46 (2001): 229–73; E. Mannix and M.A. Neale, "What Differences Make a Difference?: The Promise and Reality of Diverse Teams in Organizations," *Psychological Science in the Public Interest* 6, no. 2 (2005): 31–55.

88. D. Berend and J. Paroush, "When Is Condorcet's Jury Theorem Valid?," *Social Choice and Welfare* 15, no. 4 (1998): 481–88.

89. K.T. Dirks, L.L. Cummings, and J.L. Pierce, "Psychological Ownership in Organizations: Conditions under Which Individuals Promote and Resist Change," *Research in Organizational Change and Development*, no. 9 (1996): 1–23; J.P. Walsh and S.F. Tseng, "The Effects of Job Characteristics on Active Effort at Work," *Work & Occupations* 25, no. 1 (1998): 74–96; B. Scott-Ladd and V. Marshall, "Participation in Decision Making: A Matter of Context?," *Leadership & Organization Development Journal* 25, no. 8 (2004): 646–62.

90. Vroom and Jago, *The New Leadership*.

Chapter 7

1. HFT Investment Management Co. Ltd., "Investment Team" (Shanghai, China, 2013), www.hftfund.com (accessed June 12, 2013); Nextech Invest, "Our Values" (Zurich, Switzerland, 2013), www.nextechinvest.com (accessed June 12, 2013).

2. "Trends: Are Many Meetings a Waste of Time? Study Says So," news release (MeetingsNet, November 1, 1998); "Teamwork and Collaboration Major Workplace Trends," *Ottawa Business Journal*, April 18, 2006; "Go Teams! Firms Can't Do without Them" (American Management Association, 2008), http://amalearning.com (accessed April 21, 2010).

3. S. Wuchty, B.F. Jones, and B. Uzzi, "The Increasing Dominance of Teams in Production of Knowledge," *Science* 316 (2007): 1036–39.

4. E. Sundstrom, "The Challenges of Supporting Work Team Effectiveness," in *Supporting Work Team Effectiveness*, ed. E. Sundstrom and Associates (San Francisco: Jossey-Bass, 1999), 6–9; S.A. Mohrman, S.G. Cohen, and A.M. Mohrman Jr., *Designing Team-Based Organizations: New Forms for Knowledge Work* (San Francisco: Jossey-Bass, 1995), 39–40; M.E. Shaw, *Group Dynamics*, 3rd ed. (New York: McGraw-Hill, 1981), 8.

5. J.R. Hollenbeck, B. Beersma, and M.E. Schouten, "Beyond Team Types and Taxonomies: A Dimensional Scaling Conceptualization for Team Description," *Academy of Management Review* 37, no. 1 (2012): 82–106.

6. S.I. Tannenbaum et al., "Teams Are Changing: Are Research and Practice Evolving Fast Enough?," *Industrial and Organizational Psychology* 5, no. 1 (2012): 2–24; R. Wageman, H. Gardner, and M. Mortensen, "The Changing Ecology of Teams: New Directions for Teams Research," *Journal of Organizational Behavior* 33, no. 3 (2012): 301–15.

7. R.A. Guzzo and M.W. Dickson, "Teams in Organizations: Recent Research on Performance and Effectiveness," *Annual Review of Psychology* 47 (1996): 307–38; L.R. Offerman and R.K. Spiros, "The Science and Practice of Team Development: Improving the Link," *Academy of Management Journal* 44 (2001): 376–92.

8. P.R. Lawrence and N. Nohria, *Driven: How Human Nature Shapes Our Choices* (San Francisco: Jossey-Bass, 2002); J.R. Spoor and J.R. Kelly, "The Evolutionary Significance of Affect

in Groups: Communication and Group Bonding," *Group Processes & Intergroup Relations* 7, no. 4 (2004): 398–412.

9. M.A. Hogg et al., "The Social Identity Perspective: Intergroup Relations, Self-Conception, and Small Groups," *Small Group Research* 35, no. 3 (2004): 246–76; M. Van Vugt and C.M. Hart, "Social Identity as Social Glue: The Origins of Group Loyalty," *Journal of Personality and Social Psychology* 86, no. 4 (2004): 585–98; N. Michinov, E. Michinov, and M.C. Toczek-Capelle, "Social Identity, Group Processes, and Performance in Synchronous Computer-Mediated Communication," *Group Dynamics: Theory, Research, and Practice* 8, no. 1 (2004): 27–39.

10. S. Schacter, *The Psychology of Affiliation* (Stanford, CA: Stanford University Press, 1959), 12–19; A.C. DeVries, E.R. Glasper, and C.E. Detillion, "Social Modulation of Stress Responses," *Physiology & Behavior* 79, no. 3 (2003): 399–407; S. Cohen, "The Pittsburgh Common Cold Studies: Psychosocial Predictors of Susceptibility to Respiratory Infectious Illness," *International Journal of Behavioral Medicine* 12, no. 3 (2005): 123–31.

11. R. Cross and R.J. Thomas, *Driving Results through Social Networks: How Top Organizations Leverage Networks for Performance and Growth* (San Francisco: Jossey-Bass, 2009); R. McDermott and D. Archibald, "Harnessing Your Staff's Informal Networks," *Harvard Business Review* 88, no. 3 (2010): 82–89; J. Nieves and J. Osorio, "The Role of Social Networks in Knowledge Creation," *Knowledge Management Research & Practice* 11, no. 1 (2013): 62–77.

12. L. Buchanan, "2011 Top Small Company Workplaces: Core Values," *Inc.*, June 2011, 60–74; L. Buchanan, "Taking Teamwork to the Extreme," *Inc.*, April 18, 2013; K. Rong, "Menlo Innovations—Rich Sheridan Podcast" (YouTube, 2013).

13. M. Moldaschl and W. Weber, "The 'Three Waves' of Industrial Group Work: Historical Reflections on Current Research on Group Work," *Human Relations* 51 (1998): 347–88. Several popular books in the 1980s encouraged teamwork, based on the Japanese economic miracle. These books include W. Ouchi, *Theory Z: How American Management Can Meet the Japanese Challenge* (Reading, MA: Addison-Wesley, 1981); R.T. Pascale and A.G. Athos, *Art of Japanese Management* (New York: Simon & Schuster, 1982).

14. C.R. Emery and L.D. Fredenhall, "The Effect of Teams on Firm Profitability and Customer Satisfaction," *Journal of Service Research* 4 (2002): 217–29; G.S. Van der Vegt and O. Janssen, "Joint Impact of Interdependence and Group Diversity on Innovation," *Journal of Management* 29 (2003): 729–51.

15. R.E. Baumeister and M.R. Leary, "The Need to Belong: Desire for Interpersonal Attachments as a Fundamental Human Motivation," *Psychological Bulletin* 117 (1995): 497–529; S. Chen, H.C. Boucher, and M.P. Tapias, "The Relational Self Revealed: Integrative Conceptualization and Implications for Interpersonal Life," *Psychological Bulletin* 132, no. 2 (2006): 151–79; J.M. Feinberg and J.R. Aiello, "Social Facilitation: A Test of Competing Theories," *Journal of Applied Social Psychology* 36, no. 5 (2006): 1087–109; N.L. Kerr et al., "Psychological Mechanisms Underlying the Kohler Motivation Gain," *Personality & Social Psychology Bulletin* 33, no. 6 (2007): 828–41; A.M. Grant, "Relational Job Design and the Motivation to Make a Prosocial Difference," *Academy of Management Review* 32, no. 2 (2007): 393–417.

16. This information is from the websites of these companies, mostly on their "Careers" pages.

17. E.A. Locke et al, "The Importance of the Individual in an Age of Groupism," in *Groups at Work: Theory and Research*, ed. M.E. Turner (Mahwah, NJ: Erlbaum, 2001), 501–28; N.J. Allen and T.D. Hecht, "The 'Romance of Teams': Toward an Understanding of Its Psychological Underpinnings and Implications," *Journal of Occupational and Organizational Psychology* 77 (2004): 439–61.

18. I.D. Steiner, *Group Process and Productivity* (New York: Academic Press, 1972); N.L. Kerr and S.R. Tindale, "Group Performance and Decision Making," *Annual Review of Psychology* 55 (2004): 623–55.

19. M.W. McCarter and R.M. Sheremeta, "You Can't Put Old Wine in New Bottles: The Effect of Newcomers on Coordination in Groups," *PLoS ONE* 8, no. 1 (2013): e55058.

20. B.R. Staats, K.L. Milkman, and C.R. Fox, "The Team Scaling Fallacy: Underestimating the Declining Efficiency of Larger Teams," *Organizational Behavior and Human Decision Processes* 118, no. 2 (2012): 132–42. Brooks's law is discussed in F.P. Brooks, ed. *The Mythical Man-Month: Essays on Software Engineering*, 2nd ed. (Reading, MA: Addison-Wesley, 1995).

21. S.J. Karau and K.D. Williams, "Social Loafing: A Meta-Analytic Review and Theoretical Integration," *Journal of Personality and Social Psychology* 65 (1993): 681–706; R.C. Liden et al., "Social Loafing: A Field Investigation," *Journal of Management* 30 (2004): 285–304; L.L. Chidambaram, "Is out of Sight, out of Mind? An Empirical Study of Social Loafing in Technology-Supported Groups," *Information Systems Research* 16, no. 2 (2005): 149–68; U.C. Klehe and N. Anderson, "The Moderating Influence of Personality and Culture on Social Loafing in Typical versus Maximum Performance Situations," *International Journal of Selection and Assessment* 15, no. 2 (2007): 250–62.

22. J.R. Engen, "Tough as Nails," *Bank Director*, July 2009, 24.

23. M. Erez and A. Somech, "Is Group Productivity Loss the Rule or the Exception? Effects of Culture and Group-Based Motivation," *Academy of Management Journal* 39 (1996): 1513–37; Kerr and Tindale, "Group Performance and Decision Making"; A. Jassawalla, H. Sashittal, and A. Malshe, "Students' Perceptions of Social Loafing: Its Antecedents and Consequences in Undergraduate Business Classroom Teams," *Academy of Management Learning and Education* 8, no. 1 (2009): 42–54.

24. G.P. Shea and R.A. Guzzo, "Group Effectiveness: What Really Matters?," *Sloan Management Review* 27 (1987): 33–46; J.R. Hackman et al., "Team Effectiveness in Theory and in Practice," in *Industrial and Organizational Psychology: Linking Theory with Practice*, ed. C.L. Cooper and E.A. Locke (Oxford, UK: Blackwell, 2000), 109–29.

25. M.A. West, C.S. Borrill, and K.L. Unsworth, "Team Effectiveness in Organizations," *International Review of Industrial and Organizational Psychology* 13 (1998): 1–48; M.A. Marks, J.E. Mathieu, and S.J. Zaccaro, "A Temporally Based Framework and Taxonomy of Team Processes," *Academy of Management Review* 26, no. 3 (2001): 356–76; J.E. McGrath, H. Arrow, and J.L. Berdahl, "The Study of Groups: Past, Present, and Future," *Personality & Social Psychology Review* 4, no. 1 (2000): 95–105.

26. Wawa Inc., *Wawa Fun Fact Sheet* (Wawa, PA: November 4, 2011); B. Rose, "Cultivating a Better Corporate Culture," *Retail Leader*, January 2012, 24–28.

27. M. Kouchaki et al., "The Treatment of the Relationship between Groups and Their Environments: A Review and Critical Examination of Common Assumptions in Research," *Group & Organization Management* 37, no. 2 (2012): 171–203.

28. Sundstrom, "The Challenges of Supporting Work Team Effectiveness"; J.N. Choi, "External Activities and Team Effectiveness: Review and Theoretical Development," *Small Group Research* 33 (2002): 181–208; G. Hertel, S. Geister, and U. Konradt, "Managing Virtual Teams: A Review of Current Empirical Research," *Human Resource Management Review* 15 (2005): 69–95; G.L. Stewart, "A Meta-Analytic Review of Relationships between Team Design Features and Team Performance," *Journal of Management* 32, no. 1 (2006): 29–54; J.B. Stryker and M.D. Santoro, "Facilitating Face-to-Face Communication in High-Tech Teams," *Research Technology Management* 55, no. 1 (2012): 51–56.

29. M.A. Campion, E.M. Papper, and G.J. Medsker, "Relations between Work Team Characteristics and Effectiveness: A Replication and Extension," *Personnel Psychology* 49 (1996): 429–52; D.C. Man and S.S.K. Lam, "The Effects of Job Complexity and Autonomy on Cohesiveness in Collectivistic and Individualistic Work Groups: A Cross-Cultural Analysis," *Journal of Organizational Behavior* 24 (2003): 979–1001; N. Sivasubramaniam, S.J. Liebowitz, and C.L. Lackman, "Determinants of New Product Development Team Performance: A Meta-Analytic Review," *Journal of Product Innovation Management* 29, no. 5 (2012): 803–20; M. Valentine and A.C. Edmondson, *Team Scaffolds: How Minimal Team Structures Enable Role-Based Coordination*, Harvard Business School working paper (Boston: April 15, 2013).

30. G. Van der Vegt and E. Van de Vliert, "Intragroup Interdependence and Effectiveness: Review and Proposed Directions for Theory and Practice," *Journal of Managerial Psychology* 17, no. 1/2 (2002): 50–67; R. Wageman, "The Meaning of Interdependence," in *Groups at Work: Theory and Research*, ed. M.E. Turner (Mahwah, NJ: Erlbaum, 2001), 197–217; M.R. Barrick et al., "The Moderating Role of Top Management Team Interdependence: Implications for Real Teams and Working Groups," *Academy of Management Journal* 50, no. 3 (2007): 544–57.

31. L. Gratton and T.J. Erickson, "Ways to Build Collaborative Teams," *Harvard Business Review* (2007): 100–9; G. Anders, "Jeff Bezos Reveals His No. 1 Leadership Secret," *Forbes*, April 23, 2012, 76.

32. J. O'Toole, "The Power of Many: Building a High-Performance Management Team," *ceoforum.com.au* (2003).

33. J.R. Katzenbach and D.K. Smith, *The Wisdom of Teams: Creating the High-Performance Organization* (Boston: Harvard University Press, 1993), 45–47; S.J. Guastello, "Nonlinear Dynamics of Team Performance and Adaptability in Emergency Response," *Human Factors: The Journal of the Human Factors and Ergonomics Society* 52, no. 2 (2010): 162–72; C. Aube, V. Rousseau, and S. Tremblay, "Team Size and Quality of Group Experience: The More the Merrier?," *Group Dynamics: Theory Research and Practice* 15, no. 4 (2011): 357–75.

34. J.S. Mueller, "Why Individuals in Larger Teams Perform Worse," *Organizational Behavior and Human Decision Processes* 117, no. 1 (2012): 111–24.

35. F.P. Morgeson, M.H. Reider, and M.A. Campion, "Selecting Individuals in Team Settings: The Importance of Social Skills, Personality Characteristics, and Teamwork Knowledge," *Personnel Psychology* 58, no. 3 (2005): 583–611; V. Rousseau, C. Aubé, and A. Savoie, "Teamwork Behaviors: A Review and an Integration of Frameworks," *Small Group Research* 37, no. 5 (2006): 540–70. For a detailed examination of the characteristics of effective team members, see M.L. Loughry, M.W. Ohland, and D.D. Moore, "Development of a Theory-Based Assessment of Team Member Effectiveness," *Educational and Psychological Measurement* 67, no. 3 (2007): 505–24.

36. S. McComb et al., "The Five Ws of Team Communication," *Industrial Management* 54, no. 5 (2012): 10–13.

37. C.E. Hårtel and D. Panipucci, "How 'Bad Apples' Spoil the Bunch: Faultlines, Emotional Levers, and Exclusion in the Workplace," *Research on Emotion in Organizations* 3 (2007): 287–310; C.O.L.H. Porter et al., "Backing Up Behaviors in Teams: The Role of Personality and Legitimacy of Need," *Journal of Applied Psychology* 88, no. 3 (2003): 391–403. The bad apple phenomenon is also identified in executive team "derailers." See R. Wageman et al., *Senior Leadership Teams* (Boston: Harvard Business School Press, 2008), 97–102.

38. Kelly Services, *Effective Employers: The Evolving Workforce*, Kelly Global Workforce Index, Kelly Services (Troy, MI: November 2011); TINYpulse, *7 Vital Trends Disrupting Today's Workplace*, 2013 TINYpulse Employee Engagement Survey, TINYpulse (Seattle: December 2013); "Overwhelming Majority of Companies Say Soft Skills Are Just as Important as Hard Skills, According to a New CareerBuilder Survey," news release for CareerBuilder (Chicago: April 10, 2014).

39. D. van Knippenberg, C.K.W. De Dreu, and A.C. Homan, "Work Group Diversity and Group Performance: An Integrative Model and Research Agenda," *Journal of Applied Psychology* 89, no. 6 (2004): 1008–22; E. Mannix and M.A. Neale, "What Differences Make a Difference?: The Promise and Reality of Diverse Teams in Organizations," *Psychological Science in the Public Interest* 6, no. 2 (2005): 31–55; G.K. Stahl et al., "A Look at the Bright Side of Multicultural Team Diversity," *Scandinavian Journal of Management* 26, no. 4 (2010): 439–47; H. Haas, "How Can We Explain Mixed Effects of Diversity on Team Performance? A Review with Emphasis on Context," *Equality, Diversity and Inclusion: An International Journal* 29, no. 5 (2010): 458–90; L.M. Shore et al., "Inclusion and Diversity in Work Groups: A Review and Model for Future Research," *Journal of Management* 37, no. 4 (2011): 1262–89.

40. D.C. Lau and J.K. Murnighan, "Interactions within Groups and Subgroups: The Effects of Demographic Faultlines," *Academy of Management Journal* 48, no. 4 (2005): 645–59; S.M.B. Thatcher and P.C. Patel, "Group Faultlines: A Review, Integration, and Guide to Future Research," *Journal of Management* 38, no. 4 (2012): 969–1009.

41. B.W. Tuckman and M.A.C. Jensen, "Stages of Small-Group Development Revisited," *Group and Organization Studies* 2 (1977): 419–42; B.W. Tuckman, "Developmental Sequence in Small Groups," *Group Facilitation* (2001): 66–81.

42. G.R. Bushe and G.H. Coetzer, "Group Development and Team Effectiveness: Using Cognitive Representations to Measure Group Development and Predict Task Performance and Group

Viability," *Journal of Applied Behavioral Science* 43, no. 2 (2007): 184–212.

43. C. Lee, J.L. Farh, and Z.J. Chen, "Promoting Group Potency in Project Teams: The Importance of Group Identification," *Journal of Organizational Behavior* 32, no. 8 (2011): 1147–62.

44. B.C. Lim and K.J. Klein, "Team Mental Models and Team Performance: A Field Study of the Effects of Team Mental Model Similarity and Accuracy," *Journal of Organizational Behavior* 27 (2006): 403–18; S.W.J. Kozlowski and D.R. Ilgen, "Enhancing the Effectiveness of Work Groups and Teams," *Psychological Science in the Public Interest* 7, no. 3 (2006): 77–124; R. Rico, M. Sánchez-Manzanares, and C. Gibson, "Team Implicit Coordination Processes: A Team Knowledge-Based Approach," *Academy of Management Review* 33, no. 1 (2008): 163–84; S. McComb et al., "Temporal Patterns of Mental Model Convergence: Implications for Distributed Teams Interacting in Electronic Collaboration Spaces," *Human Factors: The Journal of the Human Factors and Ergonomics Society* 52, no. 2 (2010): 264–81.

45. L.A. DeChurch and J.R. Mesmer-Magnus, "The Cognitive Underpinnings of Effective Teamwork: A Meta-Analysis," *Journal of Applied Psychology* 95, no. 1 (2010): 32–53.

46. A.P. Hare, "Types of Roles in Small Groups: A Bit of History and a Current Perspective," *Small Group Research* 25 (1994): 443–48; A. Aritzeta, S. Swailes, and B. Senior, "Belbin's Team Role Model: Development, Validity and Applications for Team Building," *Journal of Management Studies* 44, no. 1 (2007): 96–118.

47. S.H.N. Leung, J.W.K. Chan, and W.B. Lee, "The Dynamic Team Role Behavior: The Approaches of Investigation," *Team Performance Management* 9 (2003): 84–90; G.L. Stewart, I.S. Fulmer, and M.R. Barrick, "An Exploration of Member Roles as a Multilevel Linking Mechanism for Individual Traits and Team Outcomes," *Personnel Psychology* 58, no. 2 (2005): 343–65.

48. P. de Langen, "Driving Team Building," *HRM Asia*, August 24, 2012; D. Hempstead, "Heatwave Hits Ottawa," *Ottawa Sun*, July 4, 2013; L. Robbins, "One Long Night in Puzzle City," *The New York Times*, October 13, 2013, 1; P. Swiech, "Nicor's Employees Warm Hearts, Homes," *The Pantagraph* (Bloomington, IL), May 18, 2014, A3.

49. W.G. Dyer, *Team Building: Current Issues and New Alternatives*, 3rd ed. (Reading, MA: Addison-Wesley, 1995); C.A. Beatty and B.A. Barker, *Building Smart Teams: Roadmap to High Performance* (Thousand Oaks, CA: Sage, 2004).

50. J.E. Mathieu et al., "Scaling the Quality of Teammates' Mental Models: Equifinality and Normative Comparisons," *Journal of Organizational Behavior* 26 (2005): 37–56; J. Langan-Fox and J. Anglim, "Mental Models, Team Mental Models, and Performance: Process, Development, and Future Directions," *Human Factors and Ergonomics in Manufacturing* 14, no. 4 (2004): 331–52.

51. I. Nadler, P.M. Sanderson, and H.G. Liley, "The Accuracy of Clinical Assessments as a Measure for Teamwork Effectiveness," *Simulation in Healthcare* 6, no. 5 (2011): 260–68.

52. R.W. Woodman and J.J. Sherwood, "The Role of Team Development in Organizational Effectiveness: A Critical Review," *Psychological Bulletin* 88 (1980): 166–86.

53. L. Mealiea and R. Baltazar, "A Strategic Guide for Building Effective Teams," *Personnel Management* 34, no. 2 (2005): 141–60.

54. G.E. Huszczo, "Training for Team Building," *Training and Development Journal* 44 (1990): 37–43; P. McGraw, "Back from the Mountain: Outdoor Management Development Programs and How to Ensure the Transfer of Skills to the Workplace," *Asia Pacific Journal of Human Resources* 31 (1993): 52–61.

55. D.C. Feldman, "The Development and Enforcement of Group Norms," *Academy of Management Review* 9 (1984): 47–53; E. Fehr and U. Fischbacher, "Social Norms and Human Cooperation," *Trends in Cognitive Sciences* 8, no. 4 (2004): 185–90.

56. N. Ellemers and F. Rink, "Identity in Work Groups: The Beneficial and Detrimental Consequences of Multiple Identities and Group Norms for Collaboration and Group Performance," *Advances in Group Processes* 22 (2005): 1–41.

57. K.D. Opp, "How Do Norms Emerge? An Outline of a Theory," *Mind & Society* 2, no. 1 (2001): 101–28.

58. J.J. Dose and R.J. Klimoski, "The Diversity of Diversity: Work Values Effects on Formative Team Processes," *Human Resource Management Review* 9, no. 1 (1999): 83–108.

59. S. Taggar and R. Ellis, "The Role of Leaders in Shaping Formal Team Norms," *Leadership Quarterly* 18, no. 2 (2007): 105–20.

60. D.J. Beal et al., "Cohesion and Performance in Groups: A Meta-Analytic Clarification of Construct Relations," *Journal of Applied Psychology* 88, no. 6 (2003): 989–1004; Kozlowski and Ilgen, "Enhancing the Effectiveness of Work Groups and Teams."

61. R.M. Montoya, R.S. Horton, and J. Kirchner, "Is Actual Similarity Necessary for Attraction? A Meta-Analysis of Actual and Perceived Similarity," *Journal of Social and Personal Relationships* 25, no. 6 (2008): 889–922; M.T. Rivera, S.B. Soderstrom, and B. Uzzi, "Dynamics of Dyads in Social Networks: Assortative, Relational, and Proximity Mechanisms," *Annual Review of Sociology* 36 (2010): 91–115.

62. van Knippenberg et al., "Work Group Diversity and Group Performance"; K.A. Jehn, G.B. Northcraft, and M.A. Neale, "Why Differences Make a Difference: A Field Study of Diversity, Conflict, and Performance in Workgroups," *Administrative Science Quarterly* 44, no. 4 (1999): 741–63. For evidence that diversity/similarity does not always influence cohesion, see S.S. Webber and L.M. Donahue, "Impact of Highly and Less Job-Related Diversity on Work Group Cohesion and Performance: A Meta-Analysis," *Journal of Management* 27, no. 2 (2001): 141–62.

63. E. Aronson and J. Mills, "The Effects of Severity of Initiation on Liking for a Group," *Journal of Abnormal and Social Psychology* 59 (1959): 177–81; J.E. Hautaluoma and R.S. Enge, "Early Socialization into a Work Group: Severity of Initiations Revisited," *Journal of Social Behavior & Personality* 6 (1991): 725–48.

64. B. Mullen and C. Copper, "The Relation between Group Cohesiveness and Performance: An Integration," *Psychological Bulletin* 115 (1994): 210–27; C.J. Fullagar and D.O. Egleston, "Norming and Performing: Using Microworlds to Understand the Relationship between Team Cohesiveness and Performance," *Journal of Applied Social Psychology* 38, no. 10 (2008): 2574–93.

65. Wageman et al., *Senior Leadership Teams*, 69–70.

66. M. Rempel and R.J. Fisher, "Perceived Threat, Cohesion, and Group Problem Solving in Intergroup Conflict," *International Journal of Conflict Management* 8 (1997): 216–34; M.E. Turner and T. Horvitz, "The Dilemma of Threat: Group Effectiveness and Ineffectiveness under Adversity," in *Groups at Work: Theory and Research* ed. M.E. Turner (Mahwah, NJ: Erlbaum, 2001), 445–70.

67. A.V. Carron et al., "Cohesion and Performance in Sport: A Meta-Analysis," *Journal of Sport and Exercise Psychology* 24 (2002): 168–88; Beal et al., "Cohesion and Performance in Groups"; Fullagar and Egleston, "Norming and Performing"; DeChurch and Mesmer-Magnus, "The Cognitive Underpinnings of Effective Teamwork: A Meta-Analysis."

68. W. Piper et al., "Cohesion as a Basic Bond in Groups," *Human Relations* 36 (1983): 93–108; C.A. O'Reilly, D.E. Caldwell, and W.P. Barnett, "Work Group Demography, Social Integration, and Turnover," *Administrative Science Quarterly* 34 (1989): 21–37.

69. S.M. Gully, D.J. Devine, and D.J. Whitney, "A Meta-Analysis of Cohesion and Performance: Effects of Level of Analysis and Task Interdependence," *Small Group Research* 43, no. 6 (2012): 702–25.

70. K.L. Gammage, A.V. Carron, and P.A. Estabrooks, "Team Cohesion and Individual Productivity: The Influence of the Norm for Productivity and the Identifiability of Individual Effort," *Small Group Research* 32 (2001): 3–18; C. Langfred, "Is Group Cohesiveness a Double-Edged Sword? An Investigation of the Effects of Cohesiveness on Performance," *Small Group Research* 29 (1998): 124–43; N.L. Jimmieson, M. Peach, and K.M. White, "Utilizing the Theory of Planned Behavior to Inform Change Management," *Journal of Applied Behavioral Science* 44, no. 2 (2008): 237–62. Concerns about existing research on cohesion–performance are discussed in M. Casey-Campbell and M.L. Martens, "Sticking It All Together: A Critical Assessment of the Group Cohesion–Performance Literature," *International Journal of Management Reviews* 11, no. 2 (2009): 223–46.

71. Fullagar and Egleston, "Norming and Performing."

72. D.M. Rousseau et al., "Not So Different after All: A Cross-Discipline View of Trust," *Academy of Management Review* 23 (1998): 393–404; R. Searle, A. Weibel, and D.N. Den Hartog, "Employee Trust in Organizational Contexts," in *International Review of Industrial and Organizational Psychology 2011* (Wiley, 2011), 143–91.

73. D.J. McAllister, "Affect- and Cognition-Based Trust as Foundations for Interpersonal Cooperation in Organizations," *Academy of Management Journal* 38, no. 1 (1995): 24–59; M. Williams, "In Whom We Trust: Group Membership as an Affective Context for Trust Development," *Academy of Management Review* 26, no. 3 (2001): 377–96; M. Pirson and D. Malhotra, "Foundations of Organizational Trust: What Matters to Different Stakeholders?," *Organization Science* 22, no. 4 (2011): 1087–104.

74. R.J. Lewicki, E.C. Tomlinson, and N. Gillespie, "Models of Interpersonal Trust Development: Theoretical Approaches, Empirical Evidence, and Future Directions," *Journal of Management* 32, no. 6 (2006): 991–1022.

75. Lewicki et al., "Models of Interpersonal Trust Development: Theoretical Approaches, Empirical Evidence, and Future Directions";

F.Y. Kuo and C.P. Yu, "An Exploratory Study of Trust Dynamics in Work-Oriented Virtual Teams," *Journal of Computer-Mediated Communication* 14, no. 4 (2009): 823–54.

76. E.M. Whitener et al., "Managers as Initiators of Trust: An Exchange Relationship Framework for Understanding Managerial Trustworthy Behavior," *Academy of Management Review* 23 (1998): 513–30; J.M. Kouzes and B.Z. Posner, *The Leadership Challenge*, 3rd ed. (San Francisco: Jossey-Bass, 2002), Chap. 2; T. Simons, "Behavioral Integrity: The Perceived Alignment between Managers' Words and Deeds as a Research Focus," *Organization Science* 13, no. 1 (2002): 18–35.

77. S.L. Jarvenpaa and D.E. Leidner, "Communication and Trust in Global Virtual Teams," *Organization Science* 10 (1999): 791–815; L.P. Robert, A.R. Dennis, and Y.T.C. Hung, "Individual Swift Trust and Knowledge-Based Trust in Face-to-Face and Virtual Team Members," *Journal of Management Information Systems* 26, no. 2 (2009): 241–79; C.B. Crisp and S.L. Jarvenpaa, "Swift Trust in Global Virtual Teams: Trusting Beliefs and Normative Actions," *Journal of Personnel Psychology* 12, no. 1 (2013): 45–56.

78. K.T. Dirks and D.L. Ferrin, "The Role of Trust in Organizations," *Organization Science* 12, no. 4 (2004): 450–67.

79. Two of the most important changes in teams are empowerment (evident in self-directed teams) and technology and distance (evident in virtual teams). See Tannenbaum et al., "Teams Are Changing."

80. Mohrman et al., *Designing Team-Based Organizations: New Forms for Knowledge Work*; D.E. Yeatts and C. Hyten, *High-Performing Self-Managed Work Teams: A Comparison of Theory and Practice* (Thousand Oaks, CA: Sage, 1998); E.E. Lawler, *Organizing for High Performance* (San Francisco: Jossey-Bass, 2001); R.J. Torraco, "Work Design Theory: A Review and Critique with Implications for Human Resource Development," *Human Resource Development Quarterly* 16, no. 1 (2005): 85–109.

81. P. Panchak, "Production Workers Can Be Your Competitive Edge," *Industry Week*, October 2004, 11; S.K. Muthusamy, J.V. Wheeler, and B.L. Simmons, "Self-Managing Work Teams: Enhancing Organizational Innovativeness," *Organization Development Journal* 23, no. 3 (2005): 53–66.

82. Emery and Fredenhall, "The Effect of Teams on Firm Profitability and Customer Satisfaction"; A. Krause and H. Dunckel, "Work Design and Customer Satisfaction: Effects of the Implementation of Semi-Autonomous Group Work on Customer Satisfaction Considering Employee Satisfaction and Group Performance (translated abstract)," *Zeitschrift für Arbeits-und Organisationspsychologie* 47, no. 4 (2003): 182–93; H. van Mierlo et al., "Self-Managing Teamwork and Psychological Well-Being: Review of a Multilevel Research Domain," *Group & Organization Management* 30, no. 2 (2005): 211–35; G.L. Stewart, S.H. Courtright, and M.R. Barrick, "Peer-Based Control in Self-Managing Teams: Linking Rational and Normative Influence with Individual and Group Performance," *Journal of Applied Psychology* 97, no. 2 (2012): 435–47.

83. P. LaBarre, "When Nobody (and Everybody) Is the Boss," *Fortune*, March 5, 2012; J. Mackay and R. Sisodia, *Conscious Capitalism: Liberating the Heroic Spirit of Business* (Boston: Harvard Business Review Press, 2013), 91–92.

84. Moldaschl and Weber, "The 'Three Waves' of Industrial Group Work"; W. Niepce and E. Molleman, "Work Design Issues in Lean Production from a Sociotechnical System a Perspective: Neo-Taylorism or the Next Step in Sociotechnical Design?," *Human Relations* 51, no. 3 (1998): 259–87; J.L. Cordery et al., "The Impact of Autonomy and Task Uncertainty on Team Performance: A Longitudinal Field Study," *Journal of Organizational Behavior* 31 (2010): 240–58.

85. E. Ulich and W.G. Weber, "Dimensions, Criteria, and Evaluation of Work Group Autonomy," in *Handbook of Work Group Psychology*, ed. M.A. West (Chichester, UK: Wiley, 1996), 247–82.

86. K.P. Carson and G.L. Stewart, "Job Analysis and the Sociotechnical Approach to Quality: A Critical Examination," *Journal of Quality Management* 1 (1996): 49–65; C.C. Manz and G.L. Stewart, "Attaining Flexible Stability by Integrating Total Quality Management and Socio-Technical Systems Theory," *Organization Science* 8 (1997): 59–70.

87. J. Lipnack and J. Stamps, *Virtual Teams: People Working across Boundaries with Technology* (New York: Wiley, 2001); Hertel et al., "Managing Virtual Teams"; L. Schweitzer and L. Duxbury, "Conceptualizing and Measuring the Virtuality of Teams," *Information Systems Journal* 20, no. 3 (2010): 267–95.

88. "Virtual Teams Now a Reality," news release for Institute for Corporate Productivity (Seattle: Institute for Corporate Productivity, September 4, 2008).

89. L.L. Martins, L.L. Gilson, and M.T. Maynard, "Virtual Teams: What Do We Know and Where Do We Go from Here?," *Journal of Management* 30, no. 6 (2004): 805–35.

90. "Absence Makes the Team Uneasy," news release (Menlo Park, NJ: OfficeTeam, March 6, 2008); "Go Teams! Firms Can't Do without Them"; N. Weil, "Global Team Management: Continental Divides," *CIO*, January 23, 2008.

91. J.L. Cordery and C. Soo, "Overcoming Impediments to Virtual Team Effectiveness," *Human Factors and Ergonomics in Manufacturing & Service Industries* 18, no. 5 (2008): 487–500; A. Ortiz de Guinea, J. Webster, and D.S. Staples, "A Meta-Analysis of the Consequences of Virtualness on Team Functioning," *Information & Management* 49, no. 6 (2012): 301–08.

92. G. Hertel, U. Konradt, and K. Voss, "Competencies for Virtual Teamwork: Development and Validation of a Web-Based Selection Tool for Members of Distributed Teams," *European Journal of Work and Organizational Psychology* 15, no. 4 (2006): 477–504; J.M. Wilson et al., "Perceived Proximity in Virtual Work: Explaining the Paradox of Far-but-Close," *Organization Studies* 29, no. 7 (2008): 979–1002; L.L. Martins and M.C. Schilpzand, "Global Virtual Teams: Key Developments, Research Gaps, and Future Directions," *Research in Personnel and Human Resources Management* 30 (2011): 1–72.

93. G.G. Harwood, "Design Principles for Successful Virtual Teams," in *The Handbook of High-Performance Virtual Teams: A Toolkit for Collaborating across Boundaries*, ed. J. Nemiro and M.M. Beyerlein (San Francisco: Jossey-Bass, 2008), 59–84. Also see H. Duckworth, "How TRW Automotive Helps Global Virtual Teams Perform at the Top of Their Game," *Global Business and Organizational Excellence* 28, no. 1 (2008): 6–16; L. Dubé and D. Robey, "Surviving the Paradoxes of Virtual Teamwork," *Information Systems Journal* 19, no. 1 (2009): 3–30.

94. Dubé and Robey, "Surviving the Paradoxes of Virtual Teamwork."

95. V.H. Vroom and A.G. Jago, *The New Leadership* (Englewood Cliffs, NJ: Prentice Hall, 1988), 28–29.

96. M. Diehl and W. Stroebe, "Productivity Loss in Idea-Generating Groups: Tracking Down the Blocking Effects," *Journal of Personality and Social Psychology* 61 (1991): 392–403; B.A. Nijstad, W. Stroebe, and H.F.M. Lodewijkx, "Production Blocking and Idea Generation: Does Blocking Interfere with Cognitive Processes?," *Journal of Experimental Social Psychology* 39, no. 6 (2003): 531–48; B.A. Nijstad and W. Stroebe, "How the Group Affects the Mind: A Cognitive Model of Idea Generation in Groups," *Personality & Social Psychology Review* 10, no. 3 (2006): 186–213; W. Stroebe, B.A. Nijstad, and E.F. Rietzschel, "Beyond Productivity Loss in Brainstorming Groups: The Evolution of a Question," in *Advances in Experimental Social Psychology*, ed. P.Z. Mark and M.O. James (Academic Press, 2010), 157–203.

97. B.E. Irmer, P. Bordia, and D. Abusah, "Evaluation Apprehension and Perceived Benefits in Interpersonal and Database Knowledge Sharing," *Academy of Management Proceedings* (2002): B1–B6.

98. A.D. Stajkovic, D. Lee, and A.J. Nyberg, "Collective Efficacy, Group Potency, and Group Performance: Meta-Analyses of Their Relationships, and Test of a Mediation Model," *Journal of Applied Psychology* 94, no. 3 (2009): 814–28; J. Schepers et al., "Fields of Gold: Perceived Efficacy in Virtual Teams of Field Service Employees," *Journal of Service Research* 14, no. 3 (2011): 372–89. OB experts describe team efficacy as efficacy toward a specific task, whereas team potency is the team's general efficacy.

99. D. Miller, *The Icarus Paradox: How Exceptional Companies Bring About Their Own Downfall* (New York: HarperBusiness, 1990); G. Whyte, "Recasting Janis's Groupthink Model: The Key Role of Collective Efficacy in Decision Fiascoes," *Organizational Behavior and Human Decision Processes* 73, no. 2–3 (1998): 185–209; K. Tasa and G. Whyte, "Collective Efficacy and Vigilant Problem Solving in Group Decision Making: A Non-Linear Model," *Organizational Behavior and Human Decision Processes* 96, no. 2 (2005): 119–29; H.J.M. Kooij-de Bode, D. Van Knippenberg, and W.P. Van Ginkel, "Good Effects of Bad Feelings: Negative Affectivity and Group Decision-Making," *British Journal of Management* 21, no. 2 (2010): 375–92; S.K. Lam and J. Schaubroeck, "Information Sharing and Group Efficacy Influences on Communication and Decision Quality," *Asia Pacific Journal of Management* 28, no. 3 (2011): 509–28; J.A. Minson and J.S. Mueller, "The Cost of Collaboration: Why Joint Decision Making Exacerbates Rejection of Outside Information," *Psychological Science* 23, no. 3 (2012): 219–24; K.D. Clark and P.G. Maggitti, "TMT Potency and Strategic Decision-Making in High Technology Firms," *Journal of Management Studies* 49, no. 7 (2012): 1168–93.

100. The term *brainstorm* dates back to a New York murder trial in February 1907, during which an alienist (psychiatrist) gave expert testimony that the accused had a "brain storm," which he described as a form of temporary insanity. But by the mid-1920s, a brainstorm was associated with creative thinking. For example, *Popular Science* magazine's lead article in April 1926

described innovative camera operators, one of whom received a film award for a brainstorm of filming while strapped to a windmill. Advertising executive Alex Osborn (the *O* in BBDO, the largest creative agency owned by Omnicom) first described the brainstorming process in the little-known 1942 booklet *How to Think Up* (p. 29). Osborn gave a fuller description of the brainstorming process in his popular 1948 (*Your Creative Power*) and 1953 (*Applied Imagination*) books. See A.F. Osborn, *How to Think Up* (New York: McGraw-Hill, 1942), Chap. 4; A.F. Osborn, *Your Creative Power* (New York: Scribner's Sons, 1948); A.F. Osborn, *Applied Imagination* (New York: Scribner's Sons, 1953).

101. B. Mullen, C. Johnson, and E. Salas, "Productivity Loss in Brainstorming Groups: A Meta-Analytic Integration," *Basic and Applied Psychology* 12 (1991): 2–23. The 1957 business article critiquing brainstorming is B.S. Benson, "Let's Toss This Idea Up," *Fortune*, October 1957, 145–46.

102. R.I. Sutton and A. Hargadon, "Brainstorming Groups in Context: Effectiveness in a Product Design Firm," *Administrative Science Quarterly* 41 (1996): 685–718; T. Kelley, *The Art of Innovation* (New York: Currency Doubleday, 2001); T. Kelley, *The Ten Faces of Innovation* (New York: Doubleday, 2005); K. Sawyer, *Group Genius: The Creative Power of Collaboration* (New York: Basic Books, 2007).

103. P.A. Heslin, "Better Than Brainstorming? Potential Contextual Boundary Conditions to Brainwriting for Idea Generation in Organizations," *Journal of Occupational and Organizational Psychology* 82, no. 1 (2009): 129–45; J.S. Linsey and B. Becker, "Effectiveness of Brainwriting Techniques: Comparing Nominal Groups to Real Teams," in *Design Creativity 2010*, ed. T. Taura and Y. Nagai (London: Springer London, 2011), 165–71; N. Michinov, "Is Electronic Brainstorming or Brainwriting the Best Way to Improve Creative Performance in Groups? An Overlooked Comparison of Two Idea-Generation Techniques," *Journal of Applied Social Psychology* 42 (2012): E222–E243.

104. R.B. Gallupe, L.M. Bastianutti, and W.H. Cooper, "Unblocking Brainstorms," *Journal of Applied Psychology* 76 (1991): 137–42; W.H. Cooper et al., "Some Liberating Effects of Anonymous Electronic Brainstorming," *Small Group Research* 29, no. 2 (1998): 147–78; A.R. Dennis, B.H. Wixom, and R.J. Vandenberg, "Understanding Fit and Appropriation Effects in Group Support Systems Via Meta-Analysis," *MIS Quarterly* 25, no. 2 (2001): 167–93; D.M. DeRosa, C.L. Smith, and D.A. Hantula, "The Medium Matters: Mining the Long-Promised Merit of Group Interaction in Creative Idea Generation Tasks in a Meta-Analysis of the Electronic Group Brainstorming Literature," *Computers in Human Behavior* 23, no. 3 (2007): 1549–81.

105. A.L. Delbecq, A.H. Van de Ven, and D.H. Gustafson, *Group Techniques for Program Planning: A Guide to Nominal Group and Delphi Processes* (Middleton, WI: Green Briar Press, 1986).

106. D.M. Spencer, "Facilitating Public Participation in Tourism Planning on American Indian Reservations: A Case Study Involving the Nominal Group Technique," *Tourism Management* 31, no. 5 (2011): 684–90.

107. S. Frankel, "NGT + MDS: An Adaptation of the Nominal Group Technique for Ill-Structured Problems," *Journal of Applied Behavioral Science* 23 (1987): 543–51; H. Barki and A. Pinsonneault, "Small Group Brainstorming and Idea Quality: Is Electronic Brainstorming the Most Effective Approach?," *Small Group Research* 32, no. 2 (2001): 158–205.

108. P.P. Lago et al., "Structuring Group Decision Making in a Web-Based Environment by Using the Nominal Group Technique," *Computers & Industrial Engineering* 52, no. 2 (2007): 277–95.

Chapter 8

1. E. Gibson, "Working from Home: Not Enough Contact with Others," *Southland Times* (Invercargill, NZ), October 6, 2012, 22.

2. A.H. Van de Ven, A.L. Delbecq, and R. Koenig Jr., "Determinants of Coordination Modes within Organizations," *American Sociological Review* 41, no. 2 (1976): 322–38; J.H. Gittell, R. Seidner, and J. Wimbush, "A Relational Model of How High-Performance Work Systems Work," *Organization Science* 21, no. 2 (2010): 490–506; R. Foy et al., "Meta-Analysis: Effect of Interactive Communication between Collaborating Primary Care Physicians and Specialists," *Annals of Internal Medicine* 152, no. 4 (2010): 247–58.

3. C. Barnard, *The Functions of the Executive* (Cambridge, MA: Harvard University Press, 1938), 82. Barnard's entire statement also refers to the other features of organizations that we describe in Chapter 1, namely that (a) people are willing to contribute their effort to the organization and (b) they have a common purpose.

4. M.T. Hansen, M.L. Mors, and B. Løvås, "Knowledge Sharing in Organizations: Multiple Networks, Multiple Phases," *Academy of Management Journal* 48, no. 5 (2005): 776–93; S.R. Murray and J. Peyrefitte, "Knowledge Type and Communication Media Choice in the Knowledge Transfer Process," *Journal of Managerial Issues* 19, no. 1 (2007): 111–33; S.L. Hoe and S.L. McShane, "Structural and Informal Knowledge Acquisition and Dissemination in Organizational Learning: An Exploratory Analysis," *Learning Organization* 17, no. 4 (2010): 364–86.

5. J. O'Toole and W. Bennis, "What's Needed Next: A Culture of Candor," *Harvard Business Review* 87, no. 6 (2009): 54–61.

6. W.J.L. Elving, "The Role of Communication in Organisational Change," *Corporate Communications* 10, no. 2 (2005): 129–38; P.M. Leonardi, T.B. Neeley, and E.M. Gerber, "How Managers Use Multiple Media: Discrepant Events, Power, and Timing in Redundant Communication," *Organization Science* 23, no. 1 (2012): 98–117; D.A. Tucker, P. Yeow, and G.T. Viki, "Communicating during Organizational Change Using Social Accounts: The Importance of Ideological Accounts," *Management Communication Quarterly* 27, no. 2 (2013): 184–209.

7. N. Ellemers, R. Spears, and B. Doosje, "Self and Social Identity," *Annual Review of Psychology* 53 (2002): 161–86; S.A. Haslam and S. Reicher, "Stressing the Group: Social Identity and the Unfolding Dynamics of Responses to Stress," *Journal of Applied Psychology* 91, no. 5 (2006): 1037–52; M.T. Gailliot and R.F. Baumeister, "Self-Esteem, Belongingness, and Worldview Validation: Does Belongingness Exert a Unique Influence Upon Self-Esteem?," *Journal of Research in Personality* 41, no. 2 (2007): 327–45.

8. A.M. Saks, K.L. Uggerslev, and N.E. Fassina, "Socialization Tactics and Newcomer Adjustment: A Meta-Analytic Review and Test of a Model," *Journal of Vocational Behavior* 70, no. 3 (2007): 413–46.

9. S. Cohen, "The Pittsburgh Common Cold Studies: Psychosocial Predictors of Susceptibility to Respiratory Infectious Illness," *International Journal of Behavioral Medicine* 12, no. 3 (2005): 123–31; B.N. Uchino, "Social Support and Health: A Review of Physiological Processes Potentially Underlying Links to Disease Outcomes," *Journal of Behavioral Medicine* 29, no. 4 (2006): 377–87.

10. C.E. Shannon and W. Weaver, *The Mathematical Theory of Communication* (Urbana: University of Illinois Press, 1949); R.M. Krauss and S.R. Fussell, "Social Psychological Models of Interpersonal Communication," in *Social Psychology: Handbook of Basic Principles*, ed. E.T. Higgins and A. Kruglanski (New York: Guilford Press, 1996), 655–701.

11. J.R. Carlson and R.W. Zmud, "Channel Expansion Theory and the Experiential Nature of Media Richness Perceptions," *Academy of Management Journal* 42 (1999): 153–70.

12. P. Shachaf and N. Hara, "Behavioral Complexity Theory of Media Selection: A Proposed Theory for Global Virtual Teams," *Journal of Information Science* 33 (2007): 63–75.

13. M. Hauben and R. Hauben, "Netizens: On the History and Impact of Usenet and the Internet," *First Monday* 3, no. 8 (1998); J. Abbate, *Inventing the Internet* (Cambridge, MA: MIT Press, 1999).

14. One recent study found that email was the first or second choice for almost every situation (urgency, confidentiality, accountability, integrity, and social interaction). See P. Palvia et al., "Contextual Constraints in Media Choice: Beyond Information Richness," *Decision Support Systems* 51, no. 3 (2011): 657–70.

15. N.B. Ducheneaut and L.A. Watts, "In Search of Coherence: A Review of E-Mail Research," *Human-Computer Interaction* 20, no. 1–2 (2005): 11–48; R.S. Mano and G.S. Mesch, "E-Mail Characteristics, Work Performance and Distress," *Computers in Human Behavior* 26, no. 1 (2010): 61–69.

16. W. Lucas, "Effects of E-Mail on the Organization," *European Management Journal* 16, no. 1 (1998): 18–30; D.A. Owens, M.A. Neale, and R.I. Sutton, "Technologies of Status Management Status Dynamics in E-Mail Communications," *Research on Managing Groups and Teams* 3 (2000): 205–30; N.B. Ducheneaut, "Ceci n'est pas un Objet? Talking about Objects in E-Mail," *Human-Computer Interaction* 18, no. 1–2 (2003): 85–110.

17. N. Panteli, "Richness, Power Cues and Email Text," *Information & Management* 40, no. 2 (2002): 75–86; N.B. Ducheneaut, "The Social Impacts of Electronic Mail in Organizations: A Case Study of Electronic Power Games Using Communication Genres," *Information, Communication & Society* 5, no. 2 (2002): 153–88.

18. N. Epley and J. Kruger, "When What You Type Isn't What They Read: The Perseverance of Stereotypes and Expectancies over E-Mail," *Journal of Experimental Social Psychology* 41, no. 4 (2005): 414–22.

19. J. Kruger et al., "Egocentrism over E-Mail: Can We Communicate as Well as We Think?," *Journal of Personality and Social Psychology* 89, no. 6 (2005): 925–36.

20. D. Love, "This Company Banned Email and Loved It," *Business Insider*, December 16, 2013; T.R. Weiss, "No More Email: How One Company Broke the Habit (Mostly)," *CITEworld*, August 15, 2013.

21. J.B. Walther, "Language and Communication Technology: Introduction to the Special Issue," *Journal of Language and Social Psychology* 23, no. 4 (2004): 384–96; J.B. Walther, T. Loh, and L. Granka, "Let Me Count the Ways: The Interchange of Verbal and Nonverbal Cues in Computer-Mediated and Face-to-Face Affinity," *Journal of Language and Social Psychology* 24, no. 1 (2005): 36–65; K. Byron, "Carrying Too Heavy a Load? The Communication and Miscommunication of Emotion by Email," *Academy of Management Review* 33, no. 2 (2008): 309–27; J.M. Whalen, P.M. Pexman, and A.J. Gill, "'Should Be Fun—Not!': Incidence and Marking of Nonliteral Language in E-Mail," *Journal of Language and Social Psychology* 28, no. 3 (2009): 263–80.

22. Byron, "Carrying Too Heavy a Load?"

23. G. Hertel, S. Geister, and U. Konradt, "Managing Virtual Teams: A Review of Current Empirical Research," *Human Resource Management Review* 15 (2005): 69–95; H. Lee, "Behavioral Strategies for Dealing with Flaming in an Online Forum," *The Sociological Quarterly* 46, no. 2 (2005): 385–403.

24. G.F. Thomas and C.L. King, "Reconceptualizing E-Mail Overload," *Journal of Business and Technical Communication* 20, no. 3 (2006): 252–87; S.R. Barley, D.E. Meyerson, and S. Grodal, "E-Mail as a Source and Symbol of Stress," *Organization Science* 22, no. 4 (2011): 887–906.

25. The Radicati Group, *Email Statistics Report, 2014–2018*, The Radicati Group (Palo Alto, CA: April 2014); Symantec, *Symantec Intelligence Report*, Symantec Corporation (Mountain View, CA: January 2014).

26. R.D. Waters et al., "Engaging Stakeholders through Social Networking: How Nonprofit Organizations Are Using Facebook," *Public Relations Review* 35, no. 2 (2009): 102–106; J. Cunningham, "New Workers, New Workplace? Getting the Balance Right," *Strategic Direction* 26, no. 1 (2010): 5; A.M. Kaplan and M. Haenlein, "Users of the World, Unite! The Challenges and Opportunities of Social Media," *Business Horizons* 53, no. 1 (2010): 59–68.

27. Gagen MacDonald, *Internal Social Media—a Business Driver*, Gagen MacDonald (Chicago: January 24, 2012); Microsoft, *Microsoft Survey on Enterprise Social Use and Perceptions*, Microsoft (Seattle, WA: May 29, 2013); CareerBuilder, "More Employers Finding Reasons Not to Hire Candidates on Social Media, Finds CareerBuilder Survey," news release for CareerBuilder (Chicago: June 27, 2013); Kelly Services, *Social Media and Technology*, Kelly Global Workforce Index, Kelly Services (Troy, MI: November 2013); M. Duggan and A. Smith, *Social Media Update 2013*, Pew Research Center (Washington, DC: January 2014).

28. J.H. Kietzmann et al., "Social Media? Get Serious! Understanding the Functional Building Blocks of Social Media," *Business Horizons* 54, no. 3 (2011): 241–51; J.W. Treem and P.M. Leonardi, "Social Media Use in Organizations: Exploring the Affordances of Visibility, Editability, Persistence, and Association," *Communication Yearbook* 36 (2012): 143–89.

29. S. Holtz, "Open the Door," *Communication World*, September 2010, 26; "The Coworker Network," *Kellogg Insight*, June 3, 2013.

30. Towers Watson, *Capitalizing on Effective Communication* (New York: Towers Watson, February 4, 2010).

31. J. Champy, *What I Learned from Peter Drucker* (Boston: New Word City, 2010), Chap. 4.

32. L.Z. Tiedens and A.R. Fragale, "Power Moves: Complementarity in Dominant and Submissive Nonverbal Behavior," *Journal of Personality and Social Psychology* 84, no. 3 (2003): 558–68.

33. "Body Language in the Job Interview," CareerBuilder.com, August 23, 2011. Copyright 2011 CareerBuilder, LLC. Reprinted with permission. The sample size of this survey was not stated, but is likely quite large. The same survey the previous year in the United States had a sample size of 2,500 employers. Results of the U.S. survey were similar to the more recent UK results reported here.

34. P. Ekman and E. Rosenberg, *What the Face Reveals: Basic and Applied Studies of Spontaneous Expression Using the Facial Action Coding System* (Oxford, UK: Oxford University Press, 1997); P. Winkielman and K.C. Berridge, "Unconscious Emotion," *Current Directions in Psychological Science* 13, no. 3 (2004): 120–23.

35. W.J. Becker and R. Cropanzano, "Organizational Neuroscience: The Promise and Prospects of an Emerging Discipline," *Journal of Organizational Behavior* 31, no. 7 (2010): 1055–59.

36. M. Sonnby-Borgstrom, P. Jonsson, and O. Svensson, "Emotional Empathy as Related to Mimicry Reactions at Different Levels of Information Processing," *Journal of Nonverbal Behavior* 27 (2003): 3–23; S.K. Johnson, "I Second That Emotion: Effects of Emotional Contagion and Affect at Work on Leader and Follower Outcomes," *Leadership Quarterly* 19, no. 1 (2008): 1–19; V. Vijayalakshmi and S. Bhattacharyya, "Emotional Contagion and Its Relevance to Individual Behavior and Organizational Processes: A Position Paper," *Journal of Business and Psychology* 27, no. 3 (2012): 363–74.

37. J.R. Kelly and S.G. Barsade, "Mood and Emotions in Small Groups and Work Teams," *Organizational Behavior and Human Decision Processes* 86 (2001): 99–130; T.L. Chartrand and J.L. Lakin, "The Antecedents and Consequences of Human Behavioral Mimicry," *Annual Review of Psychology* 64, no. 1 (2013): 285–308.

38. J. Fulk, "Social Construction of Communication Technology," *Academy of Management Journal* 36, no. 5 (1993): 921–50; L.K. Treviño, J. Webster, and E.W. Stein, "Making Connections: Complementary Influences on Communication Media Choices, Attitudes, and Use," *Organization Science* 11, no. 2 (2000): 163–82; B. van den Hooff, J. Groot, and S. de Jonge, "Situational Influences on the Use of Communication Technologies," *Journal of Business Communication* 42, no. 1 (2005): 4–27; J.W. Turner et al., "Exploring the Dominant Media: How Does Media Use Reflect Organizational Norms and Affect Performance?," *Journal of Business Communication* 43, no. 3 (2006): 220–50; M.B. Watson-Manheim and F. Bélanger, "Communication Media Repertoires: Dealing with the Multiplicity of Media Choices," *MIS Quarterly* 31, no. 2 (2007): 267–93.

39. Z. Lee and Y. Lee, "Emailing the Boss: Cultural Implications of Media Choice," *IEEE Transactions on Professional Communication* 52, no. 1 (2009): 61–74; D. Holtbrügge, A. Weldon, and H. Rogers, "Cultural Determinants of Email Communication Styles," *International Journal of Cross Cultural Management* 13, no. 1 (2013): 89–110.

40. R.C. King, "Media Appropriateness: Effects of Experience on Communication Media Choice," *Decision Sciences* 28, no. 4 (1997): 877–910.

41. A.K.C. Au and D.K.S. Chan, "Organizational Media Choice in Performance Feedback: A Multifaceted Approach," *Journal of Applied Social Psychology* 43, no. 2 (2013): 397–407; K.K. Stephens, A.K. Barrett, and M.J. Mahometa, "Organizational Communication in Emergencies: Using Multiple Channels and Sources to Combat Noise and Capture Attention," *Human Communication Research* 39, no. 2 (2013): 230–51.

42. K. Griffiths, "KPMG Sacks 670 Employees by E-Mail," *The Independent* (London), November 5, 2002, 19; "Shop Worker Sacked by Text Message," *The Post* (Claremont/Nedlands, Western Australia), July 28, 2007, 1, 78.

43. R.L. Daft and R.H. Lengel, "Information Richness: A New Approach to Managerial Behavior and Organization Design," *Research in Organizational Behavior* 6 (1984): 191–233; R.H. Lengel and R.L. Daft, "The Selection of Communication Media as an Executive Skill," *Academy of Management Executive* 2 (1988): 225–32.

44. R.E. Rice, "Task Analyzability, Use of New Media, and Effectiveness: A Multi-Site Exploration of Media Richness," *Organization Science* 3 (1992): 475–500.

45. R.F. Otondo et al., "The Complexity of Richness: Media, Message, and Communication Outcomes," *Information & Management* 45, no. 1 (2008): 21–30.

46. N.L. Reinsch Jr., J.W. Turner, and C.H. Tinsley, "Multicommunicating: A Practice Whose Time Has Come?," *Academy of Management Review* 33, no. 2 (2008): 391–403; A.F. Cameron and J. Webster, "Multicommunicating: Juggling Multiple Conversations in the Workplace," *Information Systems Research* 24, no. 2 (2013): 352–71.

47. Carlson and Zmud, "Channel Expansion Theory and the Experiential Nature of Media Richness Perceptions"; N. Kock, "Media Richness or Media Naturalness? The Evolution of Our Biological Communication Apparatus and Its Influence on Our Behavior toward E-Communication Tools," *IEEE Transactions on Professional Communication* 48, no. 2 (2005): 117–30.

48. V.W. Kupritz and E. Cowell, "Productive Management Communication: Online and Face-to-Face," *Journal of Business Communication* 48, no. 1 (2011): 54–82.

49. D. Muller, T. Atzeni, and F. Butera, "Coaction and Upward Social Comparison Reduce the Illusory Conjunction Effect: Support for Distraction–Conflict Theory," *Journal of Experimental Social Psychology* 40, no. 5 (2004): 659–65; L.P. Robert and A.R. Dennis, "Paradox of Richness: A Cognitive Model of Media Choice," *IEEE Transactions on Professional Communication* 48, no. 1 (2005): 10–21.

50. E.V. Wilson, "Perceived Effectiveness of Interpersonal Persuasion Strategies in Computer-Mediated Communication," *Computers in Human Behavior* 19, no. 5 (2003): 537–52; K. Sassenberg, M. Boos, and S. Rabung, "Attitude Change in Face-to-Face and Computer-Mediated Communication: Private Self-Awareness as Mediator and Moderator," *European Journal of Social Psychology* 35 (2005): 361–74; P. Di Blasio and L. Milani, "Computer-Mediated Communication and Persuasion: Peripheral vs. Central Route to Opinion Shift," *Computers in Human Behavior* 24, no. 3 (2008): 798–815.

51. Kruger et al., "Egocentrism over E-Mail: Can We Communicate as Well as We Think?"

52. R.M. Krauss, "The Psychology of Verbal Communication," in *International Encyclopedia of the Social and Behavioral Sciences*, ed. N. Smelser and P. Baltes (London: Elsevier, 2002), 16161–65.

53. H. Tsoukas, "The Missing Link: A Transformational View of Metaphors in Organizational Science," *The Academy of Management review* 16, no. 3 (1991): 566–85; G. Morgan, *Images of Organization*, 2nd ed. (Thousand Oaks, CA: Sage, 1997); J. Amernic, R. Craig, and D. Tourish, "The Transformational Leader as Pedagogue, Physician, Architect, Commander, and Saint: Five Root Metaphors in Jack Welch's Letters to Stockholders of General Electric," *Human Relations* 60, no. 12 (2007): 1839–72.

54. M. Rubini and H. Sigall, "Taking the Edge Off of Disagreement: Linguistic Abstractness and Self-Presentation to a Heterogeneous Audience," *European Journal of Social Psychology* 32 (2002): 343–51.

55. T. Walsh, "Nardelli Brags on VIP Recruits, Game Plan," *Detroit Free Press*, September 8, 2007.

56. D. Goleman, R. Boyatzis, and A. McKee, *Primal Leaders* (Boston: Harvard Business School Press, 2002), 92–95.

57. O'Toole and Bennis, "What's Needed Next: A Culture of Candor."

58. T.W. Jackson and P. Farzaneh, "Theory-Based Model of Factors Affecting Information Overload," *International Journal of Information Management* 32, no. 6 (2012): 523–32.

59. A.G. Schick, L.A. Gordon, and S. Haka, "Information Overload: A Temporal Approach," *Accounting, Organizations & Society* 15 (1990): 199–220; A. Edmunds and A. Morris, "The Problem of Information Overload in Business Organisations: A Review of the Literature," *International Journal of Information Management* 20 (2000): 17–28; R. Pennington, "The Effects of Information Overload on Software Project Risk Assessment," *Decision Sciences* 38, no. 3 (2007): 489–526.

60. D.C. Thomas and K. Inkson, *Cultural Intelligence: People Skills for Global Business* (San Francisco: Berrett-Koehler, 2004), Chap. 6; D. Welch, L. Welch, and R. Piekkari, "Speaking in Tongues," *International Studies of Management & Organization* 35, no. 1 (2005): 10–27.

61. D. Woodruff, "Crossing Culture Divide Early Clears Merger Paths," *Asian Wall Street Journal*, May 28, 2001, 9; T. Craig, "Different Strokes," *Personnel Today*, November 25, 2008, 190.

62. S. Ohtaki, T. Ohtaki, and M.D. Fetters, "Doctor–Patient Communication: A Comparison of the USA and Japan," *Family Practice* 20 (2003): 276–82; M. Fujio, "Silence during Intercultural Communication: A Case Study," *Corporate Communications* 9, no. 4 (2004): 331–39.

63. T. Hasegawa and W.B. Gudykunst, "Silence in Japan and the United States," *Journal of Cross-Cultural Psychology* 29, no. 5 (1998): 668–84.

64. D.C. Barnlund, *Communication Styles of Japanese and Americans: Images and Realities* (Belmont, CA: Wadsworth, 1988); H. Yamada, *American and Japanese Business Discourse: A Comparison of Interaction Styles* (Norwood, NJ: Ablex, 1992), Chap. 2.

65. P. Harris and R. Moran, *Managing Cultural Differences* (Houston, TX: Gulf, 1987); H. Blagg, "A Just Measure of Shame?," *British Journal of Criminology* 37 (1997): 481–501; R.E. Axtell, *Gestures: The Do's and Taboos of Body Language around the World*, rev. ed. (New York: Wiley, 1998).

66. D. Tannen, *You Just Don't Understand: Men and Women in Conversation* (New York: Ballantine Books, 1990); L.L. Namy, L.C. Nygaard, and D. Sauerteig, "Gender Differences in Vocal Accommodation: The Role of Perception," *Journal of Language and Social Psychology* 21, no. 4 (2002): 422–32; J.L. Locke, *Duels and Duets: Why Men and Women Talk So Differently* (Cambridge, UK: Cambridge University Press, 2011); M.R. Atai and F. Chahkandi, "Democracy in Computer-Mediated Communication: Gender, Communicative Style, and Amount of Participation in Professional Listservs," *Computers in Human Behavior* 28, no. 3 (2012): 881–88; N.S. Baron and E.M. Campbell, "Gender and Mobile Phones in Cross-National Context," *Language Sciences* 34, no. 1 (2012): 13–27.

67. A. Mulac et al., " 'Uh-Huh. What's That All About?' Differing Interpretations of Conversational Backchannels and Questions as Sources of Miscommunication across Gender Boundaries," *Communication Research* 25 (1998): 641–68; N.M. Sussman and D.H. Tyson, "Sex and Power: Gender Differences in Computer-Mediated Interactions," *Computers in Human Behavior* 16 (2000): 381–94; D.R. Caruso and P. Salovey, *The Emotionally Intelligent Manager* (San Francisco: Jossey-Bass, 2004), 23; D. Fallows, *How Women and Men Use the Internet*, Pew Internet and American Life Project (Washington, DC: December 28, 2005).

68. Amernic et al., "The Transformational Leader as Pedagogue, Physician, Architect, Commander, and Saint"; Microsoft, *Microsoft Survey on Enterprise Social Use and Perceptions*, May 27, 2013.

69. A. Hill, "GE's Bright Sparks Take the Lead," *Financial Times* (London), October 13, 2011, 12.

70. L.B. Comer and T. Drollinger, "Active Empathetic Listening and Selling Success: A Conceptual Framework," *Journal of Personal Selling & Sales Management* 19 (1999): 15–29; T. Drollinger, L.B. Comer, and P.T. Warrington, "Development and Validation of the Active Empathetic Listening Scale," *Psychology and Marketing* 23, no. 2 (2006): 161–80.

71. This quotation is varied slightly from the original translations by E. Carter, *All the Works of Epictetus, Which Are Now Extant*, 3rd ed., 2 vols., vol. 2 (London: J. and F. Rivington, 1768), 333; T.W. Higginson, *The Works of Epictetus* (Boston: Little, Brown, 1866), 428.

72. K. Shevory, "Office Work Space Is Shrinking, but That's Not All Bad," *The New York Times*, January 19, 2011, 8; "The Shrinking Cubicle," *Chicago Tribune*, February 9, 2011.

73. A. Leaman and B. Bordass, "Productivity in Buildings: The Killer Variables," *Building Research & Information* 27, no. 1 (1999): 4–19; T.J. Allen, "Architecture and Communication among Product Development Engineers," *California Management Review* 49, no. 2 (2007): 23–41; F. Becker, "Organizational Ecology and Knowledge Networks," *California Management Review* 49, no. 2 (2007): 42–61.

74. G. Evans and D. Johnson, "Stress and Open-Office Noise," *Journal of Applied Psychology* 85 (2000): 779–83; F. Russo, "My Kingdom for a Door," *Time Magazine*, October 23, 2000, B1.

75. D. Waisberg, "Quiet Please! . . . We're Working," *National Post*, May 30, 2007.

76. S.P. Means, "Playing at Pixar," *Salt Lake Tribune* (Utah), May 30, 2003, D1; G. Whipp, "Swimming against the Tide," *Los Angeles Daily News*, May 30, 2003, U6.

77. D. Bracken, "Open Office Plans Make 'Mine' a Thing of the Past," *News & Observer* (Raleigh, NC), March 13, 2011; "GSK Plays Musical Chairs at Work," *Business North Carolina*, June 2012; "Cost Efficient, Open-Space Office Designs: Ditching Desks—and Privacy," *Knowledge@Wharton*, June 19, 2013.

78. C. Wagner and A. Majchrzak, "Enabling Customer-Centricity Using Wikis and the Wiki Way," *Journal of Management Information Systems* 23, no. 3 (2006): 17–43; C. Karena, "Working the Wiki Way," *Sydney Morning Herald*, March 6, 2007; R.B. Ferguson, "Build a Web 2.0 Platform and Employees Will Use It," *eWeek*, June 20, 2007.

79. Canadian Management Centre, *Build a Better Workplace: Employee Engagement Edition*, Canadian Management Centre (Toronto: August 23, 2012); F. Dent, J. Rabbetts, and V. Holton, *The Ashridge Management Index 2012/2013*, Ashridge Business School (Berkhamsted, UK: May 20, 2013); United States Office of Personnel Management, *Federal Employee Viewpoint Survey Results*, Office of Personnel Management (Washington, DC: November 12, 2013); American Psychological Association, *2014 Work and Well-Being Survey*, American Psychological Association (Washington, DC: April 2014).

80. T. Fenton, "Inside the WorldBlu List: 1-800-Got-Junk?'s CEO on Why 'Being Democratic Is Extremely Important to Maintaining Our Competitive Advantage,'" *WorldBlu Blog* (Atlanta: WorldBlu, January 3, 2008). The original term is "management by *wandering* around," but this has been replaced with "walking around" over the years. See W. Ouchi, *Theory Z* (New York: Avon Books, 1981), 176–77; T. Peters and R. Waterman, *In Search of Excellence* (New York: Harper and Row, 1982), 122.

81. R. Rousos, "Trust in Leaders Lacking at Utility," *The Ledger* (Lakeland, FL), July 29, 2003, B1; B. Whitworth and B. Riccomini, "Management Communication: Unlocking Higher Employee Performance," *Communication World*, March/April 2005, 18–21.

82. K. Davis, "Management Communication and the Grapevine," *Harvard Business Review* 31 (1953): 43–49; W.L. Davis and J.R. O'Connor, "Serial Transmission of Information: A Study of the Grapevine," *Journal of Applied Communication Research* 5 (1977): 61–72.

83. S.R. Clegg and A. van Iterson, "Dishing the Dirt: Gossiping in Organizations," *Culture and Organization* 15, no. 3–4 (2009): 275–89; C. Mills, "Experiencing Gossip: The Foundations for a Theory of Embedded Organizational Gossip," *Group & Organization Management* 35, no. 2 (2010): 213–40.

84. R.L. Rosnow, "Inside Rumor: A Personal Journey," *American Psychologist* 46 (1991): 484–96; C.J. Walker and C.A. Beckerle, "The Effect of State Anxiety on Rumor Transmission," *Journal of Social Behavior & Personality* 2 (1987): 353–60; M. Noon and R. Delbridge, "News from Behind My Hand: Gossip in Organizations," *Organization Studies* 14 (1993): 23–36.

85. N. Nicholson, "Evolutionary Psychology: Toward a New View of Human Nature and Organizational Society," *Human Relations* 50 (1997): 1053–78; E.K. Foster, "Research on Gossip: Taxonomy, Methods, and Future Directions," *Review of General Psychology* 8, no. 2 (2004): 78–99; B. Beersma and G.A. Van Kleef, "Why People Gossip: An Empirical Analysis of Social Motives, Antecedents, and Consequences," *Journal of Applied Social Psychology* 42, no. 11 (2012): 2640–70.

Chapter 9

1. C. Chynoweth, "Subtle Art of Managing the Boss," *Sunday Times* (London), May 17, 2009, 1; P. Lencioni, "How to Manage Your Boss," *The Wall Street Journal*, January 3, 2009; R.C. Matuson, *Suddenly in Charge: Managing Up, Managing Down, Succeeding All Around* (Boston: Nicholas Brealey, 2011).

2. J.R. French and B. Raven, "The Bases of Social Power," in *Studies in Social Power*, ed. D. Cartwright (Ann Arbor: University of Michigan Press, 1959), 150–67; A.D. Galinsky et al., "Power and Perspectives Not Taken," *Psychological Science* 17, no. 12 (2006): 1068–74. Also see H. Mintzberg, *Power in and around Organizations* (Englewood Cliffs, NJ: Prentice Hall, 1983), Chap. 1; J. Pfeffer, *Managing with Power: Politics and Influence in Organizations* (Boston: Harvard Business School Press, 1992), 17, 30; A. Guinote and T.K. Vescio, "Introduction: Power in Social Psychology," in *The Social Psychology of Power*, ed. A. Guinote and T.K. Vescio (New York: Guilford Press, 2010), 1–18.

3. R.A. Dahl, "The Concept of Power," *Behavioral Science* 2 (1957): 201–18; R.M. Emerson, "Power-Dependence Relations," *American Sociological Review* 27 (1962): 31–41; A.M. Pettigrew, *The Politics of Organizational Decision-Making* (London: Tavistock, 1973).

4. G.A. Van Kleef et al., "Breaking the Rules to Rise to Power: How Norm Violators Gain Power in the Eyes of Others," *Social Psychological & Personality Science* 2, no. 5 (2011): 500–507.

5. J. Pfeffer and G.R. Salancik, *The External Control of Organizations* (New York: Harper & Row, 1978), 52–54; R. Gulati and M. Sytch, "Dependence Asymmetry and Joint Dependence in Interorganizational Relationships: Effects of Embeddedness on a Manufacturer's Performance in Procurement Relationships," *Administrative Science Quarterly* 52, no. 1 (2007): 32–69.

6. French and Raven, "The Bases of Social Power"; P.M. Podsakoff and C. Schreisheim, "Field Studies of French and Raven's Bases of Power: Critique, Analysis, and Suggestions for Future Research," *Psychological Bulletin* 97 (1985): 387–411; P.P. Carson and K.D. Carson, "Social Power Bases: A Meta-Analytic Examination of Interrelationships and Outcomes," *Journal of Applied Social Psychology* 23 (1993): 1150–69. The alternative models of power bases are reviewed in a recent dissertation by Heinemann, who points out that most of them parallel French and Raven's list. See P. Heinemann, *Power Bases and Informational Influence Strategies: A Behavioral Study on the Use of Management Accounting Information* (Wiesbaden, Germany: Deutscher Universitäts-Verlag, 2008). Raven subsequently proposed information power as a sixth source of power. We present information power as forms of legitimate and expert power rather than as a distinct sixth power base.

7. C. Barnard, *The Function of the Executive* (Cambridge, MA: Harvard University Press, 1938), 167–70; C. Hardy and S.R. Clegg, "Some Dare Call It Power," in *Handbook of Organization Studies*, ed. S.R. Clegg, C. Hardy, and W.R. Nord (London: Sage, 1996), 622–41.

8. A.I. Shahin and P.L. Wright, "Leadership in the Context of Culture: An Egyptian Perspective," *Leadership & Organization Development Journal* 25, no. 5/6 (2004): 499–511; Y.J. Huo et al., "Leadership and the Management of Conflicts in Diverse Groups: Why Acknowledging versus Neglecting Subgroup Identity Matters," *European Journal of Social Psychology* 35, no. 2 (2005): 237–54.

9. B. Crumley, "Game of Death: France's Shocking TV Experiment," *Time*, March 17, 2010; R.L. Parry, "Contestants Turn Torturers in French TV Experiment," *Yahoo! News*, March 16, 2010.

10. B.H. Raven, "Kurt Lewin Address: Influence, Power, Religion, and the Mechanisms of Social Control," *Journal of Social Issues* 55 (1999): 161–86.

11. A.W. Gouldner, "The Norm of Reciprocity: A Preliminary Statement," *American Sociological Review* 25 (1960): 161–78.

12. J. Renn, R. Schulmann, and S. Smith, *Albert Einstein/Mileva Maric: The Love Letters* (Princeton, NJ: Princeton University Press, 1992), xix.

13. G. Yukl and C.M. Falbe, "Importance of Different Power Sources in Downward and Lateral Relations," *Journal of Applied Psychology* 76 (1991): 416–23; Raven, "Kurt Lewin Address: Influence, Power, Religion, and the Mechanisms of Social Control."

14. P.L. Dawes, D.Y. Lee, and G.R. Dowling, "Information Control and Influence in Emergent Buying Centers," *Journal of Marketing* 62, no. 3 (1998): 55–68; D. Willer, "Power-at-a-Distance," *Social Forces* 81, no. 4 (2003): 1295–334; D.J. Brass et al., "Taking Stock of Networks and Organizations: A Multilevel Perspective," *Academy of Management Journal* 47, no. 6 (2004): 795–817.

15. S.L. Robinson, J. O'Reilly, and W. Wang, "Invisible at Work: An Integrated Model of Workplace Ostracism," *Journal of Management* 39, no. 1 (2013): 203–31.

16. M. Bolch, "Rewarding the Team," *HRMagazine*, February 2007, 91–93.

17. J.M. Peiro and J.L. Melia, "Formal and Informal Interpersonal Power in Organisations: Testing a Bifactorial Model of Power in Role-Sets," *Applied Psychology* 52, no. 1 (2003): 14–35.

18. C.R. Hinings et al., "Structural Conditions of Intraorganizational Power," *Administrative Science Quarterly* 19 (1974): 22–44. Also see C.S. Saunders, "The Strategic Contingency Theory of Power: Multiple Perspectives," *Journal of Management Studies* 27 (1990): 1–21.

19. R.B. Cialdini and N.J. Goldstein, "Social Influence: Compliance and Conformity," *Annual Review of Psychology* 55 (2004): 591–621.

20. C.K. Hofling et al., "An Experimental Study in Nurse-Physician Relationships," *Journal of Nervous and Mental Disease* 143, no. 2 (1966): 171–77.

21. C. Perkel, "It's Not CSI," *Canadian Press*, November 10, 2007; "Dr. Charles Smith: The Man Behind the Public Inquiry," *CBC News* (Toronto), August 10, 2010. Evidence-based management writers also warn against blindly following the advice of management gurus. See J. Pfeffer and R.I. Sutton, *Hard Facts, Dangerous Half-Truths, and Total Nonsense* (Boston: Harvard Business School Press, 2006), 45–46.

22. K. Miyahara, "Charisma: From Weber to Contemporary Sociology," *Sociological Inquiry* 53, no. 4 (1983): 368–88; J.D. Kudisch and

M.L. Poteet, "Expert Power, Referent Power, and Charisma: Toward the Resolution of a Theoretical Debate," *Journal of Business & Psychology* 10 (1995): 177–95; D. Ladkin, "The Enchantment of the Charismatic Leader: Charisma Reconsidered as Aesthetic Encounter," *Leadership* 2, no. 2 (2006): 165–79.

23. D.J. Hickson et al., "A Strategic Contingencies' Theory of Intraorganizational Power," *Administrative Science Quarterly* 16 (1971): 216–27; Hinings et al., "Structural Conditions of Intraorganizational Power"; R.M. Kanter, "Power Failure in Management Circuits," *Harvard Business Review* (1979): 65–75.

24. A. Bryant, "The Right Job? It's Much Like the Right Spouse," *The New York Times*, May 22, 2011, 2. The DNA acronym is from M.D. Johnson, *Brand Me. Make Your Mark: Turn Passion into Profit* (Blacklick, OH: Ambassador Press, 2008).

25. L. White, "Go for Gold with a Winning Personal Brand," *24 Hours Vancouver*, February 24, 2014, 12.

26. Hickson et al., "A Strategic Contingencies' Theory of Intraorganizational Power," 219–21; J.D. Hackman, "Power and Centrality in the Allocation of Resources in Colleges and Universities," *Administrative Science Quarterly* 30 (1985): 61–77; D.J. Brass and M.E. Burkhardt, "Potential Power and Power Use: An Investigation of Structure and Behavior," *Academy of Management Journal* 36 (1993): 441–70.

27. S.D. Harrington and B. Ivry, "For Commuters, a Day to Adapt," *The Record* (Bergen, NJ), December 21, 2005, A1; S. McCarthy, "Transit Strike Cripples New York," *Globe & Mail* (Toronto), December 21, 2005, A17.

28. M. Kennett, "Remote Control: How to Manage Homeworkers," *Management Today*, March 1, 2011, 46.

29. A. Caza, "Typology of the Eight Domains of Discretion in Organizations," *Journal of Management Studies* 49, no. 1 (2012): 144–77.

30. Kanter, "Power Failure in Management Circuits"; B.E. Ashforth, "The Experience of Powerlessness in Organizations," *Organizational Behavior and Human Decision Processes* 43 (1989): 207–42.

31. S. Wasserman and K. Faust, *Social Network Analysis: Methods and Applications*, Structural Analysis in the Social Sciences (Cambridge, UK: Cambridge University Press, 1994), Chap. 1; Brass et al., "Taking Stock of Networks and Organizations: A Multilevel Perspective."

32. M. Grossetti, "Where Do Social Relations Come From?: A Study of Personal Networks in the Toulouse Area of France," *Social Networks* 27, no. 4 (2005): 289–300.

33. Y. Fan, "Questioning Guanxi: Definition, Classification, and Implications," *International Business Review* 11 (2002): 543–61; W.R. Vanhonacker, "When Good Guanxi Turns Bad," *Harvard Business Review* 82, no. 4 (2004): 18–19; R.J. Taormina and J.H. Gao, "A Research Model for Guanxi Behavior: Antecedents, Measures, and Outcomes of Chinese Social Networking," *Social Science Research* 39, no. 6 (2010): 1195–212.

34. D. Krackhardt and J.R. Hanson, "Informal Networks: The Company Behind the Chart," *Harvard Business Review* 71 (1993): 104–11; A. Portes, "Social Capital: Its Origins and Applications in Modern Society," *Annual Review of Sociology* 24 (1998): 1–24.

35. P.S. Adler and S.W. Kwon, "Social Capital: Prospects for a New Concept," *Academy of Management Review* 27, no. 1 (2002): 17–40.

36. R.F. Chisholm, *Developing Network Organizations: Learning from Practice and Theory* (Reading, MA: Addison-Wesley Longman, 1998); W.S. Chow and L.S. Chan, "Social Network, Social Trust and Shared Goals in Organizational Knowledge Sharing," *Information & Management* 45, no. 7 (2008): 458–65.

37. R.S. Burt, *Structural Holes: The Social Structure of Competition* (Cambridge, MA: Harvard University Press, 1992).

38. M.T. Rivera, S.B. Soderstrom, and B. Uzzi, "Dynamics of Dyads in Social Networks: Assortative, Relational, and Proximity Mechanisms," *Annual Review of Sociology* 36 (2010): 91–115.

39. R. Cross and R.J. Thomas, *Driving Results through Social Networks: How Top Organizations Leverage Networks for Performance and Growth* (San Francisco: Jossey-Bass, 2009); R. McDermott and D. Archibald, "Harnessing Your Staff's Informal Networks," *Harvard Business Review* 88, no. 3 (2010): 82–89.

40. M. Kilduff and D. Krackhardt, *Interpersonal Networks in Organizations: Cognition, Personality, Dynamics, and Culture* (New York: Cambridge University Press, 2008).

41. Y. Amichai-Hamburger, G. Wainapel, and S. Fox, " 'On the Internet No One Knows I'm an Introvert': Extroversion, Neuroticism, and Internet Interaction," *CyberPsychology & Behavior* 5, no. 2 (2002): 125–28; K. Brooks, "Networking 101 for Introverts," *Psychology Today* (2010); D. Zack, *Networking for People Who Hate Networking* (San Francisco: Berrett-Koehler, 2010).

42. N.B. Ellison, C. Steinfield, and C. Lampe, "The Benefits of Facebook 'Friends': Social Capital and College Students' Use of Online Social Network Sites," *Journal of Computer-Mediated Communication* 12, no. 4 (2007): 1143–68.

43. M.S. Granovetter, "The Strength of Weak Ties," *American Journal of Sociology* 78 (1973): 1360–80; B. Erickson, "Social Networks," in *The Blackwell Companion to Sociology*, ed. J.R. Blau (Malden, MA: Blackwell, 2004), 314–26.

44. B. Uzzi and S. Dunlap, "How to Build Your Network," *Harvard Business Review* 83, no. 12 (2005): 53–60.

45. S.C. de Janasz and M.L. Forret, "Learning the Art of Networking: A Critical Skill for Enhancing Social Capital and Career Success," *Journal of Management Education* 32, no. 5 (2008): 629–50.

46. A. Mehra, M. Kilduff, and D.J. Brass, "The Social Networks of High and Low Self-Monitors: Implications for Workplace Performance," *Administrative Science Quarterly* 46 (2001): 121–46.

47. Burt, *Structural Holes: The Social Structure of Competition*.

48. B.R. Ragins and E. Sundstrom, "Gender and Power in Organizations: A Longitudinal Perspective," *Psychological Bulletin* 105 (1989): 51–88; M. Linehan, "Barriers to Women's Participation in International Management," *European Business Review* 13 (2001).

49. D.M. McCracken, "Winning the Talent War for Women: Sometimes It Takes a Revolution," *Harvard Business Review* (2000): 159–67.

50. J. Lammers, J.I. Stoker, and D.A. Stapel, "Differentiating Social and Personal Power: Opposite Effects on Stereotyping, but Parallel Effects on Behavioral Approach Tendencies," *Psychological Science* 20, no. 12 (2009): 1543–49.

51. D. Keltner, D.H. Gruenfeld, and C. Anderson, "Power, Approach, and Inhibition," *Psychological Review* 110, no. 2 (2003): 265–84; B. Simpson and C. Borch, "Does Power Affect Perception in Social Networks? Two Arguments and an Experimental Test," *Social Psychology Quarterly* 68, no. 3 (2005): 278–87; Galinsky et al., "Power and Perspectives Not Taken."

52. K. Atuahene-Gima and H. Li, "Marketing's Influence Tactics in New Product Development: A Study of High Technology Firms in China," *Journal of Product Innovation Management* 17 (2000): 451–70; A. Somech and A. Drach-Zahavy, "Relative Power and Influence Strategy: The Effects of Agent/Target Organizational Power on Superiors' Choices of Influence Strategies," *Journal of Organizational Behavior* 23 (2002): 167–79.

53. D. Kipnis, S.M. Schmidt, and I. Wilkinson, "Intraorganizational Influence Tactics: Explorations in Getting One's Way," *Journal of Applied Psychology* 65 (1980): 440–52; A. Rao and K. Hashimoto, "Universal and Culturally Specific Aspects of Managerial Influence: A Study of Japanese Managers," *Leadership Quarterly* 8 (1997): 295–312; L.A. McFarland, A.M. Ryan, and S.D. Kriska, "Field Study Investigation of Applicant Use of Influence Tactics in a Selection Interview," *Journal of Psychology* 136 (2002): 383–98.

54. C. de Gaulle, *The Edge of the Sword (Le Fil de l'epée)*, trans. G. Hopkins (London: Faber, 1960), 59.

55. Cialdini and Goldstein, "Social Influence: Compliance and Conformity."

56. Rao and Hashimoto, "Universal and Culturally Specific Aspects of Managerial Influence." Silent authority as an influence tactic in non-Western cultures is also discussed in S.F. Pasa, "Leadership Influence in a High Power Distance and Collectivist Culture," *Leadership & Organization Development Journal* 21 (2000): 414–26.

57. "Be Part of the Team If You Want to Catch the Eye," *Birmingham Post* (UK), August 31, 2000, 14; S. Maitlis, "Taking It from the Top: How CEOs Influence (and Fail to Influence) Their Boards," *Organization Studies* 25, no. 8 (2004): 1275–311.

58. A.T. Cobb, "Toward the Study of Organizational Coalitions: Participant Concerns and Activities in a Simulated Organizational Setting," *Human Relations* 44 (1991): 1057–79; E.A. Mannix, "Organizations as Resource Dilemmas: The Effects of Power Balance on Coalition Formation in Small Groups," *Organizational Behavior and Human Decision Processes* 55 (1993): 1–22; D.J. Terry, M.A. Hogg, and K.M. White, "The Theory of Planned Behavior: Self-Identity, Social Identity and Group Norms," *British Journal of Social Psychology* 38 (1999): 225–44.

59. "One-in-Four Workers Have Felt Bullied in the Workplace, CareerBuilder Study Finds," news release for CareerBuilder (Chicago: PR Newswire, April 20, 2011); "Monster Global Poll Reveals Workplace Bullying Is Endemic," *OnRec: Online Recruitment Magazine*, June 10, 2011; E. Weinbren, "Pharmacists Facing Employer Intimidation," *Chemist & Druggist*, May 19, 2012, 12; "UK's Bully Bosses," *Daily Mirror* (London), January 9, 2012, 2.

60. A.P. Brief, *Attitudes in and around Organizations* (Thousand Oaks, CA: Sage, 1998), 69–84; D.J. O'Keefe, *Persuasion: Theory and Research* (Thousand Oaks, CA: Sage, 2002).

61. These and other features of message content in persuasion are detailed in R. Petty and J. Cacioppo, *Attitudes and Persuasion: Classic and Contemporary Approaches* (Dubuque, IA: W. C. Brown, 1981); M. Pfau, E.A. Szabo, and J. Anderson, "The Role and Impact of Affect in the Process of Resistance to Persuasion," *Human Communication Research* 27 (2001): 216–52; O'Keefe, *Persuasion: Theory and Research*, Chap. 9; R. Buck et al.,

"Emotion and Reason in Persuasion: Applying the ARI Model and the CASC Scale," *Journal of Business Research* 57, no. 6 (2004): 647–56; W.D. Crano and R. Prislin, "Attitudes and Persuasion," *Annual Review of Psychology* 57 (2006): 345–74.

62. N. Rhodes and W. Wood, "Self-Esteem and Intelligence Affect Influenceability: The Mediating Role of Message Reception," *Psychological Bulletin* 111, no. 1 (1992): 156–71.

63. M.C. Bolino and W.H. Tunley, "More Than One Way to Make an Impression: Exploring Profiles of Impression Management," *Journal of Management* 29 (2003): 141–60.

64. T. Peters, "The Brand Called You," *Fast Company*, August 1997; J. Sills, "Becoming Your Own Brand," *Psychology Today* 41, no. 1 (2008): 62–63.

65. J.S. Wilson, "Personal Branding in Today's Economy," *Atlanta Journal-Constitution*, May 29, 2011, D1.

66. D. Strutton and L.E. Pelton, "Effects of Ingratiation on Lateral Relationship Quality within Sales Team Settings," *Journal of Business Research* 43 (1998): 1–12; R. Vonk, "Self-Serving Interpretations of Flattery: Why Ingratiation Works," *Journal of Personality and Social Psychology* 82 (2002): 515–26.

67. J. Foster, "Here Are Best Answers to Job Interview Questions," *The Herald* (Rock Hill, SC), April 4, 2010.

68. C.A. Higgins, T.A. Judge, and G.R. Ferris, "Influence Tactics and Work Outcomes: A Meta-Analysis," *Journal of Organizational Behavior* 24 (2003): 90–106.

69. D. Strutton, L.E. Pelton, and J.F. Tanner, "Shall We Gather in the Garden: The Effect of Ingratiatory Behaviors on Buyer Trust in Salespeople," *Industrial Marketing Management* 25 (1996): 151–62; J. O'Neil, "An Investigation of the Sources of Influence of Corporate Public Relations Practitioners," *Public Relations Review* 29 (2003): 159–69.

70. C.M. Falbe and G. Yukl, "Consequences for Managers of Using Single Influence Tactics and Combinations of Tactics," *Academy of Management Journal* 35 (1992): 638–52.

71. R.C. Ringer and R.W. Boss, "Hospital Professionals' Use of Upward Influence Tactics," *Journal of Managerial Issues* 12 (2000): 92–108.

72. G. Blickle, "Do Work Values Predict the Use of Intraorganizational Influence Strategies?," *Journal of Applied Social Psychology* 30, no. 1 (2000): 196–205; P.P. Fu et al., "The Impact of Societal Cultural Values and Individual Social Beliefs on the Perceived Effectiveness of Managerial Influence Strategies: A Meso Approach," *Journal of International Business Studies* 35, no. 4 (2004): 284–305.

73. Robert Walters Australia, *Robert Walters Employee Insights Newsletter*, Robert Walters (Sydney: August 2012); CareerBuilder, "More Than One-Third of Workers Discuss Politics at Work," news release for CareerBuilder (Chicago: March 1, 2012); "Wasting Time at Work 2012" (salary.com, 2012), www.salary.com/wasting-time-at-work-2012/slide/11/ (accessed May 28, 2014); "Nearly 70% Experience 'Workplace Politics': Poll," (Taiwan: Focus Taiwan News Channel, September 30, 2013), http://focustaiwan.tw/news/asoc/201309300033.aspx (accessed May 28, 2014); CareerBuilder, "New CareerBuilder Study Explores the Perks and Pitfalls of Working in a Desk Job vs. a Non-Desk Job," news release for CareerBuilder (Chicago: May 22, 2014).

74. This has become the generally agreed-upon definition of organizational politics over the past two decades. See G.R. Ferris and K.M. Kacmar, "Perceptions of Organizational Politics," *Journal of Management* 18 (1992): 93–116; R. Cropanzano et al., "The Relationship of Organizational Politics and Support to Work Behaviors, Attitudes, and Stress," *Journal of Organizational Behavior* 18 (1997): 159–80; E. Vigoda, "Stress-Related Aftermaths to Workplace Politics: The Relationships among Politics, Job Distress, and Aggressive Behavior in Organizations," *Journal of Organizational Behavior* 23 (2002): 571–91. However, organizational politics was previously viewed as influence tactics outside the formal role that could be either selfish or altruistic. This older definition is less common today, possibly because it is incongruent with popular views of politics and because its meaning is too ambiguous. For the older perspective of organizational politics, see J. Pfeffer, *Power in Organizations* (Boston: Pitman, 1981); Mintzberg, *Power in and around Organizations*.

75. K.M. Kacmar and R.A. Baron, "Organizational Politics: The State of the Field, Links to Related Processes, and an Agenda for Future Research," in *Research in Personnel and Human Resources Management*, ed. G.R. Ferris (Greenwich, CT: JAI Press, 1999), 1–39; Vigoda, "Stress-Related Aftermaths to Workplace Politics"; C.H. Chang, C.C. Rosen, and P.E. Levy, "The Relationship between Perceptions of Organizational Politics and Employee Attitudes, Strain, and Behavior: A Meta-Analytic Examination," *Academy of Management Journal* 52, no. 4 (2009): 779–801. The quotation is from M. Landry, "Navigating the Political Minefield," *PM Network*, March 2013, 38–43.

76. This famous quotation is attributed to both Niccolò Machiavelli and Sun Tzu. None of Machiavelli's five main books (translated) has any statement close to this quotation. Sun Tzu's *The Art of War* book (translated) does not have this quotation, either, but he makes a similar statement about spies: "Hence it is that with none in the whole army are more intimate relations to be maintained than with spies." See Sun Tzu, *The Art of War*, trans. L. Giles (Mineola, NY: Dover, 2002), 98.

77. C. Hardy, *Strategies for Retrenchment and Turnaround: The Politics of Survival* (Berlin: Walter de Gruyter, 1990), Chap. 14; G.R. Ferris et al., "Perceptions of Organizational Politics: Prediction, Stress-Related Implications, and Outcomes," *Human Relations* 49 (1996): 233–63; M.C. Andrews and K.M. Kacmar, "Discriminating among Organizational Politics, Justice, and Support," *Journal of Organizational Behavior* 22 (2001): 347–66.

78. S. Blazejewski and W. Dorow, "Managing Organizational Politics for Radical Change: The Case of Beiersdorf-Lechia S.A., Poznan," *Journal of World Business* 38 (2003): 204–23.

79. L.W. Porter, R.W. Allen, and H.L. Angle, "The Politics of Upward Influence in Organizations," *Research in Organizational Behavior* 3 (1981): 120–22; R.J. House, "Power and Personality in Complex Organizations," *Research in Organizational Behavior* 10 (1988): 305–57.

80. R. Christie and F. Geis, *Studies in Machiavellianism* (New York: Academic Press, 1970); S.M. Farmer et al., "Putting Upward Influence Strategies in Context," *Journal of Organizational Behavior* 18 (1997): 17–42; K.S. Sauleya and A.G. Bedeian, "Equity Sensitivity: Construction of a Measure and Examination of Its Psychometric Properties," *Journal of Management* 26, no. 5 (2000): 885–910.

Chapter 10

1. S. Farberov, "American Airlines Flight Delayed Four Hours after Two Female Flight Attendants Start a Fight over Cell Phone," *Mail Online* (London), September 20, 2012; "American Eagle Flight Attendants' Argument Causes 4-Hour Delay at JFK," *NBC News*, September 20, 2012; S. Grossman, "Fight or Flight?," *Time*, September 21, 2012.

2. J.A. Wall and R.R. Callister, "Conflict and Its Management," *Journal of Management* 21 (1995): 515–58; M.A. Rahim, *Managing Conflict in Organizations*, 4th ed. (New Brunswick, NJ: Transaction, 2011), 15–17; D. Tjosvold, *Working Together to Get Things Done* (Lexington, MA: Lexington, 1986), 114–15; D. Tjosvold, "Defining Conflict and Making Choices about Its Management," *International Journal of Conflict Management* 17, no. 2 (2006): 87–95.

3. For example, see R.R. Blake, H.A. Shepard, and J.S. Mouton, *Managing Intergroup Conflict in Industry* (Houston: Gulf, 1964); K.E. Boulding, "Organization and Conflict," *Conflict Resolution* 1, no. 2 (1957): 122–34; C. Argyris, "The Individual and Organization: Some Problems of Mutual Adjustment," *Administrative Science Quarterly* 2, no. 1 (1957): 1–24; L. Urwick, *The Elements of Administration*, 2nd ed. (London: Pitman, 1947).

4. Rahim, *Managing Conflict in Organizations*.

5. K.A. Jehn and C. Bendersky, "Intragroup Conflict in Organizations: A Contingency Perspective on the Conflict-Outcome Relationship," *Research in Organizational Behavior* 25 (2003): 187–242; C.K.W. De Dreu and L.R. Weingart, "A Contingency Theory of Task Conflict and Performance in Groups and Organizational Teams," in *International Handbook of Organizational Teamwork and Cooperative Working*, ed. M.A. West, D. Tjosvold, and K.G. Smith (Chichester, UK: Wiley, 2003), 151–66; L. Troyer and R. Youngreen, "Conflict and Creativity in Groups," *Journal of Social Issues* 65, no. 2 (2009): 409–27.

6. *Workplace Conflict and How Businesses Can Harness It to Thrive*, CPP Global Human Capital Report, CPP, Inc. (Mountain View, CA: July 2008).

7. F.R.C. de Wit, L.L. Greer, and K.A. Jehn, "The Paradox of Intragroup Conflict: A Meta-Analysis," *Journal of Applied Psychology* 97, no. 2 (2012): 360–90; L.L. Meier et al., "Relationship and Task Conflict at Work: Interactive Short-Term Effects on Angry Mood and Somatic Complaints," *Journal of Occupational Health Psychology* 18, no. 2 (2013): 144–56.

8. M.P. Follett, "Constructive Conflict," in *Dynamic Administration: The Collected Papers of Mary Parker Follett*, ed. H.C. Metcalf and L. Urwick (Bath, UK: Management Publications Trust, 1941), 30–49.

9. J. Dewey, *Human Nature and Conduct: An Introduction to Social Psychology* (New York: Holt, 1922), 300.

10. Although the 1970s marked a point when the benefits of conflict became widely acknowledged, a few earlier writers had also expressed this view. See H. Assael, "Constructive Role of Interorganizational Conflict," *Administrative Science Quarterly* 14, no. 4 (1969): 573–82; L.A. Coser, *The Functions of Social Conflict* (New York: Free Press, 1956); J.A. Litterer, "Conflict in Organization: A Re-Examination," *Academy of Management Journal* 9 (1966): 178–86.

11. M. Duarte and G. Davies, "Testing the Conflict-Performance Assumption in Business-to-Business Relationships," *Industrial Marketing Management* 32 (2003): 91–99; M.A. Rahim, "Toward a Theory of Managing Organizational Conflict," *International Journal of Conflict Management* 13, no. 3 (2002): 206–35; J.D. Shaw et al., "A Contingency Model of Conflict and Team Effectiveness," *Journal of Applied Psychology* 96, no. 2 (2011): 391–400.

12. P.J. Carnevale, "Creativity in the Outcomes of Conflict," in *The Handbook of Conflict Resolution: Theory and Practice*, ed. M. Deutsch, P.T. Coleman, and E.C. Marcus (San Francisco: Jossey-Bass, 2006), 414–35; P.J. Boyle, D. Hanlon, and J.E. Russo, "The Value of Task Conflict to Group Decisions," *Journal of Behavioral Decision Making* 25, no. 3 (2012): 217–27.

13. K.M. Eisenhardt, J.L. Kahwajy, and L.J. Bourgeois III, "How Management Teams Can Have a Good Fight," *Harvard Business Review* (1997): 77–85; T. Greitemeyer et al., "Information Sampling and Group Decision Making: The Effects of an Advocacy Decision Procedure and Task Experience," *Journal of Experimental Psychology: Applied* 12, no. 1 (2006): 31–42; U. Klocke, "How to Improve Decision Making in Small Groups: Effects of Dissent and Training Interventions," *Small Group Research* 38, no. 3 (2007): 437–68; K.M. Eisenhardt, J.L. Kahwajy, and L.J. Bourgeois III, "Conflict and Strategic Choice: How Top Management Teams Disagree," *California Management Review* 39 (1997): 42–62.

14. Jehn and Bendersky, "Intragroup Conflict in Organizations"; L.H. Pelled, K.M. Eisenhardt, and K.R. Xin, "Exploring the Black Box: An Analysis of Work Group Diversity, Conflict, and Performance," *Administrative Science Quarterly* 44 (1999): 1–28; H. Guetzkow and J. Gyr, "An Analysis of Conflict in Decision-Making Groups," *Human Relations* 7, no. 3 (1954): 367–82. The notion of two types of conflict dates back to Georg Simmel, who described two types of conflict: one with a personal and subjective goal, the other which has an impersonal and objective quality. See Coser, *The Functions of Social Conflict*, 112. Contemporary scholars use various labels for task and relationship conflict. We have avoided the "cognitive" and "affective" conflict labels because cognitions and emotions are interconnected processes in all human activity. A third type of conflict, process conflict, is excluded due to limited research and doubts about its distinction from task conflict.

15. C.K.W. De Dreu, "When Too Little or Too Much Hurts: Evidence for a Curvilinear Relationship between Task Conflict and Innovation in Teams," *Journal of Management* 32, no. 1 (2006): 83–107; de Wit et al., "The Paradox of Intragroup Conflict: A Meta-Analysis."

16. J.L. Farh, C. Lee, and C.I.C. Farh, "Task Conflict and Team Creativity: A Question of How Much and When," *Journal of Applied Psychology* 95, no. 6 (2010): 1173–80.

17. R.S. Lau and A.T. Cobb, "Understanding the Connections between Relationship Conflict and Performance: The Intervening Roles of Trust and Exchange," *Journal of Organizational Behavior* 31, no. 6 (2010): 898–917.

18. C.K.W. De Dreu and L.R. Weingart, "Task versus Relationship Conflict, Team Performance, and Team Member Satisfaction: A Meta-Analysis," *Journal of Applied Psychology* 88 (2003): 587–604; A.C. Mooney, P.J. Holahan, and A.C. Amason, "Don't

Take It Personally: Exploring Cognitive Conflict as a Mediator of Affective Conflict," *Journal of Management Studies* 44, no. 5 (2007): 733–58; K. Choi and B. Cho, "Competing Hypotheses Analyses of the Associations between Group Task Conflict and Group Relationship Conflict," *Journal of Organizational Behavior* 32, no. 8 (2011): 1106–26.

19. J.X. Yang and K.W. Mossholder, "Decoupling Task and Relationship Conflict: The Role of Intergroup Emotional Processing," *Journal of Organizational Behavior* 25 (2004): 589–605; B.H. Bradley et al., "Ready to Rumble: How Team Personality Composition and Task Conflict Interact to Improve Performance," *Journal of Applied Psychology* 98, no. 2 (2013): 385–92; B.H. Bradley et al., "Reaping the Benefits of Task Conflict in Teams: The Critical Role of Team Psychological Safety Climate," *Journal of Applied Psychology* 97, no. 1 (2012): 151–58.

20. P.L. Curseu, S. Boros, and L.A.G. Oerlemans, "Task and Relationship Conflict in Short-Term and Long-Term Groups: The Critical Role of Emotion Regulation," *International Journal of Conflict Management* 23, no. 1 (2012): 97–107; A. Schlaerth, N. Ensari, and J. Christian, "A Meta-Analytical Review of the Relationship between Emotional Intelligence and Leaders' Constructive Conflict Management," *Group Processes & Intergroup Relations* 16, no. 1 (2013): 126–36.

21. de Wit et al., "The Paradox of Intragroup Conflict: A Meta-Analysis."

22. A.C. Amason and H.J. Sapienza, "The Effects of Top Management Team Size and Interaction Norms on Cognitive and Affective Conflict," *Journal of Management* 23, no. 4 (1997): 495–516.

23. L. Pondy, "Organizational Conflict: Concepts and Models," *Administrative Science Quarterly* 2 (1967): 296–320; K.W. Thomas, "Conflict and Negotiation Processes in Organizations," in *Handbook of Industrial and Organizational Psychology*, ed. M.D. Dunnette and L.M. Hough (Palo Alto, CA: Consulting Psychologists Press, 1992), 651–718.

24. H. Barki and J. Hartwick, "Conceptualizing the Construct of Interpersonal Conflict," *International Journal of Conflict Management* 15, no. 3 (2004): 216–44.

25. M.A. Von Glinow, D.L. Shapiro, and J.M. Brett, "Can We Talk, and Should We? Managing Emotional Conflict in Multicultural Teams," *Academy of Management Review* 29, no. 4 (2004): 578–92.

26. J.M. Brett, D.L. Shapiro, and A.L. Lytle, "Breaking the Bonds of Reciprocity in Negotiations," *Academy of Management Journal* 41 (1998): 410–24; G.E. Martin and T.J. Bergman, "The Dynamics of Behavioral Response to Conflict in the Workplace," *Journal of Occupational & Organizational Psychology* 69 (1996): 377–87.

27. R.E. Walton and J.M. Dutton, "The Management of Conflict: A Model and Review," *Administrative Science Quarterly* 14 (1969): 73–84; S.M. Schmidt and T.A. Kochan, "Conflict: Toward Conceptual Clarity," *Administrative Science Quarterly* 17, no. 3 (1972): 359–70.

28. J.A. McMullin, T. Duerden Comeau, and E. Jovic, "Generational Affinities and Discourses of Difference: A Case Study of Highly Skilled Information Technology Workers," *British Journal of Sociology* 58, no. 2 (2007): 297–316.

29. Although this quotation is widely attributed to Thomas Jefferson, scholars suggest that the third U.S. president and a founder of the nation did not make this statement. However, Jefferson did write that young people should bring about change. According to one source, the popular quotation is a derivation of Jefferson's statement in a letter to Colonel William S. Smith on November 13, 1787, "God forbid we should ever be 20 years without such a rebellion." T. Jefferson, *Memoir, Correspondence, and Miscellanies, from the Papers of Thomas Jefferson*, 2nd ed. (Boston: Gray and Bowen, 1830), 267. See http://wiki.monticello.org.

30. Data are from the 2009 Kelly Global Workforce Index, based on information published in news releases in each country by Kelly Services in September 2009.

31. R.M. Sarala, "The Impact of Cultural Differences and Acculturation Factors on Post-Acquisition Conflict," *Scandinavian Journal of Management* 26, no. 1 (2010): 38–56.

32. T. Taylor, "Change Is an Inevitable Part of Life," *Denver Business Journal Online*, October 8, 2012.

33. P.C. Earley and G.B. Northcraft, "Goal Setting, Resource Interdependence, and Conflict Management," in *Managing Conflict: An Interdisciplinary Approach*, ed. M.A. Rahim (New York: Praeger, 1989), 161–70; K. Jehn, "A Multimethod Examination of the Benefits and Detriments of Intragroup Conflict," *Administrative Science Quarterly* 40 (1995): 245–82.

34. A. Risberg, "Employee Experiences of Acquisition Processes," *Journal of World Business* 36 (2001): 58–84.

35. Jehn and Bendersky, "Intragroup Conflict in Organizations."

36. M. Hewstone, M. Rubin, and H. Willis, "Intergroup Bias," *Annual Review of Psychology* 53 (2002): 575–604; J. Jetten, R. Spears, and T. Postmes, "Intergroup Distinctiveness and Differentiation: A Meta-Analytic Integration," *Journal of Personality and Social Psychology* 86, no. 6 (2004): 862–79.

37. Follett, "Constructive Conflict"; Blake et al., *Managing Intergroup Conflict in Industry*; T. Ruble and K. Thomas, "Support for a Two-Dimensional Model of Conflict Behavior," *Organizational Behavior and Human Performance* 16 (1976): 143–55; C.K.W. De Dreu et al., "A Theory-Based Measure of Conflict Management Strategies in the Workplace," *Journal of Organizational Behavior* 22 (2001): 645–68; Rahim, "Toward a Theory of Managing Organizational Conflict."

38. E. Knowles, *Little Oxford Dictionary of Proverbs* (Oxford, UK: Oxford University Press, 2009), 21.

39. Q. Wang, E.L. Fink, and D.A. Cai, "The Effect of Conflict Goals on Avoidance Strategies: What Does Not Communicating Communicate?," *Human Communication Research* 38, no. 2 (2012): 222–52.

40. Several studies identify the antecedents of preferred conflict style. For example, see P.J. Moberg, "Linking Conflict Strategy to the Five-Factor Model: Theoretical and Empirical Foundations," *International Journal of Conflict Management* 12, no. 1 (2001): 47–68; H.A. Shih and E. Susanto, "Conflict Management Styles, Emotional Intelligence, and Job Performance in Public Organizations," *International Journal of Conflict Management* 21, no. 2 (2010): 147–68; J.E. Barbuto Jr., K.A. Phipps, and Y. Xu, "Testing Relationships between Personality, Conflict Styles and Effectiveness," *International Journal of Conflict Management* 21, no. 4 (2010): 434–47.

41. D.W. Johnson et al., "Effects of Cooperative, Competitive, and Individualistic Goal Structures on Achievement: A Meta-Analysis," *Psychological Bulletin* 89 (1981): 47–62; G.A. Callanan,

C.D. Benzing, and D.F. Perri, "Choice of Conflict-Handling Strategy: A Matter of Context," *Journal of Psychology* 140, no. 3 (2006): 269–88; Z. Ma et al., "The Impact of Group-Oriented Values on Choice of Conflict Management Styles and Outcomes: An Empirical Study in Turkey," *International Journal of Human Resource Management* 23, no. 18 (2012): 3776–93.

42. X.M. Song, J. Xile, and B. Dyer, "Antecedents and Consequences of Marketing Managers' Conflict-Handling Behaviors," *Journal of Marketing* 64 (2000): 50–66; R.A. Friedman et al., "What Goes around Comes around: The Impact of Personal Conflict Style on Work Conflict and Stress," *International Journal of Conflict Management* 11, no. 1 (2000): 32–55; M. Song, B. Dyer, and R.J. Thieme, "Conflict Management and Innovation Performance: An Integrated Contingency Perspective," *Academy of Marketing Science* 34, no. 3 (2006): 341–56; L.A. DeChurch, K.L. Hamilton, and C. Haas, "Effects of Conflict Management Strategies on Perceptions of Intragroup Conflict," *Group Dynamics* 11, no. 1 (2007): 66–78.

43. G.A. Chung-Yan and C. Moeller, "The Psychosocial Costs of Conflict Management Styles," *International Journal of Conflict Management* 21, no. 4 (2010): 382–99.

44. C.K.W. De Dreu and A.E.M. Van Vianen, "Managing Relationship Conflict and the Effectiveness of Organizational Teams," *Journal of Organizational Behavior* 22 (2001): 309–28; Wang et al., "The Effect of Conflict Goals on Avoidance Strategies: What Does Not Communicating Communicate?"

45. *Workplace Conflict and How Businesses Can Harness It to Thrive*; "Half of Aussie Workers 'Would Rather Quit'," *Sydney Morning Herald*, 22 August 2012.

46. A. Ergeneli, S.M. Camgoz, and P.B. Karapinar, "The Relationship between Self-Efficacy and Conflict-Handling Styles in Terms of Relative Authority Positions of the Two Parties," *Social Behavior & Personality: An International Journal* 38, no. 1 (2010): 13–28.

47. J. Simms, "Blood in the Boardroom," *Director* (2009): 48.

48. C.H. Tinsley, "How Negotiators Get to Yes: Predicting the Constellation of Strategies Used across Cultures to Negotiate Conflict," *Journal of Applied Psychology* 86, no. 4 (2001): 583–93; J.L. Holt and C.J. DeVore, "Culture, Gender, Organizational Role, and Styles of Conflict Resolution: A Meta-Analysis," *International Journal of Intercultural Relations* 29, no. 2 (2005): 165–96; Z. Ma, "Conflict Management Styles as Indicators of Behavioral Pattern in Business Negotiation," *International Journal of Conflict Management* 18, no. 3–4 (2007): 260–79.

49. D.A. Cai and E.L. Fink, "Conflict Style Differences between Individualists and Collectivists," *Communication Monographs* 69 (2002): 67–87; F.P. Brew and D.R. Cairns, "Styles of Managing Interpersonal Workplace Conflict in Relation to Status and Face Concern: A Study with Anglos and Chinese," *International Journal of Conflict Management* 15, no. 1 (2004): 27–57; C.H. Tinsley and E. Weldon, "Responses to a Normative Conflict among American and Chinese Managers," *International Journal of Conflict Management* 3, no. 2 (2003): 183–94.

50. Holt and DeVore, "Culture, Gender, Organizational Role, and Styles of Conflict Resolution"; M. Davis, S. Capobianco, and L. Kraus, "Gender Differences in Responding to Conflict in the Workplace: Evidence from a Large Sample of Working Adults," *Sex Roles* 63, no. 7 (2010): 500–14.

51. K. Lewin, *Resolving Social Conflicts* (New York: Harper, 1948).

52. J.D. Hunger and L.W. Stern, "An Assessment of the Functionality of the Superordinate Goal in Reducing Conflict," *Academy of Management Journal* 19, no. 4 (1976): 591–605. M. Sherif, "Superordinate Goals in the Reduction of Intergroup Conflict," *American Journal of Sociology* 63, no. 4 (1958): 349–56.

53. Sherif, "Superordinate Goals in the Reduction of Intergroup Conflict"; Eisenhardt et al., "How Management Teams Can Have a Good Fight"; Song et al., "Antecedents and Consequences of Marketing Managers' Conflict-Handling Behaviors"; O. Doucet, J. Poitras, and D. Chenevert, "The Impacts of Leadership on Workplace Conflicts," *International Journal of Conflict Management* 20, no. 4 (2009): 340–54.

54. Lau and Cobb, "Understanding the Connections between Relationship Conflict and Performance."

55. H.C. Triandis, "The Future of Workforce Diversity in International Organisations: A Commentary," *Applied Psychology: An International Journal* 52, no. 3 (2003): 486–95.

56. D. Nebenzahl, "Managing the Generation Gap," *Montreal Gazette*, February 28, 2009, G1; D. Deveau, "L'Oréal Canada Discovers the Beauty of Motivation," *Postmedia News* (Toronto), January 24, 2011; "L'Oreal Canada Considers Inter-Generational Teams a Strength," *National Post*, May 13, 2013.

57. T. Rutledge, "No. 4 Small Company: Brookstone," *Houston Chronicle*, November 10, 2012.

58. T.F. Pettigrew, "Intergroup Contact Theory," *Annual Review of Psychology* 49 (1998): 65–85; S. Brickson, "The Impact of Identity Orientation on Individual and Organizational Outcomes in Demographically Diverse Settings," *Academy of Management Review* 25 (2000): 82–101; J. Dixon and K. Durrheim, "Contact and the Ecology of Racial Division: Some Varieties of Informal Segregation," *British Journal of Social Psychology* 42 (2003): 1–23.

59. N. Yemchenko, "I'm a Corporate Volunteer," *System Capital Management: Corporate Blog*, April 26, 2013; "About 18,000 Employees of SCM Group Clean Up 73 Ukrainian Cities," news release for S.C. Management (Donetsk, Ukraine: April 22, 2013).

60. Triandis, "The Future of Workforce Diversity in International Organisations."

61. Von Glinow et al., "Can We Talk, and Should We?"

62. L.L. Putnam, "Beyond Third Party Role: Disputes and Managerial Intervention," *Employee Responsibilities and Rights Journal* 7 (1994): 23–36; A.R. Elangovan, "The Manager as the Third Party: Deciding How to Intervene in Employee Disputes," in *Negotiation: Readings, Exercises, and Cases*, ed. R.J. Lewicki, J.A. Litterer, and D. Saunders (New York: McGraw-Hill, 1999), 458–69. For a somewhat different taxonomy of managerial conflict intervention, see P.G. Irving and J.P. Meyer, "A Multidimensional Scaling Analysis of Managerial Third-Party Conflict Intervention Strategies," *Canadian Journal of Behavioural Science* 29, no. 1 (1997): 7–18. A recent review describes 10 species of third-party intervention, but these consist of variations of the three types described here. See D.E. Conlon et al., "Third Party Interventions across Cultures: No 'One Best Choice,'" in *Research in Personnel and Human Resources Management* (Greenwich, CT: JAI, 2007), 309–49.

63. J. Myers, "When Employee Conflict Gets in the Way of Business," *Globe & Mail (Toronto)*, 29 April 2011, B15; Accountemps, "Accountemps Survey: Managers Spend Nearly a Full Day Each

Week Dealing with Staff Conflicts," News release for Accountemps (Menlo Park, CA: 15 March 2011); P. Weaver and S. Mitchell, *Lessons for Leaders from the People Who Matter*, Development Dimensions International (Pittsburgh: 16 February 2012).

64. K. Bollen, H. Ittner, and M.C. Euwema, "Mediating Hierarchical Labor Conflicts: Procedural Justice Makes a Difference—for Subordinates," *Group Decision and Negotiation* 21, no. 5 (2012): 621–36; J.A. Wall and T.C. Dunne, "Mediation Research: A Current Review," *Negotiation Journal* 28, no. 2 (2012): 217–44.

65. B.H. Sheppard, "Managers as Inquisitors: Lessons from the Law," in *Bargaining inside Organizations*, ed. M.H. Bazerman and R.J. Lewicki (Beverly Hills, CA: Sage, 1983); N.H. Kim, D.W. Sohn, and J.A. Wall, "Korean Leaders' (and Subordinates') Conflict Management," *International Journal of Conflict Management* 10, no. 2 (1999): 130–53; D.J. Moberg, "Managers as Judges in Employee Disputes: An Occasion for Moral Imagination," *Business Ethics Quarterly* 13, no. 4 (2003): 453–77.

66. R. Karambayya and J.M. Brett, "Managers Handling Disputes: Third Party Roles and Perceptions of Fairness," *Academy of Management Journal* 32 (1989): 687–704; R. Cropanzano et al., "Disputant Reactions to Managerial Conflict Resolution Tactics," *Group & Organization Management* 24 (1999): 124–53.

67. A.R. Elangovan, "Managerial Intervention in Organizational Disputes: Testing a Prescriptive Model of Strategy Selection," *International Journal of Conflict Management* 4 (1998): 301–35; P.S. Nugent, "Managing Conflict: Third-Party Interventions for Managers," *Academy of Management Executive* 16, no. 1 (2002): 139–54.

68. Bollen et al., "Mediating Hierarchical Labor Conflicts: Procedural Justice Makes a Difference—for Subordinates"; R. Nesbit, T. Nabatchi, and L.B. Bingham, "Employees, Supervisors, and Workplace Mediation: Experiences of Justice and Settlement," *Review of Public Personnel Administration* 32, no. 3 (2012): 260–87.

69. J.P. Meyer, J.M. Gemmell, and P.G. Irving, "Evaluating the Management of Interpersonal Conflict in Organizations: A Factor-Analytic Study of Outcome Criteria," *Canadian Journal of Administrative Sciences* 14 (1997): 1–13; L.B. Bingham, "Employment Dispute Resolution: The Case for Mediation," *Conflict Resolution Quarterly* 22, no. 1/2 (2004): 145–74; M. Hyde et al., "Workplace Conflict Resolution and the Health of Employees in the Swedish and Finnish Units of an Industrial Company," *Social Science & Medicine* 63, no. 8 (2006): 2218–27.

70. W.H. Ross and D.E. Conlon, "Hybrid Forms of Third-Party Dispute Resolution: Theoretical Implications of Combining Mediation and Arbitration," *Academy of Management Review* 25, no. 2 (2000): 416–27; W.H. Ross, C. Brantmeier, and T. Ciriacks, "The Impact of Hybrid Dispute-Resolution Procedures on Constituent Fairness Judgments," *Journal of Applied Social Psychology* 32, no. 6 (2002): 1151–88.

71. R. Stagner and H. Rosen, *Psychology of Union–Management Relations* (Belmont, CA: Wadsworth, 1965), 95–96, 108–10; R.E. Walton and R.B. McKersie, *A Behavioral Theory of Labor Negotiations: An Analysis of a Social Interaction System* (New York: McGraw-Hill, 1965), 41–46; L. Thompson, *The Mind and Heart of the Negotiator* (Upper Saddle River, NJ: Prentice Hall, 1998), Chap. 2.

72. K.G. Allred, "Distinguishing Best and Strategic Practices: A Framework for Managing the Dilemma between Creating and Claiming Value," *Negotiation Journal* 16 (2000): 387–97.

73. S. Doctoroff, "Reengineering Negotiations," *Sloan Management Review* 39 (1998): 63–71; D.C. Zetik and A.F. Stuhlmacher, "Goal Setting and Negotiation Performance: A Meta-Analysis," *Group Processes & Intergroup Relations* 5 (2002): 35–52.

74. B. McRae, *The Seven Strategies of Master Negotiators* (Toronto: McGraw-Hill Ryerson, 2002), 7–11.

75. A.F. Stuhlmacher, T.L. Gillespie, and M.V. Champagne, "The Impact of Time Pressure in Negotiation: A Meta-Analysis," *International Journal of Conflict Management* 9, no. 2 (1998): 97–116; C.K.W. De Dreu, "Time Pressure and Closing of the Mind in Negotiation," *Organizational Behavior and Human Decision Processes* 91 (2003): 280–95. However, one recent study reported that speeding up these concessions leads to better negotiated outcomes. See D.A. Moore, "Myopic Prediction, Self-Destructive Secrecy, and the Unexpected Benefits of Revealing Final Deadlines in Negotiation," *Organizational Behavior and Human Decision Processes* 94, no. 2 (2004): 125–39.

76. R.J. Robertson, "Defusing the Exploding Offer: The Farpoint Gambit," *Negotiation Journal* 11, no. 3 (1995): 277–85.

77. A. Tversky and D. Kahneman, "Judgment under Uncertainty: Heuristics and Biases," *Science* 185, no. 4157 (1974): 1124–31; J.D. Jasper and S.D. Christman, "A Neuropsychological Dimension for Anchoring Effects," *Journal of Behavioral Decision Making* 18 (2005): 343–69.

78. S. Kwon and L.R. Weingart, "Unilateral Concessions from the Other Party: Concession Behavior, Attributions, and Negotiation Judgments," *Journal of Applied Psychology* 89, no. 2 (2004): 263–78; R. Fells, *Effective Negotiation* (Cambridge, UK: Cambridge University Press, 2012), Chap. 8.

79. D. Malhotra, "The Fine Art of Making Concessions," *Negotiation* (2006): 3–5.

80. J.Z. Rubin and B.R. Brown, *The Social Psychology of Bargaining and Negotiation* (New York: Academic Press, 1976), Chap. 9.

81. For a critical view of the problem-solving style in negotiation, see J.M. Brett, "Managing Organizational Conflict," *Professional Psychology: Research and Practice* 15 (1984): 664–78.

82. L.L. Thompson, "Information Exchange in Negotiation," *Journal of Experimental Social Psychology* 27 (1991): 161–79.

83. S.R. Covey, *The 7 Habits of Highly Effective People* (New York: Free Press, 1989), 235–60.

84. R.J. Lewicki et al., *Negotiation*, 4th ed. (New York: McGraw-Hill/Irwin, 2003), 95; M. Olekalns and P.L. Smith, "Testing the Relationships among Negotiators' Motivational Orientations, Strategy Choices, and Outcomes," *Journal of Experimental Social Psychology* 39, no. 2 (2003): 101–17.

85. M. Olekalns and P.L. Smith, "Moments in Time: Metacognition, Trust, and Outcomes in Dyadic Negotiations," *Personality and Social Psychology Bulletin* 31, no. 12 (2005): 1696–707.

86. D.W. Choi, "Shared Metacognition in Integrative Negotiation," *International Journal of Conflict Management* 21, no. 3 (2010): 309–33.

87. J.M. Brett et al., "Sticks and Stones: Language, Face, and Online Dispute Resolution," *Academy of Management Journal* 50, no. 1 (2007): 85–99; D. Pietroni et al., "Emotions as Strategic Information: Effects of Other's Emotional Expressions on Fixed-Pie Perception, Demands, and Integrative Behavior in Negotiation," *Journal of Experimental Social Psychology* 44, no. 6 (2008):

1444–54; D. Druckman and M. Olekalns, "Emotions in Negotiation," *Group Decision and Negotiation* 17, no. 1 (2008): 1–11; M.J. Boland and W.H. Ross, "Emotional Intelligence and Dispute Mediation in Escalating and De-Escalating Situations," *Journal of Applied Social Psychology* 40, no. 12 (2010): 3059–105.

88. P.J. Carnevale and A.M. Isen, "The Influence of Positive Affect and Visual Access on the Discovery of Integrative Solutions in Bilateral Negotiation," *Organizational Behavior and Human Decision Processes* 37 (1986): 1–13; Thompson, *The Mind and Heart of the Negotiator.*

89. J.W. Salacuse and J.Z. Rubin, "Your Place or Mine? Site Location and Negotiation," *Negotiation Journal* 6 (1990): 5–10; J. Mayfield et al., "How Location Impacts International Business Negotiations," *Review of Business* 19 (1998): 21–24.

90. J. Margo, "The Persuaders," *Boss Magazine*, December 29, 2000, 38. For a full discussion of the advantages and disadvantages of face-to-face and alternative negotiation situations, see M.H. Bazerman et al., "Negotiation," *Annual Review of Psychology* 51 (2000): 279–314.

91. Lewicki et al., *Negotiation*, 298–322.

Chapter 11

1. Most of these statistics were collected in September 2013. Library of Congress data were collected in 2010.

2. Many of these perspectives are summarized in R.N. Kanungo, "Leadership in Organizations: Looking Ahead to the 21st Century," *Canadian Psychology* 39 (1998): 71–82; G.A. Yukl, *Leadership in Organizations*, 8th ed. (Upper Saddle River, NJ: Pearson Education, 2013).

3. R. House, M. Javidan, and P. Dorfman, "Project GLOBE: An Introduction," *Applied Psychology: An International Review* 50 (2001): 489–505; R. House et al., "Understanding Cultures and Implicit Leadership Theories across the Globe: An Introduction to Project GLOBE," *Journal of World Business* 37 (2002): 3–10.

4. "Leadership: The Biggest Issue," *Time*, November 8, 1976, 46.

5. J.A. Raelin, "We the Leaders: In Order to Form a Leaderful Organization," *Journal of Leadership & Organizational Studies* 12, no. 2 (2005): 18–30; C.L. Pearce, J.A. Conger, and E.A. Locke, "Shared Leadership Theory," *Leadership Quarterly* 19, no. 5 (2008): 622–28; E. Engel Small and J.R. Rentsch, "Shared Leadership in Teams: A Matter of Distribution," *Journal of Personnel Psychology* 9, no. 4 (2010): 203–11.

6. C.A. Beatty, "Implementing Advanced Manufacturing Technologies: Rules of the Road," *Sloan Management Review* (1992): 49–60; J.M. Howell, "The Right Stuff: Identifying and Developing Effective Champions of Innovation," *Academy of Management Executive* 19, no. 2 (2005): 108–19; J.M. Howell and C.M. Shea, "Effects of Champion Behavior, Team Potency, and External Communication Activities on Predicting Team Performance," *Group & Organization Management* 31, no. 2 (2006): 180–211.

7. J.W. Gardner, *On Leadership* (New York: Free Press, 1990), 138–55.

8. S. Marchionne, "Fiat's Extreme Makeover," *Harvard Business Review* (2008): 45–48.

9. C. McMorrow, *Entrepreneurs Turn Us On: 20 Years of Recognizing Bright Ideas*, EY Entrepreneur of the year—Ontario 2013,

Ernst & Young (October 2013); D. Ovsey, " 'Get out of the Way,' " *National Post*, February 18, 2014.

10. J.A. Raelin, *Creating Leaderful Organizations: How to Bring Out Leadership in Everyone* (San Francisco: Berrett-Koehler, 2003).

11. Most or all of these elements are included in W. Bennis and B. Nanus, *Leaders: The Strategies for Taking Charge* (New York: Harper & Row, 1985); N.M. Tichy and M.A. Devanna, *The Transformational Leader* (New York: Wiley, 1986); B.M. Bass and R.E. Riggio, *Transformational Leadership*, 2nd ed. (Mahwah, NJ: Erlbaum, 2006); J.M. Kouzes and B.Z. Posner, *The Leadership Challenge*, 5th ed. (San Francisco: Jossey-Bass, 2012).

12. Strategic collective vision has been identified as a key factor in leadership since Chester Barnard's seminal book in organizational behavior. See C. Barnard, *The Functions of the Executive* (Cambridge, MA: Harvard University Press, 1938), 86–89.

13. Bennis and Nanus, *Leaders*, 27–33, 89; R.E. Quinn, *Building the Bridge as You Walk on It: A Guide for Leading Change* (San Francisco: Jossey-Bass, 2004), Chap. 11; R. Gill, *Theory and Practice of Leadership* (London: Sage, 2011), Chap. 4; D. O'Connell, K. Hickerson, and A. Pillutla, "Organizational Visioning: An Integrative Review," *Group & Organization Management* 36, no. 1 (2011): 103–25.

14. J.M. Strange and M.D. Mumford, "The Origins of Vision: Effects of Reflection, Models, and Analysis," *Leadership Quarterly* 16, no. 1 (2005): 121–48; S. Kantabutra, "Toward a Behavioral Theory of Vision in Organizational Settings," *Leadership & Organization Development Journal* 30, no. 4 (2009): 319–37; S.A. Kirkpatrick, "Lead through Vision and Values," in *Handbook of Principles of Organizational Behavior*, ed. E.A. Locke (Chichester, UK: Wiley, 2010), 367–87; Gill, *Theory and Practice of Leadership*, Chap. 4.

15. J.A. Conger and R.N. Kanungo, *Charismatic Leadership in Organizations* (Thousand Oaks, CA: Sage, 1998), 173–83; M. Venus, D. Stam, and D. van Knippenberg, "Leader Emotion as a Catalyst of Effective Leader Communication of Visions, Value-Laden Messages, and Goals," *Organizational Behavior and Human Decision Processes* 122, no. 1 (2013): 53–68.

16. K.W. Parry and H. Hansen, "The Organizational Story as Leadership," *Leadership* 3, no. 3 (2007): 281–300; D.A. Waldman, P.A. Balthazard, and S.J. Peterson, "Leadership and Neuroscience: Can We Revolutionize the Way That Inspirational Leaders Are Identified and Developed?," *Academy of Management Perspectives* 25, no. 1 (2011): 60–74; S. Denning, *The Leader's Guide to Storytelling: Mastering the Art and Discipline of Business Narrative*, rev. ed. (San Francisco: Jossey-Bass, 2011).

17. L. Black, "Hamburger Diplomacy," *Report on Business Magazine,* August 1988, 30–36.

18. Canadian Management Centre, *Build a Better Workplace: Employee Engagement Edition*, Canadian Management Centre (Toronto: August 23, 2012); Kelly Services, *The Leadership Disconnect*, Kelly Services (Troy, MI: August 2012); TINYpulse, *7 Vital Trends Disrupting Today's Workplace*, 2013 TINYpulse Employment Engagement Survey, TINYpulse (Seattle: December 2013); "New Study Reveals What U.S. Employees Think about Today's Workplace," news release for Root (Sylvania, OH: March 26, 2013).

19. D.E. Berlew, "Leadership and Organizational Excitement," *California Management Review* 17, no. 2 (1974): 21–30; Bennis

and Nanus, *Leaders*, 43–55; T. Simons, "Behavioral Integrity: The Perceived Alignment between Managers' Words and Deeds as a Research Focus," *Organization Science* 13, no. 1 (2002): 18–35.

20. M. Webb, "Executive Profile: Peter C. Farrell," *San Diego Business Journal*, March 24, 2003, 32; P. Benesh, "He Likes Them Breathing Easy," *Investor's Business Daily*, September 13, 2005, A04. For a discussion of trust in leadership, see C.S. Burke et al., "Trust in Leadership: A Multi-Level Review and Integration," *Leadership Quarterly* 18, no. 6 (2007): 606–32. The survey on leading by example is reported in J.C. Maxwell, "People Do What People See," *BusinessWeek*, November 19, 2007, 32.

21. K. Tyler, "Evaluating Values," *HRMagazine*, April 2011, 57.

22. N. Augustine, *Augustine's Laws*, 3rd ed. (New York: Viking, 1986), 32.

23. Bass and Riggio, *Transformational Leadership*, 7; Kouzes and Posner, *The Leadership Challenge*, Chaps. 6 and 7.

24. W.E. Baker and J.M. Sinkula, "The Synergistic Effect of Market Orientation and Learning Orientation on Organizational Performance," *Academy of Marketing Science Journal* 27, no. 4 (1999): 411–27; Z. Emden, A. Yaprak, and S.T. Cavusgil, "Learning from Experience in International Alliances: Antecedents and Firm Performance Implications," *Journal of Business Research* 58, no. 7 (2005): 883–92.

25. Kouzes and Posner, *The Leadership Challenge*.

26. R.J. House, "A 1976 Theory of Charismatic Leadership," in *Leadership: The Cutting Edge*, ed. J.G. Hunt and L.L. Larson (Carbondale: Southern Illinois University Press, 1977), 189–207; J.A. Conger, "Charismatic Leadership," in *The Sage Handbook of Leadership*, ed. A. Bryman et al. (London: Sage, 2011), 86–102.

27. J.E. Barbuto Jr., "Taking the Charisma out of Transformational Leadership," *Journal of Social Behavior & Personality* 12 (1997): 689–97; Y.A. Nur, "Charisma and Managerial Leadership: The Gift That Never Was," *Business Horizons* 41 (1998): 19–26; M.D. Mumford and J.R. Van Doorn, "The Leadership of Pragmatism: Reconsidering Franklin in the Age of Charisma," *Leadership Quarterly* 12, no. 3 (2001): 279–309; A. Fanelli, "Bringing Out Charisma: CEO Charisma and External Stakeholders," *Academy of Management Review* 31, no. 4 (2006): 1049–61; M.J. Platow et al., "A Special Gift We Bestow on You for Being Representative of Us: Considering Leader Charisma from a Self-Categorization Perspective," *British Journal of Social Psychology* 45, no. 2 (2006): 303–20.

28. B. Shamir et al., "Correlates of Charismatic Leader Behavior in Military Units: Subordinates' Attitudes, Unit Characteristics, and Superiors' Appraisals of Leader Performance," *Academy of Management Journal* 41, no. 4 (1998): 387–409; R.E. de Vries, R.A. Roe, and T.C.B. Taillieu, "On Charisma and Need for Leadership," *European Journal of Work and Organizational Psychology* 8 (1999): 109–33; R. Khurana, *Searching for a Corporate Savior: The Irrational Quest for Charismatic CEOs* (Princeton, NJ: Princeton University Press, 2002); R.E. de Vries, R.D. Pathak, and A.R. Paquin, "The Paradox of Power Sharing: Participative Charismatic Leaders Have Subordinates with More Instead of Less Need for Leadership," *European Journal of Work and Organizational Psychology* 20, no. 6 (2010): 779–804. The effect of charismatic leadership on follower dependence was also noted earlier by U.S. government leader John Gardner. See Gardner, *On Leadership*, 34–36.

29. J. Lipman-Blumen, "A Pox on Charisma: Why Connective Leadership and Character Count," in *The Drucker Difference: What the World's Greatest Management Thinker Means to Today's Business Leaders*, ed. C.L. Pearce, J.A. Maciariello, and H. Yamawaki (New York: McGraw-Hill, 2010), 149–74.

30. A. Mackey, "The Effect of CEOs on Firm Performance," *Strategic Management Journal* 29, no. 12 (2008): 1357–67.

31. J. Barling, T. Weber, and E.K. Kelloway, "Effects of Transformational Leadership Training on Attitudinal and Financial Outcomes: A Field Experiment," *Journal of Applied Psychology* 81 (1996): 827–32.

32. A. Bryman, "Leadership in Organizations," in *Handbook of Organization Studies*, ed. S.R. Clegg, C. Hardy, and W.R. Nord (Thousand Oaks, CA: Sage, 1996), 276–92; D. van Knippenberg and S.B. Sitkin, "A Critical Assessment of Charismatic—Transformational Leadership Research: Back to the Drawing Board?," *Academy of Management Annals* 7, no. 1 (2013): 1–60.

33. B.S. Pawar and K.K. Eastman, "The Nature and Implications of Contextual Influences on Transformational Leadership: A Conceptual Examination," *Academy of Management Review* 22 (1997): 80–109; C.P. Egri and S. Herman, "Leadership in the North American Environmental Sector: Values, Leadership Styles, and Contexts of Environmental Leaders and Their Organizations," *Academy of Management Journal* 43, no. 4 (2000): 571–604.

34. A. Zaleznik, "Managers and Leaders: Are They Different?," *Harvard Business Review* 55, no. 3 (1977): 67–78; J.P. Kotter, *A Force for Change: How Leadership Differs from Management* (New York: Free Press, 1990); E.A. Locke, *The Essence of Leadership* (New York: Lexington Books, 1991); G. Yukl and R. Lepsinger, "Why Integrating the Leading and Managing Roles Is Essential for Organizational Effectiveness," *Organizational Dynamics* 34, no. 4 (2005): 361–75.

35. Bennis and Nanus, *Leaders*, 20. Peter Drucker is also widely cited as the source of this quotation. The closest passage we could find, however, is in the first two pages of *The Effective Executive* (1966) where Drucker states that effective executives "get the right things done." On the next page, he states that manual workers only need efficiency, "that is, the ability to do things right rather than the ability to get the right things done." See P.F. Drucker, *The Effective Executive* (New York: Harper Business, 1966), 1–2.

36. R.J. House and R.N. Aditya, "The Social Scientific Study of Leadership: Quo Vadis?," *Journal of Management* 23, no. 3 (1997): 409–73.

37. Yukl and Lepsinger, "Why Integrating the Leading and Managing Roles Is Essential for Organizational Effectiveness."

38. S.R. Satterwhite, "Dell's Poisonous Culture Is Sinking Its Ship—and Raises Questions for Potential Buyers," *Forbes*, April 1, 2013.

39. E.A. Fleishman, "The Description of Supervisory Behavior," *Journal of Applied Psychology* 37, no. 1 (1953): 1–6. For discussion on methodological problems with the development of these people-versus task-oriented leadership constructs, see C.A. Schriesheim, R.J. House, and S. Kerr, "Leader Initiating Structure: A Reconciliation of Discrepant Research Results and Some Empirical Tests," *Organizational Behavior and Human Performance* 15, no. 2 (1976): 297–321; L. Tracy, "Consideration and Initiating

Structure: Are They Basic Dimensions of Leader Behavior?," *Social Behavior and Personality* 15, no. 1 (1987): 21–33.

40. A.K. Korman, "Consideration, Initiating Structure, and Organizational Criteria—a Review," *Personnel Psychology* 19 (1966): 349–62; E.A. Fleishman, "Twenty Years of Consideration and Structure," in *Current Developments in the Study of Leadership*, ed. E.A. Fleishman and J.C. Hunt (Carbondale: Southern Illinois University Press, 1973), 1–40; T.A. Judge, R.F. Piccolo, and R. Ilies, "The Forgotten Ones?: The Validity of Consideration and Initiating Structure in Leadership Research," *Journal of Applied Psychology* 89, no. 1 (2004): 36–51; D.S. DeRue et al., "Trait and Behavioral Theories of Leadership: An Integration and Meta-Analytic Test of Their Relative Validity," *Personnel Psychology* 64, no. 1 (2011): 7–52; Yukl, *Leadership in Organizations*, 62–75.

41. B.A. Scott et al., "A Daily Investigation of the Role of Manager Empathy on Employee Well-Being," *Organizational Behavior and Human Decision Processes* 113, no. 2 (2010): 127–40.

42. V.V. Baba, "Serendipity in Leadership: Initiating Structure and Consideration in the Classroom," *Human Relations* 42 (1989): 509–25.

43. R.K. Greenleaf, *Servant Leadership: A Journey into the Nature of Lergitimate Power & Greatness* (Mahwah, NJ: Paulist Press, 1977; repr., 2002); D. van Dierendonck and K. Patterson, "Servant Leadership: An Introduction," in *Servant Leadership: Developments in Theory and Research*, ed. D. van Dierendonck and K. Patterson (Houndmills, UK: Palgrave Macmillan, 2010), 3–11.

44. Greenleaf, *Servant Leadership*, 27.

45. S. Sendjaya, J.C. Sarros, and J.C. Santora, "Defining and Measuring Servant Leadership Behaviour in Organizations," *Journal of Management Studies* 45, no. 2 (2008): 402–24; R.C. Liden et al., "Servant Leadership: Development of a Multidimensional Measure and Multi-Level Assessment," *Leadership Quarterly* 19, no. 2 (2008): 161–77; K.Y. Ng and C.S.K. Koh, "Motivation to Serve: Understanding the Heart of the Servant-Leader and Servant Leadership Behaviours," in *Servant Leadership: Developments in Theory and Research*, ed. D. van Dierendonck and K. Patterson (Houndmills, UK: Palgrave Macmillan, 2010), 90–104; D. van Dierendonck, "Servant Leadership: A Review and Synthesis," *Journal of Management* 37, no. 4 (2011): 1228–61.

46. J. Mattson, "'Sergeant' Means 'Servant': How NCOs Typify the Servant Leader," *NCO Journal*, May 14, 2013. For a more detailed discussion of servant leadership in the military, see D. Campbell, *The Leader's Code: Mission, Character, Service, and Getting the Job Done* (New York: Random House, 2013).

47. S.J. Peterson, B.M. Galvin, and D. Lange, "CEO Servant Leadership: Exploring Executive Characteristics and Firm Performance," *Personnel Psychology* 65, no. 3 (2012): 565–96.

48. S. Kerr et al., "Towards a Contingency Theory of Leadership Based Upon the Consideration and Initiating Structure Literature," *Organizational Behavior and Human Performance* 12 (1974): 62–82; L.L. Larson, J.G. Hunt, and R.N. Osborn, "The Great Hi-Hi Leader Behavior Myth: A Lesson from Occam's Razor," *Academy of Management Journal* 19 (1976): 628–41.

49. For a thorough study of how expectancy theory of motivation relates to leadership, see R.G. Isaac, W.J. Zerbe, and D.C. Pitt, "Leadership and Motivation: The Effective Application of Expectancy Theory," *Journal of Managerial Issues* 13 (2001): 212–26.

50. R.J. House, "A Path Goal Theory of Leader Effectiveness," *Administrative Science Quarterly* 16, no. 3 (1971): 321–39; M.G. Evans, "Extensions of a Path-Goal Theory of Motivation," *Journal of Applied Psychology* 59 (1974): 172–78; R.J. House and T.R. Mitchell, "Path-Goal Theory of Leadership," *Journal of Contemporary Business* (1974): 81–97; M.G. Evans, "Path Goal Theory of Leadership," in *Leadership*, ed. L.L. Neider and C.A. Schriesheim (Greenwich, CT: Information Age, 2002), 115–38.

51. R.J. House, "Path-Goal Theory of Leadership: Lessons, Legacy, and a Reformulated Theory," *The Leadership Quarterly* 7, no. 3 (1996): 323–52.

52. Kelly Services, *The Leadership Disconnect*.

53. J. Indvik, "Path-Goal Theory of Leadership: A Meta-Analysis," *Academy of Management Proceedings* (1986): 189–92; J.C. Wofford and L.Z. Liska, "Path-Goal Theories of Leadership: A Meta-Analysis," *Journal of Management* 19 (1993): 857–76.

54. J.D. Houghton and S.K. Yoho, "Toward a Contingency Model of Leadership and Psychological Empowerment: When Should Self-Leadership Be Encouraged?," *Journal of Leadership & Organizational Studies* 11, no. 4 (2005): 65–83.

55. R.T. Keller, "A Test of the Path-Goal Theory of Leadership with Need for Clarity as a Moderator in Research and Development Organizations," *Journal of Applied Psychology* 74 (1989): 208–12.

56. R.P. Vecchio, J.E. Justin, and C.L. Pearce, "The Utility of Transactional and Transformational Leadership for Predicting Performance and Satisfaction within a Path-Goal Theory Framework," *Journal of Occupational and Organizational Psychology* 81 (2008): 71–82.

57. B. Carroll and L. Levy, "Defaulting to Management: Leadership Defined by What It Is Not," *Organization* 15, no. 1 (2008): 75–96; I. Holmberg and M. Tyrstrup, "Well Then—What Now? An Everyday Approach to Managerial Leadership," *Leadership* 6, no. 4 (2010): 353–72.

58. C.A. Schriesheim and L.L. Neider, "Path-Goal Leadership Theory: The Long and Winding Road," *Leadership Quarterly* 7 (1996): 317–21.

59. P. Hersey and K.H. Blanchard, *Management of Organizational Behavior: Utilizing Human Resources*, 5th ed. (Englewood Cliffs, NJ: Prentice Hall, 1988).

60. R.P. Vecchio, "Situational Leadership Theory: An Examination of a Prescriptive Theory," *Journal of Applied Psychology* 72 (1987): 444–51; W. Blank, J.R. Weitzel, and S.G. Green, "A Test of the Situational Leadership Theory," *Personnel Psychology* 43 (1990): 579–97; C.L. Graeff, "Evolution of Situational Leadership Theory: A Critical Review," *Leadership Quarterly* 8 (1997): 153–70; G. Thompson and R.P. Vecchio, "Situational Leadership Theory: A Test of Three Versions," *Leadership Quarterly* 20, no. 5 (2009): 837–48.

61. Current information about situational leadership is from the company's website: www.situational.com. The 1997 figure is reported in K. Blanchard and B. Nelson, "Recognition and Reward," *Executive Excellence*, April 1997, 15.

62. F.E. Fiedler, *A Theory of Leadership Effectiveness* (New York: McGraw-Hill, 1967); F.E. Fiedler and M.M. Chemers, *Leadership and Effective Management* (Glenview, IL: Scott, Foresman, 1974).

63. F.E. Fiedler, "Engineer the Job to Fit the Manager," *Harvard Business Review* 43, no. 5 (1965): 115–22.

64. For a summary of criticisms, see Yukl, *Leadership in Organizations*, 217–18.

65. Judge et al., "The Forgotten Ones?: The Validity of Consideration and Initiating Structure in Leadership Research"; T.A. Judge, R.F. Piccolo, and T. Kosalka, "The Bright and Dark Sides of Leader Traits: A Review and Theoretical Extension of the Leader Trait Paradigm," *Leadership Quarterly* 20 (2009): 855–75.

66. N. Nicholson, *Executive Instinct* (New York: Crown, 2000).

67. This observation has also been made by C.A. Schriesheim, "Substitutes-for-Leadership Theory: Development and Basic Concepts," *Leadership Quarterly* 8 (1997): 103–08.

68. D.F. Elloy and A. Randolph, "The Effect of Superleader Behavior on Autonomous Work Groups in a Government Operated Railway Service," *Public Personnel Management* 26 (1997): 257–72; C.C. Manz and H. Sims Jr., *The New SuperLeadership: Leading Others to Lead Themselves* (San Francisco: Berrett-Koehler, 2001).

69. M.L. Loughry, "Coworkers Are Watching: Performance Implications of Peer Monitoring," *Academy of Management Proceedings* (2002): O1–O6.

70. P.M. Podsakoff and S.B. MacKenzie, "Kerr and Jermier's Substitutes for Leadership Model: Background, Empirical Assessment, and Suggestions for Future Research," *Leadership Quarterly* 8 (1997): 117–32; S.D. Dionne et al., "Neutralizing Substitutes for Leadership Theory: Leadership Effects and Common-Source Bias," *Journal of Applied Psychology* 87, no. 3 (2002): 454–64; J.R. Villa et al., "Problems with Detecting Moderators in Leadership Research Using Moderated Multiple Regression," *Leadership Quarterly* 14, no. 1 (2003): 3–23; S.D. Dionne et al., "Substitutes for Leadership, or Not," *Leadership Quarterly* 16, no. 1 (2005): 169–93.

71. J.R. Meindl, "On Leadership: An Alternative to the Conventional Wisdom," *Research in Organizational Behavior* 12 (1990): 159–203; L.R. Offermann, J.K. Kennedy, and P.W. Wirtz, "Implicit Leadership Theories: Content, Structure, and Generalizability," *Leadership Quarterly* 5, no. 1 (1994): 43–58; R.J. Hall and R.G. Lord, "Multi-Level Information Processing Explanations of Followers' Leadership Perceptions," *Leadership Quarterly* 6 (1995): 265–87; O. Epitropaki and R. Martin, "Implicit Leadership Theories in Applied Settings: Factor Structure, Generalizability, and Stability over Time," *Journal of Applied Psychology* 89, no. 2 (2004): 293–310. For a broader discussion of the social construction of leadership, see G.T. Fairhurst and D. Grant, "The Social Construction of Leadership: A Sailing Guide," *Management Communication Quarterly* 24, no. 2 (2010): 171–210.

72. R.G. Lord et al., "Contextual Constraints on Prototype Generation and Their Multilevel Consequences for Leadership Perceptions," *Leadership Quarterly* 12, no. 3 (2001): 311–38; K.A. Scott and D.J. Brown, "Female First, Leader Second? Gender Bias in the Encoding of Leadership Behavior," *Organizational Behavior and Human Decision Processes* 101 (2006): 230–42; S.J. Shondrick, J.E. Dinh, and R.G. Lord, "Developments in Implicit Leadership Theory and Cognitive Science: Applications to Improving Measurement and Understanding Alternatives to Hierarchical Leadership," *Leadership Quarterly* 21, no. 6 (2010): 959–78.

73. S.F. Cronshaw and R.G. Lord, "Effects of Categorization, Attribution, and Encoding Processes on Leadership Perceptions," *Journal of Applied Psychology* 72 (1987): 97–106; J.L. Nye and D.R. Forsyth, "The Effects of Prototype-Based Biases on Leadership Appraisals: A Test of Leadership Categorization Theory," *Small Group Research* 22 (1991): 360–79.

74. Meindl, "On Leadership: An Alternative to the Conventional Wisdom," 163; B. Schyns, J.R. Meindl, and M.A. Croon, "The Romance of Leadership Scale: Cross-Cultural Testing and Refinement," *Leadership* 3, no. 1 (2007): 29–46; J. Felfe and L.E. Petersen, "Romance of Leadership and Management Decision Making," *European Journal of Work and Organizational Psychology* 16, no. 1 (2007): 1–24.

75. J. Pfeffer, "The Ambiguity of Leadership," *Academy of Management Review* 2 (1977): 102–12.

76. R. Weber et al., "The Illusion of Leadership: Misattribution of Cause in Coordination Games," *Organization Science* 12, no. 5 (2001): 582–98; N. Ensari and S.E. Murphy, "Cross-Cultural Variations in Leadership Perceptions and Attribution of Charisma to the Leader," *Organizational Behavior and Human Decision Processes* 92 (2003): 52–66; M.L.A. Hayward, V.P. Rindova, and T.G. Pollock, "Believing One's Own Press: The Causes and Consequences of CEO Celebrity," *Strategic Management Journal* 25, no. 7 (2004): 637–53.

77. The history of the trait perspective of leadership, as well as current research on this topic, is nicely summarized in S.J. Zaccaro, C. Kemp, and P. Bader, "Leader Traits and Attributes," in *The Nature of Leadership*, ed. J. Antonakis, A.T. Cianciolo, and R.J. Sternberg (Thousand Oaks, CA: Sage, 2004), 101–24.

78. R.M. Stogdill, *Handbook of Leadership* (New York: Free Press, 1974), Chap. 5.

79. J. Intagliata, D. Ulrich, and N. Smallwood, "Leveraging Leadership Competencies to Produce Leadership Brand: Creating Distinctiveness by Focusing on Strategy and Results," *Human Resources Planning* 23, no. 4 (2000): 12–23; J.A. Conger and D.A. Ready, "Rethinking Leadership Competencies," *Leader to Leader* 32 (2004): 41–47; Zaccaro et al., "Leader Traits and Attributes." For a recent discussion on leadership traits and evolutionary psychology, see Judge et al., "The Bright and Dark Sides of Leader Traits."

80. This list is based on S.A. Kirkpatrick and E.A. Locke, "Leadership: Do Traits Matter?," *Academy of Management Executive* 5 (1991): 48–60; R.M. Aditya, R.J. House, and S. Kerr, "Theory and Practice of Leadership: Into the New Millennium," in *Industrial and Organizational Psychology: Linking Theory with Practice*, ed. C.L. Cooper and E.A. Locke (Oxford, UK: Blackwell, 2000), 130–65; D. Goleman, R. Boyatzis, and A. McKee, *Primal Leaders* (Boston: Harvard Business School Press, 2002); T.A. Judge et al., "Personality and Leadership: A Qualitative and Quantitative Review," *Journal of Applied Psychology* 87, no. 4 (2002): 765–80; T.A. Judge, A.E. Colbert, and R. Ilies, "Intelligence and Leadership: A Quantitative Review and Test of Theoretical Propositions," *Journal of Applied Psychology* 89, no. 3 (2004): 542–52; Zaccaro et al., "Leader Traits and Attributes."

81. M. Popper et al., "The Capacity to Lead: Major Psychological Differences between Leaders and Nonleaders," *Military Psychology* 16, no. 4 (2004): 245–63; R.G. Lord and R.J. Hall, "Identity, Deep Structure and the Development of Leadership Skill," *Leadership Quarterly* 16, no. 4 (2005): 591–615; D.V. Day, M.M. Harrison, and S.M. Halpin, *An Integrative Approach to Leader Development: Connecting Adult Development, Identity, and Expertise* (New York: Routledge, 2009); D.S. DeRue and

S.J. Ashford, "Who Will Lead and Who Will Follow? A Social Process of Leadership Identity Construction in Organizations," *Academy of Management Review* 35, no. 4 (2010): 627–47.

82. Carroll and Levy, "Defaulting to Management: Leadership Defined by What It Is Not."

83. J. Adonis, "Richard Branson's Leadership Tips," *Sydney Morning Herald*, August 20, 2010.

84. R. Davidovitz et al., "Leaders as Attachment Figures: Leaders' Attachment Orientations Predict Leadership-Related Mental Representations and Followers' Performance and Mental Health," *Journal of Personality and Social Psychology* 93, no. 4 (2007): 632–50.

85. J.B. Miner, "Twenty Years of Research on Role Motivation Theory of Managerial Effectiveness," *Personnel Psychology* 31 (1978): 739–60; House and Aditya, "The Social Scientific Study of Leadership: Quo Vadis?"

86. The large-scale studies are reported in C. Savoye, "Workers Say Honesty Is Best Company Policy," *Christian Science Monitor*, June 15, 2000; J. Schettler, "Leadership in Corporate America," *Training & Development*, September 2002, 66–73; Kouzes and Posner, *The Leadership Challenge*, Chap. 2.

87. J. Hedlund et al., "Identifying and Assessing Tacit Knowledge: Understanding the Practical Intelligence of Military Leaders," *Leadership Quarterly* 14, no. 2 (2003): 117–40; R.J. Sternberg, "A Systems Model of Leadership: WICS," *American Psychologist* 62, no. 1 (2007): 34–42.

88. J.M. George, "Emotions and Leadership: The Role of Emotional Intelligence," *Human Relations* 53 (2000): 1027–55; Goleman et al., *Primal Leaders*; Lord and Hall, "Identity, Deep Structure and the Development of Leadership Skill"; C. Skinner and P. Spurgeon, "Valuing Empathy and Emotional Intelligence in Health Leadership: A Study of Empathy, Leadership Behaviour and Outcome Effectiveness," *Health Services Management Research* 18, no. 1 (2005): 1–12.

89. B. George, *Authentic Leadership* (San Francisco: Jossey-Bass, 2004); W.L. Gardner et al., "'Can You See the Real Me?' A Self-Based Model of Authentic Leader and Follower Development," *Leadership Quarterly* 16 (2005): 343–72; B. George, *True North* (San Francisco: Jossey-Bass, 2007), Chap. 4; M.E. Palanski and F.J. Yammarino, "Integrity and Leadership: Clearing the Conceptual Confusion," *European Management Journal* 25, no. 3 (2007): 171–84; F.O. Walumbwa et al., "Authentic Leadership: Development and Validation of a Theory-Based Measure," *Journal of Management* 34, no. 1 (2008): 89–126.

90. W.G. Bennis and R.J. Thomas, "Crucibles of Leadership," *Harvard Business Review* 80, no. 9 (2002): 39–45; R.J. Thomas, *Crucibles of Leadership: How to Learn from Experience to Become a Great Leader* (Boston: Harvard Business Press, 2008).

91. R. Jacobs, "Using Human Resource Functions to Enhance Emotional Intelligence," in *The Emotionally Intelligent Workplace*, ed. C. Cherniss and D. Goleman (San Francisco: Jossey-Bass, 2001), 161–63; Conger and Ready, "Rethinking Leadership Competencies."

92. R.G. Lord and D.J. Brown, *Leadership Processes and Self-Identity: A Follower-Centered Approach to Leadership* (Mahwah, NJ: Erlbaum, 2004); R. Bolden and J. Gosling, "Leadership Competencies: Time to Change the Tune?," *Leadership* 2, no. 2 (2006): 147–63.

93. Six of the Project GLOBE clusters are described in a special issue of the *Journal of World Business* 37 (2000). For an overview of Project GLOBE, see House et al., "Project GLOBE: An Introduction"; House et al., "Understanding Cultures and Implicit Leadership Theories across the Globe."

94. J.C. Jesuino, "Latin Europe Cluster: From South to North," *Journal of World Business* 37 (2002): 88. Another GLOBE study, of Iranian managers, also reported that "charismatic visionary" stands out as a primary leadership dimension. See A. Dastmalchian, M. Javidan, and K. Alam, "Effective Leadership and Culture in Iran: An Empirical Study," *Applied Psychology: An International Review* 50 (2001): 532–58.

95. D.N. Den Hartog et al., "Culture Specific and Cross-Cultural Generalizable Implicit Leadership Theories: Are Attributes of Charismatic/Transformational Leadership Universally Endorsed?," *Leadership Quarterly* 10 (1999): 219–56; F.C. Brodbeck et al., "Cultural Variation of Leadership Prototypes across 22 European Countries," *Journal of Occupational and Organizational Psychology* 73 (2000): 1–29; E. Szabo et al., "The Europe Cluster: Where Employees Have a Voice," *Journal of World Business* 37 (2002): 55–68. The Mexican study is reported in C.E. Nicholls, H.W. Lane, and M.B. Brechu, "Taking Self-Managed Teams to Mexico," *Academy of Management Executive* 13 (1999): 15–25.

96. G.N. Powell, "One More Time: Do Female and Male Managers Differ?," *Academy of Management Executive* 4 (1990): 68–75; M.L. van Engen and T.M. Willemsen, "Sex and Leadership Styles: A Meta-Analysis of Research Published in the 1990s," *Psychological Reports* 94, no. 1 (2004): 3–18.

97. R. Sharpe, "As Leaders, Women Rule," *BusinessWeek*, November 20, 2000, 74; M. Sappenfield, "Women, It Seems, Are Better Bosses," *Christian Science Monitor*, January 16, 2001; A.H. Eagly and L.L. Carli, "The Female Leadership Advantage: An Evaluation of the Evidence," *The Leadership Quarterly* 14, no. 6 (2003): 807–34; A.H. Eagly, M.C. Johannesen-Schmidt, and M.L. van Engen, "Transformational, Transactional, and Laissez-Faire Leadership Styles: A Meta-Analysis Comparing Women and Men," *Psychological Bulletin* 129 (2003): 569–91.

98. A.H. Eagly, S.J. Karau, and M.G. Makhijani, "Gender and the Effectiveness of Leaders: A Meta-Analysis," *Psychological Bulletin* 117 (1995): 125–45; J.G. Oakley, "Gender-Based Barriers to Senior Management Positions: Understanding the Scarcity of Female CEOs," *Journal of Business Ethics* 27 (2000): 821–34; N.Z. Stelter, "Gender Differences in Leadership: Current Social Issues and Future Organizational Implications," *Journal of Leadership Studies* 8 (2002): 88–99; M.E. Heilman et al., "Penalties for Success: Reactions to Women Who Succeed at Male Gender-Typed Tasks," *Journal of Applied Psychology* 89, no. 3 (2004): 416–27; A.H. Eagly, "Achieving Relational Authenticity in Leadership: Does Gender Matter?," *The Leadership Quarterly* 16, no. 3 (2005): 459–74.

Chapter 12

1. K. Linebaugh, D. Searcey, and N. Shirouzu, "Secretive Culture Led Toyota Astray," *The Wall Street Journal*, February 10, 2010; Toyota North American Quality Advisory Panel, *A Road Forward* (Washington, DC: Toyota North American Quality Advisory Panel, May 23, 2011); F. Meier, "Toyota to Pay $17.35 Million for Recall Delay," *USA Today*, December 19, 2012, B2; D. Hechler,

"Lost in Translation," *Corporate Counsel*, April 2013; "Leadership Shake-up at Toyota Brings Ex-GM Executive Aboard," *The Commercial Appeal* (Memphis, TN), March 7, 2013, 2.

2. S. Ranson, R. Hinings, and R. Greenwood, "The Structuring of Organizational Structure," *Administrative Science Quarterly* 25 (1980): 1–14; J.E. Johanson, "Intraorganizational Influence," *Management Communication Quarterly* 13 (2000): 393–435; K. Walsh, "Interpreting the Impact of Culture on Structure," *Journal of Applied Behavioral Science* 40, no. 3 (2004): 302–22.

3. H. Mintzberg, *The Structuring of Organizations* (Englewood Cliffs, NJ: Prentice Hall, 1979), 2–3.

4. E.E. Lawler III, *Motivation in Work Organizations* (Monterey, CA: Brooks/Cole, 1973); M.A. Campion, "Ability Requirement Implications of Job Design: An Interdisciplinary Perspective," *Personnel Psychology* 42 (1989): 1–24.

5. G.S. Becker and K.M. Murphy, "The Division of Labor, Coordination Costs, and Knowledge," *Quarterly Journal of Economics* 107, no. 4 (1992): 1137–60; L. Borghans and B. Weel, "The Division of Labour, Worker Organisation, and Technological Change," *The Economic Journal* 116, no. 509 (2006): F45–F72.

6. Mintzberg, *The Structuring of Organizations*, Chap. 1; D.A. Nadler and M.L. Tushman, *Competing by Design: The Power of Organizational Architecture* (New York: Oxford University Press, 1997), Chap. 6; J.R. Galbraith, *Designing Organizations: An Executive Guide to Strategy, Structure, and Process* (San Francisco: Jossey-Bass, 2002), Chap. 4.

7. J. Stephenson Jr., "Making Humanitarian Relief Networks More Effective: Operational Coordination, Trust and Sense Making," *Disasters* 29, no. 4 (2005): 337.

8. A. Willem, M. Buelens, and H. Scarbrough, "The Role of Inter-Unit Coordination Mechanisms in Knowledge Sharing: A Case Study of a British MNC," *Journal of Information Science* 32, no. 6 (2006): 539–61; R.R. Gulati, "Silo Busting," *Harvard Business Review* 85, no. 5 (2007): 98–108.

9. Borghans and Weel, "The Division of Labour, Worker Organisation, and Technological Change."

10. T. Van Alphen, "Magna in Overdrive," *Toronto Star*, July 24, 2006.

11. Galbraith, *Designing Organizations*, 66–72; D. Aaker, *Spanning Silos: The New CMO Imperative* (Cambridge, MA: Harvard Business Press, 2008), 95–96; A. Pike, *Brands and Branding Geographies* (Cheltenham, UK: Edward Elgar, 2011), 133.

12. S.M. Sapuan, M.R. Osman, and Y. Nukman, "State of the Art of the Concurrent Engineering Technique in the Automotive Industry," *Journal of Engineering Design* 17, no. 2 (2006): 143–57; D.M. Anderson, *Design for Manufacturing: How to Use Concurrent Engineering to Rapidly Develop Low-Cost, High-Quality Products for Lean Management* (Boca Raton, FL: CRC Press/Taylor & Francis, 2014), Chap. 2.

13. A.H. Van De Ven, A.L. Delbecq, and R.J. Koenig Jr., "Determinants of Coordination Modes within Organizations," *American Sociological Review* 41, no. 2 (1976): 322–38.

14. "One-Third of Employees Feel Micromanaged by Boss," news release (Skillman, NJ: BlessingWhite, October 27, 2008); T. Gould, "How Employees Really Feel about Their Bosses," *HR Morning*, July 2, 2011; Kelly Services, *Effective Employers: The Evolving Workforce*, Kelly Global Workforce Index, Kelly Services (Troy, MI: November 2011); Society for Human Resource Management, *SHRM Poll: Intergenerational Conflict in the Workplace*, Society for Human Resource Management (Alexandria, VA: April 29, 2011); "Something to Talk about," news release (Toronto: Accountemps, October 22, 2013).

15. Y.M. Hsieh and A.T. Hsieh, "Enhancement of Service Quality with Job Standardisation," *Service Industries Journal* 21 (2001): 147–66.

16. B. Davison, "Management Span of Control: How Wide Is Too Wide?," *Journal of Business Strategy* 24, no. 4 (2003): 22–29; N.A. Theobald and S. Nicholson-Crotty, "The Many Faces of Span of Control: Organizational Structure across Multiple Goals," *Administration Society* 36, no. 6 (2005): 648–60; R.M. Meyer, "Span of Management: Concept Analysis," *Journal of Advanced Nursing* 63, no. 1 (2008): 104–12.

17. D.D. Van Fleet and A.G. Bedeian, "A History of the Span of Management," *Academy of Management Review* 2 (1977): 356–72; H. Fayol, *General and Industrial Management*, trans. C. Storrs (London: Pitman, 1949); D.A. Wren, A.G. Bedeian, and J.D. Breeze, "The Foundations of Henri Fayol's Administrative Theory," *Management Decision* 40, no. 9 (2002): 906–18.

18. D. Drickhamer, "Lessons from the Leading Edge," *Industry Week*, February 21, 2000, 23–26.

19. S. Nix et al., *Span of Control in City Government Increases Overall*, Office of City Auditor, City of Seattle (Seattle, WA: September 19, 2005); "FedEx 2008 Shareowners Meeting," (Memphis, TN: FedEx, September 29, 2008); J. McLellan, *Administrative Review: An Agenda for Business Improvement*, Multnomah County (Portland, OR: May 19, 2009); D. Thompson, "More on the Span of Control Issue," *Statesman Journal Blog* (Oregon), May 16, 2011; Iowa State Legislative Services Agency, *Span of Control*, Fiscal Note, Iowa State (Des Moines: Iowa Legislature, March 10, 2011); Western Management Consultants, *Service Efficiency Study Program Management Span of Control Review Report to the City Manager*, City of Toronto (Toronto: October 31, 2012); United States Postal Service, *Supervisor Workhours and Span of Control: Management Advisory* (Washington, DC: United States Postal Service, April 4, 2013).

20. G. Anders, "Overseeing More Employees—with Fewer Managers—Consultants Are Urging Companies to Loosen Their Supervising Views," *The Wall Street Journal*, March 24, 2008, B6.

21. J. Greenwald, "Ward Compares the Best with the Rest," *Business Insurance*, August 26, 2002, 16.

22. J.H. Gittell, "Supervisory Span, Relational Coordination and Flight Departure Performance: A Reassessment of Postbureaucracy Theory," *Organization Science* 12, no. 4 (2001): 468–83.

23. M. Guadalupe, J. Wulf, and H. Li, "The Rise of the Functional Manager: Changes Afoot in the C-Suite," *European Business Review* (2012); G.L. Neilson and J. Wulf, "How Many Direct Reports?," *Harvard Business Review* 90, no. 4 (2012): 112–19.

24. S. Marchionne, "Navigating the New Automotive Epoch," *Vital Speeches of the Day* (2010): 134–37.

25. T.D. Wall, J.L. Cordery, and C.W. Clegg, "Empowerment, Performance, and Operational Uncertainty: A Theoretical Integration," *Applied Psychology: An International Review* 51 (2002): 146–69.

26. J. Morris, J. Hassard, and L. McCann, "New Organizational Forms, Human Resource Management and Structural Convergence? A Study of Japanese Organizations," *Organization Studies* 27, no. 10 (2006): 1485–511.

27. J. Denby, "Leaders in African Electricity," *African Business Review*, May 11, 2010; "Q1 2012 Sandvik AB Earnings Conference Call," news release for Sandvik AB (Stockholm, Sweden: CQ FD Disclosure, April 27, 2012).

28. The variations of decentralization within a company are discussed in G. Masada, "To Centralize or Decentralize?," *Optimize*, May 2005, 58–61. The 7-Eleven example is described in J.G. Kelley, "Slurpees and Sausages: 7-Eleven Holds School," *Richmond* (VA) *Times-Dispatch*, March 12, 2004, C1; S. Marling, "The 24-Hour Supply Chain," *InformationWeek*, January 26, 2004, 43.

29. Mintzberg, *The Structuring of Organizations*, Chap. 5.

30. W. Dessein and T. Santos, "Adaptive Organizations," *Journal of Political Economy* 114, no. 5 (2006): 956–95; A.A.M. Nasurdin et al., "Organizational Structure and Organizational Climate as Potential Predictors of Job Stress: Evidence from Malaysia," *International Journal of Commerce and Management* 16, no. 2 (2006): 116–29; C.J. Chen and J.W. Huang, "How Organizational Climate and Structure Affect Knowledge Management—the Social Interaction Perspective," *International Journal of Information Management* 27, no. 2 (2007): 104–18.

31. T. Burns and G. Stalker, *The Management of Innovation* (London: Tavistock, 1961).

32. J. Tata, S. Prasad, and R. Thom, "The Influence of Organizational Structure on the Effectiveness of TQM Programs," *Journal of Managerial Issues* 11, no. 4 (1999): 440–53; A. Lam, "Tacit Knowledge, Organizational Learning and Societal Institutions: An Integrated Framework," *Organization Studies* 21 (2000): 487–513.

33. W.D. Sine, H. Mitsuhashi, and D.A. Kirsch, "Revisiting Burns and Stalker: Formal Structure and New Venture Performance in Emerging Economic Sectors," *Academy of Management Journal* 49, no. 1 (2006): 121–32.

34. Mintzberg, *The Structuring of Organizations*, 106.

35. Mintzberg, *The Structuring of Organizations*, Chap. 17; R.M. Burton, B. Obel, and G. DeSanctis, *Organizational Design: A Step-by-Step Approach*, 2nd ed. (Cambridge, UK: Cambridge University Press, 2011), 61–63.

36. Galbraith, *Designing Organizations*, 23–25; Burton et al., *Organizational Design*, 63–65.

37. E.E. Lawler III, *Rewarding Excellence: Pay Strategies for the New Economy* (San Francisco: Jossey-Bass, 2000), 31–34.

38. The evolutionary development of the divisional structure is described in J.R. Galbraith, "The Evolution of Enterprise Organization Designs," *Journal of Organization Design* 1, no. 2 (2012): 1–13.

39. These structures were identified from corporate websites and annual reports. These organizations typically rely on a mixture of other structures, so the charts shown have been adapted for learning purposes.

40. M. Goold and A. Campbell, "Do You Have a Well-Designed Organization?," *Harvard Business Review* 80 (2002): 117–24. Others have added factors such as economies of scale and what resources need to be controlled the most. See G. Kesler and A. Kates, *Leading Organization Design: How to Make Organization Design Decisions to Drive the Results You Want* (San Francisco: Jossey-Bass, 2011), Chap. 3.

41. J.R. Galbraith, "Structuring Global Organizations," in *Tomorrow's Organization*, ed. S.A. Mohrman et al. (San Francisco: Jossey-Bass, 1998), 103–29; C. Homburg, J.P. Workman Jr., and O. Jensen, "Fundamental Changes in Marketing Organization: The Movement toward a Customer-Focused Organizational Structure," *Academy of Marketing Science Journal* 28 (2000): 459–78; T.H. Davenport, J.G. Harris, and A.K. Kohli, "How Do They Know Their Customers So Well?," *Sloan Management Review* 42 (2001): 63–73; J.R. Galbraith, "Organizing to Deliver Solutions," *Organizational Dynamics* 31 (2002): 194–207.

42. Burton et al., *Organizational Design*, 65–68.

43. Valve Corporation, *Valve Handbook for Employees* (Bellevue, WA: Valve Press, 2012); M. Abrash, "Valve: How I Got Here, What It's Like, and What I'm Doing," *Ramblings in Valve Time*, April 13, 2012, http://blogs.valvesoftware.com/abrash; J. Cook, "Valve Designer Greg Coomer: How Getting Rid of Bosses Makes for Better Games," *GeekWire*, October 29, 2012; N. Wingfield, "Game Maker without a Rule Book," *The New York Times*, September 9, 2012.

44. J.R. Galbraith, E.E. Lawler III, and Associates, *Organizing for the Future: The New Logic for Managing Complex Organizations* (San Francisco: Jossey-Bass, 1993); R. Bettis and M. Hitt, "The New Competitive Landscape," *Strategic Management Journal* 16 (1995): 7–19.

45. P.C. Ensign, "Interdependence, Coordination, and Structure in Complex Organizations: Implications for Organization Design," *Mid-Atlantic Journal of Business* 34 (1998): 5–22.

46. M.M. Fanning, "A Circular Organization Chart Promotes a Hospital-Wide Focus on Teams," *Hospital & Health Services Administration* 42 (1997): 243–54; L.Y. Chan and B.E. Lynn, "Operating in Turbulent Times: How Ontario's Hospitals Are Meeting the Current Funding Crisis," *Health Care Management Review* 23 (1998): 7–18.

47. R. Cross, "Looking before You Leap: Assessing the Jump to Teams in Knowledge-Based Work," *Business Horizons* 43, no. 5 (2000): 29–36; M. Fenton-O'Creevy, "Employee Involvement and the Middle Manager: Saboteur or Scapegoat?," *Human Resource Management Journal* 11 (2001): 24–40; C. Douglas and W.L. Gardner, "Transition to Self-Directed Work Teams: Implications of Transition Time and Self-Monitoring for Managers' Use of Influence Tactics," *Journal of Organizational Behavior* 25 (2004): 47–65; G. Garda, K. Lindstrom, and M. Dallnera, "Towards a Learning Organization: The Introduction of a Client-Centered Team-Based Organization in Administrative Surveying Work," *Applied Ergonomics* 34 (2003): 97–105.

48. S.M. Davis and P.R. Lawrence, *Matrix* (Reading, MA: Addison-Wesley, 1977); J.R. Galbraith, *Designing Matrix Organizations That Actually Work* (San Francisco: Jossey-Bass, 2009).

49. "Organizational Structure and Business Activities" (Melbourne, Australia: Macquarie Group, 2013), www.macquarie.com.au/mgl/au/about-macquarie-group/profile/organisation-structure (accessed June 7, 2013). Other global matrix structures are also discussed in Kesler and Kates, *Leading Organization Design*, Chap. 7.

50. Deloitte U.S. Chinese Services Group, *Balancing Flexibility and Control: Optimizing Your Organizational Structure in China*, Board Brief China (New York: Deloitte, 2008).

51. R.C. Ford and W.A. Randolph, "Cross-Functional Structures: A Review and Integration of Matrix Organization and Project Management," *Journal of Management* 18 (1992): 267–94.

52. R. Muzyka and G. Zeschuk, "Managing Multiple Projects," *Game Developer*, March 2003, 34–42.

53. J.X.J. Qiu and L. Donaldson, "Stopford and Wells Were Right! MNC Matrix Structures *Do* Fit a 'High-High' Strategy," *Management International Review (MIR)* 52, no. 5 (2012): 671–89; D. Ganguly and M. Mitra, "Survive the Matrix," *Economic Times* (Mumbai, India), March 29, 2013.

54. G. Calabrese, "Communication and Co-operation in Product Development: A Case Study of a European Car Producer," *R&D Management* 27 (1997): 239–52; T. Sy and L.S. D'Annunzio, "Challenges and Strategies of Matrix Organizations: Top-Level and Mid-Level Managers' Perspectives," *Human Resource Planning* 28, no. 1 (2005): 39–48; J. Wolf and W.G. Egelhoff, "An Empirical Evaluation of Conflict in MNC Matrix Structure Firms," *International Business Review* 22, no. 3 (2013): 591–601.

55. D. Ganguly, "Matrix Evolutions," *Economic Times* (Mumbai, India), February 18, 2012.

56. Nadler and Tushman, *Competing by Design*, Chap. 6; M. Goold and A. Campbell, "Structured Networks: Towards the Well-Designed Matrix," *Long Range Planning* 36, no. 5 (2003): 427–39.

57. D. Ciampa and M. Watkins, "Rx for New CEOs," *Chief Executive*, January 2008.

58. L. Donaldson, *The Contingency Theory of Organizations* (Thousand Oaks, CA: Sage, 2001); J. Birkinshaw, R. Nobel, and J. Ridderstråle, "Knowledge as a Contingency Variable: Do the Characteristics of Knowledge Predict Organizational Structure?," *Organization Science* 13, no. 3 (2002): 274–89.

59. P.R. Lawrence and J.W. Lorsch, *Organization and Environment* (Homewood, IL: Irwin, 1967); Mintzberg, *The Structuring of Organizations*, Chap. 15.

60. Burns and Stalker, *The Management of Innovation*; Lawrence and Lorsch, *Organization and Environment*.

61. Mintzberg, *The Structuring of Organizations*, 282.

62. D.S. Pugh and C.R. Hinings, *Organizational Structure: Extensions and Replications* (Farnborough, UK: Lexington Books, 1976); Mintzberg, *The Structuring of Organizations*, Chap. 13.

63. Galbraith, *Designing Organizations*, 52–55; G. Hertel, S. Geister, and U. Konradt, "Managing Virtual Teams: A Review of Current Empirical Research," *Human Resource Management Review* 15 (2005): 69–95.

64. C. Perrow, "A Framework for the Comparative Analysis of Organizations," *American Sociological Review* 32 (1967): 194–208; D. Gerwin, "The Comparative Analysis of Structure and Technology: A Critical Appraisal," *Academy of Management Review* 4, no. 1 (1979): 41–51; C.C. Miller et al., "Understanding Technology-Structure Relationships: Theory Development and Meta-Analytic Theory Testing," *Academy of Management Journal* 34, no. 2 (1991): 370–99.

65. R.H. Kilmann, *Beyond the Quick Fix* (San Francisco: Jossey-Bass, 1984), 38.

66. A.D. Chandler, *Strategy and Structure* (Cambridge, MA: MIT Press, 1962).

67. D. Miller, "Configurations of Strategy and Structure," *Strategic Management Journal* 7 (1986): 233–49.

Chapter 13

1. H. Blodget, "Mark Zuckerberg, Moving Fast and Breaking Things," *Business Insider*, October 14, 2010; K. Ladendorf, "For Facebook Workers, It's Not Just a Job," *Austin American-Statesman*, May 1, 2011, E1; M. Swift, "Facebook Landing Team Transports Company Culture," *San Jose Mercury News* (CA), March 25, 2011; K. Raghav, " 'We Paint the Walls,' " *LiveMint*, June 10, 2011.

2. A. Williams, P. Dobson, and M. Walters, *Changing Culture: New Organizational Approaches* (London: Institute of Personnel Management, 1989); E.H. Schein, "What Is Culture?," in *Reframing Organizational Culture*, ed. P.J. Frost et al. (Newbury Park, CA: Sage, 1991), 243–53.

3. M. Lagace, "Gerstner: Changing Culture at IBM," *HBS Working Knowledge*, September 12, 2002.

4. B.M. Meglino and E.C. Ravlin, "Individual Values in Organizations: Concepts, Controversies, and Research," *Journal of Management* 24, no. 3 (1998): 351–89; B.R. Agle and C.B. Caldwell, "Understanding Research on Values in Business," *Business and Society* 38, no. 3 (1999): 326–87; S. Hitlin and J.A. Pilavin, "Values: Reviving a Dormant Concept," *Annual Review of Sociology* 30 (2004): 359–93.

5. N.M. Ashkanasy, "The Case for Culture," in *Debating Organization*, ed. R. Westwood and S. Clegg (Malden, MA: Blackwell, 2003), 300–10.

6. B. Kabanoff and J. Daly, "Espoused Values in Organisations," *Australian Journal of Management* 27, Special issue (2002): 89–104.

7. "Norway Criticizes BP, Smedvig over Safety," *Energy Compass*, January 3, 2003; J.A. Lozano, "BP Refinery Had History of Dangerous Releases, Report Finds," *Associated Press*, October 28, 2005; S. McNulty, "A Corroded Culture?," *Financial Times* (London), December 18, 2006, 17; U.S. Chemical Safety and Hazard Investigation Board, *Investigation Report: Refinery Explosion and Fire* (Texas City, Texas: BP, March 23, 2005); U.S. Chemical Safety Board (Washington, DC: March 2007); S. Greenhouse, "BP Faces Record Fine for '05 Refinery Explosion," *The New York Times*, October 30, 2009; L.C. Steffy, *Drowning in Oil: BP and the Reckless Pursuit of Profit* (New York: McGraw-Hill, 2011).

8. S. Stern, "The Lofty View from Davos Could Just Be a Mirage," *Financial Times* (London), January 28, 2008; Deloitte Touche Tohmatsu, *Core Beliefs and Culture*, Deloitte Touche Tohmatsu (New York: 2012). *2013 Culture and Change Management Survey*, (New York: 9 November 2013).

9. C. Ostroff, A.J. Kinicki, and R.S. Muhammad, "Organizational Culture and Climate," in *Handbook of Psychology,* 2nd ed., ed. I.B. Weiner (Wiley, 2012), 643–76.

10. C.A. O'Reilly III, J. Chatman, and D.F. Caldwell, "People and Organizational Culture: A Profile Comparison Approach to Assessing Person–Organization Fit," *Academy of Management Journal* 34 (1991): 487–516; J.J. van Muijen, "Organizational Culture," in *A Handbook of Work and Organizational Psychology: Organizational Psychology*, ed. P.J.D. Drenth, H. Thierry, and C.J. de Wolff (East Sussex, UK: Psychology Press, 1998), 113–32; P.A. Balthazard, R.A. Cooke, and R.E. Potter, "Dysfunctional

Culture, Dysfunctional Organization: Capturing the Behavioral Norms That Form Organizational Culture and Drive Performance," *Journal of Managerial Psychology* 21, no. 8 (2006): 709–32; C. Helfrich et al., "Assessing an Organizational Culture Instrument Based on the Competing Values Framework: Exploratory and Confirmatory Factor Analyses," *Implementation Science* 2, no. 1 (2007): 13. For reviews of organizational culture survey instruments, see T. Scott et al., "The Quantitative Measurement of Organizational Culture in Health Care: A Review of the Available Instruments," *Health Services Research* 38, no. 3 (2003): 923–45; D.E. Leidner and T. Kayworth, "A Review of Culture in Information Systems Research: Toward a Theory of Information Technology Culture Conflict," *MIS Quarterly* 30, no. 2 (2006): 357–99; S. Scott-Findlay and C.A. Estabrooks, "Mapping the Organizational Culture Research in Nursing: A Literature Review," *Journal of Advanced Nursing* 56, no. 5 (2006): 498–513.

11. J. Martin, P.J. Frost, and O.A. O'Neill, "Organizational Culture: Beyond Struggles for Intellectual Dominance," in *Handbook of Organization Studies*, ed. S. Clegg et al. (London: Sage, 2006), 725–53; N.E. Fenton and S. Inglis, "A Critical Perspective on Organizational Values," *Nonprofit Management and Leadership* 17, no. 3 (2007): 335–47; K. Haukelid, "Theories of (Safety) Culture Revisited—an Anthropological Approach," *Safety Science* 46, no. 3 (2008): 413–26.

12. G. Hofstede, "Identifying Organizational Subcultures: An Empirical Approach," *Journal of Management Studies* 35, no. 1 (1990): 1–12; J. Martin and C. Siehl, "Organizational Culture and Counterculture: An Uneasy Symbiosis," *Organizational Dynamics* (1983): 52–64; E. Ogbonna and L.C. Harris, "Organisational Culture in the Age of the Internet: An Exploratory Study," *New Technology, Work and Employment* 21, no. 2 (2006): 162–75.

13. H. Silver, "Does a University Have a Culture?," *Studies in Higher Education* 28, no. 2 (2003): 157–69.

14. A. Sinclair, "Approaches to Organizational Culture and Ethics," *Journal of Business Ethics* 12 (1993); T.E. Deal and A.A. Kennedy, *The New Corporate Cultures* (Cambridge, MA: Perseus Books, 1999), Chap. 10; A. Boisnier and J. Chatman, "The Role of Subcultures in Agile Organizations," in *Leading and Managing People in Dynamic Organizations*, ed. R. Petersen and E. Mannix (Mahwah, NJ: Erlbaum, 2003), 87–112; C. Morrill, M.N. Zald, and H. Rao, "Covert Political Conflict in Organizations: Challenges from Below," *Annual Review of Sociology* 29, no. 1 (2003): 391–415.

15. J.S. Ott, *The Organizational Culture Perspective* (Pacific Grove, CA: Brooks/Cole, 1989), Chap. 2; J.S. Pederson and J.S. Sorensen, *Organizational Cultures in Theory and Practice* (Aldershot, UK: Gower, 1989), 27–29; M.O. Jones, *Studying Organizational Symbolism: What, How, Why?* (Thousand Oaks, CA: Sage, 1996).

16. A. Furnham and B. Gunter, "Corporate Culture: Definition, Diagnosis, and Change," *International Review of Industrial and Organizational Psychology* 8 (1993): 233–61; E.H. Schein, "Organizational Culture," *American Psychologist* (1990): 109–19; E.H. Schein, *The Corporate Culture Survival Guide* (San Francisco: Jossey-Bass, 1999), Chap. 4.

17. M. Doehrman, "Anthropologists—Deep in the Corporate Bush," *Daily Record* (Kansas City, MO), July 19, 2005, 1.

18. C.J. Boudens, "The Story of Work: A Narrative Analysis of Workplace Emotion," *Organization Studies* 26, no. 9 (2005): 1285–306; S. Denning, *The Leader's Guide to Storytelling* (San Francisco:

Jossey-Bass, 2005); T.E. Deal and A.A. Kennedy, *Corporate Cultures* (Reading, MA: Addison-Wesley, 1982), Chap. 5.

19. J.C. Meyer, "Tell Me a Story: Eliciting Organizational Values from Narratives," *Communication Quarterly* 43 (1995): 210–24; W. Swap et al., "Using Mentoring and Storytelling to Transfer Knowledge in the Workplace," *Journal of Management Information Systems* 18 (2001): 95–114; A.L. Wilkins, "Organizational Stories as Symbols Which Control the Organization," in *Organizational Symbolism*, ed. L.R. Pondy et al. (Greenwich, CT: JAI Press, 1984), 81–92; R. Zemke, "Storytelling: Back to a Basic," *Training* 27, no. 3 (1990): 44–50.

20. D. Roth, "My Job at The Container Store," *Fortune* (January 10, 2000): 74–78.

21. R.E. Quinn and N.T. Snyder, "Advanced Change Theory: Culture Change at Whirlpool Corporation," in *The Leader's Change Handbook*, ed. J.A. Conger, G.M. Spreitzer, and E.E. Lawler III (San Francisco: Jossey-Bass, 1999), 162–93.

22. G. Smith, *Why I Left Goldman Sachs: A Wall Street Story* (New York: Grand Central Publishing, 2012); R. Blackden, "Goldman Sachs in Hunt for 'Muppet' Email," *The Telegraph*, March 22, 2012.

23. A.C.T. Smith and B. Stewart, "Organizational Rituals: Features, Functions and Mechanisms," *International Journal of Management Reviews* 13 (2011): 113–33.

24. "The Ultimate Chairman," *Business Times Singapore*, September 3, 2005.

25. Churchill apparently made this statement on October 28, 1943, in the British House of Commons, when London, damaged by bombings in World War II, was about to be rebuilt.

26. G. Turner and J. Myerson, *New Workspace New Culture: Office Design as a Catalyst for Change* (Aldershot, UK: Gower, 1998).

27. K.D. Elsbach and B.A. Bechky, "It's More Than a Desk: Working Smarter through Leveraged Office Design," *California Management Review* 49, no. 2 (2007): 80–101.

28. "Define Core Values First," *National Post*, February 7, 2011, JV1; "Sharing a Vision with Clearly Contacts CEO Roger Hardy," *PeopleTalk*, Spring 2013, 50.

29. R. Barrett, *Building a Values-Driven Organization: A Whole System Approach to Cultural Transformation* (Burlington, MA: Butterworth-Heinemann, 2006); J.C. Collins and J.I. Porras, *Built to Last: Successful Habits of Visionary Companies* (London: Century, 1994); J.M. Kouzes and B.Z. Posner, *The Leadership Challenge*, 4th ed. (San Francisco: Jossey-Bass, 2007), Chap. 3; Deal and Kennedy, *The New Corporate Cultures*.

30. C. Siehl and J. Martin, "Organizational Culture: A Key to Financial Performance?," in *Organizational Climate and Culture*, ed. B. Schneider (San Francisco, CA: Jossey-Bass, 1990), 241–81; G.G. Gordon and N. DiTomaso, "Predicting Corporate Performance from Organizational Culture," *Journal of Management Studies* 29 (1992): 783–98; J.P. Kotter and J.L. Heskett, *Corporate Culture and Performance* (New York: Free Press, 1992); C.P.M. Wilderom, U. Glunk, and R. Maslowski, "Organizational Culture as a Predictor of Organizational Performance," in *Handbook of Organizational Culture and Climate*, ed. N.M. Ashkanasy, C.P.M. Wilderom, and M.F. Peterson (Thousand Oaks, CA: Sage, 2000), 193–210; A. Carmeli and A. Tishler, "The Relationships between Intangible Organizational Elements and Organizational Performance," *Strategic Management Journal* 25 (2004): 1257–78; S. Teerikangas and P. Very,

"The Culture–Performance Relationship in M&A: From Yes/No to How," *British Journal of Management* 17, no. S1 (2006): S31–S48.

31. L. Carapiet, "NAB's John Stewart Knows His ABCs," *Australian Banking & Finance*, December 2007, 6; J.H. Want, *Corporate Culture: Key Strategies of High-Performing Business Cultures* (New York: St. Martin's Press, 2007), 38.

32. Y. Wiener, "Forms of Value Systems: A Focus on Organizational Effectiveness and Cultural Change and Maintenance," *Academy of Management Review* 13, no. 4 (1988): 534–45; J.A. Chatman and S.E. Cha, "Leading by Leveraging Culture," *California Management Review* 45 (2003): 20–34; M. Alvesson, *Understanding Organizational Culture*, 2nd ed. (London: Sage, 2013).

33. B. Ashforth and F. Mael, "Social Identity Theory and the Organization," *Academy of Management Review* 14 (1989): 20–39.

34. Heidrick & Struggles, *Leadership Challenges Emerge as Asia Pacific Companies Go Global*, Heidrick & Struggles (Melbourne: August 2008).

35. M.R. Louis, "Surprise and Sensemaking: What Newcomers Experience in Entering Unfamiliar Organizational Settings," *Administrative Science Quarterly* 25 (1980): 226–51; S.G. Harris, "Organizational Culture and Individual Sensemaking: A Schema-Based Perspective," *Organization Science* 5 (1994): 309–21.

36. J.W. Barnes et al., "The Role of Culture Strength in Shaping Sales Force Outcomes," *Journal of Personal Selling & Sales Management* 26, no. 3 (2006): 255–70.

37. D. Frith, "Follow the Leader," *Business Review Weekly*, April 19, 2012, 18.

38. C.A. O'Reilly III and J.A. Chatman, "Culture as Social Control: Corporations, Cults, and Commitment," *Research in Organizational Behavior* 18 (1996): 157–200; B. Spector and H. Lane, "Exploring the Distinctions between a High Performance Culture and a Cult," *Strategy & Leadership* 35, no. 3 (2007): 18–24.

39. Kotter and Heskett, *Corporate Culture and Performance*; J.P. Kotter, "Cultures and Coalitions," *Executive Excellence* 15 (1998): 14–15; B.M. Bass and R.E. Riggio, *Transformational Leadership*, 2nd ed. (New York: Routledge, 2006), Chap. 7. The term *adaptive culture* has a different meaning in organizational behavior than it has in cultural anthropology, where it refers to nonmaterial cultural conditions (such as ways of thinking) that lag the material culture (physical artifacts). For the anthropological perspective see W. Griswold, *Cultures and Societies in a Changing World*, 3rd ed. (Thousand Oaks: Pine Forge Press (Sage), 2008), 66.

40. T. Krisher and D.A. Durbin, "General Motors CEO Akerson Leads Comeback from Bankruptcy by Ruffling Company's Bureaucracy," *Associated Press Newswires*, December 17, 2011.

41. W.E. Baker and J.M. Sinkula, "The Synergistic Effect of Market Orientation and Learning Orientation on Organizational Performance," *Academy of Marketing Science Journal* 27, no. 4 (1999): 411–27; Z. Emden, A. Yaprak, and S.T. Cavusgil, "Learning from Experience in International Alliances: Antecedents and Firm Performance Implications," *Journal of Business Research* 58, no. 7 (2005): 883–92.

42. Lockheed Martin, "Culture" (Bethesda, MD: Lockheed Martin, 2014), www.lockheedmartin.com.au/us/who-we-are/culture.html (accessed June 8, 2014).

43. M. Pascoe, "Worst Is Yet to Come for Murdoch," *Sydney Morning Herald*, July 18, 2011; "News International and Phone-Hacking," ed. UK House of Commons: Culture Media and Sport Committee (London: The Stationary Office Limited, 2012).

44. M.L. Marks, "Adding Cultural Fit to Your Diligence Checklist," *Mergers & Acquisitions* 34, no. 3 (1999): 14–20; Schein, *The Corporate Culture Survival Guide*, Chap. 8; Teerikangas and Very, "The Culture–Performance Relationship in M&A: From Yes/No to How"; G.K. Stahl and A. Voigt, "Do Cultural Differences Matter in Mergers and Acquisitions? A Tentative Model and Examination," *Organization Science* 19, no. 1 (2008): 160–76.

45. "KPMG Identifies Six Key Factors for Successful Mergers and Acquisitions," news release for KPMG (New York: PR Newswire, November 29, 1999); D. Henry, "Mergers: Why Most Big Deals Don't Pay Off," *BusinessWeek*, October 14, 2002; M.L. Sirower, *The Synergy Trap: How Companies Lose the Acquisition Game* (New York: Free Press, 1997); J. Krug, *Mergers and Acquisitions: Turmoil in Top Management Teams* (Williston, VT: Business Expert Press, 2009); C. Cook and D. Spitzer, *World Class Transactions*, KPMG (London: 2001).

46. C.A. Schorg, C.A. Raiborn, and M.F. Massoud, "Using a 'Cultural Audit' to Pick M&A Winners," *Journal of Corporate Accounting & Finance* (2004): 47–55; W. Locke, "Higher Education Mergers: Integrating Organisational Cultures and Developing Appropriate Management Styles," *Higher Education Quarterly* 61, no. 1 (2007): 83–102.

47. A.R. Malekazedeh and A. Nahavandi, "Making Mergers Work by Managing Cultures," *Journal of Business Strategy* (1990): 55–57; K.W. Smith, "A Brand-New Culture for the Merged Firm," *Mergers and Acquisitions* 35 (2000): 45–50.

48. M. Joyce, "AirTran Employees Getting New Culture," *Dallas Business Journal*, July 8, 2011.

49. Hewitt Associates, "Mergers and Acquisitions May Be Driven by Business Strategy—but Often Stumble over People and Culture Issues" (Lincolnshire, IL: PR Newswire, 1998).

50. J. Martin, "Can Organizational Culture Be Managed?," in *Organizational Culture*, ed. P.J. Frost et al. (Beverly Hills, CA: Sage, 1985), 95–98.

51. A.S. Tsui et al., "Unpacking the Relationship between CEO Leadership Behavior and Organizational Culture," *Leadership Quarterly* 17 (2006): 113–37; Y. Berson, S. Oreg, and T. Dvir, "CEO Values, Organizational Culture and Firm Outcomes," *Journal of Organizational Behavior* 29, no. 5 (2008): 615–33; B. Schneider, M.G. Ehrhart, and W.H. Macey, "Organizational Climate and Culture," *Annual Review of Psychology* 64, no. 1 (2013): 361–88.

52. E.H. Schein, "The Role of the Founder in Creating Organizational Culture," *Organizational Dynamics* 12, no. 1 (1983): 13–28; R. House, M. Javidan, and P. Dorfman, "Project GLOBE: An Introduction," *Applied Psychology: An International Review* 50 (2001): 489–505; R. House et al., "Understanding Cultures and Implicit Leadership Theories across the Globe: An Introduction to Project GLOBE," *Journal of World Business* 37 (2002): 3–10.

53. M. De Pree, *Leadership Jazz: The Essential Elements of a Great Leader*, 2nd ed. (New York: Broadway Business, 2008).

54. B. O'Connor, "CEO Credits Quicken Loans' Culture for Firm's Success," *Detroit News*, May 1, 2013, C2.

55. M. De Pree, *Leadership Is an Art* (East Lansing: Michigan State University Press, 1987).

56. J. Kerr and J.W. Slocum Jr., "Managing Corporate Culture through Reward Systems," *Academy of Management Executive* 1 (1987): 99–107; J.M. Higgins et al., "Using Cultural Artifacts to Change and Perpetuate Strategy," *Journal of Change Management* 6, no. 4 (2006): 397–415; H. Hofstetter and I. Harpaz, "Declared versus Actual Organizational Culture as Indicated by an Organization's Performance Appraisal," *International Journal of Human Resource Management* (2011): 1–22.

57. Deloitte Touche, *Core Beliefs and Culture: Chairman's Survey Findings* (New York: Deloitte Touche, 2012). http://www. deloitte.com/print/en_US/us/About/Leadership/1fe8be4ad25e7310 VgnVCM1000001956f00aRCRD.htm (accessed 26 July 2012).

58. R. Charan, "Home Depot's Blueprint for Culture Change," *Harvard Business Review* (2006): 61–70.

59. B. Schneider, "The People Make the Place," *Personnel Psychology* 40, no. 3 (1987): 437–53; B. Schneider et al., "Personality and Organizations: A Test of the Homogeneity of Personality Hypothesis," *Journal of Applied Psychology* 83, no. 3 (1998): 462–70; T.R. Giberson, C.J. Resick, and M.W. Dickson, "Embedding Leader Characteristics: An Examination of Homogeneity of Personality and Values in Organizations," *Journal of Applied Psychology* 90, no. 5 (2005): 1002–10.

60. T. Hsieh, *Delivering Happiness: A Path to Profits, Passion, and Purpose* (New York: Business Plus, 2010); K. McGee, "Education for Life: Companies Offer Different Corporate Culture," *Las Vegas Business Press*, July 30, 2012, S22.

61. Taleo Research, "Talent Management Processes," (Dublin, CA: Taleo, 2010), www.taleo.com (accessed 2 June 2010); "Thirty-Seven Percent of Companies Use Social Networks to Research Potential Job Candidates, According to New Careerbuilder Survey," News release for Careerbuilder (Chicago: 18 April 2012); Cubiks International, *Cubiks International Survey on Job and Cultural Fit*, Cubiks International (Guildford, UK: July 2013); Kelly Services, *Engaging Active and Passive Job Seekers*, Kelly Global Workforce Index, Kelly Services (Troy, MI: May 2014).

62. T.A. Judge and D.M. Cable, "Applicant Personality, Organizational Culture, and Organization Attraction," *Personnel Psychology* 50, no. 2 (1997): 359–94; D.S. Chapman et al., "Applicant Attraction to Organizations and Job Choice: A Meta-Analytic Review of the Correlates of Recruiting Outcomes," *Journal of Applied Psychology* 90, no. 5 (2005): 928–44; A.L. Kristof-Brown, R.D. Zimmerman, and E.C. Johnson, "Consequences of Individuals' Fit at Work: A Meta-Analysis of Person-Job, Person-Organization, Person-Group, and Person-Supervisor Fit," *Personnel Psychology* 58, no. 2 (2005): 281–342; C. Hu, H.C. Su, and C.I.B. Chen, "The Effect of Person-Organization Fit Feedback via Recruitment Web Sites on Applicant Attraction," *Computers in Human Behavior* 23, no. 5 (2007): 2509–23.

63. P. Nunes and T. Breene, "Reinvent Your Business before It's Too Late," *Harvard Business Review* 89, no. 1/2 (2011): 80–87.

64. A. Kristof-Brown, "Perceived Applicant Fit: Distinguishing between Recruiters' Perceptions of Person-Job and Person-Organization Fit," *Personnel Psychology* 53, no. 3 (2000): 643–71; A.E.M. Van Vianen, "Person-Organization Fit: The Match between Newcomers' and Recruiters' Preferences for Organizational Cultures," *Personnel Psychology* 53 (2000): 113–49.

65. D.M. Cable and J.R. Edwards, "Complementary and Supplementary Fit: A Theoretical and Empirical Integration," *Journal of Applied Psychology* 89, no. 5 (2004): 822–34.

66. J. Van Maanen, "Breaking In: Socialization to Work," in *Handbook of Work, Organization, and Society*, ed. R. Dubin (Chicago: Rand McNally, 1976).

67. S.L. McShane, G. O'Neill, and T. Travaglione, "Managing Employee Values in Values-Driven Organizations: Contradiction, Façade, and Illusions" (paper presented at the 21st Annual ANZAM Conference, Sydney, Australia, December 2007); S.L. McShane, G. O'Neill, and T. Travaglione, "Rethinking the Values-Driven Organization Process: From Values Engineering to Behavioral Domain Training," (paper presented at the Academy of Management 2008 Annual Meeting, Anaheim, CA, 2008).

68. D.G. Allen, "Do Organizational Socialization Tactics Influence Newcomer Embeddedness and Turnover?," *Journal of Management* 32, no. 2 (2006): 237–56; A.M. Saks, K.L. Uggerslev, and N.E. Fassina, "Socialization Tactics and Newcomer Adjustment: A Meta-Analytic Review and Test of a Model," *Journal of Vocational Behavior* 70, no. 3 (2007): 413–46.

69. G.T. Chao et al., "Organizational Socialization: Its Content and Consequences," *Journal of Applied Psychology* 79 (1994): 450–63; H.D. Cooper-Thomas and N. Anderson, "Organizational Socialization: A Field Study into Socialization Success and Rate," *International Journal of Selection and Assessment* 13, no. 2 (2005): 116–28.

70. N. Nicholson, "A Theory of Work Role Transitions," *Administrative Science Quarterly* 29 (1984): 172–91; A. Elfering et al., "First Years in Job: A Three-Wave Analysis of Work Experiences," *Journal of Vocational Behavior* 70, no. 1 (2007): 97–115; B.E. Ashforth, D.M. Sluss, and A.M. Saks, "Socialization Tactics, Proactive Behavior, and Newcomer Learning: Integrating Socialization Models," *Journal of Vocational Behavior* 70, no. 3 (2007): 447–62; T.N. Bauer, "Newcomer Adjustment during Organizational Socialization: A Meta-Analytic Review of Antecedents, Outcomes, and Methods," *Journal of Applied Psychology* 92, no. 3 (2007): 707–21.

71. J.M. Beyer and D.R. Hannah, "Building on the Past: Enacting Established Personal Identities in a New Work Setting," *Organization Science* 13 (2002): 636–52; H.D.C. Thomas and N. Anderson, "Newcomer Adjustment: The Relationship between Organizational Socialization Tactics, Information Acquisition and Attitudes," *Journal of Occupational and Organizational Psychology* 75 (2002): 423–37.

72. L.W. Porter, E.E. Lawler III, and J.R. Hackman, *Behavior in Organizations* (New York: McGraw-Hill, 1975), 163–67; Van Maanen, "Breaking In: Socialization to Work," 67–130; D.C. Feldman, "The Multiple Socialization of Organization Members," *Academy of Management Review* 6 (1981): 309–18.

73. B.E. Ashforth and A.M. Saks, "Socialization Tactics: Longitudinal Effects on Newcomer Adjustment," *Academy of Management Journal* 39 (1996): 149–78; J.D. Kammeyer-Mueller and C.R. Wanberg, "Unwrapping the Organizational Entry Process: Disentangling Multiple Antecedents and Their Pathways to Adjustment," *Journal of Applied Psychology* 88, no. 5 (2003): 779–94.

74. Porter et al., *Behavior in Organizations*, Chap. 5.

75. Louis, "Surprise and Sensemaking."

76. S.L. Robinson and D.M. Rousseau, "Violating the Psychological Contract: Not the Exception but the Norm," *Journal of Organizational Behavior* 15 (1994): 245–59.

77. D.L. Nelson, "Organizational Socialization: A Stress Perspective," *Journal of Occupational Behavior* 8 (1987): 311–24; Elfering et al., "First Years in Job."

78. J.P. Wanous, *Organizational Entry* (Reading, MA: Addison-Wesley, 1992); J.A. Breaugh and M. Starke, "Research on Employee Recruitment: So Many Studies, So Many Remaining Questions," *Journal of Management* 26, no. 3 (2000): 405–34.

79. J.M. Phillips, "Effects of Realistic Job Previews on Multiple Organizational Outcomes: A Meta-Analysis," *Academy of Management Journal* 41 (1998): 673–90.

80. Y. Ganzach et al., "Social Exchange and Organizational Commitment: Decision-Making Training for Job Choice as an Alternative to the Realistic Job Preview," *Personnel Psychology* 55 (2002): 613–37.

81. C. Ostroff and S.W.J. Koslowski, "Organizational Socialization as a Learning Process: The Role of Information Acquisition," *Personnel Psychology* 45 (1992): 849–74; Cooper-Thomas and Anderson, "Organizational Socialization: A Field Study into Socialization Success and Rate."; A. Baber and L. Waymon, "Uncovering the Unconnected Employee," *T&D* (2008): 60–66.

82. S. Nifadkar, A.S. Tsui, and B.E. Ashforth, "The Way You Make Me Feel and Behave: Supervisor-Triggered Newcomer Affect and Approach-Avoidance Behavior," *Academy of Management Journal* 55, no. 5 (2012): 1146–68.

83. N. Singh, "Buddies Build Bonds, Leadership Skills at Companies," *Times of India*, March 5, 2013; R.E. Silverman, "First Day on Job: Not Just Paperwork," *The Wall Street Journal*, May 29, 2013, B10.

Chapter 14

1. S. Lohr, "Even a Giant Can Learn to Run," *The New York Times*, January 1, 2012, 3.

2. M. Haid et al., *Ready, Get Set . . . Change!: The Impact of Change on Workforce Productivity and Engagement* (Philadelphia, PA: Right Management, 2009).

3. D. Howes, "Future Hinges on Global Teams," *Detroit News*, December 21, 1998.

4. J. Welch, *Jack: Straight from the Heart* (New York: Warner Business Books, 2001), 432.

5. K. Lewin, *Field Theory in Social Science* (New York: Harper & Row, 1951).

6. D. Coghlan and T. Brannick, "Kurt Lewin: The 'Practical Theorist' for the 21st Century," *Irish Journal of Management* 24, no. 2 (2003): 31–37; B. Burnes, "Kurt Lewin and the Planned Approach to Change: A Re-appraisal," *Journal of Management Studies* 41, no. 6 (2004): 977–1002.

7. "Ogilvy & Mather Corporate Culture" (New York, 2011), www.ogilvy.com/About/Our-History/Corporate-Culture.aspx (accessed May 17, 2011).

8. J. Mouawad, "Largest Airline Has Bigger Troubles," *International Herald Tribune*, November 30, 2012, 14; M. Mecham, "Not Yet United," *Overhaul & Maintenance*, April 2012, 46; M. Brownell, "Here's Why United Was Just Named America's Worst Airline," *Daily Finance*, June 18, 2013.

9. D. Howell, "Nardelli Nears Five-Year Mark with Riveting Record," *DSN Retailing Today* 9 (May 2005): 1, 38; R. Charan, "Home Depot's Blueprint for Culture Change," *Harvard Business Review* (2006): 61–70; R. DeGross, "Five Years of Change: Home Depot's Results Mixed under Nardelli," *Atlanta Journal-Constitution*, January 1, 2006, F1.

10. Some experts suggest that resistance to change should be restated in a more positive way by its opposite: readiness for change. See M. Choi and W.E.A. Ruona, "Individual Readiness for Organizational Change and Its Implications for Human Resource and Organization Development," *Human Resource Development Review* 10, no. 1 (2011): 46–73.

11. S. Chreim, "Postscript to Change: Survivors' Retrospective Views of Organizational Changes," *Personnel Review* 35, no. 3 (2006): 315–35.

12. J.K. Galbraith, *Economics, Peace, and Laughter* (Boston: Houghton Mifflin, 1971), 50.

13. E.B. Dent and S.G. Goldberg, "Challenging 'Resistance to Change,'" *Journal of Applied Behavioral Science* 35 (1999): 25–41; D.B. Fedor, S. Caldwell, and D.M. Herold, "The Effects of Organizational Changes on Employee Commitment: A Multilevel Investigation," *Personnel Psychology* 59, no. 1 (2006): 1–29.

14. B.J. Tepper et al., "Subordinates' Resistance and Managers' Evaluations of Subordinates' Performance," *Journal of Management* 32, no. 2 (2006): 185–209; J.D. Ford, L.W. Ford, and A. D'Amelio, "Resistance to Change: The Rest of the Story," *Academy of Management Review* 33, no. 2 (2008): 362–77.

15. D. Miller, "Building Commitment to Major Change—What 1700 Change Agents Told Us Really Works," *Developing HR Strategy*, no. 22 (2008): 5–8; W. Immen, "When Leaders Become Glory Hounds," *Globe & Mail* (Toronto), March 5, 2010, B15; Towers Watson, *Capitalizing on Effective Communication*, Towers Watson (New York: February 4, 2010); Futurestep, *The Innovation Imperative*, Futurestep (Los Angeles: June 2013).

16. D.A. Nadler, "The Effective Management of Organizational Change," in *Handbook of Organizational Behavior*, ed. J.W. Lorsch (Englewood Cliffs, NJ: Prentice Hall, 1987), 358–69; R. Maurer, *Beyond the Wall of Resistance: Unconventional Strategies to Build Support for Change* (Austin, TX: Bard Books, 1996); P. Strebel, "Why Do Employees Resist Change?," *Harvard Business Review* (1996): 86–92; D.A. Nadler, *Champions of Change* (San Francisco: Jossey-Bass, 1998).

17. S. Oreg et al., "Dispositional Resistance to Change: Measurement Equivalence and the Link to Personal Values across 17 Nations," *Journal of Applied Psychology* 93, no. 4 (2008): 935–44.

18. R.R. Sharma, *Change Management: Concepts and Applications* (New Delhi: Tata McGraw-Hill, 2007), Chap. 4; I. Cinite, L.E. Duxbury, and C. Higgins, "Measurement of Perceived Organizational Readiness for Change in the Public Sector," *British Journal of Management* 20, no. 2 (2009): 265–77; A.A. Armenakis and S.G. Harris, "Reflections: Our Journey in Organizational Change Research and Practice," *Journal of Change Management* 9, no. 2 (2009): 127–42; S. Jaros, "Commitment to

Organizational Change: A Critical Review," *Journal of Change Management* 10, no. 1 (2010): 79–108.

19. D.T. Holt et al., "Readiness for Organizational Change: The Systematic Development of a Scale," *Journal of Applied Behavioral Science* 43, no. 2 (2007): 232–55; G. Bohner and N. Dickel, "Attitudes and Attitude Change," *Annual Review of Psychology* 62, no. 1 (2011): 391–417.

20. R. de la Sablonnière et al., "Profound Organizational Change, Psychological Distress and Burnout Symptoms: The Mediator Role of Collective Relative Deprivation," *Group Processes & Intergroup Relations* 15, no. 6 (2012): 776–90.

21. S. Oreg, M. Vakola, and A. Armenakis, "Change Recipients' Reactions to Organizational Change: A 60-Year Review of Quantitative Studies," *Journal of Applied Behavioral Science* 47, no. 4 (2011): 461–524.

22. D. Grosse Kathoefer and J. Leker, "Knowledge Transfer in Academia: An Exploratory Study on the Not-Invented-Here Syndrome," *Journal of Technology Transfer* 37, no. 5 (2012): 658–75; A.L.A. Burcharth, M.P. Knudsen, and H.A. Søndergaard, "Neither Invented nor Shared Here: The Impact and Management of Attitudes for the Adoption of Open Innovation Practices," *Technovation* 34, no. 3 (2014): 149–61.

23. V. Newman, "The Psychology of Managing for Innovation," *KM Review* 9, no. 6 (2007): 10–15.

24. *Bosses Want Change but Workers Want More of the Same!*, Talent 2 (Sydney: June 29, 2005).

25. R. Davis, *Leading for Growth: How Umpqua Bank Got Cool and Created a Culture of Greatness* (San Francisco: Jossey-Bass, 2007), 40.

26. C. Lawton and J. Lublin, "Nokia Names Microsoft's Stephen Elop as New CEO, Kallasvuo Ousted," *The Wall Street Journal*, September 11, 2010; C. Ziegler, "Nokia CEO Stephen Elop Rallies Troops in Brutally Honest 'Burning Platform' Memo? (Update: It's Real!)," *Engadget*, February 8, 2011.

27. J.P. Kotter, *A Sense of Urgency* (Boston: Harvard Business School Press, 2008); S.H. Appelbaum et al., "Back to the Future: Revisiting Kotter's 1996 Change Model," *Journal of Management Development* 31, no. 8 (2012): 764–82.

28. L.D. Goodstein and H.R. Butz, "Customer Value: The Linchpin of Organizational Change," *Organizational Dynamics* 27 (1998): 21–35.

29. D. Miller, *The Icarus Paradox: How Exceptional Companies Bring about Their Own Downfall* (New York: HarperBusiness, 1990); S. Finkelstein, *Why Smart Executives Fail* (New York: Viking, 2003); A.C. Amason and A.C. Mooney, "The Icarus Paradox Revisited: How Strong Performance Sows the Seeds of Dysfunction in Future Strategic Decision-Making," *Strategic Organization* 6, no. 4 (2008): 407–34. Richard Goyder's quotation is from "Sustaining High Performance (Richard Goyder: Wesfarmers)," *CEO Forum*, September 2006.

30. T.F. Cawsey and G. Deszca, *Toolkit for Organizational Change* (Los Angeles: Sage, 2007), 104.

31. J.P. Kotter and L.A. Schlesinger, "Choosing Strategies for Change," *Harvard Business Review* (1979): 106–14.

32. M. Meaney and C. Pung, "Creating Organizational Transformations: McKinsey Global Survey Results," *McKinsey Quarterly*, July 2008, 1–7; A.E. Rafferty, N.L. Jimmieson, and A.A. Armenakis, "Change Readiness: A Multilevel Review," *Journal of Management* 39, no. 1 (2013): 110–35.

33. J.P. Kotter and D.S. Cohen, *The Heart of Change* (Boston: Harvard Business School Press, 2002), 83–98; J. Allen et al., "Uncertainty during Organizational Change: Managing Perceptions through Communication," *Journal of Change Management* 7, no. 2 (2007): 187–210; T.L. Russ, "Communicating Change: A Review and Critical Analysis of Programmatic and Participatory Implementation Approaches," *Journal of Change Management* 8, no. 3 (2008): 199–211; M. van den Heuvel et al., "Adapting to Change: The Value of Change Information and Meaning-Making," *Journal of Vocational Behavior* 83, no. 1 (2013): 11–21.

34. G. Jones, "Chemical Reaction," *Smart Business Pittsburgh*, February 2011, 10.

35. Towers Watson, *2013–2014 Change and Communication Roi—the 10th Anniversary Report*, Towers Watson (New York: December 2013). These statistics are interpolated from data on high and low effectiveness companies provided in the most recent survey (2013–2014) as well as from total sample results provided in corresponding earlier surveys. High and low effectiveness company results were very similar for most categories.

36. D.M. Herold and S.D. Caldwell, "Beyond Change Management: A Multilevel Investigation of Contextual and Personal Influences on Employees' Commitment to Change," *Journal of Applied Psychology* 92, no. 4 (2007): 942–51; D.T. Holt and J.M. Vardaman, "Toward a Comprehensive Understanding of Readiness for Change: The Case for an Expanded Conceptualization," *Journal of Change Management* 13, no. 1 (2013): 9–18.

37. K.T. Dirks, L.L. Cummings, and J.L. Pierce, "Psychological Ownership in Organizations: Conditions under Which Individuals Promote and Resist Change," *Research in Organizational Change and Development* 9 (1996): 1–23; E.A. Lofquist, "Doomed to Fail: A Case Study of Change Implementation Collapse in the Norwegian Civil Aviation Industry," *Journal of Change Management* 11, no. 2 (2011): 223–43; L.K. Lewis and T.L. Russ, "Soliciting and Using Input during Organizational Change Initiatives: What Are Practitioners Doing," *Management Communication Quarterly* 26, no. 2 (2012): 267–94.

38. S.G. Bamberger et al., "Impact of Organisational Change on Mental Health: A Systematic Review," *Occupational and Environmental Medicine* 69, no. 8 (2012): 592–98.

39. N.T. Tan, "Maximising Human Resource Potential in the Midst of Organisational Change," *Singapore Management Review* 27, no. 2 (2005): 25–35; A.E. Rafferty and S.L.D. Restubog, "The Impact of Change Process and Context on Change Reactions and Turnover during a Merger," *Journal of Management* 36, no. 5 (2010): 1309–38.

40. M. McHugh, "The Stress Factor: Another Item for the Change Management Agenda?," *Journal of Organizational Change Management* 10 (1997): 345–62; D. Buchanan, T. Claydon, and M. Doyle, "Organisation Development and Change: The Legacy of the Nineties," *Human Resource Management Journal* 9 (1999): 20–37.

41. T. Wakefield, "No Pain, No Gain," *Canadian Business*, January 1993, 50–54; M. Cash, "StandardAero Back on the Sale Block," *Winnipeg Free Press*, December 14, 2010.

42. D. Nicolini and M.B. Meznar, "The Social Construction of Organizational Learning: Conceptual and Practical Issues in the Field," *Human Relations* 48 (1995): 727–46.

43. E.E. Lawler III, "Pay Can Be a Change Agent," *Compensation & Benefits Management* 16 (2000): 23–26; Kotter and Cohen, *The Heart of Change*, 161–77; M.A. Roberto and L.C. Levesque, "The Art of Making Change Initiatives Stick," *MIT Sloan Management Review* 46, no. 4 (2005): 53–60.

44. Lawler III, "Pay Can Be a Change Agent."

45. Goodstein and Butz, "Customer Value: The Linchpin of Organizational Change"; R.H. Miles, "Leading Corporate Transformation: Are You up to the Task?," in *The Leader's Change Handbook,* ed. J.A. Conger, G.M. Spreitzer, and E.E. Lawler III (San Francisco: Jossey-Bass, 1999), 221–67.

46. R.E. Quinn, *Building the Bridge as You Walk on It: A Guide for Leading Change* (San Francisco: Jossey-Bass, 2004), Chap. 11; D.M. Herold et al., "The Effects of Transformational and Change Leadership on Employees' Commitment to a Change: A Multilevel Study," *Journal of Applied Psychology* 93, no. 2 (2008): 346–57.

47. P. Ingrassia, "Ford's Renaissance Man," *The Wall Street Journal*, February 28, 2010; C. Tierney, "Ford Sets Ambitious Global Plan for Growth," *Detroit News*, June 8, 2011, A1; J. McElroy, "Mulally Is Simplifying Ford," *Ward's Auto World*, May 1, 2012, 18; B.G. Hoffman, *American Icon: Alan Mulally and the Fight to Save Ford Motor Company* (New York: Crown, 2012).

48. M.S. Cole, S.G. Harris, and J.B. Bernerth, "Exploring the Implications of Vision, Appropriateness, and Execution of Organizational Change," *Leadership & Organization Development Journal* 27, no. 5 (2006): 352–67; S. Kirkpatrick, "Leading through Vision and Values," in *Handbook of Principles of Organizational Behavior: Indispensable Knowledge for Evidence-Based Management*, ed. E. Locke (Hoboken: Wiley, 2010), 367–87; V. Lundy and P.P. Morin, "Project Leadership Influences Resistance to Change: The Case of the Canadian Public Service," *Project Management Journal* 44, no. 4 (2013): 45–64.

49. Kotter and Cohen, *The Heart of Change*, 61–82; D.S. Cohen and J.P. Kotter, *The Heart of Change Field Guide* (Boston: Harvard Business School Press, 2005).

50. J.P. Kotter, "Leading Change: Why Transformation Efforts Fail," *Harvard Business Review* (1995): 59–67.

51. J.B. Cunningham and S.K. James, "Implementing Change in Public Sector Organizations," *Management Decision* 47, no. 2 (2009): 330.

52. S. Keller and C. Aiken, *The Inconvenient Truth about Change: Why It Isn't Working and What to Do about It*, McKinsey & Company (New York: 2008).

53. A. De Bruyn and G.L. Lilien, "A Multi-Stage Model of Word-of-Mouth Influence through Viral Marketing," *International Journal of Research in Marketing* 25, no. 3 (2008): 151–63; J.Y.C. Ho and M. Dempsey, "Viral Marketing: Motivations to Forward Online Content," *Journal of Business Research* 63, no. 9/10 (2010): 1000–06; M. Williams and F. Buttle, "The Eight Pillars of WOM Management: Lessons from a Multiple Case Study," *Australasian Marketing Journal (AMJ)* 19, no. 2 (2011): 85–92.

54. L. Herrero, *Homo Imitans* (Beaconsfield Bucks, UK: meetingminds, 2011).

55. M. Beer, R.A. Eisenstat, and B. Spector, *The Critical Path to Corporate Renewal* (Boston: Harvard Business School Press, 1990).

56. J. Riel, "Building a Design Thinking Organization from Within," in *Design of Business: Why Design Thinking Is the Next Competitive Advantage*, ed. R. Martin (Boston: Harvard Business Press, 2009), 166–86.

57. Beer et al., *The Critical Path to Corporate Renewal,* Chap. 5; R.E. Walton, "Successful Strategies for Diffusing Work Innovations," *Journal of Contemporary Business* (1977): 1–22; R.E. Walton, *Innovating to Compete: Lessons for Diffusing and Managing Change in the Workplace* (San Francisco: Jossey-Bass, 1987).

58. E.M. Rogers, *Diffusion of Innovations*, 4th ed. (New York: Free Press, 1995).

59. P. Reason and H. Bradbury, *Handbook of Action Research* (London: Sage, 2001); Coghlan and Brannick, "Kurt Lewin: The 'Practical Theorist' for the 21st Century"; C. Huxham and S. Vangen, "Researching Organizational Practice through Action Research: Case Studies and Design Choices," *Organizational Research Methods* 6 (2003): 383–403.

60. V.J. Marsick and M.A. Gephart, "Action Research: Building the Capacity for Learning and Change," *Human Resource Planning* 26 (2003): 14–18.

61. L. Dickens and K. Watkins, "Action Research: Rethinking Lewin," *Management Learning* 30 (1999): 127–40; J. Heron and P. Reason, "The Practice of Co-operative Inquiry: Research 'with' Rather Than 'on' People," in *Handbook of Action Research*, ed. P. Reason and H. Bradbury (Thousand Oaks, CA: Sage, 2001), 179–88.

62. D.A. Nadler, "Organizational Frame Bending: Types of Change in the Complex Organization," in *Corporate Transformation: Revitalizing Organizations for a Competitive World*, ed. R.H. Kilmann, T.J. Covin, and Associates (San Francisco: Jossey-Bass, 1988), 66–83; K.E. Weick and R.E. Quinn, "Organizational Change and Development," *Annual Review of Psychology* 50 (1999): 361–86.

63. T.M. Egan and C.M. Lancaster, "Comparing Appreciative Inquiry to Action Research: OD Practitioner Perspectives," *Organization Development Journal* 23, no. 2 (2005): 29–49.

64. N. Turner, J. Barling, and A. Zacharatos, "Positive Psychology at Work," in *Handbook of Positive Psychology*, ed. C.R. Snyder and S. Lopez (Oxford, UK: Oxford University Press, 2002), 715–30; K. Cameron, J.E. Dutton, and R.E. Quinn, eds., *Positive Organizational Scholarship: Foundation of a New Discipline* (San Francisco: Berrett-Koehler, 2003); S.L. Gable and J. Haidt, "What (and Why) Is Positive Psychology?," *Review of General Psychology* 9, no. 2 (2005): 103–10; M.E.P. Seligman et al., "Positive Psychology Progress: Empirical Validation of Interventions," *American Psychologist* 60, no. 5 (2005): 410–21.

65. D.K. Whitney and D.L. Cooperrider, "The Appreciative Inquiry Summit: Overview and Applications," *Employment Relations Today* 25 (1998): 17–28; J.M. Watkins and B.J. Mohr, *Appreciative Inquiry: Change at the Speed of Imagination* (San Francisco: Jossey-Bass, 2001).

66. D. Meinert, "Positive Momentum," *HRMagazine* 58, no. 6 (2013): 68–74.

67. D.L. Cooperrider and D.K. Whitney, *Appreciative Inquiry: A Positive Revolution in Change* (San Francisco: Berrett-Koehler, 2005). Recent writing has extended this list to eight principles. See D.K. Whitney and A. Trosten-Bloom, *The Power of Appreciative Inquiry: A Practical Guide to Positive Change*, 2nd ed. (San Francisco: Berrett-Koehler, 2010).

68. F.J. Barrett and D.L. Cooperrider, "Generative Metaphor Intervention: A New Approach for Working with Systems Divided by Conflict and Caught in Defensive Perception," *Journal of Applied Behavioral Science* 26 (1990): 219–39; Whitney and Cooperrider, "The Appreciative Inquiry Summit: Overview and Applications"; Watkins and Mohr, *Appreciative Inquiry: Change at the Speed of Imagination*, 15–21.

69. Z. Pedersen, "Using Appreciative Inquiry to Focus on Positives, Transform Workplace Culture," *Canadian HR Reporter*, August 13, 2012, 10–12; Z. Pedersen, *Appreciative Inquiry and Changing Workplace Culture* (Toronto: YouTube, 2012); M.K. McCarthy, M.J. McNally, and K. Sabo, "Toronto Western Hospital Positive Leadership Program: Creating a Culture of Excellence," in *National Health Leadership Conference* (Niagara Falls, Ontario: Canadian College of Health Leaders, 2013).

70. T.F. Yaeger, P.F. Sorensen, and U. Bengtsson, "Assessment of the State of Appreciative Inquiry: Past, Present, and Future," *Research in Organizational Change and Development* 15 (2004): 297–319; G.R. Bushe and A.F. Kassam, "When Is Appreciative Inquiry Transformational? A Meta-Case Analysis," *Journal of Applied Behavioral Science* 41, no. 2 (2005): 161–81.

71. G.R. Bushe, "Five Theories of Change Embedded in Appreciative Inquiry" (paper presented at the 18th Annual World Congress of Organization Development, Dublin, Ireland, July 14–18 1998).

72. T.C. Head and P.F. Sorenson, "Cultural Values and Organizational Development: A Seven-Country Study," *Leadership and Organization Development Journal* 14 (1993): 3–7; R.J. Marshak, "Lewin Meets Confucius: A Review of the OD Model of Change," *Journal of Applied Behavioral Science* 29 (1993): 395–415; C.M. Lau, "A Culture-Based Perspective of Organization Development Implementation," *Research in Organizational Change and Development* 9 (1996): 49–79; C.M. Lau and H.Y. Ngo, "Organization Development and Firm Performance: A Comparison of Multinational and Local Firms," *Journal of International Business Studies* 32, no. 1 (2001): 95–114.

73. M. McKendall, "The Tyranny of Change: Organizational Development Revisited," *Journal of Business Ethics* 12 (1993): 93–104; C.M.D. Deaner, "A Model of Organization Development Ethics," *Public Administration Quarterly* 17 (1994): 435–46.

74. G.A. Walter, "Organization Development and Individual Rights," *Journal of Applied Behavioral Science* 20 (1984): 423–39.

75. The source of this often-cited quotation was not found. It does not appear, even in other variations, in the books that Andrew Carnegie wrote (such as *Gospel of Wealth,* 1900; *Empire of Business,* 1902; and *Autobiography,* 1920). However, Carnegie may have stated these words (or similar ones) elsewhere. He gave many speeches and wrote numerous articles, parts of which have been reported by other authors.

Photo Credits

Contents

Page viii: Plush Studios/DH Kong/Blend Images/ Getty Images RF; p. ix (top): Andy Roberts/ Getty Images RF, (bottom): donskarpo/ iStock/360 RF; p. x: Design Pics/Kristy-Anne Glubish RF; p. xi (top): Big Cheese Photo/ Jupiterimages RF, (bottom): Ingram Publishing RF; p. xii: Jorg Greuel/Getty Images RF; p. xiii: Barbara Penoyar/Getty Images RF.

Chapter 1

Opener: Tomwang112/iStock/360/Getty Images RF; p. 4: © ColorBlind Images/Blend Images LLC RF; p. 5: Ghislain & Marie David de Lossy/ The Image Bank/Getty Images; p. 6: Plush Studios/DH Kong/Blend Images/Getty Images RF; p. 9: Goodluz/iStock/360/Getty Images RF; p. 10: © Wavebreakmedia Ltd PH26L/Alamy; p. 11: sam74100/iStock/360/Getty Images RF; p. 13: Bloomberg via Getty Images; p. 15: John Harrelson/Getty Images for NASCAR; p. 17: © 2014 Zappos.com; p. 18: Siede Preis/Getty Images RF; p. 21: © Hero Images/Getty Images.

Chapter 2

Opener: Robert Daly/OJO Images/Getty Images RF; p. 25: Courtesy of the United States Navy/U.S. Navy photo by Mass Communication Specialist 3rd Class Darien G. Kenney/Released; p. 25: Pylone/Shutterstock Images LLC RF; p. 27: Squaredpixels/iStock/360/Getty Images RF; p. 28 (left): LinkedIn, the LinkedIn logo, the IN logo and InMail are registered trademarks of LinkedIn Corporation and its affiliates in the United States and/or other countries; p. 28 (middle): Facebook © 2014; p. 28 (right): Twitter.com; p. 29: Kenneth Sponsler/Hemera/360/Getty Images RF; p. 32 (middle): Associated Press RF; p. 32 (bottom): Christin Gilbert/age footstock; p. 35: Image Source/ Getty Images RF; p. 36: DNY59/iStock/360/Getty Images RF; p. 37: Tuomas Kujansuu/E+/Getty Images RF; p. 38: Image Source/Getty Images RF; p. 41: © Robert Daly/age fotostock.

Chapter 3

Opener: Jacobs Stock Photography/Jupiterimages RF; p. 44: © Deborah Baic/The Globe and Mail/ The Canadian Press; p. 45: © Alex Stojanov/ Alamy RF; p. 46: Spark Studio/Getty Images RF; p. 47: Maria Taglienti-Molinari/Brand X Pictures/ Jupiterimages RF; p. 49: Adam Gault/Getty Images RF; p. 50: Design Pics/Don Hammond RF; p. 51: Aluma Images/Photographer's Choice RF/Getty Images RF; p. 53: Juice Images/Glow Images RF; p. 55: © PeskyMonkey/iStock RF; p. 56: Imagee-gamI/iStock RF; p. 58: Ingram Publishing RF.

Chapter 4

Opener: Ingram Publishing RF; p. 62: Richard Nelson/Cutcaster RF; p. 65: Google and the Google logo are registered trademarks of Google Inc., used with permission; p. 66: Jonnie Miles/ Getty Images RF; p. 68: Jose Luis Pelaez Inc/Blend Images LLC RF; p. 69: Jack Hollingsworth/Blend Images LLC RF; p. 71: Ingram Publishing RF; p. 73: Monty Rakusen/Getty Images RF; p. 75: donskarpo/iStock/360 RF; p. 77: Jose Luis Pelaez

Inc/Getty Images RF; p. 79: Associated Press RF; p. 81: © Hero Images/Getty Images.

Chapter 5

Opener: Jack Hollingsworth/Getty Images RF; p. 84: DHL Express Sub-Saharan Africa; p. 85: K-PHOTOS/Alamy; p. 87: Design Pics/ Kristy-Anne Glubish RF; p. 88: Royalty-Free/ Corbis; p. 93: Courtesy of Deloitte; p. 94: Tim Teebken/Photodisc/Jupiterimages RF; p. 96: © Stockbyte/Getty Images RF; p. 99: © Stock-byte/PunchStock RF; p. 100: Antenna/Getty Images RF; p. 105: © Hero/Corbis/Glow Images.

Chapter 6

Opener: © Image Source/Alamy RF; p. 109: Ilya Rozhdestvensky/Getty Images RF; p. 110: Google and the Google logo are registered trademarks of Google Inc., used with permission; p. 112: Jonathan Evans/Photodisc/Getty Images RF; p. 113: gemphotography/iStock/360 RF; p. 114: © Ned Frisk/Blend Images LLC RF; p. 115: Jonathan Evans/Getty Images RF; p. 117: Brand X Pictures/ PunchStock RF; p. 118: Brand X Pictures RF; p. 121: © ansonsaw/E+/Getty Images RF; p. 122: Courtesy of Brasilata SA Embalagens Metalicas; p. 125: © Sam Edwards/age fotostock.

Chapter 7

Opener: Design Pics/Don Hammond RF; p. 129: © BananaStock Ltd. RF; p. 131: Radius Images/360/Getty Images RF; p. 132: Ron Riccio/ Wawa, Inc.; p. 135: Ingram Publishing RF; p. 136: Blend Images/SuperStock RF; p. 138: © John Lund/Sam Diephuis/Blend Images LLC RF; p. 139: Design Pics/Kristy-Anne Glubish RF; p. 142: Courtesy of Whole Foods Market. "Whole Foods Market" is a registered trademark of Whole Food Market IP, LP; p. 143: Creative Crop/Getty Images RF; p. 144: Lane Oatey/Getty Images RF; p. 146: Simon Potter/Getty Images RF.

Chapter 8

Opener: Image Source RF/Cadalpe/Getty Images RF; p. 151: Jorg Greuel/Getty Images RF; p. 153: pictafolio/Getty Images RF; p. 156: © Chris Ryan/ age fotostock RF; p. 157: © David J. Green - life-style themes/Alamy; p. 158: Jose Luis Pelaez Inc/ Blend Images LLC RF; p. 160: Steve Cole/Getty Images RF; p. 162 (top): Lane Oatey/Getty Images RF; p. 162 (bottom): Stockdisc RF; p. 164: Copyright GlaxoSmithKline. Used with permission; p. 165: Rawpixel/iStock/360 RF; p. 166: Blend Images/ Getty Images RF; p. 167: © Image Source, all rights reserved.

Chapter 9

Opener: Image Source/Getty Images RF; p. 169: Henglein and Steets/Getty Images RF; p. 172: © Yami 2; p. 173: © JGI/Blend Images LLC RF; p. 174: Andy Roberts/Getty Images RF; p. 175 (top): © CJ Burton/Corbis; p. 175 (bottom): Helder Almeida/Shutterstock Images LLC RF; p. 177: Dimitri Vervitsiotis/Getty Images RF; p. 178: Image Source/Getty Images RF; p. 180: Ingram Publishing RF; p. 181: Big Cheese Photo/Jupiterimages RF; p. 184: Jon Schulte/iStockphoto RF.

Chapter 10

Opener: Eric Audras/Photoalto/PictureQuest RF; p. 189: Big Cheese Photo/Jupiterimages RF; p. 190: Rubberball/Getty Images RF; p. 191: Barbara Penoyar/Getty Images RF; p. 193: Creatas/PunchStock RF; p. 196 (top): Abel Mitja Varela/Getty Images RF; p. 198: BananaStock/ PictureQuest RF; p. 199: ATIC12/iStock/360/ Getty Images RF; p. 202 (top): Ryan McVay/ Getty Images RF; p. 202 (bottom): Getty Images RF; p. 205: © Rachel Frank/Corbis/Glow Images.

Chapter 11

Opener: Cultura/Getty Images RF; p. 208: mood-board/Getty Images RF; p. 210: Barbara Penoyar/ Getty Images RF; p. 211: altrendo images/Getty Images; p. 212: © Image Source/PunchStock RF; p. 214: SSG George Gutierrez/U.S. Army Forces Command/dvidshub.net; p. 216: Blend Images/ Ariel Skelley/Getty Images RF; p. 217: andres_/ iStock RF; p. 218: Tomasz Trojanowski/Shutter-stock Images LLC RF; p. 219: © Jose Luis Pelaez Inc/Blend Images LLC RF; p. 221: Helder Almeida/ Shutterstock Images LLC RF; p. 222: © Jose Luis Pelaez Inc/Blend Images LLC RF.

Chapter 12

Opener: Giorgio Fochesato/Getty Images RF; p. 226: © Jose Luis Pelaez, Inc/Getty Images RF; p. 227: Royalty-Free/Corbis; p. 228: © age fotostock Spain, S.L./Alamy; p. 230: © ColorBlind Images/Blend Images LLC RF; p. 231 (top): Alex Staroseltsev/ Shutterstock Images LLC RF; p. 231 (bottom-left): Comstock Images/Alamy RF; p. 231 (bottom-right): Steven P. Lynch RF; p. 233: Helder Almeida/ Shutterstock Images LLC RF; p. 235 (top): © Stuart Isett. All Rights Reserved; p. 235 (bottom): Tom Grill/Corbis/Punchstock RF; p. 237: © Flying Colours Ltd/Getty Images RF; p. 239: Digital Vision/ PunchStock RF; p. 241: © Robert Daly/age fotostock.

Chapter 13

Opener: LEGO® is a trademark of the LEGO Group of Companies, used here by permission. © 2014 The LEGO Group; p. 245: Flying Colours Ltd/Photodisc/Getty Images RF; p. 246: Image Source/Getty Images RF; p. 247: Royalty-Free/ Corbis; p. 248: © Brendan McDermid/Reuters/ Corbis; p. 250: Big Cheese Photo/Jupiterimages RF; p. 251: Dole08/iStock RF; p. 254 (left): sdominick/iStock/360 RF; p. 254 (right): © 2014 Zappos.com; p. 257: © PhotoAlto RF; p. 259: © Hero/Corbis/Glow Images.

Chapter 14

Opener: Vladitto/iStock/360 RF; p. 263 (man): Yuri Arcurs/Shutterstock Images LLC RF; p. 263 (blocks): Steve Mason/Getty Images RF; p. 263 (right): ©/Michael Stravato/AP Images; p. 264: © Brand X Pictures/PunchStock RF; p. 266: Dean Mitchell/iStock/360 RF; p. 269 (top): Pixtal/age fotostock RF; p. 269 (bottom): © Comstock Images/ PictureQuest RF; p. 270: Bloomberg via Getty Images; p. 272: Monty Rakusen/Getty Images RF; p. 274: © Colin Anderson/Blend Images LLC RF; p. 275: © Digital Vision/Alamy RF; p. 276: Ryan McVay/Getty Images RF.

Index

Note: Page numbers followed by n indicate material found in footnotes or source notes.

Introduction to the Field of Organizational Behavior

SUMMARY

LO1 Define organizational behavior and organizations, and discuss the importance of this field of inquiry.

Organizational behavior is the study of what people think, feel, and do in and around organizations. Organizations are groups of people who work interdependently toward some purpose. OB theories help people (a) make sense of the workplace, (b) question and rebuild their personal mental models, and (c) get things done in organizations. OB knowledge is for everyone, not just managers. OB knowledge is just as important for the organization's financial health.

LO2 Debate the organizational opportunities and challenges of globalization, workforce diversity, and emerging employment relationships.

Globalization, which refers to various forms of connectivity with people in other parts of the world, has several economic and social benefits, but it may also be responsible for work intensification, reduced job security, and lessening work–life balance. Workforce diversity is apparent at both the surface level (observable demographic and other overt differences in people) and deep level (differences in personalities, beliefs, values, and attitudes). There is some evidence of deep-level diversity across generational cohorts. Diversity may be a competitive advantage that improves decision making and team performance on complex tasks, but it also imposes numerous challenges, such as dysfunctional team conflict and lower team performance. Work–life balance—minimizing conflict between work and nonwork demands—is an emerging employment trend. Another is virtual work, particularly working from home (telework). Working from home potentially increases employee productivity and reduces employee stress, but it also may lead to social isolation, reduced promotion opportunities, and tension in family relations.

LO3 Discuss the anchors on which organizational behavior knowledge is based.

The multidisciplinary anchor states that the field should develop from knowledge in other disciplines (e.g., psychology, sociology, economics), not just from its own isolated research base. The systematic research anchor states that OB knowledge should be based on systematic research, consistent with evidence-based management. The contingency anchor states that OB theories generally need to consider that there will be different consequences in different situations. The multiple levels of analysis anchor states that OB topics may be viewed from the individual, team, and organizational levels of analysis.

LO4 Compare and contrast the four perspectives of organizational effectiveness.

The open systems perspective views organizations as complex organisms that "live" within an external environment. They depend on the external environment for resources, then use organizational subsystems to transform those resources into outputs, which are returned to the environment. Organizations receive feedback from the external environment to maintain a good "fit" with that environment. Fit occurs by adapting to the environment, managing the environment, or moving to another environment. According to the organizational learning perspective, organizational effectiveness depends on the organization's capacity to acquire, share, use, and store valuable knowledge. Intellectual capital consists of human capital, structural capital, and relationship capital. Knowledge is retained in the organizational memory; companies also selectively unlearn.

KEY TERMS

corporate social responsibility (CSR) organizational activities intended to benefit society and the environment beyond the firm's immediate financial interests or legal obligations.

deep-level diversity differences in the psychological characteristics of employees, including personalities, beliefs, values, and attitudes.

ethics the study of moral principles or values that determine whether actions are right or wrong and outcomes are good or bad.

evidence-based management the practice of making decisions and taking actions based on research evidence.

globalization economic, social, and cultural connectivity with people in other parts of the world.

high-performance work practices (HPWPs) a perspective that holds that effective organizations incorporate several workplace practices that leverage the potential of human capital.

human capital the stock of knowledge, skills, and abilities among employees that provide economic value to the organization.

intellectual capital a company's stock of knowledge, including human capital, structural capital, and relationship capital.

open systems a perspective that holds that organizations depend on the external environment for resources, affect that environment through their output, and consist of internal subsystems that transform inputs to outputs.

organizational behavior (OB) the study of what people think, feel, and do in and around organizations.

organizational effectiveness a broad concept represented by several perspectives, including the organization's fit with the external environment, internal subsystems configuration for high performance, emphasis on organizational learning, and ability to satisfy the needs of key stakeholders.

organizational efficiency the amount of outputs relative to inputs in the organization's transformation process.

organizational learning a perspective that holds that organizational effectiveness depends on the organization's capacity to acquire, share, use, and store valuable knowledge.

organizations groups of people who work interdependently toward some purpose.

relationship capital the value derived from an organization's relationships with customers, suppliers, and others.

stakeholders individuals, groups, and other entities that affect, or are affected by, the organization's objectives and actions.

structural capital knowledge embedded in an organization's systems and structures.

surface-level diversity the observable demographic or physiological differences in people, such as their race, ethnicity, gender, age, and physical disabilities.

values relatively stable, evaluative beliefs that guide a person's preferences for outcomes or courses of action in a variety of situations.

virtual work work performed away from the traditional physical workplace by using information technology.

work–life balance the degree to which a person minimizes conflict between work and nonwork demands.

The high-performance work practices (HPWPs) perspective identifies a bundle of systems and structures to leverage workforce potential. The most widely identified HPWPs are employee involvement, job autonomy, development of employee competencies, and performance- or skill-based rewards. HPWPs improve organizational effectiveness by building human capital, increasing adaptability, and strengthening employee motivation and attitudes. The stakeholder perspective states that leaders manage the interests of diverse stakeholders by relying on their personal and organizational values for guidance. Ethics and corporate social responsibility (CSR) are natural variations of values-based organizations because they rely on values to determine the most appropriate decisions involving stakeholders. CSR consists of organizational activities intended to benefit society and the environment beyond the firm's immediate financial interests or legal obligations.

chapter two

Individual Behavior, Personality, and Values

SUMMARY

LO1 Describe the four factors that directly influence individual behavior and performance.

Four variables—motivation, ability, role perceptions, and situational factors (represented by the MARS acronym)—directly influence individual behavior and performance. Motivation represents the forces within a person that affect his or her direction, intensity, and persistence of voluntary behavior; ability includes both the natural aptitudes and the learned capabilities required to successfully complete a task; role perceptions are the extent to which people understand the job duties (roles) assigned to them or expected of them; situational factors include conditions beyond the employee's immediate control that constrain or facilitate behavior and performance.

LO2 Summarize the five types of individual behavior in organizations.

There are five main types of workplace behavior. Task performance refers to goal-directed behaviors under the individual's control that support organizational objectives. Organizational citizenship behaviors consist of various forms of cooperation and helpfulness to others that support the organization's social and psychological context. Counterproductive work behaviors are voluntary behaviors that have the potential to directly or indirectly harm the organization. Joining and staying with the organization refers to agreeing to become an organizational member and remaining with the organization. Maintaining work attendance includes minimizing absenteeism when capable of working and avoiding scheduled work when not fit (i.e., low presenteeism).

LO3 Describe personality and discuss how the "Big Five" personality dimensions and four MBTI types relate to individual behavior in organizations.

Personality is the relatively enduring pattern of thoughts, emotions, and behaviors that characterize a person, along with the psychological processes behind those characteristics. Personality traits are broad concepts about people that allow us to label and understand individual differences. Personality is developed through hereditary origins (nature) as well as socialization (nurture). The Big Five personality dimensions include conscientiousness, agreeableness, neuroticism, openness to experience, and extraversion. Conscientiousness and emotional stability (low neuroticism) predict individual performance in most job groups. Extraversion is associated with performance in sales and management jobs, agreeableness is associated with performance in jobs requiring cooperation, and openness to experience is associated with performance in creative jobs.

Based on Jungian personality theory, the Myers-Briggs Type Indicator (MBTI) identifies competing orientations for getting energy (extraversion vs. introversion), perceiving information (sensing vs. intuiting), processing information and making decisions (thinking vs. feeling), and orienting to the external world (judging vs. perceiving). The MBTI improves self-awareness for career development and mutual understanding but is more popular than it is valid.

LO4 Summarize Schwartz's model of individual values and discuss the conditions where values influence behavior.

Values are stable, evaluative beliefs that guide our preferences for outcomes or courses of action in a variety of situations. Compared to personality traits, values are evaluative

KEY TERMS

ability the natural aptitudes and learned capabilities required to successfully complete a task.

achievement-nurturing orientation cross-cultural value describing the degree to which people in a culture emphasize competitive versus cooperative relations with other people.

collectivism a cross-cultural value describing the degree to which people in a culture emphasize duty to groups to which they belong and to group harmony.

conscientiousness a personality dimension describing people who are organized, dependable, goal-focused, thorough, disciplined, methodical, and industrious.

counterproductive work behaviors (CWBs) voluntary behaviors that have the potential to directly or indirectly harm the organization.

extraversion a personality dimension describing people who are outgoing, talkative, sociable, and assertive.

five-factor model (FFM) the five broad dimensions representing most personality traits: conscientiousness, emotional stability, openness to experience, agreeableness, and extraversion.

individualism a cross-cultural value describing the degree to which people in a culture emphasize independence and personal uniqueness.

mindfulness a person's receptive and impartial attention to and awareness of the present situation as well as to one's own thoughts and emotions in that moment.

moral intensity the degree to which an issue demands the application of ethical principles.

moral sensitivity a person's ability to recognize the presence of an ethical issue and determine its relative importance.

motivation the forces within a person that affect his or her direction, intensity, and persistence of voluntary behavior.

Myers-Briggs Type Indicator (MBTI) an instrument designed to measure the elements of Jungian personality theory, particularly preferences regarding perceiving and judging information.

neuroticism a personality dimension describing people who tend to be anxious, insecure, self-conscious, depressed, and temperamental.

organizational citizenship behaviors (OCBs) various forms of cooperation and helpfulness to others that support the organization's social and psychological context.

personality the relatively enduring pattern of thoughts, emotions, and behaviors that characterize a person, along with the psychological processes behind those characteristics.

power distance a cross-cultural value describing the degree to which people in a culture accept unequal distribution of power in a society.

role perceptions the degree to which a person understands the job duties assigned to or expected of him or her.

uncertainty avoidance a cross-cultural value describing the degree to which people in a culture tolerate ambiguity (low uncertainty avoidance) or feel threatened by ambiguity and uncertainty (high uncertainty avoidance).

(rather than descriptive), more likely to conflict with each other, and are formed more from socialization than heredity. Schwartz's model organizes several dozen values into a circumplex of 10 dimensions along two bipolar dimensions: openness to change to conservation and self-enhancement to self-transcendence. Values influence behavior when the situation facilitates that connection and when we actively think about our values and understand their relevance to the situation. Values congruence refers to how similar a person's values hierarchy is to the values hierarchy of another source (organization, person, etc.).

LO5 Describe three ethical principles and discuss three factors that influence ethical behavior.

Ethics refers to the study of moral principles or values that determine whether actions are right or wrong and outcomes are good or bad. Three ethical principles are utilitarianism, individual rights, and distributive justice. Ethical behavior is influenced by the degree to which an issue demands the application of ethical principles (moral intensity), the individual's ability to recognize the presence and relative importance of an ethical issue (moral sensitivity), and situational forces. Ethical conduct at work is supported by codes of ethical conduct, mechanisms for communicating ethical violations, the organization's culture, and the leader's behavior.

LO6 Describe five values commonly studied across cultures.

Five values commonly studied across cultures are individualism (valuing independence and personal uniqueness); collectivism (valuing duty to in-groups and to group harmony); power distance (valuing unequal distribution of power); uncertainty avoidance (tolerating or feeling threatened by ambiguity and uncertainty); and achievement-nurturing orientation (valuing competition vs. cooperation).

SUMMARY

LO1 Describe the elements of self-concept and explain how each affects an individual's behavior and well-being.

Self-concept includes an individual's self-beliefs and self-evaluations. It has three structural characteristics—complexity, consistency, and clarity—all of which influence employee well-being, behavior, and performance. People are inherently motivated to promote and protect their self-concept (self-enhancement) and to verify and maintain their existing self-concept (self-verification). Self-evaluation consists of self-esteem, self-efficacy, and locus of control. Self-concept also consists of both personality identity and social identity. Social identity theory explains how people define themselves in terms of the groups to which they belong or have an emotional attachment.

LO2 Outline the perceptual process and discuss the effects of categorical thinking and mental models in that process.

Perception involves selecting, organizing, and interpreting information to make sense of the world around us. Perceptual organization applies categorical thinking—the mostly nonconscious process of organizing people and objects into preconceived categories that are stored in our long-term memory. Mental models—knowledge structures that we develop to describe, explain, and predict the world around us—also help us make sense of incoming stimuli.

LO3 Discuss how stereotyping, attribution, self-fulfilling prophecy, halo, false consensus, primacy, and recency influence the perceptual process.

Stereotyping occurs when people assign traits to others based on their membership in a social category. This assignment economizes mental effort, fills in missing information, and enhances our self-concept, but it also lays the foundation for prejudice and systemic discrimination. The attribution process involves deciding whether an observed behavior or event is caused mainly by the person (internal factors) or the environment (external factors). Attributions are decided by the perceived consistency, distinctiveness, and consensus of the behavior. This process is subject to self-serving bias and (possibly) fundamental attribution error. A self-fulfilling prophecy occurs when our expectations about another person cause that person to act in a way that is consistent with those expectations. This effect is stronger when employees first join the work unit, when several people hold these expectations, and when the employee has a history of low achievement. Four other perceptual errors commonly noted in organizations are the halo effect, false-consensus effect, primacy effect, and recency effect.

LO4 Discuss three ways to improve perceptions, with specific application to organizational situations.

One way to minimize perceptual biases is to become more aware of their existence. Awareness of these biases makes people more mindful of their thoughts and actions, but this training sometimes reinforces rather than reduces reliance on stereotypes and tends to be ineffective for people with deeply held prejudices. A second strategy is to become more aware of biases in our own decisions and behavior. Self-awareness increases through formal tests such as the Implicit Association Test (IAT) and by applying the Johari Window, which is a process in which others provide feedback to you about your behavior, and you offer disclosure to them about yourself. The third strategy is meaningful interaction, which applies the contact hypothesis that people who interact will be less

KEY TERMS

attribution process the perceptual process of deciding whether an observed behavior or event is caused largely by internal or external factors.

categorical thinking organizing people and objects into preconceived categories that are stored in our long-term memory.

confirmation bias the process of screening out information that is contrary to our values and assumptions and to more readily accept confirming information.

contact hypothesis a theory stating that the more we interact with someone, the less prejudiced or perceptually biased we will be against that person.

empathy a person's understanding of and sensitivity to the feelings, thoughts, and situations of others.

false-consensus effect a perceptual error in which we overestimate the extent to which others have beliefs and characteristics similar to our own.

fundamental attribution error the tendency to see the person rather than the situation as the main cause of that person's behavior.

global mindset an individual's ability to perceive, appreciate, and empathize with people from other cultures, and to process complex cross-cultural information.

halo effect a perceptual error whereby our general impression of a person, usually based on one prominent characteristic, colors our perception of other characteristics of that person.

Johari Window a model of mutual understanding that encourages disclosure and feedback to increase our own open area and reduce the blind, hidden, and unknown areas.

locus of control a person's general belief about the amount of control he or she has over personal life events.

mental models knowledge structures that we develop to describe, explain, and predict the world around us.

perception the process of receiving information about and making sense of the world around us.

positive organizational behavior a perspective of organizational behavior that focuses on building positive qualities and traits within individuals or institutions as opposed to focusing on what is wrong with them.

primacy effect a perceptual error in which we quickly form an opinion of people based on the first information we receive about them.

recency effect a perceptual error in which the most recent information dominates our perception of others.

selective attention the process of attending to some information received by our senses and ignoring other information.

self-concept an individual's self-beliefs and self-evaluations.

self-efficacy a person's belief that he or she has the ability, motivation, correct role perceptions, and favorable situation to complete a task successfully.

self-enhancement a person's inherent motivation to have a positive self-concept (and to have others perceive him or her favorably), such as being competent, attractive, lucky, ethical, and important.

self-fulfilling prophecy the perceptual process in which our expectations about another person cause that person to act more consistently with those expectations.

self-serving bias the tendency to attribute our favorable outcomes to internal factors and our failures to external factors.

self-verification a person's inherent motivation to confirm and maintain his or her existing self-concept.

social identity theory a theory stating that people define themselves by the groups to which they belong or have an emotional attachment.

stereotyping the process of assigning traits to people based on their membership in a social category.

prejudiced or perceptually biased toward one another. Meaningful interaction is strongest when people work closely and frequently with relatively equal status on a shared meaningful task that requires cooperation and reliance on one another. Meaningful interaction helps improve empathy, which is a person's understanding and sensitivity to the feelings, thoughts, and situations of others.

LO5 Outline the main features of a global mindset and justify its usefulness to employees and organizations.

A global mindset refers to an individual's ability to perceive, know about, and process information across cultures. This includes (1) an awareness of, openness to, and respect for other views and practices in the world; (2) the capacity to empathize and act effectively across cultures; (3) an ability to process complex information about novel environments; and (4) the ability to comprehend and reconcile intercultural matters with multiple levels of thinking. A global mindset enables people to develop better cross-cultural relationships, to digest huge volumes of cross-cultural information, and to identify and respond more quickly to emerging global opportunities. Employees develop a global mindset through self-awareness, opportunities to compare their own mental models with people from other cultures, formal cross-cultural training, and immersion in other cultures.

SUMMARY

LO1 Explain how emotions and cognition (logical thinking) influence attitudes and behavior.

Emotions are physiological, behavioral, and psychological episodes experienced toward an object, person, or event that create a state of readiness. Emotions differ from attitudes, which represent a cluster of beliefs, feelings, and behavioral intentions toward a person, object, or event. Beliefs are a person's established perceptions about the attitude object. Feelings are positive or negative evaluations of the attitude object. Behavioral intentions represent a motivation to engage in a particular behavior toward the target.

Attitudes have traditionally been described as a purely rational process in which beliefs predict feelings, which predict behavioral intentions, which predict behavior. We now know that emotions have an influence on behavior that is equal to or greater than that of cognition. This dual process is apparent when we internally experience a conflict between what logically seems good or bad and what we emotionally feel is good or bad in a situation. Emotions also affect behavior directly. Behavior sometimes influences our subsequent attitudes through cognitive dissonance.

LO2 Discuss the dynamics of emotional labor and the role of emotional intelligence in the workplace.

Emotional labor consists of the effort, planning, and control needed to express organizationally desired emotions during interpersonal transactions. It is more common in jobs requiring a variety of emotions and more intense emotions, as well as in jobs where interaction with clients is frequent and has a long duration. Cultures also differ on the norms of displaying or concealing a person's true emotions. Emotional dissonance is the psychological tension experienced when the emotions people are required to display are quite different from the emotions they actually experience at that moment. Deep acting can minimize this dissonance, as can the practice of hiring people with a natural tendency to display desired emotions.

Emotional intelligence is the ability to perceive and express emotion, assimilate emotion in thought, understand and reason with emotion, and regulate emotion in oneself and others. This concept includes four components arranged in a hierarchy: self-awareness, self-management, awareness of others' emotions, and management of others' emotions. Emotional intelligence can be learned to some extent, particularly through personal coaching.

LO3 Summarize the consequences of job dissatisfaction as well as strategies to increase organizational (affective) commitment.

Job satisfaction represents a person's evaluation of his or her job and work context. Four types of job dissatisfaction consequences are quitting or otherwise getting away from the dissatisfying situation (exit), attempting to change the dissatisfying situation (voice), patiently waiting for the problem to sort itself out (loyalty), and reducing work effort and performance (neglect). Job satisfaction has a moderate relationship with job performance and with customer satisfaction. Affective organizational commitment (loyalty) is the employee's emotional attachment to, identification with, and involvement in a particular organization. This contrasts with continuance commitment, which is a calculative bond with the organization. Companies build loyalty through justice and support, shared values, trust, organizational comprehension, and employee involvement.

KEY TERMS

affective organizational commitment an individual's emotional attachment to, involvement in, and identification with an organization.

attitudes the cluster of beliefs, assessed feelings, and behavioral intentions toward a person, object, or event (called an attitude object).

cognitive dissonance an emotional experience caused by a perception that our beliefs, feelings, and behavior are incongruent with one another.

continuance commitment an individual's calculative attachment to an organization.

emotional dissonance the psychological tension experienced when the emotions people are required to display are quite different from the emotions they actually experience at that moment.

emotional intelligence (EI) a set of abilities to perceive and express emotion, assimilate emotion in thought, understand and reason with emotion, and regulate emotion in oneself and others.

emotional labor the effort, planning, and control needed to express organizationally desired emotions during interpersonal transactions.

emotions physiological, behavioral, and psychological episodes experienced toward an object, person, or event that create a state of readiness.

exit–voice–loyalty–neglect (EVLN) model the four ways, as indicated in the name, that employees respond to job dissatisfaction.

general adaptation syndrome a model of the stress experience, consisting of three stages: alarm reaction, resistance, and exhaustion.

job satisfaction a person's evaluation of his or her job and work context.

psychological harassment repeated and hostile or unwanted conduct, verbal comments, actions, or gestures that affect an employee's dignity or psychological or physical integrity and that result in a harmful work environment for the employee.

service profit chain model a theory explaining how employees' job satisfaction influences company profitability indirectly through service quality, customer loyalty, and related factors.

stress an adaptive response to a situation that is perceived as challenging or threatening to the person's well-being.

stressors environmental conditions that place a physical or emotional demand on the person.

trust positive expectations one person has toward another person in situations involving risk.

LO4 Describe the stress experience and review three major stressors.

Stress is an adaptive response to a situation that is perceived as challenging or threatening to a person's well-being. The stress experience, called the general adaptation syndrome, involves moving through three stages: alarm, resistance, and exhaustion. Stressors are the causes of stress and include any environmental conditions that place a physical or emotional demand on a person. Three stressors that have received considerable attention are harassment/incivility, work overload, and low task control.

LO5 Identify five ways to manage workplace stress.

Many interventions are available to manage work-related stress, including removing the stressor, withdrawing from the stressor, changing stress perceptions, controlling stress consequences, and receiving social support.

SUMMARY

LO1 Define employee engagement.

Employee engagement is an individual's emotional and cognitive (rational) motivation, particularly a focused, intense, persistent, and purposive effort toward work-related goals. It is emotional involvement in, commitment to, and satisfaction with the work, as well as a high level of absorption in the work and sense of self-efficacy about performing the work.

LO2 Explain how drives and emotions influence employee motivation and summarize Maslow's needs hierarchy, McClelland's learned needs theory, and four-drive theory.

Motivation consists of the forces within a person that affect his or her direction, intensity, and persistence of voluntary behavior in the workplace. Drives (also called primary needs) are neural states that energize individuals to correct deficiencies or maintain an internal equilibrium. They are the "prime movers" of behavior, activating emotions that put us in a state of readiness to act. Needs are goal-directed forces that people experience from activated drives and emotions. They are influenced by the individual's self-concept (including personality and values), social norms, and past experience.

Maslow's needs hierarchy groups needs into a hierarchy of five levels and states that the lowest needs are initially most important, but higher needs become more important as the lower ones are satisfied. Although popular, the theory lacks research support because it wrongly assumes that everyone has the same hierarchy. Instead, needs hierarchies likely vary from one person to the next according to their personal values. McClelland's learned needs theory argues that needs can be strengthened through learning. The three needs studied in this respect have been need for achievement, need for power, and need for affiliation. Four-drive theory states that everyone has four innate drives—the drives to acquire, bond, comprehend, and defend. These drives activate emotions, and the motivation of conscious emotions are regulated through the individual's skill set of social norms, past experience, and personal values. The main recommendation from four-drive theory is to ensure that jobs and workplaces provide a balanced opportunity to fulfill the four drives.

LO3 Discuss the expectancy theory model, including its practical implications.

Expectancy theory states that work effort is determined by the perception that effort will result in a particular level of performance (E-to-P expectancy), the perception that a specific behavior or performance level will lead to specific outcomes (P-to-O expectancy), and the valences that the person feels for those outcomes. The E-to-P expectancy increases by improving the employee's ability and confidence to perform the job. The P-to-O expectancy increases by measuring performance accurately, distributing higher rewards to better performers, and showing employees that rewards are performance-based. Outcome valences increase by finding out what employees want and using these resources as rewards.

LO4 Outline organizational behavior modification (OB Mod) and social cognitive theory and explain their relevance to employee motivation.

Organizational behavior modification states that people alter their behavior to maximize positive consequences and minimize adverse consequences. Antecedents are

KEY TERMS

autonomy the degree to which a job gives employees the freedom, independence, and discretion to schedule their work and determine the procedures used in completing it.

distributive justice perceived fairness in the individual's ratio of outcomes to contributions relative to a comparison other's ratio of outcomes to contributions.

drives hardwired characteristics of the brain that correct deficiencies or maintain an internal equilibrium by producing emotions to energize individuals.

employee engagement individual's emotional and cognitive motivation, particularly a focused, intense, persistent, and purposive effort toward work-related goals.

equity theory a theory explaining how people develop perceptions of fairness in the distribution and exchange of resources.

expectancy theory a motivation theory based on the idea that work effort is directed toward behaviors that people believe will lead to desired outcomes.

four-drive theory a motivation theory based on the innate drives to acquire, bond, learn, and defend that incorporates both emotions and rationality.

goal setting the process of motivating employees and clarifying their role perceptions by establishing performance objectives.

job characteristics model a job design model that relates the motivational properties of jobs to specific personal and organizational consequences of those properties.

job design the process of assigning tasks to a job, including the interdependency of those tasks with other jobs.

job enlargement the practice of adding more tasks to an existing job.

job enrichment the practice of giving employees more responsibility for scheduling, coordinating, and planning their own work.

job specialization the result of division of labor in which work is subdivided into separate jobs assigned to different people.

Maslow's needs hierarchy theory
a motivation theory of needs arranged in a hierarchy, whereby people are motivated to fulfill a higher need as a lower one becomes gratified.

motivation forces within a person that affect the direction, intensity, and persistence of voluntary behavior.

motivator-hygiene theory Herzberg's theory stating that employees are primarily motivated by growth and esteem needs, not by lower-level needs.

need for achievement (nAch) a learned need in which people want to accomplish reasonably challenging goals and desire unambiguous feedback and recognition for their success.

need for affiliation (nAff) a learned need in which people seek approval from others, conform to their wishes and expectations, and avoid conflict and confrontation.

need for power (nPow) a learned need in which people want to control their environment, including people and material resources, to benefit either themselves (personalized power) or others (socialized power).

needs goal-directed forces that people experience.

organizational behavior modification (OB Mod) a theory that explains employee behavior in terms of the antecedent conditions and consequences of that behavior.

procedural justice perceived fairness of the procedures used to decide the distribution of resources.

scientific management the practice of systematically partitioning work into its smallest elements and standardizing tasks to achieve maximum efficiency.

self-reinforcement reinforcement that occurs when an employee has control over a reinforcer but doesn't "take" it until completing a self-set goal.

skill variety the extent to which employees must use different skills and talents to perform tasks within their jobs.

social cognitive theory a theory that explains how learning and motivation occur by observing and modeling others as well as by anticipating the consequences of our behavior.

strengths-based coaching a positive organizational behavior approach to coaching and feedback that focuses on building and leveraging the employee's strengths rather than trying to correct his or her weaknesses.

task identity the degree to which a job requires completion of a whole or identifiable piece of work.

task significance the degree to which a job has a substantial impact on the organization and/or larger society.

environmental stimuli that cue (not necessarily cause) behavior. Consequences are events following behavior that influence its future occurrence. Consequences include positive reinforcement, punishment, negative reinforcement, and extinction. The schedules of reinforcement also influence behavior.

Social cognitive theory states that much learning and motivation occurs by observing and modeling others as well as by anticipating the consequences of our behavior. It suggests that people typically infer (rather than only directly experience) cause–effect relationships, anticipate the consequences of their actions, develop self-efficacy in performing behavior, exercise personal control over their behavior, and reflect on their direct experiences. The theory emphasizes self-regulation of individual behavior, including self-reinforcement, which is the tendency of people to reward and punish themselves as a consequence of their actions.

LO5 Describe the characteristics of effective goal setting and feedback.

Goal setting is the process of motivating employees and clarifying their role perceptions by establishing performance objectives. Goals are more effective when they are SMARTER (specific, measurable, achievable, relevant, time-framed, exciting, and reviewed). Effective feedback is specific, relevant, timely, credible, and sufficiently frequent. Strengths-based coaching (also known as *appreciative coaching*) maximizes employee potential by focusing on their strengths rather than weaknesses. Employees usually prefer nonsocial feedback sources to learn about their progress toward goal accomplishment.

LO6 Summarize equity theory and describe ways to improve procedural justice.

Organizational justice consists of distributive justice (perceived fairness in the outcomes we receive relative to our contributions and the outcomes and contributions of others) and procedural justice (fairness of the procedures used to decide the distribution of resources). Equity theory has four elements: outcome/input ratio, comparison other, equity evaluation, and consequences of inequity. The theory also explains what people are motivated to do when they feel inequitably treated. Companies need to consider not only equity of the distribution of resources but also fairness in the process of making resource allocation decisions.

LO7 List the advantages and disadvantages of job specialization and describe three ways to improve employee motivation through job design.

Job design is the process of assigning tasks to a job, including the interdependency of those tasks with other jobs. Job specialization—subdividing work into separate jobs for different people—tends to increase work efficiency because employees master the tasks more quickly, spend less time changing tasks, require less training, and are better matched to jobs requiring their skills. However, job specialization may reduce work motivation, create mental health problems, lower product or service quality, and increase costs through higher dissatisfaction and turnover.

The five core job dimensions of the job characteristics model are skill variety, task identity, task significance, autonomy, and job feedback. Contemporary job design strategies try to motivate employees through job rotation, job enlargement, and job enrichment. Organizations introduce job rotation to reduce job boredom, develop a more flexible workforce, and reduce the incidence of repetitive strain injuries. Job enlargement involves increasing the number of tasks within the job. Two ways to enrich jobs are clustering tasks into natural groups and establishing client relationships.

Decision Making and Creativity

SUMMARY

LO1 Describe the rational choice paradigm of decision making.

Decision making is a conscious process of making choices among one or more alternatives with the intention of moving toward some desired state of affairs. The rational choice paradigm relies on subjective expected utility to identify the best choice. It also follows the logical process of identifying problems and opportunities, choosing the best decision style, developing alternative solutions, choosing the best solution, implementing the selected alternative, and evaluating decision outcomes.

LO2 Explain why people differ from the rational choice paradigm when identifying problems/opportunities, evaluating/choosing alternatives, and evaluating decision outcomes.

Stakeholder framing, perceptual defense, mental models, decisive leadership, and solution-oriented focus affect our ability to objectively identify problems and opportunities. We can minimize these challenges by being aware of the human limitations and discussing the situation with colleagues.

Evaluating and choosing alternatives is often challenging because organizational goals are ambiguous or in conflict, human information processing is incomplete and subjective, and people tend to satisfice rather than maximize. Decision makers also short-circuit the evaluation process when faced with an opportunity rather than a problem. People generally make better choices by systematically evaluating alternatives. Scenario planning can help make future decisions without the pressure and emotions that occur during real emergencies.

Confirmation bias and escalation of commitment make it difficult to accurately evaluate decision outcomes. Escalation is mainly caused by self-justification, self-enhancement effect, the prospect theory effect, and sunk costs. These problems are minimized by separating decision choosers from decision evaluators, establishing a preset level at which the decision is abandoned or reevaluated, relying on more systematic and clear feedback about the project's success, and involving several people in decision making.

LO3 Discuss the roles of emotions and intuition in decision making.

Emotions shape our preferences for alternatives and the process we follow to evaluate alternatives. We also listen to our emotions for guidance when making decisions. This latter activity relates to intuition—the ability to know when a problem or opportunity exists and to select the best course of action without conscious reasoning. Intuition is both an emotional experience and a rapid, nonconscious analytic process that involves both pattern matching and action scripts.

LO4 Describe employee characteristics, workplace conditions, and specific activities that support creativity.

Creativity is the development of original ideas that make a socially recognized contribution. The four creativity stages are preparation, incubation, insight, and verification. Incubation assists divergent thinking, which involves reframing the problem in a unique way and generating different approaches to the issue.

Four of the main features of creative people are intelligence, persistence, expertise, and independent imagination. Creativity is also strengthened for everyone when the work environment supports a learning orientation, the job has high intrinsic motivation, the

KEY TERMS

anchoring and adjustment heuristic a natural tendency for people to be influenced by an initial anchor point such that they do not sufficiently move away from that point as new information is provided.

availability heuristic a natural tendency to assign higher probabilities to objects or events that are easier to recall from memory, even though ease of recall is also affected by nonprobability factors (e.g., emotional response, recent events).

bounded rationality the view that people are bounded in their decision-making capabilities, including access to limited information, limited information processing, and tendency toward satisficing rather than maximizing when making choices.

creativity the development of original ideas that make a socially recognized contribution.

decision making the conscious process of making choices among alternatives with the intention of moving toward some desired state of affairs.

divergent thinking reframing a problem in a unique way and generating different approaches to the issue.

employee involvement the degree to which employees influence how their work is organized and carried out.

escalation of commitment the tendency to repeat an apparently bad decision or allocate more resources to a failing course of action.

implicit favorite a preferred alternative that the decision maker uses repeatedly as a comparison with other choices.

intuition the ability to know when a problem or opportunity exists and to select the best course of action without conscious reasoning.

prospect theory effect a natural tendency to feel more dissatisfaction from losing a particular amount than satisfaction from gaining an equal amount.

organization provides a reasonable level of job security, and project leaders provide appropriate goals, time pressure, and resources. Three types of activities that encourage creativity are those that redefine the problem, associative play, and cross-pollination.

LO5 Describe the benefits of employee involvement and identify four contingencies that affect the optimal level of employee involvement.

Employee involvement refers to the degree that employees influence how their work is organized and carried out. The level of participation may range from an employee providing specific information to management without knowing the problem or issue to complete involvement in all phases of the decision process. Employee involvement may lead to higher decision quality and commitment, but several contingencies need to be considered, including the decision structure, source of decision knowledge, decision commitment, and risk of conflict.

SUMMARY

LO1 Explain why employees join informal groups, and discuss the benefits and limitations of teams.

Teams are groups of two or more people who interact and influence each other, are mutually accountable for achieving common goals associated with organizational objectives, and perceive themselves as a social entity within an organization. All teams are groups because they consist of people with a unifying relationship; not all groups are teams, however, because some groups do not exist to serve organizational objectives.

People join informal groups (and are motivated to be on formal teams) for four reasons: (1) They have an innate drive to bond, (2) group membership is an inherent ingredient in a person's self-concept, (3) some personal goals are accomplished better in groups, and (4) individuals are comforted in stressful situations by the mere presence of other people. Teams have become popular because they tend to make better decisions, support the knowledge management process, and provide superior customer service. Teams are not always as effective as individuals working alone. Process losses and social loafing drag down team performance.

LO2 Outline the team effectiveness model and discuss how task characteristics, team size, and team composition influence team effectiveness.

Team effectiveness includes the team's ability to achieve its objectives, fulfill the needs of its members, and maintain its survival. The model of team effectiveness considers the team and organizational environment, team design, and team processes. Three team design elements are task characteristics, team size, and team composition. Teams tend to be better suited for situations in which the work is well structured, yet complex with enough task interdependence to require teams. Teams should be large enough to perform the work, yet small enough for efficient coordination and meaningful involvement. Effective teams are composed of people with the abilities and motivation to perform tasks in a team environment. Team member diversity has advantages and disadvantages for team performance.

LO3 Discuss how the four team processes—team development, norms, cohesion, and trust—influence team effectiveness.

Teams develop through the stages of forming, storming, norming, performing, and eventually adjourning. Within these stages are two distinct team development processes: developing team identity and developing team mental models and coordinating routines. Team development can be accelerated through team building—any formal activity intended to improve the development and functioning of a work team. Teams develop norms to regulate and guide member behavior. These norms may be influenced by initial experiences, critical events, and the values and experiences that team members bring to the group.

Team cohesion—the degree of attraction people feel toward the team and their motivation to remain members—increases with member similarity, smaller team size, higher degree of interaction, somewhat difficult entry, team success, and external challenges. Cohesion increases team performance when the team has high interdependence and its norms are congruent with organizational goals. Trust refers to positive expectations one person has toward another person in situations involving risk. People trust others on the basis of three foundations: calculus, knowledge, and identification.

KEY TERMS

brainstorming a freewheeling, face-to-face meeting where team members aren't allowed to criticize but are encouraged to speak freely, generate as many ideas as possible, and build on the ideas of others.

brainwriting a variation of brainstorming whereby participants write (rather than speak about) and share their ideas.

Brooks's law the principle that adding more people to a late software project only makes it later.

electronic brainstorming a form of brainstorming that relies on networked computers for submitting and sharing creative ideas.

evaluation apprehension a decision-making problem that occurs when individuals are reluctant to mention ideas that seem silly because they believe (often correctly) that other team members are silently evaluating them.

nominal group technique a variation of brainwriting consisting of three stages in which participants (1) silently and independently document their ideas, (2) collectively describe these ideas to the other team members without critique, and then (3) silently and independently evaluate the ideas presented.

norms the informal rules and shared expectations that groups establish to regulate the behavior of their members.

process losses resources (including time and energy) expended toward team development and maintenance rather than the task.

production blocking a time constraint in team decision making due to the procedural requirement that only one person may speak at a time.

role a set of behaviors that people are expected to perform because they hold certain positions in a team and organization.

self-directed teams (SDTs) cross-functional work groups that are organized around work processes, complete an entire piece of work requiring several interdependent tasks, and have substantial autonomy over the execution of those tasks.

LO4 Discuss the characteristics and factors required for success of self-directed teams and virtual teams.

Self-directed teams (SDTs) complete an entire piece of work requiring several interdependent tasks, and they have substantial autonomy over the execution of their tasks. Members of virtual teams operate across space, time, and organizational boundaries and are linked through information technologies to achieve organizational tasks. Virtual teams are more effective when the team members have certain competencies, the team has the freedom to choose the preferred communication channels, and the members meet face-to-face fairly early in the team development process.

LO5 Identify four constraints on team decision making and discuss the advantages and disadvantages of four structures aimed at improving team decision making.

Team decisions are impeded by time constraints, evaluation apprehension, conformity to peer pressure, and overconfidence (excessive team efficacy). Four structures potentially improve decision making in team settings: brainstorming, brainwriting, electronic brainstorming, and nominal group technique.

SUMMARY

LO1 Explain why communication is important in organizations, and discuss four influences on effective communication encoding and decoding.

Communication refers to the process by which information is transmitted and understood between two or more people. Communication supports work coordination, organizational learning, decision making, changing others' behavior, and employee well-being. The communication process involves forming, encoding, and transmitting the intended message to a receiver, who then decodes the message and provides feedback to the sender. Effective communication occurs when the sender's thoughts are transmitted to and understood by the intended receiver. The effectiveness of this process depends on the similarity of the sender's and receiver's codebooks, the sender's proficiency at encoding the message to the audience, the sender's and receiver's motivation and ability to transmit messages through that particular communication channel, and their common mental models of the communication context.

LO2 Compare and contrast the advantages of and problems with electronic mail, other verbal communication media, and nonverbal communication.

The two main types of communication channels are verbal and nonverbal. Various forms of Internet-based communication are widely used in organizations, with email being the most popular. Although efficient and a useful filing cabinet, email is relatively poor at communicating emotions; it tends to reduce politeness and respect; it is an inefficient medium for communicating in ambiguous, complex, and novel situations; and it contributes to information overload. Social media are emerging communication tools that include Internet- or smartphone-based channels that allow users to generate and interactively share information. Social media are more conversational and reciprocally interactive than traditional channels. They are "social" by encouraging collaboration and the formation of virtual communities. Nonverbal communication includes facial gestures, voice intonation, physical distance, and even silence. Unlike verbal communication, nonverbal communication is less rule-bound and is mostly automatic and nonconscious. Some nonverbal communication is automatic through a process called emotional contagion.

LO3 Explain how social acceptance and media richness influence the preferred communication channel.

The most appropriate communication medium partly depends on its social acceptance and media richness. Social acceptance refers to how well the communication medium is approved and supported by the organization, teams, and individuals. This contingency includes organization and team norms, individual preferences for specific communication channels, and the symbolic meaning of a channel. A communication medium should also be chosen for its data-carrying capacity (media richness). Nonroutine and ambiguous situations require rich media. However, technology-based lean media might be almost as effective as rich media for transferring information. This particularly occurs where users can multicommunicate and have high proficiency with that technology, and where social distractions of high-media-richness channels reduce the efficient processing of information through those channels. These contingencies are also considered when selecting the best channels for persuasion.

KEY TERMS

communication the process by which information is transmitted and understood between two or more people.

emotional contagion the nonconscious process of "catching" or sharing another person's emotions by mimicking that person's facial expressions and other nonverbal behavior.

grapevine an unstructured and informal communication network founded on social relationships rather than organizational charts or job descriptions.

information overload a condition in which the volume of information received exceeds the person's capacity to process it.

management by walking around (MBWA) a communication practice in which executives get out of their offices and learn from others in the organization through face-to-face dialogue.

media richness a medium's data-carrying capacity—that is, the volume and variety of information that can be transmitted during a specific time.

persuasion the use of facts, logical arguments, and emotional appeals to change another person's beliefs and attitudes, usually for the purpose of changing the person's behavior.

LO4 Discuss various barriers (noise) to effective communication, including cross-cultural and gender-based differences in communication.

Several barriers create noise in the communication process. People misinterpret messages because of misaligned codebooks due to different languages, jargon, and use of ambiguous phrases. Filtering messages and information overload are two other communication barriers. These problems are often amplified in cross-cultural settings where the previously mentioned problems occur along with differences in meaning of nonverbal cues, silence, and conversational overlaps. There are also some communication differences between men and women, such as the tendency for men to exert status and engage in report talk in conversations, whereas women use more rapport talk and are more sensitive than are men to nonverbal cues.

LO5 Explain how to get your message across more effectively, and summarize the elements of active listening.

To get a message across, the sender must learn to empathize with the receiver, repeat the message, choose an appropriate time for the conversation, and be descriptive rather than evaluative. Listening includes sensing, evaluating, and responding. Active listeners support these processes by postponing evaluation, avoiding interruptions, maintaining interest, empathizing, organizing information, showing interest, and clarifying the message.

LO6 Summarize effective communication strategies in organizational hierarchies, and review the role and relevance of the organizational grapevine.

Some companies try to encourage communication through workspace design, as well as through Internet-based communication channels. Some executives also meet directly with employees, such as through management by walking around (MBWA) and town hall meetings, to facilitate communication across the organization.

In any organization, employees rely on the grapevine, particularly during times of uncertainty. The grapevine is an unstructured and informal network founded on social relationships rather than organizational charts or job descriptions. Although early research identified several unique features of the grapevine, some of these features may be changing as the Internet plays an increasing role in grapevine communication.

SUMMARY

LO1 Describe the dependence model of power and describe the five sources of power in organizations.

Power is the capacity to influence others. It exists when one party perceives that he or she is dependent on the other for something of value. However, the dependent person must also have countervailing power—some power over the dominant party—to maintain the relationship, and the parties must have some level of trust.

There are five power bases. Legitimate power is an agreement among organizational members that people in certain roles can request certain behaviors of others. This power has restrictions represented by the target person's zone of indifference. It also includes the norm of reciprocity (a feeling of obligation to help someone who has helped you) as well as control over the flow of information to others. Reward power is derived from the ability to control the allocation of rewards valued by others and to remove negative sanctions. Coercive power is the ability to apply punishment. Expert power is the capacity to influence others by possessing knowledge or skills that they value. An important form of expert power is the (perceived) ability to manage uncertainties in the business environment. People have referent power when others identify with them, like them, or otherwise respect them.

LO2 Discuss the four contingencies of power.

Four contingencies determine whether these power bases translate into real power. Individuals and work units are more powerful when they are nonsubstitutable, that is, there is a lack of alternatives. Employees, work units, and organizations reduce substitutability by controlling tasks, knowledge, and labor, and by differentiating themselves from competitors. A second contingency is centrality. People have more power when they have high centrality: the number of people affected is large and people are quickly affected by their actions. The third contingency, visibility, refers to the idea that power increases to the extent that a person's or work unit's competencies are known to others. Discretion, the fourth contingency of power, refers to the freedom to exercise judgment. Power increases when people have freedom to use their power.

LO3 Explain how people and work units gain power through social networks.

Social networks are social structures of individuals or social units (e.g., departments, organizations) that are connected to each other through one or more forms of interdependence. People receive power in social networks through social capital, which is the goodwill and resulting resources shared among members in a social network. Three main resources from social networks are information, visibility, and referent power.

A person's social capital tends to increase with the number of network ties. Strong ties (close-knit relationships) can also increase social capital because these connections offer more resources and offer them more quickly. However, having weak ties with people from diverse networks can be more valuable than having strong ties with people in similar networks. Weak ties provide more resources that we do not already possess. Social capital tends to increase with the person's centrality in the network. Network centrality depends on the extent to which you are located between others in the network (betweenness), how many direct ties you have (degree), and the closeness of these ties. People also gain power by bridging structural holes—linking two or more clusters of people in a network.

KEY TERMS

centrality a contingency of power pertaining to the degree and nature of interdependence between the power holder and others.

charisma a personal characteristic or special "gift" that serves as a form of interpersonal attraction and referent power over others.

coalition a group that attempts to influence people outside the group by pooling the resources and power of its members.

countervailing power the capacity of a person, team, or organization to keep a more powerful person or group in the exchange relationship.

impression management actively shaping through self-presentation and other means the perceptions and attitudes that others have of us.

influence any behavior that attempts to alter someone's attitudes or behavior.

inoculation effect a persuasive communication strategy of warning listeners that others will try to influence them in the future and that they should be wary of the opponent's arguments.

legitimate power an agreement among organizational members that people in certain roles can request certain behaviors of others.

Machiavellian values the beliefs that deceit is a natural and acceptable way to influence others and that getting more than one deserves is acceptable.

norm of reciprocity a felt obligation and social expectation of helping or otherwise giving something of value to someone who has already helped or given something of value to you.

organizational politics behaviors that others perceive as self-serving tactics at the expense of other people and possibly the organization.

persuasion the use of facts, logical arguments, and emotional appeals to change another person's attitudes and behavior.

power the capacity of a person, team, or organization to influence others.

referent power the capacity to influence others on the basis of an identification with and respect for the power holder.

social capital the knowledge and other resources available to people or social units (teams, organizations) from a durable network that connects them to others.

social networks social structures of individuals or social units that are connected to each other through one or more forms of interdependence.

structural hole an area between two or more dense social network areas that lacks network ties.

substitutability a contingency of power pertaining to the availability of alternatives.

upward appeal a type of influence in which someone with higher authority or expertise is called on in reality or symbolically to support the influencer's position.

LO4 Describe eight types of influence tactics, three consequences of influencing others, and three contingencies to consider when choosing an influence tactic.

Influence refers to any behavior that attempts to alter someone's attitudes or behavior. The most widely studied influence tactics are silent authority, assertiveness, information control, coalition formation, upward appeal, impression management, persuasion, and exchange. "Soft" influence tactics such as friendly persuasion and subtle ingratiation are more acceptable than "hard" tactics such as upward appeal and assertiveness. However, the most appropriate influence tactic also depends on the influencer's power base; whether the person being influenced is higher, lower, or at the same level in the organization; and personal, organizational, and cultural values regarding influence behavior.

LO5 Identify the organizational conditions and personal characteristics associated with organizational politics, as well as ways to minimize organizational politics.

Organizational politics refers to influence tactics that others perceive to be self-serving behaviors at the expense of others and sometimes contrary to the interests of the organization. It is more common when ambiguous decisions allocate scarce resources and when the organization tolerates or rewards political behavior. Individuals with a high need for personal power and strong Machiavellian values have a higher propensity to use political tactics. Organizational politics can be minimized by providing clear rules for resource allocation, establishing a free flow of information, using education and involvement during organizational change, supporting team norms and a corporate culture that discourage dysfunctional politics, and having leaders who role-model organizational citizenship rather than political savvy.

chapter ten

Conflict and Negotiation in the Workplace

SUMMARY

LO1 Define conflict and debate its positive and negative consequences in the workplace.

Conflict is the process in which one party perceives that its interests are being opposed or negatively affected by another party. The earliest view of conflict was that it was dysfunctional for organizations. Even today, we recognize that conflict sometimes or to some degree consumes productive time, increases stress and job dissatisfaction, discourages coordination and resource sharing, undermines customer service, fuels organizational politics, and undermines team cohesion. But conflict can also be beneficial. It is known to motivate more active thinking about problems and possible solutions, encourage more active monitoring of the organization in its environment, and improve team cohesion (where the conflict source is external).

LO2 Distinguish task from relationship conflict and describe three strategies to minimize relationship conflict during task conflict episodes.

Task conflict occurs when people focus their discussion around the issue while showing respect for people with other points of view. Relationship conflict exists when people view each other, rather than the issue, as the source of conflict. It is apparent when people attack each other's credibility and display aggression toward the other party. It is difficult to separate task from relationship conflict. However, three strategies or conditions that minimize relationship conflict during constructive debate are (1) emotional intelligence on the part of the participants, (2) team cohesion, and (3) supportive team norms.

LO3 Diagram the conflict process model and describe six structural sources of conflict in organizations.

The conflict process model begins with the five structural sources of conflict: incompatible goals, differentiation (different values and beliefs), interdependence, scarce resources, ambiguous rules, and communication problems. These sources lead one or more parties to perceive a conflict and to experience conflict emotions. This, in turn, produces manifest conflict, such as behaviors toward the other side. The conflict process often escalates through a series of episodes.

LO4 Outline the five conflict-handling styles and discuss the circumstances in which each would be most appropriate.

There are five known conflict-handling styles: problem solving, forcing, avoiding, yielding, and compromising. People who use problem solving have a win–win orientation. Others, particularly forcing, assume a win–lose orientation. In general, people gravitate toward one or two preferred conflict-handling styles that match their personality, personal and cultural values, and past experience.

The best conflict-handling style depends on the situation. Problem solving is best when interests are not perfectly opposing, the parties trust each other, and the issues are complex. Forcing works best when you strongly believe in your position, the dispute requires quick action, and the other party would take advantage of a cooperative style. Avoiding is preferred when the conflict has become emotional or the cost of resolution is higher than its benefits. Yielding works well when the other party has substantially more power, the issue is less important to you, and you are not confident in the logical soundness of your position. Compromising is preferred when the parties have equal power, they are under time pressure, and they lack trust.

KEY TERMS

best alternative to a negotiated settlement (BATNA) the best outcome you might achieve through some other course of action if you abandon the current negotiation.

conflict the process in which one party perceives that its interests are being opposed or negatively affected by another party.

negotiation the process whereby two or more conflicting parties attempt to resolve their divergent goals by redefining the terms of their interdependence.

relationship conflict a type of conflict in which people focus on characteristics of other individuals, rather than on the issues, as the source of conflict.

superordinate goals goals that the conflicting parties value and whose attainment requires the joint resources and effort of those parties.

task conflict a type of conflict in which people focus their discussion around the issue while showing respect for people who have other points of view.

third-party conflict resolution any attempt by a relatively neutral person to help conflicting parties resolve their differences.

win–lose orientation the belief that conflicting parties are drawing from a fixed pie, so the more one party receives, the less the other party will receive.

win–win orientation the belief that conflicting parties will find a mutually beneficial solution to their disagreement.

LO5 Apply the six structural approaches to conflict management and describe the three types of third-party dispute resolution.

Structural approaches to conflict management include emphasizing superordinate goals, reducing differentiation, improving communication and understanding, reducing interdependence, increasing resources, and clarifying rules and procedures. Third-party conflict resolution is any attempt by a relatively neutral person to help the parties resolve their differences. The three main forms of third-party dispute resolution are mediation, arbitration, and inquisition. Managers tend to use an inquisition approach, although mediation and arbitration might be more appropriate, depending on the situation.

LO6 Describe the bargaining zone model and outline strategies skilled negotiators use to claim value and create value in negotiations.

Negotiation occurs whenever two or more conflicting parties attempt to resolve their divergent goals by redefining the terms of their interdependence. The bargaining zone model identifies three strategic positions for each party (initial, target, resistance) and shows how each party moves along a continuum in opposite directions with an area of potential overlap. All negotiations consist of two divergent objectives: claiming value (getting the best personal outcome) and creating value (discovering ways to achieve mutually satisfactory outcomes for both parties). Skilled negotiators claim more value by preparing and setting goals, knowing their alternatives to the negotiation (BATNA), managing time to their advantage, and managing first offers and concessions. Skilled negotiators create more value by gathering information, using offers and concessions to discover issue priorities, and building relationships with the other party. The situation is also an important consideration in negotiations, including location, physical setting, and audience characteristics.

SUMMARY

LO1 Define leadership and shared leadership.

Leadership is defined as the ability to influence, motivate, and enable others to contribute toward the effectiveness and success of the organizations of which they are members. Leaders use influence to motivate followers and arrange the work environment so that they do the job more effectively. Shared leadership views leadership as a role rather than a formal position, so employees throughout the organization act informally as leaders as the occasion arises. These situations include serving as champions for specific ideas or changes as well as filling leadership roles where needed.

LO2 Describe the four elements of transformational leadership and explain why they are important for organizational change.

Transformational leadership begins with a strategic vision, which is a positive representation of a future state that energizes and unifies employees. A vision is values-based, a distant goal, abstract, and meaningful to employees. Transformational leaders effectively communicate the vision by framing it around values, showing sincerity and passion toward the vision, and using symbols, metaphors, and other vehicles that create richer meaning for the vision. Transformational leaders model the vision (walk the talk) and encourage employees to experiment with new behaviors and practices that are potentially more consistent with the visionary future state. They also build employee commitment to the vision through the above activities as well as by celebrating milestones to the vision. Some transformational leadership theories view charismatic leadership as an essential ingredient of transformational leadership. However, this view is inconsistent with the meaning of charisma and at odds with research on the dynamics and outcomes of charisma in leader–follower relationships.

LO3 Compare managerial leadership with transformational leadership and describe the features of task-oriented, people-oriented, and servant leadership.

Managerial leadership includes the daily activities that support and guide the performance and well-being of individual employees and the work unit toward current objectives and practices. Transformational and managerial leadership are dependent on each other, but differ in their assumptions of change versus stability and their macro versus micro focus.

Task-oriented behaviors include assigning employees to specific tasks, clarifying their work duties and procedures, ensuring they follow company rules, and pushing them to reach their performance capacity. People-oriented behaviors include showing mutual trust and respect for subordinates, demonstrating a genuine concern for their needs, and having a desire to look out for their welfare.

Servant leadership defines leadership as serving others toward their need fulfillment and personal development and growth. Servant leaders have a natural desire or "calling" to serve others. They maintain a relationship with others that is humble, egalitarian, and accepting. Servant leaders also anchor their decisions and actions in ethical principles and practices.

KEY TERMS

authentic leadership the view that effective leaders need to be aware of, feel comfortable with, and act consistently with their values, personality, and self-concept.

Fiedler's contingency model a leadership model stating that leader effectiveness depends on whether the person's natural leadership style is appropriately matched to the situation (the level of situational control).

implicit leadership theory a theory stating that people evaluate a leader's effectiveness in terms of how well that person fits preconceived beliefs about the features and behaviors of effective leaders (leadership prototypes) and that people tend to inflate the influence of leaders on organizational events.

leadership influencing, motivating, and enabling others to contribute toward the effectiveness and success of the organizations of which they are members.

leadership substitutes a theory identifying conditions that either limit a leader's ability to influence subordinates or make a particular leadership style unnecessary.

managerial leadership a leadership perspective stating that effective leaders help employees improve their performance and well-being toward current objectives and practices.

path–goal leadership theory a leadership theory stating that effective leaders choose the most appropriate leadership style(s), depending on the employee and situation, to influence employee expectations about desired results and their positive outcomes.

servant leadership the view that leaders serve followers, rather than vice versa; leaders help employees fulfill their needs and are coaches, stewards, and facilitators of employee development.

shared leadership the view that leadership is a role, not a position assigned to one person; consequently, people within the team and organization lead each other.

situational leadership theory
a commercially popular but poorly supported leadership model stating that effective leaders vary their style (telling, selling, participating, delegating) with the motivation and ability of followers.

transformational leadership
a leadership perspective that explains how leaders change teams or organizations by creating, communicating, and modeling a vision for the organization or work unit and inspiring employees to strive for that vision.

LO4 Discuss the elements of path–goal theory, Fiedler's contingency model, and leadership substitutes.

Path–goal theory of leadership takes the view that effective managerial leadership involves diagnosing the situation and using the most appropriate style for the situation. The core model identifies four leadership styles—directive, supportive, participative, and achievement-oriented—and several contingencies relating to the characteristics of the employee and of the situation.

Two other contingency leadership theories include the situational leadership theory and Fiedler's contingency theory. Research support is quite weak for both theories. However, a lasting element of Fiedler's theory is the idea that leaders have natural styles and, consequently, companies need to change the leaders' environments to suit their style. Leadership substitutes theory identifies contingencies that either limit the leader's ability to influence subordinates or make a particular leadership style unnecessary.

LO5 Describe the two components of the implicit leadership perspective.

According to the implicit leadership perspective, people have leadership prototypes, which they use to evaluate the leader's effectiveness. Furthermore, people form a romance of leadership; they want to believe that leaders make a difference, so they engage in fundamental attribution error and other perceptual distortions to support this belief in the leader's impact.

LO6 Identify eight personal attributes associated with effective leaders and describe authentic leadership.

The leadership attributes perspective identifies the characteristics of effective leaders. Research suggests that effective leaders have specific personality characteristics, positive self-concept, drive, integrity, leadership motivation, knowledge of the business, cognitive and practical intelligence, and emotional intelligence. Authentic leadership refers to how well leaders are aware of, feel comfortable with, and act consistently with their self-concept. This concept consists mainly of two parts: self-awareness and engaging in behavior that is consistent with one's self-concept.

LO7 Discuss cultural and gender similarities and differences in leadership.

Cultural values also influence the leader's personal values, which in turn influence his or her leadership practices. Women generally do not differ from men in the degree of people-oriented or task-oriented leadership. However, female leaders more often adopt a participative style. Research also suggests that people evaluate female leaders on the basis of gender stereotypes, which may result in higher or lower ratings.

chapter twelve

Designing Organizational Structures

SUMMARY

LO1 Describe three types of coordination in organizational structures.

Organizational structure is the division of labor, as well as the patterns of coordination, communication, workflow, and formal power that direct organizational activities. All organizational structures divide labor into distinct tasks and coordinate that labor to accomplish common goals. The primary means of coordination are informal communication, formal hierarchy, and standardization.

LO2 Discuss the role and effects of span of control, centralization, and formalization, and relate these elements to organic and mechanistic organizational structures.

The four basic elements of organizational structure are span of control, centralization, formalization, and departmentalization. The optimal span of control—the number of people directly reporting to the next level in the hierarchy—depends on what coordinating mechanisms are present other than formal hierarchy, whether employees perform routine tasks, and how much interdependence there is among employees within the department.

Centralization occurs when formal decision authority is held by a small group of people, typically senior executives. Many companies decentralize as they become larger and more complex, but some sections of the company may remain centralized while other sections decentralize. Formalization is the degree to which organizations standardize behavior through rules, procedures, formal training, and related mechanisms. Companies become more formalized as they get older and larger. Formalization tends to reduce organizational flexibility, organizational learning, creativity, and job satisfaction.

Span of control, centralization, and formalization cluster into mechanistic and organic structures. Mechanistic structures are characterized by a narrow span of control and a high degree of formalization and centralization. Companies with an organic structure have the opposite characteristics.

LO3 Identify and evaluate five types of departmentalization.

Departmentalization specifies how employees and their activities are grouped together. It establishes the chain of command, focuses people around common mental models, and encourages coordination through informal communication among people and subunits. A simple structure employs few people, has minimal hierarchy, and typically offers one distinct product or service. A functional structure organizes employees around specific knowledge or other resources. This structure fosters greater specialization and improves direct supervision, but it weakens the focus on serving clients or developing products.

A divisional structure groups employees around geographic areas, clients, or outputs. This structure accommodates growth and focuses employee attention on products or customers rather than tasks. However, this structure also duplicates resources and creates silos of knowledge. Team-based structures are very flat, with low formalization, and organize self-directed teams around work processes rather than functional specialties. The matrix structure combines two structures to leverage the benefits of both types. However, this approach requires more coordination than functional or pure divisional structures, may dilute accountability, and increases conflict.

KEY TERMS

centralization the degree to which formal decision authority is held by a small group of people, typically those at the top of the organizational hierarchy.

divisional structure an organizational structure in which employees are organized around geographic areas, outputs (products or services), or clients.

formalization the degree to which organizations standardize behavior through rules, procedures, formal training, and related mechanisms.

functional structure an organizational structure in which employees are organized around specific knowledge or other resources.

matrix structure an organizational structure that overlays two structures (such as a geographic divisional and a product structure) in order to leverage the benefits of both.

mechanistic structure an organizational structure with a narrow span of control and a high degree of formalization and centralization.

organic structure an organizational structure with a wide span of control, little formalization, and decentralized decision making.

organizational strategy the way the organization positions itself in its setting in relation to its stakeholders, given the organization's resources, capabilities, and mission.

organizational structure the division of labor as well as the patterns of coordination, communication, workflow, and formal power that direct organizational activities.

span of control the number of people directly reporting to the next level in the hierarchy.

team-based organizational structure an organizational structure built around self-directed teams that complete an entire piece of work.

LO4 Explain how the external environment, organizational size, technology, and strategy are relevant when designing an organizational structure.

The best organizational structure depends on whether the environment is dynamic or stable, complex or simple, diverse or integrated, and hostile or munificent. Another contingency is the organization's size. Larger organizations need to become more decentralized and more formalized. The work unit's technology—including variability of work and analyzability of problems—influences whether it should adopt an organic or mechanistic structure. These contingencies influence but do not necessarily determine structure. Instead, corporate leaders formulate and implement strategies that shape both the characteristics of the contingencies and the organization's resulting structure.

chapter thirteen

Organizational Culture

SUMMARY

LO1 Describe the elements of organizational culture and discuss the importance of organizational subcultures.

Organizational culture consists of the values and assumptions shared within an organization. Shared assumptions are nonconscious, taken-for-granted perceptions or beliefs that have worked so well in the past that they are considered the correct way to think and act toward problems and opportunities. Values are stable, evaluative beliefs that guide our preferences for outcomes or courses of action in a variety of situations.

Organizations differ in their cultural content, that is, the relative ordering of values. There are several classifications of organizational culture, but they tend to oversimplify the wide variety of cultures and completely ignore the underlying assumptions of culture. Organizations have subcultures as well as the dominant culture. Subcultures maintain the organization's standards of performance and ethical behavior. They are also the source of emerging values that replace misaligned core values.

LO2 Describe four categories of artifacts through which corporate culture is deciphered.

Artifacts are the observable symbols and signs of an organization's culture. Four broad categories of artifacts include organizational stories and legends, rituals and ceremonies, language, and physical structures and symbols. Understanding an organization's culture requires assessment of many artifacts because they are subtle and often ambiguous.

LO3 Discuss the importance of organizational culture and the conditions under which organizational culture strength improves organizational performance.

Organizational culture has three main functions: a form of social control, the "social glue" that bonds people together, and a way to help employees make sense of the workplace. Companies with strong cultures generally perform better than those with weak cultures, but only when the cultural content is appropriate for the organization's environment. Also, the culture should not be so strong that it drives out dissenting values, which may form emerging values for the future. Organizations should have adaptive cultures so that employees support ongoing change in the organization and their own roles.

LO4 Compare and contrast four strategies for merging organizational cultures.

Organizational culture clashes are common in mergers and acquisitions. This problem can be minimized by performing a bicultural audit to diagnose the compatibility of the organizational cultures. The four main strategies for merging different corporate cultures are integration, deculturation, assimilation, and separation.

LO5 Describe five strategies for changing and strengthening an organization's culture, including the application of attraction–selection–attrition theory.

An organization's culture begins with its founders and leaders, because they use personal values to transform the organization. The founder's activities are later retold as organizational stories. Companies also introduce artifacts as mechanisms to maintain or change the culture. A related strategy is to introduce rewards and recognition practices that are consistent with the desired cultural values. A fourth method to change and strengthen an organization's culture is to support workforce stability and communication.

KEY TERMS

adaptive culture an organizational culture in which employees are receptive to change, including the ongoing alignment of the organization to its environment and continuous improvement of internal processes.

artifacts the observable symbols and signs of an organization's culture.

attraction–selection–attrition (ASA) theory a theory that states that organizations have a natural tendency to attract, select, and retain people with values and personality characteristics that are consistent with the organization's character, resulting in a more homogeneous organization and a stronger culture.

bicultural audit a process of diagnosing cultural relations between companies and determining the extent to which cultural clashes will likely occur.

ceremonies planned displays of organizational culture, conducted specifically for the benefit of an audience.

organizational culture the values and assumptions shared within an organization.

organizational socialization the process by which individuals learn the values, expected behaviors, and social knowledge necessary to assume their roles in the organization.

realistic job preview (RJP) a method of improving organizational socialization in which job applicants are given a balance of positive and negative information about the job and work context.

reality shock the stress that results when employees perceive discrepancies between their preemployment expectations and on-the-job reality.

rituals the programmed routines of daily organizational life that dramatize the organization's culture.

Stability is necessary because culture exists in employees. Communication activities improve sharing of the culture. Finally, companies strengthen and change their culture by attracting and selecting applicants with personal values that fit the company's culture, by encouraging those with misaligned values to leave the company, and by engaging in organizational socialization—the process by which individuals learn the values, expected behaviors, and social knowledge necessary to assume their roles in the organization.

LO6 Describe the organizational socialization process and identify strategies to improve that process.

Organizational socialization is the process by which individuals learn the values, expected behaviors, and social knowledge necessary to assume their roles in the organization. It is a process of both learning and adjustment. During this process, job applicants and newcomers develop and test their psychological contract—personal beliefs about the terms and conditions of a reciprocal exchange agreement between that person and another party (the employer).

Employees typically pass through three socialization stages: preemployment, encounter, and role management. To manage the socialization process, organizations should introduce realistic job previews (RJPs) and recognize the value of socialization agents in the process. RJPs give job applicants a realistic balance of positive and negative information about the job and work context. Socialization agents provide information and social support during the socialization process.

chapter fourteen

Organizational Change

SUMMARY

LO1 Describe the elements of Lewin's force field analysis model.

Lewin's force field analysis model states that all systems have driving and restraining forces. Change occurs through the process of unfreezing, changing, and refreezing. Unfreezing produces disequilibrium between the driving and restraining forces. Refreezing realigns the organization's systems and structures with the desired behaviors.

LO2 Discuss the reasons why people resist organizational change and how change agents should view this resistance.

Restraining forces are manifested as employee resistance to change. The main reasons why people resist change are the negative valence of change, fear of the unknown, not-invented-here syndrome, breaking routines, incongruent team dynamics, and incongruent organizational systems. Resistance to change should be viewed as a resource, not an inherent obstacle to change. Change agents need to view resistance as task conflict rather than relationship conflict. Resistance is a signal that the change agent has not sufficiently strengthened employee readiness for change. It is also seen as a form of voice, so discussion potentially improves procedural justice.

LO3 Outline six strategies for minimizing resistance to change, and debate ways to effectively create an urgency to change.

Organizational change requires employees to have an urgency for change. This typically occurs by informing them about driving forces in the external environment. Urgency to change also develops by putting employees in direct contact with customers. Leaders often need to create an urgency to change before the external pressures are felt, and this can occur through a vision of a more appealing future.

Resistance to change may be minimized by keeping employees informed about what to expect from the change effort (communicating); teaching employees valuable skills for the desired future (learning); involving them in the change process; helping employees cope with the stress of change; negotiating trade-offs with those who will clearly lose from the change effort; and using coercion (sparingly and as a last resort).

LO4 Discuss how leadership, coalitions, social networks, and pilot projects assist organizational change.

Every successful change also requires transformational leaders with a clear, well-articulated vision of the desired future state. They also need the assistance of several people (a guiding coalition) who are located throughout the organization. Change also occurs more informally through social networks. Viral change operates through social networks using influencers.

Many organizational change initiatives begin with a pilot project. The success of the pilot project is then diffused to other parts of the organization. This occurs by applying the MARS model, including motivating employees to adopt the pilot project's methods, training people to know how to adopt these practices, helping clarify how the pilot can be applied to different areas, and providing time and resources to support this diffusion.

KEY TERMS

action research a problem-focused change process that combines action orientation (changing attitudes and behavior) and research orientation (testing theory through data collection and analysis).

appreciative inquiry an organizational change strategy that directs the group's attention away from its own problems and focuses participants on the group's potential and positive elements.

force field analysis Kurt Lewin's model of systemwide change that helps change agents diagnose the forces that drive and restrain proposed organizational change.

refreezing the latter part of the change process, in which systems and structures are introduced that reinforce and maintain the desired behaviors.

unfreezing the first part of the change process, in which the change agent produces disequilibrium between the driving and restraining forces.

LO5 Describe and compare action research and appreciative inquiry as formal approaches to organizational change.

Action research is a highly participative, open systems approach to change management that combines an action orientation (changing attitudes and behavior) with a research orientation (testing theory). It is a data-based, problem-oriented process that diagnoses the need for change, introduces the intervention, and then evaluates and stabilizes the desired changes.

Appreciative inquiry embraces the positive organizational behavior philosophy by focusing participants on the positive and possible. Along with this positive principle, this approach to change applies the constructionist, simultaneity, poetic, and anticipatory principles. The four stages of appreciative inquiry include discovery, dreaming, designing, and delivering.

Large-group interventions are highly participative events that view organizations as open systems (i.e., involve as many employees and other stakeholders as possible) and adopt a future and positive focus of change. Parallel learning structures rely on social structures developed alongside the formal hierarchy with the purpose of increasing the organization's learning. They are highly participative arrangements, composed of people from most levels of the organization who follow the action research model to produce meaningful organizational change.

LO6 Discuss two cross-cultural and three ethical issues in organizational change.

One significant concern is that organizational change theories developed with a Western cultural orientation potentially conflict with cultural values in some other countries. Also, organizational change practices can raise one or more ethical concerns, including increasing management's power over employees, threatening individual privacy rights, and undermining individual self-esteem.